STUDIES IN BRITISH ART

Seventeenth-Century Interior Decoration in England, France and Holland

Peter Thornton

Published for the Paul Mellon Centre
for Studies in British Art
by
Yale University Press
New Haven and London

Library of Congress catalog card number: 77-91067
International standard book number: 0-300-021933 (cloth)
0-300-02776-1 (paper)

Designed by John Nicoll and set in Monophoto Bembo.
Printed in Great Britain by BAS Printers Limited, Over Wallop, Hampshire.
Colour illustrations printed in Great Britain by Jolly and Barber Limited, Rugby, Warwickshire.

Published in Great Britain, Europe, Africa, and Asia (except Japan) by Yale University Press, Limited, London. Distributed in Australia and New Zealand by Book & Film Services, Artarmon, N.S.W., Australia; and in Japan by Harper & Row, Publishers, Tokyo Office.

TO ANN, MY WIFE

IL SAVIO SA TROVAR TUTTO NEL POCO

To the wise man a trifle may reveal all

Inscription painted in the seventeenth century on the corridor-wall at Skokloster in Sweden

FOREWORD

UNDERLYING the survey of seventeenth-century interior decoration encompassed in these pages is a special way of looking at historic houses. It is an approach that my colleagues and I in the Department of Furniture and Woodwork in the Victoria and Albert Museum have as a group adopted and which is finding increasing favour with a number of other people who work in this general field. For my own part, my inclination towards treating the subject in this way springs from contacts with Scandinavian museum curators in the late 1940s, most notably with Dr Tove Clemmensen of the National Museum in Copenhagen who each summer used to take a small team of collaborators out to some country house where they spent several weeks studying, recording and photographing the rooms and their contents in great detail. The result was that they saw a great deal of antique furniture of all kinds in its intended context, and came to understand much about its purpose and the settings against which it was supposed to be seen. In the Scandinavian approach, much stress was laid on the study of contemporary illustrations and old photographs that provided information about the conventions governing decoration and the arrangement of furniture in the past.

The difficulty of applying this method to houses in England was largely one of scale (although money also came into it); there are so many more houses, they are larger and their contents are more numerous. Nevertheless, due largely to the enthusiastic and determined activities of John Hardy and Clive Wainwright, a remarkable survey has been made over the past decade or so. It is less thorough and consistent than the Danish version but is far more extensive and no less informative. It has been an essential factor in our growing understanding of the arrangement of rooms in the past and of the décor against which these arrangements were contrived.

A feature that became increasingly obvious (it is one of which most people are still only dimly aware) was how the rooms in ancient houses had not always been furnished with a random scattering of antique items, as they so often are today. There had been conventions, there had been a plan, there had been a host of special requirements that governed these matters—and these ground rules were quite different from those which have prevailed in recent times. None of this was explained as one went round English country houses, and there was no readily accessible literature to guide one. Although the architectural shell differed in each case and one might distinguish a specific piece of furniture here or a painting there, room after room had come to look very much alike. There seemed to be endless strings of drawing-rooms and very few interiors had any distinct character of their own. Certainly there were none which conveyed any genuine impression as a whole of an eighteenth-century room let alone one from the seventeenth century. All were presented according to aesthetic principles that have been paramount since about 1910. There was nothing inherently wrong with this; most people liked it that way. But it was rather monotonous and it did little to help the visitors to understand how these buildings came into being, what purposes they had served at various stages, what were the aspirations of those who built them.

The number of questions on these matters that reached us at the Victoria and Albert Museum began to increase. We also wanted to know for our own purposes. Here was a field that seemed in need of more purposeful tilling. Considerable impetus was given to our own craving for information in this area by our having in our care Ham House, a delightful seventeenth-century villa on the Thames about an hour's hard row upstream from Westminster, and Osterley Park, a magnificent Adam house near London Airport. Both had remained largely untouched, respectively since the 1670s and 1770s. Both contained the actual furniture provided for them at these stages. Moreover, in both cases inventories of the periods existed that help us the better to envisage how the respective rooms must originally have looked. And, finally, very little furniture from later periods remained in the two houses, so there was no reason why we should not strive to present them as nearly as possible in their original guises. At any rate, we needed to know more about furnishing in those two periods and the reader will very quickly become aware that the experience of myself and my colleagues with Ham House has been of immense importance to our appreciation of the background to, as well as many details of, seventeenth-century interior decoration. In my work as Keeper in charge of Ham House, I have been most ably supported by Maurice Tomlin. We have learned an enormous amount about the house while working together and many observations originally made by him are recorded in this volume. Indeed, I cannot adequately express my gratitude to the colleagues in my Department for the help they have given me over the years because, among other things, it takes the form of a protracted conversation in which these questions are discussed first from one angle and then from another. Theories are put forward, adjusted, refined. Fresh information comes pouring in daily. New opinions are voiced, criticisms are levelled against the wilder assumptions. The results are evident to ourselves and those who know us well, and we believe these results to be in every way worthwhile. But it is often impossible to recall who first came up with an idea, who first drew attention to some important point. All I can now do is thank them as a group of which I am proud to be a member, and list them in order of seniority— Simon Jervis, John Hardy, Maurice Tomlin, Clive Wainwright, Julia Raynsford, Gillian Walkling, Lisa Clinton, Frances Cooper and Griselda Chubb.

We have of course not been alone in thinking that the workings of historic houses needed more serious investigation. A scholar who is bringing about a fundamental change in our attitude to the country house is Dr Mark Girouard, an architectural historian whose stimulating talks on the radio and whose essays about the workings of the great Elizabethan houses and on the Victorian country house have already borne impressive fruit, and whose Slade lectures, delivered at Oxford University in 1976, are shortly to be published by the Yale University Press when they will undoubtedly have a very considerable impact. Another scholar who has thought a great deal about these matters and who has always been exceedingly generous in sharing his knowledge with those who are interested is John Nevinson. His many admirers eagerly await the publication of his study of the astonishing collection of Elizabethan textiles at Hardwick Hall. Equally stimulating and enjoyable have been the discussions I have had over the last few years with Gervase Jackson-Stops of the National Trust. Once again it is fervently hoped that the publication of his study of Daniel Marot and his contemporaries will not be too long delayed as it will clearly be of the greatest importance to our understanding of late seventeenth-century decoration.

From what has been said it will be seen that very little of a general nature has so far been published on the subject of historic interior decoration in this country, and one has had to turn to foreign authorities for serious information in this field. No one can afford to ignore, for example Henry Havard's *Dictionnaire de l'ameublement* which appeared in Paris between 1887 and 1890. It is a rich source from which not a few of my quotations have been culled. William Karlson's *Ståt och Vardag i Stormaktidens herremanshem* (Lund, 1948) is a thorough survey of the contents of Swedish seventeenth-century country houses which is unfortunately only accessible to the relatively few people who can read Swedish. It was only brought to my attention fairly recently, but I was much relieved to discover that we had reached identical conclusions on many points, and that there were happily very few details over which we disagree. Another useful work is Walter Stengel's *Alte Wohnkultur* which appeared in 1958 in the depressing atmosphere of post-war Berlin, the result of a life-long study of life and domestic arrangements in and around that city in former times. Dreary in appearance and limited in its scope, this work was nonetheless a potent source of inspiration during the early stages of my own work.

However, a change is taking place in this country and as evidence one may cite John Fowler and John Cornforth's *English Decoration in the 18th Century* which appeared in 1974. It is a pioneering work that has laid a respectable foundation for further studies and we are naturally gratified that it incorporates, as the authors generously acknowledge, a number of ideas originally conceived in my Department as well as several discoveries made by myself and my colleagues. Their book and mine complement each other in considerable measure, especially as the authors have touched upon a certain number of seventeenth-century matters by way of introduction to their main theme.

Enough has been said to make it clear that a fresh way of studying historic houses has developed in this country in the past decade or so, and that the Fowler-Cornforth book and the present volume are early manifestations of this approach. Because the machinery for carrying out studies in this direction did not exist, my colleagues and I were forced to devise systems of self-help within the Department and I want to record with gratitude the imaginative assistance that has been given to us over the years by the Marc Fitch Fund, which has in all kinds of ways enabled us to achieve much that would otherwise have had to be left undone. We are especially grateful to Francis Steer, the former Secretary to the fund, whose work on the interpreting of inventories has incidentally been so useful to us all, and whose constant interest and encouragement have been so valuable to us.

While the present book was actually being written, it became clear to me that I needed to make a further visit to Holland. It was due to the assistance generously given me by the British Academy that I was enabled to accomplish this at the right moment and with special success. I would like to record my thanks to the Research Fund Committee for giving me this support.

Which brings me to the publication of this book. This would not have been possible without the assistance of the Paul Mellon Centre for Studies in British Art and I am very conscious of the debt of gratitude I owe the Centre and its Director, Christopher White, for the vote of confidence they have given me and my work by stepping in and sponsoring publication at the crucial moment. I should also like to thank my Director, Dr Roy Strong for the encouragement he has given me. The imaginative approach he has adopted in conservation matters has done a great deal to draw attention to problems that urgently need attention all over Britain, and this has in turn enabled me and my Department to give greater help to others in this direction, and has been a deep source of encouragement to us in the task that we find so fascinating. Friends and colleagues all over the world have given me much help over the years during which this book was in preparation. I hope I have recorded my appreciation in the appropriate places and hope to be forgiven for any omissions in this respect. I am also sincerely grateful to the owners of the objects illustrated in this work who have given me permission to publish them here. Acknowledgement is given at the end of the book, in the appropriate note to the illustration concerned.

Lastly, I want to mention Louisa Warburton-Lee, my assistant. Not only did she turn my manuscript from a nightmare scribble into a neat body of typing that in other circumstances, could perfectly well have been printed as it stood; she also saved me from a great deal of trouble and from making numerous mistakes. She achieved this, moreover, not merely with hard work, but with patience and good humour. My debt to her is immense.

Victoria & Albert Museum,   Peter Thornton
London
July 1977

For the second printing of this book I would like to record my gratitude to several friends and colleagues who have drawn my attention to various mistakes in the first edition which have now been corrected.

Since the book first went to press, Mark Girouard's *Life in the English Country House, A Social and Architectural History* (New Haven and London, 1978) has been published. Having read the manuscript before publication, I was able to refer to certain points in his work in support of my own arguments, but the reader is strongly urged to study Girouard's book for the wider background it provides to the present offering.

Because the planning of Renaissance and Baroque houses was so closely integrated with the formal gardens, surrounding the houses, the story of these gardens runs parallel to that surveyed in this volume. For this reason the reader will find much complementary information in Roy Strong's *The Renaissance Garden in England* (London and New York, 1979).

June 1979   P.K.T.

CONTENTS

Introduction

THE seventeenth century saw England and Northwestern Europe discarding the last vestiges of a mediaeval way of life and adopting in its stead one that has formed the basis of the western tradition ever since. An educated man of the seventeenth century would be surprised by many aspects of our life today but we would be able to discuss with him most of our daily problems and could expect to find his manner of thinking very similar to our own. This would not be the case if one of our mediaeval ancestors were to reappear amongst us.

Science, by the middle of the seventeenth century, had moved from the hesitant, secretive, tradition-bound gropings of the age of Copernicus to a level-headed inquisitiveness that sought to systematise knowledge, to discover order and regularity in every facet of the universe. Symbolic of this new attitude was the widespread adoption in the last years of the century of the pendulum clock—a piece of mechanism that not only intrigued our ancestors on account of the regularity which the pendulum imparted to the timepiece but was to set in motion what a modern historian has described as 'the remorseless subjection of humanity to the Clock'.[1] Although the working day of the labourer was still regulated by the hours of daylight, the day was no longer divided by the liturgical hours and governed by the ringing of a church bell. Regularity, precision and order came, indeed, to fire the imagination of those with an intellectual cast of mind, to such a degree that the world itself seemed, in Boyle's phrase, like 'a great piece of clockwork'.

Horrifying outrages were still perpetrated during the seventeenth century in the name of religion but, as the fearful stresses set up by the Reformation and the reaction against it were gradually resolved, men for the most part decided that it was better to be tolerant than to kill one another or to destroy each other's means of survival. This not only affected their attitude to spiritual matters but brought a hitherto unknown measure of peace, safety and profit into their everyday activities. In the Protestant countries particularly, this more liberal approach soon led to the questioning of entrenched beliefs in every field, to the rooting out of old-established practices that could be shown to have become outworn, to the revision of ancient organisations, and the introduction of new methods and techniques.

In this new atmosphere commerce thrived. Energetic, enterprising and determined men had better opportunities for growing rich than ever before—and often did so. On the other hand the cost of living had risen enormously in the sixteenth century and, although wages had been increased, the labouring classes found their living standards had declined by the beginning of the seventeenth century. Sporadic famines and furious epidemics, together with the appalling upheavals brought about by the wars of religion and the revolutions of the middle of the century brought widespread distress to the working population. The social division between them and the ruling classes now became marked, and the latter came to fear trouble less from other members of their class than from the many distressed elements of the workforce. Indeed, the seventeenth century saw the ruling classes coming increasingly to hang together in support of each other. A great lord was no longer simply the head of a family, governor of a large household with which he maintained personal contact, owner of estates, head of an extensive business enterprise, and surrounded with people who supported him and might even, if need be, fight for him. He was now a member of a class.

The great landed families were in fact able to entrench themselves ever more securely and they profited from the rise in prices to reinforce their position on the land. In a period of inflation the value of land is usually maintained and often increased. The merchant or banker who had made good in the seventeenth century was no less conscious of this than is his successor today, and many invested their freshly-won capital in country estates. Owning land became an important avenue to a rise in social rank and, in time and with luck, to political office. Socially this development was of course reactionary and did nothing to resolve the pressures that were building up in the labouring section of the population; but it established the landed aristocracy the more firmly and backed up this aristocracy with a substantial landed gentry, all of whom shared roughly identical interests.

If ownership of land was a source of power, an unmistakable symbol of that power was to have standing on one's own land a magnificent building, richly furnished, with the family's coat of arms much in evidence, and portraits of members of the royal and other great families prominently displayed as a reminder of one's connections. As Dr Mark Girouard has explained, by keeping up a handsome and impressive establishment, you could hope to make people feel it was 'a good thing to come in on your side'.[2] As he has also pointed out such advertising of your resources and of the potential support you could muster meant that the government tended to give you jobs and perquisites; so your income increased yet again while other members of the ruling class sought alliances with your family through marriage and you thus acquired even greater leverage for getting better jobs and perquisites—in fact, more influence and more power.

However, great families almost invariably also had an imposing house in the capital city. These houses were rarely as large as their country residences because the price of land in the cities was high and, as we shall see, they did not need to be so large. But these establishments were often even more grandly appointed than the country houses. What is more, some families found the journeys to their often distant country places so arduous that they could not visit them all that often, so they built themselves small *pieds-à-terre* in the countryside a few hours' ride from the capital. In seventeenth-century England, for instance, such sub-urban 'villas' sprang up along the banks of the Thames where they were equally convenient for getting into London or paying a visit to the Court when it was at Windsor or Hampton Court. Certain French noble families created similar small residences on the outskirts of Paris.

Yet, however powerful the aristocracy may have been on their estates, however imposing their country houses, however luxurious their sub-urban residences, it was at Court that offices and favours were acquired. And in France and England it was from the monarch that aspirants obtained positions of power—be it a political, clerical or military post. For, in order to protect the wider national interest in the face of growing hardship and unrest, the state had increasingly, during the sixteenth century, felt compelled to intervene in domestic affairs. This had led to tighter centralised control from the capital or seat of government—of which the monarch was head. This, and the fact that the nobility had rather too often proved unreliable in serving the interests of the state, encouraged monarchs to turn absolutist and speak more openly of the Divine Right of Kings,[3] setting up at the same time a middle-class administration steered by men who owed their position entirely to the monarch and whose allegiance was therefore hopefully beyond doubt. These men might belong to the gentry but were rarely of exalted birth. As they incidentally often came to wield great power, they were frequently able to amass great wealth, and could in consequence set themselves up in great luxury.

The monarchy in its turn found it essential to surround itself with a splendour that was even greater than that of its most wealthy subjects, so that everyone might be reminded of its close personal association with the divine power on high—or, failing that, of the yet more substantial wealth and power it could command through the state machinery.[4] In this respect it was the French monarchy that set the pattern that other kings strove to emulate. In England, although royal power was totally in eclipse during the period of the Commonwealth and was somewhat circumscribed after the Restoration, the later Stuart monarchs established themselves in considerable splendour in their royal palaces—St James's, Windsor, Holyrood, Hampton Court and Kensington—but the arrangements they made were for the most part based on French precepts.

Arrangements in the houses of the great noble families were closely modelled on those adopted by the respective royal households, the aim always being first and foremost to advance the power and status of their owners. As one moved down the social scale, so the splendour decreased but the standards of behaviour and taste set by the ruling families were recognised by all, and people adopted them as best they could, according to their means.

Great houses were built not merely for show, not merely as evidence of one's power or good taste. They were also intended as settings in which one could entertain one's equals or, if one were fortunate, one's superiors.[5] In town houses this did not require more space than the company would fill for the occasion. But, in a country house, suitable accommodation was needed for the visitors who might often stay quite a while (the journey there was rarely easy) and who were not infrequently accompanied by a substantial retinue. Important apartments had to be available for grand guests while lodgings of less splendour had to be provided for the supporting cast, each according to his degree. What is more, the owner's staff might itself be of considerable size and had likewise to be accommodated within the building—there being a permanent staff that always remained in residence as well as the retinue that habitually accompanied him from the capital or one of his other estates. The country residences of the principal noble families therefore tended to be extensive buildings, with a series of apartments, guest-rooms and accommodation for staff, as well as rooms for entertainment and ceremonial occasions.

The mediaeval lord had ruled by personal contact with those who supported him.[6] If necessary he was prepared to make his point with physical force, and evidence of valour in the field was at a premium. Holding estates that were often widely separated from one another meant that he had to visit each in order to supervise their management and, incidentally, to assert his authority by his presence and obvious signs of power. In many cases the lord was anyway forced to move on

3

because the quantity of provisions he and his accompanying retinue required was very substantial indeed and no neighbourhood could sustain so many people indefinitely. Thus the lord and his supporters tended to move from one great house to the next, travelling on when the provisions ran out, making his presence felt at each place ('showing the flag' as Girouard has called it) as well as seeing to his affairs.

This unsettled way of life among the seigneurial class dictated the form of furnishings that a great lord would take with him as he moved from one castle to the next, or from house to house. Some rugged pieces of furniture of no great value will have remained at each place, ready for use, but the more important furnishings had to be mobile,[7] they had to be capable of being packed onto a cart in the baggage-train, and set forth again at the next place of sojourn. Tapestries, that could be rolled up, and folding chairs met this requirement admirably; so did trestle-tables, folding beds and cushions. Hangings that could be used to transform a bare hall into an impressive setting for ceremony, a cosy bower or a charming bedchamber were likewise particularly in demand.

By the seventeenth century all this had changed. Grand people still travelled but they mostly travelled with only a few companions. They did not normally carry all their most treasured possessions with them. Their houses remained furnished all the time (even if the richest beds and wall-hangings were removed to the wardrobe-room and the rest was under cover when the family was not in residence).[8] Most of the old forms of furniture thus became obsolete. Tapestries and folding chairs happened to retain their importance as status symbols but no longer had any practical value; as for the rest, they were supplanted by new forms of furniture which were evolved to suit the new, static circumstances—the massive bed, the elaborate buffet, the writing-cabinet on a stand and the draw-table, for example. That these lost their massive character and became more delicate and graceful during the seventeenth century had to do with aesthetics and notions of comfort, and hardly at all with practical considerations.

Once the use of gunpowder had become widespread and artillery had become really effective, a lord could no longer hope to defend his castle against large-scale assault, and far less elaborate defences were adequate to cope with the sort of trouble that dissatisfied farm-labourers or resentful tenants might offer. The requirements of defence therefore gradually ceased to dictate the appearance and lay-out of seigneurial residences, and new types of buildings came to be devised—buildings with windows of more generous proportions that let in more light, for instance, and buildings arranged to accommodate rather more adequately the increasingly refined domestic arrangements that were gradually being adopted. Moreover, since there were severe practical limits to how far one could adapt an ancient castle to suit the new mode of life, it was quickly found to be easier to start afresh with an entirely new building.

For all the reasons given above, and no doubt for many others, there was incentive enough to build and the spate of significant building activity which started in France and England during the sixteenth century continued with only occasional losses of momentum right through the seventeenth century.[9] But we are beginning to trespass too deeply into the field of the architectural historian and the reader is referred to the works of such highly competent authorities as Sir Anthony Blunt and Sir John Summerson for surveys of this aspect of the matter.[10]

To whom could a nobleman or successful merchant turn when seeking to erect a new mansion in the seventeenth century? Sixteenth-century contracts to build were usually between the client and a contractor—a mason or a carpenter. There would not be any stipulation that the work had to satisfy a third party—an architect. Indeed, in 1600 there were still very few architects in France and hardly any in England, so that only extremely important buildings were erected with the aid of such a professional, a man versed in the mysteries of design and familiar with all aspects of building, who could co-ordinate the whole enterprise and ensure that each of its components met proper standards.[11] But as the principles of Italian Renaissance architecture came to be more widely assimilated in northern Europe, as a sense of order, regularity and discipline came to be an admired feature in a house, so any ambitious building enterprise came to require a governing mind to which the various craftsmen had to subordinate themselves. Even then an architect would mostly expect the individual contractors to submit designs for those features they were to construct; the notion that the architect should provide designs for all the required features was still not generally accepted even by the mid-seventeenth century, and most houses, even quite impressive ones, continued to be erected by craftsmen working on their own or in association, right through the century. The client therefore often had to steer the enterprise himself—or had to see that his agent did—and it is remarkable how many of them had an excellent grasp of the subject and were able to guide those working for them into creating harmonious and accommodating buildings.

Members of the nobility had of course often travelled abroad; some had even been to Italy and seen for themselves examples of the new style of building, and a few had sufficient understanding of these matters to enable them to recreate in their own country very creditable imitations, either for themselves or by way of providing guidance for other members of their class who were about to build. Sir Roger Pratt, who was himself one of the most influential of English architects in the middle of the century, advised those wishing to build at least to 'get some ingenious gentleman who has seen much of that kind abroad and been somewhat versed in the best authors of Architecture . . . to do it for you, and to give you a design of it in paper'.[12] The result will certainly be better than any builder can provide, he insists. His mention of 'the best authors of Architecture' reminds us that the sixteenth century had seen the publication in Italy of the first manuals of architecture and books of designs—just another aspect of the Renaissance demand for order, for codifying information. Such works appeared in increasing numbers during the seventeenth century,[13] and architects, both professional and amateur, who could procure these guides were greatly helped in their endeavours to bring order and discipline into their creations. But most patrons told their builders to copy an existing building or features from various buildings they admired. Certain buildings which were regarded as particularly successful therefore came to exert enormous influence on the history of architecture.[14]

What has all this to do with interior decoration, the reader may ask. One must not think that architects and gentlemen amateurs merely concerned themselves with questions of proportion, of how to draw correctly the different Classical orders of columns and other strictly architectural details. They were also interested in planning buildings so they would be more convenient for the sort of life that now had to be lived in them, and so as to provide greater comfort. Sir Henry Wotton, who was an ardent devotee of the new Italian taste in architecture, had this in mind when he explained in 1624 that 'Well building hath three Conditions—Commoditie, Firmness and Delight.' He places commodity, or convenience, first. However, it was the French who were to humanise the formalism of Italian house-planning and it is the French contribution in this field which remains paramount in countries north of the Alps throughout the seventeenth century.

The vital French contribution to the history of interior decoration during this period is the subject of the next chapter and is, indeed, the *leitmotif* in this book. Suffice it here to say that it was French architects who first insisted on controlling every aspect of creating an interior, who first thought it perfectly proper to provide designs for all the components, and who could then ensure that the various elements came together into a unified whole—the ultimate application of Renaissance principles to the creation of a building as an entity. Yet even in France it was only a handful of royal architects who took up such a dictatorial stance while, in England and Holland, it was only Daniel Marot who came to play such a role before the end of the century. Otherwise, it was not until the eighteenth century that leading architects, faced with an important commission, felt it necessary or desirable to attend to every detail of a scheme of interior decoration.

An important seventeenth-century house, then, might be the creation of an architect who would provide the ground-plan and elevations of the façades. When it came to the interior he might ask the various contractors for suitable designs for the features they were to provide—for example the plasterer who was to do the ceiling, the mason who was to create the chimneypiece, and the paviour or joiner who had to lay the floor. And he had to regulate the work of all these tradesmen as building proceeded. But the final appearance of any important seventeenth-century room depended largely on the contribution made by the upholsterer, who provided all the hangings (for walls, beds, windows, etc.) as well as coverings for seat-furniture, tables, floors, etc., and knew where to obtain furnishings of all kinds to complete the effect. Given the architectural shell, a great upholsterer could unaided provide a complete scheme of interior decoration and, although a handful of architects might presume to direct his contribution, the task was in most cases left to him. To a very large extent it was therefore still the upholsterer who governed fashion in this field and this is why he and his creations loom so large in the chapters that follow.

CHAPTER I
France and Aristocratic Fashion

MANUALS of deportment and polite behaviour had been published in the sixteenth century but European manners, even among the ruling classes, were still very rough when the new century opened in 1600. In France responsibility for bringing about the change to a less rude way of life has often been laid at the door of the Marquise de Rambouillet (1588–1665). It would of course be ludicrous to give her sole credit for this, but she clearly gave considerable impetus to this development and her rôle in it was no doubt exceedingly important. The famous *salon* she established at her house in Paris, the Hôtel de Rambouillet, became extremely influential and, while the subjects discussed were mainly literary, a pattern of well-mannered behaviour was forged there which spread right through the beau-monde and finally set the pattern for civilised behaviour throughout France and, ultimately, the whole of Europe. As Sir Harold Nicolson has said, 'In the history of French civility she remains a pioneer of wise and serious originality.'[1]

Her mother was a member of one of the oldest noble families in Rome (she was born a Princess Savelli) where her father was for a while French Ambassador. She herself was born in Rome and spent much of her childhood there. As a result she was atuned to Italian thinking and Italian behaviour before she came to live in Paris, and she must also have been familiar with some of the more advanced Italian ideas on questions of taste and manners at the turn of the century. Many aspects of life in Paris must have struck her as crude or provincial, but her husband's position as *Grand Maître de la Garde-Robe du Roi*, and her own very considerable fortune, enabled her to take up a central position in Parisian cultural life in the second decade of the century from which she was able to exert great influence on her entourage and material surroundings.

In 1619 she set about remodelling her father's old house which now came to be known as the Hôtel de Rambouillet. She took a lively personal interest in the enterprise and is said herself to have supplied such drawings and designs for it as were required.[2] We have noted that it was still in those days exceptional for someone setting out to build a house to engage an architect, and that a client who was well-informed in these matters might steer the undertaking himself, sketching ground-plans and details if he could, pointing to designs in pattern-books that appealed to him, and vetting sketches submitted to him by the mason or the carpenter. But that a woman should do so probably struck people as unusual and that the result turned out such a success was certainly thought remarkable at the time.[3] Moreover, because she came to have such enormous influence during the 1620s and 1630s, the arrangements this highly intelligent woman made in her house came to occupy an important position in the history of taste and interior decoration. For the presence of these features in her house[4] was a more certain advertisement for them than their presence in less celebrated buildings could ever have been.

In what directions did the advances made actually lie? Probably towards convenience and comfort on one hand, and harmony on the other.

7

Apart from its magnificence, what particularly struck the Parisians about her house was its 'régularité'. They also spoke of 'des agrémens, des commodités, des perfections',[5] and observed how the rooms were 'proportionnés & ordonnés avec tant d'art, qu'ils imposent à la vue, & paroissent beaucoup plus grands qu'ils ne sont en effet' [proportioned and ordered with such art, that they impress the onlooker, and seem much larger than they actually are].[6] This sense of spaciousness, these delightful aspects, seem to have been contrived by applying to the interior of this house the standard precepts of Italian Renaissance architecture—order, regularity and proportion—and these were matters the Marquise was well qualified to understand, intellectually and through her upbringing.

She may also have been more consistent than her predecessors in creating a unified effect in important rooms and this in turn added to the sense of order and harmony. We know that the famous *Chambre Bleue* where she regularly held her literary soirées was painted blue,[7] that the walls were covered with a blue material, and that the chair-covers and other textile components were also blue.[8] Occasionally bedchambers in the Middle Ages had been provided with wall-hangings and floor-coverings that were en suite with the bed-hangings, thus producing a totally uniform dressing for the room,[9] but it remained exceptional until early in the seventeenth century to have uniformity in the décor of a room as a whole, and it seems to be only from about 1625 onwards that this becomes a dominant feature of fashionable French interior decoration (Plates 1 and 2). It could well be that Madame de Rambouillet played a significant part in bringing this about.

But she may perhaps have made an even more personal contribution to what the French call *commodité*—to questions of convenience, ease and comfort. For she seems to have been prepared to scrap conventions in order to achieve this quality. This is reflected in the way she converted an old dressing-room into a small and private bedchamber (she suffered greatly from the cold and this little room could easily be kept warm).[10] She then turned her main bedchamber—the celebrated *Chambre Bleue*—into what we would call a drawing room. It is only when one comes to understand how rigid were the conventions that governed house-planning and room sequence at this period (see Chapter III) that one can appreciate what independence of mind such a move betrays.

Whatever the innovations to be seen at the Hôtel de Rambouillet may have been, we learn from contemporaries that features of the décor and arrangement soon came to be imitated 'dans tous les logis propres & superbes' [in all well-ordered and splendid houses].[11] Even the Queen Mother, Marie de Medici, is said to have 'ordered the architects to go and look at the Hôtel de Rambouillet' when she was building the Palais du Luxembourg and, while we do not know which particular aspects they went to see, we are told that 'ce soin ne leur fut pas inutile' [this precaution was not without benefit].[12] The architectural shell of the Luxembourg already existed by the time Madame de Rambouillet was starting to rebuild her house on the other side of the river Seine,[13] so it must have been in matters of detail that the Queen's designers were interested. Whatever the case, the Luxembourg was itself to exert a powerful influence on French architecture, particularly on account of its rich interior decoration.

Madame de Rambouillet brought to French manners a feminine pattern of elegance and it was principally through the women in her circle that she exerted her

1. Upper-class Parisian girls in a fashionable interior of about 1640. The covers of the chairs are en suite with the fitted table-carpet. The single curtains to each window are pulled respectively to the left and right for the sake of symmetry.

2. Parisian interior of the 1630s. The covers of the chair and its cushion on the left are en suite with the bed-hangings.

influence. If, as seems likely, the innovations she made in the field of interior planning and decoration were chiefly of a practical nature leading to ease and greater comfort, it will have been to women that they first and foremost appealed. At any rate it was to a large extent women who created the distinctive character of French interior arrangements and decoration in the seventeenth century (Plates 3 and 4). As Christopher Wren noted when he was in Paris in 1665, 'the Women, as they make here the Language and Fashions, and meddle in Politicks and Philosophy, so they sway also in Architecture'.[14] Italian sixteenth-century architects had demonstrated, both in their buildings and in their published designs, how to produce order and clarity in an interior, but convenience and comfort were concepts that hardly came into their calculations at all. The French genius lay in adapting the formal schemes of Italian architectural theory in order to create interiors that were practical and comfortable as well as harmonious and imposing; indeed, this was to be the chief French contribution to European architecture during the seventeenth century and the influence of women on this development can scarcely be overrated. In the more public domain this is reflected in the enormous amount of attention given by the French to questions of planning in architecture—in working out how most conveniently to bring visitors up to the reception rooms, how to route them through the rooms so they saw the decoration to best advantage, how to lay out rooms so as to provide maximum comfort, how to ensure that servants could come and go with minimum disturbance, how to secure privacy for the family and how to contrive a means of retreat if one wanted to get away from unwelcome visitors. In the more personal field the feminine contribution lay in their insisting on having a high degree of comfort in their private rooms, particularly in their closets (*cabinets*). Closets had existed before but the elegant small rooms of retreat which became such a notable feature of well-appointed French houses at this period were a new development (see Chapter XII). They were the forerunners of the *petits appartements* so dear to the eighteenth century, ranges of private rooms set behind the more formal rooms of reception. Moreover, the luxurious comfort first contrived for private rooms gradually came to pervade and soften the formality of the grander, more public rooms—the *antichambres*, the *salons*, and so on. True comfort, as we understand it, was invented by the French in the seventeenth century.

However, the luxurious form of comfort evolved in Paris towards the end of the seventeenth century did not come to be widely adopted in Europe until well into the next century. What at the time principally struck foreigners about important French buildings was their magnificence. And it was particularly the details of their sumptuous interior decoration which impressed them. Writing to a correspondent in Paris to obtain information on 'what is to be found in the most distinguished town houses and more particularly in the State Apartment at Versailles', the Swedish architect Nicodemus Tessin remarked that in 'tout ce que concerne le dedans des appartements . . . on raffine en France de jour en jour et [c'est en quoy] où l'on reuscit avec beaucoup de succés' [all that concerns the interior of apartments . . . is improved upon daily in France and it is there they achieve such great success].[15]

After the building and decorating of the Luxembourg, the next important landmark in Parisian interior decoration was the embellishment of the mansion built for himself by the powerful minister, Cardinal Mazarin, right in the centre of Paris. At the Palais Mazarin, as it was called, richness and magnificence of quite a new

3. Feminine comforts in Paris, about 1640. In the corner is a daybed.

4. A Parisian woman receiving female friends in her bedchamber in the 1630s.

order were to be seen and it came to be regarded as one of the principal wonders of the city in its day. It was decorated between 1645 and 1647. One of the most impressive rooms was the *Galerie Mazarine*, the ceiling of which was painted by the great Roman artist G. F. Romanelli; this was to have a profound influence on Le Brun when he came to decorate the *Galerie d'Apollon* at the Louvre (commissioned in 1663). The chief decorative enterprises in the French capital until the 1660s were still for the most part entrusted to foreign artists. This had been so at the Luxembourg, and Mazarin is said likewise to have 'constraint presque toutes les Nations de la Terre à contribuer à l'ornement' [constrained most of the Nations of the Earth to contribute to the decoration] of the Galerie Mazarine which 'l'Art et la Nature semblent avoir pris plaisir à enrichir' [Art and Nature seem to have taken pleasure in adorning].[16]

But a truly national style of aristocratic interior decoration—based on Italian formulae, it is true, but with a quite distinctive flavour of its own—was being evolved in France and was embodied on a grand scale for the first time in the Château of Vaux-le-Vicomte which was built with unusual rapidity and decorated in a most sumptuous manner between 1657 and 1661 for the wealthy *Surintendant des Finances*, Nicolas Fouquet, to the designs of the famous architect, Louis Le Vau. It has been said of Fouquet that he was 'the actual founder of a school of French decorative art in the building and furnishing of his château of Vaux',[17] but the architecture itself was not all that remarkable; what was important about the house, what gave the château its special character, was its interior decoration which was conceived as a magnificent whole by Charles Le Brun and executed by a team of artists and craftsmen working under his personal and enormously talented direction (Plate 5). Here at last was a totally French achievement, conjured up by a French architect-decorator and carried out entirely by Frenchmen.

Unfortunately for Fouquet this spectacular building was altogether too blatant evidence of his growing power and the wealth he had somewhat dubiously amassed. Jealous and uneasy, Louis XIV therefore in 1661 had Fouquet arrested and charged with embezzlement. Shortly afterwards Le Brun and his team were engaged in the royal service. In 1664 Le Brun was created *Premier peintre du Roi* as well as *Directeur de la Manufacture Royale des Meubles de la Couronne*, the establishment at the Gobelins which produced not only superb tapestries woven to his designs but furnishings of all kinds created under his personal supervision. When he had in addition been made director of the *Académie Royale de Peinture et de Sculpture*, it was fair to say, as the *Mercure Galant* did at the time, that 'all the Arts are carried on under him' and that 'there is no aspect that he is not concerned with' (Plates 6–10).[18]

Le Brun's first major work of interior decoration for the King was the *Galerie d'Apollon* at the Louvre, begun in 1663, but his great achievement was the internal decoration of the Château de Versailles which Le Vau had started to extend for his royal master in 1669. It was Le Brun, more than anyone else, who helped Louis create the grandeur and magnificence with which the King there surrounded himself—the glorious setting against which were enacted the dazzling ceremonies and entertainments that advertised unmistakably the King's absolute power (Plates 11 and 12). Uncomfortable, impractical and not especially distinguished as architecture, this vast palace overawed all who saw it. It served not only as an indication of French might, however; it also furnished a pattern for palace

12

5. Design by Charles Le Brun for a candlestand, probably intended for Vaux-le-Vicomte although not necessarily executed. About 1660.

6. Furnishings designed by Le Brun about 1670. Scene woven in tapestry 1671–6 at the Gobelins after a composition by Le Brun, depicting an audience given by Louis XIV in 1664. The candlestand on the left is similar to that shown in Plate 8.

7. Preliminary design for a candlestand by Le Brun. About 1670?

8. Drawing, probably by a Parisian silversmith, of a candlestand based on the design by Le Brun reproduced in Plate 7 with alternative feet.

architecture, and more particularly for palatial interior decoration, that has been followed in its essentials all over Europe ever since.[19]

The ceremonial that Louis XIV introduced at Versailles was actually retrogressive. He re-imposed and formalised ancient customs that had almost fallen out of use, and enforced this elaborate and inflexible structure on court life. But this oppressive ceremonial had its reverse side which took two forms—diversion in the form of entertainments on the one hand, and the development of elegant, luxurious and comfortable retreats on the other. These two developments at the French Court in the seventeenth century pointed the way towards the graceful informality of the Rococo period and were therefore of more profound significance than the pomp and circumstance for which Versailles is mostly renowned.

In the park at Versailles were erected various pavilions or *maisons de plaisance* to which one could make excursions or which might form the focal point of some entertainment for the courtiers and the many visitors from abroad—ballets, collations, firework-displays and diversions of all kinds (Plate 13). In these places a playfulness and informality could be allowed to reign, both in the manners allowed there and in the décor. It was on a drawing with proposed ornaments for the little pleasure-house at the *Ménagerie* that Louis commented to his architect in 1699 that he felt something more youthful would be appropriate.[20] But something of the same spirit existed long before that. The arrangements at the *Trianon de Porcelaine*, for example, must have come as a delightful surprise to those who were invited there.

14

9. Preliminary
design for a
console-table by
Le Brun. 1670s?

10. Two designs
for console-tables,
probably executed
by a Parisian
silversmith, and
perhaps intended
for the *Grands
Appartements* at
Versailles. The
left-hand section of
the top proposal is
presumably based
on Le Brun's
sketch reproduced
as Plate 9.

11. (right) Contemporary view of one end of the *Grande Galerie* (the *Galerie des Glaces*) at Versailles showing Le Brun's ceiling and the array of silver furniture including vases with orange trees.

12. (below) The setting for this masquerade is probably based on a knowledge of similar scenes at the French court. Note the display of massive silver vessels at the sideboard, the orange trees in silver urns, and the crystal chandeliers.

13. (far right) Display of precious vessels on a *buffet*, perhaps set up in some *bosquet* near one of the royal *maisons de plaisance*. Some of the silver can apparently be identified with items in the French royal inventories and A. F. Desportes, who painted this scene in about 1700, is known to have assisted with the decoration at several of the French royal châteaux including Marly.

14. The bed set up in 1672 in the *Chambre des Amours* at the *Trianon de Porcelaine*. The French royal inventory described it as 'un lit extraordinaire'. This astonishing blue and white confection was no state bed but was the central feature of a royal love-nest where fantasy could be allowed free reign.

15. Presumably the second bed at the *Trianon de Porcelaine* (see Plate 14).

Begun already in 1670, this charming building consisted of little more than two bedchambers in which stood two fantastic beds (Plates 14–16), while the rest of the décor was exotic and whimsical in character. It was an attempt to conjure up a sort of fairyland and, although it was swept away not many years later, this little building was the ancestress of all those chinoiserie pavilions that were to be so fashionable in the eighteenth century.[21] Different styles of fantasy and informality prevailed at the other small pleasure-palaces to be found in the grounds—the *Ménagerie*, and (later) the *Trianon de Marbre* (Plate 17) which we know as the *Grand Trianon*—but all were created to counterbalance the overpowering character of the public rooms in the main Château which was being done over in the 1660s and was then greatly extended to its present guise in the 1670s.[22] The same purpose, incidentally, lay

16. A French engraving showing a fashionable lady resting on a small bed (possibly a daybed) similar in conformation to the bed shown in Plate 15.

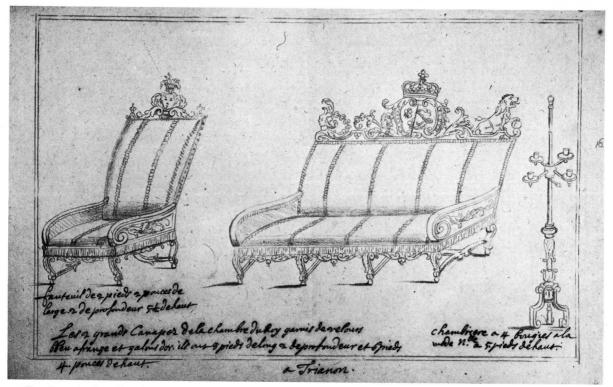

17. Furniture in the *Chambre du Roi* at the *Trianon de Marbre* (the Grand Trianon) probably drawn early in the 1690s.

18. Furniture in the most private rooms at the Château de Marly probably dating from the early 1680s.

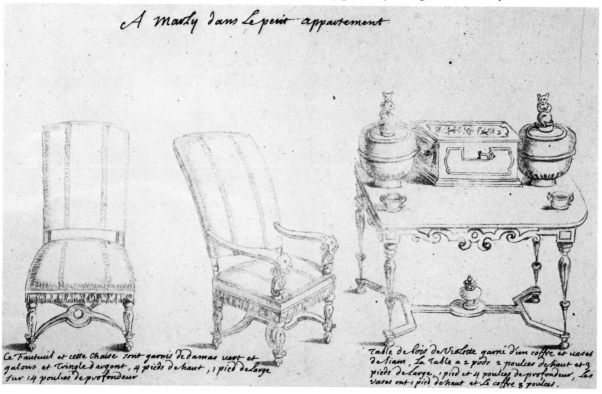

Buffet Execute a Marly

19. One of the eight fixed *buffets* installed at Marly in 1699–1700 when the château was radically altered.

behind the creation of the little Château de Marly which was built some miles from Versailles.[23] To be among those invited by the King to spend a few days there was regarded as an immense privilege, and considerable lack of formality characterised the stay.[24] Eventually the King spent too much on Marly; it became almost as sumptuous as Versailles itself and the early carefree atmosphere seems to have evaporated (Plates 18 and 19).[25]

However, it is often forgotten that in the main building at Versailles there were numerous private rooms in which the King or other members of the royal family could relax. He had his own private apartment behind the official rooms of reception—the *Grand Appartement*—to which he could retire and this included a private bedchamber where he frequently slept. The Dauphin likewise had a luxurious apartment on the ground floor where the décor was of an advanced character and considerable informality reigned. Moreover, each of the King's successive *maitresses en titre* was provided with a private suite of rooms close to the *Petit Appartement* of the King. The arrangement and decoration of Madame de Maintenon's apartment are well known to us through Saint-Simon's descriptions and it is clear that, for all her high-minded and austere way of life, a very considerable measure of comfort and ease was to be found there, so it is not surprising that the King during her 'reign', spent much of his time in this relaxed atmosphere, while she hardly left the rooms at all for weeks on end. Of her predecessor, Madame de Montespan's private apartment we know less but, judging from such evidence as is provided by her small château at Clagny, a stone's throw from Versailles, her surroundings were characterised by great charm and some novelty (Plate 20).[26] Moreover, immediately below the *Grand Appartement*, the

21

principal state rooms of the Palace, there was a luxury flat known as the *Appartement des Bains* which comprised not merely a sumptuous bathing room (Plate 21) but a whole suite of rooms that are said to have been of great beauty and must indeed have been delightful, for the King and Madame de Montespan spent many a long and happy hour in the relaxed atmosphere of this secluded retreat during the years when their liaison was at its height.[27]

At any rate, it needs to be borne in mind that an informal atmosphere, and a light-hearted and sometimes playful décor to go with it, existed side by side with the overpowering grandeur and formality of official French court life at this period. Madame de Rambouillet and her circle had shown the way to ease and comfort in the first quarter of the century. The last quarter of the century saw her ideas carried to a high degree of perfection within the orbit of the King himself (Plate 22 and 23).

20. (left) Probably the most luxuriously appointed house in its day, the 1670s, with furnishings in the most advanced taste—Madame de Montespan's Château de Clagny, just outside the park at Versailles. She reclines *en negligée* on an extremely elaborate canopied daybed. In the Gallery stand Oriental lacquer cabinets with porcelain massed on top.

21. Sketch for the scheme finally accepted for the *Cabinet des Bains* at Versailles; 1672. The walls were completely faced with marble of several sorts—apparently an early exercise in such treatment.

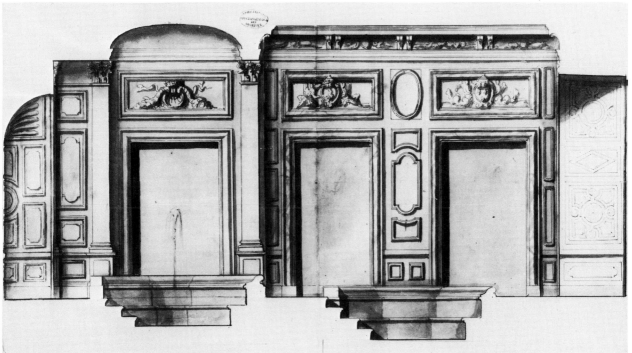

22. Seat-furniture in the *Antichambre* of the Dauphin's Apartment at Versailles in the 1690s. It was furnishings such as these that made the Dauphin's rooms one of the special marvels of the Palace. The colour-scheme was blue and gold, the loosely-hanging material on the walls, with its capping, presumably being en suite with the blue damask and 'brocard d'or piqué et d'or' on the *canapé* and *chaise*(s).

23. The Dauphin in his Closet at Meudon; about 1699. Decorated to the designs of Jean Bérain, the prince's personal and greatly appreciated interior architect. Several bronze-founders collaborated over the intricate mounts, including the *ébéniste et fondeur*, André-Charles Boulle, who presumably also provided the desk and glazed bookcases. Indeed, this is the kind of setting against which boullework is meant to be seen.

CHAPTER II
The Spread of the French Ideal

BY 1660 there was no longer any doubt that it was the French who set the pattern of civilised life indoors. The lay-out and arrangement of their buildings was widely studied, the details of their interior decoration was imitated, and the pattern of life led in such surroundings was copied. As has already noted, we have the word of the great Swedish architect, Nicodemus Tessin, for the fact that, as far as the interior of grand houses was concerned, here was a field in which the French were continually making admirable refinements (see p. 10). This was in 1694, but Christopher Wren implied much the same thing when he wrote from Paris in 1665 that the Palais du Louvre had so much to offer that it was 'for a while my daily Object' because not only was there much to be learned about the vast undertakings then in progress at the palace 'where no less than a thousand Hands are constantly employ'd in the Works' but he could also watch the artists and craftsmen engaged 'in Carving, Inlaying of Marbles, Plaistering, Painting, Gilding &c. Which altogether make a School of Architecture, the best probably, at this Day in Europe'.[1] He must be referring to the great programme of interior decoration then being carried out under Le Brun's direction including the decking out of the *Galerie d'Apollon*. At any rate there is evidence aplenty that what was being done in France in this field was being noted in many parts of Europe—not least in England and Holland, which are the countries that concern us here.

One must of course not think that French influence was in any way co-ordinated or was applied systematically. The impulses arrived haphazardly and in many various ways. Travellers to France took note of what they saw and the better-informed were often able to convey and interpret new French ideas to their own countrymen. Those architects who went abroad (and they now more frequently went to Paris as well as Rome, indeed, Wren never went to Italy at all) usually came back with notebooks full of observations and sketches that helped them introduce innovations to their homeland and it was increasingly often French ideas that caught their imagination. Engraved plans and proposals for ornament were published in Paris in ever growing quantity and, as they became more readily available abroad, so they came to constitute a powerful source of inspiration (e.g. Plates 27 and 28). The services of French artists and craftsmen likewise came into great demand; the emigration of large numbers of, for the most part, exceptionally capable Huguenot craftsmen and designers gave enormous impetus to the spread of French taste and techniques towards the end of the century (Plates 50 and 144), while francophile monarchs and aristocrats occasionally invited French artists to their countries to carry out specially important tasks.

Wren himself tells us that he had bought numerous engravings of the buildings he had seen in and around Paris 'that I might not lose the Impression of them'.[2] In fact he told his correspondent that he would 'bring you all France in Paper' and this gives one a measure of how great was the variety of engravings available in Paris already in the 1660s. He actually explains that those he was bringing home would 'give our

25

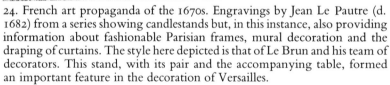

24. French art propaganda of the 1670s. Engravings by Jean Le Pautre (d. 1682) from a series showing candlestands but, in this instance, also providing information about fashionable Parisian frames, mural decoration and the draping of curtains. The style here depicted is that of Le Brun and his team of decorators. This stand, with its pair and the accompanying table, formed an important feature in the decoration of Versailles.

25. Drawing of a candlestand (*guéridon*) by Claude Ballin, the most renowned of Louis XIV's silversmiths, which was procured and sent in some triumph to Stockholm in 1693 at the request of the Swedish royal architect, Nicodemus Tessin. A drawing of the table which was flanked by two such stands was dispatched with it. The set must have constituted a spectacular feature of one of the principal state rooms at Versailles in the 1670s—which is presumably why Le Pautre chose to illustrate it (Plate 24).

26. (right) Engraving of about 1665 providing information about modern Parisian bedchambers with one of the newly fashionable alcoves that has a raised *parquet* and is fronted by a balustrade.

Country-men Examples of Ornament and Grotesks, in which the Italians themselves confess the French to excel'.

Already in the sixteenth century the French were publishing engravings of ornament suited to interior decoration. The most famous work that included proposals in this line was Jacques Androuet Du Cerceau's *Les plus excellents bastiments de France* of 1576 and 1579 (it was in two volumes). The other French books on architecture which came to be widely known in the seventeenth century—the works of de l'Orme, Le Muet, Fréart, Jean Marot—concentrated on purely architectural matters, on façades, the Classical orders, pediments, etc.,[3] but of course the ground plans given in these books were a great help to those who were about to build and provided tips not merely on orderly planning but also on practical questions of access and so forth. This was particularly the case with Le Muet's treatise, which was found so useful in England that it was translated into English.[4] Incidentally, a book the importance of which may have been underrated by historians (perhaps because it is not illustrated) is Louis Savot's little handbook entitled *L'Architecture Françoise des bastimens particuliers* which first appears in 1624 but which Blondel re-issued in 1673 with comments. It is full of useful hints on the planning and arrangement of rooms—on which way particular rooms should face, on where to set the fireplace—as well as on such questions as rigging up a bathroom or building an ice-house. It also gives advice on how to order slates, quarry-tiles and window-glass, and makes observations on the merits of the respective architectural treatises then available.

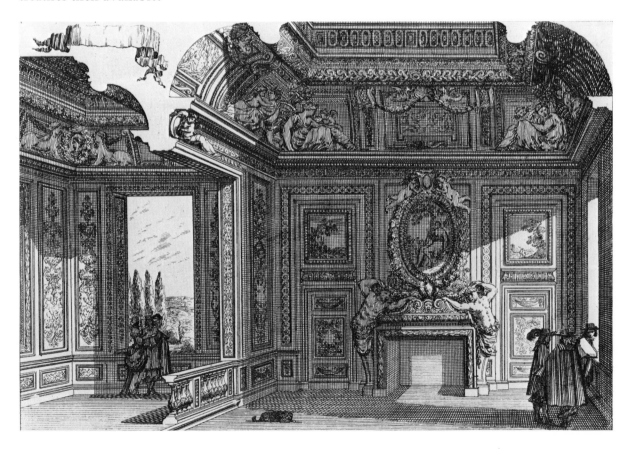

27 & 28. Engravings by Jean Le Pautre from about 1660 showing bed-alcoves in which stand fashionable beds of the period.

Those decorating houses, on the other hand, could obtain inspiration from the astonishing number of engravings for ornament of various kinds that began to appear in Paris from the 1630s onwards. These usually took the form of sets of engravings devoted to a particular class of ornament or feature—panelling, doors, chimneypieces, ceilings, candlestands, tables, bed-alcoves, frames, vases, and every other sort of ornamental detail (Plates 24, 26 and 27). They were sold in sets or singly; sometimes various sets were combined and sold in a single volume. These prints, moreover, would often convey far more information about prevailing French tastes than the title of each set would imply. For example, the designs for a chimneypiece might show the latest form of fire-dog as well; there might also be a *garniture* of vases or a clock on the mantel-shelf, and the opening of the fireplace might be fitted with a decorated chimney-board (Plate 252). An illustration of a candlestand would be surrounded by a handsomely moulded frame, and the representation of one of the new bed-alcoves would indicate how to drape a curtain and would tell an intelligent observer much about balustrades and new forms of panelling (Plate 26 and 28). As a famous eighteenth-century printseller commented on the engravings of Jean Le Pautre, that most prolific artist whose delightful compositions (e.g. Plate 36) made the style of Charles Le Brun known to the world in the 1660s and 1670s, 'ce qu'il mettoit au jour étoit moins receu comme des modèles que comme des idées propres à échauffer le génie' [the things that he published were taken up less as [direct] models than as ideas gauged to fire the imagination].[5] One might say the same of many other Parisian designers of ornament. Jean Barbet's proposals for chimneypieces (Plates 65 and 66), for instance, were adapted by Inigo Jones in England and by the craftsmen working at Skokloster some forty miles north of Stockholm.[6] Indeed, they were found so useful that they were redrawn and slightly altered and then issued in Amsterdam not long after they had first appeared in Paris (Plate 67).[7] In the same way, Le Pautre's proposals for bed-alcoves (Plate 28) were copied (rather tamely) and published in London by Robert Pricke in 1674, about a decade after their publication in Paris.[8] In any case, this enormous output of engraved ornament in Paris, and the fact that others bothered to issue re-engraved copies, betokens a great need for information in this field. By feeding this need, the French generated yet more demands for what they had to offer.

French taste in these matters was also transmitted by means of genre scenes. The charming views of interiors by Abraham Bosse (1602–76) showing members of the Parisian *haute bourgeoisie* going about their daily lives in fashionable settings did much to convey an impression of how the various elements went together (Plates 1–4 and 84). They showed not only the new forms of bed or chair, but indicated how they should stand in the room. The way a harmonious atmosphere could be imparted by a unified décor also became clear from such illustrations. Indeed, the pattern of interior living evolved by Madame de Rambouillet and her friends is surely reflected in these scenes, even if the settings depicted by Bosse are perhaps rather less magnificent.

They must have done a great deal to help spread the civilised, graceful and comfortable way of life for which Paris was becoming renowned when these prints were new—in the 1630s and early 1640s. Later in the century many more prints were published showing fashionable people in various situations—a lady taking

29. (above) A Parisian fashion-plate of the 1690s giving details of contemporary interior decoration.

30. (upper right) A Parisian fashion-plate showing one of the new *cabarets* for serving chocolate.

31. (right) Fashion-plate showing a lady affixing a patch on her cheek, standing at her dressing-table which is *en forme de bureau* and would normally have been flanked by a pair of candlestands. The illustration also shows a sash-window.

32. Fan-leaf with a scene of the marriage of Louis XIV to Maria Theresa of Spain in 1660. Even such small ephemeral objects carried a message about fashionable French décor—the way the curtains of the canopy could be tied back with cats-whisker bows, the fancy dressing of a *lit à la Romaine*, the court ladies seated on *pliants*, etc.

33. The scene of an important royal event carrying information about fashionable French interior decoration in the 1640s. Note the magnificent rock-crystal chandeliers, the marquetry floor, the form of the state bed.

34. (left) Even the almanack for the year 1682 brings information about fashions at the French court; note the mirror-backed sconces, the *garniture de cheminée*, the chandeliers (probably of glass), and the upholstered *tabouret*.

35 & 36. (above) Two designs of the 1660s for bed-alcoves masquerading as scenes from Classical history (here respectively of Cleopatra and Alexander the Great). A bed of the sort shown in Plate 35 might perhaps not be suitable for a state bedchamber, but might very well be seen in the bedchamber of a royal mistress (see Plate 20).

chocolate, a couple playing cards, a girl washing her feet, a woman at her dressing-table—but all also serving as an excuse for illustrating current fashions in interior decoration, or aspects of it (Plates 30, 289 and 304). Thus one learns about the latest form of day-bed, the new *cabarets* used when serving chocolate, how to arrange flowers in vases or great 'cisterns'. Some of these scenes may be regarded as early fashion-plates, for often they concentrated particularly on the details of dress and *coiffure*. Related in this respect to genre scenes and fashion-plates are the scenes of some historical event in Classical history—the death of Cleopatra, the Rape of the Sabines–which offered a splendid excuse for illustrating an especially flamboyant setting. Such a design would probably not be considered at all suitable for a grand room but might provide ideas for settings where fantasy could be allowed free rein— in the rooms of a courtesan, for instance, or in some *maison de plaisance* (Plate 35).

French engravings were obtainable through printsellers in Amsterdam and London but a far wider selection, including the latest sets, was of course available in Paris and it was those who visited the French capital who got a more balanced idea of what French taste in the field really comprised. Indeed, Sir Roger Pratt remarked in 1660 that the man who 'deserves the name of an Architect' must have seen the old buildings of Rome 'as likewise the more modern of Italy and France' because it can never 'be supposed that anything should be in the Intellect, which was never in the senses'. The aspirant can study designs but, however good these may be, 'never having seen anything in its full proportions it is not to be thought that he can conceive of them as he ought'.[9] Go and see for yourself and then do as Wren was to do, bring back some engravings so as not to 'lose the Impression of them'. And many did go.

However, a visit of a few weeks was not really sufficient. Those who stayed longer had the advantage. Among those whose sojourn tended to last several years and whose duties brought them into contact with the grandest and most fashionable aspects of French life were the foreign ambassadors. Having once acquired a taste for

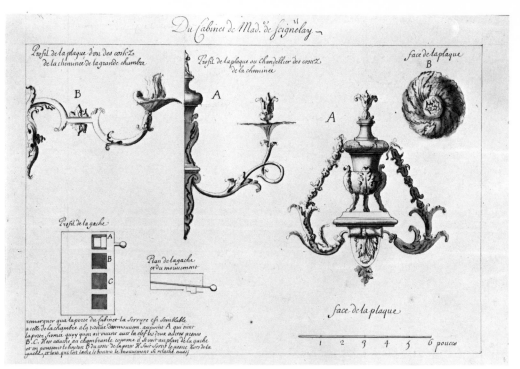

37. Evidence of the widespread interest shown in fashionable French décor is this drawing of cut steel ornaments in the newly-decorated closets of Mme. de Seignelay which were specially drawn in 1693 and sent to the architect to the Swedish Crown in Stockholm, Nicodemus Tessin, whose agent in Paris kept him informed of all the latest innovations in the French capital.

the new aristocratic pattern of life in Paris and at the French court, they were apt to try and introduce it to their homeland after their return, remodelling or rebuilding their residences along French lines, decorating them in the French style, bringing over French furniture with which to deck them out (Plates 38 and 39). Sometimes they even brought French artists and craftsmen over in order to carry out their schemes.[10] Moreover, they were often the recipients of handsome diplomatic gifts and these might also help spread notions of French magnificence and of French artistic and technical mastery. Louis XIV, for example, sometimes presented ambassadors with a splendid state bed and its associated kit of chairs and stools (Plate 41).[11] Gifts direct to foreign monarchs were also intended to convey the same message—we, the French, know how to do these things better than anyone else—and the message was widely believed.

I have discussed some of the ways in which knowledge of fresh developments in the field of interior decoration might be spread abroad from the French capital. I shall now briefly consider how this knowledge came to be assimilated in Holland and in England.

In the field of interior decoration, Dutch (also Flemish and North-German) taste during the first quarter of the seventeenth century was still entirely dominated by the kind of Mannerism embodied in the widely famed works of Hans Vredeman de Vries (1527–1604), notably in his *Variae Architecturae Formae* which was published at Antwerp in 1560. It was a style that borrowed elements from the works of the Italian authorities on Classical architecture but which relied greatly on the use of applied ornament that was often grotesque in character (Plates 42 and 43). It was a restless style, open to abuse and not readily lending itself to the creation of harmonious

38. (above left) Old photograph (1904) of one of a set of Parisian chairs brought back from Paris by an ambassador in 1682, showing their original upholstery.

39. (above centre) Chair from another set acquired in Paris by the same ambassador as that shown in Plate 38.

40. (above right) One of a set of chairs of markedly French conformation at Ham House which may have been procured from Paris in the 1670s when the building was being modernised in an advanced taste. It is even possible that they were a gift to the powerful Duke of Lauderdale from Louis XIV although no evidence for this suggestion has come to light. They still sport their original silk covers.

41. (left) State bed given to an ambassador by Louis XIV in about 1682. Such specimens of high-quality Parisian craftsmanship gave powerful impetus to the spread of French fashions and techniques.

effects.[12] A provincial and for the most part rather clumsy version of this Netherlandish Mannerist style reigned in England at the same time. In neither Holland nor England was there any real understanding of the basic principles of Classical architecture—exterior or interior. It was not appreciated that well-proportioned space and a well-developed sense of order were the key-notes of the style, and that no amount of plastering surfaces with Classical pediments, pilasters and friezes would produce the right effect.

At the beginning of the century, anyone in England wanting guidance on how to build had to read such architectural treatises as existed in their original language.[13] If one could not read Italian or French one was lost. Admittedly a Dutch version of Serlio was published in Antwerp in 1553 and new versions came out in Amsterdam in 1606 and 1616. The work was moreover re-translated into English in 1611 as *The First Book of Architecture made by Sebastian Serly*. For the rest one was obliged to fall back on the works of Hans Vredeman de Vries which purported to give information about Classical ornaments but left the builder to 'arrange them to his contentment according to the opportunity of his work', as the author himself disarmingly explained.[14]

The buildings which Inigo Jones erected in England between about 1620 and 1640 or so must therefore have seemed absolutely astonishing to contemporaries, for here suddenly was an architect who had absorbed the Italian Renaissance ideal and could create buildings in the Classical idiom that would have appealed even to his great Italian contemporaries. However, the Italian treatises of Scamozzi and Palladio that he so greatly admired cannot have been of much help when it came to decorating the interior of his buildings. He could produce Classical mural decoration, perhaps, and an Italian structure to the ceiling; but, as far as the details were concerned, he must have had to rely mostly on artists and craftsmen trained in the Netherlandish tradition.[15] What a help it must have been when engravings of French ornamental details began to appear on the market. He found particularly useful the designs for chimneypieces by Jean Barbet, published in 1632, which he copied freely as we have already noted. He also seems to have derived inspiration from the ceiling designs of Jean Cotelle (Plate 44 and Colour Plate V),[16] and there is a strong French flavour about much of his interior detailing. What is more, since some of the enterprises for which he was responsible were for Queen Henrietta Maria, the sister of Louis XIII of France and daughter of Marie de Medici, it is likely that the rooms concerned were furnished in something very like the current French manner (Plates 1–4), perhaps even with a certain amount of actual French furniture.

A central figure in cultural developments in England and Holland in the 1620s was Sir Henry Wotton (1568–1639). Much travelled, of an intellectual cast of mind, friend of Francis Bacon, Donne and Isaak Walton, this intelligent man was appointed Ambassador to the Venetian Republic in 1604 and was engaged in diplomatic duties in Venice with occasional breaks until 1624. He played an important part in bringing Francis Cleyn to England, having made Cleyn's acquaintance in Venice. Although Cleyn was a painter (he was thought by some to be 'il famosissimo pittore, miracolo del secolo') and is now mainly known as the chief designer at Charles I's tapestry manufactory at Mortlake, he was also able to turn his hand to interior decoration although his rôle in this field has not yet been properly evaluated.[17] It may well have been quite important. Wotton also wrote a

42. A Netherlandish interior decorated in the Mannerist style; about 1620. Although much of the ornament is Classical in derivation, the effect is made restless by the intrusive grotesque features (in this case, notably on the interior porch and buffet). The scale is misrepresented in this scene; the figures in front are too small, as the position of the door-handle shows.

43. A Dutch interior of about 1621 in the same style as that shown in Plate 42 but rather less grand.

44. A ceiling design drawn by Jean Cotelle (1607–76) in an album that may have been in Inigo Jones'
drawing-office. Perhaps a proposal for the Hôtel de Rohan in Paris, drawn in the 1630s.

guide to builders entitled *the Elements of Architecture* which was published in 1624 but
was reprinted many times and clearly met a need in its day. Not surprisingly
Wotton's book was a plea for the Italian form of architecture but he lists as the
qualities of a good building that it should possess 'Commoditie, Firmness, and
Delight'. He is here using commodity in the French sense meaning convenience, and
it was this same word that was used to describe the arrangements at Madame de
Rambouillet's house in Paris.[18] Clearly this need for practical yet well-ordered
architecture was becoming widely felt in the 1620s. In fact, he has sensible things to
say about planning.

Wotton's handbook was translated into Dutch, perhaps at the instigation of the
brilliant Constantijn Huygens (1596–1687) and certainly with his encouragement.[19]
During his boyhood at The Hague, Wotton had for a while been a neighbour and
had taught him to play the lute. Huygens visited England in 1618 and again for
seventeen months in 1621–3. He moved in court circles and can hardly have avoided
meeting Inigo Jones. He was certainly present when Jones' Banqueting House was
first used and records having seen several important works by Jones in London
including the famous galleries at Lord Arundel's house.[20] At any rate Huygens
seems to have sought to introduce 'ceste egalité regulière de part de l'autre . . . que

38

45. Design by John Webb, former pupil and assistant of Inigo Jones, for 'the Alcove in his Mats. Bedchamber, Greenwich 1665' which is clearly based on French proposals like those reproduced in Plates 27 and 28.

vous sçavez avoir tant pleu aux Anciens, et que les bons Italiens d'aujourd'huij recherchent encor aveq tant de soin' [that regular equivalance between one part and the other . . . which as you know formerly so appealed to the Ancients [i.e. in Classical Rome] and which the good Italians today so painstakingly seek to revive][21] into his own house which he built in the 1630s and of which he later sent an engraving that he hoped would convince Inigo Jones that 'le Bon Vitruve n'est pas du tout exclu d'Hollande' [the good Vitruvius is not totally excluded from Holland].[22]

Classical forms were being used with understanding in certain quarters in Holland by the 1630s (Plate 46) although it would seem that nothing so thoroughly Italian in conception as the buildings of Inigo Jones in England was produced there. On the other hand, certain French elements were apparently being introduced into Dutch architecture at this time, largely due to the personal intervention of the Stadholder, Frederik Hendrik, Prince of Orange (succeeded 1625, died 1647), to whom Constantijn Huygens was secretary. The Prince had strong leanings towards France. His mother was French and they had stayed a year in Paris together in 1598 at the court of Henri IV who was his godfather. He was extremely interested in architecture and later visited Paris again to study the latest developments. By 1630

46. This princess of the House of Orange-Nassau is portrayed in a Classical interior; she is Maria Stuart, daughter of Charles I and married to Willem II. Painted in the 1640s. Note the silver throne under a richly trimmed velvet canopy, and the splendid Persian carpet. The throne is of silver.

47. (far right) A portrait by the same artist as Plate 46 depicting a Dutch girl of a well-to-do family. This could well give an impression of a House of Orange interior in the 1640s.

the Stadholder's position was very strong and he set about re-planning the centre of The Hague along French lines.[23] Huygens' house and the well-known Mauritshuis, which is strongly French in character, formed part of this scheme. An English visitor to The Hague at this period (1634) noted 'The ladies and gentlemen here all Frenchified in French fashion.'[24] One may assume that the furnishing of these houses within the Stadholder's orbit was likewise based on French models, information about which was beginning to become more freely available at this stage, as we have already noted (Plate 47). A further instance of French influence on taste at the Stadholder's court is provided by the little Palace of Honselaarsdijk which the Prince started to build in 1621. Although much smaller, it had several features in common with the Palais du Luxembourg, Marie de Medici's residence that had been started only six years before—a building that has already been mentioned (see p. 8)—and it may well be that the plans for Honselaarsdijk were obtained from Paris. What is more, in 1634, the Prince secured the services of Jacques de la Vallée as his personal architect and the latter was the son of Marie de Medici's master of works at the Luxembourg.[25]

The court at The Hague of the Princes of Orange-Nassau, who became hereditary Stadholders of the United Provinces of the Free Netherlands, was the main avenue along which French influence was brought to bear on Dutch culture from about 1625 until the end of the century. Princely, almost royal at times, it remained none the less modest by comparison with the great royal courts of France, Vienna, Madrid and London. Indeed, the whole tenor of Dutch life in the seventeenth century

48. The pride and self-assurance of the Dutch middle-classes is admirably conveyed by paintings such as this. There is no ostentation; their dress and furnishings are costly but sober. The bed is tucked away into a corner; it does not dominate the centre of the room in the 'aristocratic' manner. About 1665. See also Colour Plate XIII.

remained anti-aristocratic. For the power lay with the Protestant élite in the cities, successful traders who came to form a self-perpetuating ruling caste—an upper middle class social and political dictatorship that was strongly opposed to the regal pretension of the House of Orange with which it waged an often bitter and sometimes bloody feud throughout the century. The regent or magistrate class in the chief cities at first led an austere life, without ostentation or pomp although they were imbued with a strong measure of self-assurance and civic pride that is embodied very clearly in the reticent but unmistakable magnificence of the Town Hall in Amsterdam (begun in 1648). Writing of Holland in the 1660s, Sir William Temple stated that

of the two chief officers in my time, Vice-Admiral de Ruyter and Pensioner de Witt . . . I never saw the first in clothes better than the commonest sea-captain . . . and in his own house neither was size, building, furniture or entertainment at all

42

exceeding the use of every common merchant or tradesman ... Nor was this manner of life used only by these particular men, but was the general fashion or mode among all the magistrates of the State.[26]

Such men viewed Frenchified ways with suspicion but, as commerce prospered and riches were amassed, a fresh generation grew up which drew its income from investments, land and houses; and this *rentier* class gradually came to demand the luxuries that French culture was known to be so skilful in devising. 'The old severe and frugal way of living is now almost out of date in Holland,' wrote Sir William Temple in 1673,[27] and greater opulence does indeed begin to pervade the scenes of interiors painted by the more fashionable Dutch artists at this time (Colour Plate I).

In 1672 France invaded Holland. After violent upheavals at home, the Dutch nation fell in behind the Stadholder, William III, Prince of Orange, who defended Holland with determination and skill. But although he had been the national leader in the war against France, he was a child of his time; for him Paris was still the centre of civilised life and the House of Orange remained the chief transmitter of French culture to the Dutch. A new phase in this movement began when thousands of Huguenot refugees arrived from France as a result of the fresh bout of persecutions that received official sanction in 1685 when the Edict of Nantes, which had granted French Protestants a measure of religious freedom, was revoked by Louis XIV.

Among the refugees were many who were prominent members of their trades and the effect their arrival had on the commercial and artistic life of the countries in which they settled was profound. As far as artistic developments in Holland are

49. Design for a study or small library by a Dutchman showing strong French influence (even the title is in French) and probably daring from the 1680s. The style is that of Jean Le Pautre and seems to owe nothing to Daniel Marot; it may have been composed before the latter arrived in Holland in 1684.

SECOND. LIURE DAPPARTE...
...par Marot Architecte du Roy Guillaume III...
...

50. A complete, co-ordinated scheme of decoration designed by Daniel Marot, about 1695. The furbelows of the bed's tester are echoed in the pelmet-like cappings of the wall-hangings, while the festoons on the headcloth are repeated as 'pilasters' that divide the wall-hangings into panels. Waved falls edge both the bed-curtains and the hangings.

51. (right) Drawing by Daniel Marot for a pier-glass, table and pair of candlestands (only one is shown) for Het Loo, the House of Orange residence near Apeldoorn. Dated 1700.

concerned, the assimilation of the latest French style was given immense encouragement by the appearance on the scene of the Parisian designer Daniel Marot (1661–1752). Son of the architect Jean Marot, he had fled his native land already in 1684 and soon entered the service of the Stadholder. He was an exceptionally capable designer and could turn his hand to all branches of the decorative arts. He not only designed complete houses but could provide drawings for the decorations and all the furnishings (Plate 51). The small palace at Het Loo (begun in 1692) was perhaps his greatest triumph but his *oeuvre* was enormous and his influence extensive (Plates 141–4). The style he brought with him was that of Paris of 1680 although, once separated from the stimulating atmosphere of his native city which he must have understood so well, and forced to rely largely on his own inspiration or what he could glean from the latest French prints, his style evolved in a personal manner different from the main line in France. But he was a designer of international stature. What is more he was backed by a whole range of excellent craftsmen who were quick to pick up his style. As is well known, the master he served became King William III of England and Marot also provided designs for a

44

La Largeur 40 pouces

la mesure ne doit avoir que 96 pouces de hauteur a qui est 8 pied

Les paneaux est fait de la hauteur marqué par la Lettre A.A et je le pouray faire plus haut pour ajuster la proportion de cette grande glace, a la Lettre B.B.

paneaux

Moulure de la Croisée

Croy

la de sus de la table est de Marbre blanc

Lambris 32 pouces 2 pi 7·8

2 pied 7 pied

D Marot fecit à la Haye ce 20 de N Mu on estei 170 à chevé et passe den le mois d'oust 1701

good deal of work in this country in the 1690s, notably at Kensington Palace and at Hampton Court. At this point the artistic development of Holland and England ran parallel. But we must return to the England of Charles I to see how the British had accepted French influence in the meantime.

The purposeful francophile sentiments of Frederik Hendrik, Prince of Orange, were not strongly echoed at the English court. Charles I does not seem to have displayed any exceptional interest in French taste and it is difficult to judge how much the taste of his queen, the French princess Henriette Marie (1609–69), influenced artistic developments in this country. She was only sixteen when she arrived in England in 1625 and it is well known that Charles, a year later, dismissed her retinue of French personal attendants. However, she may have been rather more interested in art and decoration than is generally supposed. She would certainly have known something of her mother's great building enterprise, the Palais du Luxembourg. It may have been through her personal intervention that Inigo Jones was provided through the French Ambassador with a French design for a chimneypiece that he was to imitate for a fireplace in the Queen's apartment at Somerset House in the 1630s (see also Plate 64).[28] Furthermore, a French gardener, André Mollet, laid out her gardens at St James's Palace and later at Wimbledon House and was retained out of her privy purse. She may have had French furniture brought over for her rooms, and, if she had a French gardener, she may equally well have secured the services of a French upholsterer to help do up her apartments. Her mother came over in 1638, admittedly as a refugee banished by her son Louis XIII but presumably still able to give impetus to any latent inclinations her daughter may have had towards introducing French ways at the English court.

By and large, however, the Queen must have been too pre-occupied with the acute political troubles that centred on her husband to give much thought to matters of decoration before the outbreak of the Civil War. She was in fact forced to leave the country in 1644, when she was still only thirty-five. She was provided with an apartment, first at Saint-Germain and then at the Louvre. While in France she naturally picked up fresh notions on fashionable French tastes and, on her return to England in 1660, she initiated changes in her apartment at Somerset House where, among other things, she had some parquetry floors laid which must have been inspired by floors in certain important rooms that she will have known in Paris (Plate 87).[29] It is unlikely that any English joiners would have been capable of executing such work in the 1660s and it may have been for this reason that some French joiners were working at the time at Somerset House.[30] We can see a new French fashion actually spreading in this case, for John Evelyn writes in his *Account of Architects and Architecture* that 'not to be forgotten are the Floorings of Wood which Her Majesty the Queen Mother has just brought into use in England at her Palace of Somerset-House, the like whereof I directed to be made in a Bed-chamber at Berkeley House; the French call it Parquetage'.

A childhood friend of Charles I was William Murray (1561–1654/5) who was appointed Gentleman of the Bedchamber in 1626 and had been among that band of constant companions of the future king who had formed the so-called 'Whitehall Group' of connoisseurs and art-collectors that included the Duke of Buckingham and Sir Balthazar Gerbier who will be mentioned again shortly. Murray redecorated Ham House, his villa on the Thames, in the late 1630s. As it probably remained

46

virtually untouched right through the period of the Civil War the inventory of about 1654, which has recently come to light, is likely to give some indication of what the house was like once Murray's new schemes were completed.[31] It would seem that the house was most fashionably appointed and that the chief rooms were decorated in a unified manner, with complete matching suites of upholstery (the full *ameublement*) in the principal rooms.[32] If the décor at Ham in some measure reflects tastes at the English court in the 1630s, as seems probable, this indicates that the basic principles of the new French thinking on interior decoration were by that date well understood in fashionable English circles (Colour Plate II).

A curious figure now appears on the stage who in a way symbolises the complexity of the network of influences being brought to bear on English taste at this time. Sir Balthazar Gerbier (1592–1663), born in Holland of French emigré parents, was connoisseur, painter, diplomat, adventurer, pamphleteer and architect. He was familiar with everything and everyone in France, Holland and England, and was for a while the English ambassador in Brussels, so also knew the Spanish Netherlands. He came to England with the Dutch ambassador in 1616 and entered the service of the Duke of Buckingham whom he assisted in the acquisition of pictures for his famous collection. He was thus a key figure of the 'Whitehall Group' of connoisseurs, and accompanied the Duke and the future king Charles I on their famous visit to Spain in 1623. He was with the Duke in Paris in 1625 and shortly afterwards designed the Thames-side water-gate for York House, the Duke's chief residence, which he modelled on the Medici Fountain in the Gardens at the Palais du Luxembourg—a building whose seminal importance has already been mentioned. As Gerbier is said to have helped 'in contriving' some of the Duke's houses, he is very likely to have had a say in the decoration of their interiors, in which case he could have fallen back on his knowledge of Dutch and French practice and fashions. After a rather distressing interlude as ambassador in Brussels he was created Master of Ceremonies at court, in which capacity he may to some extent have been able to influence decorative arrangements in the royal residences. Certainly, after the restoration of the monarchy, he designed the triumphal arches that were needed for Charles II's coronation. In the 1660s, as an old man, he worked for the Earl of Craven, who had spent much time in Holland, and built for him a large country house (Hamstead Marshall, long ago demolished) and perhaps also the charming hunting-lodge at Ashdown—both of which echo the Franco-Dutch style of the 1640s. And, finally, Gerbier published in 1662 his *Brief Discourse concerning the Three principles of Magnificent Building*, a rambling and not particularly helpful little essay, and a year later his *Counsel and Advise to All Builders* which is, on the other hand, full of useful information. It seems to have been inspired by Louis Savot's work of 1624 with which it has many features in common. It may possibly be of some significance that Gerbier dedicated his work to (among others) Henrietta Maria, who was by then the Queen Mother.

Gerbier knew something of the latest fashions in building and decoration in Paris between 1625 and the outbreak of the English Civil War but his sympathies really lay with the Netherlandish tradition which was itself being shaped by French influence by that time. This was essentially the position right through the middle decades of the seventeenth century in England. The Mannerist tradition still had much impetus over here[33] and Dutch Classicism, evolved under Italian and French influence, then gradually came to affect English tastes. Direct inspiration from France was not apparent to any really noticeable extent outside a narrow court circle until after 1675 or so.

The fact that many upper-class Englishmen and women found it convenient to absent themselves from their country during the Commonwealth period on account of their royalist sympathies, or simply because life in England seemed uncongenial to them,[34] was of course to have great significance after the Restoration, for these people had learned about fashions on the Continent and could not fail to bring back with them many fresh ideas. It was not merely that the future Charles II and his court were exiled in Holland (Plate 257) and in France and had been able to study the Frenchified manners adopted by the House of Orange, as well as the genuine article at the Louvre and Saint-Germain; quite a few people who were not members of the court were also abroad. Sir Ralph Verney was an example and it is of interest to recall that he brought back with him in 1653 some Venetian mirrors and some ebony and tortoiseshell cabinets which he had purchased in Holland.[35] He proceeded to do over his family house shortly after his return. John Evelyn and Robert Boyle went abroad at this time; so did Sir Roger Pratt who took the opportunity to study architecture in France, Italy and the Low Countries on an extended tour lasting from 1642 to 1649. As a result he acquired an excellent understanding of these matters and put this to good use on his return. He was one of the three Commissioners appointed to supervise the rebuilding of the City of London after the Great Fire in 1666 and designed two highly influential houses, Coleshill in Berkshire and Clarendon House in Piccadilly (see p. 337). He favoured the French style and paid attention to details of interior furnishing—the most convenient height for bookshelves, how to contrive locks for windows so that 'women and short folk' might reach them.[36] One of the surveyors appointed to carry out the rebuilding of London after the Fire was Robert Hooke (1635–1703), the scientist and, like Pratt, an 'amateur' architect. Hooke records in his diary that he habitually purchased books on architecture and prints from France and Holland and some of his buildings betray marked French influence. Evelyn noted, for instance, that Montagu House (1675–9), which Hooke had designed, was 'built after the French pavilion-way'.[37]

But if Pratt and Hooke inclined to the French taste, Hugh May and William Winde preferred the Dutch style.[38] Hugh May (1622–84) has been described by H. M. Colvin as 'one of the two or three men who determined the character of English domestic architecture after the Restoration'. He accompanied Lely (who was of course Dutch) to Holland in 1653 and spent the years of the Commonwealth there. Later he was to give the brilliant Dutch carver, Grinling Gibbons, his first important commissions in this country. On the other hand, he was assisted at Windsor Castle by the decorative painter Antonio Verrio who worked in the French Baroque style of Le Brun which he had picked up while in France during the early 1670s.[39] Moreover, he collaborated with Evelyn on the translation of Fréart's *Parallèle de l'architecture antique et de la moderne* in 1664. William Winde (c. 1642–1722), for his part, was actually born in Holland while his royalist parents (his father had been Gentleman of the Privy Chamber to Charles I) were in exile there. Although a rather dashing cavalry officer, he could turn his hand to military architecture and Sir Balthazar Gerbier addressed to him one of the dedications of his *Counsel and Advise to*

All Builders of 1663. He had for a while served Elizabeth of Bohemia, daughter of James I and a friend of the Earl of Craven for whom Winde completed Hampstead Marshall after Gerbier's death and rebuilt Combe Abbey. But as Colvin remarked 'Winde's indebtedness to the Netherlands for his architectural ideas has sometimes been exaggerated.'

The other important figure on the architectural scene during the second half of the seventeenth century in this country was of course Sir Christopher Wren, but he towers so high above the others and the main lines of his career are so well known that I need not go into the matter here. However, it is worth recalling how impressed he had been with French interior decoration during his visit to Paris in 1665 and that he had on that occasion acquired a lot of engravings of French buildings and ornament. He will certainly have studied with interest any French engravings of this class of which he could subsequently gain a view and, as these were fairly readily available in London after about 1670, he will have been au fait with the main developments in his field during the last decades of the century.

Mention should also be made of Sir William Bruce, one of the most sensitive architects of the period, who built a number of charming houses in Scotland during the last part of the century (Plate 317) and carried out a major extension to the palace of Holyrood for Charles II. He had been in Holland in 1658 but the style he adopted with such success strongly reflects French mid-century taste with which he became familiar during a visit to France in 1663. Bruce was well-connected and influential; for example, he was a cousin of William Murray's daughter, Elizabeth Dysart, who was to marry the Duke of Lauderdale in 1672. It was from the Duke, whom Charles II had created Secretary for Scotland after the Restoration, that he received the commission for the work at Holyrood, which in turn led to his appointment as Surveyor-General of the King's Works in Scotland. He was friendly with Lauderdale, advising him on architectural matters of all kinds in connection with the Duke's several houses in Scotland and also with Ham House, on the Thames, which the Lauderdales were doing over in the latest fashion between 1672 and 1680 or so. As Elizabeth Dysart also went to France in 1670 it is hardly surprising that there are many French features among the decorations at Ham from that period (Plate 77).

While English architects at this stage concerned themselves with planning and the fixed elements of the interior, there is no evidence that they exerted any influence on the loose furnishings even of important rooms. They may sometimes have given a tip here, from their experience, or a sketch there. For the rest, this was something they were content to leave to the upholsterer. I shall discuss his rôle more fully in Chapter IV, but he provided many of the most prominent features of a room—the wall-hangings, the window-curtains, the seat-furniture which stood in serried ranks along the walls, the towering bed (if it was a bedchamber), and much else—and his part in creating the final appearance of such a room was all but paramount. It is therefore important to note that many of the chief upholsterers of the Stuart period bore French names and were presumably Frenchmen. John Casbert, John Poitevin (Paudevine), 'Monsieur La Grange', Francis La Pierre and Philip Guibert are names that appear prominently in the English royal accounts during the last three decades of the century, for instance (Colour Plate XII).[40] Some actual specimens of Parisian upholstery were to be seen in England and these of course demonstrated unmistakably the great superiority of the French in this field at the time. Particularly spectacular was the Parisian bed of Queen Catherine of Braganza at Hampton Court which, as Evelyn tells us in his diary, had cost £8,000, 'being a present made by the States of Holland when his Majesty returned' (presumably in 1660, that is).[41] Far less spectacular but none the less providing excellent examples of the new French line in comfort will have been chairs like those which Lord Montagu brought back from Paris in the 1670s.[42]

Carvers, who did so much to deck out a richly decorated room during the Restoration period, tended to work in the Dutch style and the best craftsmen in this field were at first Dutch. Grinling Gibbons is the best-known example but there was Anthony Verhuyck who also worked for the royal household. At the end of the century, however, the most prominent carvers were Frenchmen—Jean Pelletier and Robert Derignée, for instance, who were particularly well able to interpret the new style currently being introduced at some of the royal residences by Daniel Marot (Plate 51). Carvers produced not only ornamental cornices, door-frames and chimneypieces; they also made candlestands, tables, and supports for cabinets, and worked up elaborate chair-frames. Actual carved furniture found its way to England from Holland and France, and no doubt provided fresh inspiration. For example, it would seem that a carved table and accompanying candlestands at Ham House were acquired from Holland by the Duke of Lauderdale in 1672,[43] and some similar furniture at Hampton Court and elsewhere are also likely to be Dutch imports. The exceptionally handsome carved and gilt tables and stands at Knole, which were probably a gift from Louis XIV, cannot but have made a deep impression on anyone who saw them when they were newly arrived in 1671.[44]

The most exquisite cabinet making during this period, on the other hand, was produced in Paris and there is one of the most superb examples at Drumlanrig, Dumfriesshire, in the form of a marquetry cabinet which is believed to have been given by Louis XIV to Charles II.[45] However, it was Dutch cabinetmaking that had the most fundamental influence on English practice and, once again, some of the foremost practitioners in this country seem to have been Dutch or Flemish. Thomas Mallin, for instance who worked for Charles II in the 1660s may well have been a Fleming. Later in the century there were Cornelius Gole and Gerreit Jensen, both Dutch but working by that time in the French style. Indeed the intricacies of the network of influences being brought to bear on Holland and England at this stage are admirably brought out by these very men. Cornelis Golle, to give him his correct Dutch name, was the son of the celebrated cabinetmaker, Pierre Golle (d. 1684), whose name occurs prominently in the French royal accounts during the Louis XIV period. Cornelis presumably learned his trade in Paris and came over to England in the 1680s to serve Charles II. His brother Adriaan was cabinetmaker to the Princess of Orange (later Queen Mary of England); he had come from Paris to work in Amsterdam. To cap it all, their sister Catherine married Daniel Marot. But the links are even more remarkable for we find Pierre Golle in Paris owing money on his death to Gerreit Jensen in London for sending him a consignment of English glue, which was apparently especially efficacious.[46]

As far as we know, the Frenchman Daniel Marot was the first architect in Holland who attempted to co-ordinate all the decorative elements of a room (Plate 50) in the way Le Brun had done at Vaux-le-Vicomte and at the French royal palaces under Louis XIV. He apparently effected a similar form of co-ordination over certain schemes of decoration at Kensington Palace and Hampton Court but it was to be some while before any native English architect exerted a similar all-embracing influence on the décor of important rooms. However, that is an eighteenth century story and does not concern us here.

CHAPTER III

The Architectural Framework

IN ERECTING a building, the architect or whoever was responsible for the enterprise, created a shell the inside of which then had to be decorated and furnished. Although the rôle of the architect was still being defined during the seventeenth century, most really important buildings were being designed by such a professional, and he sought to co-ordinate the activities of the various contractors who were master-craftsmen of their respective trades. Designing a building at first consisted mainly in working out a suitable ground-plan and contriving tasteful elevations. When it came to the detailed features, these were discussed with the individual contractors concerned; they might provide a sketch of what they proposed to do and the architect could then either approve it or suggest something different. But, as a greater measure of unity was sought in the decoration of important rooms, it became necessary for the architects themselves to provide designs for the fixed decorative features and this was an aspect of their work which increasingly came to occupy their attention during the century. What is more, in the cases where an architect was trying to achieve a truly integrated scheme of interior decoration in a room, he tended also to concern himself with the design of the movable furniture, or at least the more eye-catching items. There was no consistent movement in this direction but once Le Brun had demonstrated at the French royal palaces and in certain Parisian *hôtels* how much more satisfactory a unified concept could be, ambitious architects began to try to exert an influence along the same lines. As far as we know, Daniel Marot was the first architect to apply this unifying principle to interior decoration in England and Holland, but the generation before—men like Sir William Bruce and Hugh May, for instance—seem to have taken a lively interest in interior embellishment and, even if they had to work through others (e.g. May supervised Verrio, and his team of decorators that included Grinling Gibbons, on the embellishment of important schemes at Windsor Castle), they may well have influenced the final appearance more than we can appreciate at present. One suspects that Inigo Jones, back in the 1620s and 1630s, cannot have been content to have his neatly ordered schemes ruined by the introduction of the ordinary run of clumsy Jacobean furniture. Something more elegant and in keeping must surely have been devised. The stools to be seen in the well-known view of the Earl of Arundel's famous sculpture gallery are Italian in form and may have been imported from Italy but Jones would have been perfectly capable of designing furniture of that kind, just as he could devise theatrical settings or costumes for masques. And there is evidence that suggests he may have relied quite considerably on men like Francis Cleyn to

I. (above right) The Dutch *haute bourgeoisie* adopted increasingly Frenchified ways in the third quarter of the century. There is a strong measure of French elegance in this scene of about 1670 showing the interior of a Dutch house in the country.

II. (right) Views of English seventeenth-century interiors are extremely rare but this charming picture of about 1638 is one of the earliest representations in colour of a suite of furniture (bed and seat-furniture) decorated in a unified manner.

contrive detailed decoration and even furniture that was suitable for the novel kind of interior architecture he was introducing (Plate 52).[1]

This is a big question that needs a great deal more investigation by architectural historians, but especially by those who can think of how buildings looked when they were completely finished, with all their furnishings in place. It is not sufficient for this purpose to view buildings merely as compilations of building materials rigged up according to certain rules into façades and spatial units. Architecture is far more than that and the seventeenth century architect was aware of it. Studying Vitruvius was all very well but people had to live in the buildings architects contrived. As Sir Francis Bacon so sensibly observed, 'Houses are built to Live in, and not to Looke on: Therefore let Use bee preferred before Uniformitie; Except where both may be had.'[2]

Even when it comes to the planning of houses, architectural historians have tended to think primarily in spatial terms and all too rarely help us understand how the great houses they study were actually supposed to be used. The rooms have different names but what purpose did each type of room serve? Were visitors to the house meant to see them in any particular order and, if so, why? These and related questions are only beginning to be answered. A seminal essay was H. Murray Baillie's on 'Etiquette and the Planning of the State Apartments in Baroque Palaces'.[3] This explains why the sequence of rooms in seventeenth-century royal palaces in England, France and Germany followed certain patterns and how these patterns varied in points of detail in the three countries as a result of variations in ceremonial at the respective courts. The subject has been greatly extended by

52. A chair from Holland House, said by Horace Walpole 'undoubtedly' to have been designed by Francis Cleyn. Such Italianate furniture would have suited the kind of Classical interior being devised for the English court and its immediate circle during the second quarter of the century by Inigo Jones and those, like Cleyn, who were associated with him.

III. (left) The State Bedchamber at Ham House as it must have looked in 1680. A small-scale reconstruction based on a careful study of the contemporary inventories, supported by the kind of evidence that is presented in this book. As the state bed, the balustrade, the tapestries and the chairs no longer survive, it is not possible to restore the room itself to its original guise.

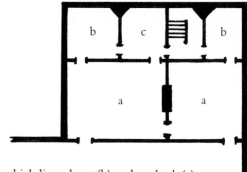

53. The basic formula for an apartment, with bedchamber (a) behind which lie a closet (b) and *garderobe*(c).

54. Approach to a state bedchamber through a sequence of rooms with doors *en enfilade*. Note how the chimneypieces face one as one progresses. The bed was considered so important that its position is commonly shown on plans of the period, as here. *Salle* (a), antechamber (b), bedchamber (c), closet (d), *garderobe* (e). There is a smaller apartment on the other side of the staircase with only a bedchamber (f) and closet (g). In the symmetrical wing beyond the Gallery (h) lies a chapel (j).

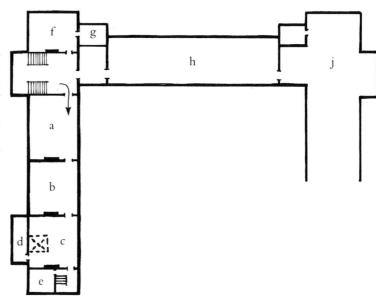

55. Twin principal apartments as shown in a French book of architecture in 1647. Vestibule (a), antechambers (b), bedchambers (c), closets (d), *garderobe* (e) which has a bed in it, presumably for a lady-in-waiting. A subsidiary apartment has an antechamber serving as *salle à manger* (g) with bedchamber (h) which has an alcove and *garderobe* (j) beyond. The gallery (f) occupies the opposite wing.

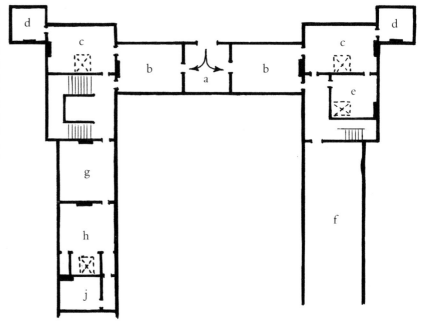

Girouard who, in his entertaining and informative book on great country houses,[4] has surveyed the whole organisation of these buildings and how this affected their planning from mediaeval times down to the present day. A chapter has also been devoted to the matter in Fowler and Cornforth's *English Decoration in the 18th Century*.[5] The reader is referred to these works for information on this fascinating and still not at all well understood subject. Here I shall only discuss it in so far as it affects interior decoration.

The arrangements made at court set the pattern for the great aristocratic families, and their arrangements were in turn imitated by those beneath them in rank—each according to his means. In royal palaces, the king had an apartment, a suite of rooms in which he resided. The principal room was the bedchamber which visitors approached through other rooms to which they were admitted according to their status and where the ceremonial of court life was performed (Plate 60). Behind the bedchamber were private rooms to which the monarch could retire. The high estate of the monarch was symbolised by the State Bed that formed the focal point of the State Bedchamber, and also by a throne and canopy (sometimes called 'an Estate' or 'Cloth of State') in the Presence Chamber. In the houses of the great nobility, where one might expect to have the king or queen coming to stay, a State Apartment had to be provided and it was arranged along similar lines, with a great symbolic bed at the culminating point of its sequence of rooms (Plates 54 and 59). Unless the monarch or an ambassador, or someone else of exceptionally high rank, were staying in the house, the State Bed was apparently not slept in, although the State Apartment was used for ceremonial occasions by the owner of the house—he 'held state' there.[6]

'You cannot have a Perfect Pallace,' wrote Francis Bacon, 'except you have two sevrall Sides; a Side for the Banquet ... And a Side for the household; the One for Feasts and Triumphs and the Other for Dwelling.'[7] Bacon is here saying that one side of a house should contain the State Apartment while the other should house the family. One should separate the ceremonial section in a grand house from the domestic part. The former was decked out in as impressive a manner as possible while the domestic quarters were rather less splendid but, depending on the inclinations and circumstances of the owner, might still be furnished with considerable opulence. These two distinct sets of rooms were actually more often to be found on different floors rather than in separate wings. In the sixteenth century and seventeenth century the State Apartments were normally on the first or even on the second floor, the domestic and family rooms being below. In the eighteenth century, this order was usually reversed so that the state rooms came to be on the raised *piano nobile*, with a view over the grounds, and the family then actually lived upstairs or sometimes in a wing. There were several permutations but all that needs concern us here is that there was this differentiation between the state and domestic apartments, and this difference in the status of the rooms came to be reflected in their décor.

In a royal palace an apartment was also set aside for the queen (Plate 61) and, because she usually symbolised an alliance with another country, she had to be treated with great respect and accorded much dignity. Her apartment was therefore usually almost as large and as grand as that of her husband. In some very large country houses, where they expected to have to entertain both the king and the

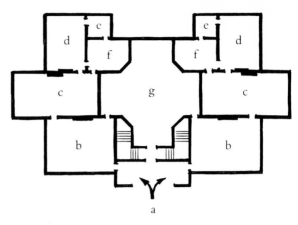

56. French principles of planning applied to a Dutch *maison de plaisance* (the Huis ten Bosch) built by Frederik Hendrik, Prince of Orange, and his consort, Amalia van Solms, in the second quarter of the century. Entrance hall (a), antechambers (b), bedchambers (c), great closets (d), little closets (e), *garderobes* (f) and saloon (g) (the *Oranjezaal* decorated with allegorical paintings honouring the House of Orange).

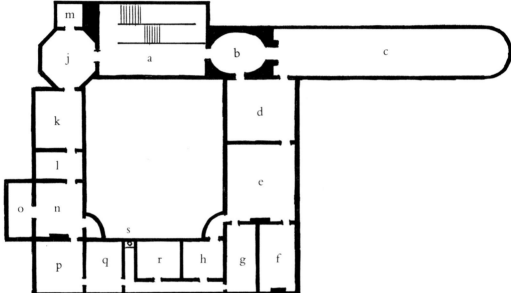

57. At the Hôtel Lambert in Paris, begun about 1640, ingenious planning enabled magnificence to be combined with great convenience. In spite of its complexity, the conventional sequence is maintained for the two principal apartments. Staircase (a), vestibule (b), gallery (c) decorated by Le Brun, antechamber (d), bedchamber (e), closet—the famous *Cabinet des Muses* decorated by Le Sueur (f), closet (g) and *garderobe* (h). Also antechamber (j), bedchamber (k), closet (l), *garderobe* (m). A subsidiary apartment (n–q) lies behind, as does a 'chambre pour les domestiques malades' (r) and a close-stool room (s).

queen, two equal State Apartments were provided[8] but most large houses were content to have just the single 'Great Apartment', as it was sometimes called (Plate 54). However, the owner and his wife also had an apartment each,[9] in the family section of the house. These consisted of the same general sequence of rooms leading to a grand bedchamber but they were naturally rather less formal than the rooms of the State Apartments. Faced with the need to incorporate such twin apartments in the ground-plan of a great house, the architects who were seeking to bring Classical order to their buildings seized upon the genial idea of making them into two equal apartments disposed symmetrically about a large central room lying on the central axis of the house (Plate 55). This plan was even adopted in quite small houses like

Ham House (as altered in the 1670s) where the Duke and Duchess had similar suites to either side of a central room, in this case a dining room, on the ground floor.

As well as the State Apartment and the suites of the owner and his wife, there would often be several other less important apartments[10] in a grand house—which could be used, for instance, by the eldest son, or the widowed mother, or an unmarried sister. The younger sons and the officers of the household—the steward, comptroller, tutor, gentleman usher, gentlewoman of the bedchamber, gentleman of the horse, etc.—had rooms that were a good deal less splendid but might still have closets attached so that they were essentially small private suites. The status of any room could readily be estimated by the richness of its appointment. The value of the textiles used for the upholstery in each case was usually the best indication but the rest of the furnishings tended to be commensurate. At Ham House, which still furnishes us with such excellent examples of seventeenth-century practice to this day, we find the most important rooms are those for which silver-handled fire-irons were provided; less important rooms have fire-irons with brass handles, or simply of iron.

Ordinary servants slept all over the place, often close to their place of work. The porter, whose job it was to guard the main door, slept alongside it. At Ham he had a bed in a chest that he could open out at night. In the early part of the century, personal servants frequently slept on a pallet bed[11] at the doors that gave access to their master's or mistress's bedchambers, thus forming a veritable bodyguard. Other servants slept in all kinds of small cubbyholes that we would today not think fit for human habitation—mere broom-cuboards! The seamstresses, the laundrymaids and other female members of the staff tended to sleep herded together in dormitories in the attic. The furnishing of the rooms occupied by the lower servants was sparse and inexpensive. Few had curtains to their beds, for instance.

Servants were much in evidence during the early part of the century but gradually they were swept away behind the scenes. The higher servants were no longer culled from the gentry and minor nobility; they rose from the ranks. The differentiation between the family and the servants became increasingly apparent and they now began to live apart. But, in order that servants should be able to attend to the wants of the family, a whole system of access-passages had then to be provided.

Let us return to the main rooms and see how they were organised. Girouard has described how the principal rooms in the great mediaeval house had been the hall, where the household dined, and a bedchamber beyond, where the master slept. Gradually this pattern changed so that, by the end of the sixteenth century, there was the hall at the entrance where the servants ate, supervised by the steward who was the chief officer of the household. Behind the hall was a parlour where the lord and his family dined but, on ceremonial occasions or if the lord considered himself especially grand, they would dine in the 'Great Chamber' which was now a large room upstairs. It had long ago lost its bed but the symbolism of high estate might still be embodied by a canopy suspended (in lieu of the bed, as it were) over the lord's 'high chair' or chair of state (Plates 166 and 46). Behind the Great Chamber there was a 'Withdrawing Chamber' to which the fine company could withdraw after a banquet. Here one could relax to some extent, perhaps waiting while the Great Chamber was cleared for dancing or some other form of entertainment. Behind the Withdrawing Chamber lay the State Bedchamber which contained the symbolic

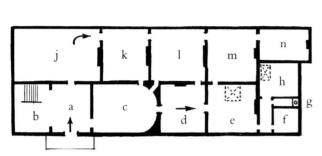

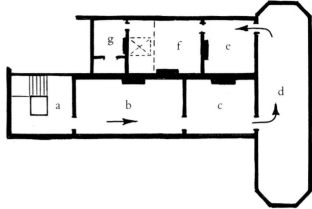

58. A late seventeenth-century project for a Parisian hôtel incorporating a *grand cabinet* (l) among the reception rooms. The direction of progress is indicated by the facing chimneypieces (j–n). Vestibule (a), staircase (b), *salle à manger* (c), antechamber (d), bedchamber (e), *petit garderobe* (f), *le lieu* (so named) for the close-stool (g), *garderobe* (h). Alongside run the receptions rooms: the *Grande salle* (j), antechamber (k), *grand cabinet* (l), *cabinet* (m), and *arrière cabinet* (n).

59. Diagram of the state-room sequence at Ham House. The sequence of the 1630s comprised the staircase (a), great dining room (b), with-drawing room (c), and gallery (d). To this was added in the 1670s a modern sequence with an antechamber (e), state bedchamber (f), called 'The Queens Bedchamber', and closet (g) with an alcove for the sleeping chairs, see Colour Plate XVI, opposite p. 290.

State Bed (Plate 54). And behind that were more private rooms called closets. The family used these grand rooms on formal occasions (the main meal of the day was often a formal occasion surrounded with much ceremony)[12] but had their own lodgings downstairs, while lesser lodgings for people of varying rank were tucked into the remaining spaces.

This was the picture around 1600: between the Great Chamber and the State Bedchamber there was already one room, a withdrawing chamber. The tendency thereafter was to increase the number of reception rooms between the Great Chamber, which now came to be renamed 'The Saloon', and the bedchamber. In a royal palace such rooms might be called 'presence chambers' and 'audience chambers' and might have thrones with canopies set up in them (Plate 60), but in the great aristocratic houses they were called antechambers (Plates 54–59). An important house from the 1670s onwards, therefore, would be entered via a hall, which was no longer used for dining (even by the lower servants who had by this time been moved out of sight to a 'servants' hall'), up a grand staircase on which architects now began to bestow much ingenuity, through a saloon, a withdrawing room, an antechamber (so called because it came *before* the bedchamber), to the bedchamber with its great bed and its small private rooms beyond—closets, *garderobes* and dressing-rooms. Naturally there were variations on this pattern at different houses, and architects were kept busy thinking out clever ways of arranging the different rooms to best advantage (Plates 57 and 58).

Each room in this sequence was more elegantly appointed than that which lay before it, so anyone progressing through the sequence found the décor increasingly magnificent until the culmination was reached in the splendour of the bedchamber.[13] The impact of this sequence of splendour could be enhanced by

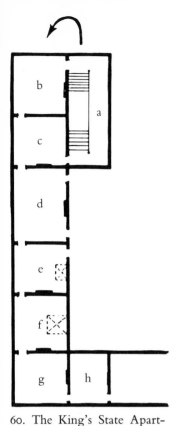

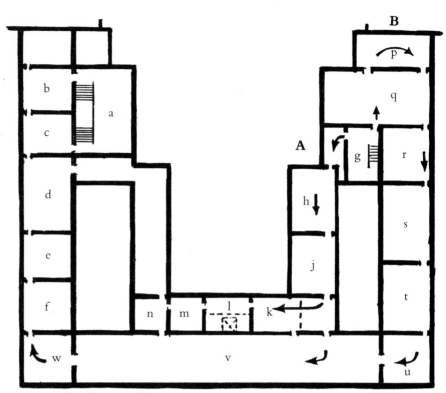

60. The King's State Apartment (*Les Grands Appartements*) at Versailles as built in the 1670s. The room-sequence advanced to the State Bedchamber (f), and a canopy or cloth of estate (see p. 57) was set up in the Antechamber (e). Louis XIV at this stage actually slept in a small bedchamber behind this sequence (h). Main staircase, *Escalier des Ambassadeurs* (a); reception room, *Salon de Vénus* (b); reception room, *Salon de Diane* (c), guardchamber, *Salon de Mars* (d); Antechamber or Throne Room, *Salon de Mercure* (e); State Bedchamber, *Salon d'Apollon* (f); great closet, *grand Cabinet*, served as Privy Council Chamber (g); King's Private bedchamber (h) with minor closets attached.

61. The King's and the Queen's Apartments (**A** & **B**) at Versailles at the end of the century. The approach was now from the 'Queen's Staircase' (g) whence one could enter the King's Apartment (A: h–n) or the Queen's (B: p–t). Added was the *Grande Galerie* (v) with *salons* at each end, linking both apartments with the old sequence of *Grands Appartements* (a–f; see Plate 60) through which one now progressed in reverse, the ceremonial roles of (e) and (f) then being exchanged. The King now actually slept in his state bedchamber (l) which lay at the axial centre of the palace.

The King's Apartment (**A**): King's Guardchamber (h); *Antichambre du grand couvert* (j) where the King dined in public; *Antichambre de l'Oeil de Boeuf* (k) until 1701 comprising the King's Bedchamber and a smaller antechamber; the King's Bedchamber from 1701 (l) formerly the *Salon du Roi*; the Great Closet or Privy Council Chamber, *Cabinet de Conseil* (m); the King's gemstone collection, *Cabinet des Thermes* (n).

The Queen's Apartment (**B**); the Queen's Guard chamber, at this stage divided up as an apartment for Mme de Maintenon (p); the Great Guard Chamber (q); Antechamber (r); Great Closet (s) (with a canopy); curiously this closet came *before* the Queen's Bedchamber (t).

62. Design for a chimney piece by Pierre Collot, probably from his *Pieces d'architecture où sont comprises plusiers sortes de cheminées . . .* published in Paris in 1633. Such French suites of engraved proposals for architectural details were immensely influential.

63. French design for a chimneypiece by Jean Cotelle, which is included in a book of designs that probably belonged to Inigo Jones (see Plate 44). Coloured red and blue with touches of gold, this design is a reminder of how colourful French, and no doubt most, interiors were around 1630.

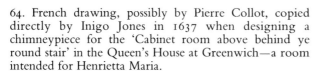

64. French drawing, possibly by Pierre Collot, copied directly by Inigo Jones in 1637 when designing a chimneypiece for the 'Cabinet room above behind ye round stair' in the Queen's House at Greenwich—a room intended for Henrietta Maria.

arranging the rooms in a line so that the connecting doorways were *en enfilade* and one could look right down the whole row of rooms (Colour Plate IV, Plate 54).[14] This was the commonest arrangement from about 1630 onwards. The doorways were placed close to the windows so that the main part of the room lay to one side as one proceeded along the line. There could be no doubt about the direction in which such a sequence was to be viewed because the chimneypieces were always set on the wall facing one—if they were not on the wall opposite the windows (e.g. Plates 54 and 60).[15] At any rate they were never to be found on the 'back' wall that one left behind as one proceeded, except when the architect had had to adapt an existing building. For it is no simple matter to move a fireplace: the flue is built into the masonry of the wall and there is often a massive, protruding chimney-breast as well. One can shift a chimneypiece a few feet to one side or the other, perhaps; but one cannot easily move it to the opposite side of the room. When Louis XIV reversed the direction of approach to the *Grand Appartement* at Versailles, the chimneypieces in three of the principal rooms (including the State Bedchamber and Throne Room) could not be seen by a visitor advancing through the sequence unless he turned and looked behind him (cf. Plates 60 and 61).

Having worked out a satisfactory ground plan, the architect could then proceed to think of the interior architecture. If he was good at his job he would consider the proportions of each important room as a spatial unit and he would try and dispose the fireplace, doors, windows and other essential fixed features in harmonious arrangements. Architectural historians deal with these matters in their works and what follows in this chapter is intended mainly to supplement their findings. It is not meant to be a consistent survey of the fixed elements of interior architecture and their decoration.

Since the chimneypiece was the principal feature of the room—the seat of warmth, light and therefore, by implication, of life itself—it is hardly surprising that architects took a lot of trouble to make it as striking as possible (Colour Plate V). In consequence this was a field in which demand for fresh inspiration was particularly strong. De l'Orme had included some designs for chimneypieces in his great architectural treatise of 1567[16] but separate sets of designs for these features began to become available in Paris in the 1630s. The most famous was that of Jean Barbet (Plates 65 and 66, see also Plate 1) but other selections were published from that point onwards.[17] So popular, indeed, was Barbet's *Livre d'architecture,* which first came out in Paris in 1632, that it was re-issued already in 1641 in both Paris and Amsterdam[18] while a set of simplified proposals based on his designs appeared under the title *Poorten en Schoorsteen-mantels en Autare* [Doorways, Chimney-mantels and Altars] at about the same time (Plate 67).[19] It must not, incidentally, be thought that every room had a fireplace in the seventeenth century. The Princess Palatine complained that, at the Château de Saint-Cloud, 'many of the rooms my people are lodged in have no fireplaces, which makes them unbearable in winter'.[20]

Sixteenth-century chimneypieces were massive structures, composed of architectural elements, with a large opening which was apt to be draughty. The seventeenth century saw the evolution in France of a form that was light and elegant, and totally lacked the overpowering character of its antecedants. This was brought about by a general refinement of the individual elements making up the whole. First, the great weight of sculptural ornament on the chimneybreast was tidied up. There

65 & 66. (above) Two designs for chimneypieces from Jean Barbet's *Livre d'architecture*, first published in 1632 and so popular that a second edition (from which the present reproductions are taken) was brought out in Paris and Amsterdam in 1641. Barbet's book was dedicated to Cardinal Richelieu and claimed to show 'ce qu'il y a de beau dans Paris'. Inigo Jones used this work as a source of inspiration. See also Plate 1.

67. A simplified version of a Parisian design published in Amsterdam, presumably early in the 1640s. See Plate 160 where a chimneypiece in this style is depicted.

68. (above left) an example of the less over-powering form of chimneypiece that was beginning to be installed in fashionable Parisian houses in the 1650s. Engraving from Jean Le Pautre's *Cheminées à la moderne*, 1661.

69. (above right) The massive form of chimneypiece, albeit now more compact, continued in favour well into the third quarter of the century, as this title-page of a suite of designs for *Cheminées à l'Italienne* dated 1665 shows.

70. A chimneypiece of the compact model evolved towards the end of the century, with a panel of glass in the chimney-breast. Designs like this not only helped to spread the new fashion but gave information about fire-dogs, fire-backs and *garnitures de cheminées*.

71. Daniel Marot helping to spread the French
fashion. The title-page of his *Nouvelle cheminées à
panneaux de glace à la manière de France . . .,*
published in Amsterdam about 1695.

72. Daniel Marot modernising the Dutch
over-hanging form of chimneypiece late in
the century. From his *Nouveaux lievre de
cheminées à la Hollandoise.*

is still a certain lack of cohesion in Jean Barbet's designs of 1632 which are based on
what was then recently completed work in Paris (Plates 65 and 66).[21] By 1665,
however, the process had reached a point where Jean Le Pautre could publish a set of
'cheminées à l'italienne' which are proposals for compact chimneypieces of the
sculptural type, usually with a central frame (oval, rectangular or fancily shaped)
flanked by two figures (Plate 69). This form, also known as *à la Romaine,* was by now
distinguishable from the new French form, *à la Moderne,* for which Le Pautre had
brought out some designs in 1661 (Plate 68).[22] These reflect the new tendency
towards lower openings for the fireplace, and often generally smaller openings, as
well as a great simplification of the ornament of the chimneybreast, which
ultimately came to be decorated with a simple panel en suite with those of the walls
alongside, while the fireplace surround became a simple if bold moulding. As
Blondel remarked in 1683 'l'on faisoit cy-devant beaucoup de dépense pour la
structure & les ornmens des cheminées que l'on chargeoit excessivement: Mais
presentement on les rend beaucoup plus legères, & l'on les trouve plus belles dans leur
simplicité' [formerly one spent much on the building and decoration of
chimneypieces which were excessively loaded with ornament; but today they are far
less massive and, with their simple lines, seem much more graceful].[23]

   The great breakthrough in lightening the chimneypiece, however, was brought
about by means of mirror-glass. A Venetian looking-glass had apparently been set
into the panelling above a fireplace at Fontainebleau as early as 1601 but this seems to
have been an isolated phenomenon. Glasses were not otherwise embedded in the
chimney-breast until very late in the seventeenth century. Fiske Kimball suggested
that the earliest executed scheme incorporating such a feature was the new *Chambre
du Roi* at Versailles that was carried out in 1684 (Plate 82).[24] Once glass was being

66

73. One of Marot's *Nouvelle cheminées faittes en plusiers en droits de la Hollande et autres provinces*. The design on the title-page has a fire-back displaying the royal arms of England and Marot describes himself as 'Architecte des appartements de sa Majesté Britannique'.

74. Inscribed in the corner 'cheminée à l'angloise' and perhaps showing a chimneypiece for one of the English palaces for which Marot devised schemes of decoration. Note the royal crown.

used to face walls in fashionable rooms (Plate 80), it quickly crept out onto the chimney-breast, but such a feature is not shown in published engravings earlier than the 1690s, notably in Pierre Le Pautre's *Cheminées et Lambris à la mode* (Plate 70) which the title explains have been 'executez dans les nouveaux Bâtiments de Paris' [erected in the most recent buildings in Paris]. In 1697 the Swedish architect Nicodemus Tessin, was advising Countess Piper on how to do up her house in Stockholm in the latest French taste and recommended 'pour les chiminées je les ferrois de glaces . . . du haut en bas; c'est le goust qui regne et qui est d'autant mieux fondé qu'avec 2 ou 4 bougies un appartement par la reverbération se trouve plus éclairé et plus guay qu'un autre avec 12' [for the chimneypieces I would make them with mirrors . . . from top to bottom; that is the taste that prevails here and which is all the more justified since with two or four candles a room, on account of the reflection, is lighter and more cheerful than another with twelve].[25] The magical effect of candles reflected in numerous panels of glass was still something of a novelty at this time, since relatively large plates of glass could not be produced at all easily.

At the end of the century, Daniel Marot, the Parisian emigré architect working in Holland for William of Orange, published a set of engravings in his personal variant of current French taste which he entitled *Nouvelle cheminées à panneaux de glace à la manière de France*, and there are chimneypieces in this style to be seen at Hampton Court and Kensington Palace, as well as in Holland (Plate 71). He also published a *Nouveaux lievre de cheminées à la Hollondoise* at about the same time; this will have been to satisfy conservative tastes in Holland, for they are all of the traditional Dutch type with a boldly protruding chimney-breast (with a mantelshelf) forming a large hood above the fireplace which is open on three sides (Plate 72). The French form was only open to the front.

75. French design for a ceiling signed by Jean Cotelle and dated 1647 (see also Colour Plate VI). It is signed by two master craftsmen at least one of whom was employed on Crown buildings in France. The crown above the cipher seems to be a royal one. This is from the album of drawings which was probably once in Inigo Jones' drawing office. Many of the other Cotelle ceiling-designs in the album are those actually published in his *Livre des divers ornemens pour Plafonds* . . .

The large Dutch openings lent themselves well to facing with tiles which were both decorative and easy to clean. There are numerous illustrations of such fireplaces in Dutch paintings (Plate 198) and they need no description here, but the practice of using tiles in this way spread into northern France and to England. Pepys had several fireplaces 'done with Dutch tiles' in the 1660s[26] and there are fireplaces faced with Dutch delftware tiles still to be seen at Ham House, dating from the 1670s. It is noteworthy that some of the Ham fireplaces have undecorated white tiles (i.e. without the blue patterns that one so readily associates with this kind of tile) which, however, are haphazardly tinted and range from the normal creamy white of the tin-oxide glaze to pale mauve, pink and grey—very different from the harsh, even whiteness of modern bathroom tiles. These 'white' tiles are by no means set up in the least important rooms; for instance the Duchess of Lauderdale had them in her own bedchamber and Sir Roger Pratt ordered 'white tyles' for his withdrawing room in the 1660s.[27] But English interest in using Dutch tiles for lining fireplaces started well before the Civil War, for we find Sir William Brereton took a good deal of trouble, during his stay in Amsterdam in 1634–5, to acquire a set of such tiles which were decorated with soldiers of various kinds, and then made careful note of how they were to be assembled back in England. 'Yesterday', he wrote, 'we bought four-score painted stones for one chimney; these postures of foot-men for the back of the chimney: care to be taken these to be placed half on one side of the hob[hearth], half on the other; half faces one way on one side, and so on the other side; drummers and officers to be placed in the most eminent places.' With the infantry thus marshalled facing each other, he could lay the 'Horsemen's postures for an hearth; fifty to be placed with as much care and in same manner as the other.' Brereton also bought a set of fifty flowered tiles and another of fifty birds for two more fireplaces. 'The horsemen and footmen cost nine gilders an hundred; the birds and flowers cost four gilders an hundred.'[28]

After the chimneypiece, the most noticeable feature of a room was usually the ceiling, and architects certainly gave much thought to the devising of striking ceilings in the seventeenth century. I will not say much about them because this is an aspect of interior decoration that has received much attention from art historians already.[29] However, let it just be said that here too the French published sets of designs to assist architects. The compositions of Jean Cotelle, for instance, seem to have inspired Inigo Jones and his followers (Colour Plate VI and Plates 44 and 75),[30] and Jean Le Pautre's ceiling designs were likewise influential.

While we know a good deal about the form modelled plasterwork ceilings could take in the seventeenth century we are still far from certain how they were decorated. Today we almost invariably see them painted white but were they originally so? In humbler houses, where the modelling was fairly simple, they no doubt were just white—but the white was far from pure and would almost certainly be regarded as a very light grey today. Grander ceilings sometimes had gilded elements—crowns and coronets, ciphers, ribbons binding festoons and wreaths, and similar features. And then there were even more elaborate schemes with

76. An architect's suggestion for the decoration of a ceiling. Inscribed 'for ye vault of ye Ceelings of ye Roomes East and West end' at Wilton, 1649, in the handwriting of John Webb, Inigo Jones' pupil and successor. Such a drawing would be used as a basis for large-scale drawings from which the actual painting was to be executed—in this case by Matthew Gooderick or Emmanuel de Critz.

77. The early Le Brun style of ceiling-painting translated to England. The ceiling of the Duchess of Lauderdale's magnificent 'White Closet' at Ham House dating from the latter 1670s, painted by Antonio Verrio who had worked in Paris for a while around 1671. The marbled surround is red and white, precisely echoing the actual marble on the fireplace and window-sill in this charming little room.

polychrome effects, fruit and foliage being coloured naturalistically. This is a big subject that needs a great deal of careful study but useful indications of contemporary practice may be found from studying the *trompe l'oeil* imitations of plasterwork ceilings that are painted on flat ceilings faced with canvas or boards, many of which survive in Sweden although examples may also be seen in Holland and no doubt elsewhere. The white of the Swedish ceilings of this class, at any rate, is invariably grey.

When it comes to mural decoration, one can once again say that a good deal has been written about panelling and about the better sorts of decorative painting, but something more should be said about the finishing treatment given to panelling, even though a great deal more work needs to be done on this aspect of the matter.

The two principal timbers used for panelling in the seventeenth century were pine and oak. Deal was almost invariably painted[31] but oak was more often left uncovered except sometimes for a sealing coat of varnish.[32] In England and Holland, the grain and colour of oak was generally admired and it was mostly left to speak for itself although, during the first half of the century the bare wood often served as a background for painted or gilded ornament (arabesques, strapwork, coats of arms), while during the second half particularly rich panelling might have gilded details on carved mouldings and enrichments. If Evelyn can be trusted there ought to be less bold veining in oak panelling of the later part of the century, for he tells us that 'curiously veined' oak panels were 'of much esteem in former times, till the finer grain'd Spanish and Norway timber came among us'.[33] In France in the seventeenth century, on the other hand, oak panelling was usually painted (i.e. it was treated in the same way as deal, without ceremony) although in a few fashionable houses at the end of the century one might find rooms boisé à la capucine, which was the term used to describe varnished oak panelling because it seemed as stark as the walls of the cell of a Capucin monk.[34] Possibly this is an example of English influence on France.

A number of rooms in Elizabethan England were faced with unpainted oak panelling that was inlaid with patterns of contrasting woods. The fashion for decorating wood panels with such intarsia work originated in Italy in the late fifteenth century and was subsequently adopted in Germany and the Low Countries. German panelling of this class could be immensely elaborate but English examples were mostly rather simple. An exception seems to have been the panelling in the High Great Chamber in the old house at Chatsworth which was 'set forth with planets' executed 'in coulored woods markentrie'—the planets rendered in marquetry (or intarsia) of coloured woods.[35] Another room was 'very fayre waynscotted with coulored woods set out with portals [i.e. arcading or arched patterns] and some albaster and other stone'. Some detached panels of intarsia representing formalised architecture now preserved at Hardwick Hall may be from this room. Like most work of this sort, dirt and fading has effaced the contrast between the woods so it is difficult to visualise the original effect.[36] Such work went out of fashion in the seventeenth century but a certain amount of simply inlay (e.g. star-shaped patterns) was used in panelling late in the century. Panelling of oak with decoration carved in relief in the centre of each field was admired in France in the sixteenth century. It may well be that the 'French pannell' mentioned in the inventories of Chatsworth and Cockesden of, respectively, 1601 and 1610 was of this type.[37] During the seventeenth century the carving on panelling in France was for the most part confined to the surrounding mouldings while the fields remained plain and therefore lent themselves especially well to painted decoration—landscapes, portraits, etc.

Apart from oak and pine, other timbers were occasionally used for wall-panelling in the seventeenth century. The hall at Chippenham was 'wanscoated with wallnut tree, the pannells and rims round with mulberry tree that is a lemon coullour, and the mouldings beyond it round are of a sweete outlandish wood not much differing from cedar but of finer graine'.[38] The Great Chamber in the Mauritshuis at The Hague, built in about 1633, was panelled in 'a most rare Indian wood' that probably

71

78. Design for mural decoration, perhaps of a closet since the scale seems to be small. The lozenge-shaped mascle was the device of the Princesse de Rohan who was carrying out important schemes of interior decoration in Paris in the 1630s. The blank panels were probably to be filled with inset paintings. This is one of the designs that are likely to have been known to Inigo Jones, indeed, there is no reason why he should not actually have been responsible for procuring them from France.

79. (right) Proposal for mural decoration, perhaps by Jean Cotelle; 1630s? Once again this is from the collection that was probably in Inigo Jones' drawing-office. It seems to be for a closet, the owner of which sported a coronet and had the initials R.M.

came from Brazil.[39] However most of the exotic timber effects were obtained by means of graining (i.e. painted imitation of a timber) executed on deal panelling which was in itself relatively inexpensive. Thus one finds imitations of olive-wood and cedar at Ham House (Plate 314), a parlour at Broadlands was 'wanscoated and painted a cedar coullour',[40] while Sir Roger Pratt mentions also the imitation of 'prince's wood' which was a form of rosewood.[41] However, more commonly the imitations were of oak and walnut rather than of the fancy woods just mentioned.

The only type of wood Sir Balthazar Gerbier mentions in his list of prices for particular forms of paintwork is walnut; the other woods are merely 'timber colour'.[42]

Closely related to graining, of course, is marbling and this was equally popular in the seventeenth century. Indeed, these deceits might be practised in very grand settings. For instance, the Queen's attiring chamber at Denmark House had a chimney-piece painted in 1610–11 'with divers culloured stones as rance [i.e. red-and-white marble], white and black marble, serpentine and purfire'.[43] At Newby, Celia Fiennes noted that 'the best roome was painted just like marble, few roomes were hung' (i.e. with textiles), while at Barmiston there was a parlour 'with plaine wanscoate painted in veines like marble with white streaks'.[44] Remarkable examples of seventeenth-century marbling may still be seen at Dyrham, Ham House (Colour Plate XVI and Plate 77) and Belton.

A lot of work is currently being done on ancient paintwork and we shall soon be a great deal better informed about the composition of seventeenth-century paints and the techniques used in their application.[45] Nothing really useful can be said about colours in the space available here beyond propounding the general rule that colours were at first bold, and often in the primary range, becoming less strident towards the end of the century. Tessin was informed in 1693 that in Paris 'On ne peint les chambres boisées, les portes, les volets, les jassis [chassis], les plafonds, les portes, etc. que de blanc avec le filet d'or ou sans or' [One no longer paints panelled rooms, doors, shutters, window-frames, ceilings, doors, etc. anything but white with or without narrow gilded mouldings],[46] but this fashion did not reach other countries until into the next century.

Before moving on from the subject of panelling, it should be noted that certain important rooms at Hardwick which were hung with textile materials had the sections of wall beneath the windows faced with panelling, presumably because any hangings put there might easily be damaged by rain or condensation. In the same way, Sir Roger Pratt stipulated that there should be 'wainscote under ye window' in his own and his wife's bedchamber when he was building Ryston Hall.[47]

Localised protection of walls could also be obtained by means of tiles. The Dutch frequently fitted a line of delftware tiles along the bottom of a plastered wall so as to form a shallow skirting that could not be marked by boots and chair-legs. Sometimes a similar line of tiles was set vertically on each side of a door-case to ward against finger-marks. Occasionally larger areas were faced with tiles. We have already spoken of tiled fireplaces and one sometimes sees in Dutch paintings a section of wall panelled with tiles.[48] Queen Mary II of England had a complete room faced with tiles, a dairy at Hampton Court which was built shortly before her death in 1694 and had large blue and white Delft tiles handsomely decorated with ornament designed by Daniel Marot.[49] The Trianon de Porcelaine, incidentally, which was built in the park at Versailles in 1670–71, was faced outside with tiles of delftware (i.e. faience, not porcelain) but the interior was of plasterwork painted in imitation of Chinese blue and white porcelain and tiles were, it seems, used only rather sparingly inside.[50]

We have already considered the use of mirror-glass in connection with the evolution of the chimneypiece in the late seventeenth century. Now something must be said about its use as a facing for walls in general.

Catherine de Medici (1519–89) had a *Cabinet de Miroirs* faced with 109 'miroirs plains de Venise . . . enchassez dans le lambris' [plain Venetian mirrors . . . set into the panelling].[51] The plates must have been quite small and the woodwork of the panelling into which they were set probably still remained the predominant feature. This little room seems to have been unique and, although we noted that Marie de Medici had a Venetian looking-glass[52] set into the chimney-breast of a fireplace at Fontainebleau in 1601, it seems that, for a while, those who wanted to achieve a striking effect with mirrors did so with looking-glasses suspended in front of the panelling or textile hangings. Francis Bacon spoke in 1624 of 'Rich Cabinets, Daintily Paved, Richly Hanged, Glased with Crystalline Glasse . . .',[53] indicating that the walls were clad with striking textiles and suggesting that the glass element was therefore subsidiary—just possibly inset but more probably loose in front. A ball was given at the Hôtel de Chevreuse in 1633 in a room that was 'tous revêtus de grands miroirs d'argent, de tapisseries exquises et garnis d'autres meubles dont la richesse ne trouve point ailleurs de comparaison' [completely dressed with large silver-framed looking-glasses and exquisite tapestries, and adorned with other furniture the richness of which has no comparison anywhere].[54] The looking-glasses with silver frames in this sumptuous interior must also have been hanging on the walls along with the tapestries (probably in front of them), but the effect was none the less impressive. The delightful effect such mirrors produced is indeed conveyed in a verse about a party given by the Archbishop of Sens in 1651.

> Cinquante miroirs de Venise,
> Des plus riches et des plus beaux
> Servoient d'agréables tableaux
> Pour representer les figures,
> Les grimaces, les grâces, les apas,
> Les ris, les mains et les bras
> De toute la belle cabale,
> Qu'on festoyoit dans cette sale.[55]

[Fifty of the richest and most beautiful Venetian mirrors serve as delightful pictures displaying the faces, the expressions and poses, the smiles, the graces, the charms, the bosom, the hands and arms of all the fine company that is entertained in this room.]

When 'La Grande Mademoiselle' (Anne, Duchess of Orléans, niece of Louis XIII) was sent into exile at Saint-Fargeau in 1653 she had her closet decorated 'avec quantité de tableaux et mirrors et je croyais avoir fait le plus beau chef d'oeuvre du monde' [with a quantity of pictures and mirrors and I believe it has made the finest masterpiece in the world].[56] She was no doubt putting a brave face on her situation and was trying to imitate effects with which she had been familiar in Paris (Plate 80).

By 1670 or so, however, one could see several rooms in France and England with large areas of wall entirely panelled with mirror-glass. Probably the earliest surviving example is a closet at the Château de Maisons of about 1660 (Plate 81). When, in 1668, Louis XIV did up a luxurious apartment for his new mistress, Madame de la Vallière, he had her *Grand Cabinet* faced with mirror-glass and we can be sure that this represented the most advanced taste of the day.[57] The Duchess of Portsmouth (Louise de Querouaille) and Nell Gwynne, the mistresses of Charles II, both had closets decorated in this new way, but already in 1667 Sir Samuel Morland

80. The closet attached to the principal bedchamber at the Hôtel Lauzun, Paris; about 1660. Instead of paintings inset in the middle band of decoration, panes of mirror-glass are here inserted—still in rather a primitive manner.

81. (right) The *Cabinet aux Miroirs* at the Château de Maisons. François Mansart's architectonic use of mirror-glass in this elegant little room, must have given rise to delighted astonishment when it was new, around 1660. Sir Thomas Browne saw it in 1664 and noted that 'whatsoever way you turn yourself you see an army of your owne selfe' reflected in the 'looking glasses quite round'. Note the elaborate marquetry floor which is apparently contemporary.

had had a room at his house at Vauxhall faced in the same manner.[58] Since it was not yet possible to produce plates of any great size, large areas were faced with abutted plates held in place by studs with large heads overlapping the corners. As was later explained to Tessin, one could fill panels 'de quarrés de glaces de telle grandeur que la depense que vous y voudriez faire permettroit, toutes les dites glaces sans bizeaux proprement jointes et ne composant pour aincy dire qu'une grande glace' [with panes of glass of such a size as the expenditure you have in mind will permit, all the panes being without bevelled edges, neatly juxtaposed so as to make as it were a single large glass].[59] Celia Fiennes saw something like this at Chippenham at the end of the century, describing it as '4 pannells of glass in length and 3 in breadth set together in the wanscoate' while the dining room 'had this looking-glass [i.e. with

panels set together] on the two piers between the three windows; it was from top to bottom 2 pannells in breadth and 7 in length' which means that each pier was faced with fourteen abutting panels forming one large pier-glass.[60]

What struck Celia Fiennes as so amazing about these composite mirrors at Chippenham, however, was that 'it shows one from top to toe'. It seemed incredible to people in the seventeenth century that one should be able to see the whole of oneself in a mirror. This is why rooms like the *Galerie des Glaces* at Versailles were considered so astonishing, for there one could see not only oneself, but the whole splendid company and the superb adornments reflected in the mirror-glass facing of this enormous room (Plate 11).

In 1684 Louis XIV planned a *Petite Galerie* at Versailles which was to be extensively faced with mirror-glass and was to have small brackets fixed to the glazed walls on which his fabulous collection of gemstone vessels could be displayed (Plate 236). The panels were rigged up at the Gobelins but were never erected at Versailles. Is it possible that the young Daniel Marot saw these panels before he was forced to go into exile in Holland? At any rate he created in Holland and England a number of rooms for the display of Mary II's large collection of Oriental porcelain. The engravings published in a suite entitled *Nouvelle cheminées faittes en plusier en droits de la Hollande et autres Provinces, du dessein de D. Marot, Architecte des appartements de sa Majesté Britannique* may perhaps show chimneypieces in rooms at the palaces favoured by the House of Orange in this country and in Holland (Plate 73; see also Plate 238). One engraving has a fire-back with the English royal arms while another is in addition described as 'à l'angloise' (Plate 74). They all have panels of mirror-glass in the French manner, and porcelain on small brackets is much in evidence. When Tessin visited the little palace of Honselaarsdijk, outside The Hague, in 1687, he saw one of the closets of the Princess of Orange (later Queen Mary II of England) which had probably been created the year before by Daniel Marot; it had a ceiling of mirror-glass and the walls were of Oriental lacquer.[61]

Large plates of glass were extremely difficult to make and were therefore very expensive. A plate had only to be a few inches larger to double in cost, so great were the hazards of trying to increase the size.[62] Until the 1660s almost all plate glass came from Venice[63] and when one is told that only something like two hundred cases of this costly material were imported into France each year, one can begin to appreciate why the first glazed closets caused such a sensation. By 1665 the demand for mirror-glass had so increased in France that a *Manufacture des Glaces de Venise* was established in Paris. The factory soon changed its title to *Manufacture Royale des Glaces de Miroirs*, reflecting the royal patronage it enjoyed.[64] It was able to fulfil official orders for mirror-glass by 1670 but the glass, as with all other plate-glass at this time, was produced by the blown method which placed a severe limitation on the size of plate that could be produced. To make larger plates, a new technique had to be invented.

Experiments in the casting of glass plate were carried out in the 1680s and a factory was set up in Paris in 1688 to make glass by this method which seemed to hold much promise. However, it was not until 1691 that four unblemished mirrors of this sort could be presented to Louis XIV. The casting process was laborious and attended by great risk of breakage; the polishing operation was unpleasant and noisy; and the silvering was difficult. By 1700 the French claimed to be able to make a plate 100 × 60 *pouces* in size (a *pouce* was about an inch), but between 1688 and 1699

82. Design for the chimney wall of the *Chambre du Roi* at Versailles; 1684. The large panels of mirror-glass set into the chimney-breast make this one of the earliest examples of what was to become the characteristic French chimneypiece in which the use of glass imparts lightness and grace. In order to obtain a sufficiently large area of glass, several plates had to be juxtaposed.

only eleven mirrors of 80 × 45 *pouces* had been produced and the breakage-rate during manufacture was enormous. Yet, by 1697, the Venetians had recognised that the French were the masters in this field and decided henceforth to confine their production to plates of 20 × 45 *pouces* and below.[65] By contrast, the French plate-glass manufactory was only permitted, by its letters patent of 1688, to produce glass of 60 × 40 *pouces* or more. At first it was allowed to sell broken pieces to foreigners but this was soon seen to be bad for business. In 1691 the firm moved to St. Gobain in Picardy and was shortly after amalgamated with the royal manufactory. Most of the large plates of glass produced right through the next century came from this single factory in Picardy. To the high cost of the product itself, had to be added the cost of transporting it from the point of manufacture to where it was to be set up.

It is hardly surprising that other nations tried to emulate the French but it was a long while before rivals captured any appreciable slice of the market. England, for instance, had sought to prohibit the importation of Venetian glass in 1620 in order to support home production[66] but this was clearly not successful as the prohibition had to be re-introduced in 1664 when the Worshipful Company of Looking-glass makers was incorporated. The Duke of Buckingham's 'glass-house' at Vauxhall enjoyed a certain amount of success. Evelyn claimed that they produced 'looking-glasses far larger and better than any that came from Venice' but they were still using the blown method so only small sizes of plate were obtainable. Robert Hooke, the scientist and architect is said to have taken out a patent for casting glass in 1691 but there is no evidence that any glass was ever produced by his method.[67]

Glass plates might be decorated in several ways. Slips of glass with bevelled edges,

83. Multiple interior shutters in a Parisian house early in the century, with leaded lights.

sometimes cut into fancy shapes, might be applied to the face of the mirror with screws or rivets. These slips were in some cases coloured.[68] One might engrave patterns at the edges that reflected the light in an interesting way.[69] And one could paint compositions on the glass. Catherine de Medici's *Cabinet de Miroirs* had a portrait of her husband painted on the glass that was set over the fireplace.[70] The glass walls of the *Apartement des Attiques*, built at Versailles in 1676, were painted with scenes by Bon Boulogne,[71] and at the end of the century we find Claude Audran painting with arabesques the borders of the mirror-glass panels of the Duchesse de Bouillon's closet.[72] The fashion also spread to England. Jean-Baptiste Monnoyer, who had been brought to England by Lord Montagu but who eventually came to work for Queen Mary, painted a glass at Kensington Palace that was 'tastefully decorated with festoons of flowers'.[73]

I have been discussing glazed wall-panels as part of a survey of fixed mural ornament contributing to the shell of interior architecture. Windows affect mural concepts as well but architectural historians mostly think of windows in terms of façades and their 'fenestration'. They rarely say much about the effect of windows on the interior. Yet again one has to admit that this is a large subject and that one can only touch upon certain aspects here. Madame de Rambouillet has been credited with introducing the tall 'French window' which reached right down to the floor. These 'fenêtres sans appui, qui regnent de haut en bas, depuis son plat-fond jusqu'à son parterre' make a room 'très gaie' and permit 'jouir sans obstacle de l'air, de la vue & du plaisir du jardin' [These windows without sills, which extend from top to bottom, from ceiling to the ground, make a room extremely cheerful and permit one to enjoy without hindrance the air, the view, and the pleasures of the garden].[74] However, this form of window must have been invented some while after the Marquise rebuilt her family house (started 1619).[75]

The question of how light fell in a room was of course of paramount importance and there is good evidence that architects gave much thought to it. Savot explains why libraries, for instance, should face south while Wotton insisted that 'All the principal Chambers of Delight, All Studies and Libraries, be towards the East, for the Morning is a friend to the Muses.' Galleries and 'Repositories for works of rarity in Pictures or other Arts,' on the other hand, should face north as they 'require a steady light'.[76] Dutch painters were obviously interested in the play of light through windows and have recorded the many delightful effects that could be achieved by various combinations of shutters, open or closed, or with curtains drawn across one section (e.g. Plates 110 and 267). For windows during the first half of the century might have tiers of interior shutters (anything up to four tiers, one above the other (Plate 42) although one only fitted shutters up to a height that one could reach—any tier above that would have to have a curtain, if one wanted to exclude light or retain warmth). Indeed, interior shutters served both as insulation and as sun-blinds. Multiple interior shutters remained popular in Holland until the middle of the century but went out of fashion in France rather earlier (Plate 83). Windows with two tiers may be seen in engravings of Parisian interiors by Abraham Bosse, dating from the 1630s (Plate 84).

The earliest shutters consisted of a single leaf swinging on hinges at one side (Plate 133). This simple form had the great disadvantage that it projected into the room and clearly constituted quite a hazard. One could halve this projection by having pairs of shutters swinging from each side so as to meet in the middle of the window when closed, and this form could be made even more compact by arranging that each leaf could be folded back upon itself before it was folded away into a recess in the thickness of the window reveal. Bosse shows this stage evolving with a two-tiered system (Plate 84), but soon shutters of this type running the full height of the window were introduced. These were so much part of the architecture that they no longer appear in inventories. The earlier forms do, on the other hand, sometimes get listed—as 'window shutes', 'shute windows' and 'window leaves'.[77] The 'drawinge windowes' at Hatfield Priory in 1629 were probably also interior shutters and it would seem that they could be lifted off their hinges and stored in summer, for several were stacked in the 'wash-house', others were to be found in the apple loft and more were in the 'Folding Chamber'.[78]

Against the heat of the day one might fit blinds of various kinds, and these are dealt with in Chapter VI, but an effective measure adopted in parts of France was to fit abat-jours—slatted external shutters which excluded sun yet let through a current of air. On bright, sunny days they make a pleasant light indoors. A French edict of 1693 governed the amount abat-jours might project into the street so as not to inconvenience passers-by.[79] To exclude cold, on the other hand, one could fit curtains or mats inside a window, but in the present chapter we need only consider double windows which were certainly known in the late seventeenth century. The Duchess of Lauderdale had them in her closet which is in a rather exposed, eastern

Jey viennent à la haste,   La Cuisine les attire,
Les Enfans de Mardy gras   Soit par coustume, ou par jeu;
Mettre la main à la paste,   Et les bignets les font rire,
S'escrimant à tour de bras. Tandis qu'ils sont pres du feu.

L'HYVER

Monsieur, dict vne Maistresse, Mais cette picotterie,
Si vous touchez mon tetin,   Se termine incontinent,
Je repandray de la graisse   Et toute leur raillerie,
Sur vostre habit de satin.   Est de Caresme-prenant.

84. Two-tiered, folding interior shutters in a Parisian house of the 1630s. The quarries of leaded glass are arranged in fancy patterns. Strengthening bars are fitted across the width.

corner at Ham House[80] and there were such windows at the *Orangerie* at Versailles in 1687, while Celia Fiennes saw some at Ashstead at the end of the century. She called them 'double sashes' and explains that they were 'to make the house warmer for it stands pretty bleake'.[81]

All houses of any pretensions had glazed windows by 1600,[82] but glass was still quite expensive and could only be obtained in relatively small pieces. The lattice-window, which only required small 'quarries' of glass, set in lead 'cames', therefore remained popular until larger panes of glass became more freely available (Plates 83 and 286). In 1613 it was still worth bringing out a pattern-book for the use of glaziers faced with the problem of devising varied patterns of lattices.[83] Occasionally a quarry was omitted and the space filled by an openwork panel of lead which served to ventilate the room[84] and many city-dwellers had small devices (usually their coats of arms) executed in stained glass set into their leaded windows. This was particularly popular in Holland during the first half of the century (Plate 232).

The opening of windows with leaded lights always posed problems. One could only have small opening sections as this delicate type of window was easily damaged

82

85. A sash window in a Parisian house of about 1640? Abraham Bosse, who drew and engraved this scene, is usually so accurate on points of detail that this apparent representation of a sash window was unlikely to be mere artistic license.

by the buffeting of winds. A window that banged was apt to lose some of its quarries. It helped to have the section opening inwards, with the attendant inconvenience that also attached to the early single-leafed interior shutters. When the wooden framed window came into general use, with its larger, rectangular 'panes', it became possible to have windows opening outwards with reasonable safety. This form is so well known that nothing more need be said about it here, but on the other hand it is necessary to say something about the so-called 'sash window' which should strictly speaking be called the 'double sliding-sash window'.

The French term for any frame, and particularly any window-frame, is *chassis*—from which word comes our 'sash'. The word ought not to bear any implication that the frame can slide. Indeed, the French term for a 'sash window' is *fenêtre à chassis à coulisse* but luckily they have never been all that popular in France so they have not had to use this mouthful very often. Babelon claims that sash windows were used on staircases and other not easily accessible positions quite early in the century[85] and some of Bosse's scenes of Parisian interiors of the late 1630s and early 1640s seem to show this kind of window used in quite grand rooms (Plates 85 and 131). One is

83

certainly illustrated in a fashion-plate of the 1690s which indicates that the form was by then *à la mode* even if it did not sweep other types of window from the scene (Plate 31). In 1692 a tariff of dues payable on windows with fixed and sliding *chassis* was published in France and the latter were then described as being with a 'chassis à carreaux de verre à coulisse' [Window-frame with panes of glass that slides].[86]

Daniel Cronström wrote to Tessin in Stockholm in 1693 that 'Je vous envoiroy aussi, Monsieur [a drawing of] un invention de contre pieds [sic] nouveau pour les jassis de fenestre qui fait que les jassis demeure à la hauteur ou on le léve sans l'accrocher. Rien n'est plus commode et plus simple' [I will send you, Sir, a drawing of an invention of counter-weights for window-frames which make the frame stay at the height to which it is raised without fastening it. Nothing is more convenient or simpler].[87] But Tessin replied that 'J'ay vû une invention des contrepieds pour des jassis à [the Dutch palace of Het] Loo. Je seroy ravy de voir . . . si c'est la mesme ou non' [I have seen an invention of counter-weights for window frames at Loo. I shall be delighted to see . . . if it is the same or not]. When Tessin visited Het Loo in 1687 he did in fact record having seen the sliding sash windows.

> The upper section of the window which is of 5 large panes in height and the same in breadth is fixed. The lower section, which is just as large, goes all the time up and down with cords to which weights are hanging that run up over small pulleys and are fixed to small slots on each side of the window halfway up its height, so that the cords do not rub and yet cannot be seen. The two weights are proportioned to the weight of the window and are of lead, flat and rather like a small hand in size. They have holes at the top through which the cord is tied. It is to be noticed that all the window surrounds have two flat pieces of wood screwed into place forming a channel on one side of the window; this can be unscrewed so that one can get out an entire window and clean it. Large French window panes are fitted into the oak *chassis* and are fixed not with lead but with a certain compound.[88]

At the very same period, a sash-window with a counter-balancing system was being installed at Windsor Castle, but this was the period when Daniel Marot was architect to William III so any novelty of this kind in a Dutch or English palace would have been known within a short while in both countries.[89] Hitherto, one had had to lock the sash in position by means of small swivelling quadrants that engaged in a notched bead at the side of the window.[90] The occasional references to sashes with 'lines and pullies' prior to the 1680s may concern cords that facilitated the pulling up of the sliding sash (it was probably only the lower section that moved in the earliest forms of this type of window) as no mention is made of weights. This may have been the purpose of the '4 pairs of clock strings' that the Duke of Lauderdale bought in London in 1674 'to make strings for sash windows', and even the 'very strong shasses with their frames and brass pullies and very good lines to them' provided by a joiner for Whitehall Palace in November 1685 may have been of this early sort.[91] The Duke of Hamilton had sash windows fitted at Hamilton Palace in 1690 but his wright was sent to London three years later to inspect the new form of sash window—presumably because the Duke knew there was something better than the type with catches available by then.[92] The Maréchal de Lorge showed Dr Lister 'his great sash windows' in 1699 and demonstrated proudly 'how easily they might be lifted up and down and stood at any height; which contrivance he said he had out of

England by a small model brought on purpose thence, there being nothing of this poise in windows in France before'.[93]

In the 1570s, Harison explained that 'only the clearest glass is the most esteemed' and went on to say that 'we have divers sorts, some brought out of Burgundy, some out of Normandy, much out of Flanders, besides which it is made in England'.[94] This suggests that English glass was still of no consequence in his time. When Sir Roger Pratt was writing, almost a century later, the best glass from Newcastle was costing sevenpence per square foot while glass from Normandy cost seventeen pence and was considered much superior.[95] Indeed, during the seventeenth century Dutch and English privateers found it well worth trying to capture the shipments of Normandy glass that were regularly being sent from the factory at Tourlaville, via Cherbourg and up the Seine to Paris. So troublesome were their activities that the French had to send an armed escort to convoy the glass-boats.

Floors are of course also an important feature of the architectural shell which affect the appearance of an interior. We need not concern ourselves with how floors were supported and the other more purely structural aspects of the matter, but something needs to be said of the surfacing of floors in the present context.

86. Examples of paviour-work in various types of marble.

'Roomes on moist grounds do well to be paved with marble because the boarding otherwise is subject to rot,' wrote Sir Balthazar Gerbier in 1664[96] but not a few important rooms were paved with marble for the grand effect this produced. Much consideration was given by paviours (and perhaps also by the architects who were guiding their activities) to the patterns one could produce by combining stone 'quarries' of two or more colours (Plate 86). Several illustrations here show how intricate a pattern could be produced by using black and white quarries alone; it was particularly the Dutch who favoured floors of this kind, and Dutch marble was apparently exported in some quantity for this purpose (Colour Plate XIII and Plate 108).

The Dutch also exported thick tiles for flooring which were faced with a coloured lead glaze.[97] These were no longer a particularly fashionable type of flooring but tiles of some sort were laid as late as 1660 under the lantern in the Long Gallery at Knole (presumably because it leaked) and it was considered acceptable merely to renew old tile-work at Versailles in 1677 when the Château was being extended.[98] These are likely to have been of the more decorative kind—tiles of delftware (or maiolica) which have patterns executed in a limited range of colours on a white, tin-oxide ground. Italians had made much use of maiolica tiles in the sixteenth century and, when the potters of the Low Countries began to imitate Italian maiolica, tiles of this material were among their products. Indeed, Netherlandish maiolica tiles were exported all over northern Europe.[99] Moreover, Flemish potters versed in the techniques of producing this attractive ware emigrated and established themselves in many parts of Europe. Some settled in Norwich and, in 1567, proposed to make 'gally paving tiles and vessels for apothecaries and others'.[100] Strangely enough this was not to be a common form of flooring in the seventeenth century, however. The thin, and therefore rather delicate, delftware tiles by then being manufactured in Holland (at Rotterdam and elsewhere, apart from at Delft itself) were not really suitable for large floor areas although they lent themselves well to purposes like skirtings, fire-surrounds and even hearths.

In the three countries that primarily concern us here, wooden floors were primarily made of oak and it was considered noteworthy when Sir Bulstrode Whitelocke, who had been the English ambassador to Sweden in 1653, introduced the Scandinavian practice of having floors of deal when he had some boards of this timber imported and laid as a floor at Fawley Court.[101] The Scandinavians kept floors of this wood smooth and white, one method of doing this being to rub the floor with cold water and slaked lime, using a pad of straw knotted in a figure of eight.[102] The English method involved the use of wet sand, sometimes mixed with Fuller's earth. Floors were 'dry sanded' between-times and, in some parts of nineteenth-century America, a thin layer of sand was left on the floor and swept into decorative patterns—a practice which very probably reflects a much more ancient one stemming from northern Europe.[103]

IV. (right) Enfilade on the principal floor of the Hôtel Lauzun, Paris. View from the *Premier Salon*, through the *Salon de Musique* (antechamber) and *Chambre à alcove* to the *Cabinet* (see Plate 80). Built about 1656–7, probably by Louis Le Vau, for a financier, this gives a good idea of the kind of decoration to be seen in the most fashionable Parisian *hôtels* at about the time of Cardinal Mazarin's death.

Oak floors, on the other hand, were waxed. Cronström had to explain to Tessin in Stockholm how the floor of the *Grande Galerie* (the *Galerie des Glaces*) at Versailles was treated. They should be rubbed, he said with 'un peu de cire jaune . . . de sorte que les bois de chesne a sa couleur naturelle, à cela près que la cire le rend un peu plus jaune'[a little yellow wax . . . so that the oak wood keeps its natural colour, or perhaps the wax will make it a little yellower].[104] The almost black parquet one sees today in many old French houses is of course saturated with dirt that has become embedded in the wax over the centuries. Tessin was told that the floor needed to be polished with 'une brosse à frotter le parquet' [a brush for polishing the parquet] and a specimen of this implement was dispatched to him three months later.

In 1693 Tessin was also informed that, at Versailles 'il y a une frize ou bande de marbre noir de 8 pouces environ . . . qui regne tout au tour des lambris en bas' [there is a frieze or band of black marble about 8 inches wide . . . which runs right round the bottom of the panelling] while, at the Trianon, 'où il n'y a point de lambris de marbre, les parquets touchent aux lambris. Il n'y a qu'une seule piece à Versailles dont le parquet soit par quarrés . . . tout le reste est en lozanges à la nouvelle manière' [where the walls do not have panels of marble, the parquet floors reach the panelling. There is only one room at Versailles where the parquet is laid in squares . . . all the others are [laid] in lozenges in the new manner] (Plate 94).[105] Parquet laid diagonally *en lozanges* is still called *parquet de Versailles* in the trade.

Technically similar but far more elaborate were the floors which stemmed from the famous parquetry floors laid for Marie de Medici at the Luxembourg in 1620s, a type of floor-decoration that originated in Italy, as a contemporary noted.[106] Richard Symonds, who was in Paris in 1649, described the floor of the Queen's closet as being 'wrought in little workes all Sevvall forms pitcht in with Silver.'.[107] Such work would only be entrusted to joiners of the utmost capability; the Luxembourg floors were apparently laid by a man named Du Hancy and his skill was such that Martin Lister could still remark on their astonishing 'firmness, duration and intirenes' when he saw them in 1699, three quarters of a century later.[108] The floors of the next Queen of France, Anne d'Autriche, at the Palais Royal were furnished by the highly competent Jean Macé who would now qualify for the title of cabinet maker (Plates 33 and 81).[109] And her successor had floors laid by Pierre Golle who was nothing less than *ébéniste du roi*—cabinetmaker to His Majesty. A drawing of a floor laid by him in one of the Dauphin's closets shows how intricate such floors could be (Plate 90). In the record of payment to Golle it is justly called a 'parquet marqueté'. The famous cabinetmaker, André-Charles Boulle created another floor of this kind for the Dauphin in 1682–3.[110] No illustration of it survives but it is known to have been of extreme delicacy.

Around 1650 the Princess of Orange fitted out a closet at the Huis ten Bosch near The Hague where she had Oriental lacquerwork set into the panelling and the floor was of palisander wood with a large star in the middle, executed in woods of several colours; the whole was noted as being 'very curious'.[111] By French standards this floor was probably relatively simple, as was the roughly contemporary floor at Sir

V. (left) An imposing French chimneypiece bearing the arms of France and Navarre and intertwined L's for Louis XIII, who assumed power from his regent mother, Marie de Medici, in 1617 and died in 1643.

87. The patterns of parquetry floors laid in the apartment of Henrietta Maria, the Queen Mother, at Somerset House in 1661.

88 & 89. (far right) Patterns of parquetry. Presumably designs to be seen in the 1690s in important French buildings including the royal palaces (note the *fleur de lys*). One design has roundels with marquetry scenes.

John Danvers' house in Chelsea which John Aubrey described as being 'chequered like a chess board of box and ewgh[yew] panels of about six inches square'.[112] Plate 87 shows the patterns of floors laid very early in the 1660s in the apartment of Queen Henrietta Maria at Somerset House, which work was said to have been 'a curiosity never practised before in England'. The Queen returned to England from exile in France in 1660 and will have seen, not only her mother's floors at the Luxembourg, but also some of the more recent manifestations of this form of decoration (e.g. Plate 33.).

A floor with an intricate strapwork pattern and with the crowned ciphers of the Duke and Duchess of Lauderdale may still be seen in the State Bedchamber and its attendant Closet at Ham House, which dates from 1673 (Colour Plate XVI).[113] Probably of about the same date are the remains of an elaborate marquetry floor now mounted on a late seventeenth-century table at Boughton; it may have come from a closet at Montagu House which was built in the 1670s and damaged by fire in 1680. That it was thus re-used suggests it was prized in its day.[114] At Belton there is a closet with a floor painted black, red and brown in imitation of a floor of this kind; it may well give a truer indication of the original striking appearance of such floors than the mellow-toned survivals of the genuine article.[115]

The French term *parquet* comes from the small, fenced-in 'park' from which kings or other exalted persons had formerly administered justice. The floor of these small areas, which was usually raised, was often treated in some special manner in order to stress their separate character, and floors of *parquet* were presumably first used in such a context. Certainly, the very elaborate 'marquetry' floors were only laid in small

90. The 'parquet marqueté' of the Dauphin's *Cabinet Doré* at Versailles executed by the famous *ébéniste*, Pierre Golle, who was paid 7,500 *livres* for the work in 1682. The floor was taken up in 1688. The Dauphin's *Grand Cabinet* next door had a floor executed by the no less famous André-Charles Boulle, but floors of such complexity were exceptional.

rooms like closets, or in special areas like the raised step of the alcove in some grand bedchamber.[116] On the other hand, parquet, in the sense that we understand the term, had been widely adopted for all the principal rooms in important new French buildings by the end of the century, and this fashion was spreading to England and Holland by 1700.

Once the architectural shell existed, it had to be furnished. Just as one could rely on the plasterer to provide a suitable ceiling, and the marble contractor might supply a handsome chimneypiece in the prevailing style, so one could expect a fashionable upholsterer to provide hangings, beds and seat-furniture that would blend satisfactorily with the surroundings. But an ambitious architect, striving to create a special effect for some important commission, might guide the upholsterer by providing him with sketches of what he wanted. And he might do the same with the cabinetmaker, the joiner, the metalworkers and the other contractors engaged on the project. This is a matter that needs more investigation but a few comments are appropriate here.

Architects of the seventeenth century certainly did not concern themselves with the ordinary run of furniture; they will only have taken an interest in pieces which formed a salient feature in an important scheme of decoration on which they were engaged. Leading Italian architects were apparently already designing specially important pieces of furniture in the sixteenth century—a fancily inlaid marble table and its supporting frame, a cabinet to stand in some particularly eye-catching position, a candlestand, a state bed—and this tendency became more marked in the seventeenth century (Plates 7 and 51).[117] If Francis Cleyn really did design the shell-backed *sgabelli*-type chairs for Holland House (Plate 52) and for Ham House, it may well be that he was inspired to do so because he was following a practice that he had come across in Italy when he had stayed there early in the century.[118] Cleyn seems anyway to have worked within the circle where Inigo Jones was the presiding genius, and the latter is very likely to have wanted furniture in a style that needed to be specially created for the interiors he was devising for Charles I and his court in the 1620s and 1630s. Like Cleyn, he will also have known about current Italian practice and could well have provided sketches for furniture himself. Whether he actually did so is another matter. What we do know, however, is that his pupil and protégé, John Webb, did design an alcove with a state bed standing in it, for Charles II's apartment at Greenwich Palace (Plate 45). The drawing is dated 1665. The bed itself is a fairly straightforward structure of the type fashionable at the time, but Webb seems to have added an extra finial (cup with plumes of ostrich feathers) that distinguishes it from the more sketchy beds one sees in Jean Le Pautre's otherwise rather similar representations of alcoves (Plates 27 and 28), on which Webb's composition was no doubt based. Le Pautre's engravings, for their part, probably show the co-ordinated effects executed in Paris around 1660 by an important French architect.

We get on to rather firmer ground when Charles Le Brun appears on the scene. We have already discussed the superbly integrated schemes for which he was responsible, first at Vaux-le-Vicomte and then at the French royal palaces. Already at Vaux (i.e. around 1660) he was providing designs in sketch form for individual pieces of furniture (Plate 5) that the various craftsmen could develop into working drawings, and he continued this practice when he became director of the Gobelins, that incredible group of workshops, staffed by the best craftsmen of the day, which provided sumptuous furnishings of all kinds for the French royal household. For instance, a sketch from le Brun's own hand survives for what is believed to be one of the imposing silver tables that stood in the state rooms at Versailles (Plate 9), and a more finished drawing of the same table also exists, probably representing the silversmith's final conception deriving from Le Brun's inspirational sketch (Plate 10). The table itself, along with many other pieces of silver furniture, was constructed in the 1670s but all the silver furniture at Versailles was melted down in 1689 to help bolster up the then ailing French exchequer.[119]

The table in question was a console-table that was intended to stand against a window-pier, presumably with a mirror above and flanked by a pair of candlestands—an ensemble that became highly fashionable during the last two decades of the century (Plate 218).[120] The candlestands were later dispensed with (they got in the way of curtains and must always have been getting knocked over) but the mirror and its accompanying table were already then an essential part of the

91 & 92. Examples of designs for furniture published by architects to meet the need for unity of style in an interior. The joiners who bought this book, Paul Vredeman's *Verscheyden Schrynwerck* or *Plusiers Menuiseries*, could be sure that the 'doorcases, clothes-presses, buffets, beds, tables, chests, chairs, benches, stools, roller-towel holders, mirror-frames and works of many other kinds' would be in a fashionable style consonant with the interior architecture of the rooms in which they were to be set up.

architecture, so it is not surprising that architects paid special attention to this feature. A design by Daniel Marot for such a 'triad' (the term is modern) that was to be set up at Het Loo exists and shows the care he bestowed on its proportions (Plate 51). For, of course, an ensemble of this sort was designed to stand in a particular position in a special room; such furniture was not interchangeable, although it might still look very impressive even if moved from its intended surroundings. For the most part, however, such triads were produced by cabinetmakers or carvers to their own designs in a fashionable style that would blend perfectly adequately with the general décor of any newly decorated room. Such furniture was in these instances bought for a specific position but it was not actually designed for it.

In designing such important pieces (or groups) of furniture, master-craftsmen could turn to publish designs for inspiration. These were often composed by men who called themselves architects even though some of them seem to have concentrated on design as such rather than on erecting actual buildings. Nevertheless they will all have recognised that practising architects needed to have furniture

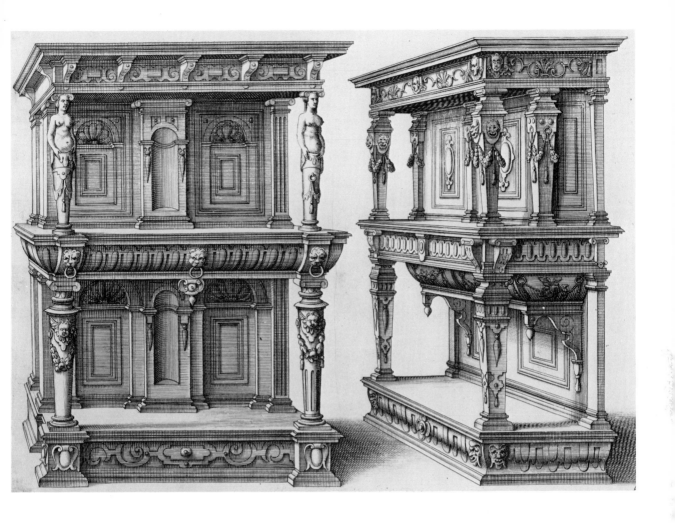

that was consonant in style with the architecture they were creating (Plates 91 and 92). The furniture that is illustrated in the published works of architects (e.g. Du Cerceau, Hans Vredeman, Jean Marot and Daniel Marot) may therefore be called 'architectural furniture', for the designs were put forward with the needs of the architect in mind. State beds, which formed the focal point of an important bedchamber and embodied such potent symbolism, therefore received a good deal of attention in such works. So, in the sixteenth century and the first half of the seventeenth century, did the great buffets on which valuable plate could be displayed, although these subsequently went out of fashion. The handsome draw-leaf dining table, with its associated stools, also figured in works of the early seventeenth century but the only kind of table that interested late seventeenth-century architects was the console-table which we have already discussed. Candlestands, urns, perfume-burners, thrones, cabinets, day-beds, clocks—all were the subject of such published designs: all therefore have claims to being called 'architectural furniture'.

95

Daniel Marot is a case rather on his own, as he practised as an architect but was also capable of designing all the furnishings and interior decoration—and, indeed, published many designs in this field (Plates 95 and 143). He no doubt found it necessary to spread as quickly as possible the style he introduced to Holland from Paris when he emigrated in 1684, so that his clients became familiar with it and would soon demand work only in that taste, and so that a supporting cast of craftsmen would spring up that could provide furnishings in the new style with a minimum of additional guidance.

In Daniel Marot's oeuvre the distinction between 'architectural furniture' and furniture in general is obscured by his versatility, but the distinction was never all that clear-cut. There was never a class of furniture that was invariably architect-designed. There were, however, certain classes of furniture for which architects occasionally took it upon themselves to provide the designs.

CHAPTER IV
The Upholsterer's Task

THE seigneurial pattern of life on the Middle Ages had involved frequent moves from one residence to another, as we have already noted. One of the purposes of these moves was to demonstrate a lord's power and high status. This was achieved by a display of wealth and luxury which clearly set him apart from lesser beings. It was also achieved through the performance of complicated ceremonial and the lavish entertainment of large numbers of people against a magnificent background. Devising suitable settings for these various activities seems to have been the responsibility of the *fourrier* in those days.[1] He carried out his task primarily with the aid of furnishings made of textile materials—wall-hangings, cushions, carpets, bed-hangings, padded chairs and canopies—with which he could quickly transform a bare interior into one of accommodating comfort and visual delight, and could contrive settings appropriate to each occasion. As these largely textile furnishings were made of extremely valuable materials that were conspicuous evidence of the lord's wealth, they were carefully protected and were not normally left at a residence once the lord had moved on elsewhere; they were taken along on the journey in the baggage train. Textile furnishings were of course particularly well suited to this way of life because they could be folded into manageable form for packing or they could be rolled up for stowing in the carts.[2]

Using these materials, the *fourrier* with the help of his staff could, for instance, divide off part of the great hall to make a smaller, more intimate compartment, he could rig up a daïs and canopy where the lord could sit in state, he could dress the staging of the buffet with a cup-board cloth on which the lord's collection of rich plate (his 'cups') could be proudly displayed. He might dress up a charming bower for my lady, strewing the seats with rich cloths and cushions, and he could furnish equally suitable lodgings for the rest of the family and for grand visitors—each according to his status. He knew the form for weddings, for christenings, for mournings, and could dress the house and chapel to an appropriate degree for each occasion. He could fix up a setting for a tournament and would remember to hang rich carpets and table-covers from the balconies when there was a parade. As we have said, he did all this primarily with the aid of textile materials made up in various ways.

When aristocratic life became more static, after 1500 or so, rich textile furnishings remained the symbol of high estate and still constituted the most conspicuous element of the décor in any house of importance. It took a long while before wooden furniture came into any great evidence and, even when it did, it was often largely masked with textiles. It was the hangings that were the most prominent part of the great carved beds of the sixteenth century; tables were covered with handsome 'carpets', and the massive buffets were dressed with their 'cupboard cloths'.

By the sixteenth century, responsibility for disposing the furnishings in a suitable manner for each occasion in a large household lay with the Gentleman Usher

93. Hangings still being used in the mediaeval manner. The verdure tapestries are nailed to the walls along the top edge and clad the walls down to the floor. They are roughly pulled back to disclose the door when necessary.

(*huissier*).[3] He was a senior member of the household (as the name indicates, he was classed as a gentleman and normally came from the ranks of the lesser nobility or gentry) and he was supported in his task by two Yeoman Ushers, who were respectively responsible for the arrangements in the Great Chamber and in the Hall, and they were in turn assisted by a staff of Grooms.[4] The furnishings were cared for by the Yeoman of the Wardrobe[5] who gave instructions to a bevy of seamstresses, laundry maids, joiners and so forth.[6]

The hierarchy of gentleman and yeoman servants in a household withered away during the seventeenth century (except in royal households where these posts lingered on vestigially) and the ordinary usher gradually became a waiter or flunkey. They could still arrange the furniture in the ordinary way but anything special had to be carried out by a man called an upholder or upholsterer.[7] Such a person might

98

be attached to a great household[8] but he was more often brought in to attend to the now for the most part fixed textile furnishings that still formed so important a part of the décor (Plate 94).

The upholsterers had come up in the world since the Middle Ages. It seems they had originally been dealers in second-hand household goods and clothing but their status gradually improved and, by the beginning of the seventeenth century, they were involved entirely with the provision of new furnishings for houses or for doing over existing furnishings, but they were particularly concerned with those which had components of textile materials—beds, seat-furniture, wall-hangings, carpets.[9] It was no doubt in recognition of the altered character of the trade that the upholsterers' Company of the City of London, which had been in being since 1459 at least, was granted a fresh charter in 1626 but, as the document was burned in the Great Fire of London, we do not know anything of its provisions. By 1747, the upholsterer was being described as 'a Connoisseur in every article that belongs to a House'—he was an interior decorator.

In furnishing houses, the upholsterer had of course to visit the site so as to receive his instructions and take measurements. He might also have to return for further consultations and to check progress. He came to know about life in high society, and

94. The importance of upholstery. The bed-hangings, chair-covers, *portière* and table-carpet are en suite in a red material (velvet?) with gold trimmings. The sun-curtains match. The tapestries are fitted to the walls. Note the ostrich-feather plumes and aigrettes forming finials above the tester of the bed.

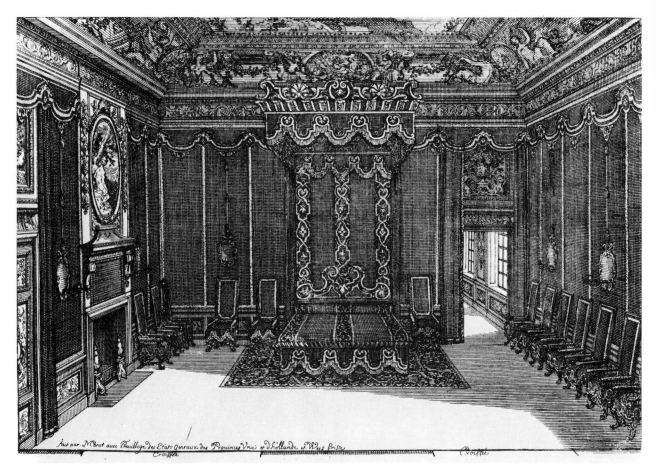

95. A scheme of decoration unified by upholstery. The flying-tester bed sets the key and all the other elements are en suite—the wall-hangings with their capping, the *portière*, and the chair-covers with their deep skirts (*pentes*). Design by Daniel Marot of about 1690.

to understand the aspirations and requirements of the rich. The top members of the trade saw for themselves what was fashionable and were able to help spread fashions; they gave advice to customers who found these matters bewildering or could not make up their minds. What is more they placed considerable orders with tradesmen of many different kinds for the wares they needed in order to make up their own goods, so they were to a large extent able to dictate what should be made by these craftsmen and how it should look. For instance, they patronised the silk mercer who dealt in silken goods and the finest of the woollen materials, and thus could have a say in what colours and patterns were produced. They could also guide the production of the *passementier*, the maker of trimmings who created the laces, fringes, tassels and galloons that played such an important part in the make-up of seventeenth-century upholstery (Plates 99 and 100). They likewise dealt with the embroiderer who could execute fancy needlework (Plates 98 and 106), the feather-dresser who not only provided stuffing for mattresses and pillows but also made the ostrich plumes that formed such spectacular finials on grand beds (Plate 94), the saddler who curled horsehair for stuffing chairs, the linen draper who dealt in linings and backing-materials, the blacksmith who made all the hooks and hinges that were

96. A late-seventeenth-century French design for a bed-head decorated with appliqué work. An upholsterer would have had such a drawing made to indicate what was desired from the embroiderers who would in turn have made full-scale drawings from which to work.

97. The upholsterer's art. The bed-head of the state bed of the first Earl of Melville; about 1695. Such an elaborate confection can only have been made by one of the leading London upholsterers, and very probably by one of French extraction like Guibert or Lapierre.

98. The counterpoint of the Melville Bed (see Plate 97).

99. Detail of the valance of a bed made in France for Queen Ulrika Eleonora of Sweden in 1680, showing the rich trimming incorporating the Queen's crowned monogram. The various kinds of gold thread would originally have been as bright as the detail in the bottom left-hand corner.

100. Tattered but still conveying an impression of richness, the valances and a finial (cup) of a 'French bed' of about 1665. Probably English.

101. Cups from a rich bed; probably French about 1660. Most of the bell-tassels have fallen away. The velvet is black, with a pale-blue ground. The undersides are of yellow silk as are the trimmings.

necessary as well as the curtain-rods and rings that were needed for bed-hangings, and they had to deal with the carver and gilder in connection with the more showy of the wooden components of beds and chairs. As the upholsterer gradually came to be entrusted with complete schemes of decoration, so he was forced to bring in other contractors—paviours for marble floors, cabinetmakers, painters, dealers in mirror-glass, joiners specialising in the laying of parquet, plasterers and so on (Plate 102). On all these people the upholsterer could bring his influence and tastes to bear. At a time when the architect still only occasionally took over total control of a building enterprise and only rarely attempted to dictate how the interior arrangements should look, the upholsterer still had matters very much his own way. It was therefore largely he who created the most eye-catching features of new schemes of interior decoration in the seventeenth century and it was invariably he who did so if it was merely a question of doing over existing rooms— which was something grand people were in the habit of having done frequently.

It is not surprising, therefore, that several seventeenth-century upholsterers became rich and some became famous. The name of Simon de Lobel, the principal *tapissier* to Louis XIV, was a household word around 1680, for instance. In the eighteenth century it was still a great deal more profitable to be an upholsterer than a mere cabinetmaker.[10]

Upholsterers (or their equivalent) brought a measure of unification to important rooms long before architects started to integrate the various elements into a cohesive scheme of decoration. Already in the Middle Ages, certain grand bedchambers were being completely hung with the same material as that which was used for the hangings of the bed. Such unity was not apparently common, however, until early in the seventeenth century. It became the convention when the concept of *regularité*,

103

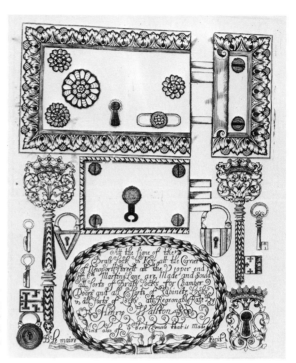

102. Among the many sub-contractors from whom an upholsterer might commission work was the locksmith. This bill-head of a London locksmith was drawn by a Frenchman, judging by his name which is inscribed in the bottom corner.

with which the name of Madame de Rambouillet is associated, came to be accepted as the basis for good taste in interior architecture. Sir Henry Unton, who had been ambassador to France and must have known what was fashionable in Paris in the late sixteenth century, does not seem to have had any properly unified suites of furnishings, *ameublements* as the French called them, in his houses when inventories were taken in 1595, and this suggests that they were not yet common in France, even in smart circles. However, at Ingatestone five years later we find two chairs and a stool all covered 'sutable unto the bedd' or 'sutelike', although the rest of the furniture did not match.[11] The Earl of Northampton, in 1614, had most of the furnishings of his bedchamber 'all suteable to the bed' which had hangings of purple velvet trimmed with silver lace,[12] and in 1625 a French bedchamber is described as having a fine embroidered bed 'avec garniture de la chambre pareille' [with the furnishings of the room to match].[13] When Lady Leicester was in Paris in 1640 she notes that '6 chears of on sorte, 6 of on other, and 6 stooles . . . is just the number that is used hear to all good beds', which implies that this set of furniture was decorated en suite.[14] The Ham House inventory of about 1654, which probably reflects the state of the house prior to the outbreak of the Civil War, shows that several rooms there were unified in their *ameublement*. For instance, one bed had two 'great chaires', eight stools, two table-covers and the window-curtains all en suite.[15] Indeed, by the 1640s, it must have been a commonplace in grand circles to have the textile furnishings of important rooms matching (Colour Plate II). Already in 1641, even a mere squire living in Devonshire might have the 'blew hangings' of his Little Parlour Chamber matching the bed which had 'curtaynes of the same'.[16] Nor was it solely the furnishings of bedchambers that could be en suite although it was at first primarily in this important room that such refinements were to be seen: at Easton Lodge in 1637 there were 'one high Chayer, one Low Chayer and three Low stooles all of Gillt Leather sutable to the hangings in the Clossett in the Chappell'.[17] Later inventories abound with descriptions of whole rooms decorated with textile furnishings decorated en suite.[18] When window-curtains became fashionable, and no longer simply served a utilitarian purpose, they were brought into the schemes and came to play an important rôle in the décor. Firescreens might also be en suite.

A careful reading of the three inventories of Ham House during the Lauderdale period (i.e. in the years around 1680)[19] shows how frequently changes were made to the furnishings of rooms at the time. In important rooms beds and their accompanying chairs were given new upholstery twice in five years, whole *ameublements* were transferred to another room and adapted to the new surroundings.[20] Some sets were taken off to the wardrobe for storing and there was usually some spare material in store against the time when hangings needed repairing or altering. Presumably the new sets were provided by prominent London upholsterers but much of the work of adaptation and maintenance must have been done by the household staff. Upholsterers provided a cleaning service but the staff was supposed to see that the hangings were kept in proper order.

The cost of the materials of which upholstery was made was high. The raw materials (notably silk) had to be brought from distant parts of the world, and the process of weaving anything like a complicated pattern was laborious and slow.[21] The creating of intricate trimmings was also time-consuming. The making up by the upholsterer had then to be added to these prime costs. Once someone had paid for such expensive confections he took good care to protect them. All grand beds were provided with protective 'case curtains' (Plate 144); all expensive chair-covers had 'cases' to protect them or were themselves removeable.[22] Many of Cardinal Mazarin's most sumptuous wall-hangings had specially made bags in which they could be stored.[23] Indeed, valuable upholstery was often removed to the wardrobe-room and laid flat on shelves, at rest as it were, and seems only to have been put up when the family was in residence or on gala occasions.[24] For much of the year, the interiors of all grand houses must have been swathed in dust-covers.[25] It is only our own antique-besotted generation that expects what remains of these precious objects to be constantly on show—prey to the merciless ravages of light, to repeated fingering, to battering by assiduous cleaning staff, to corrosive dust, to rotting damp, and to the strains of hanging in one position, day after day, as they slowly tear themselves apart with their own weight. People in the past took enormous care although some of the instructions given to household staff do not always indicate this. Mazarin's servants, for instance, were expected to attend each day to the wall-hangings—'les bien ballayer et vergetter tous les jours pour en oster la poudre et empescher que les araignées ne s'y mettent et prendre garde que les souris ne gastent les tapisseries' [to brush them well and beat them every day so as to remove the dust, and to take care that the mice do not gnaw the tapestries].[26] That rats and mice might indeed attack the hangings is borne out by a Swedish inventory of 1672 where it is noted that the fringes of some fine hangings were 'något sönder skurit af rotter'—somewhat gnawed by rats.[27]

Hangings of tapestry or velvet and other thick materials are warm in character and are particularly suitable for clothing a room in wintertime. But in the summer heat they can seem hot and dusty. For this reason, particularly grand rooms were sometimes hung differently in summer and in winter. The State Bedchamber at

Ham House, a room decorated in the late 1670s, was provided with a set of tapestry hangings for the walls in winter while the bed was hung with a blue and gold velvet and the chairs were covered to match.[28] The 'Summer Furniture' (i.e. the complete *ameublement*) for the room was of plain silk and must have seemed a lot cooler. There can be little doubt that this feature at Ham, which was merely the Lauderdales' suburban villa, reflected the practice in Paris. Indeed, the future Duchess (she was married to the Duke in 1672) may have seen something similar on her visit to the French capital in 1670 and there is a hint in a parody of 1674 of the opera *Alceste* suggesting that Parisian audiences were entirely familiar with such changes, for a character is mocked because 'vos rideaux sont d'esté et vos pentes d'hyver' [your bed-curtains are from the summer set, the valances from the winter set].[29] What may have been sets of winter and summer furniture were the alternative suites of hangings provided for the High Great Chamber at Hardwick, presumably in the 1590s. These consisted respectively of a set of tapestries (these are now on the walls the whole year through) and 'an other sute of of hangings for the same chamber being eight pieces of woollen cloth stayned with frett and storie and silk flowers', which have long ago disappeared.[30] These painted hangings seem to have had a fretted strapwork border, scenes from some story, and silk flowers that were probably embroidered. It was perhaps even more sensible to provide beds with two sets of hangings. Gabrielle d'Estrées, the mistress of Henri IV, had summer hangings on her bed of *taffetas de Chine* which must have seemed highly exotic in the Paris of 1599.[31] The parody on *Alceste* of 1674 shows that beds might then have alternative summer and winter sets of hangings sufficiently often to extract a laugh of recognition from a Parisian audience. Whether the two sets of hangings for the bed in the Duke's Chamber at Cockesden in 1626 served the same seasonal purpose, one cannot say, but there was certainly a second set for the 'great bed' in the cypress chest that stood in the room.[32]

With textiles playing so vital a rôle in seventeenth-century interior decoration, the task of the upholsterer was unending. That he drifted into providing services of many other kinds such as undertaking and furniture hire is hardly surprising. Moreover that his influence on taste and on the appearance of the seventeenth-century interior could be immense seems to be beyond doubt. We must now consider more specifically some of the things he provided and the materials he used.

CHAPTER V
The Upholsterer's Materials

UPHOLSTERERS used a very wide range of materials to make up the goods they created. In this chapter I shall review the different classes of materials available to them in the seventeenth century; in subsequent chapters, we shall see how they were used.

As far as the textile materials are concerned, scholars have no difficulty in defining the main classes but it is far from easy for them to agree about the identity of individual materials mentioned in contemporary documents. For example, there is as yet no general agreement as to what 'dornix' and 'mohair' were like although both terms occur frequently in seventeenth-century inventories. Dornix was clearly very different in character in the seventeenth century from what it became in the nineteenth. Mohair was the name of a woollen material with a distinctive finish in earlier times but by the late seventeenth century the name was undoubtedly used in reference to a silk material to which the same finish had been applied. As for the simpler forms of woollen materials, what was technically the same material could have several different names according to its weight, its quality, or the scale of its pattern, or due to some additional finish. Unfortunately no glossary of seventeenth-century textile terms exists as yet[1] and what follows must not be taken as anything more than a general guide, designed to help the reader understand the later chapters of this book. It should however be borne in mind when dealing with the names given to textile materials in household inventories that these names reflect differences that were easily recognised by normally intelligent people at the time. Although the differences might in the first place depend on some technical feature, these will not have been distinctions that only a textile historian can now detect; they will have been clearly visible to any casual observer.

TAPESTRIES, TAPISSERIES DE BERGAME AND DORNIX

Weaving tapestry is laborious and therefore expensive.[2] Like all weaving the technique requires a loom and, for the weaving of large tapestry hangings, the loom has to be correspondingly large. However the technique can be used for small, delicate wares, in which case the resulting material can have a superficial resemblance to some sorts of needlework with which tapestry-weaving otherwise has absolutely no connection.

There was no particular point in making firescreens and other small panels in this technique although it became fashionable to do so late in the seventeenth century (Colour Plate XIV). On the other hand, the comparatively robust and flexible character of larger tapestry-woven panels had made them particularly suitable for the mediaeval way of life in aristocratic circles. They could withstand the constant taking down from the walls, the bundling into carts and the fixing up again in some new setting that went with this mobile manner of living among the upper classes. Indeed, it can only have been because tapestry was so firmly associated in everyone's consciousness with aristocratic settings that it remained in fashion long after its practical advantages as a material had ceased to be of any real significance. For, in the largely static interior arrangements pertaining from the sixteenth century onwards, tapestry hangings tended to be fixed to the walls as permanent decoration and, if one simply wanted a picture on the wall, one executed in paint would have been far more satisfactory than one composed in this cumbersome technique. But an astute man like Colbert would never have established the extensive tapestry-weaving *ateliers* at the Gobelins in the mid-1660s if tapestries had not still been highly fashionable and had looked as if they would long remain so; nor would numerous high-class *ateliers* have been kept going in Brussels right through the sixteenth and seventeenth century. Incidentally, tapestry was often still called 'arras' in the early seventeenth century although particularly fine tapestries were no longer being woven at Arras.

Tapestries could be woven in huge panels; they did not have to be made up from several widths of material, as would have been the case if a panel of the same large size was to be made out of some other class of textile. Tapestries were normally made of wool but the highlights in a pictorial composition might be executed in silk in hangings of fine quality, and certain passages might be woven in gold thread in the most expensive quality of all. Because of the freedom this technique allowed the designer, it was well suited to large pictorial compositions, but formal and even repetitive patterns might also be produced by it although there was no practical advantage in doing so.

What might be called 'poor man's tapestry' was a class of rather coarse materials of wool which had large patterns that made them suitable for wall-hangings and other large-scale upholstery work. They were known as *Tapisseries de Bergame*.[3] The patterns were sometimes elaborate and were always repetitive rather than pictorial (Colour Plate VII). These materials were woven in a relatively straightforward manner on a wide loom, and large panels were made up by stitching widths together. The warps, which ran vertically, were usually of hemp which made these cloths very robust. The grandest sort might have passages rendered in metal thread or in silk but these materials were mainly intended for secondary rooms and offices in important buildings, and for a middle-class clientèle that could not afford real tapestries.[4] Their patterns included formal 'pomegranate' designs, flame-like *point d'Hongrie* and a related fish-scale form called *écaille*, and also crowned 'Ls' alternating with *fleurs-de-lis* in reference to a King Louis, and more likely to the fourteenth rather than to the thirteenth or later kings of that name.[5] Narrower border-widths of these weaves were available; with these one could frame widths of the main material and so make up hangings of any size.

Tapisseries de Bergame were made at Rouen and Elbeuf, and were sometimes called *tapisseries de Rouen*.[6] They were no doubt made elsewhere—at some of the other places noted for the production of woollen upholstery materials like Lille, Roubaix, Amiens and Tournai, for instance.[7] Moreover, it seems that these hangings were widely exported from France and Flanders,[8] and there is no reason to doubt that they were also brought into England.[9] Chambers' *Dictionary* of 1786 lists 'Bergamot' as a 'coarse tapestry' but the term does not seem to occur in seventeenth-century inventories.

It may well be that the 'dornix' which is so frequently mentioned in seventeenth-century inventories was identical with *tapisserie de Bergame* although, since we know that dornix came in several classes,[10] the term probably embraced a whole range of rather coarse, comparatively large-patterned upholstery materials that were readily distinguishable even if their patterns varied considerably.[11] Collections of ancient textiles usually contain examples of such materials; they have not so far attracted much attention from textile historians but it seems likely that at least some of them would have been recognised as dornix by a clerk compiling an inventory in the seventeenth century (Colour Plate VIII b and c). Dornix, at any rate, derived its name from Tournai (Doornik) in the Low Countries which was a centre of tapestry-weaving and of the manufacture of woollen upholstery materials. It would be very natural if its products included the sort of material under discussion. As with *tapisserie de Bergame*, dornix was found in secondary rooms.[12]

Another rather coarse woollen material that was readily identifiable was 'Kidderminster stuff'. It is mentioned in inventories from about 1630 onwards, and remained in favour in the eighteenth century.[13] It was boldly patterned in a simple way. The same may be said of 'Scotch pladd' which was being used for the complete *ameublements* of several rooms at Tart Hall in 1641 and at Dyrham at the end of the century.[14]

TURKEYWORK AND ORIENTAL CARPETS

When we speak of a carpet, we are usually thinking of a sturdy class of woven cloth with a thick pile surface that is easily recognisable, but the word 'carpet' simply meant a cover that lay flat, in the seventeenth century.[15] On the other hand, we tend to call all small carpets rugs but a 'rugg' was a coarse and often shaggy form of coverlet to our seventeenth-century ancestors, and they referred to all Oriental carpets or rugs as 'carpets'.

Oriental carpets have a pile that is produced by tying knots in rows as the fabric is being woven.[16] Most of the knotted-pile rugs brought to Europe in the seventeenth century came from Anatolia, the modern Turkey; these were usually boldly patterned in a few strong colours (Colour Plates XI and XIII). That they are frequently to be seen in early seventeenth-century portraits must, however, not be taken to mean that there were numerous rugs of this sort in every house at that date; the 'sitter' (who is usually standing in such portraits) was very likely painted with the rug because it was a prized possession.[17] Some of these small carpets were prayer-rugs, with a prayer-niche forming the chief feature of their design, and it would seem that these were sometimes called *mosquets* in French inventories and 'Musketta carpetts' in England.[18] Anatolian rugs were manufactured for the European market in considerable quantities and a lively trade in these exotic coverings grew up during the seventeenth century. Dutch paintings of the middle of the century show that they were relatively common, at least in Holland, by that stage.

Finer in quality, more subtle in design, and usually much larger, were Persian carpets (Plate 108). The finest of these, notably those made with a silk pile and with passages brocaded with gold thread, were often courtly presents from the Shah to people of influence,[19] and Persian carpets were not at all common in the seventeenth century.[20] Such weaves came from important centres; the ordinary rugs woven in the villages of Persia and by nomadic tribesmen—the equivalent of the Anatolian rugs—probably reached Europe only very rarely. On the other hand, the large Turkish court carpets woven at Ushak and the distinguished carpets from Cairo seem to have reached Europe in some quantity.[21] Large carpets of a Persian character were also commissioned in India for European consumption by the East India Company.[22] Suffice it to say that large Eastern carpets were expensive and still comparatively rare in Western Europe during the seventeenth century.

So greatly were Near Eastern carpets admired, however, that attempts to imitate them were made in several parts of Europe. Carpet-weaving had been introduced into Spain by the Moors in the Middle Ages and Spanish carpets had been widely famed right down to the sixteenth century but the industry had withered away by the seventeenth century. However, rugs with Anatolian patterns and using the Turkish technique were woven at Cuenca, although there is no indication that they were much exported and they hardly concern us here.[23] Carpets very similar in character, imitating Turkish patterns and constructed by Turkish methods, were being woven in England by the time of Elizabeth, as is proved by some famous specimens at Boughton, dated 1584 and 1585 and bearing the Montagu arms inwoven. There is also a panel with the royal arms of England and the date 1600 in the Victoria and Albert Museum.[24] Early in the seventeenth century carpets 'façon de Turquie' were also being made in Paris, and an *atelier* was established under the *Grande Galerie* of the Louvre in 1618 'travaillant pour le Roy en ouvrage de Turquie' [producing work in the Turkish manner for the King] (see Plate 6).[25] A decade later the famous workshops at Chaillot, set up in an old soap-factory (*savonnerie*), were established and the two factories were later amalgamated out there. The fact that they produced carpets 'façon de Perse' need not necessarily be taken to imply that the patterns of these weaves were Oriental in character, for some of the thirteen 'grand tapis . . . façon de Levant, faits à la Savonnerie pour servir à la Gallerie d'Apollon du Louvre' [large carpets woven in the Levantine manner, made at the *Savonnerie* for the *Galerie d'Apollon* at the Louvre] still exist and are decorated with designs that are entirely in the European tradition.[26] Indeed, during the middle decades of the seventeenth century, the Savonnerie designers evolved a characteristic form of carpet-design, composed of naturalistic flowers in a formal framework based on the repertoire of Classical ornament, that has remained in favour for European carpets ever since.[27] However, as few Savonnerie carpets were exported, and then only as presents, and no other country was able to emulate the French example until well into the next century, this French development remained an isolated one in the seventeenth century.

In England, the local imitations of Turkish rugs went by the name of 'turkeywork'[28] but one cannot always be sure that what is described as a 'Turkie carpett' was not in fact a rug woven in England. For example, the Earl of Northampton had in 1614 'a large Turkie carpett of Englishe worke with the Earle of Northampton his armes, being 5 yeardes and 3 quarters large',[29] and Lady Dorchester spoke of 'my fower white turkey carpetts, and the long one that John Frithe wrought' in 1638.[30] At Ingatestone in 1600 there was an 'old Turkey foote carpett' that was probably woven in England because the pattern is indicated by the phrase 'the worke roses', which suggests a European style.[31]

Just as in France the Savonnerie weavers developed designs that owed nothing to Eastern traditions, so the English weavers of turkeywork gradually abandoned

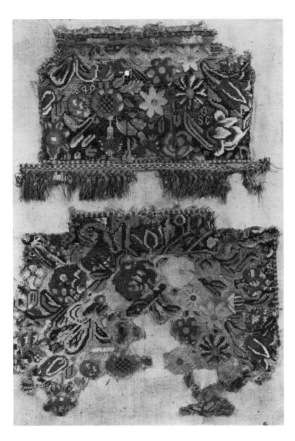

103. Fragments of English turkeywork panels made for covering chairs, one dated 1649 and trimmed with a worsted fringe. The panels have a 'barber's pole' border woven in the pile technique also used for the main pattern, showing that the panels were specially made for mounting on chairs of a standard size and no doubt of the 'farthingale' type.

Anatolian patterns and turned instead to the repertoire of the needleworker. Few traces of Eastern influence remained after 1625 or so; the patterns were now scaled-up and simplified versions of current fashions in embroidery (Plate 103).[32] Turkeywork was made on a large scale at Norwich and the industry was already well established there by the end of the sixteenth century.[33] Some turkeywork kneelers bearing the city arms were made for Norwich Cathedral in 1651 and provide well-documented specimens of what the local weavers could produce.[34] They also made carpets (Colour Plate II) but their main production consisted of panels suitable for upholstering the seats and backs of chairs. It is not always realised that English turkeywork (probably from Norwich) was exported to the Continent and colonies in substantial quantity. A French tariff of import-duties issued in 1664 makes it clear that a duty of a hundred *sols* was payable on each piece of 'tapis de Turquie, d'Angleterre ou d'ailleurs' while thirty *sols* was payable on 'tapis dudit pays d'Angleterre, pour faire chaises et emmeublement' [pile carpet from England, used for chairs and for upholstery].[35] Turkeywork appears to have been woven in Ireland as well, for 'an Irish turkey work carpott' is listed in an inventory of 1684 and there was an Irish carpet four yards long and two and three-quarter yards wide at Kilkenny Castle in the same year.[36]

WOOLLEN VELVETS

The pile of a velvet is produced mechanically by the weaving process and is not knotted into the weave, as in a carpet.[37] We are here concerned with moquette and other velvets with a woollen pile. Silk-pile velvets are dealt with under silks; velvets

111

with a cotton pile did not come into widespread use until the mid-eighteenth century.

Woollen velvets are robust materials yet they are soft and yielding. They were popular in the nineteenth century—for instance, for the seats in railway-carriages. By that time the material was often called 'plush'. Woollen velvets were also much used in the seventeenth century, but the material is very vulnerable to attack by moths; it then quickly becomes unsightly and tends to be discarded. As a result, comparatively little ancient material of this class survives (Colour Plate VIII a). Moquette was also known in France as *moucade* (hence the English 'mockado').[38] It was made principally at Lille, Tournai, Abbeville and Rouen but weavers of this material established themselves in various other parts of Europe during the sixteenth and seventeenth centuries. It came with fancy patterns making it suitable for carpeting (in the tougher range) or the covering of seat-furniture; it could also be plain, and the plain material could have a pattern stamped onto it with heated metal plates (*gauffré*). In Holland and France both the plain and the patterned varieties went by the name of *trippe* or *trijp*.[39] A version was called *peluche* (hence 'plush') which may have had an especially long pile; and plain woollen velvets also seem to have been known as *pannes*.[40]

In England this class of material was not only called 'mockado' but we find 'vallure' (velure) and 'caffoy' or 'capha'.[41] The latter has a Dutch derivation: *Caffa werkers* were apparently weavers of this material. The Dutch made especially good materials of this class.[42] This may be why the misleading term 'Utrecht velvet' or *velours d'Utrecht* has come to be attached to it, but it seems these fabrics were never made at Utrecht; the term may derive from the fact that the figured versions were woven on a draw-loom and were thus a *velours de trek* (i.e. *à la tire*, drawn). The terminology within this whole class of materials is immensely confusing and deserves serious investigation. One might then be able to identify the different varieties, including 'tuft moccado' which was on some stools in 1585.[43]

RUGGS, BLANKETS AND FLEDGES

Ruggs, Blankets and Fledges were woollen materials, made up in recognisable forms, that one could place on a bed for warmth, although ruggs and fledges might sometimes also be used on the floor.

A rugg was a cloth of coarsely-woven material (*rug* means rough in Scandinavian) that served as a form of coverlet.[44] 'Irish ruggs' seem to have had a shaggy pile and may have resembled the *ryer* of Swedish and Finnish peasant-culture which were bed-hangings with a long pile, boldly patterned. In Ireland these ruggs were also used as cloaks[45] and one sees people wearing this shaggy garment in contemporary illustrations. Irish ruggs are sometimes described as being 'chequered', which presumably means they had a tartan effect in their weave.[46] They were apparently identical with the 'caddows' which Cotgrave explains was a type of 'couverture velouté' [coverlet with a pile] that we know could be checked.[47] In 1610 it was noted that Ireland produced 'course wool caddowes . . . or coverlets'.[48]

Irish ruggs were often to be seen on beds in grand English houses in England in the sixteenth and early seventeenth century[49] but the fact that someone could speak of 'outlandish caddows' in 1681 suggests that they had by then long disappeared from the fashionable scene.[50] Ruggs, on the other hand, continue to be mentioned among lists of bedclothes and the word had presumably come simply to mean a coarse woollen coverlet, as it does today. They tended to be colourful.

Exactly how a rugg differed from a blanket is not clear but most of the time there may have been no more difference than there is today. Superior to ordinary blankets were 'Spanish blankets'[51] which in France were often known as *catalonnes* or *castelognes* because they came from Catalonia.[52] However, these highly regarded bed-coverings were also referred to as ruggs—an inventory of 1603, for instance, included 'a large tawny Spanish rugge'.[53] By the middle of the century, fine blankets were being made in England. Cardinal Mazarin, who was highly discriminating in all such matters, had several sets of 'couvertures de laine trés fine d'Angleterre, ayant quatre couronnes bleues au quatre coins' [fine woollen coverlets [or blankets] from England, with four blue crowns in the four corners].[54] Blankets were apparently also woven on large estates for local use; the inventory of Ingatestone Hall of 1600 includes some 'home-made' blankets, one pair of which had black selvedges ('broad black lists').[55]

Blankets were normally of wool but the term comes from the mediaeval French word *blanchet* (pronounced *blanquet* in the west of France) which was a form of bed-clothing made of white linen,[56] and some seventeenth century blankets were in fact not of wool but of silk. The Duchess of Lauderdale, for example, had a silk blanket on her bed at Ham House,[57] while two that were 'quilted both sides' were bought in 1699 for a royal bed at Hampton Court [58]. William III's 'low bed' (i.e. his personal bed rather than his bed of state) had a pair of 'India sattan blankets'.[59] These were exceptional, however. Commonly referred to in lists of bedclothes are 'fustian blankets' or often simply 'fusteans'. Fustian in the seventeenth century seems to have been a material of cotton and linen but some fustians were classed with woollen materials.[60] It clearly had a fuzzy, napped surface which was distinctive. Some pillows at Ingatestone had 'the napp syde of the fustian outwarde'.[61]

In 1554 a fustian blanket was valued at 5s. 10d., a woollen blanket at 1s. 8d., and a 'fledge blanket' at only 12d.[62] Fledge was a material of which 'fledges' were made.[63] They are mentioned in the inventories of Hardwick and Chatsworth of 1601 when they were to be found on beds or on the floor round the bed. It has been suggested that fledges were eiderdowns or quilts filled with feathers (*flèches*) but it seems more likely that the material of which they were made, and from which they derived their name, had a distinctive feather-like pattern—a herringbone effect in the weave.[64] They do not appear in inventories much after the beginning of the seventeenth century.

WORSTED DAMASK AND PRINTED PARAGON

Damask is woven on a draw-loom with a pattern contrived by means of two contrasting weaves that catch the light in different ways. A damask can be of silk, of linen (see below), or of wool—or rather of worsted, which is spun from an especially long and well-combed woollen fibre so as to produce a particularly tough, smooth and shiny yarn. Damasks of worsted woven with large patterns suitable for hangings came into fashion in the late seventeenth century. Celia Fiennes saw a bed and wall-hangings at Ashstead Park 'of a fine damaske made of worsted. It looks pretty and with a gloss like camlett.'[65] 'Camlet', with its tougher relation, 'paragon' (*baracan* in French), was a ribbed worsted cloth but they could both be 'watered' (i.e. crushed so that the ribbed weave reflected light unevenly and so produced the characteristic wavy pattern of watering or *moirage*, as the French call it, giving a *moiré* or watered effect), or they could be printed with hot plates against a wooden block carved in intaglio with a pattern. The resulting 'printed paragon' was much used for hangings in the seventeenth century. A closet still hung with what is presumably this material is to be seen at Knole. The pattern is very similar to that which one might have found on a contemporary damask of worsted or silk. All are materials of a single colour with a pattern produced by the play of light on contrasting surfaces.

WOOLLEN STUFFS WITH LITTLE OR NO PATTERN

There was a very wide range of woollen stuffs with little or no pattern available in the seventeenth century. They came in many qualities, some of them far better than anything normally available today. There were numerous different types of weave and each had a different name. Some were given yet another name merely on account of a variation in quality or scale of pattern, while additional effects like 'watering' could also lead to their acquiring a fresh name. Moreover, the textile industry itself sometimes invented new names in order to promote sales. The main sorts were, however, fairly easy to recognise and their names occur in the inventories where they were presumably used properly. All the same, there was plenty of room for confusion at the time and the compilers of many inventories avoided the difficulty simply by calling all such materials 'stuffs' or 'cloth' (*drap* in French), and occasionally we find 'worsted stuff'.

Nevertheless, we must try and distinguish the chief sorts—not in a way that will satisfy the textile historian but sufficiently to give a general sense of the varieties that were available.

A material very commonly used in upholstery was 'serge' which has a pronounced twill (i.e. is woven in such a way as to produce a diagonal ribbed effect). London serges were admired but the principal centre of production, as with most woollen or worsted materials, was North-eastern France (Châlons, Rheims, Amiens). They also came from Chartres and from as far afield as Florence, Athens and Smyrna. 'Say(e)' was a light-weight form of serge;[66] in France it was known as *sayette* and it came chiefly from Amiens, but it was also woven at Norwich and at Sudbury in Suffolk. 'Shalloon' (named after Châlons) was also a form of serge. A tougher form of twilled worsted was 'perpetuana', known in French as *sempiterne*; some samples in a Swedish collection have a marked basket-like effect in the weave that is superimposed, as it were, on the twill ground.[67]

A common material at the time was 'kersey', which was flannel-like, but it was not much used in upholstery. The same applies to 'linsey woolsey', a coarse and often homespun cloth. Very similar to modern baize were the 'bays' of the seventeenth century although some had a longer nap. They came in many qualities but the finest bays were made at Colchester and bays from there and other towns in Essex were exported in large quantities. They were chiefly used for linings but were also suitable for making protective covers for furniture. 'Frieze' was a material that is usually associated with heavy outer clothing but some hangings of this heavily-napped stuff were to be seen in rather grand rooms at the Earl of Arundel's Tart Hall in 1641.[68] 'Homespun' was presumably woven locally and appears among the contents of unimportant rooms as 'wadmole' or 'woodmeale'.[69]

'Tammy' was a rather ordinary sort of worsted material in the eighteenth century, with a plain weave and a rather springy texture. It was originally called 'stamin' or 'stammel'; this was a corruption of the French term for the material, *estamine*. This in turn derives from the Italian for a strainer, *stamigna*, which indicates that it had an open weave[70]. Lady Leicester's 'best bed' had hangings of this material in 1634, it was obviously a very respectable material in her day.[71]

'Camlet' was a very important upholstery material. It had a ribbed effect and was raspy to the touch. It was very robust. Camlet could be 'watered', 'waved' or 'figured'.[72] A tougher form of camlet was 'paragon' which came in the same three forms, the 'figured' type being called 'printed paragon', as has already been noted.

SILKS, BROCATELLE AND HALF-SILKS

The most sumptuous and the most costly class of silk material was silk velvet[73] which could be plain (Plate 41) or figured. The type known as 'Genoa velvet', which had bold patterns rendered in one or more colours in silk pile against a plain or satin ground, was the most expensive of all in the seventeenth century (Colour Plate XI). Genoa was famous for its silk furnishing materials, of which the large-patterned velvets were the most spectacular, but 'Genoa velvet' was also woven elsewhere, notably at Lyons, from the middle of the century onwards. No other centre ever quite succeeded in improving on the Genoese product, however. Silk damask[74] came next in precedence but was probably the most popular of the luxury materials used for upholstery purposes. Once again, silk damasks with bold patterns suitable for this purpose were woven in great quantity at Genoa but were imitated in other centres of silk-weaving (Plate 38). Damasks were normally of a single colour but could be executed in two or more colours on occasion. If there were passages of gold in the pattern (or small areas of any second colour, for that matter) these would be 'brocaded' so as to save material. Brocading consisted of expressly inserting these passages with a separate bobbin of the required thread; this section of pattern did not appear automatically through the main weaving process.[75]

Silks of any sort could be brocaded. A handsome brocaded satin[76] dating from the 1670s is to be seen on the walls of the Queen's Closet at Ham House and on the two armchairs that belong there (Colour Plate XVI). A 'brocade' was strictly speaking any silk material incorporating brocading but in the seventeenth century it was more loosely used in reference to any silk material in which passages brocaded with gold or silver thread played a notable part.[77] 'Cloth of gold' was a term loosely used to describe any silk material where gold was much in evidence, either from heavy brocading with gilt thread of one or more kinds (Plate 140),[78] or because it was woven into the ground as part of the main weaving process. 'Cloth of silver' was similar but a material called 'tissue' seems to have been one with much silver woven into the ground.[79] Likewise 'tinsell' may have been the silk material, of which many specimens survive, which has strips of gold thread woven into the ground that made it sparkle (*étinceler*).[80]

Far more common, naturally, were the plain silken materials. I have mentioned plain velvet. Satin was also usually plain. Silk woven in plain weave was called 'taffeta' and a thin version of this, suitable for linings and sun-curtains, was known as 'sarcenet'.[81] A ribbed plain silk like *gros de Tours* was 'tabby' (*tabis* in French). It came plain or watered, but could also have a small pattern (probably self-coloured) when it came to be known as *tabis à fleurs*.[82] The 'spotted sad colour tabby' of the summer hangings in the Queen's Bedchamber at Ham House may have been of this last type.[83] Closely related to tabby was 'mohair' which some modern authorities insist was a woollen material, but the contexts in which mohair occurs in seventeenth-century inventories make this inconceivable, and it is actually called 'mohair silke' in some documents.[84] Taffetas might be 'changeable' which merely meant that they were what would now be called 'shot silks', with warps and wefts of two different colours which produces changing effects according to how the light falls on folds in the material. Satins (and taffetas later) might also be 'clouded' which is today called *chiné*; it is not easy to explain this process which involves dying the pattern onto the warps before they are woven. This produces a hazy pattern which can be very attractive.

Brocatelle (sometimes given as 'brocadillo') was specially designed for use as rich wall-hangings. It appears on the face to be all of silk and has large patterns similar to those on furnishing damasks and velvets. But the warps are of linen which make it robust and helped to take the weight of long 'drops' of the material when hung on a wall. Since it does not drape well, it was rarely used for other purposes. 'Brocatelle de Venise' was a very fashionable material in the late seventeenth century.

There were other half-silk materials available in the seventeenth century, and some had large patterns that made them suitable for upholstery. One finds specimens in large collections of historic textiles but, as with 'dornix' with which some of these materials have affinities, little serious study has so far been devoted to them. Common in the sixteenth and early seventeenth century was 'Bruges Satin' (rendered as 'Brydges satten' in some documents) which seems to have had a silk warp and linen weft (the latter probably only appeared on the face when there was a pattern).

COTTON AND LINEN MATERIALS, CANVAS AND TICKING

European cotton materials were not much used for upholstery in the seventeenth century.[85] On the other hand the delightful Indian painted cottons known as 'pintadoes' or 'chintes' were to be seen in some of the most fashionable settings during the second half of the century (Plate 115 and colour Plate XIII). These exotic materials were beginning to reach Europe in the late sixteenth century.[86] By 1609 the English East India Company was engaged in a lively trade in them[87] and, by 1620, was placing orders in India for specific types.[88] The Countess of Arundel so admired these materials that she had three whole rooms (including her own bedchamber) hung with them.[89] All the same, Pepys had to explain what 'a chinke' was when he bought some to hang his wife's study in 1663.[90] By the 1680s, however, plenty of these colourful materials were to be seen in every grand house in England, Holland and France. The 'Calleco Chamber' at Cowdray in 1682 was in no way exceptional. Not only the wall-hangings of this room were of 'painted caleco', but also the window-curtains, the table-covers and the hangings of the bed.[91]

Attempts were made in Europe to imitate these attractive Indian products. Patterns of an exotic character were printed (not painted) with wood blocks on cotton and on linen—but chiefly on the latter—in the seventeenth century; European printed cottons (*indiennes*) only really came into their own after about 1730.

Linen played little part in the more showy aspects of upholstery. Bed-hangings were very occasionally made of linen[92] but otherwise linen tended to be hidden away in the form of backings, inner coverings of chairs over which a finer material was fitted, and protective loose covers. Window-curtains were occasionally made of linen materials like 'buckram' and 'soultwich' (often rendered as 'southege') which must have been translucent so they acted as sun-blinds (Colour Plate I).[93] In the form of bed-linen and table-linen however the material truly came to the fore.

Sheets in the seventeenth century came in several qualities ranging from 'coarse' or 'towen' through 'flaxen' and 'dowlas' to 'Holland'.[94] Holland sheets were the finest—and whitest. In Elizabethan times, distinction was still being made between sheets of Holland and of Cambrick,[95] but Cambrai fell behind in the competition.

Table-linen also came in various qualities, with flaxen and towen at the coarse end and the linen damasks at the other. Some of the coarse grades were off-white and even brown (i.e. unbleached). Next came 'diaper' which had a regular all-over pattern,[96] with 'hucaback' which was even finer. There was 'French diaper' and 'Holland diaper', which was superior. Likewise there was 'course' and 'fine' damask, the latter almost certainly coming from Haarlem where the best linen-damasks were woven, although the weavers of Courtrai were scarcely less skilful.[97]

Mattresses, pillows and bolsters were usually composed of a bag made of canvas 'ticking' or 'tick' (*coutil* in French). Ticking was normally striped (Plate 116) and this was probably why it was possible to distinguish 'Bruxhill [Brussels] ticke' from 'Britanie ticke', or 'Flanders tick' from 'Dutch tike of small stripe';[98] for until quite recently, there were national preferences in the colour of ticking-stripes, the French preferring brown and white while the English liked black and white. However, 'tick' came also to mean the bag itself. There was at Ingatestone, for example, a 'fustian tick' filled with down whereas the other down mattresses were covered with 'ticke fyne . . . with blew stripes'.[99]

The padding of chairs was built up on an even coarser material—sackcloth. In the seat it would be supported on 'girthweb'—the webbing bands of which saddle-girths are made.[100] These materials were also commonly striped brown and white.

MATTING AND MATS

During the second half of the sixteenth century and the first three decades of the seventeenth century it was normal to have the floors of the grandest rooms fitted with an all-over covering of matting. This was made of rushes braided in strips, herringbone fashion, and could be stitched together to form what was presumably the earliest form of fitted carpet (Colour Plate XI). Such floor-coverings may be seen in several Elizabethan portraits. The matting at Ingatestone came from Cornwall.[101] Cornish mats were famous in the eighteenth century and Dr Johnson stated that 'the women and children of Cornwall make mats of small bents there growing which serve to cover floors and walls.'[102] The 'natte anglaise tres fine' which was used in 1771 to protect a staircase in Paris was perhaps a Cornish product.[103] But matting had gone out of fashion for covering floors in important rooms by the mid-seventeenth century and one thereafter finds it in less noticeable places—'a flore matt & piece of corse cloth to cover ye stairs' and '2 church flore matts' being typical examples.[104]

This matting was plain, but mats could also have a coloured pattern. There were some 'fayre matts black and white' at Hardwick in 1601, and at the Nassau residence in Brussels in 1618 there were in store some 'marchepieds de joncqz d'Espagne grandz, de couleur noire et jaulne' [large [long?] runners of Spanish rushes, black and yellow coloured], and Cardinal Mazarin had 'un tapis de natte de Hollande, façonné de diverse couleurs' [a Dutch patterned mat of various colours].[105] A black and white mat is also visible in the portrait of a Spanish princess at Knole (Plate 117), and what could well be a Dutch mat is to be seen on the floor in a well known painting by Jan Steen (Plate 116). Such mats were clearly acceptable in fashionable settings. Some of them could well have been made in North Africa whence thin and colourful mats are still imported. Pepys saw 'a very fine African mat' in London in 1666 and maintained that it was entirely suitable 'to lay upon the ground under a bed of state'.[106] Under the bed of the Duchess of Ormonde at Kilkenny Castle in 1684 there was a 'Tangier mat' which could well have been similar to what Pepys saw.[107] In the Drawing Room at Kilkenny, moreover, there were some 'Portugal mats'. These must have been distinctive for they are mentioned in quite a few late seventeenth-century inventories of important houses. They were usually in the bedchamber and it would seem that it became the fashion to have grand beds standing on them (Plate 95).[108] Already in 1641 we find the Countess of Arundel's bed at Tart Hall standing on an 'Indian matt' and there was a roll of this material, comprising fourteen pieces, in the North Gallery which also sported many Turkish and Persian carpets.[109] Presumably we here have a transitional stage, with the Elizabethan tradition of a matted floor on which Oriental rugs could be placed, now carried out with exotic matting while an individual exotic mat is being placed in a strategic spot, as was to become the fashion later in the century. Matting and mats were, at any rate, to be seen in the grandest houses throughout the century.

The mattresses of beds were also frequently laid on mats supported on a network of ropes. Thick rush mats could also serve as insulation for windows in winter.

LEATHER

'Gilt leather' was extensively used for wall-hangings during the seventeenth century (Colour Plate XIII and Plates 47, 104 and 227). It was also used for covering chairs during the second half of the century. 'Gilt leather' was not in fact gilt at all; it was made with 'skins' (of calves) that were faced with tin-foil. During the second half of the century these prepared skins might be embossed by pressing into a wooden mould carved in intaglio with a pattern. In all cases, however, the ground was then punched with small sub-patterns that would reflect the light, and the main pattern was then painted in one or more colours. Those parts of the tin-foil ground that had not been painted were then glazed with a markedly yellow varnish which imparted a golden look to the tin-foil.[110]

The skins could be made up into hangings of any required size. Border-patterns

104. Gilt leather providing a striking form of wall-decoration in a Dutch house; about 1640. Whole skins bearing a formal Renaissance pattern alternate in bands with a narrow border-pattern. A similar bordering is used at top and bottom.

were available and narrow strips of the material could be provided for disguising the nails that held the hangings in place on the walls.[111]

'Gilt leather' was first produced by the Islamic peoples, and Moorish Spain developed the technique. Indeed, this material has become so closely identified with Spain that some authorities still call it 'Spanish leather',[112] although the term is not commonly used to describe this material in seventeenth-century inventories. By this time the centre of production had anyway passed to the Low Countries—Malines (Mechlin) and Amsterdam being particularly famed for their gilt leathers. However, the material was also produced in France, and to a lesser extent in England, Brandenburg, Italy and Portugal. In the mid-seventeenth century some large pictorial hangings imitating tapestries were made in this technique (Plate 105) but, in most cases, each individual skin bore a complete repeat of the pattern concerned or was one of a set of four which made up a full repeat.

Chairs were sometimes covered with gilt leather (although not to the extent that some antique dealers and collectors would have us believe), but plain leather was much more commonly used (Plates 149 and 164). 'Russia leather' is mentioned frequently in this connection and 'Turkey leather' also appears; 'Morocco leather' only seems to make an appearance late in the century.[113] In Italy and Spain chairs

105. Gilt leather hangings with large-scale pictorial decoration, framed with widths of a border-pattern. Flemish; 1660s.

with leather backs that were heavily tooled and gilt, in the manner of rich book-bindings, were greatly in favour but this fashion was not widely accepted in the north. The 'couche of crimson leather printed border wise' mentioned in an inventory of 1614 probably had a tooled leather cover like this.[114] At Hardwick in 1601 there was 'a chare of black leather guilded'[115] which might also have been tooled and gilded, although the gilding could have been applied on some form of priming. In certain Dutch paintings, notably some by Vermeer, one sees chairs with what look like black leather backs that have gilded diamond-shaped patterns (Plate 227).

———————————

VI. (right) Design for a ceiling by Jean Cotelle; French, 1640s. This drawing may well have been procured from Paris for Inigo Jones and is likely to concern an important commission, perhaps in a French royal palace.

'Scorched leather' was a reddish-brown leather onto which a pattern was scorched with the aid of a hot plate applied to the face, and a mould applied under pressure to the back. The effect somewhat resembled that of damask (Plate 299) and there can be little doubt that the 'leather damask' of the inventories was in fact leather of this type, especially as 'to damask' also meant to stamp patterns on a material (see p. 124). It was much used for making protective covers—'cases' and 'carpets'—for furniture.

PRINTED, PAINTED AND FLOCKED HANGINGS

We have already mentioned several printed, painted and flocked materials. We discussed printed linens and cottons, the imprinting of patterns on woollen velvets, on paragon and camlet, on ribbed silks, and on scorched leather. We also discussed Indian painted cottons (chintzes), and painted gilt-leather panels.

Large hangings that were painted with scenes similar to those woven into tapestries were not all that rare in the sixteenth and seventeenth centuries but not many specimens survive (Colour Plate IX). They varied enormously in quality—from the 'paynted clothes about ye chamber' valued at 6s. 8d. to be seen in an Oxfordshire farmhouse in 1579,[116] which were substitutes for genuine tapestry, to the sumptuous and delicately executed hangings that were provided for the *Grande Galerie* at Versailles (presumably soon after 1680) which were described as 'une tenture de tapisserie peinte sur un fonds de toile d'argent trait, représentant partie de l'Histoire du Roy, dessein de Mr. Le Brun' [a tapestry [like] hanging, painted on a ground of drawn silver thread with a representation of part of the History of the King, designed by Mr. Le Brun].[117] At Hardwick the famous High Great Chamber was not only furnished with a set of tapestry hangings depicting the Story of Ulysses but had also 'another sute of hangings', no doubt for use in summer, which were of 'woollen cloth stayned [i.e. painted] with frett [strapwork patterns?] and storie and silk flowers.'[118] The Hardwick hangings very probably came from Flanders for the English industry was in decline in Elizabethan times.[119] At the end of the century there were painted satin hangings in a room at Dyrham[120] but these are likely to have been Chinese, since Chinese painted silk hangings were by then just coming into fashion.

In 1634, one Jerome Lanyer sought letters patent for 'by affixinge Wooll, Silke and other Material of divers Cullors, upon Lynnen, Cloath, Silke, Cotton, Leather, and other substances with Oyle, Size, and other Ciments, to make useful and serviceable Hangings'.[121] He was referring to hangings which had their patterns executed in flock of various kinds, but usually of wool flock (*tontisse*, in French). Flock applied in this way produced a tolerably good imitation of velvet and, since real velvet was both desirable and expensive, this cheap substitute was eagerly sought.

Flock hangings of some sort were already available in the sixteenth century and the Painter-Stainers Company of London claimed in 1626 that 'flock work' was one

VII. (left) *Tapisserie de Bergame*; probably woven in Northern France in the middle of the seventeenth century. Although rather coarse, such colourful, large-patterned materials were suitable for wall-hangings in all but the grandest settings. As this panel shows, separate borderings were available so that panels of any size could be made up.

of their monopolies.[122] How Lanyer's patent of a few years later differed is not clear now. A Scotsman visiting Amsterdam in 1693 reported that 'there is a . . . velvett and guilded leather [here] that is exported from this [country] to England',[123] and there is a late seventeenth-century model chair in the Saffron Walden Museum which is covered in a flocked gilt leather which might be a specimen of this Dutch product.[124] The famous Parisian decorative painter, Claude Audran III, organised 'une manufacture de tapisseries composées de laine hachée ou pilée, sur toile ciré' [a manufactory of hangings [with patterns] composed of chopped or crushed wool on [a ground of] oiled cloth] at the end of the century.[125] Audran's hangings are said to have become popular in Paris, probably because of the charm of Audran's designs rather than the technique in which they were rendered. Sadly, none seems to survive.

The Painter-Stainers' monopoly may primarily have concerned flocked *paper* hangings. Their monopoly only extended to England, of course, but they probably did not at this stage feel that the factory at Rouen producing *papier velouté* offered any serious competition.[126] Nevertheless, the industry was to wax, and flock wallpaper ('caffoy paper') was to become an English speciality in the eighteenth century.

Not all wallpaper was flocked, but wallpapers were not otherwise much used in the seventeenth century. It was still necessary for a writer in 1699 to explain that 'they are managed like wollen hangings' and are called 'paper tapestry'.[127] However, shops dealing in wallpaper existed in London from the time of Charles II onwards[128] and it had become worth levying a tax on wallpaper by 1712.

Pepys's wife had hangings of 'counterfeit damask' on the walls of her closet.[129] As it was an imitation of damask rather than velvet, it will not have been flocked. But the process involved printing for the word 'damask' also meant 'to stamp rude draughts on waste paper, etc.'[130] When books were censored, it was not unusual for the offending pages to be used as a ground for printing such patterns. In 1673 the Bishop of London, for instance, ordered the Master and Wardens of the Stationers' Company 'to damask or obliterate whatever sheets you have seized of a book called *Leviathan*'.[131] Luckily some copies of Hobbes' book escaped the net and 'the greatest, perhaps the sole, masterpiece of political philosophy in the English language' is therefore still known to us.

NEEDLEWORK

Wall-hangings, chair-covers, table-carpets and most of the other confections that the upholsterer handled had to be assembled with the aid of a needle. Materials were made up into the desired form, trimming was applied, and the requisite hooks, rings and tapes were stitched in place. Upholstery has in this respect not changed in its essentials since the seventeenth century and there is no need to elaborate on this aspect here. What was created as a result of such labours can, however, best be studied from looking at contemporary illustrations including those in this book.

Needlework was also involved at a more artistic level in creating appliqué work which consists of taking ornamental shapes cut out (*découpé*) of one material and applying them to a ground material (Plates 96 and 107). One of the most striking examples of *appliqué* work in England is the 'Spangled Bed' at Knole which is traditionally associated with James I.[132] This has hangings of red satin to which a pattern of strapwork ornament cut from white silk has been applied. The edges of the *découpé* ornament are trimmed with silk cord that is 'couched', or stitched onto the surface. The spangles which have earned the bed its name are sequins stitched along the centre-line of the strapwork. Bold effects can readily be achieved by means of *appliqué* work, and there is a certain three-dimensional quality to materials assembled in this way. What may be regarded as an extension of *appliqué* work was the stitching to the face of a textile hanging or a chair-cover, of a braid or 'galloon' so as to form an inner border (Plate 162). This type of decoration could be quite elaborate, incorporating intricate scrollwork, and might be worked with two different widths of braid so that a counterpoint effect was achieved.

Actual embroidery, that is to say patterns worked with the needle on a textile ground (e.g. Plates 106 and 203),[133] came in many forms during the seventeenth century and the reader is referred to some of the numerous books on the subject which survey the technical and artistic aspects of this craft.[134] It was a highly versatile medium in which a needlewoman living, for instance, deep in the country could create decorative panels suitable for many purposes—cushion-covers, firescreen panels, coverlets, chair-covers, etc. She might copy a motif from one of the many pattern-books available, or she might get someone skilled with a pencil to draw a design for her to work—she might even do this herself if she felt she had the talent. Alternatively, she might imitate in needlework the pattern on a woven textile that was available to copy. At any rate, the panels created domestically in this way were rarely very big; the production of large hangings, table-carpets, and coverlets was on the whole left to the professional 'broderers', working in *ateliers* in the cities. They usually had access to skilful designers who could compose patterns suitable for any given purpose. The capabilities of individual professional embroiderers of course varied immensely, but the most skilful were able to produce work of the very greatest delicacy and beauty. The designs worked in the principal ateliers tended to be international in character, based on engraved compositions by Italian, Flemish, German or Parisian artists.

106. An embroidered bed-valance of about 1600. Executed in coloured silks and gold thread on cream-coloured silk and trimmed with two sorts of gold lace bordering. Although probably made in Germany, the pattern is in a style that was fashionable all over Europe at the time.

While the patterns executed with a needle might be described by someone making an inventory, they never specify what stitch was employed although the various kinds of stitches all had individual names that were known to embroiderers. It is therefore puzzling that inventories often mention 'Irish stitch',[135] until one realises that this was a pattern rather than a stitch. It was in fact the same as *point d'Hongrie,* the flame-like zig-zag pattern that was also executed as a woven pattern in materials like *tapisserie de Bergame.* It was a favourite pattern in the seventeenth century and has no other name in English inventories. Some hangings of this pattern survive at Chastleton that can with a fair degree of certainty be equated with the 'hangings of Irish stitch' mentioned in the inventory of 1633.[136]

Large hangings executed entirely in embroidery were anyway quite exceptional. Large pieces were more frequently decorated with bands of embroidery, with applied ornaments of embroidery, or with open patterns in which much ground was allowed to show between the elements. In fact, for large-scale work, embroidery was a form of embellishment and rarely served as a means of overall decoration.

The finest sorts of professional embroidery, executed perhaps in several kinds of gold thread with details worked with coloured silks, could be a most impressive form of decoration. Such work was also very expensive. Domestic work, on the other hand, was mostly worked or 'wrought' by the lady of the house or by the women of her entourage whose labour was free, so the only expense involved would lie in the purchasing of the materials.[137]

TRIMMINGS

Trimming serves two purposes. It can be used to finish off edges of upholstery work and to disguise seams, or it may serve merely as embellishment. In the seventeenth century it often did both at the same time.

To achieve a rich effect two or more materials could be assembled in a variety of ways, material could be decorated with *appliqué* work or with embroidery, or it could be loaded with trimmings of various kinds. Indeed, this last was the principal means by which the seventeenth-century upholsterer achieved his effects (Plate 95 and 193). By and large, seventeenth-century upholstery was not very well executed but failings could be disguised by these eye-catching ornaments. Trimmings were piled onto the richer kinds of seventeenth-century upholstery in great profusion, as contemporary descriptions sometimes prove and many illustrations show (Plate 140 and Colour Plate XII). Surviving specimens of seventeenth century upholstery, on the other hand, have so often lost their complement of trimming that they no longer give anything like a true impression of how such confections looked when new. The contribution of the *passementier,* as the French called the maker of trimmings, to the final appearance of seventeenth-century upholstery must not be underestimated.

Randle Holme, writing in the middle of the century, explained that hangings might have 'inch fringe, caul fring, tufted fring, snailing fring, gimp fring with tufts and buttons, vellem fring, etc.',[138] but there were many sorts and some were of

107. (left) French appliqué work of about 1680. The headcloth of the Bielke Bed (see Plate 41). Strapwork of white silk, with foliate ornament in blue silk, all edged with couched silk cord, applied to crimson velvet. The tendrils are also rendered in the couched technique.

immense complexity. His list in fact seems to be arranged in increasing order of richness, the 'inch fringe' being a simple, straightforward fringe (Plate 40) while examples of what must be vellum fringe (because narrow strips of vellum are used to help produce loops and thus a three-dimensional build-up) show it to have been of extreme richness (Plate 100).[139] 'Snailing' was produced with a spiralling core; the fringe was usually uncut, and thus had loops rather than whiskers, as it were. 'Caul' means net, and fringes with a wide band of netting at the top were popular during the first half of the century (Colour Plate II and Plate 136). The strands were gathered into tassel-like bunches along the lower edge. 'Tufted fringe' had small bell-like tufts which led the French to call them *campanes* (Plate 38). In English this became 'campaign fringe'.[140]   The terms used for fringes in France are most confusing. 'Lorsque la frange est tout-à-fait basse on l'apelle mollet; quand les fils en font plus longe que l'ordinaire & que la tête est large & ouvragée à jour, on lui donne le nom crépine' [When the fringe is quite short it is called *mollet*; when the threads are much longer than usual and the heading is wide and of open-work, it is known as *crépine*.] says Savary at the beginning of the eighteenth century.[141] But he is speaking of the well-established practice of the period of having long fringes, *crépines*, only in positions where they could hang straight down (i.e. along lower edges, or along top edges if affixed to hang downwards instead of upwards), while one had short fringes of the same pattern along the vertical edges and along the top, if the fringe at the top was not reversed.[142] On the other hand, as he also implies, *crépine* was the name given to any openwork fringe. It need not even display what we would understand by fringing; it could be an intricate network of metal thread (Plate 99) but used where *crépine* (or long fringe) would have been used.[143]

Rich fringes might be of gold thread, less commonly of silver, but were not infrequently of silver and gold together. Fringes were even more often made of silk, sometimes of two colours alternating along their length (Plate 40). Fringes on woollen or worsted hangings were often none the less of silk, but worsted (called 'crewel') fringe was also available (Plate 103). The heading of fringes could be plain or embellished in fancy ways, if a richer effect was required.

Another form of trimming was lace, which could be of silk, or of silver or gold thread.[144] It was applied in bands as inset bordering or so as to break up large areas of material into panels (Plate 2).[145] In inventories this is sometimes described as being 'striped with lace'.[146] Braids and galloons could be applied in the same way, as has already been noted.

The *passementier* also made up tassels, rosettes, cords and ribbons with which upholstery work could be completed.

FILLINGS AND STUFFING

The upholsterer required soft materials with which to fill mattresses, bolsters and pillows, and to pad chairs and other forms of seat-furniture. I shall consider the various types of mattress in use in the seventeenth century when I come to discuss beds, but the fillings of mattresses ranged from swansdown and eiderdown, through ordinary feathers, wool clippings or flock, to straw and chaff.

Less common were cotton wool, beech leaves, and goose feathers. During the second half of the century, horsehair began to be used for mattresses.

Horsehair was not much used for padding seat-furniture before the 1660s (Plate 180).[147] The padding was otherwise achieved with the aid of down or of straw.

Securing stuffing so that it did not collect at one end of a mattress, or did not slide away from the pressure-points of a chair presented problems for the upholsterer. For coverlets and then mattresses, quilting provided the answer. This involved stitching right through the sandwich—cover, filling, cover—so that the stuffing was locked in position. Quilting is of course a form of needlework and the stitching could be organised into decorative patterns. It was not practical for thicker forms of mattress or squabs, however. For this purpose, what we would now call 'buttoning' was devised. Here the materials were secured by means of strong thread passed through at isolated spots with a long needle. The threads placed a considerable strain on the surface-material so the thread was looped over a tuft of linen which helped to spread the load (Plate 304). The tufts served the same purpose as buttons which were, however, not introduced until the late eighteenth century. Compared with the deep buttoning of the nineteenth century, incidentally, seventeenth and eighteenth century tufting or buttoning was quite shallow. The padding of chairs was also at first held in place by quilting (Plate 172) but, in the late seventeenth century, a few important pieces of French seat-furniture had their stuffing secured in position by tufting (Plate 170).

CHAPTER VI
The Upholsterer's Furnishings

HAVING surveyed the materials with which furnishings were made in the seventeenth century, we can now consider how the upholsterer made them up into 'furniture'—a term that embraced all the loose furnishings of a room, and not merely the wooden items, as it does today. In this chapter, I shall deal in turn with wall-hangings, portières, window-curtains and floor-coverings. Beds and seat-furniture constitute such important classes that separate chapters are devoted to them.

WALL-HANGINGS

Generally speaking, tapestries were the most valuable form of wall-covering in the seventeenth century and people tended to hang them in the most important rooms—in the Great Chamber, the Salon or Withdrawing Room, or the main bedchambers. There were two principal types of tapestry available. On the one hand were the pictorial kind with a three-dimensional scene. These are variously described as 'histories', 'of imagery' or 'with personages' (Plate 2 and 12).[1] Related to them were 'landskips (Plates 1, 93 and 94). On the other hand there were the essentially two-dimensional hangings with ornamental motifs like 'grotesques' and those displaying armorial bearings. One should perhaps class with these the so-called 'verdure tapestries' which show massed foliage and undergrowth (Plate 108). They often appear two-dimensional although they are in fact a variant of the landscape type. They were usually described as being of 'fforrest worke' and the 'buskedge' hangings, occasionally met with in English inventories are also likely to have been of this type.[2]

On rare occasions a set of tapestries would be designed with a special room in mind and then of course they would exactly fit the particular walls concerned.[3] Rather more commonly, a rich man might order a set of tapestries from a well-known series[4] and have them made so that they fitted a specific room. More modest people would buy a set of tapestries ready-made and adapt them to the walls of the room where they were to hang. A certain amount of adjustment could be obtained by playing around with the borders, which were usually separate weaves sewn on around the central panel (Plate 108). Part of the main scene could be folded under at one end and the border could be re-attached to make up the hanging tidily. Sometimes the piece that was not required was actually cut off. On other occasions a piece from a different scene was added to one side of the main panel to extend it. If such measures seemed too drastic, hangings could simply be taken past a corner of a room and round onto a bit of the next wall. As long as the walls were totally clad with the material, it did not matter too much that each panel did not precisely fit an individual wall (Plate 33). If a hanging obscured a doorway, it could be looped up out of the way at that place, with the aid of cords or hooks (Plate 93). It was preferable to arrange the hangings so that two abutted in line with the handle side of

108. Window with a single curtain pulled to one side and held up with a cord or ribbon. Note the rings attached with tapes. Dutch; 1660s.

the door (Plate 48); but, if necessary, a slit could even be cut in the hangings. If there was a narrow gap between the top of the hanging and the cornice, a narrow band of a neutral colour could be specially woven and stitched onto the top edge. The permutations were numerous; all that needs to be stressed is that, for all its associations with an aristocratic way of life, and in spite of its high cost, tapestry was not treated with all that much respect in the seventeenth century. No one thought twice about hanging pictures or a mirror in front of tapestries (Plates 1 and 311). A large nail was quite often driven straight through the hanging into the wall and that was that.

It was very much easier to adjust 'grotesques' and verdure tapestries. One could subtract a piece of the latter without spoiling the effect at all, while the open, symmetrical patterns of grotesque compositions could quite easily be trimmed or extended by adjusting both sides equally.

Most other materials were rather more easy to adjust to a particular wall because they came in narrower widths and therefore had anyway to be made up into panels of the requisite size.

Coarse hangings like *tapisseries de Bergame* could be three or four feet wide but still needed to be joined to form a hanging of any great size. One could obtain lengths of bordering which could be sewn, not only round the edges of the whole hanging in the ordinary way (Colour Plate VII), but might be interposed between each width of the main material so as to make up a hanging with several rectangular panels. This was a very common formula for wall-hangings in the seventeenth century because it allowed almost infinite flexibility. Special borders were also available for gilt-leather hangings (Plate 104) and for brocatelle.[5] Few other materials had special bordering but one could make up borders with a different material and this was the commonest method used at the time (Colour Plate XVI). It would be pointless to try to list the many combinations that occur in seventeenth-century inventories but it was common in grand rooms to have two or three widths of a rich silk material—say, damask—framed into panels or 'panes'[6] with, for instance, a striped silk, or with a plain silk with an embroidered pattern, or with damask of another colour. Worsted materials might be treated in the same way. For a while in the middle of the century it seems to have been fashionable to have a worsted panel framed with gilt leather.[7]

Hangings could of course be made up simply with one material, and often were; but a paned effect could then be achieved by couching onto the surface lines of lace (of metal or coloured silks) which broke up the surface in much the same way. For the purposes of making an inventory, it was not usually necessary to describe every detail, so a bald statement that some hangings were of, say, blue damask often gives no indication that they in fact had various embellishments which one did not need to mention in order simply to identify the hangings.

With particularly ambitious sets of hangings, the sections of bordering interposed between the panels might be fashioned like columns or pilasters. Cardinal Mazarin had some especially rich hangings of 'brocart d'argent avec figures de chasseurs, d'animaux, oiseaux, fontaines, de soies de divers couleurs' [silver brocade with figures of hunters, animals, birds, fountains, executed in silks of various colours] and these had 'colonnes de brocart d'or' [columns of gold brocade] to go between them.[8] At the end of the century it became highly fashionable in Paris to have hangings decorated with applied *colonnes torses* [spiral columns].[9] With *découpage* one could, moreover, easily have panels of fancy shape, as some splendid *appliqué* hangings at Penshurst show (Colour Plate X).

Round most hangings one could expect to see a trimming of fringe.[10] These ranged from the straight fringe, the simple form that we understand by the term today, to extremely complicated confections like the *campane* or 'campaign fringe' which had a mass of small bell-like tassels. A hanging would normally be trimmed with two different lengths of the fringe concerned—a long version for the horizontal edges where the fringe could hang straight down, and a shorter version for the vertical edges where a long fringe would otherwise droop in an unfortunate way. Along the top edge of a hanging, one could either have a short fringe facing upwards, as it were; or one could have a long fringe reversed to hang downwards from the edge. Intricate edgings could also be made up with the aid of a needle. At Ham House, for instance, there is a fragment of a rich border trimmed with small gathered puffs of pink silk, all edged with a very narrow fringe. Even now, the effect is charming.

Some particularly splendid hangings had what amounted to a pelmet running along the top. At Tart Hall, for instance, there was 'a long valence for a roome' in store in 1641.[11] Daniel Marot included such a feature in several of his proposals for rooms at the end of the century and the Dauphin had a straight valance round the top of the red camlet hangings in one of his rooms at Versailles (Plates 22 and 95). An example survives at Rosenborg Castle, in Copenhagen, dating from the early years of the eighteenth century.[12]

All these applied details helped to give rich seventeenth-century hangings that lively, frothy appearance which was so greatly admired at the time. Straightforward hangings, of a single material, without any trimming at all, can only have been seen in the very humblest of homes. For the rest, it must have been the wall-hangings more than anything which gave each room in a seventeenth-century house its individual character. It is difficult for us today to envisage how enormous was the variety of effects that could be achieved by clever combinations of materials and by the subtle application of trimmings.

Reading through inventories gives one a general impression of the materials that were commonly used for wall-hangings and those which were more rarely so used. Tapestries were to be found in most important houses, usually in the principal rooms, but other kinds of expensive material might equally well be found in the same locations. Silk damask, for instance, was favoured for grand settings right through the century, crimson damask being particularly popular at the end of the period. Plain silk velvet was relatively common and was usually to be found in combination with another material, but it would seem that the large-patterned and very expensive Genoa velvets were by no means prevalent.[13] Mohair (which I have argued was a silk material; see p. 115) was to be found in many fashionable rooms during the last two decades of the century.

Gilt leather hangings were greatly in favour during the seventeenth century and provided a truly striking effect (Plate 227) but they were going out of fashion in Paris by the end of the century.[14] Coming into favour at that time were worsted damask and camlet. Chintz, which had been seen in a few rooms before the middle of the century, became popular after that in rooms of a not too formal character.

Down the scale somewhat came the *tapisseries de Bergame* and other coarse woollen upholstery materials, for instance dornix, which were to be found in rooms of secondary importance during most of the century (Colour Plates VII and VIII). The same may be said of 'Irish stitch'.

Worsted materials of various kinds were to be seen on the walls in rather humbler rooms. Perpetuana, camlet and paragon might be found in quite grand surroundings, Kidderminster stuffs in rather less so, and the many types of relatively inexpensive materials, often just called 'woollen stuff', were used in rooms of lower status.

Exceptional but rather grand must have been rooms hung with turkeywork and moquette.[15] The rooms at Tart Hall hung with frieze trimmed with gold lace seem to have been unique and it is difficult to imagine what they were like although it is clear that they were very splendid.[16] Rooms hung with Scots 'pladd' were not common but must have been striking; presumably they had a checked, tartan effect.[17] And then there was wallpaper, which was still rare at the end of the century although flock papers imitating velvet seem to have found a ready market.

The *Dictionnaire de Trévoux* of 1704 tells us that 'Il n'y a pas longtemps que toutes les murailles des maisons etoient tapissées de nattes' [It is not long since all the walls of houses were hung with mats] and it seems that it was the practice in the Middle Ages to use matting as insulation in winter, fitting *paillassons* against windows and doors.[18] At Saint-Germain-en-Laye in 1548 there were still 'nattes faictes de neuf contre les murs . . . tant contre des deux pans de murs au deux costez de la dicte Gallerye, que aux deux boutz d'icelle' [mats newly fitted to the walls . . . on the two sections of walls at the sides of the said Gallery, as well as at the two ends of it].[19] Galleries were always difficult rooms to keep warm; they by no means always had a fireplace. As late as 1669 mats were being fitted 'devant les croissées du grand salon des Thuilleries' [in front of the windows of the great *salon* at the Tuileries].[20] They had inner facings of *toile* which were no doubt neat and colourful. The practice of insulating with mats must have been known in England. Evelyn, anyway, advised gardeners in 1664 to 'keep the doors and windows of your conservatories well matted'.[21] In order to prevent children of high rank from hurting themselves, the walls and floors of their nurseries had in former times also been padded with matting. This practice was maintained in France in the seventeenth century, the apartments of royal children up to the age of twelve being padded with thick Savonnerie carpeting or with Gobelins tapestry 'qu'en jouent ils ne puissent se blesser'.[22]

Important hangings seem usually to have been kept in the Wardrobe and were only put up when the family was in residence. If there were summer and winter hangings for a room, at least one of the sets would have to be stored away at any given time. Delicate hangings also needed frequent attention—fringes repairing, wrinkles adjusting, etc. So hangings of any degree of richness must have been readily detachable from the walls. Some velvet and silk damask hangings at Ham House which are still on the walls for which they were created in the 1670s (and are not now taken down very often) have an arrangement of hooks and eyes. Very heavy hangings must have been nailed to battens fixed to the walls. Sometimes hangings were fixed to frames like picture-stretchers.[23] Wallpaper was usually pasted directly onto the wall but might first be pasted onto canvas.[24] Sometimes it was nailed with the pieces overlapping to hide the nails.

PORTIÈRES

It was common in especially grand rooms during the second half of the century to have hangings in front of the doors (Plate 94) These were usually en suite with the wall-hangings although they might be decorated with even greater elaboration. Such *portières* contributed to the unified appearance of the room. They are mentioned in the French royal inventories and in those of Cardinal Mazarin's collection,[25] for instance, and one can see them in some of the illustrations of rooms by Daniel Marot. Occasionally a *portière* might form a contrast to the wall-hangings, on the other hand. Such would seem to have been Mazarin's two pieces of 'tapisserie de Portugal servans de dessus de porte' [Portuguese tapestry for use over the door]; it seems unlikely that they were simply panels to be fitted as over-doors (i.e. above the door-case).

Although *portières* might form an important feature of the decoration, their original purpose was functional—they served to exclude draughts—and most *portières* were erected primarily with this in mind. The 'piece of old tapestry over the door' in Lady Teynham's Old Chamber at Cowdray must have been there as a draught-excluder and the Countess of Shrewsbury had a coverlet hung in front of one door in her bedchamber at Hardwick and 'a counterpoynt of tapestrie before another dore'.[26]

Portières tended to get dirty rather quickly as they had to be pushed aside each time someone passed through the doorway. The richest *portières*, like some of those in Mazarin's collection, therefore had to have their own protective curtains. Hitching up a *portière* always posed a problem. In one Elizabethan house there was a curtain of green kersey 'wth. a curtyn rod of iron wh. is to hand afore the dore, wth. a greate hooke to putt it up when it is not drawn.'[27] This hook must have been a primitive 'hold-back'. The same result could be achieved with a smaller hook and a cord. In many cases the wall-hangings themselves were carried in front of a door and matters would then be so arranged that the junction between two abutting hangings lined up with the handle side of the door. To prevent an awkward hitching-up of the hanging over the door when it was opened, one could extend the door with battens right up to the cornice so that the whole section of hanging above the doorway also would swing out from the wall. Such an arrangement may still be seen at Ham House.

What must have served as a double door was the frame covered in tapestry ['un chassis à tapisserie servant sur les portes'] which was in Mazarin's house.[28] Celia Fiennes certainly saw some double doors at Chippenham Park at the end of the century but they were lined, and served 'to prevent noise'.[29] At Dyrham, incidentally, there was 'an engine for closing the door' in one room.[30]

WINDOW-CURTAINS AND BLINDS

Window-curtains were by no means fitted to every window in the seventeenth century but they were not uncommon in rooms of any importance, particularly in rooms set aside for dining, as well as in bedchambers and in closets—in all of which a higher degree of comfort was required than in other types of room. Curtains were primarily fitted to exclude draughts or sunlight. Privacy was hardly a consideration at all because most important rooms were up on the first and second floor. Only in towns might it present a problem. It may well be that shutters were more common in city houses than in the country; if so, this might be due primarily to the wish to have a measure of privacy rather than from any desire for security or insulation.

A clear distinction was almost invariably made in seventeenth-century inventories between the curtains listed among the hangings of a bed and those provided for a window which are almost always specified as such.[31]

Mats were sometimes fitted into window-embrasures in winter as protection against the cold. One could presumably also hang a cloth to serve the same purpose, and the references to 'window pieces' and 'window cloths' which occur from the

109. Screening curtain in a doctor's surgery with taped rings, and cords for drawing backwards and forwards. A screen of wicker (with a handle) is inserted in the lower half of the window as an additional aid to privacy.

110. (right) Symmetry achieved at windows with single fitted curtains, by pulling them to opposite sides. The lower sections of the windows are dark because the outside shutters have been closed.

111. (far right) At present this appears to be the earliest known representation of divided window-curtains. The office of the Steward at the Danish royal castle, Rosenborg, in 1653.

Middle Ages down into the early seventeenth century seem to concern something of the kind.[32] Perhaps they were hooked in place at night or when it was particularly cold. Curtains that could be drawn (i.e. that had a rod and rings, or the equivalent) had occasionally been fitted to windows already in the Middle Ages.[33] They remained utilitarian until well into the seventeenth century. Curtains might be made of a pretty material but the rods and rings were not disguised and only a single curtain would be fitted to each window.[34] At that stage few people were worried about symmetry and a curtain that was simply pulled to one side did not offend the eye at all (Plate 1 and 108). Nor was it common to have the window-curtains matching the hangings until towards the middle of the century,[35] or so it would seem, although the wealthier citizens of Antwerp are said to have already had matching curtains by the middle of the sixteenth century.[36]

When the demand for greater order in interior architecture began to manifest itself, it was recognised that the single window-curtain could spoil the symmetry of a scheme of mural decoration. If there were two windows, one could pull the single curtains to opposite sides of the windows (Plate 110), and this would of course work with any even number of windows. But many rooms had an odd number so the solution was not fully satisfactory (Plate 219). Then the idea of dividing the single curtain down the middle was developed, so that the halves could be drawn to opposite sides of the window-opening during daytime. There were divided window-curtains at Ham House by the middle of the seventeenth century [37] and there is a picture of the steward at Rosenborg Castle, in Copenhagen, doing his accounts in 1653, in which one may discern a set of divided curtains suspended by rings from a rod (Plate 111). In 1673 the *Mercure Galant*, which kept Parisians informed of the latest gossip and fashions, told its readers of what it claimed was a new invention. 'Il n'y a pas jusques au rideaux qu'on met devant des fenestres, qui ne

soient aussi sujets aux caprices de la mode. Ils sont presentement fendus par le milieu, et au lieu qu'on ne les tiroit que d'une coste, on les tire maintenant des deux costez: et l'on a introduit cette mode parce qu'ils incommoderoient moins, et que les fenestres en recevoient plus d'ornement.' [Even the curtains which are put in front of the windows are also subject to the caprices of fashion. They are now divided down the middle, and instead of pulling them to one side only they are now pulled to each side; and this fashion has been introduced because they are less inconvenient, and because the windows become more decorative.][38] Can it really be that divided curtains were unknown in France before that date? One suspects that, if they were to be seen at Ham in the 1640s, one could also by then have seen the device in certain places in France. But the French were placing much more emphasis on curtains and other hangings by the 1670s and it may well be that the *Mercure Galant* was merely pointing out that the old type of single curtain could no longer be tolerated in a fashionable interior. At any rate, thereafter the device was quickly adopted in fashionable circles. Dublin Castle, which was so elegantly appointed in the time of the Duke of Ormonde, certainly had divided curtains by 1679[39] and the curtains in the principal rooms at Ham House, fitted during the redecoration of the 1670s, were all of the divided type (Plate 112).

At about this time a new form of curtain was invented in France. This was the 'pull-up' curtain which, as its name implies, could be pulled up to the window-head by means of cords, and was so organised as to hang in festoons (Plate 238).[40] This form of curtain may have been developed from the 'tie-up' curtains used on beds of the *lit à housse* type (see p. 165), with which upholsterers would have been generally familiar by the middle of the century (Plate 132). Such curtains looked particularly good from inside the room and looked best if not pulled up too tightly against the top of the window. The fact that Louis XIV on one occasion gave explicit instructions as to how the holes for the pulleys at the top of the window-embrasure should be pierced is an indication of how important a contribution this type of curtain was thought to make to the decoration.[41] The new form was eagerly espoused by Daniel Marot in Holland and England, as several of his engravings show; he had no doubt seen early examples in Paris before he emigrated in 1684 (Plate 303). Pull-up curtains were anyway being installed in the English royal palaces at the end of the century, as an estimate for upholstery work at Hampton Court makes clear.[42]

It seems that pull-up curtains at first were fitted so as to pull up against the under-surface of the top of the window-embrasure. Later, a projecting board, pierced for the pulleys, came to be fitted at the window-head and the curtain was nailed to the front edge of this pulley-board, simply with a ruffled heading rising an inch or two above the board. The next development was to mask the pulley-board with a box-like window-cornice which might be of quite a fancy shape. This wooden box was often faced with the same material as that of the curtain below it.[43] Ordinary 'hanging' curtains were also thought to require a more decorative finish at the top and pelmets (called 'valances') were therefore added. An early reference to such a feature is one made in 1673 to curtains 'avec les petites pentes du haut' [with little valances at the top] while another in 1680 concerned 'deux rideaux et deux pentes de sarge violette pour les fenestres . . .' [two curtains and two valances of violet coloured serge for the windows].[44] Some of the curtains illustrated by Daniel Marot

112. Divided window-curtains in a Dutch house in 1674. The red curtains are probably of thin silk (sarsnet). The lower half of the window is fitted with painted double-fold interior shutters.

have complicated pelmets with gathered pleats falling into festoons and tails. Celia Fiennes saw some white silk damask curtains at Lady Donegal's at the end of the century which had 'furbellows of callicoe printed [with] flowers'.[45]

Against the cold one chose a woollen material for one's window-curtains. Particularly popular in even the grandest settings during the first half of the century was dornix, which was warm and colourful.[46] Window-curtains of saye and other serges are mentioned frequently. Paragon was often used later in the century. Rather less common were Kidderminster stuff, shalloon, linsey-wolsey, pladd, and

139

wadmole. The last was sufficiently thick to be 'unlyned'.[47] Tapestry was never used for curtains as it was too thick to draw backwards and forwards conveniently but it was still being used for window-cloths during the first decades of the century.[48]

An important bedchamber at Hardwick in 1601 had 'curtins of darnix for the windowes' against the cold, but also had 'curtins of damask and sarcenet for the windowes'.[49] The second set must have been there to reduce the amount of light coming into the room. The 'two great southege curtyons for ye great windowe' in the Great Chamber at Hengrave Hall must have served the same purpose; the cold was excluded by a 'window-cloth' of 'arras'.[50] Likewise there was a large curtain and rod in a window at Hatfield Priory a quarter of a century later but the additional 'rodds within the window' had three buckram curtains.[51] Southege and buckram, like the silk damask and sarcenet, would have been translucent, as must have been the curtains of 'greene cotten' at Cockesden in 1610 and the 'ffour ffrench green cotton window curtaines' at Edington in 1665.[52]

Window-curtains of silk are rarely mentioned in English inventories before the middle of the century. There were some at Hardwick at the beginning of the century, as we noted, but they were apparently exceptional. Very striking must have been the 'streamed tafata curtaines . . . without any lyning' which were hanging in the nine windows of the South Gallery at Tart Hall, one of the Arundels' magnificent residences, shortly before the outbreak of the Civil War.[53] After 1650, silk curtains are mentioned in the inventories of most grand houses.[54] They were effective as blinds against the sun and they were decorative. If they were to serve as blinds they were mostly of white silk[55] but, as window-curtains came increasingly to be embraced in the decoration of the room, the tendency was to have them matching the rest of the upholstery—the rest of the *ameublement*.

At Cowdray there were some window-curtains of Indian painted callico—of chintz. They were en suite with the rest of the textile furnishings of the room which was appropriately named 'The Calleco Chamber'.[56] The effect of the light coming through the chintz must have been charming. A somewhat similar effect will have been seen in the room at Dyrham which had curtains of painted satin—presumably painted in China with exotic birds and foliage—at the end of the century.[57]

The *Mercure Galant* once again acquired a niche in the history of window-curtains when, in 1686, it brought news of some white damask curtains destined for the Château de Versailles which were brocaded in gold thread (which is heavy) with monograms and lyres, 'mais seulement d'espace en espace, parce ce qu'on ne doit pas trop charger d'or un rideau qui doit estre aisé à manier' [monograms and lyres of gold, but only here and there, because one must not overload a curtain which must be easy to manage].[58] However, if curtains were particularly delicate or very heavy, or were somehow awkward to manoeuvre, one might fix cords to the top and draw them backwards and forwards by pulling on these instead of tugging at the bottom of the hanging. Cardinal Mazarin, for instance, had some white taffeta curtains with 'cordons de soie blanche' attached, 'servans à couller les rideaux' [cords of white . . . used for drawing the curtains].[59] At Kilkenny Castle in 1684 some white shalloon curtains (which were hanging on a rod so were not of the pull-up kind) also had 'strings to draw'[60] and one occasionally sees curtains fitted with draw-strings in contemporary illustrations (Plates 94 and 109). Curtain-rings, incidentally, were usually of iron but could be of horn. Brass rings were not introduced until the eighteenth century.[61] The rings were sometimes sewn directly to the top edge, or to the back with a gathered heading. Not infrequently they were also attached with loops of tape which made the top of the curtain hang well below the rod (Plates 108 and 109). This presumably helped to prevent the ring binding on the rod. Rods were of iron and were sometimes gilded. They seem usually to have had loops at each end which fitted down onto hooks driven into the wall. Alternatively a rod might have a loop at one end only while the other end was fed through a ring like a modern screw-eye set in the wall at that end. During the second half of the century, curtains in luxurious settings were often trimmed with fringe (Plates 16 and 31).

Against the heat of the sun one might have blinds of straw or matting on rollers which could be pulled up by means of cords.[62] From this it was a simple step to adapt the roller to take a textile material and so produce a roller-blind. Such devices were being fitted to windows at Stockholm Palace in 1713[63] and it is reasonable to suppose that similar features could be seen in other parts of Europe. There were makers of 'window blinds' in London, at any rate by 1726 when a certain John Brown advertised that he could supply blinds of various materials 'the best painted of any in London'.[64] When Tessin was at Versailles in 1687 he noted that the pictures in the Dauphin's Closet were protected by blinds of a painted satin on rollers, fitted with a spring that held the blind down in front of the picture.[65] If one wanted to look at the picture, one raised the blind by means of a cord. The modern roller-blind with a spring, which seems to have been evolved in the eighteenth century, of course works the other way round. Slatted blinds (Venetian blinds or *jalousies à la persienne*) also seem to have been introduced in the eighteenth century but we have seen that *abat-jours* (outside slatted shutters) were much in evidence in parts of France in the late seventeenth century and Havard cites a reference of 1659 to what could possibly be an early form of *persienne*.[66] In Sweden, incidentally, it was customary to whitewash the inside of glass windows to protect the curtains from the sun in summer. Dexterous housemaids were able to produce decorative scrolls with the whiting-brush. This custom may have been widespread. It is not long since the glass of greenhouses was regularly whitewashed to reduce the heat in summer.

In his book on *The Art of Painting in Oyl*, published in 1687, John Smith devotes a whole chapter to 'The manner of painting cloth or sarsnet shash-windows'. I discussed windows with sliding sashes in Chapter III and noted that the word 'sash' derives from the French word for a frame—*chassis*. The sashes or frames to which Smith was referring were not fitted with panes of glass but were stretchers for paper, silk or linen which could be varnished and thus made transparent.[67] They were fitted inside glazed windows and acted as sun-blinds. Smith explains how one could mix verdegris with the varnish to make a green light that is 'very comfortable to the sight'. On the paper or silk one might 'paint upon them what fancy you please, but a landskip is most common and natural'.[68] Such 'transparencies' could be very decorative; one does occasionally see windows fitted with such 'sashes' in contemporary illustrations (Plates 113 and 114). The *chambre du Roi* at Fontainebleau was fitted with a 'grand chassis à verre et à pappier' in about 1640. This would seem to have been a 'double-window' with glass in the outer frame and a transparent paper sash inside.[69] Sashes were fitted inside windows at Skokloster, Count Wrangel's great country house north of Stockholm; in 1669 and in 1678 a Stockholm bookbinder charged a member of the Stenbock family for making up

De quel que façon que ie pense
A ce qui flatte nos desirs,
Ie ne treuue point de plaisirs
Plus charmans que ceux de l'Enfence.

Ces passetemps sans artifice
Diuertissent innocemment;
Et sont exempts esgallement
De passion et de malice.

LES
IIII. AAGES DE
l'Homme
faites par Bosse
Et se Vend chez Je Blond
Auec Priuilege du Roy.1636.

Selon que l'humeur les conuie,
Les enfans suiuent diuers ieux,
Et nous-mesme auons fait côme eux
Aux premiers ans de nostre vie.

Pour moy, connoissant leur aage
Bannit le chagrin et le dueil,
Ie voudrois usques au cercueil
Pouuoir iouer leur personnage.

113. Painted sashes fitted into windows in a loggia. Scenes from *Genesis* painted probably on oiled silk stretched on frames that formed transparencies for the light from the windows to shine through.

114. What appear to be hinged painted sashes fitted inside windows at a House of Orange residence close to The Hague, depicted in 1697.

two 'paper windows' and oiling them.[70] References to sashes are not all that common in English inventories or accounts but the fact that Smith thought it worth informing his readers how to make them suggests there was a steady demand for these fittings. Anthony Wood did, however, note that 'in most of the lower windows' of Oxford colleges numerous candles were placed on festive occasions and that, in one instance, there were 'severall emblems painted in colours on paper pasted on frames with mottoes under or neare describing them'.[71] Steele writing in 1712, told how his eye had been caught 'by the face of a very fair girl . . . fixed at the chin to a painted sash made part of the landscape'.[72] He must have seen the girl looking out of a window over the top of a transparency painted with a landscape in the manner described by John Smith.

FLOOR-COVERINGS

In the Middle Ages it had been the practice to strew loose rushes and straw on the floor. This seems to have been done in the grandest of houses and the French might still say of a very rich man in the seventeenth century that he was 'dans la paille jusques au ventre' [waist-deep in straw].[73] Nevertheless, rushes and straw were probably only used in this way on stone floors, which means that the family's more luxurious and private rooms, which were usually upstairs, would not have had such floor-coverings. It is even less probable that the floors of splendid rooms were strewn with rushes or straw in the late sixteenth century and early seventeenth century—in Elizabethan times—as it often claimed. This misconception probably springs from the apparent mis-translation of a statement made by Paul Hentzner who came to England in 1598. Hentzner was Swiss and he wrote his travel-account in Latin. His comments were translated and published nearly two centuries later by Horace Walpole, who makes him say of the royal palace of Greenwich that he found 'the floor, after the English fashion, strewed with hay'.[74] Walpole was translating the word 'faeno' but adds the comment that 'He probably means rushes,' and it was in fact a practice greatly favoured in this country to strew such greenery on the floor. Levinus Lemnius, writing in 1560, states that

> the better to qualifie and mitigate the heate, it shall be very good to sprinckle on the pavements and cool the floors of our houses or chambers with the springing water, and then strew them over with sedge, and to trimme up our parlours with green boughs, freshe herbes and vine leaves; which thing, although in the Low Country it be frequented, yet no nation more decently, more trimmely, nor more sightly than they doe in Englande.[75]

It will be noted that Lemnius was writing about a method of keeping a room fresh and cool in hot weather—with succulent, green foliage and not with dry straw—and it was probably to this practice, which the English had somehow perfected, that Hentzner was referring; hence his remark about it being 'after the English fashion'.[76]

Had Hentzner said that the floors were laid with straw mats, no one would subsequently have been misled. For it was a common practice in his day to lay rush matting on the floor. There is plenty of evidence that this was also the case in France in the sixteenth century and early seventeenth century.[77] A popular mid-sixteenth-century French poem refers to a 'chambre natée en toute place' (the French for a mat

115. Fitted rush matting in 1635. The plaited strips are sewn together; the stitching is clear. Even in this tragic scene recording the death of a wife in childbirth (note the wicker cradle draped with black and the black bed-hangings), some treasured possessions have been included—the valuable lute, the colourful globe and the exotic chintz on the table.

116. (right) A rush mat beside a Dutch bed in 1663. Thin mats of this kind are still imported from the East and, while this may possibly be a Dutch product, it is more likely to be an example of the class known as 'Tangier mats' imported from North Africa and perhaps related to the more elaborate 'Portugal mats' of the late seventeenth century. Note the Turkish carpet on the table.

being *natte*). This implies that the matting was fitted to the shape of the room which was made readily possible because it was plaited in strips about six inches wide. Fitted matting seems to have been quite common in England as well (Plate 115). The 'Best Chamber' at Walton, for instance, was 'matted under foote' when an inventory was taken in 1624 and the Gallery had three pieces of 'new matt'. At Chatsworth there was likewise a 'Matted Gallerie'.[78] Just fifteen years after Hentzner's visit to Greenwich Palace, the Duke of Saxe-Weimar visited Hampton Court and remarked on the fact that the floors of all the lodgings and galleries were fitted with plaited matting.[79] Maybe matting was used less frequently in Germany but it is more likely that he was impressed by the large number of rooms in the

144

English royal palace that were thus furnished. There is anyway no doubt that aristocratic Elizabethans and Jacobeans were very happy to be portrayed standing in a room laid with matting, even if they sometimes gilded the lily by laying a Turkish carpet on top of the matting (colour Plate XI).

Rush matting went out of fashion in the middle of the century. There was still matting in a bedchamber at Cowdray in 1682 but the house was by then appointed in an old-fashioned manner.[80] The Long Gallery at Ham House was still being called 'The Matted Gallery' in the inventory of 1677 although no mats are listed and it is very unlikely they were still present at that date. Thereafter, rush matting was mainly used in inconspicuous places—on landings, in the chapel, etc.[81] Mats were sometimes coloured (Plate 117) but those which were are likely to have been imported. Pepys' remark about an African mat being suitable to go under a bed of state suggests they were a very respectable form of floor-covering.[82]

'Portugal mats' and their relations were actual mats and probably had at least a border if not an overall pattern (Plate 95).[83] Rush matting, on the other hand, came in plaited strips and so could be made up into any size and fitted to the room, as already explained. It must have been the earliest form of fitted carpeting. Actual fitted carpet, that is to say, widths of pile carpeting sewn together into the shape of the room, does not seem to have been evolved until sometime in the second half of the eighteenth century but widths of moquette (see p. 112) were being joined and made up into carpets which were so large that they must have been for laying on the floor.[84] In the Chapel at Versailles, moreover, there was a large carpet of crimson velvet.[85] In this connection one should also mention 'fledges' which were made up of a material called 'fledge' (see p. 113). The Countess of Shrewsbury had fledges on the floor round her bed at Hardwick so it is clearly a fairly robust material although she also had some on the bed.[86] As for the 'peece of woolin hangeinge with birds and beasts under the beddes feett' at Cockesden in 1626,[87] this may well have been a hanging of dornix. Single widths of material of various kinds were also used on the floor as runners. There was 'a piece of corse cloath to cover ye stairs' at Dyrham, and borders of Savonnerie carpet were set aside 'pour servir aux marchepieds qui sont autour du sallon du billard de Trianon' [to serve as runners round the billiard room at the Trianon].[88]

The word 'carpet' had the same meaning in the seventeenth century as it has today but it was also used in reference to other large covers that lay flat—either on tables, as decoration, or as protective covers for delicate table-tops, marquetry floors, and so on. Table-carpets are discussed in Chapter IX but I shall here consider carpets of various kinds that were laid on the floor. In fact, a distinction was usually made between table-carpets and floor-carpets (or 'foot carpets'). The French likewise tended to speak of a *tapis à pied* or *tapis de pied*.[89]

I have already surveyed the various kinds of Oriental carpet that were available in Europe in the seventeenth century and we have discussed the European imitation of such pile-surfaced materials—principally turkeywork and Savonnerie carpets. Carpets were expensive and were therefore treated with respect. The Elector of Brandenburg was so proud of his Turkish carpets that, in 1617, he was still keeping them in his Cabinet of Curiosities—his *Wunderkammer* (see p. 302).[90] One gets the impression that carpets were commonly kept in store and only brought out on important occasions or when the family was in residence.[91] Large carpets had to be placed on the floor but small ones made a good show lying on a table, so there was a tendency first of all to place them there.[92] Only when carpets became fairly common, after the middle of the century, did it become rare in England and France to have pile carpets on tables, but the Dutch so liked the effect that they maintained the practice right through the century (Plate 108 and Colour Plate XIII).

Oriental carpets came in something like standard sizes. Occasionally commissions were placed through agents in the East for a carpet with some special feature—with the owner's coat-of-arms woven into the pattern, or of an unusual shape. However, it was easier to get special orders carried out in Europe. Turkeywork carpets might be made to fit a special position—usually a table-top but also, say, a space by a bed or in an alcove. They also not uncommonly had the owner's arms inwoven.[93] As for the carpets produced at the Savonnerie works, they were invariably ordered with a special position in mind[94] but, because they were all produced for royal consumption in France and nothing comparable was being made elsewhere in the seventeenth century, they constitute an exceptional form of floor-covering which hardly affects the general picture at all.

Tapestries were rarely laid on the floor[95] but carpets produced in the tapestry-weaving technique existed in the seventeenth century, although probably not in

117. Black and white rush matting illustrated in a Spanish painting of about 1620. Probably an African mat, an elaborate version of that to be seen in Plate 116.

large quantities. Cardinal Mazarin had a *tapis* of Brussels *haute-lisse* (which meant tapestry to the layman at the time)[96] and Savary des Bruslons tells us that, anyway by 1723, tapestry carpets were being woven at Rouen, Arras and Felletin.[97] The Aubusson factory, which has since given its name to tapestry-woven carpets as a class, was not started until 1743.

Blankets and 'ruggs' of various kinds might also be used on the floor in bedrooms, placed round the bed. Such materials came ready-made to size, although 'fledge blankets' were apparently made up from widths of a material known as 'fledge'.

Judging by inventories, embroidered floor-carpets were not at all common in the seventeenth century. On the floor round a bed at Hengrave Hall in Elizabethan times were three embroidered carpets 'of Englishe worke', and Lady Dorchester owned 'a black footcloth of cloth imbroydered round in borders with silk fringe' valued at £8.[98] Louis XIV had 'un petit tapis de toile de cotton blanche brodé . . . en or et argent' [a small carpet of white cotton . . . embroidered with gold and silver] and another quilted in small squares, but it is not certain that they were meant to go on the floor.[99]

When leather carpets are mentioned in seventeenth-century inventories, the reference is usually to a protective cover of some sort. These might lie on the floor, like the 'two leather Covers for the Stepp' which protected the elaborate marquetry of the daïs in the Queen's Bedchamber at Ham House,[100] in which case they were probably of scorched leather. But there do seem to have been actual carpets of leather which could be left in position even on grand occasions. For example, one closet at Tart Hall was 'covered with a carpett of yellow leather' while another had one of white leather.[101] One might perhaps think they there served as protection for elaborate floors (although no marquetry floors had apparently been made in England by that date) but the Earl of Arundel's bed also stood on a yellow leather floor-cover and this can only have been removable in exceptional circumstances. Cardinal Mazarin also owned 'un tapis de cuir rouge imprimé' which could have been 'printed' like a tooled book-binding.[102] It is listed among the other splendid *tapis* in his collection and certainly does not seem to have been merely a protective cover. Furs had been used on the floor in the Middle Ages but were rarely to be seen there in fashionable circles during the seventeenth century. William III had 'one baires skeen with the haire on' on the floor of his Great Closet at Kensington Palace and there was another bearskin on the floor of the Chapel,[103] but these seem to have been rarities.

CHAPTER VII
Beds, Cloths of Estate and Couches

ALL but the humblest beds in the seventeenth century had hangings. Being therefore large pieces of furniture, they automatically came to occupy a prominent position in the room where they stood. But the beds in important bedchambers also embodied a high degree of symbolism, coming thus to constitute the focal point of the bedchamber they occupied. For these reasons, a great deal of attention was paid to the design and decoration of beds in the seventeenth century and no further excuse need be made for devoting a separate chapter to them. Moreover, since canopies, or 'cloths of estate', were related to hung beds, both symbolically and structurally, it seems sensible to discuss them together. However, we must first survey the various types of bed; then we can consider bed-hangings and bed-clothes.

THE VARIOUS TYPES OF BED

The terms used for the various components of a seventeenth-century bed are set out in the key to the accompanying diagram of an imaginary bed (Plate 118). Only the word 'tester' needs special explanation. This was the word used throughout the century for the flat, roof-like component supported above the bed by the posts, although the mediaeval word 'ceilour' was still very occasionally used in reference to this component in early seventeenth-century inventories.[1] Most beds, incidentally, stood with their heads to the wall so that three sides were exposed. I shall discuss the exceptions to this rule later.

The simplest form of bed consists of a frame with four short posts at the corners forming legs. Greater rigidity can be obtained by carrying up the posts some inches above the frame and by fitting a cross-piece or board across at the head—the 'headboard'. Such beds existed in earliest times. In the seventeenth century, they were known in French as *couches* or *couchettes*, according to their size.[2] While a *couche* could be a simple structure, used by people of humble station, it could also be a very grand piece of furniture, perhaps with an elaborate headboard or with its posts extended to form notable features. The 'couch beddstead, the head posts, post[s], and feete thereof richly guilt' that belonged to Charles I (or perhaps to Henrietta Maria) was of this type, as must have been the 'couche de bois de chesne à pilliers tournez' [bed with an oak bedstock, with turned posts] mentioned in a French inventory of 1556.[3] Molière's 'couche à pieds d'aiglon, peints de bronze vert, avec un dossier peint et doré, sculpture et dorure' [*couche* with eagle's feet, painted a green bronze colour [i.e. bronzed], with painted and gilt headboard, carved and gilded] may also have been of this sort although it may equally well have been the sort of couch that we would now call a 'day-bed'.[4] Couches and day-beds are discussed below (see p. 172).

This basic form of bed could have hangings suspended round it; indeed, this was how bed-hangings first evolved in the early Middle Ages. The hangings had at first been held up on rods stretching across the room or by means of cords attached to hooks in the ceiling. At the Château de Turenne in 1615 there was what must have

118. Diagram showing the parts of a seventeenth-century bed with the main bed-curtains omitted for the sake of clarity.

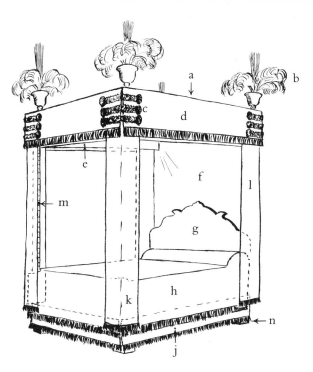

- a. Tester.
- b. Cup with plumes (ostrich feather *panaches*, and *aigrettes*).
- c. Buttons and loops (originally linked the valances but became decorative, as here).
- d. Outer valance (*pente*).
- e. Inner valance (*pente*).
- f. Headcloth (*dossier*).
- g. Headboard.
- h. Counterpoint.
- j. Base valance (*pente* or *soubassement*).
- k. Cantoon (*cantonnière*).
- l. Bonegrace (*bonnegrâce*).
- m. Post with its case.
- n. Feet, the lowest part of the bedstock.

119. An elaborate version of the *couche* or *couchette* with a separate canopy suspended over it. This is probably the daybed of a fashionable French lady (compare with Madame de Montespan's couch shown in Plate 20).

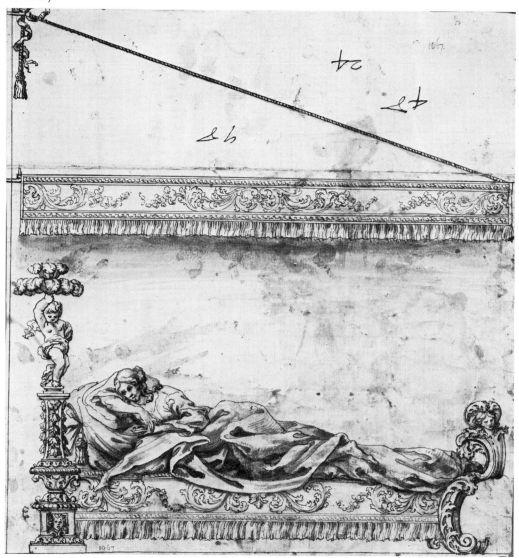

been a folding bed, intended for travelling, which is described as a 'couchette de bois de noyer . . . montant à vis' which was 'faictes à pavillon' [a *couchette* of walnut wood . . . that screws together . . . with a canopy].[5] The travelling-bed of Henri IV's mistress, Gabrielle d'Estrées, which will have had hangings of great refinement, was likewise called a *couchette*[6] and the bed shown in Plate 14, which stood in the *Trianon de Porcelaine* at Versailles, and has hangings of the greatest complexity, is described in the royal inventory as 'un lit extraordinaire dont le bois est une couchette' [an extraordinary bed of which the bedstock is a *couchette*]. The form of bed known as a *lit à la romaine* should presumably also be classed with the *couches* and *couchettes*: they too could have separate hangings (Plate 121).

At the other end of the social scale was the 'trundle-bedstead', or 'truckle bed', which was also a simple bedstead. It was mounted on wheels and could be stowed under the main bed in the room.[7] An inventory of 1513 mentions a *couchette* that was 'soud ledict grant lit' [beneath the aforesaid large bed] while one of 1572 refers to a bed 'au-dessous duquel y a une couchette' [under which is a *couchette*].[8] Personal

120. Seen from the foot-end, this magnificent bed must have been similar to that shown in Plate 119 but has a much more complicated canopy with a scene of Venus discovering Cupid painted or embroidered on the headcloth. Thought to date from 1669 and to be by Le Brun.

121. Two proposals for *lits à la Romaine* by Jean Le Pautre, probably published about 1670. Such *couches* were meant to have separate canopies as Plate 119 shows.

122. A very elaborate late sixteenth-century travelling bed (field bed), now lacking its bed-curtains and valances. The bedstock is held together with bolts (the heads of two may be seen at the foot end) while the head- and foot-boards are secured with hooks. The crestings are hinged and the posts can be dismantled.

123 & 124. (below) A seventeenth-century field bed that folds into itself and forms a travelling-box. The top section of the posts at the head are missing. Webbing straps ran lengthwise and were secured by a cord at the headboard.

servants could then sleep close to their masters.[9] A variant was the *couchette* on trestles (*sur pliant*) which was to be seen in a French country-house in 1688.[10] It had a *pavillon*—a suspended canopy—of serge.

The mediaeval form of bed-hangings, which were suspended with cords from the ceiling, somewhat resembled a hovering sparrowhawk and was therefore called an *épervier*. This was rendered as 'sparver' in English. A few beds of this kind seem to have lingered on into the seventeenth century. There was 'a fayre lardge sparver and beds' head with double vallance of cloth of golde' at Hardwick early in the century, while the 'furniture for a sparver bed' (consisting of a tester, headcloth, valances and five curtains) was in store at Knole in 1645.[11] But occasionally an additional canopy was suspended over a bed that already had its own tester (Plate 136). For example, in 1641 we find the Earl of Arundel had 'a great sparver about over the bed of the like stuff [as the bed], tyed up with yellow silk strings.'[12] Cardinal Mazarin had something similar—a bed complete with posts supporting the tester and valances, and with an additional *daïs* suspended above by means of silk cords.[13] As we shall see, the word *daïs* in French means a canopy.

Beds with posts supporting the tester (and therefore the curtains, valances and headcloth) had been evolved by the fifteenth century. The earliest form of bed with posts is likely to have been the so-called 'field bed' (*lit de camp*) which could be folded and was used, not only by military gentlemen in the field, but by all people of rank when travelling.[14] When travelling, one could not expect always to find convenient places in the ceiling from which to suspend the bed-hangings in the usual way, so it was necessary to provide posts with the bed to hold them up instead (Plate 122).

Field beds were first and foremost practical pieces of furniture. When dismantled they were stowed in a bag or a box (Plates 123 and 124).[15] They slotted together and the components were held in place by hooks or screws. They tended to be simple in outline but luxurious versions were made for rich people, with expensive hangings and decorated headboards.[16] Their testers did not have cornices, which could get damaged, but might have valances of intricate shape hanging from them.[17] Field beds might be rectangular, brick-shaped structures but some had hipped, pyramid-shaped testers.[18] Many seem to have had one end sloping (Plate 125) and some even

125. A Parisian field bed of the 1690s. It folds into a small bundle of wooden members and hangings which no doubt fitted into a bag. Such a bed might have been called a 'slope bedstead' in England.

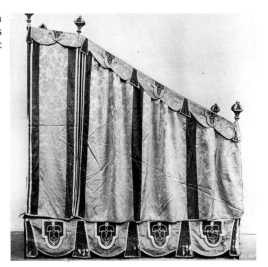

had both ends sloping.[19] The term 'slope bedstead' which occurs in several seventeenth-century inventories, must refer to beds of this form.[20] Randle Holme explains that a 'cant bed' can fit under a sloping roof, and many beds of this shape may merely have been simple beds used by relatively humble members of a household, living in rooms high under the roof.[21] Apart from the fact that such beds could not readily be dismantled, there would be little difference between them and the field bed version. Grand field beds must have been prized possessions and they were often set up in quite important rooms in the owner's house, particularly in the early part of the century.[22] Later, they become rarer. There was a 'camp bed' at Dyrham at the end of the century and Dr Martin Lister tells of a certain retired French field-marshal who in 1699 'very obligingly showed us his own apartment . . . and in his chamber his little red damask field bed, which he lay in now, and which had also served him when he commanded on the Rhine'.[23]

As aristocratic life became more static during the sixteenth century, the principal beds in a house could be allowed to remain where they were placed, year in, year out. There was no longer any need for them to be easily dismantled, and important beds could therefore be constructed in a far more substantial manner. The massive bed, with strikingly decorated wooden components, thus came to be developed, reaching the high point of its evolution shortly before 1600 (Plate 126). It is a form which is familiar to everyone, since, being robust, so many specimens have survived. It will, however, become clear that it was not the only form of bed that was in fashion at the time.

Such an obtrusive piece of furniture, standing in a prominent position in an important room, quickly gained the attention of the architect and those decorating interiors, and a number of designs for such beds were published in engraved form in the sixteenth century (Plate 91).[24] These proposals chiefly concerned the wooden components of the bed, incidentally; the design of the hangings was still in most cases left to the upholsterer. Nevertheless, these beds became architectural in character and, generally speaking, their ornament was made consonant with that of the rooms in which they were to stand.

Writers of inventories sometimes noted that a bed was of oak or of walnut, and we can usually then safely assume that the bed was of the massive sort, with the wooden members showing prominently. Otherwise beds in the seventeenth century were normally identified by the nature of their hangings (e.g. 'the green velvet bed'), so it would normally only be where the woodwork was especially prominent that it would be mentioned. The fact that the tester of such a bed was of wood (usually panelled) was also noteworthy.[25] On the other hand, the elaborate headboards, with their panelled and carved ornament, do not seem to have attracted much attention. Inlay, carving, painting and gilding are mentioned, however.[26] Far more care was taken in describing the hangings and we need to be reminded that, for all the ebullience of their wooden parts, the most conspicuous parts of these beds

VIII. (right) Seventeenth-century woollen (worsted) upholstery materials of the more elaborate sort.
    a. Two small pieces of woollen velvet made up as a panel about 32 cms high.
    b. Part of a woollen hanging (here shown partly reversed) which may be of 'dornix'. The yellow sprigs are about 7 cms high.
    c. Three specimens of wool and linen material which may also loosely have been classed as 'dornix' at the time.

154

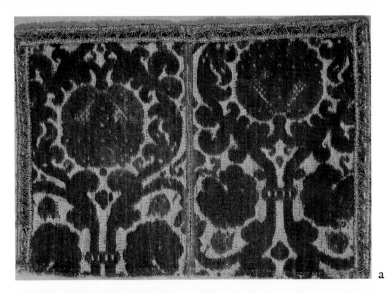

a

b

c

remained their textile components, for the headboard would largely have been in shadow and the posts were masked by the curtains.

The term 'standing bed' occurs frequently in inventories from the first decades of the seventeenth century. It may refer to a specific type of bed[27] but it seems more probable that it was used in reference to any substantial and essentially immovable bed—including the massive type I have been discussing.[28] But clearly the standing bed with 'a tester of redde velvet and gold' at Sir Henry Unton's house in 1595[29] cannot have been of the type with a wooden tester. Moreover, one of the two standing beds in the nursery at Marton Hall is described as being 'with poulles' (i.e. poles or columns, rather than 'with posts' which implies carving) while the other was 'without poules'.[30] The latter would seem to have been a *couche* with only low posts at the corners. Whatever the case, it was presumably not intended that any of these beds were to be moved in the ordinary course of events.

IX. (left) A rare survival: a fine example of a painted hanging. Part of a set of canvas wall-hangings with scenes from the life of Alexander the Great signed by Jan and Daniel Smit of Amsterdam. Separate borderings were obtainable with which to trim a panel to any size required. This hanging is of unusually fine quality.

126. A bed of the massive kind, showing how the hangings masked much of the woodwork. A bed of the same general class as the Great Bed of Ware but with a hipped roof and finials. From a Danish engraving of 1645.

The massive type of bed, with its architectural form, had a bold cornice round the edges of the tester below which a valance of a textile material was invariably attached (Plate 126). Without this feature, the proportions of the whole structure are altered. As surviving beds of this class are today mostly shown without hangings, the impression now given is somewhat misleading, for not only does the tester look wrong without its valances but the carved posts were not meant to be so obtrusive; they were meant to peep out from a rich tumble of hangings and bedclothes.

This type of bed also seems normally to have had a flat top in France and England, but in Holland, Germany and Scandinavia domed or hipped testers were favoured (Plate 126). Beds with domed testers are also occasionally mentioned later in the century. The Duchess of Ormonde had one at Kilkenny in the 1680s. At the same time her husband had a 'pillar bedstead with a rising tester' which was presumably hipped.[31]

In the Netherlands a box-like form of bed was popular. It was enclosed with panelling on all sides but one, where there was a curtain over the opening (Plates 127 and 198)).[32] This form usually stood against the wall and in, some cases such beds were actually built into the wall or were incorporated into the scheme of panelling. Beds tended anyway to be placed in the corners of the room in the Low Countries, the 'aristocratic' position with the bed standing out from the central point of a wall being only gradually adopted, as far as one can judge—presumably as Frenchified ways came to be accepted.

Scholars have often been misled by the term 'canopy bed' which occurs frequently in inventories from the first half of the century. The 'canopy' was suspended over the head of the bed (which was of *couche* form) by means of a cord attached to the ceiling (Plates 36, 113 and 128). It usually consisted of a cone-shaped or domed 'bowl'[33] with a valance all round, and with two or three large curtains that were often called 'trains' because they had to drag (*trainer* in French) on the ground, in order to be long enough to reach out and also encompass the foot-end of the bed (Plate 129).[34] The French called such canopies *pavillons*.[35] The coat of arms of the Upholsterers' Company of London bears '3 pavilions ermine, lined azure, garnished or . . .' and, apart from the central tent-poles, these pavilions resemble the

127. (upper left) A Dutch box-bed with panelled wooden ends and base; 1624. Only one side was open and fitted with curtains. Note the warming-pan hanging at the foot end, and the striped bed-clothes. On the floor lies a farthingale, the padded waist-ring that was at this time fast going out of fashion.

128. (lower left) A 'canopy bed' showing the bowl suspended by a cord from the ceiling. Dutch; 1660s.

129. (right) Diagram of a canopy bed with its 'trains' tied back. The smaller sketch shows how the trains reached out to cover the foot end. The detail shows a 'soft' bowl depicted in several paintings by Terborch.

130. (far right) One of the three pavilions represented in the coat of arms of the Upholders' Company of London. When originally granted in 1465 the device was described as a 'sparver'.

131. What may be a 'lit à housse'. It has pairs of cords (the outer cords are clearly shown) by means of which the curtains can be tied up out of the way (see Plate 132). Note the *cantonnières* at the corners.

pavillons or canopies of 'canopy beds', with a fancy conical bowl topped by a finial, and depending curtains (Plate 130).[36] The top of such a canopy might of course be square instead of round, in which case it could be classed as a 'sparver' (see p. 153). The Upholsterers' bearings were actually called sparvers in the original grant of arms in 1465.[37] Jean Le Pautre was clearly fascinated by this type of bed and published a number of engravings depicting elaborate structures of this class in the middle of the century (Plate 36).

The type of bed which became far more popular than any other in the seventeenth century was that known all over Europe as a 'French bed' although its popularity between about 1620 and 1680 was such that most references to beds of an unspecified nature probably concern this type (Plate 136). They are to be seen in numerous illustrations of the period but hardly any specimens have survived because the wooden components were of such simple character that they were not considered worth preserving once the hangings had become soiled and tattered, and the bed was out of date.

The simple wooden framework of this type of bed supported the hangings so as to form a plain, rectangular box. There was no cornice running round the top; the

32. Tying up the curtains of a bed of a similar type to that shown in Plate 131. This bed does not have *cantonnières*. Note how the post is encased with a textile sheath trimmed en suite with the curtains.

curtains hung straight down from the top rails. In the simplest form of such beds, there were three curtains, one to each of the exposed sides, nailed to the top rails. These curtains could be tied up out of the way by means of pairs of cords hanging down from the same top rails, rather like the tapes used for tying up the door of a tent (Plates 2 and 131). An engraving by Bosse shows a servant in the act of tying up a curtain on such a bed, and the cords may be seen in several other contemporary illustrations (Plate 132). A bed in Charles I's possession must have been of this type as it had eighteen 'tassells with stringes', six to each side, so the curtains will have hung in four festoons on each side, when tied up[38].

The more complicated and common form of such beds had curtains that moved horizontally on rods in the usual way. In this case the rods and rings were masked by valances but there was still no cornice and the outline was still essentially brick-shaped (Plates 133–6). Both the pull-up and the sliding forms, however, had their outlines enlivened by four prominent finials on the flat top. The status of the bed was otherwise entirely demonstrated by the cost of the hangings and the degree of richness of the trimmings. No wooden components were visible; even the posts were encased in material.

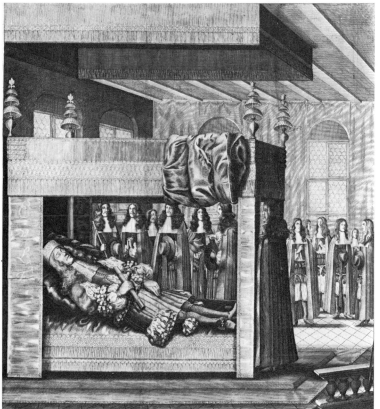

133. (upper far left) A Parisian engraving of about 1614 showing a fully-developed 'French bed'. It does not appear to have *cantonnières* but details are not drawn with much care in this picture.

134. (lower far left) A Dutch bedchamber in 1624 with a 'French bed' installed. On the quilted counter-point lie piled cushions and some bridal crowns.

135. (above) Two 'French beds' set up in a Danish bedchamber in 1645. Instead of draught-excluding *cantonnières*, these beds have their curtains joined with ribbons at the corners.

136. (left) A German prince lying in state on a 'French bed' above which an additional canopy is suspended. The *cantonnières* and *bonnegrâces* are clearly shown. The curtains have been slung up out of the way onto the top of the tester. The hangings appear to be of watered silk.

138. Even in the State Bedchamber of Louis XIV himself the bed would be simple in outline, as this proposal for the *Chambre du Roi* at Versailles of 1679 shows. In France, magnificence in state beds was achieved by means of sumptuous materials, rich trimmings and splendid *panaches*. Only in informal settings was the fancy given a free rein (see Plate 14). Note the alcove protected by its balustrade.

139. Sketch of Louis XIV's State Bed at Versailles in the early 1680s (based on contemporary illustrations) showing the rectilinear shape favoured for formal beds in France. Only a small cornice breaks the severe lines; richness is effected by the elaborate valances.

137. (left) A Parisian bed of 1680, still simple in outline but richly trimmed with gold lace. It has a slight doming in the tester which can hardly be seen from the front. The bed appears to have been cut down somewhat; the *pentes* of the counterpoint would normally have been deeper and the curtains longer to correspond.

These two related forms of bed were probably evolved from the field bed which also had a simple wooden structure and an uncomplicated outline. The shape must have struck someone as resembling a fine bed with its protective cover of an inexpensive material draped over it. At any rate, it seems at first to have been called a *lit à housse*, (the French for a loose-cover being *une housse*).[39] The link with the field bed is indicated by the 'lict de campagne à housse' which belonged to Gabrielle d'Estrées at the end of the sixteenth century.[40] This may have had curtains of the pull-up type. The 'lit carré' [rectangular bed] she also owned may have been of the more usual type of 'French bed' with sliding curtains.[41] But, once this sort of bed had become the most common form, there would no longer have been any reason to be specific and one could simply call it *un lit*—a bed.

Beds of this kind (both variants) were from an early date provided with *cantonnières* and *bonnegrâces* ('cantoons' and 'bonegraces', in English) which were narrow curtains at the corners that closed the gaps between the main curtains (Plate 118). If these features were at first peculiar to 'French beds', as seems possible, then it is perhaps worth noting that the earliest recorded reference to a bed with *bonnegrâces* seems to be in a French royal inventory of 1589, while *cantonnières* are at any rate mentioned early in the seventeenth century.[42] They must at first only have been fitted to beds of great luxury. There should, technically speaking, only be a pair of each on a bed but the terms were sometimes confused; the early reference of 1589, for instance, is to four *bonnegrâces*, two of which would normally have been called *cantonnières*, while a bed at Ham House was described in 1679 as having four 'cantoons'.[43] It would anyway seem that the 'French bed' was being evolved during the last decades of the sixteenth century. Three 'French beds' are listed in the inventory of Sir Henry Unton in 1596; although he had been ambassador to France in 1591–2, it is evident from the context that the references are to a class of bed. An early illustration of such a bed is to be seen in Salomon de Caus' *Perspective*, published in 1612, although it appears to lack *bonnegrâces* (perhaps because it seems to be a fairly humble bed) and its base is boxed in. An engraving published in Paris some two years later shows this kind of bed in its fully developed form (Plate 133).

Beds grew taller during the second half of the century (Plates 137 and 140). The French continued to favour the rectilinear form, even for the grandest settings,[44] the only concession to a lively outline being in the fancy contours given to the valances which, however, remained essentially two-dimensional (Plates 139 and 140). Moreover, the richness of the trimming continued to increase (Plate 137). The English and the Dutch, on the other hand, preferred a more elaborate form of tester with a cornice. These flaring cornices were often pierced and were generally covered with the same materials as the bed-hangings (Plate 142). Daniel Marot published many designs for beds of this sort, the complicated lineaments of which were in great contrast to the contemporary French form (Plate 50). However, the latter was current at the same time in England (and no doubt in Holland as well),[45] whereas the Marot type of bed does not seem to have found favour in France at all, at any rate, not for beds of a formal nature. But Marot may have been familiar with certain fantastic beds that had been created for light-hearted settings, such as the beds at the *Trianon de Porcelaine* (Plates 14 and 15), before he left his native country in 1684 to go into exile in Holland and England. These wild exercises were *tours de force* of the upholsterer's art and may have made a strong impression on the young artist who then subsequently applied similar features to state beds—a notion that would surely have struck stay-at-home Frenchmen as highly inappropriate!

Right from the beginning of the century there had been half-tester beds which were often called 'half-headed' (Plate 145).[46] Since the tester only covered the head-half of the bed, it would seem that many 'canopy-beds' were also described as 'half-headed', as a canopy (i.e. *pavillon*) is mentioned immediately afterwards.[47] Such beds were used by persons of secondary status—children of the family, tutors, ladies in waiting, etc. Towards the middle of the century a new form of grand bed became fashionable. This was the *lit d'ange* which had a flying tester suspended over the whole sleeping surface of the bed (Plate 141). Because the tester was suspended (with cords or chains) it in some respects resembled a canopy bed with its bowl hanging from a cord. The Dutch compiler of an inventory of the Palace at the Noordeinde at The Hague in 1633 recognised this when he explained that the Princess's bed had summer hangings 'op de maniere van een pavillioen, anders genaent een lict à l'ange' [in the manner of a *pavillon*, otherwise known as a *lit d'ange*].[48] Tessin saw the State

---

140. (right) State bed probably made for James II about 1685. This shows a late stage in the development of the grandest type of 'French bed', with valances of fancy outline, and with the increased height favoured late in the century. The form is still essentially rectilinear, however. Conflicting evidence makes it difficult to decide whether this actual bed was made in Paris or by a French upholsterer working for the Crown in London. This is the most splendid of the few surviving seventeenth-century beds. It is accompanied by a set of armchairs and squab-frames (in this view only the chair behind the bed is en suite; see Plate 152).

Bed of Louis XIV at Versailles in 1687 and described it minutely[49] 'Le lict est en forme de lict d'ange et admirablement beau', he wrote, 'le pavillon est suspendu au toict avec des cordons et houppes d'or, qui les soustiennent par les petits enroullements dorés au coins du pavillon.' [The bed is in the form of a *lit d'ange* and is astonishingly beautiful . . . the tester is suspended from the ceiling by means or cords and tassels of gold which are held by little gilt scrolls at the corners of the tester.][49] Five years later it was said that the ability to judge 'le grand art de retrousser les rideaux d'une lit d'ange' [the great art of tying up the curtains of a *lit d'ange*] was the sign of a true courtier,[50] and the tying back of the curtains did indeed offer the Parisian upholsterers of the day plenty of scope to display their skills. The tester of the *lit d'ange* at Versailles was called an *impériale* by Tessin although the whole ensemble he calls a *pavillon*. Indeed, such beds might be called 'lits à impériale'.[51] The bed Celia Fiennes saw in the Duke of Norfolk's apartment at Windsor Castle at the end of the century was presumably a *lit d'ange* and is likely to have been in the style Daniel Marot was then publicising in England and Holland (Plates 141–4). She called it 'a half bedstead as the new mode'.[52]

In inventories from the early part of the century, reference is often made to 'livery bedsteads'. They must have been fairly simple as they were to be found in relatively humble rooms in large houses. Sometimes they had their own separate canopy (Plate 146).[53] Maybe this was just a form of *couchette* that could be set up (*livré*) where required, for servants or guests. I have already discussed the *couchette* and its wheeled

168

141. (far left) Design for a state bed with a flying tester by Daniel Marot. Anglo-Dutch; about 1690. The iron rod running rather incongruously outside the tester is for the protective curtain (see Plate 144). The *portière* is en suite. This form of bed owes much to the Parisian *lits à la Romaine* or *couchettes* with canopies from the middle of the century (see Plates 14, 15, 119, 120 and 121).

142. (centre left) An English state bed of the 1690s. Note the pierced and flaring cornice so characteristic of English beds at this period. See Plates 97 and 98 for details from this bed which was made for the first Earl of Melville.

143. (left) Proposals by Marot for beds with flying testers; about 1700.

version, the trundle bed (p. 151). Beds for servants were tucked away into odd corners and various devices were adopted to hide away the bedding during the daytime. Squares of ticking or canvas, filled with straw, and called pallets could be laid directly on the floor or set out on some sort of board. Personal servants often slept by the doors to their master's or mistress's apartment and acted as a kind of bodyguard. On the landing outside the main entrance to the Countess of Shrewsbury's rooms at Hardwick stood 'a bedsted to turne up like a chest' while there were pallets by many of the other doors.[54] There was a 'trunke bedstead' at the Countess of Leicester's house and a 'settle bedstead' at Tart Hall.[55] Dean Goodwin had a 'press bedstead' which must have been similar to the 'banc à coucher en forme d'armoire' [sleeping-bench in the form of a cupboard] mentioned in a French inventory.[56] The porter at Ham House slept by the front door that he controlled; his bed was described as 'one presse bed of walnutree' and its bedding.[57]

When the famous hospital, the Hôtel de Dieu, was established in 1623, it was equipped with bedsteads of iron so they would be easier to keep clean and free of vermin. But the box-like hangings were of course still of a textile material so the gain can only have been partial.[58] Since wicker chairs were quite common in England in the seventeenth century one would expect to find beds of this material over here, too, but this is not the case. There was a basketwork bed (*Korbbette*) at Copenhagen Castle in 1638, however.[59] Hammocks were not unknown, on the other hand. There was a 'cotton hamocke' at Knole in 1645 and Prince Maurice of

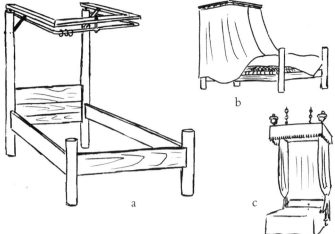

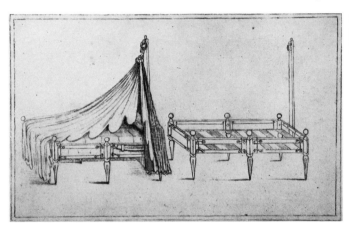

145.
a. Sketch of a simple bed with a half-headed tester at Hardwick Hall dating from the seventeenth century.
b. How the bed presumably looked when furnished with hangings.
c. Sketch of a grander type of half-tester with the chains suspending the tester from the ceiling indicated.

146. Sketch of a French folding bed, perhaps for servants or guards, or possibly for travelling.

147. Eighteenth century drawing of a ceremonial couch of state at Hardwick. The wooden structure of the couch itself survives (Plate 148), but this drawing indicates how it was originally dressed, under its canopy and flanked by a pair of stools. The arrangement is the same as that adopted for a more common form of chair of state like those shown in Plates 168 and 169.

144. (far left) Drawing by Marot of a bed with informative notes in his handwriting. For example, the iron rod (*verger d'assier*) encircling the tester is for a curtain that is a 'surtout, pour conserver le lict contre la poussier' which may be pulled 'jusque au millieu' (i.e. to meet in the middle at the foot end). The main bed-curtains run between 'les 2 campanes du lict marqué A'. The bed is of crimson velvet lined with an 'Estof d'or ou d'argent'.

Nassau (1604–79) once presented the King of France with 'un lit à la chinoise, fait de rezeaux de corde de fil vert pour estre suspendu' [a bed in the Chinese manner, made from a network of green fibre cords, which can be suspended].[60]

The 'clothes of estate' or canopies that were suspended over the principal seat of honour in a room set out for ceremonial use were formed like a tester of the period, with valances, curtains and a back-cloth (Plates 147 and 166). We have already noted that they might be suspended above the tester of an important bed (Plate 136). More often a canopy was hung over a chair of state or throne. Occasionally, they were hung above the portrait or the sculptured bust of some absent person who was being honoured (Plate 12). In England, it seems that anyone over the rank of earl rated a canopy when he or she was seated in state, and there might be more than one canopy set up in an important house.[61] The practice varied from country to country, however.[62] The chair of state, which was usually covered en suite with the canopy and might not only have a footstool but also one or more pairs of stools to flank it,[63] was normally placed on a raised platform or daïs. It should, incidentally, be noted that this word was used by the French to denote the cloth of estate, or the whole ensemble and not simply the raised platform.[64]

Chairs of state are discussed more fully in the next chapter but something should here be said about couches, a variant of which might serve as a ceremonial seat of estate.

We have seen that a *couche* or *couchette* was a simple form of bed, and it of course lent itself not only to sleeping on at night but could also be used as a day-bed. Day-beds seem already to have existed in the late Middle Ages and were certainly to be found in fashionable houses in France and England by 1600 (Plate 205). The couch must have acquired a high degree of symbolism because it was evidence of conspicuous luxury and therefore of presumed wealth and power, for only the very grand could spend time during the day lolling about. At any rate, a version of the couch was adopted to serve as a seat of state under a canopy, and we find several references to couches with canopies in inventories of the second quarter of the seventeenth century.[65] Judging from the surviving ceremonial couch at Hardwick, which is illustrated still standing under its square canopy in an eighteenth-century drawing, these formal pieces of seat-furniture stood with one side against the wall so that the ends of the *couche* now formed arms (Plate 147). The ends were made to slope outwards so as to accommodate large cushions against which one could lean.[66] The *couche* serving as a day-bed (a *lit de repos*), on the other hand, seems normally to have had a single end or head-board (Plate 208).[67]

The distinction between the two forms was probably quite clear at the time, as an exchange in John Fletcher's play *Rule a Wife and Have a Wife* of 1624 suggests:

MARGARITA: Is the great couche up, the Duke of Medina sent?
ALTEA: 'Tis up and ready.
MARGARITA: And day-beds in all chambers?
ALTEA: In all, lady.

Here the ceremonial 'great couch' was erected, complete with canopy; the day-beds presumably had no canopies although they could be so furnished—with a *pavillon* rather than a square canopy of state.[68] No doubt the essentially informal day-bed ensemble was smaller in scale than the ceremonial variant but we now have only the

172

148. The remains of the ceremonial couch illustrated in Plate 147. Painted red. Only the top inner faces of the sloping ends are decorated since these areas were not masked by the upholstery. The scrolling floral ornament no doubt imitates that which was on the covers of the cushions, squab and valances, decorated with a scroll pattern executed in embroidery. On the ends are also painted the arms of the second Earl of Devonshire and his wife who inherited Hardwick in 1625–6 and probably first set up this couch of state, soon afterwards.

149. Couch with hinged arm-rests, that may be adjusted by means of iron rods. Covered with gilt leather. English; 1640s. Presumably this was a ceremonial seat that stood under a canopy like that shown in Plate 147.

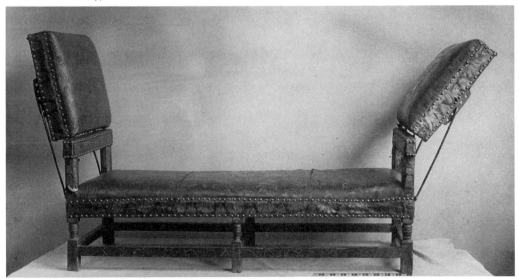

150. Sumptuously upholstered couch with hinged arm-rests that are adjusted by irons at the back. This famous piece of furniture at Knole is often called a sofa although it would probably have been known as a 'couch chair' when new, in the second quarter of the seventeenth century.

context to guide us in deciding whether a reference to a couch and canopy concerns the one form or the other.

Some double-ended couches had hinged ends so that these arm-supports could better accommodate the large cushions one leant against. There was a leather-covered couch with hinged ends secured by ratchets at Forde Abbey earlier in this century (Plate 149).[69] The *reposoir* in a French mansion in 1621, described as being 'à vice dorées' (with gilt screws) probably had some form of adjusting mechanism like this.[70] Single-ended day-beds might also be fitted with such an adjustment (Plate 207). Day-beds, which relate also very closely to sofas, are discussed in the next chapter.

BED-HANGINGS

There might be anything from two to six main curtains on a bed but four was the commonest number. Only half-headed and canopy beds had two curtains or 'trains'. It was chiefly beds with curtains of the pull-up variety that had three, while only exceptionally splendid beds had six curtains. Curtains other than those of the pull-up sort hung from rings running on iron rods exactly like those used for window-curtains. The rings might be of iron, or horn or copper.

174

51. The fleur-de-lis on the crestings of this magnificent piece of late-seventeenth-century seat-furniture suggests it was designed to stand in some royal setting in France. With its double ends this recalls the ceremonial couches of earlier in the century (Plate 147). Can this form have been a 'lit de repos en canapée'?

A fine bed might have paired valances (inner and outer) which could be of equal depth or might have the inner set shallower than the outer. The outer valances were often more richly decorated than the curtains hanging below. Early in the century the valances, tester and head-cloth of a grand bed might even be of a different material from the curtains.[71] The base valances ('bases' or *soubassements*), which hung down between the legs, were usually fairly plain.

The massive wooden beds of the early part of the century had intricate headboards but other sorts of bed, notably the 'French beds' that became so fashionable after 1620 or so, had headcloths which might constitute a fairly simple hanging, perhaps with the owner's arms embroidered on it. From the middle of the century a low headboard of fancy outline and covered with material was customarily fitted in front of the headcloth. In beds of the Marot type the headboard could be a very complicated piece of ornament with pierced scrollwork and rich trimming, the material of the hangings being pasted to the carved wooden backing.

Together with the tester, it was the 'counterpoint' (counterpane) that was most elaborately decorated, usually with needlework or patterns contrived with applied trimming.[72] Its pattern was often reflected more simply on the underside of the tester. The counterpoint was often shaped so as to fit round the posts at the foot end and so as to encompass the bolster at the head. It also had *pentes*, the three panels falling down the sides of the bed.[73] The counterpoint was meant to lie flat and be squared at the edges. In order to make sure this happened, Cardinal Mazarin had a set of 'trois tringles couvertes de lames d'argent avec broquettes d'argent, servans à mettre sous la courte pointe pour la rendre quarrée et unie' [three rods covered with silver plate with silver fastenings, used to put under the counterpoint so as to make it square and flat].[74] The servant making the bed might use a *baton de lit* to aid the process of flattening or tucking the counterpoint in under the bolster (if the counterpoint did not have a built-in bag).

Bed-hangings were mostly lined, usually with a light-weight material that contrasted in colour with that of the main material. If decorated, it was in a comparatively restful manner. The counterpoint and headcloth were frequently faced with the lining material.

To cap off the whole edifice, finials were usually fitted above the tester, over the posts. As they were to be viewed from the front only, the two rearmost finials on late seventeenth century beds were sometimes halved, as if split down the middle so that the resulting flat face was nearest the wall at the back. Finials might be simple turned knobs, perhaps gilded, but often they were faceted and vase-shaped, in which case the material of the hanging was usually pasted to the wooden core and the edges were trimmed with braid.[75] Such 'cupps' might have 'spriggs' or *aigrettes* of egret feathers rising stiffly from a socket at the top. More showy were the *bouquets de plume* which consisted of a bunch of ostrich plumes (*panaches*), sometimes centred on an *aigrette*, which were fixed in a vase-like finial.[76] Plumes were usually white but could be coloured.[77] Sometimes the *bouquets* were made to resemble actual flowers, either in the form of silk or metal artificial flowers, or carved as a compact composition and gilded.[78] 'French beds' of the third quarter of the century seem often to have had tiered finials like those shown in Plate 136.[79]

Most of the materials that were used for wall-hangings or window-curtains could also be used for the hanging of beds (see Chapter V and p. 139). Tapestry, however, was far too heavy to be used at all commonly[80] although coverlets of 'arras' are sometimes mentioned.[81] Brocatelle, which did not drape well on account of its structure (see p. 116), was also rarely used on beds[82] and the same applies to turkey-work and gilt leather (pp. 109 and 118). Embroidered hangings, on the other hand, were common on beds (they were usually called 'wrought' or 'worked' beds) and it is noteworthy that they mostly belonged to ladies.[83] Although the quality of the needlework on such ladies' beds may often have been high, it was probably 'domestic' in character—that is to say, it was mostly executed by the women of the household and as a result lacked some of the finesse to be seen in the best professional work.[84] The patterns, moreover, will mostly have been charming rather than elegant. Professional embroidery, on the other hand, tended to be worked to patterns from the main line of current ornamental motifs, often with the lavish use of gold or silver thread of various kinds. The distinction was of course not always as clear cut as is here implied but when men had beds with embroidered hangings, it will probably have been of the professional kind, and this effectively means that only men of considerable wealth had needlework beds because professional embroidery was very expensive. It is incidentally widely supposed that a common type of embroidered bed-hanging in the second half of the seventeenth century was the so-called 'crewel work hanging' which has large-leafed patterns executed usually in dark green and blue crewels (worsted thread) on a cream-coloured cotton and linen ground. Because the material is robust, many specimens survive but references to what could be hangings of this class are not all that common in seventeenth-century inventories.[85] What is more, they were probably not to be found in the grandest surroundings, where something more splendid would have been used.

As for trimmings, the same varieties were used on bed-hangings as on other forms of upholstery (see p. 127), and they were made up in ways similar to those employed for wall-hangings. Peculiar to bed-hangings, however, were the 'buttons and loops' which were applied straps of braid that linked the valances together at the corners. Originally there really was a loop at one end of each strap that was hitched over the corresponding 'button' or toggle, but soon the junction was made with disguised hooks and eyes, and the feature became purely decorative. It was standard on 'French beds' of the grander sort but was no doubt used on other types of bed as well.

I have already mentioned the fact that very important beds might have two sets of hangings, one for summer and one for winter (p. 106), and that bed-hangings might be stored in the Wardrobe Room except when the family was in residence. Indeed, since people had spent so much money on a rich bed, every precaution was naturally taken to protect the fragile and valuable textiles and their delicate trimmings. I have already given some examples of beds being covered with sheets or with loose-covers but, towards the end of the seventeenth century when the upholstery of a great bed might be of immense complexity, special 'case-curtains' were provided as a permanent feature. Daniel Marot shows such curtains on several of his engravings of beds and on a drawing (Plate 144) actually states that the curtain was fitted 'pour conserver le lit contre la poussière' [to protect the bed from dust]. The curtain ran on an iron rod fixed to the top of the tester and running round some six or eight inches out from the cornice. It does not seem to have worried anyone that the iron bar was rather obtrusive, judging from the illustrations, but maybe a certain satisfaction was derived from demonstrating in this way that the hangings of one's bed required such special protection. A protective cover round a bed was in French called a *tour de lit* (*un tour*, a circuit). A bed at Ham House in 1683 had a 'tower de leet' which must have been a feature of this nature.[86]

BEDCLOTHES

Seventeenth-century bedclothes were not really all that different from those we use today, except that they did not have sprung or foam mattresses, and a decent bed therefore had several soft mattresses.[87] However, I shall deal with each layer separately, starting with the lowest.

The mattresses might lie on boards ('lath bottoms') or on cords stretched across the frame of the bedstock,[88] or could be supported by a 'sack-cloth bottom'. If cords were used, a 'bed matt' was placed over them to provide a bearing surface.[89]

The 'featherbed' so often met with in seventeenth-century inventories was of course a mattress, a bag of canvas ticking or *coutil* filled with feathers. In France this was known as a *couette* or *coite*. It was normally of ordinary feathers(*de plume*) but the finest featherbeds were filled with swansdown.[90] 'Eiderdowns' (bags filled with the feathers of the Eider duck which was fairly common round the Baltic) existed in

Germany and Scandinavia but were used as an overlay, not as a mattress, and did not come into common use in France and England until the eighteenth century.[91]

The *matelas* was a mattress filled with wool. The best were filled with *bourrelanisse* or *laveton* which were the cheap clippings of wool or flock.[92] In England we find the same distinction being made between the 'feather bed' and the 'flock bed' (sometimes called 'wool bed'). The 'dust bedds' mentioned as being on some beds in Devonshire farmhouses in the middle of the century were probably cheap flock beds, and such mattresses were no doubt very dusty at the best of times.[93] It is possible that some mattresses were filled with cotton wool.[94]

The commonest (in both senses) form of mattress was straw-filled. The 'straw bed' or *paillasse* (which in English became 'paliasse') was of course the oldest form of underbedding of all. The Vikings, for example, spoke disparagingly of a 'straw death' when a warrior had had the misfortune to die in bed; a true hero expired on the battlefield and was then carried off by the Valkyries to Valhalla. On the other hand, the Swiss Guard at Versailles slept on straw mattresses called *baudets* which must have been similar to the 'pallets' used by servants in England (see p. 169). People of high standing did not normally sleep directly on straw-filled mattresses in France and England in the seventeenth century[95] although a straw bed might constitute the lowest of a set of mattresses forming the underlay of a grand bed.

Mattresses filled with horsehair seem to have come into use in France during the middle of the seventeenth century. Molière had two mattresses on his bed; one of flock and one 'rempli de crin' [filled with horsehair].[96] Horsehair, although rather hard, was thought to be hygienic.

All but the very humblest beds seem to have had sheets of some kind in the seventeenth century. We have already discussed the various qualities of linen sheeting and the coarse sheets made of canvas. The finest linen sheets came from Holland and most of the best bed-linen probably had decorated edges. Certainly the top sheet, which had to be turned down, often had a wide band of decoration along the top edge. For example, some sheets 'de toille d'Ollande' at the Château de Turenne, early in the century, were enriched with 'gaze blanche' (white gauze, which could be of linen or silk) embroidered with black silk and silver roses,[97] while the top sheet on the bed occupied on his wedding night by the Duc de Bourgogne was trimmed with *point de Venise* lace a yard deep.[98] Louis XIV had some strange sheets which were 'peints tout autour d'une frize et cinq fleurons au milieu et dans les quatre coins' [painted all round with a border and with five flowers at the centre and in the four corners].[99] On the Continent bed-linen was quite often striped and might sometimes be checked,[100] but in the higher strata of society people wanted their sheets to be as white as possible. An exception was the great prince mentioned by Brantôme in his *Dames Galantes* who made his mistresses sleep between sheets of black taffeta 'afin que leur blancheur et delicatesse de chair parust bien mieux parmy ce noir, et donnant plus d'esbat' [so that their whiteness and delicacy of skin appeared even better against the black, and providing more entertainment].

On top of the sheets one might lay one or more blankets or a 'rugge'. Blankets were normally of wool but fustian blankets (often listed as 'fusteans') were presumably of cotton with a heavy nap, while a few exceptional 'blankets' were of silk. Ruggs were rough so Lady Beauchamp had 'one rugge with a false cotton cover' (i.e. a loose cover of cotton).

Uppermost lay one or more quilts. There were serviceable quilts, provided for warmth, and there was the decorative counterpoint, or counterpane, which lay on top and often formed part of the suit of bed-hangings. The word 'counterpoint' comes from *contre point* (often rendered as *courte-pointe*) because the quilting was executed by 'piquure faite pointe contre pointe'.[101] It would seem that the counterpoint was often left on the bed while the occupant was in it although Lord Montague instructed the Yeoman of his Wardrobe in 1595 to remove the quilts from the beds in the guest-rooms at night and replace them with Irish ruggs. Whether this was a general practice throughout the house or whether it only applied to guest-rooms is not clear.

Quilts that were decorative presumably lay on top of the more utilitarian quilted 'coverlets'—those of linen or of cotton.[102] The Dutch exported fine quilts of cotton in large quantity and they are mentioned in many inventories.[103] Marseilles quilts seem to have been distinctive; many are listed in the French royal inventories and Lady Dorchester's 'French quilt' may have been of this class.[104]

Pillows and bolsters were usually filled with feathers.[105] In England, few beds had more than two pillows[106] but on the Continent it was a sign of rank to have a large number. The Comtesse de Soissons is said to have had 'des oreillers dans son lit, de toutes les grandeurs imaginables; il y en en avait même pour son pouce' [pillows in her bed, of every imaginable size; there was even one for her thumb].[107] The bolster stretched right across the full width of the bed and the pillow rested against it. Husband and wife normally had separate beds (indeed, they usually had separate apartments, see p. 58) but one does occasionally see contemporary illustrations of beds prepared for two people, with a pair of pillows lying against the bolster (Plate 2).

Randle Holme mentions 'bed-staves' as being necessary to a bed and illustrates one (Plate 319 [81]), describing it as 'a Bed staffe, of some termed a Burthen staffe'.[108] They are occasionally mentioned in inventories; they seem to have come in sets of six and were sometimes kept in a case. They could be coloured.[109] Samuel Johnson in fact furnishes us with an explanation of how bed-staves were used, for in his *Dictionary* of 1755 he states that a bedstaff was 'a Wooden pin stuck anciently on the sides of a bedstead to hold the cloathes from slipping either side'. Presumably they were stuck vertically down the sides of the bed, two to each exposed flank, between the mattresses and the wooden rails of the bedstock. Swedish peasants had a similar device which they called a *Sänghäst* (a bed horse); it was comb-like but served the same purpose, for there was nothing else to prevent the multiple quilts from sliding off the bed.

CHAPTER VIII
Upholstered Seat-furniture

CUSHIONS AND SQUABS

CUSHIONS, like tapestries, can be easily moved about. For this reason they were much prized in the Middle Ages among the seigneurial classes. A window-seat of stone or a bench made of a plank fixed to the wall in a castle could be transformed into a comfortable seat in a trice by draping a cloth over it and placing a cushion upon it. With a cushion, the top of a chest could be made accommodating, and the hard seats of wooden stools and chairs made soft. Cushions were a symbol of luxury and ease and soon therefore became associated also with high status and dignity. In Dutch, the phrase 'op het kussen zitten' still means to hold high office. Since they were so important, much attention was paid to the decoration of cushions and this tradition lasted deep into the seventeenth century. The long and loving descriptions of the numerous cushions at Hardwick are eloquent evidence of this.[1] In Elizabethan portraits, moreover, great pains were taken by the artist to depict accurately the long cushions that lie across the arms of the chairs of state that are so often shown in the background.

In the sixteenth century a cushion-cover consisted of two rectangles of material, more or less richly decorated, laced together round the edges to produce an envelope for the stuffed inner bag (sometimes called 'the pillow'). The lace might be highly decorative and its zig-zag course through the eyelets, with the material of the bag inside peeping through, was itself an attractive feature. The lacing might be replaced by rows of buttons and loops. However, the modern envelope-like cushion, with an opening only at one end, existed by 1600. After about 1630 less trouble was taken to embroider cushions richly and more attention was paid to their trimming with fringes and galloon. Moreover, most fine cushions were furnished with four large tassels at the corners—prominent and expensive features. Cushions were not normally tightly stuffed and remained out of shape when squashed. The corners of a fat cushion might sometimes be pulled in so that the tassels nestled in the resulting indentations. At any rate, seventeenth century cushions did not as a rule have aggressively pointed corners. Cane-seated and 'rush-bottomed' chairs and couches were often provided with cushions or 'squabs' (Plate 320).[2] The latter were less yielding and might be constructed like a mattress, with vertical sides and even with 'tufting', i.e. primitive buttoning (see p. 128).[3] Cushions and squabs might have 'ribbons to tie at the corners', as did some at Kilkenny,[4] and French and Dutch caned chairs with caned backs sometimes had quilted padding tied to the inside back for additional comfort. Squabs were called *carreaux* in French, because they were often square although they could also be oblong.[5] The squared cushion that fitted into the bucket-seat of a late seventeenth century easy chair might also be called a *carreau* and this was the term used for the squabs normally provided for cane chairs.[6]

A large cushion might be provided for a chair of state instead of a footstool (Plate 166), but there was otherwise no tradition of using cushions on the floor in northern

Europe at the beginning of the seventeenth century. In Spain, on the other hand, the Moorish tradition had lingered on, and this ancient Eastern custom was adopted in fashionable circles in France during the sixteenth century. Since these floor-cushions were squab-like, they were called *carreaux* but the compiler of an inventory in Marseilles in 1583 felt it necessary to explain that the 'trois carreaux' he was listing were 'aureliers de tapisserie, doublés de cuir rouge, pour s'assessoir dessus' [pillows of tapestry, lined with red leather, for sitting upon]. The 'leather lining' was probably his way of describing the leather facing of the underside, provided to better withstand abrasion from the floor.[7] Catherine de Medici had many *carreaux* but the fashion does not seemed to have gained ground all that quickly, for Anne d'Autriche was still described in her time as being seated on 'des carreaux à la mode d'Espagne, au milieu de ses dames' [*carreaux* in the Spanish fashion, surrounded by her ladies].[8] On the other hand this may be a reference to a modification of the *carreau* which involved supporting it on a low stool—a *porte-carreaux* (Plate 152), for the *carreau* tended to be too low (Plate 153). They could be made more comfortable by using two, one piled on top of the other, but it was even better if they could be lifted off the ground by something more solid. One can see pairs of *carreaux* on such supporting stools in Plate 289. All this trouble to make this rather awkward form of seating comfortable can only have been taken because it was fashionable and, indeed, there are many references to *carreaux* in the literature describing life in high society at the time. Moreover, grand beds were often provided with a couple of *carreaux* as part of their complement of accompanying seat-furniture. The great cloth-of-gold state bed at Knole for instance has a pair, each with two squabs (Plate 152). There is a walnut squab-frame with a caned top at Knole which has for years masqueraded as a footstool[9] but has now regained one of its *carreaux* from which it had become

152. (below) A squab-frame (*porte-carreaux*) supporting one of its two squabs (compare with Plate 289). The top of the frame is caned. Originally gilded; now black. The apron-piece has largely broken away. One of a pair *en suite* with the state bed shown in Plate 140.

153. (right) Lady seated on a large *carreau*. Sitting upright on such a squab, with one's legs out to the side and with the then fashionable sharp-pointed corset digging into one's abdomen cannot have been all that comfortable. Small wonder that ladies tried to avoid sitting on *carreaux* except in informal circumstances where a decorous posture was not expected.

separated. In the same way, 'two small squob frames carv'd & guilt' at Ham House, which had long been upholstered as footstools, have now been recognised for what they are.[10] They originally had two cushions each. Sometimes on each *porte-carreau* one cushion was covered with the main material of the bed-hangings and the other cushion was covered with the lining, thus maintaining unity even here.

FORMS, BENCHES AND STOOLS

The most rudimentary type of form was constructed on the principle of the milking-stool, with a thick wooden seat drilled with large holes into which the legs were jammed. A six-legged form in the Pantry at Ingatestone in 1600, described as being 'with iiiiii stake feete', must have been of this class, as may have been the 'ploncke fformes' in the Hall at Hatfield Priory in 1629 which were distinguished from some 'Joyned fformes' that must have been of the more elaborate type, produced by the joiner using mortice and tenon joints to make a form of what one might call the 'school-room' variety.[11]

Forms were used with the long tables that had stood in the halls of great houses in earlier times but, with the advent of the draw-table (see p. 226), the form came to be dropped from politer settings and its place was taken by a multitude of stools. For, although the leaves of the draw-table could be pushed shut so that the length was halved, a form could not be shortened. Stools allowed great flexibility and forms were thenceforth only to be seen in old-fashioned halls, churches, school-rooms, alongside billiard-tables, and so forth. Occasionally a form was padded (Plate 155) like the four in Cardinal Mazarin's possession which were 'enbourrées de crin couvertes de moquette' [stuffed with horsehair and covered with plush].[12]

Randle Holme illustrates a plain form and describes it as 'a joynt forme or bench'[13] but normally a bench was a form which had a back-support. Indeed, the back-support could itself be called 'a bench'.[14] There was, anyway, no doubt in the minds of the members of the London Company of Joyners as to the distinction when they ordered one of their number to provide 'two forms at 2s. per foot and some benches at 22d. per foot', while the Ipswich carpenter who had to make 'a joyned forme of 4 foot long and a binch behind the table' presumably knew what was expected of him.[15]

A bench might have a panelled back[16] and might also have the space between the legs enclosed so it became what we would call a settle.[17] There were two 'close benches' at Ingatestone, and the *archebanc* met with in French inventories no doubt belonged to the same class.[18] Sometimes these disguised a bed.[19]

Garden-benches existed in the seventeenth century; a very handsome pair of carved oak may still be seen at Ham House. They date from the 1670s.

Randle Holme illustrates the varieties of stool to be found in England in the second quarter of the seventeenth century (Plate 319[71–76]). The 'staked stool', or 'countrey stoole' as he calls it, was only to be found in humble settings by his time. The 'turned stool', with its triangular boarded seat (Plate 197), remained popular in the Netherlands but was not any longer to be seen in fashionable surroundings (Plate 154). The type of stool with trestle ends had gone out of use by the early seventeenth century and was replaced by the 'joined stool' or 'joynt stoole', which had turned legs in the form of columns or balusters and, later, might have spiral twists. Any

154. Turned stools with T-shaped backs. A common form in Holland early in the seventeenth century, evolved from the common three-legged turned stool with a triangular wooden seat (see Plate 197). By this time such stools were normally supplied with a cushion, as here in a scene of fine company at an inn.

stool might be furnished with cushions but the 'joint stools' that were so commonly to be seen in the rooms of great houses around 1600 were mostly upholstered (Plates 84 and 133). The French called this form a *tabouret*. As Nicot, in his *Thresor de la langue française*, wrote in 1606, 'Tabouret signifie ce petit siège bas, embourré, couvert de tapisserie de point ou autre estoffe ou les femmes s'asséent tenans leurs cacquetoire ou faisant leur ouvrage.': it was stuffed, covered with needlework or some other material, and was sat on by women when chatting or doing their embroidery. Randle Holme states that in Cheshire a 'joynt stoole' was called a 'buffit stoole' (Plate 319[72]) but buffet stools are met with in inventories from all over the country.[20] Presumably they were primarily associated with the dining table, near which there would usually be a buffet (see p. 238).

Stools were often made en suite with a set of chairs for use round a dining-table. It is curious that many sets of stools comprised some that were 'high' while others are called 'low', yet the implication is that they went round the same table. Presumably the difference in height was minimal but still reflected the relative status of the sitters. Apparently the low version of the *tabouret* might in France be called a *respect* for this reason.[21] The upholstered *tabouret* continued in fashionable favour right through the century (Plates 133 and 199).

Randle Holme illustrates a nursing stool, for use when tending a baby (Plate 319[76]), and it is worth noting that grand people usually had a stool placed in the bath-tub so that they could sit on it while carrying out their ablutions (see p. 319).

155. Assorted Parisian seat-furniture of the 1630s. In the background, an upholstered bench, a 'farthingale chair' and a '*pliant*'. The mother on the right sits on a low nursing chair while the fostermother swaddling the baby may possibly be sitting on a seat similar to those shown in Plates 197 and 198.

156. A *perroquet* and a rush-bottomed chair—a 'Dutch chair'. The latter is here shown apparently with a boarded seat but the illustration occurs in a treatise on perspective where such details were immaterial. On the right is a bed-stock with a hipped tester. The placing of a chamber-pot on a chair alongside a bed seems to have been normal practice (see Plate 127).

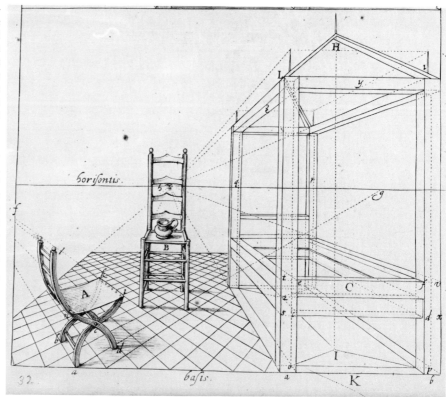

The French were fond of the folding stool with an X-frame which they called a *pliant* (Plates 1 and 155). Although seemingly a humble piece of furniture, it was to be seen in the grandest settings right through the century. It does not seem to have been very popular in England but a pair of mutilated specimens can still be seen at Knole.[22] The seat was formed by girth-webbing and was then covered with material, often richly. Sometimes the wooden members were painted; in other instances they were closely encased in the same material as that of the seat (the Knole specimen is thus decorated). The French royal inventories list several X-frame stools with silver mounts ('garnis d'argent cizelée') and a bed is mentioned which was accompanied by 'six sièges plians d'argent massif, cizelez et tres delicatement travaillez' [six folding seats of solid silver, chased and delicately worked].[23] The fact that such stools took up very little room may partly account for their popularity in France, but it may also have to do with the notion that such seats were associated by tradition with the mobile aristocratic life of former times. We still call them camp stools.

CHAIRS

A version of the folding stool, the *pliant* just discussed, was known as a *perroquet*.[24] It had a back, and the finials, which were often hooked forward, made it resemble a parakeet. The X-frame was hinged transversely so that the chair folded fore-and-aft (Plate 156), unlike the standard *pliant* where the sides came together. The *perroquet* came into fashion in France during the first half of the seventeenth century and was principally used at the dining table. Cardinal Richelieu had a set round his circular dining table with which, like King Arthur, he sought to overcome the problems of precedence.[25] They do not seem to have found favour in England, but why this should be so is difficult to explain.

Another form of chair which was essentially a stool with a back was Italian in origin and would today be called a *sgabello* although the term was in fact applied to stools of many kinds and not just to those with a back. This was a form of trestle-stool with a richly carved board of fancy shape forming the front 'legs' while the inside face of the back is equally richly worked. The seat was of wood and had a circular depression on top. The form may have been known in France but what is curious is that a pair can be seen in the background to the portrait of the Countess of Arundel, painted around 1617 or so, while chairs of this sort with shell-shaped backs were to be seen at Holland House and at Ham House, at both of which houses Francis Cleyn worked as a decorator (Plate 52). So this Italian form seems to have enjoyed a measure of favour within circles close to the court of Charles I and his architect, Inigo Jones (see pp. 53 and 93).

Also in a sense related to the stool, because it was essentially a *tabouret* with a back added, was the so-called 'back stool'. This was a simple form of upholstered chair but it was by far the commonest type of relatively comfortable chair in use between about 1615 and the 1660s, and it remained popular long after that. Randle Holme illustrates a 'back stool' and describes it as such (he shows one with finials which was seemingly an unusual feature on this class of chair), and they are to be seen in numerous illustrations of the period.[26] The back consisted of a rectangular pad attached to upright extensions of the back legs (Plate 158). These chairs tended to be

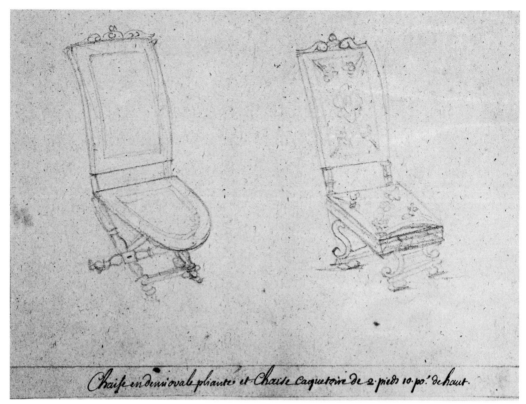

Chaise en demi ovale pliante et Chaise Caquetoire de 2 pieds 10 po.^s de haut.

157. Sketches from the 1690s presumably showing chairs to be seen in French court circles at the end of the seventeenth century. The 'chaise en demi ovale' appears to be a folding occasional seat evolved from the *perroquet*. The 'chaise caquetoire' may not have been very different from the chair shown in Plate 162 although it had a cresting and strange legs.

lower than other forms of seat-furniture[27] and were often used by women—for which reason they were sometimes called *chaises à demoiselles*.[28] As they had no arms and there was a gap between the lower edge of the back-pad and the seat, they were easy for women to sit in while wearing a farthingale—that large padded ring which women in about 1600 wore round their hips in order to hold out their voluminous skirts, like a barrel (Plate 127). Back-stools are often called 'farthingale chairs' by dealers and collectors but the term does not seem to occur in contemporary English inventories. On the other hand, *chaises à vertugadin* are quite often mentioned in French inventories of the period, and the meaning was the same, for a farthingale was called a *vertugadin* in French.[29] The term *chaise caquetoire* is also met with in French inventories at the time and probably refers to chairs of the 'farthingale' type rather than to an all-wooden form of armchair, as is often supposed; for references to *chaises caquetoires* (literally 'prattling chairs' or 'nattering chairs') usually mention upholstery and it is clear that they were low.[30]

When chair-backs became higher, at the end of the century, the form retained its name although the back was no longer low. The chair shown in Plate 157, drawn at the end of the century, is entitled 'un caquetoire' and Furetière, writing at this time, explains that a *caquetoire* is a 'chaise basse qui à le dos fort haut et qui n'a point de bras, où l'on babille à l'aise auprès du feu' [low chair with a very high back which has no arms, on which one chats at ease by the fireside].[31] The *chaises du four* [fireside chairs]

158. The so-called 'farthingale chair', the commonest form of chair in the seventeenth century, used all over Europe. Numerous variants of this basic form were produced. This example is shown in a Dutch drawing of 1672. In England they were commonly called 'back stools'. Note the domed padding on the seat of this simple specimen.

one also finds in French inventories were probably of this class as well.[32] Every now and then one comes across references in English inventories to 'back *chairs*' and one is probably once again dealing with chairs of this sort.[33] Maybe some people felt that they were so obviously chairs and not stools that it was misleading to call them 'back *stools*'. Nevertheless this was their common name throughout the period of their popularity. From about 1670 onwards, however, it seems that any chair without arms could be called a 'back stool'.[34] For this reason it is convenient to retain the term 'farthingale chair' for this once ubiquitous form of chair that I have been discussing (Plates 159, 162 and 164). Incidentally, the legs and stretchers of such chairs were left exposed and might simply have their wooden surfaces polished or varnished. Grand versions, however, had these parts painted or gilded. The two short sections of upright between the seat and the back-rest, on the other hand, were usually encased in the same material as these components.[35]

Although the farthingale chair was much used for relaxing in comfortable circumstances, it was the standard chair of its time and was also used for dining—in which case it was often covered in leather or in turkeywork (Plates 164 and 165). En suite with a set of farthingale dining-chairs there would often be a 'great chaire' which was a scaled-up version with arms. This was in turn the standard form of armchair during the middle of the century. The arms were usually covered with material, as were the short lengths of upright at the back (Plates 183). In the classical

X. (far right) Daybed and chairs upholstered en suite with appliqué wall-hangings, in a style fashionable in Paris late in the seventeenth century. The furniture, however, is English. The magnificent chandeliers are of about the same date.

159. (right) A middling grand farthingale chair of about 1630, with the remains of its original upholstery—a blue woollen cloth decorated with applied ornament executed in coloured silks. The remains of a red and blue fringe may be seen running round the lower edge of the seat-rails. Note the sheathed uprights to the back. The upholsterer attempted to square the padding of the seat. The lower ends of the legs have been cut off, no doubt because they were damaged.

160. The outside back of most seventeenth-century chairs was left uncovered (see also Plate 93). Only very grand seat-furniture had this part covered. The uprights to the back were covered, however.

161. (upper left) A grand version of the farthingale chair in 1663. Note the nail-patterning, the inset braid, the short fringe round the top and sides of the back, the braided sheath of the upright, and the long netted fringe along the lower edge of the back-rest and seat.

162. (above) Late-seventeenth-century chair evolved from the 'far-thingale' form, with the high back then fashionable. Note the rounded padding of seat and back. Trimmed with broad galloon round the outer edge. In England such a chair would doubtless still have been called a 'back stool'.

163. (left) A Dutch 'farthingale' chair of the late 1660s. Note the domed padding of the seat. The larger armed version of this type of chair is to be seen in the pendant portrait repro-duced in Plate 186.

XI. (far left) An English portrait of 1616 showing a Turkish carpet laid on a floor covered with rush matting that is fitted to the room (or it may be a tent, the armour perhaps indicating that the portrait was painted in the field). The red velvet table-carpet is richly embroidered with gold thread. However, it is still the clothes which are the most splendid items at this stage.

version, the arms consisted of two plain bars meeting at right-angles, but earlier versions had more substantial arm–rests sweeping downwards and showing that this form of chair supplanted the old form of all-wooden 'great chair' or 'high chair', which was itself probably not to be seen in fashionable surroundings after 1610 or so. The fact that so many all-wood Jacobean and Carolean 'great chairs' survive is due to their being robust and obviously showy pieces that seem valuable. Chairs of the scaled-up farthingale type (Plate 183) rarely seemed worth keeping once the upholstery had become worn and unsightly. The all-wooden 'great chair' of the seventeenth century belonged in the smaller country-house and the large farmhouses of the squirarchy.

The 'great chair' (of whatever type) was a seat of honour but was not in itself a symbol of rank. It reflected precedence in the context concerned. So, while a monarch might sit enthroned on a chair of state as his subjects stood around him, a mere squire would occupy the 'great chair' in his own house, honour being due to him as master of the household. However, if someone of superior rank paid the squire a visit, the latter would normally be bound to defer to the visitor and yield the seat of honour to him.[36] Questions of precedence bedevilled life at court in the seventeenth century but do not really concern us here. Honour was signified by raising the person to be honoured above the rest of the company. The 'high table' stood on a daïs at one end of the hall; a chair of state or throne likewise stood on a daïs. The seat of honour would also usually be of imposing proportions (hence 'great chair') and was often accompanied by a footstool—not merely to support the feet because the seat was higher than normal, but because the raising of the feet off the

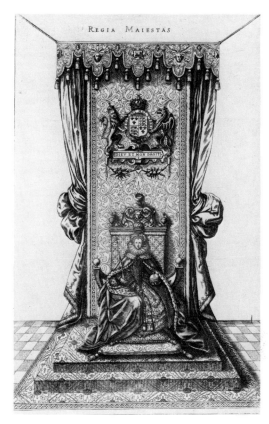

164 (far left) Two disparate 'back stools' covered with gilt leather. English, mid-seventeenth-century. The legs of the right-hand chair have been shortened.

165. (left) The back-stool remained in favour right to the end of the century. The backs grew taller late in the century as this chair, acquired for Christ Church, Oxford, in 1692, shows. Made locally, a set of twelve cost £6. It is covered in 'Russia leather'. The leather extends in one piece down the front edge of the uprights.

166. (right) Queen Elizabeth enthroned: an engraving of 1608 showing (seemingly none too accurately) an X-frame chair of state. However, the canopy (cloth of estate) is clearly depicted, as are the cushions that serve as a foot-rest. The canopy is suspended 'sparver fashion' by means of cords attached to hooks in the ceiling.

ground was in itself a symbol of authority. One might further distinguish a principal seat of honour by raising a canopy over it.

The 'chair of state' in the seventeenth century might be of conventional armchair form but the ancient folding-chair (Plate 168), which people still associated with the aristocratic way of life in former times, remained in favour as a seat of authority in England, right through to the middle of the century[37] and several seem still to have been used at the French court later in the century (Plate 170). Crude versions are, moreover, to be seen in many Dutch pictures of the seventeenth century, so the form must have remained popular even in relatively humble houses in Holland well into the century (Plate 268). But it was probably always a seat of honour. With its folding X-frame, it had been a practical piece of furniture, well suited to the mobile life of the aristocracy in mediaeval times but sixteenth and seventeenth-century examples were massive and could only fold slightly, if at all.[38] In the Middle Ages, this kind of chair was called a *fauldesteuil* in French (from the Latin *faldestolium*). Nicot (1606) explains that a *fauldesteuil* was 'une espèce de chaire à dossier et à accouldoirs, ayant le siège de sangles entrelacées, laquelle se plie pour plus commodément la porter d'un lieu a l'autre; et est un chaire de parade, laquelle on tenoit anciennement auprès d'un lict de parade' [a kind of chair with a back and arm-rests, having a seat formed with interlaced webbing, which folds so it may the more easily be carried from one place to the other; it is a chair of state which in ancient times stood close to a state bed].[39] The word *chaire* implies that it was a kind of 'great chair' or chair of state. Mary, Queen of Scots' 'twa auld faulding stuillis of cramosis velvot'[40] must have been of this type, and the Germans called them *faltstühle*. The French, on the other hand,

67. (left) To underline the fact that the lady here portrayed was of high rank (she was Countess of Denbigh) she is shown standing by a chair of state, a symbol of exalted status. This X-frame chair was entirely covered with red velvet. Note the long cushion lying across the armrests.

68. (above left) An X-frame chair of state from Hampton Court. It has an X-frame foot-stool en suite. Probably about 1620. Although fixed cross-members in the back and seat have always made this chair rigid, the crossing of the legs has still been made in the traditional manner to articulate scissor-wise. The woodwork is entirely masked with upholstery—red woollen cloth covered with a red and silver silk (probably 'silver tissue'), trimmed with silver braid and netted fringe.

69. (above right) The exposed woodwork of this X-frame chair of state gives a clue to its original appearance. Painted red with diagonal lines of simulated silver lace, inspection behind the present rather plausible and itself ancient covering revealed the former covering—red velvet laid vertically with silver lace, the impression of which is still to be seen in the pile. Finials are lacking and the original loose cushion has been built in when the present cover was put on.

shortened the word to *fauteuil*[41] which came to be the term used in reference to any important-looking armchair and then eventually to all fully upholstered armchairs.

It is difficult to trace how this transfer of meaning took place, but the two chairs with curtained cubicles shown in Plates 170 and 171 may throw light on the problem. Both chairs were probably to be seen somewhere in French court circles in the 1690s but neither need have been new at the time (see Plate 17). The Dauphin gave Madame de Maintenon a specially comfortable chair for use when she came to stay at his residence at Meudon. It was described as being 'un fauteuil à commodité apellé confessional' [an easy chair called 'a confessional'].[42] Could this chair have looked like one of those in the illustrations? Their curtained cubicles might indeed be likened to confessionals. At any rate, the term *fauteuil de commodité* had come by the 1680s to be applied to truly easy chairs, often with some contrivance for making them especially comfortable.[43] For example, the French royal inventory of 1687 lists

170. Sketches of important and probably royal French seat-furniture in the 1690s. On the right an X-frame chair with attached canopy. Was it a throne or a *fauteuil de commodité*? On the left, a rush-seated chair—probably one of the many 'petites chaises de paille' often mentioned in the French royal inventories in the time of Louis XIV. The other chair has 'tufted' upholstery.

thirty 'grands fauteuils de commodité à cremillière' [i.e. with *cremaillières* or ratchets] which suggests that they had adjustable backs like the so-called 'sleeping chairs' at Ham House which date from about 1678 (Plate 181).[44] Important bedchambers and closets were often furnished with an easy chair in which the occupant of the apartment could relax, perhaps in front of the fire; indeed, one such chair, or even a pair, became a standard part of the complement of seat-furniture that accompanied an important bed from about 1695 onwards. For example, 'six grands fauteuils de commodité' were supplied 'pour servir dans les chambres des seigneurs' [for use in the rooms of noblemen] in the French palaces at about this time.[45] Around 1700, the phrase *à commodité* was dropped and the accommodating armchair came simply to be called *un fauteuil*.

The earliest forms of adjustable chair seem to have been those devised for some illustrious invalid (Plate 172 and 175). They might have hinged backs, leg-supports, built-in reading desks, and even casters. 'Sleeping chairs' were evolved from such furniture. Evelyn saw something of the sort in Rome in 1644 which he described as a 'conceited chayre to sleepe in with legs stretch'd out with hooks & pieces of wood to draw out longer & shorter'.[46] Charles I had a 'sleepeinge chayre' covered in red velvet but it was valued at only £1 so cannot have been very elaborate.[47] The chair with ratchet-adjustments shown in Plate 178 would seem to date from the 1660s or early 1670s and may resemble the 'sleeping chair' provided by Richard Price for Windsor Castle in 1675 that was designed 'to fall in the back of iron worke'.[48] Two years later John Paudevine (Poitevin) supplied for 'Her Mats. Bed Chamber' at one of the royal palaces 'a sleeping chaire neatly carved and with the irons all gilt with gold' at a cost of £6. It may have been he that supplied the pair of 'sleeping chayres' for Ham House a year or so later. They have gilded iron quadrants drilled with a series of holes through which gilt pegs are pushed to lock the back at the desired

171. On the right, an easy chair with a canopy-like enclosure, perhaps a *'fauteuil en confessional'*, drawn at about the same time as Plate 170. Left, an arm-chair with a curved back; and, centre, 'tufted' upholstery on a strange chair with paw-and-ball feet.

172 & 173. The invalid chair of Philip II of Spain who died in 1598. Note the quilted upholstery, padded arms, hinged back and footrest, and spherical casters. The padding is stated to be of horsehair.

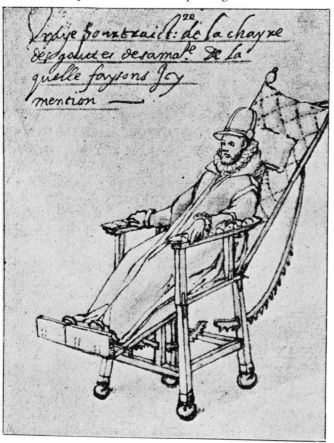
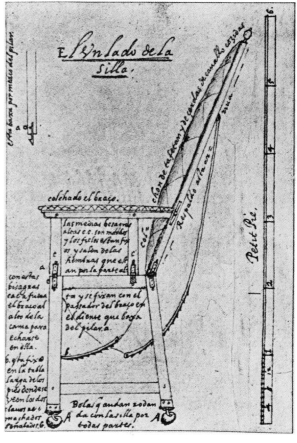

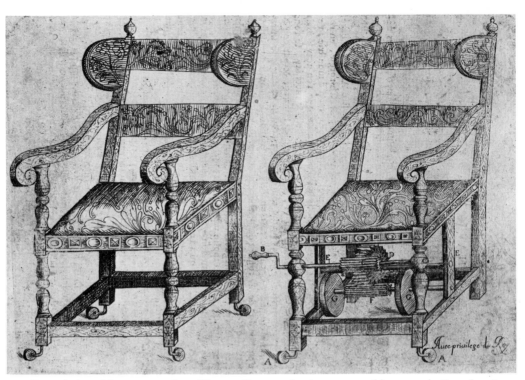

174. Easy chairs with casters, and a self-propelling mechanism operated by a crank. French, 1620s.

angle (Plate 182). A third 'sleeping chair' seems formerly to have been in the Duke's Closet at Ham; it has a different form of adjustment, one that is built into the armrests, and is in addition fitted with casters (Plate 179). It had a canopy[49] but this may not have been a ceremonial structure associated with the fact that its occupant was a Duke (for this chair stood in a closet, which was an informal location) but may rather have served the same purpose as the cubicles rising from *fauteuils de commodité*, like those shown in Plate 171. However, we know that the Duke's canopy was a separate item; it was not attached to the chair.

If the easy chair, with its wings and accommodating form (Colour Plate X), was developed from primitive invalid chairs, the more common type of upholstered armchair was evolved from the scaled-up, armed version of the 'farthingale' form that we have already discussed (p. 187 and Plate 183). It is reasonable to suppose that the 'French chairs' which are mentioned in English chairmakers' accounts from the 1660s and through the 1670s were representatives of this phase, because the French were at this stage leading the development towards greater comfort in this field.[50] The term 'French chair' first occurs in the royal accounts in the early 1660s and clearly meant something specific (Plate 186). In 1660–1 the London upholsterer, John Casbert, provided for royal use a 'crimson velvet french chair covered all over with gold and silver fringe and [with] a bagg [i.e. a cushion or squab] filled with downe'.[51] There can be no doubt the chair was intended to be comfortable, with its expensive cushioning of down. In 1674 Casbert supplied a 'French chaire hollow in ye back and quilted . . . of crimson damask . . .'. Chairs were occasionally given a concave (trough-like) curve to the back at this period the better to accommodate the sitter (Plate 177).[52] Backs also were made to slope backwards more pronouncedly to

198

175 & 176. The invalid chair of Charles X of Sweden who died in 1660. The hinged back and footrest are linked by straps running through the armrests and therefore move together. Note the crook in the back, probably a novel feature at this time. The seat lifts to reveal a compartment containing a close-stool pan that can be removed by a trap-door on one side. There is a further compartment on the other side. In the armrests are extension rods that can support an adjustable reading-desk. Originally all covered in velvet. The conformation of the spiral-turned legs suggests a Dutch provenance.

177. An English invalid chair with features similar to that shown in Plates 175 and 176. From the 1670s.

178. An English sleeping chair of 1665–75 with a hinged back adjusted by means of iron ratchets. Note the rods for supporting a reading-desk. The leather cover of the back, at least, seems to be original.

179 & 180. An English sleeping chair, perhaps that which stood in the Duke of Lauderdale's closet at Ham House, under a canopy. Mentioned in an inventory of 1679. The hinged back is adjusted by fore and aft movement of the armrest which can be held in the desired position by pegs passing through holes into the upright supports. Note the near spherical casters of *lignum vitae*, and the horsehair padding.

181. One of the pair of splendid sleeping chairs in the Queen's Closet at Ham House which were acquired between 1677 and 1679. Here shown with its back swung backwards to the full extent of the quadrant (see Plate 182), in which position the chair is liable to fall over.

182. (lower left) Adjustment of the Ham House sleeping chairs is made by pegs inserted through a quadrant in the direction of the black arrow.

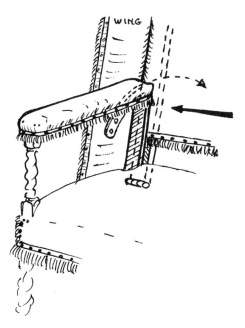

183. (right) Remains of an important 'great chaire'. Essentially a scaled-up version of a 'farthingale chair' (with a set of which it was no doubt en suite). The exposed parts of the wooden structure are gilded and painted with flowers. The chair will originally have had finials at the top of the uprights to the back. The dark line across the original red velvet of the back shows where a line of silver-gilt fringe once ran. More fringe will have trimmed the lower edges of the back-rest and the seat.

184. (right) Chair shown in a portrait of Sir Arthur Onslow (1622–88). The whole chair above the seat-rail is covered in velvet trimmed with a looped fringe (long, plain fringe along lower edges). Note the oval-headed nails on the seat-rail.

185. (far right) From an engraved portrait of Catherine of Braganza from the 1660s. The padding of the seat is highly domed. Note how some pendant fringe also trims the top edge of the back-support.

increase the comfort. In 1674 Richard Price, another royal upholsterer, provided a 'large chaire of Estate with a very crooked back'.[53] And once the back was thus tilted, most English chairmakers decided it was advisable either to rake the back legs backwards or to shape them so that they were crooked to make heels—'compass heeles', as they were called.[54] The French, on the other hand, did not rake their chair-legs backwards, relying on the weight to provide stability (cf. Plates 181 and 188). As for the arms, while these had consisted merely of a horizontal bar, there had been an incentive to cover them with material (Plate 186) but, once the arms began to be shaped (sweeping downwards in a comfortable curve and providing scope for decorative carving), they ceased to be covered. It was only the true 'easy chairs' that normally had padded arms.

Chairs with caned seats became popular in England after the Restoration (Plate 177). The Cane-Chair Makers Company, probably around 1680 or so, claimed that 'about the year 1664, cane-chairs came into use'. They were liked 'for their Durable, Lightness, and Cleanness from Dust, Worms and Moths which inseparably attend Turkey-work, Serge and other stuff chairs and couches, to the spoiling of them and all furniture near them'.[55] They were trying to counter the claim of the woollen manufacturers, made in a petition to Parliament, that the woollen industry would suffer greivously if cane chairs became popular. The cane-chair makers insisted that the number of people involved was not really so great and that, anyway, cane seats needed cushions (or 'quilts', as they are also called in this statement), the making of which provided much work for the woollen industry. Certainly cushions are often mentioned in connection with cane chairs in contemporary inventories, and it may be that, where no mention is made, the fact was merely overlooked because the fitting seemed an integral part of the chair. The cane chair makers also claimed that a great many cane chairs were exported 'into almost all parts of the world where heat renders turkey-work . . . useless'. Presumably, in hot countries, such chairs had to be used without squabs or this particular advantage would have been lost. Cane-seated chairs were popular in Holland but did not gain much favour in France before 1720 or so.[56] However, the sofa and chair shown in Plate 195, which have caned seats, show that such furniture was known (and presumably made) in France in the late seventeenth century although these actual pieces are described as being 'à l'Anglaise'.

Simple chairs with seats made of rushes were being produced in most parts of Europe during the eighteenth and nineteenth centuries, and are still being made in

186. (above left) The upholstered armchair becomes more refined in the 1660s. This pattern became international (here shown in a Dutch portrait). References to 'French chairs' in English documents at this period probably concern chairs of this type.

187. (above right) A French armchair of the 1670s with carved and gilt uprights to the armrests which appear to be padded. The velvet covering is of the slip-over variety, secured with hooks and eyes at the base of the back-rest, and at the four corners of the seat.

188. (right) Although curved the back legs of this grand French armchair of about 1675 are essentially upright and have forward-pointing feet in the characteristic French manner. Note the two lengths of fringe. The covers are of the slip-over kind.

189. A Dutch armchair of the 1680s showing the un-covered outside back and the domed seat covered with needlework. The covers are nailed in place through the bell-fringe, which is double banked. Very similar chairs were being made in England at the same time.

190. (right) Parisian armchair of the 1680s. The cover is of the slip-over variety. The armrests are not padded.

191. (far right) A fashionable Parisian armchair of 1687. An early example of the back with rounded corners. A broad galloon runs round the edge of the cover. It seems to be trimmed with a metal edging.

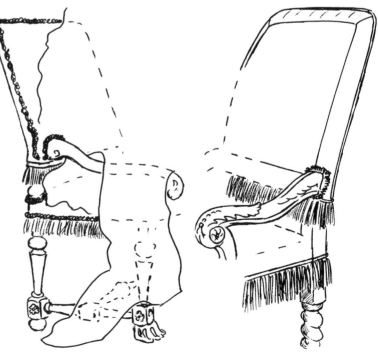

192. (above left) English armchair of the 1680s with slip-over covers of needlework in the French taste. The lower edge of the seat-cover was almost certainly trimmed with a heavy fringe hanging down to mask the square block of the front leg. A similar fringe will have run along the lower edge of the back.

193. (above right) Old photograph of an English armchair of about 1695 showing the original upholstery prior to restoration. The slip-over covers of red and silver silk are trimmed with an elaborate fringe—a long version along the scalloped lower edges, a short version round arms and uprights, and in a wavy line around the inside back. Knotted tassels are attached at strategic points like the indentations of the scalloping.

194. (left) A late-seventeenth-century Parisian armchair with arms padded—not seemingly a common feature at this date.

some rural areas today. The products of each area have their individual characteristics but the general conformation is the same. The uprights are usually turned on a lathe, and it was members of the guilds of Turners who mostly produced this sort of chair. Such chairs were certainly being made in Italy in the sixteenth century and it seems that there was a considerable export of them from Pisa. The inventory of a house at Marseilles taken in 1578, for example, refers to 'huit cheres de paille servant à femmes, à la fasson de Pise' [eight straw chairs for use by women, of Pisan type].[57] These chairs were clearly distinctive; the turned uprights of the back may have had quite fancy profiles and there may have been multiple spindles in the back. The woodwork may even have been stained. The implication of 'servant à femmes' is that they were low in the seat like the *chaises à vertugadin*.

The rush-seated chair was being made in Flanders by the beginning of the seventeenth century[58] and came to be produced in great quantities in Holland during the century. At first these may have had multiple spindles in the back but the Dutch seem to have developed the ladder-back form which has several shaped slats fitted across the back, like a ladder (Plates 127, 156 and 196). Such chairs are often to be seen in Dutch illustrations from the 1620s onwards and also appear in French and English scenes later in the century. No doubt they were made in France as well but many were apparently exported from Holland. Frequent reference is made in English inventories to 'Dutch chairs' or 'Holland chairs'; occasionally the fact that they had rush-seats is noted and we find also 'Dutch matted chairs' and 'Dutch flagg-chaires'.[59] A chair of this sort at Cowdray was described as being green, and Lady Rivers actually mentions a 'Greene Dutch chayre' in her will of 1644, which suggests she placed a certain value on it.[60] But most chairs of this sort were left with the wood in its natural state, which explains why fashionable people in France sometimes called them 'chaises à la capucine', as if they were only fit for the monastic life. This did not prevent them introducing such chairs to quite grand surroundings. Many 'petites chaises de paille' are, for instance, mentioned in the French royal

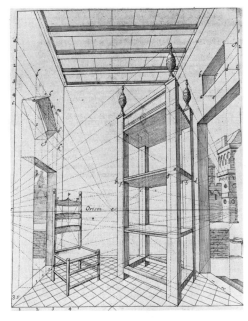

195. (far left) Caned furniture in fashionable French circles late in the seventeenth century. The large seat is described as a 'Sopha d'anglaise en caquetoire', the seat being 'de jonque'. The smaller chair is a 'Banquette d'anglaise'.

196. (left) A Dutch turned chair with a ladder-back shown in a work on perspective published in 1625. The seat will have been 'rush bottomed'.

inventories from the time of Louis XIV.[61] Some had arms and some were japanned ('façon de verny de la chine').[62] Plate 170 probably shows such a chair that was to be seen in one of the French palaces in the 1690s. Many had squabs and loose quilted padding tied to their backs.[63] A chair with such a padded overlay may be seen in the painting of a Dutch doll's house, reproduced in Plate 320.

There seems to be no evidence that rush-bottomed chairs were made in England before 1700 but, as so many were made here in the eighteenth century, it is probable that the industry was established in this country before the end of the seventeenth century. The English, on the other hand, developed the 'milking stool' formula of legs ('stakes') jammed into holes bored through a thick wooden seat and evolved what came to be known as the 'Windsor chair'. As there were 'staked stools' and forms with 'stake feete' in English houses in Elizabethan times, it is reasonable to suppose that backed versions (i.e. chairs) were being evolved during that century to become the ancestors of the ubiquitous 'Windsor chair' of the mid-eighteenth century. Mrs Agius noted references to 'rodden' or 'rodd' chairs in Oxford inventories of the seventeenth century.[64] In one case, such a chair is mentioned directly after one made of wicker, which indicates that there was a distinction between the two.

Chairs of wicker were, anyway, common all over Europe in the seventeenth century, not least in England, and they were to be found in quite smart surroundings. Lady Rivers, for example, mentions in her will the 'great wicker chare with the cushion usually lying in it in my chamber'.[65] Wicker chairs had arms (not only for comfort but because they made the structure more rigid) and many had a hood rising up over the sitter like the later porter's chairs.[66] Randle Holme explains that 'chairs called Twiggen chaires . . . are made of owsiers and withen twigs; having round covers over the heads of them like a canopy. These are principally used by sick and infirm people and such women as have bine lately brought to bed.'[67] The extremely comfortable wicker armchair, with its 'winged'

207

197. A Dutch wickerwork swaddling seat, known as a *bakermat*. The Frenchwoman swaddling a baby in Plate 155 may be seated in a similar piece of furniture or she may simply be sitting on the floor. The *bakermat* must have been a practical aid to nursery routine. Note the three-legged, turned stool.

hood, not only made an excellent invalid chair but must have been the model for the great 'easy chairs' of the later decades of the seventeenth century and it was when the latter became common in grand circles that the wicker chair was relegated to humbler surroundings. A tray-like wicker seat with a low back was used in Holland for nursing and swaddling babies (Plates 197 and 198). The sitter's back was supported while her legs were stretched straight out to form a trough in which the baby lay safely as the swaddling proceeded. In Dutch they were called *bakermats*.[68] It may be that the 'one nurse twige chayre' in an English inventory of 1673 was of this class.[69]. There was a 'strowe chair' in the Master's Bedchamber at Gilling Castle in 1624[70] and it is possible that this was made of coils of plaited straw, as certain 'pouffes' still are today, but it is more likely to have been a wicker chair or a chair with a rush seat.

At Knole there was a 'Spanish chair wth. elbowes' in 1645 which was in some way distinctive; the term is frequently found in Dutch inventories of the early part of the century.[70] The twelve 'great Italian chairs with guilt frames covered with crimson velvet, with 12 stooles suteable, with brass tops' in Lady Dorchester's possession must have made an impressive show; they seem to have been of a well-known type,

98. A *bakermat* with a rather higher back than that shown in Plate 197 and with a handle. One is shown hanging on the wall by its handle in Plate 320 (top left-hand room). About 1670?

solid, fully upholstered and with small brass finials on the crest-rail.[72] At Tart Hall in 1641 there was an exotic group comprising an 'Indian chayre & 3 other India chayres' which were clearly Oriental in origin.[73] And what were 'Flanders chairs'? They are mentioned in many sixteenth and early seventeenth-century inventories both in England and France; some were covered with leather, others had rush seats.[74] They must have been distinctive, perhaps with turned members, but cannot yet be positively identified. And then there were 'scrowle chairs' which was probably the name for a small, upholstered chair of the early seventeenth century which had a back with a marked backwards scroll that is to be seen in several Netherlandish and German pictures.[75]

There were all kinds of scaled-down chairs for children, as well as a pulpit-like seat in which an infant could be placed before it could walk properly (Plate 231). In the Victoria and Albert museum there is a cage composed of turned members on swivelling casters into which a child could be locked until it learned to walk properly.

SOFAS AND DAYBEDS

I have already discussed how the simple form of bed, the *couche* or *couchette*, evolved in two ways—into the single-ended day-bed and into the double-ended ceremonial couch—and that the word 'couch' in English could be used for either type (see Plates 147 and 207, and p. 172). As the double-ended couch seems to have stood against the wall, usually under a canopy, it came to be a sort of backless sofa. The ends sloped outwards and were softened by two large cushions against which one could lean. The ends of later models were sometimes hinged so they could either be vertical, or inclined outwards for greater comfort. It was no doubt because one sat

199. Seat-furniture, probably in a French royal palace in the 1690s. The sofa is described as a 'Grand Canapé' and is six *pieds* in length. The chair is stated to be 'à la mode' and the stool is a 'banquette à la romaine'.

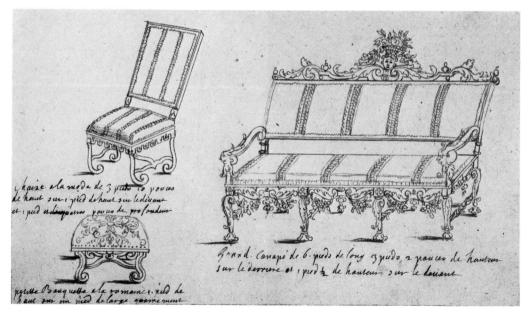

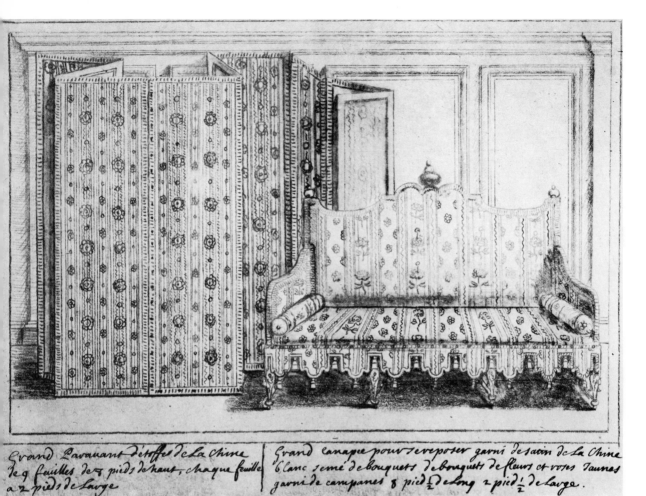

Grand Paravant d'etoffes de la Chine de 9 fouilles de 7 pieds de haut, chaque feuille a 2 pieds de large

Grand canapée pour se reposer garni de satin de la Chine blanc semé de bouquets de bouquets de fleurs et roses jaunes garni de campanes 8 pied ½ de long 2 pied ½ de large.

200. This French sofa of the 1690s is described as a 'Grand canapée pour se reposer' which may imply that the piece could open forward to form a bed. Note the galloon round the edge and forming bands, the cylindrical bolsters, and the lappets with bell-like tassels called 'campanes'. The covering is of Chinese white brocaded satin. The screen is of nine leaves, seven feet high, and is covered with a Chinese silk.

rather than lay on such couches that they were sometimes called 'couch chayres' (see p. 172). Once this stage had been reached (perhaps about 1630) it was a logical step to provide this form of seat with a back, and it then became a sofa in everything but name. A famous backed couch with hinged 'ends' or arm-rests is to be seen at Knole and represents this phase (Plate 150).[76]

The French seem to have called both types of couch (i.e. single- and double-ended) *lits de repos* or *reposoirs*. A 'reposoir à vice dorées' [couch with gilt screws] in a house in 1621 is likely to have been a double-ended couch with hinged arm-rests since the plural of the adjective suggests it had more than one screw-adjustment,[77] but normally there is no indication that a *lit de repos* in a French inventory was not of the single-ended variety like that shown in Plate 205, which were day-beds on which one could recline, informally and at ease.

In her bedchamber in 1684, Madame de Maintenon had a 'lit de repos en canapée.[78] It had two bolsters and three valances so was evidently double-ended and stood with one long side to the wall. Perhaps this term was confined to the double-ended couch (Plate 151) and may reflect the fact that the ceremonial form had in earlier times had a canopy?[79] Insufficient evidence is at present to hand and all we

211

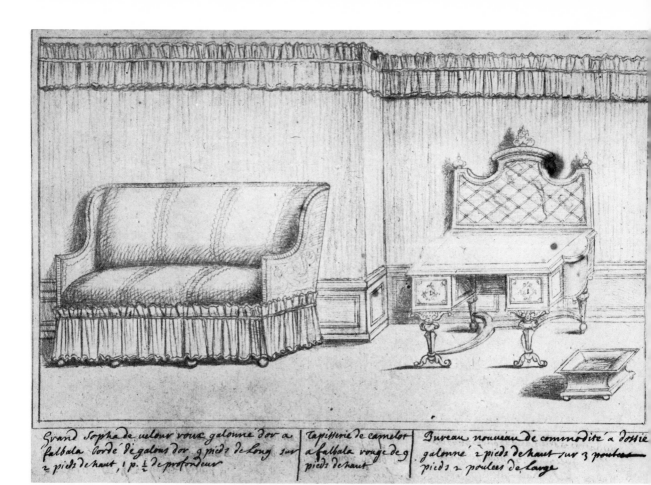

Grand Sopha de velour roux galonné d'or a
falbala bordé de galons d'or 9 pieds de long sur
2 pieds de haut, 1 p. ½ de profondeur | *Tapisserie de camelot*
a falbala rouge de 9
pieds de haut | *Bureau nouveau de commodité a dossie*
galonné 2 pieds de haut sur 3 poulces
pieds 2 poulces de large

201. A truly comfortable 'Grand Sopha' covered with a russet velvet trimmed with galloon and with a skirt 'à falbala[s
(with furbellows, which are echoed in the wall-hangings of red camlet). It may be that the filled-in arms and cheeks mak
this a 'sofa' rather than a 'canapée'. The *bureau* is described as being 'nouveau' and 'de commodité'.

can now say is that another *canapé* (so described) was provided for royal use in the
mid-1680s,[80] while the term was being used in the 1690s to describe what we would
call a sofa, as the inscriptions under the drawings reproduced in Plates 17 and 199
show (they refer to 'grands canapés'). But two of the pieces are called *sophas* (Plate
201) although there does not seem to be any obvious difference between them and
those labelled as *canapés*. The fact that in 1692 someone explained that 'Un sofa [est]
une éspèce de lit de repos à la manière des Turcs' does not help to clarify the
problem[81] as far as the two sofas in question are concerned, although one could
understand it if the exotic double-seated affair shown in Plate 287 were called a *sopha
à la turque* (note the turban on a stand alongside). Unfortunately the inscription
below this drawing is indecipherable. But, even at the time, there seems to have been
some confusion. For example, Cronström, writing back to Stockholm from Paris in
1695, spoke of 'les sophas ou canappés', of which he said 'Il n'y a maintenant point de
chambre où il n'y en ait icy.' [There is now no room here where there is not one.][82]
What he says can, incidentally, only have been true of rooms (he cannot have meant
only *bed*-chambers) in houses of the most fashionable sort, and it may well be that
canapés and sofas were still at that period in some degree symbolic of high status and
may even occasionally have stood under canopies.[83]

212

Couches that can only have been day-beds (i.e. single-ended) had been furnished with canopies earlier in the century, presumably for the sake of comfort. The Duke of Lauderdale had a canopy over the sleeping-chair in his closet at Ham House around 1680 (Plate 180), as we have already noted, and we have illustrations of what must be French sleeping-chairs with attached canopies dating from the end of the century (Plate 171). Moreover, the *canapé* shown in Plate 200 is described as a 'grand canapé pour se reposer' (large *canapé* to sleep on) which may indicate that its base could pull out (and perhaps swing up and over) to form a bed-frame. If this is so, then it must be the direct ancestor of the sort of sofa-couches converting into beds that are illustrated in the works of Chippendale and of Ince and Mayhew in the middle of the next century.[84] These could have canopies, as the splendid Genoa velvet specimen at Holkham, installed in 1758, so magnificently shows.[85]

Sofas were by no means common in England before 1700 but some 'sophas in the Long Gallery' at Hampton Court were repaired in that year and were at the time described as being old.[86] The close resemblance between the opulent sofa made for the Duke of Leeds, now at Temple Newsam House near Leeds and some of those shown in the French drawings of furniture from the 1690s is not surprising if one realises that the leading upholsterers in London at that time were French or of French extraction.[87] The name of the maker of the Leeds sofa recently came to light and the same man, Philip Guibert, made what sounds like a very similar piece for William III in 1697 which was described in the bill as 'a fine black soffa of a new fashion, filled up with downe, the frieze and cheeks all molded and fringed'.[88] The Leeds sofa is accompanied by a no less magnificent day-bed upholstered en suite (Colour Plate

202. A strange sofa with rounded back in a closet panelled with mirror-glass (a 'Grand Cabinet de Glace' which is 'vue du grand Chambre'). French; 1690s.

CONTENTEMENT D'VNE DAME NOBLE.

SONNET EMBLEMATIQVE.

C'Eſt vn contentement & vne douce vie
　　De voir la Damoiſelle ainſi dans ſa maiſon,
Prendre ſon Luth en main, eſtudier ſa leçon,
Et marier ſa voix auec ſon harmonie.

Elle banniſt de ſoy toute melancolie,
　　Elle trouue repos en toute la ſaiſon;
Elle chaſſe de ſoy de l'amour le tiſon,
Et ne ſçait ce que c'eſt de l'infernale enuie.

Si quelqu'vn la vient voir dans le deuoir d'honneur,
　　On voit rougir ſon front teſmoin de ſa pudeur,
Et à peine peut-on entendre ſa parole:

Mais celle-là qui va, & qui court çà & là,
　　Qui à baſtons rompus parle par cy par là,
Monſtre des actions d'vne perſonne fole.

3

203. (upper far left) An English sofa of the 1690s formed like two adjacent easy chairs—a conformation frequently adopted in England. It may be that such sofas served a more formal, even ceremonial, purpose than we at present suppose. The red woollen material is superbly embroidered in coloured silks—no doubt professional work executed in London. The legs were originally gilded.

204. (lower far left) An English sofa of the late seventeenth century with integrated back and wings (note the line of the trimming on the armrests). Such imposing pieces of furniture are likely to have carried the implication that their owners held high rank. Made for the first Earl of Conyngsby about 1695.

205. (left) An early illustration of a daybed in a Parisian publication of about 1614. It has a drop-in squab and a large, shaped bolster.

206. A Dutch daybed; 1636. There must be some sort of upright head supporting the pillow. It has a loose coverlet.

207. Daybed with an adjustable head-rest organised in a similar manner to the double-ended couch shown in Plate 149. There is no indication that this piece ever had a hinged rest at the opposite end, so it must always have been a daybed, but a double-ended couch is en suite with it.

208. A French sofa and daybed in the 1690s. The daybed is described as a 'Lit de repos' with a headboard or backrest 'à la siamoise' (it is in fact decorated with appliqué work similar to that shown in Plate 96). The sofa is called a 'Grand Canapée', the paned covers (panels of gold brocade on green velvet) are stated to be 'à la mode'.

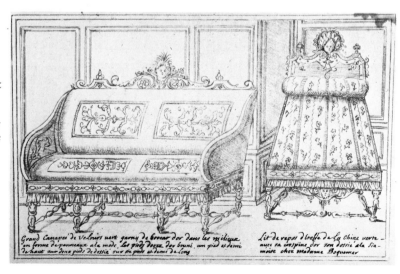

XII). Indeed, sofas and day beds were the two kinds of furniture on which the leading upholsterers of the day could display all their talents.

UPHOLSTERY

Before 1600, comfortable seating was generally achieved with the aid of cushions, and chairs with fixed upholstery were still something of a rarity. Moreover, such upholstery as was to be seen on seat-furniture at that period was of a most rudimentary kind. The devising of truly comfortable seat-furniture by means of cunningly placed padding and covering was left to the upholsterers of the seventeenth century and the technical advances made, particularly between 1660 and 1700, were immense. Nevertheless, it needs to be said that seventeenth century upholstery on seat-furniture was very poor when compared with that of the nineteenth century; it lacked firmness, it was often irregular and the workmanship can rarely have stood up to close inspection. One might say that it did the job, but the high traditions that one sees embodied in the best nineteenth-century upholstery had still to be evolved. The seventeenth century upholsterer achieved his effects with rich materials and by loading the confection with trimmings.

It is a comparatively simple matter to place a pile of padding (straw, hair, feathers, etc.) on a seat and to hold it down by nailing a cover over it. The result is a domed seat, and many seventeenth century upholstered chair-seats were of this simple shape (Plates 158, 163 and 186). To achieve anything more subtle required more elaborate techniques: the padding had to be stitched down and located in the desired position.

The earliest attempts to secure padding probably relied on attached quilted overlays to chair-backs and seats. Cane-seated and backed chairs were still being fitted with such overlays at the end of the seventeenth century and later. They were tied on with ribbons but the next step was to fix such padding to the framing with nails. Chairs with fixed quilting were apparently being made in both Spain and Italy before 1600; the invalid-chair of Philip II of Spain (d. 1598) seems to have this kind of padding (Plate 172). The stitching formed a lozenge pattern in this case but more decorative designs, such as scale-patterns, could be executed in this technique. It may be no accident that many of these early essays in fixing the padding of chairs were executed in leather, for it was probably the saddlers who first showed the way in this field.[89] They had perforce to make sure the padding of saddles stayed in place under the most rigorous conditions and, once evolved, such techniques could of course easily be applied to chairs. Maybe these techniques were first tried out on the seats of carriages and sedan chairs, for the saddlers and the carriage-makers naturally worked in close association.

Vermeer often painted a chair (it was presumably in his studio) which had padding stitched in such a way as to form long ridges round the edge and a cross in the middle (Plate 210). The technique seems primitive and probably reflects a Netherlandish practice from the early part of the century. Such padding could, however, never be very thick and it had to wait until buttoning (or tufting, see p. 128) had been evolved before anything more substantial could be fitted (Plates 170 and 171). This did probably not happen much before 1660.

Attempts were made from about 1630 onwards to produce squared edges to seats and backs but, as the distorted seat of the farthingale chair illustrated in Plate 159

217

shows, the techniques for securing such shapes rigidly had not been evolved and were not mastered until well into the eighteenth century. A certain squaring could be indicated by means of piped or corded edges but the essentially domed forms could not all that easily be disguised.

The padded back-rests of ordinary chairs remained rectangular until the end of the century and there was therefore always a gap between the lower edge of the rest and the top of the seat which no amount of fringing quite masked. Invalid chairs and easy chairs, on the other hand, often had no gap at the back.[90] On chairs of the farthingale type and the scaled-up armchair version made between about 1620 and 1670 the short sections of upright between the seat and the back-rest were often encased in material (Plates 160 and 184), as were the arms of the armchairs. There was a measure of padding on the top surfaces of the arm-rests in later models but the uprights and arm-rests of armchairs made after about 1670 tended to be left uncovered (Plate 191), it being left to the easy chair to take on the full padding of all surfaces.

Some X-frame chairs of state and some *pliants* had had their wooden members totally encased in material early in the century (Plate 168) but legs were mostly left natural, or were painted or gilded. When painted, the appearance of the textile covering material was often imitated. There is, for instance, an X-frame chair at Knole which has its legs painted red with a lace-pattern in white over it (Plate 169). Close inspection shows that the chair was originally covered in red velvet to which a silver lace was applied, so the paintwork on the legs would simply have carried on the decoration in a different medium.[91] Some farthingale chairs at Knole, dating from the 1620s and covered with red velvet trimmed with fringe, have their legs painted with translucent red varnish over a gold ground.[92] The red covering is reserved so as to leave the gold showing in a pattern of moresques but it also shows through the varnish to give the whole a brilliant effect. The same technique is used on 'Queen Elizabeth's Virginals', a Venetian spinet of about 1570 in the Victoria and Albert Museum. By and large, the colour of the painted woodwork formed an extension of the upholstered decoration but occasionally contrasting effects were sought—like the marbled stools in Cardinal Mazarin's collection.[93] Black, however, was much in favour for the wooden members of chairs right through the century. Many chairs with black leather covers to be seen in illustrations from the first third of the century seem to have their wooden members stained black; numerous cane chairs from the last third of the century had black frames as did some rush-seated chairs; and it was apparently fashionable for chairs in the 1680s and 90s to have black frames with gilt details (Colour Plate XII)[94] In fact, references to totally gilt seat-furniture are rare in the seventeenth century while references to silvered furniture occur rather more frequently than might be supposed from reading the average book on antique furniture.[95] Of course a gilded look could be achieved by applying a yellow varnish to a silvered finish—as was sometimes done on the stands of cabinets and to other carved work of the Restoration period.

But let us return to the actual upholstery. The padding of the seat was laid on a lattice of girth-webbing nailed across the seat-frame—just as it still is on many chairs today. Karin Walton has drawn attention to the fact that the French practice was to lace broad webs so closely as to form an unbroken surface, whereas the English preferred to use a narrow web spaced to form an open network.[96] This was certainly

209. (far left) Sketch of early stitched padding forming four mounds on a chair-seat, based on a painting of about 1625. The moulded seat-rails are faced with velvet as well. The chair is otherwise of a standard Netherlandish type.

210. (left) Stitching forming ridges in padding on a Dutch mid-seventeenth-century chair in Vermeer's studio.

true of chairs in the eighteenth century but these divergent practices may have become established well before 1700. The padding of the back was attached to a canvas or linen backing nailed to the front face of the back (the inside back as upholsterers call it). The covering material is then taken round the sides of the back-frame and nailed in position. A modern upholsterer will invariably cover the outside back with material so as to hide the wooden framing and the canvas or linen backing, but most seventeenth century chairs were left with these structural features exposed (Plates 160 and 189). After all, chairs were designed normally to stand with their backs to the wall, so there seemed little point in wasting money on decorating what was not often seen.[97] Only exceptionally grand chairs had coverings on the outside back as well. In some cases, late in the century, material was fitted closely to the wooden members at the back and then across the back of the canvas backing—that is to say, there was a rectangular recess covered in the fine material at the back.

The outer covering had to be fixed with nails and a virtue was often made out of this necessity by having the nails play a decorative part, in which case nails with gilded heads were used. 'Close-nailing' (i.e. with the nails close-set) was not used in the seventeenth century; they preferred a more open spacing with the nails hammered through a braid or the heading of a fringe. Sometimes nails with heads of fancy shapes were used, and it was not uncommon to have nails of two quite different sizes used in combination to form patterns (Plate 168). On the other hand, the material might be held with iron tacks that were not meant to be seen; in such cases, fringes of various kinds (notably the spiralling *mollet*, see p. 128) would be used to mask them.

Great freedom was allowed the upholsterer in the application of trimming (Plate 204), although there were in practice several conventions that most of them observed. These can best be understood by studying contemporary illustrations. The fact that silk materials of the period tended to be about twenty inches wide posed problems for the upholsterer when chair-backs and seats (not to speak of sofas) became wider and the material had to be seamed. Placing a decorative stripe at the join was one way of disguising it. Another was to have a rectangle of galloon applied to the back and to the seat.

When not in use, expensively covered chairs would invariably be protected against dust, light and fingering, and most will have been provided with loose covers of a less expensive material, often of serge or bays, or even taffeta. They often had vents at the sides of the back, or in the middle of the outside back, so that they were not too tight to put on, and they were then tied tight and secured with tapes or laces.[98] Later, hooks and eyes were used.[99]

The process might also be reversed so that it was the slip-over covering that was of the expensive material while a cheaper material remained fixed to the chair. Such 'slip-over' covers could be removed to the wardrobe room except when the family was in residence. Something of the kind may have been used quite early in the century[100] but the practice was well established by the 1670s, the 'dolphin chairs' at Ham House still providing excellent examples with their slip-over covers of 'rich brocard' (Plate 40).[101] These *housses* might have deep skirts. Cardinal Mazarin had eight armchairs 'en housse' in the 1650s which had 'pantes' (i.e. *pentes* or valances)[102] but it was left to the upholsterers of the 1690s to develop the heavy-skirted look, as several of Daniel Marot's engravings show (Plate 143).

Casters that swivelled had been evolved before 1600 and seem at first to have been applied to invalid chairs (Plate 173). They were later put on some easy chairs, for example that which stood in the Duke of Lauderdale's closet at Ham House in the 1670s (Plate 180), and the Duke of Ormonde had a 'crimson velvet easy chair on wheels' at Kilkenny Castle in 1684.[103] Such fittings were certainly not common, however. The wheels tended to be globular at this early stage. The Lauderdale chair has casters with sockets fitting over the ends of the legs.

As for the materials used for the covering of chairs, one might use almost any material as long as it was sufficiently strong. But, in practice, the commonest covering materials were plain silk velvet and silk damask at the upper end of the scale, and woollen cloths like serge at the lower end. Leather, which came in many forms, plain or decorated, was widely used—being strong, pliant and easy to clean, it was much in favour for dining chairs. Turkeywork and the various forms of woollen velvet were also very popular because they combined a yielding pile surface with bright colours. But let us consider these materials and their application to chairs in a little more detail.

Chair-covers of tapestry were uncommon in the seventeenth century although cushion-covers specially woven for the purpose were produced in great quantities, notably in Holland.[104] An armchair in the royal castle at Copenhagen in 1638 was covered in 'Flemish' ('mit flamsch überzogen') which indicates that it had a tapestry-woven material on it, tapestry being known as 'flamsk vaevning', Flemish weaving, in Scandinavia.[105] However, this material does not seem to have been used at all frequently for the covering of seat-furniture. The only English examples that can at present be cited are the tapestry-woven loose-covers for the large japanned squab-frames that already stood in the Gallery at Ham House in 1679 and are still there today.[106] In 1695 Daniel Cronström wrote from Paris advising Countess Piper in Stockholm that, if she wanted to do up her house in the latest Parisian fashion, she should have the chairs in her bedchamber covered with damask or *hautelisse* (by which he meant tapestry), or in Venetian brocatelle.[107] But he was no doubt recording the fashions current in a very thin stratum of Parisian society and there is no other indication that chairs covered with tapestry were to be seen at all frequently even there. Nor, for that matter, was it common to use brocatelle which was a rather stiff half-silk (see p. 116).

Dornix, which was so much used for hangings, was presumably too loosely woven to be suitable for chair-covering.[108] Another distinctive woollen material must have been 'Scotch pladd' which presumably had tartan checks. There was a room completely hung with this material at Tart Hall in 1641 and the couch, with its cushions and canopy, were of the same material, as were two small chairs and a table-carpet that completed the suite.[109] Right at the end of the century, there was a 'Plod' chamber at Dyrham which had hangings of 'Scots Plod' and seat-furniture covered en suite.[110] But this material does not seem to have been at all common, either. The woollen (or worsted) materials that were used for chair-covers in really substantial quantity were 'Cloth, Serge, Perpetuanoes, Chamlets, Bays, Kersies, Norwich Cheniis & Kidderminster Prints' with which, it was claimed (admittedly by members of the woollen industries) 240,000 new chairs were covered each year around 1685 or so.[111] Serge and dyed linen were, incidentally, often used for the fixed coverings of expensive chairs that had slip-over covers of a richer material.

Little need be said about silken materials, as far as their application to chair-covers is concerned, but it is interesting to note that grand people in the seventeenth century were not averse to having on chairs silken materials that were brocaded with gold or silver thread (Plates 168 and 181). In the eighteenth century, it was quite exceptional to use such materials, their scratchiness presumably being considered unacceptable for the purpose. The large-patterned 'Genoa velvets' do not seem to have been much used for chair-covering until the very end of the century (Colour Plate XII), when they began to enjoy a period of high favour that lasted into the middle of the next century. Sarsnet, that thin taffeta so suitable for sun-curtains, was only applied to chair-covers in the form of loose covers of the more expensive sort.

The various kinds of woollen velvet (see p. 111) were greatly favoured right through the seventeenth century for the covering of seat-furniture. For example, a 'chaize de bois à dam[ois]elle' [a woman's chair of wood] and twenty-one armchairs in a room at a house in Rheims in 1621 were covered in 'moquette de diverse couleurs' which was fixed with gilt nails, while a house at Marseilles in 1636 had 'trois tamboretz [tabourets] garnis de tripe de velours' [three stools covered with woollen velvet].[112] In a room at the Noordeinde residence at The Hague in 1632 were two old armchairs covered in *caffa*, and seat-furniture covered with this material and the related 'flowered trippe' are frequently mentioned in House of Orange inventories towards the end of the century.[113] In 1678 the *Académie Française* was provided with a set of walnut chairs covered with *moquade*.[114] There were numerous chairs and stools at Marly and Meudon covered with *tripe* and the 'six grand fauteuils de commodité' mentioned on p. 196 were covered splendidly in 'panne d'Hollande couleur de feu'.[115] At about the same time some chairs at Dyrham were being covered in 'stript plush' while at Tredegar House in South Wales a couch and some cane chairs were acquired which had cushions of 'flowered plush'.[116]

While technically different from the woollen velvets, turkeywork also had a woollen pile and was therefore popular for the same reason, namely that it had a comfortable resilient surface. The pile was usually rather coarser but it was also more robust. In the 'Little Dyning Chamber' at Hardwick in 1601 there was 'a chare of Turkie worke' with a stool covered en suite.[117] The other seat-furniture in the room consisted of 'joint stools'. It is not clear whether this room was used by the Countess of Shrewsbury as a private dining-room, or whether it was used by her steward or senior staff, but one can say that the seat of turkeywork was a fairly grand piece of furniture, inferior only to the opulent pieces in the state rooms. Many stools were covered in turkeywork during the early part of the century but the material really came into its own as covering for farthingale chairs which were produced in large quantities from about 1630 onwards.[118] Panels specially woven to go on such chairs were being made by the middle of the century (Plate 103). The royal household continued to order this simple but comfortable type of chair for use in offices and the like right into the eighteenth century.[119]

Technically related to turkeywork was Savonnerie carpeting and, likewise, it made excellent chair-covers. However, it was extremely expensive and its production was anyway under the king's control, so it was only to be found on seat-furniture in rather exceptional circumstances. Cardinal Mazarin had a whole set of furniture covered in this material—twelve armchairs, twelve ordinary chairs, a couch and two carpets—but then he always surrounded himself with objects of the most conspicuous luxury.[120] The Dauphin had some forms at Meudon in 1702 which were covered in yellow Savonnerie carpeting and a set of stools with Savonnerie covers that must have been specially designed as seat-covers because they each had inwoven a rose at the centre and a dolphin (*dauphin*) at each corner.[121]

Leather had been used for chair-seats and chair-backs since time immemorial; its properties make it particularly suitable for the purpose. Folding chairs and stools could have leather seats (and backs) which needed no further strengthening or padding, although they could of course have both. Moreover, leather can be decorated in various ways, and it is easy to keep clean—for which reason it was popular for dining-chairs. Most seventeenth century leather chair-seats were plain, made of 'Russia leather' which was relatively coarse, or of 'Turkey leather' which seems to have been finer. Towards the end of the century, 'Morocco leather' came into use for the purpose. Black leather with a certain amount of gilt tooling was popular in the Netherlands during the first half of the century,[122] but tooled and gilded leather was not unknown in England at the time, as several documents prove.[123] No doubt leather chair-backs and seats were sometimes painted, like so much other leatherwork of the period, such as the fire-buckets at Ham House, dating from the 1670s, which are painted with the Lauderdale's coat of arms. So-called 'gilt leather' was used to some small extent for chairs (Plate 164). There were eighteen chairs so covered in the 'Guilt Leather Room' at Cowdray in 1682, several sets at Ham House in the middle of the century had seats and backs covered with cloth bordered with gilt leather, while at the princely court at Groeningen in 1633 there were eight 'men's chairs' of gilt leather and a 'large English gilt leather chair'.[124] The material seems, however, to have gone out of fashion in England for the covering of chairs (it was never apparently favoured in France for this purpose and was not much used in Holland either) but it was put to this use in Germany and Scandinavia until well into the eighteenth century.

Embroidery, as has already been explained, could be executed in so many

XII. (right) Although made in London, this sumptuous daybed and its accompanying sofa exemplify better than any other surviving pieces the French style in luxurious seat-furniture at the end of the century. Richly carved, painted black and partly gilded, covered with polychrome Genoa velvet, and trimmed with bell-fringe, this furniture was made for the Duke of Leeds about 1700.

different ways and was so infinitely flexible as a medium for producing decorated textile covers for seat-furniture (Plates 189 and 204) that nothing can be gained by making generalisations here. However, one form of embroidery needs to be mentioned, because it was much used for the coverings of seat-furniture in the seventeenth century, and that is *point d'Hongrie* or 'Irish stitch' (see p. 127). I have also discussed the distinction between domestic and professional embroidery, explaining however that the distinction was by no means always clearly defined. But rich chair-covers worked by professional embroiderers could be very expensive, as Cronström pointed out when comparing them with covers of tapestry. 'Les chaises de haute lisse couteront mesme ou un peu moins que celles à l'aiguille' [Chairs with *hautelisse* will cost the same or rather less than those with needlework], he wrote in 1695. He explained that the high cost of needlework was due to the fact that 'Il n'y a qu'une personne qui puisse travailler à chaque morceau' at a time and that therefore 'cela vas plus lentement.' [Only one person can work at each piece, which goes much more slowly.] What is more, he added, 'ces animaux de tapissiers' [those beasts of upholsterers] were always terribly slow and would invent reasons for late delivery. In Paris a finely embroidered chair-cover might then have cost 22 *écus*.[125]

Between June 1660 and Michaelmas of the following year, John Casbert supplied Charles II with a considerable amount of seat-furniture. Although based in London and working for the Royal Wardrobe, Casbert was probably a French upholsterer and his productions are likely to have been in the latest French taste. Indeed, he described several pieces in his account as 'french Chaires'.[126] He lists the various materials that he used for making up this furniture—sackcloth, girthweb, black tacks (i.e. of iron, as opposed to gilded nails), lining for the backs, crimson serge to cover the chairs, 'milland [Milan] fustion for baggs' (i.e. cushions), down to fill them with, 'curled haire to fill the chaire backs', 'gilt nailes for garnishing', and gold and silver fringe. He then charged for 'making and covering the chairs with crimson serge' and 'fitting false cases of crimson damaske'—these were detachable slip-over covers of the rich material. This is one of the earliest references to the use of horsehair (*crin*) in upholstery. Horsehair seems to have been used for padding the back of Philip II's gout-chair (Plate 173) in the late sixteenth century and Cardinal Mazarin had some forms stuffed with hair in the 1650s.[127] It will be noted that Casbert used horsehair only in the backs; presumably it was especially practical for this task as it was easier to keep in place than other forms of padding. Later it was used all over chairs where firm, springy padding was needed (Plate 179). For real softness, seventeenth-century upholstery relied on down and the accommodating *fauteuils de commodité* and *canapés* of the 1690s acquired their luxurious character through the lavish use of down in conjunction with forms carefully designed to support the human frame in maximum comfort. So great was the use of down for upholstery at the end of the century that an increase in the number of sufferers from piles in Paris was actually attributed to the too liberal use of down 'dans les chaises, les carrosses et autres sièges qui servoient à la commodité, au lieu de crin, dont on se servoit autrefois' [in sedan chairs and other seats which provided comfort, in place of horsehair, which was used formerly].[128]

XIII. (left) A looking-glass canted forward; the common method of hanging large framed items in the seventeenth century. The painting behind has a green protective curtain. Note also the vase of flowers. Dutch, 1678.

CHAPTER IX
Tables and Cup-boards

TABLES that could be dismantled or folded up had suited the mobile life of the ruling classes during the Middle Ages. As a more static life came to be adopted, a parallel development to that which we noted with beds took place—massive, heavy tables were evolved that were virtually impossible to move and therefore remained constantly in one position. But the mobile forms of table continued in favour for occasional use. The servants might bring one in so that dinner could be taken in warmth and comfort by the fire in winter, or they might set one up in the garden so that a meal could be eaten al fresco. Occasional tables were needed for all kinds of purposes—serving food, shaving, washing, accommodating extra people at meals, and so forth. Military gentlemen still needed such equipment on campaigns (Plate 211), moreover, and the rich might still have a folding table to go with the field-bed and the folding chairs when they travelled.

A simple and well-known form of portable table had two or more loose trestles each of which were hinged at the top and opened out into inverted V-shaped stands.[1] A development of this had trestle-like legs fixed with hinges to the underside of the table; the legs were locked in the open position with long iron hooks (Plate 213). This form seems to have been evolved in Spain and at any rate remained popular in that country for a long while.[2] It was known as a 'Spanish table' in the seventeenth century.[3] They are frequently mentioned in English inventories but were inexpensive and uninteresting pieces of furniture, so hardly any specimens have survived (Plate 212).[4] There were doubtless several other types of readily portable table; some were merely small, others had folding tops (Plates 214 and 215), while yet others must have stood on X-frame stands.[5]

Although the artistocracy in the mediaeval period carried their folding tables and trestle-tables with them, they often also had non-portable tables set up in their castles and residence. The long and heavy tables with their massive trestles that usually stood in the hall of great houses were fixtures of this kind[6] but by 1600 it was only the lower servants who would dine at such tables.[7] They would usually be presided over by the steward who would often sit at a draw-table—a table which had draw-leaves at each end by means of which the table area could be doubled at will.[8] The draw-table was itself somewhat massive and so tended to be kept in one place.

The draw-table was also the form commonly used by the owner and his family in their dining parlours or in other rooms where they frequently took meals (Plates 232 and 242).[9] It remained in favour until the middle of the century when the round or oval table with hinged flaps and a swinging gate-leg made its appearance.[10] These rounded shapes were convenient in the smaller and more intimate dining-rooms that were coming into fashion. They enabled the servants to circulate more easily, and questions of precedence were rarely much of a problem in such relatively informal surroundings. The gate-leg form could fold into a narrow compass and could then be placed out of the way against the wall (together with the dining chairs) or in an adjacent passageway.

211. A trestle table with folding, inverted 'V' trestles set up in a military tent. Note the velvet table-carpet. A folding X-frame chair may be seen in the background; at this date it would not only have been a practical piece of furniture to take on campaign but would in addition have underlined the owner's high estate.

212. A folding table of oak. This is likely to be an example of the 'Spanish tables' so often listed in English seventeenth-century inventories. The iron struts brace the folding legs when the table is in use.

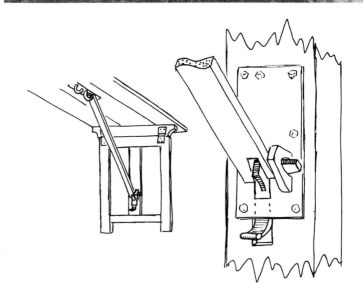

213. The locking action of the table shown in Plate 212. Pulling the spring-loaded catch downwards enables the strut to be un-hooked sideways from the protruding lug.

214 A late-seventeenth-century pinewood occasional table that can be folded. Provided for the use of a Queen of Sweden. The top folds upwards longitudinally; the gate-legs swing round outwards upon the other half-trestles which in turn fold up against the leaf (the trestle at one end is hinged from a deep block to allow the opposite trestle to fold under first).

215. An occasional table of pinewood dated 1696. Such simple furniture has very rarely survived. When in use it would normally have been covered with a cloth.

216. A tea-table of Javanese lacquer raised to a height suitable for Europeans by a Carolean joiner. About 1680.

217. Tea-table with markedly Dutch characteristics provided for royal use in a Danish palace, probably in 1696.

In the 'Great Dining Room' at Ham House in the 1670s there were eight folding tables of cedarwood.[11] They were no doubt humble structures that were usually hidden by the four Oriental screens that were also in the room. It is probable that they were rectangular and could be set out next to each other so as to make up a single table as large as circumstances at each meal required.[12] Extension-pieces were also known in the seventeenth century.[13]

There were of course many specialised forms of table. One type that must have been distinctive was an 'oyster table' at which one did in fact eat oysters, then a relatively inexpensive food. They were apparently circular, with a hole in the centre under which stood a basket for the empty shells.[14] They could be folded away[15] but a certain Mr Hastings, a squire living in Dorset who died in 1650, had in his parlour an 'oyster table at the lower end' which was 'of constant use twice a day all the year round'.[16] They were relatively common in the first half of the century but there was still 'a little oyster table' standing in the hall at Ham House in 1679.[17]

Tables specially designed for the taking of tea only made their appearance late in the century. A specimen at Rosenborg Castle in Copenhagen has a tray-like top with splayed sides, all covered with floral marquetry. It stands on four spiral-turned legs. It may have been made in Copenhagen by a Dutch cabinetmaker or it may have been imported from Holland (Plate 217). Also with a tray-like top is the East Indian lacquerwork tea-table at Ham House which is presumably to be equated with the 'Tea-Table carved and guilt' that stood in the Duchess of Lauderdale's private closet in 1683 (Plate 216).[18] There are similar tables at Dyrham and Lyme Park, and several more are to be seen at Schloss Charlottenburg, Berlin.[19] Since the latter was at that period the residence of a Dutch princess, it may well be that all these East Indian tables were acquired from a dealer in Amsterdam. The Lauderdales certainly bought furniture in Amsterdam although there is no evidence that this particular table came from Holland. By the turn of the century, the familiar form of tea-table with a tip-up top with a pillar and a tripod stand had been devised, probably in Holland.[20] One may be discerned standing in the corner of a room in the painting of a doll's house of about 1700 (Plate 320). Its painted top faces out into the room. The early models had a raised, moulded rim but it was soon found easier to have no rim so that a tea-tray could, so to speak, be slid onto the top.

The French, who were supreme masters in the creation of comfort in the seventeenth century, even devised small tables for taking meals in bed. At the end of the century there were six tables 'pour servir à manger sur le lit' at the Château de Marly, a royal residence where informality and relaxation were *de rigueur*.[21] But almost a century before there had been a 'table à metre devant madame lors qu'elle mange dans le lict' [table for placing before my lady when she takes a meal in bed] at the Château de Turenne.[22] No doubt other examples from the intervening decades could be found from a careful search in inventories.

In contemporary illustrations from about 1630 onwards, one often sees ladies at their *toilette* but no examples of dressing-tables from before about 1675 seem to survive, nor are references at all common in the documents. There were 'sixteene little dressinge Tables of severall sizes' at Easton Lodge in 1637 and there was one at Ham House in the middle of the century.[23] In many of the principal bedchambers at Ham in the 1670s there were small cedarwood tables which may well also have served this purpose, and one has to remember that the fashionable furniture ensemble of the 1670s and 1680s, comprising a side-table, looking-glass and pair of candlestands, might be used as a grand dressing-suite (see Plate 94), although such a triad was normally set up in a room just for show. Indeed, it was the principal fashionable furnishing unit of the period (Plate 218)[24] The group was commonly set against a pier between windows (Plate 273) and thus became the ancestor of the eighteenth century pier-glass and console-table (Plate 219). In that position it of course served well as a dressing-table for the light from the windows fell on the face of the lady in the daytime, while at night the light from the candles on the stands did the same. The looking-glass had to be canted forward so that the sitter could see her reflection. The tables initially associated with such groups tended to be rather insubstantial and therefore unsteady but in the 1680s the French introduced a more sturdy form of table with shorter legs and a knee-hole (Plate 31). This form is today often called a *bureau Mazarin* but, while some may actually have served as writing-desks, many were certainly dressing-tables.[25]

Elaborately decorated tables of various kinds were made right through the seventeenth century for purely decorative purposes—prized possessions of their owners. They were very naturally placed in prominent positions but, since each was unique and since they constituted such exceptional items there is no need to discuss them in the present context.[26]

One must not be misled by the term 'a pair of tables' which occurs in many early seventeenth-century inventories. This meant a games board which, at the time, usually took the form of a box with two tray-like halves hinged so as to open out to form a backgammon (*tric-trac*) board. On the outside faces were the boards for two other games—chess or draughts, and Nine-Men's Morris (Plate 160)[27] When closed, the box held the requisite 'men'. But, while chess-boards were not actual tables, there were several forms of table used for specific games—tables for billiards and *Trou-Madame*, and shovelboards. A mid-seventeenth century billiard-table is still to be seen at Knole and is probably the one mentioned in the inventory of 1645.[28] The drawing of a later example that stood at Chantilly is reproduced in Plate 225. It was faced with green cloth, just as it would be today, but there was a pillar with small bells at the top (*le but*) standing up in the centre. Shovelboards, being very long, are mostly to be found among the furnishings of galleries.[29] *Trou-Madame* was roughly like the modern bagatelle (Plate 83).[30] Some card-tables made for the Dauphin and the Prince de Condé are illustrated in Plates 223 and 224.

A form of table that remains a mystery was something called a 'brushing board' although it was easily recognisable for what it was in the early seventeenth century. In a room where some of the maids slept at Ingatestone, there was a 'brushing bourde of two breadthes lying upon a frame', while at Chatsworth there was 'a playne borde to brush on' in one small room.[31] The purpose of such tables is clear but their nature is not.

Finally, we must discuss cup-boards, a term that embraces a variety of forms, the common purpose of which was to provide a stage (or board) on which precious vessels ('cups') could be displayed.[32] Such furniture was usually to be found in rooms where grand company dined, but cup-boards might also sometimes be placed in bedchambers. Cup-boards had originally taken the form of a simple table but gradually acquired extra shelves or staging on which larger quantities of plate could be shown.[33] Eventually, the lower sections came to be enclosed, with a door in

Jean le Pautre inv. et fecit

218 (left) The fashionable ensemble of the second half of the seventeenth century shown in a Parisian engraving of about 1670. From a suite entitled *Livre de Miroirs, Tables et Guéridons*. For convenience such a group is here called a 'triad'.

219. (above) A Dutch engraving of 1697 shows the eighteenth-century console-table and pier-glass evolving from the late-seventeenth-century 'triad'. The unstable candlestands have already been dispensed with.

front, and thus the term 'cupboard', as we understand it, gained its modern meaning.[34] Cup-boards in the form of *étagères* with enclosed cupboard-sections (i.e. with doors) were not uncommon in the sixteenth century (Plate 92). Being useful for other purposes as well as mere display, now that they could house objects and provide a measure of security, the cupboard came to be used in other rooms—notably in the bedchamber where it served also as a place in or on which to place the 'livery' of food or drink that was issued to important members of the household and guests for the night,[35] although this practice was fast going out of fashion by 1600.[36] The 'livery cupboard' seems finally to have acquired a generally recognisable form and, when it was placed in other rooms (for example, the dining parlour), it was still given this name even though it was presumably never expected to house liveries there. The cup-board with multiple stages (sometimes now with a small cupboard forming a centre section) evolved in England and came to be known as a 'court cupboard', presumably because it was a form that had in the first place been used at court.[37] At any rate, livery cupboards and court cupboards are frequently mentioned in English inventories of the first half of the seventeenth century. As both could have cupboard-sections and neither was invariably confined respectively to the bedchamber and the dining parlour, there was room for confusion at the time and it is no longer possible always to be sure which type of furniture was being described in a particular case.

220. (above) One of the massive silver tables at Versailles. Made by Claude Ballin (1615–78) in the 1670s. This actual table seems to be in the foreground of the view of the *Grande Galerie*, to which room it must have been moved early in the 1680s. Although the piece is there shown used as a pier-table, it appears to be a centre-table (i.e. with four decorated faces).

221. (right) The only surviving piece of silver furniture which faithfully conveys to us how the massive pieces at Versailles must have looked is this font, made by a French silversmith specially brought to Stockholm to execute important commissions for the Swedish Crown.

223. (far right) The Dauphin's card-table at Versailles late in the seventeenth century. The armchair was occupied by the Dauphin (note the dolphin armrests) while the rest of the company will have sat on circular *tabourets* like that illustrated.

222. Tables at Versailles late in the seventeenth century. From a suite of engravings entitled *Livre de tables qui sont dans les apartemens du Roy sur lesquelles sont posées les bijoux des Cabinet des Medailles*. This may be understood to mean that the tables stood in the *Cabinet de Medailles* (completed 1685) which certainly housed part of Louis XIV's collection of gemstone vessels. But the closet could hardly have contained so many tables (ten are illustrated) and we are probably meant to understand that the tables stood in the *Grands Apartments* but that the vessels are here merely shown standing on them. If so, the tables will be those of gilded wood that replaced the massive silver furniture that was melted down in 1689.

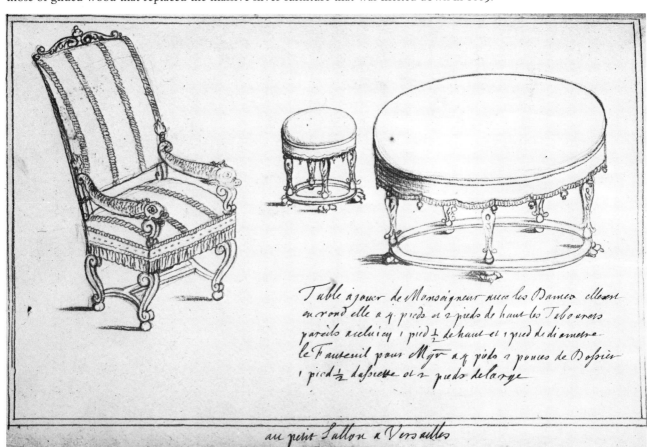

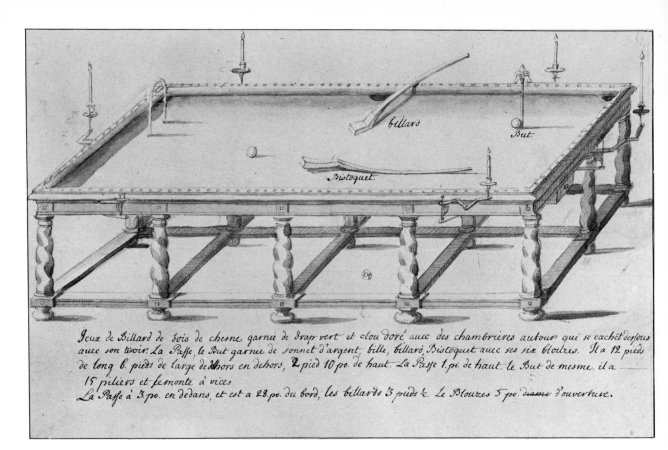

Jeux de Billard de bois de chesne garnie de drap vert et clou doré auec des chambrieres autour qui se cachét dessous auec son tiroir. La Passe, le But garnie de sonnet d'argent, bille, billard, Bistoquet auec ses six blouzes. Il a 12 pieds de long 6. pieds de large dehors en dehors, 2 pied 10 po. de haut. La Passe 1. pi. de haut. le But de mesme, il a 15 piliers et semonte à vices

La Passe à 3. po. en dedans, et est à 28. po. du bord, les billards 3 pieds ½. Le Blouzes 5 po. diame d'ouverture.

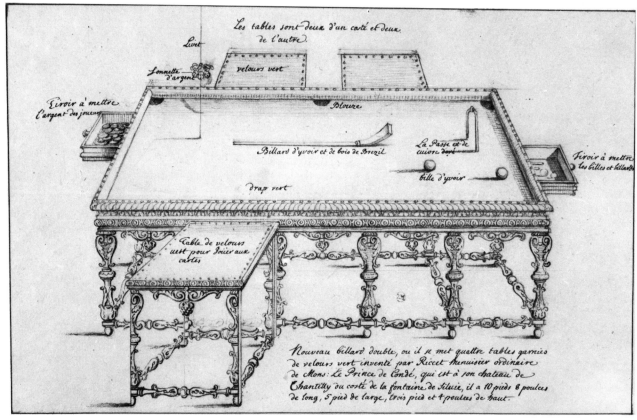

Les tables sont deux d'un coté et deux de l'autre.

Livet

velours vert

Sonnette d'argent

Tiroir à mettre l'argent des joueurs

Blouze

Billard d'yvoir et de bois de Brezil

La Passe et de cuivre doré

bille d'yvoir

Tiroir à mettre les billes et billards

drap vert

Table de velours uert pour joüer aux cartes

Nouveau billard double, ou il se met quattre tables garnies de velours vert inventé par Riccet menuisier ordinaire de Mons: le Prince de Condé, qui est à son chateau de Chantilly du costé de la fontaine de Siluie, il a 10 pieds 6 poulces de long, 5 pied de large, trois pied et 4 poulces de haut.

224 & 225. (left) Two late-seventeenth-century French billiard-tables. The goal (*but*) is fitted with bells that will have rung when the post was struck. There is also a hoop (*passe*). The first table is covered with green cloth, the second, which stood at Chantilly, with green velvet. The latter is stated to be a new model by the Prince de Condé's joiner, Riccet (Ricetti?). A card-table is shown in front.

226. (above) The plain tables set against the window wall in this scene of an English royal banquet given in 1672 are described as 'court cupboards' in the contemporary key to the engraving.

227. An undressed *buffet* with superimposed staging for display of plate. The lower section must comprise two cupboard sections. Opposite stands a draw-table. The presence of these two pieces of furniture indicates that the room commonly served as a dining room.

The *étagère* type of court cupboard went out of fashion in the middle of the century but the term 'court cupboard' was still apparently used after that to describe a straightforward table used as a sideboard (Plate 226).[38] As Randle Holme stated, 'side-tables or court cubberts' were essential in a dining room.[39] The term 'side-board' occurs in the inventory of Hatfield Priory already in 1629, while a 'side-board table' is mentioned in the mid-century inventory of Ham House.[40] The buffet with stages, conceived as a single piece of furniture, went out of fashion in the middle of the century, and was replaced by the sideboard. On very special occasions, when it was still desired to have a rich display of plate, a special side-table with staging entirely masked with a cloth was easily contrived (Plate 229).

The French called the cup-board with staging a *dressoir* (hence our 'dresser') in the Middle Ages, presumably because one dressed it with plate.[41] Later the common term for such a piece of furniture was *un buffet*, because from it one often dispensed drink (Plates 92 and 227).[42] Occasionally, it was also known as a *dessert*, perhaps because the dessert stood on it prior to being brought to the table.[43]

Continental buffets were altogether more elaborate than their English counterparts; they often had highly decorated back-boards, and many comprised cupboards in the lower stage. However, the more skeletal form (which the English called a 'court cupboard') was also known, at least in France, judging by two shown in an illustration in De Breuil's treatise on perspective of 1642–9.[44]

The various forms of buffet so far mentioned were movable (even if they were

238

228. A *buffet* or cup-board covered with a cupboard cloth and dressed with plate. Dutch; 1602. The master of the house has a 'great chair' with arms; his wife and children have less impressive forms of seating.

rarely moved because they were very heavy) but built-in buffets came into fashion late in the century. Plate 19 shows one of eight counter-like buffets of this sort that were provided for the central, octagonal Salon at the Château de Marly in 1699–1700. In the latter year, Jean Bérain, designer to the *Menus Plaisirs*, the organisation that provided ephemeral equipment and decoration for the numerous elaborate festivities and ceremonies at the French Court, invented a special buffet which was 'fort propre pour les festes' [very suitable for banquets]. It was set in a niche and had sliding doors assisted by counterweights. It was decorated with 'figures à la Chine'.[45] In Holland, and also to some extent in England, buffets might be contrived in arched niches at one end of a dining-room.[46] Such buffet-niches were to become a common feature of Dutch interiors in the eighteenth century.

The seventeenth-century tables that one sees in museums and country houses today are almost all left bare—uncovered. This gives a false impression of their original appearance, for at that period they were, almost without exception, covered with a cloth of some kind (Plate 231). Draw-tables and other forms of table that stood in prominent places invariably had special 'table carpets' that were more or less splendid according to the depth of the owner's purse (Plate 232). Dining-tables were, moreover, covered with linen tablecloths at mealtimes.[47] When cup-boards or buffets were dressed with plate, a 'cup-board cloth' covered at least the uppermost stage and often the whole structure (Plate 228). Even the very splendid tables, decorated elaborately with inlay or marquetry and designed specially for show,

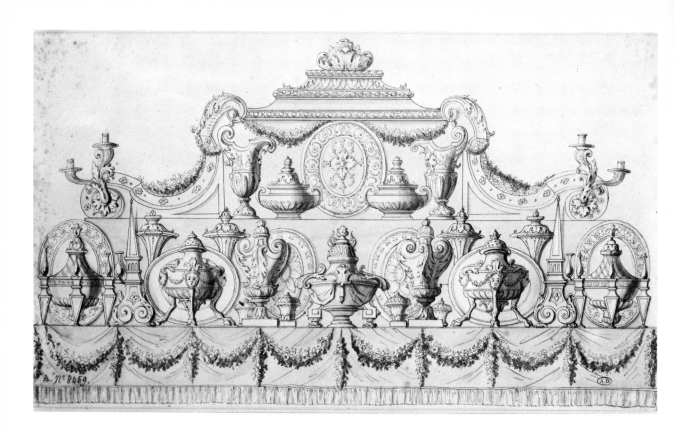

A. N.º 8459.

Plan, Elevation et Profil d'vn Buffet de Marbre et de Bronze, au milieu du quel est vn Tableau et aux côtez deux
Niches, dans lesquelles il y a des Cascades. Ce Buffet est executé chez Monsieur Thevenin a Paris.

I. Mariette excudit.

3.

229. (upper left) Proposal for dressing a *buffet* by Jean Bérain (1640–1711), showing an impressive array of plate including two perfume-burners (*casolettes*) with their pierced lids. The legs of this piece of furniture are not shown.

230. (lower left) End wall of a Parisian dining room late in the seventeenth century with a fixed *buffet* of marble flanked by niches containing fountains.

231. (above) The table-carpet constituted a prominent element in the décor of a room. Here is a relatively plain example, of woollen or silken velvet trimmed with fringe, on a table in Gerard Terborch's house in 1665.

would normally have been covered with a protective cover, only to be revealed in their full glory on festive occasions. However, such protective covers could be quite decorative in their own right as they had to be seen for much of the time.[48] Others, it must be admitted, were more purely utilitarian.[49]

In the seventeenth century, a 'table cloth' was a cover (usually of linen) that was placed over a table for dining. A 'table carpet', on the other hand, was a much more substantial covering. The equivalent in France was a *tapis de table*. The finest table-carpets were prized possessions that were treated with great care and perhaps were only displayed on special occasions. As tables with intricate marquetry decoration on their top surfaces became commoner, in the second half of the century, so the great age of the table-carpet receded into history. After that, the only form of table which was still in most cases covered with a 'carpet' was the dressing-table.

Table-carpets mostly consisted of a plain material (woollen cloth, or silk or woollen velvet) trimmed all round with a fringe.[50] Materials with a pile that was soft to the touch were of course in great favour for this purpose (Plate 211). During the first half of the century Turkish rugs, which were expensive and valued possessions were far more often to be seen on tables than on the floor, and this fashion

241

232. A draw-table with a table-carpet that fits it precisely. Maybe both were of standard sizes, or perhaps one was made to fit the other. This table-carpet is a characteristic product of Dutch tapestry-weaving *ateliers* of the second quarter of the seventeenth century. The cushions, pelmet round the chimneypiece, and bed-hangings are all en suite with the carpet.

continued in Holland right through the century (Colour Plate XIII and Plate 242).[51] Table-carpets of turkeywork were used in the same way as Oriental rugs.[52] Moquette, with or without pseudo-Oriental patterns,[53] was much used for table-covers, or so it seems. In Holland table-carpets were produced specially for the purpose in the tapestry-weaving technique; one may be seen in Plate 232 where it forms part of a complete suite comprising cushion-covers, bed-hangings and a pelmet round the over-hanging chimneypiece.[54] The class of material known as dornix was also used for covering tables on occasion.[55] I have considered covers for tables made of protective leather but table-carpets were also occasionally made of this material for show.[56] Gilt-leather, which is not pliant, could only be used for this purpose if the table-carpet was specially shaped (i.e. had four flaps or *pentes* that hung down the sides of the table from the rectangular top),[57] or if the central panel was of some less rigid material and only the borders were of gilt leather.[58] Occasionally one comes across references to unusual table-carpets, like the 'cubberd cloth of Indyan stuff' which was on a 'fayer court cubbard' at Cockesden in 1610, and the 'Indian twilt' (quilt?) on a small table at Tart Hall.[59] There is a chintz on the table to be seen in Plate 115.

Many table-carpets were embroidered and, as has been explained, needlework could be as varied in its delicacy and elaboration as the skills of each individual embroiderer permitted. Thus many quite plain cloths might have a simple border embroidered on them by one of the ladies of the household. At the other end of the scale were the sumptuous table-carpets worked by the professional 'broderers' working in some metropolitan *atelier* with all the facilities for obtaining expensive materials (silks of all kinds and a variety of gold and silver threads) and designs of advanced taste at their doorstep (Colour Plate XI).[60]

On cup-boards and sideboards, it was usual to place a cupboard-cloth of linen when it was to be dressed with plate (Plate 228). Such cloths are usually listed with the household linen.[61] They tended to have lace edges which hung down over the sides of the shelf. As for the carpets on dining-tables, these were sometimes left in place under the linen tablecloth, when the table was being laid for a meal, but the practice seems to have varied from one country to another.[62]

Until the last years of the century, all dressing-tables were simple structures which required no decoration as they were entirely hidden by a 'carpet'. The carpet was at first protected from damage by powder and other cosmetics by a small linen cloth— a *toilette*—but this gradually became a more important feature until the *toilette* evolved as a richly trimmed cloth in its own right and might be of velvet or silk (Plates 29, 131 and 289).[63] Eventually, the word came to embrace the complete dressing-set which could comprise not just the cloth but comb-cases, brushes, mirrors, patch-boxes, flasks, trays and much else, as well as a container for it all, a dressing-gown and a pair of slippers. Such ensembles were given as expensive presents at the end of the century,[64] especially in connection with important weddings. About 1700 it became fashionable in Paris to have gauze or muslin covers, gathered in furbellows, laid over a silk *toilette*.[65] If there was a dressing-glass on the table, this would sometimes be provided with a 'scarf' of the same flimsy material which was fixed at the top of the frame and fell down the sides over the edge of the table.

CHAPTER X
Other Furniture and Decorative Features

ORNAMENTAL CABINETS

THE ornamental cabinet played a prominent part in the decoration of grand rooms during the seventeenth century (Plate 241). As the massive buffets and other varieties of cup-board went out of fashion, their place was taken on the one hand by straightforward tables that could assume the buffet's practical rôle by serving as sideboards, and on the other hand by the decorative cabinet which became *par excellence* the fashionable class of carcass-furniture of the period 1625–85. Its place was ultimately taken by the chest of drawers, the bureau-bookcase and the other highly decorative forms that were to dominate in the eighteenth century.

In the sixteenth century, cabinets had been sufficiently small to be portable and could therefore be placed on a table or some other piece of furniture at the owner's convenience.[1] They came in several qualities but the craftsmanship displayed in these small confections was generally of a much higher order than that bestowed on most other classes of furniture.[2] The exquisite workmanship of the best cabinets was a source of wonder and delight, and the proud owner tended to keep such valuable objects in the *Wunderkammer* or in his private study. But as the prestige and popularity of the cabinet grew, the tendency was to place it in more prominent positions: in the main bedchamber, in the withdrawing room or the gallery. In such positions, it was the decorative qualities of cabinets that came to the fore. In order to present a larger surface for ornament, the cabinet grew in size and eventually required a stand of its own (Plate 234). Soon the ornamental potential of this unit became widely apparent and considerable care was taken over the design of important specimens which came to be the subject of special commissions. Among the drawings at the Ashmolean Museum are several for imposing cabinets, one of which bears the cipher of Marie de Medici, and cannot therefore date from later than 1630 when she was deprived of her power (Plate 233).

The delicate work of the skilled cabinetmakers of Augsburg and Paris was beyond the means of all but the wealthiest clientèle; nevertheless there were many people who well appreciated the prestige that owning a handsome cabinet could bestow on its owner. As a result a lively industry sprang up in the Netherlands (notably at Antwerp but also at Amsterdam) which did a brisk business in what may be described as the second-class cabinet field (Plate 241).[3] The products of this trade are still to be found, now often sadly battered, in country houses all over Europe. They are showy objects on which the maximum decorative effect is achieved at relatively small expense;[4] they are typical confections of the Baroque age and must have given great pleasure when they were new.

Cabinets of an exotic character were greatly prized and were conspicuous evidence of wealth (Plate 20). In the principal bedchamber at Ham House stood a large ivory cabinet that still survives at the house. It is entirely faced with short lengths of ivory decorated with wave-moulding. To us it may seem rather a dull

233. An imposing French ornamental cabinet apparently intended for Queen Marie de Medici who was deprived of her power in 1630. A double M cipher under a royal crown occurs several times in this composition. The cabinet was probably to be faced entirely with ebony and set with gilt mounts, like the very similar cabinet recently acquired by the Victoria and Albert Museum. The drawing is here attributed to the architect Pierre Collot.

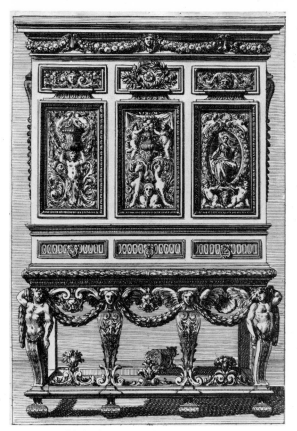

234. A published French design for an ornamental cabinet; about 1660. Such a piece was entirely for show.

235. Curiosities in a cabinet. Although the painting is German, this gives a vivid impression of the variety of goods one might expect to find in such a piece of furniture. Apart from the works of art, they include a baby's skull, sea shells and a document. Note the cup-hooks from which several items hang.

object but, if one considers how many elephants had to be sacrificed in order to clad this piece of furniture with ivory, one may start to appreciate why it was so highly rated and was placed in the most important room in the house.[5] There are at Ham also several Oriental cabinets faced with black lacquer which have carved and gilded stands that were specially made for them in Europe. They also stood in prominent positions in the main rooms.[6] Already in 1614 the Earl of Northampton had owned a 'china guilt cabonette upon a frame', but this must have been one of the earliest specimens to have made its appearance in England.[7] Cardinal Mazarin, who owned many cabinets, only seems to have had one Oriental piece although this was most certainly a curiosity, for it took the form of a pagoda.[8] With their more firmly established links with the Far East, the Dutch seem to have been able to procure Oriental lacquer cabinets slightly more easily than their neighbours. At the Prince of Orange's residence at The Hague there were several pieces by 1632[9] and, by the middle of the century, there were sufficient for it to be possible to cut them up and panel an entire closet with lacquer in the Huis ten Bosch. It should be added that not all Eastern cabinets were faced with lacquer; one cabinet in the Princess of Orange's closet was covered with Persian silk with a gold ground brocaded with flowers and had a gilt stand resembling a stool.[10] Towards the end of the century exotic cabinets became quite familiar in well-appointed houses. By 1688 the first handbook on how to paint imitation lacquer-work had made its appearance in London and 'Japanners'

246

were at work in most important cities, turning out fairly plausible renderings of these Oriental wares to satisfy the demand from those who could not afford the real thing—or who could not tell the difference.[11]

Since cabinets made such handsome and telling features in a room, and as they were increasingly displayed in the main (and therefore larger) rooms, they were sometimes made in pairs so as to contribute even more effectively to a symmetrical scheme of decoration (Plate 20).[12] In some cases cabinets came with a table decorated en suite: a cabinet veneered with red tortoiseshell in the Victoria and Albert Museum is still accompanied by its associated table, and there is a similar group decorated with floral marquetry at Ham House.[13] Cabinets seem also occasionally to have been accompanied by a pair of candlestands.[14] Flickering candlelight shining on the often gilded embellishments of a richly decorated cabinet would have produced a supremely decorative effect and, even if the cabinet did not have candlestands en suite, it is probable that candles were often placed flanking cabinets when a truly stunning effect was required after dark.

Cabinets mostly had flat tops that provided a convenient surface on which other decorative objects could be placed—clocks, small works of sculpture, caskets and boxes of all kinds, and vessels of precious metal or porcelain (Plates 291 to 293). Indeed, when the craze (no other word will do) for massed displays of Chinese porcelain gripped fashionable society in Europe, not only were porcelain vessels crammed onto the tops of cabinets but more vessels of this exotic ware were ranged between the legs of their stands. It was of course particularly cabinets of Oriental lacquer that were involved in these presentations of 'China ware'.

While cabinets could serve 'simplement d'ornement dans les chambres, galleries, ou autres appartements' [simply as ornaments in bedchambers, galleries or other rooms], as Savary des Bruslons pointed out early in the eighteenth century, he reminds us that they might also be receptacles in which 'les choses les plus precieuses' [objects of the most precious kind] could be kept (Plate 235).[15] Viscountess Dorchester had two cabinets 'in the roome, next my ladies Chamber' in which she kept, for example, some items of silver, six pairs of embroidered gloves and twelve plain pairs, some cups and dishes of amber, a looking-glass with a gold frame, a prayer-book with an embroidered cover, eleven purses and some caps.[16] Another detailed list of the contents of a cabinet is included in a French inventory of 1693. In it the owner kept not only several important documents but also various trinkets, some small boxes, reliquaries, watches, some precious balsam and some artificial flowers.[17] A similar miscellaneous collection of valued objects was to be found in a cabinet in Breda Castle in 1619—a cross and some bowls of rock crystal, some jewellery, a casket of mother-of-pearl, a little basket of silver filigree, two flasks and some medals.[18]

MASSED PORCELAIN AND SIMILAR FORMAL DISPLAYS

By the late sixteenth century Italian architects were organising collections of precious vessels and the like in formal arrangements on the wall, each piece standing on a separate bracket.[19] Such schemes conformed to the Renaissance sense of order that was already so strikingly embodied in the current Italian architecture and, as the Italian formula for orderly interior arrangements spread northwards across the Alps,

236. Precious vessels set on brackets arranged in formal patterns on the walls. Proposal for the mural decoration of the *Petite Galerie* at Versailles drawn by Lassurance in 1684. The room was to house Louis XIV's magnificent collection of gemstone vessels.

237. A collection of sculpture arranged formally. A display of François Girardon's works (and that of certain other sculptors, note the Chinese Dog of Fo under the table) in the gallery of his house in Paris at the end of the seventeenth century. Girardon (1628–1715) was the chief sculptor engaged at the Château de Versailles in the time of Louis XIV.

it is hardly surprising that formal displays of this kind gradually came to be adopted in the more northerly countries of Europe. However, it is not easy to plot the spread of this fashion.

The inventory of the Stadholder's residence at The Hague, taken in 1632, provides us with our earliest impression of a carefully organised scheme of this sort.[20] There pottery of various apparently valuable kinds was displayed on shelves in massed arrangements round the room.[21] There were a few intrusive items (a cup of rhinoceros horn, two Oriental trays, some Eastern basketwork boxes and two vases of alabaster) but otherwise the assemblages were of a consistent nature and must have been striking.

There may have been other rooms in Holland decorated in this manner at the time, for the Earl and Countess of Arundel had what they called their 'Dutch Pranketing Room' rigged up in a similar manner at this period and this suggests that it was recognised as a characteristically Dutch form of decoration. The Arundels'

248

Banqueting Room was apparently a separate building standing in the garden at Tart Hall (rebuilt 1638–40) and a separate inventory of it survives which describes the various groups of rarities that were assembled in seemingly formal arrangements there—groups of glassware, basketwork and brassware as well as porcelain vessels and figures.[22] The groups comprising large numbers of objects were displayed between the windows, on a dresser, in the corners of the room, on the jambs of the chimneypiece, above the door, and on structures with up to seven shelves which, in the inventory, are called 'classes'. One such structure was 'a narrow classe in manner of a columne'.

The list of porcelain in the possession of Amalia van Solms, widow of Frederik Hendrik, Prince of Orange, in the middle of the century is very long and its relative importance may be judged from the fact that it follows immediately after that of her gold and silver plate, and before the objects of rock crystal, amber and semi-precious stones.[23] Amalia van Solms had caused a number of valuable Oriental lacquer cabinets to be dismembered and the resulting panels used to face the walls of a closet at her small villa, the Huis 'ten Bosch, outside The Hague. Some valuable Oriental lacquer screens suffered a similar fate when another closet was fitted out in the little palace of Honselaarsdijk in 1686, probably to the designs of Daniel Marot. Marot may have been inspired by what he had seen of a rich closet that was being created at Versailles for the Dauphin at the very time that the young designer was forced to emigrate in 1684.[24] The Swedish architect, Nicodemus Tessin saw the room at Honselaarsdijk the year after it was completed and carefully described its walls of Chinese lacquerwork, its ceiling of mirror-glass, and the massed porcelain on the chimney-piece.[25] We do not know much about the appearance of the Dauphin's closet but we have an inventory of his palace at Meudon, made in 1702, which informs us that in the Gallery, for instance, there were 'sur le cheminée & sous les cabinets, quatre porcelaines, six autres de Siam, neuf bronzes donnez par le Roy, [et] deux autre bronzes' [on the chimneypiece and beneath the cabinets, four porcelain vessels, six others from Siam, nine bronzes presented by the King and two other bronzes]. In the closet set aside for the use of Louis XIV when he paid a visit to his son, there were 'dessus et dessous des bureaux, quatre porcelaines de siam' [on and under the desks, four pieces of Siamese porcelain].[26] In another room porcelain stood both on and under a table, and so on.

Curiously enough, while his son derived much pleasure from porcelain, Louis XIV did not seem to care for it all that much, but he liked to have his treasures marshalled in an orderly manner that contributed to the mural schemes and the décor of his rooms as a whole. The Cabinet of Curiosities he built in 1684 to house his fabulous collection of hardstone vessels had these treasures set on brackets in a formal arrangement up the walls,[27] and Plate 236 shows a proposal of the same year for the Petite Galerie at Versailles that was to be dressed with valuable items of a similar nature, perched on brackets set in regular formation against panels of mirror-glass.

The porcelain cabinets that Daniel Marot began to create for Mary, Princess of Orange and soon to be Queen of England, shortly after his arrival in Holland combined Parisian stylishness in the most up-to-date fashion with the Dutch love of massed porcelain (Plates 72, 73 and 238). She brought the style to England, her appartment at Kensington Palace being decked out with very large numbers of

238. Massed arrays of porcelain integrated with the architecture. View of a 'China Closet' by Daniel Marot; about 1690. The triad against the window-pier closely resembles Marot's design of 1700, reproduced in Plate 51, which was to form part of the decoration at the Dutch palace of Het Loo; but, by the end of the century, rooms like this were to be seen in most of the House of Orange residences—Hampton Court, The Hague, Oranienburg, Leeuwarden, Kensington, etc.

porcelain vessels while several rooms at Hampton Court were dressed in a similar manner.[28]

All over northern Europe during the last half of the seventeenth century it was members of the House of Orange-Nassau who formed nucleii from which the china mania spread. Amalia van Solms' daughter, Luise Henriette, married the Elector of Brandenburg and seems to have introduced the fashion to that north-German state. At any rate, when her son Frederick I of Prussia rebuilt her small palace (appropriately named Schloss Oranienburg) between 1688 and 1695, he created a china closet dressed entirely with porcelain, using an architect (I. B. Broebes) who had been a pupil of Jean Marot (the father of Daniel) who was one of the principal designers in Paris during the third quarter of the century.[29] And when Albertina Agnes of Orange-Nassau had built Schloss Oranienstein (note the allusive name once more) on the Lahn near Koblenz, a task completed in about 1683, she began to collect porcelain on a large scale and soon amassed huge quantities which she too arranged in the new fashion.[30]

In the various House of Orange porcelain rooms at the end of the century there was the now obligatory stacking of vessels on top of cabinets, on chimneypieces, over doors and under tables. At Oranienstein more porcelain was set on *tablets* which

239. The hanging bookshelf, suspended merely on ribbons, was a common seventeenth century feature—apparently called a 'tablette' in France. This mid-seventeenth-century French still-life shows treasured objects including Chinese porcelain, a silver-gilt ewer and basin (for hand-washing) and a Japanese lacquer casket.

were pairs of hanging shelves separated by balusters. Some of the shelves were gilded (Plate 239). At Oranienburg there were some gilded *étagères* backed with mirror-glass that still survive although the room itself has long since gone. At Kensington there were special pedestals on which stood 'one fine Jar & cover [and] two fine large beakers' and there were 'two round black shelves to putt china on, ye under side covered with looking glass' which again were stacked with porcelain. Vessels were, moreover, combined in fanciful compositions. There were in a closet two 'fine basons of a sorte, one upon ye other, one fine little dish upon the bason; all this in one stand,' while nearby were 'two stands, each stand maide up with three jarrs & one china platt on the top'.[31] Marot's engraving of a china closet (Plate 238) gives a good impression of how such rooms looked. It will be seen how the porcelain is set so as to accentuate architectural features—up pilasters, in pyramid forms over the fireplace, along cornices, and so forth.

Defoe recorded how fashionable people in England fell over themselves trying to imitate the form of decoration Queen Mary had made so very much her own, 'till it became a grievance in the expence of it'.[32] It would be unfair to blame the Queen entirely for the porcelain mania, however, as such schemes were certainly known in these islands before she returned to England as William III's consort.[33] Her

251

arrangements differed from earlier essays in this field of decoration chiefly in scale and probably also in the elegance of the presentation, for which Daniel Marot was largely responsible.

THE HANGING OF PICTURES AND LOOKING-GLASSES

As with precious vessels, paintings were sometimes already being hung in regular formations on walls in Italy in the sixteenth century.[34] In this way, the group of pictures formed part of the mural decoration, part of the architecture, and it was the rhythmic arrangement of rectangular, but sometimes round or oval, frames that formed the essential decorative element; the contents of the frame were in this respect of secondary importance. In important rooms of a formal nature paintings continued to be disposed on the walls in such regular arrangements, right through the seventeenth century (Plate 241). This fashion came to full fruition in the neo-classical period of the eighteenth century.

Most people in the seventeenth century did not however hang their pictures in such rigid patterns. In illustrations of Dutch interiors, which mostly show middle-class surroundings, paintings are hung in every conceivable position—high up under the cornice, in several tiers, haphazardly, tightly packed—no rules seem at first to have existed. Yet certain conventions must have governed these matters although it is difficult to get a clear impression of what they were.

Large paintings and looking-glasses, for instance, were rarely hung flat against the wall; they were mostly canted forward so that the top of the frame stood out several inches from the wall (Colour Plate XIII and Plate 94). If there were several rows of pictures, one above the other, the top row might be canted forward more than the lower rows but, once again, this does not invariably seem to have been the case. Experiments carried out at Ham House with the single row of portraits in the Gallery indicate that they were probably hung at a lower level than one might expect today. There was very little furniture in galleries in those days and pictures did not therefore have to be raised above cabinets and so forth; they could be set quite low.

Large pictures and looking-glasses were normally suspended from two rings or hooks at the back of the frame, from which one could either have two cords rising to be attached to two hooks under the frieze, or one could have a single cord running up to and over a single hook or nail in what is still the common fashion today (Plate 240). Inspection of the backs of seventeenth-century frames will show where the rings or hooks were originally fixed. In the case of frames that were meant to be canted forward, the hitching-point was quite far down from the top. This automatically threw the frame forward when it was hung from these points. Small frames would normally have a central ring at the top which fitted over a hook driven straight into the wall—if necessary, right through the wall-hangings (Plate 311). Hooks in the wall and rings on frames were often disguised by bows of silk ribbon (Plate 246),[35] and the cords might be masked with lengths of ribbon although cords might be made so decorative that they formed an embellishment in their own right. Sometimes the cords were organised in a decorative manner so that a tail ending in a tassel could hang down on each side of the frame (Plate 241). The permutations were numerous, it will be seen.

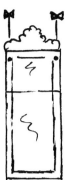

240. Diagram of the four principal ways of hanging framed objects in the seventeenth century. Here demonstrated with looking-glasses. Top left: canted forwards by having the hitching-points set low. Top right: with two cords, hanging flat. Lower left: small glass hanging on a single hook. Lower right: with a length of cord from a single hook. Bows were commonly used to disguise hooks and rings.

241. Various forms of picture hanging. Above the cornice are paintings set into frames in the wall. Against the chimneybreast is a large painting canted forward. Flanking the cabinet are two paintings hanging from hooks disguised by bows (the rings seem to be ornamental). The looking-glass probably rests on top of the cabinet and its angle of canting is adjusted by the cord attached to a single hook; the flanking cords and tassels are purely decorative. The ornamental cabinet, made in Antwerp, is decorated with paintings inside the doors. Flemish picture; 1660s.

An artist's handbook of 1675 explained which subjects were most suitable for the different classes of room.

> Let the *Hall* be adorned with Shepherds, Peasants, Milk-maids, Flocks of sheep and the like . . . Let the *Staircase* be set off with some admirable monument or building, either new or ruinous, to be seen and observed at a view passing up . . . Let landskips, Hunting, fishing, fowling, histories and antiquities be put up in the *Great Chamber* . . . In the Inward or *Withdrawing* Chambers put . . . draughts of the life, of Persons of Honor, intimate or special friends and acquaintance . . . in *Banqueting-rooms* put cheerful and merry paintings of Bacchus, Centaurs, satyrs, syrens and the like, but forbearing all obscene pictures. Histories, grave stories, and the best works become *Galleries*; where one may walk and exercise their senses in viewing, examining, delighting, judging and censuring . . . in the *Bedchamber* put your own, your wives and childrens pictures; as only becoming the most private room, and your modesty; lest (if your wife be a beauty) some wanton and libidinous guest should gaze too long on them and commend the work for her sake.[36]

The mention of a 'Great Chamber' suggests these rules were formulated earlier in the century. Certainly the Duke and Duchess of Lauderdale did not adhere to them when Ham House was done over the 1670s. Nevertheless there will have been conventions that led people to feel that one sort of picture was more appropriate than another in a given position. The inventory of pictures at Ham indicates in which room each item used to hang and, since most of the pictures concerned are still in the house, is a most revealing document.[37] Large portraits of high-ranking friends and relations were hung in the Long Gallery but there were many other portraits scattered throughout the house. In the Duke's Bedchamber the pictures embedded in the panelling were masculine in character (seascapes with men-o'-war and other shipping) while his wife had 'feminine' paintings (of birds) in hers.[38] In the closets, which were small rooms of an intimate and personal character, the pictures were correspondingly small ('cabinet pictures') and were often of high quality since they could be studied close to, an important consideration as many hours were spent in these places. In many of the rooms the over-door paintings are still in position and Ham therefore provides us with an especially good opportunity of studying 'furnishing pictures' that were designed for the actual spaces concerned. Some of them are good pictures but many are not.

A few people collected paintings for their own sake in the seventeenth century but most owners of houses bought pictures in the same way as they might acquire a fine cup of rock crystal, a splendidly inlaid cabinet, or a Persian carpet. These were valuable objects that projected the right image; they were acquired with an eye on the effect they would make. People might therefore often be content with a copy of a famous painting, and the quality of a picture tended to matter less than the subject it portrayed. Today, with the vast apparatus of scholarship in this field at our command, with comparative photographs to guide us, and the acute necessity of being able to differentiate forced upon us by overpowering commercial pressures, it is difficult to envisage how a seventeenth-century owner, living deep in the country, could be quite content with what would today be regarded as a mediocre assemblage. These things had significance for him; to understand this we need to consider the original context very carefully.[39]

Paintings that were particularly valued were sometimes provided with protective curtains of thin silk which hung from a rod fixed along the top of the frame (Colour Plate XIII). The Dauphin had roller-blinds on some of his pictures but this was certainly unusual (see p. 141). Since pictures were in many cases hung so as to contribute to the décor, their frames assumed great importance. An excellent frame might well be put round a painting that would today be rated as being of no great consequence.

SCREENS

The English word 'screen' should normally be rendered as *paravent* in French, while the French term *écran* is principally used in reference to firescreens. The *paravent* is usually a large structure which serves to keep off draughts, as the name indicates. When no specific indication is given in seventeenth-century inventories, one can assume that the term screen is being applied to a *paravent* but one cannot be altogether certain.[40]

There was a 'great foulding skreene of seaven foulds' in the Great Chamber at Hengrave Hall in 1603 but most seventeenth-century screens (*paravents*) had an even number of sections [41]. One of nine is, however, shown in Plate 200.

Early folding screens may have had detachable 'screen-cloths'[42] but most covers were nailed to the framing, the nails being driven through a tape running round the edge that prevented fraying (Plate 242). It would seem that these screens were usually covered on one side only.[43]

One could use almost any material for covering a screen. Worsted cloth of some

242. A simple folding screen (*paravent*) consisting of a wooden frame to which green cloth is nailed through a red tape.

243. An adjustable wickerwork firescreen with an oak stand, at Hardwick Hall. This may well date from around 1600.

244. Stand for a screen-cloth to hang over, at Hardwick Hall. In 1601 such a screen was in the Best Bedchamber sporting a cloth of carnation-coloured velvet embroidered with gold thread and trimmed with gold fringe.

kind was the most usual[44] but silk was also used to some extent, especially towards the end of the century when the decorative potential of the screen began to be appreciated more widely.[45] There was a 'skrine [i.e. the wooden frame] & cloth of fine tapestrie' at Ham House in a room hung with tapestry during the middle of the century, but this was not a material commonly used for the purpose until the eighteenth century.[46] Gilt leather screens became popular at the end of the century and were extremely decorative.[47] European embroidery was not much to be seen on screens but there was a screen of embroidered Indian sarsnet at Ham in the 1670s.[48] A few particularly expensive folding screens were covered in Savonnerie carpetting, a material that would not seem especially well suited for the purpose but promised to be durable.[49]

Oriental screens were prized to quite a different degree and were indeed highly decorative. Already in 1614 a ship had arrived in the Port of London carrying 'Japanese Wares, as ritch scritores, trunckes, beoubes ... of a most excellent varnish.'[50] The merchandise was put up for sale and one of the lots consisted of 'a biobee or skreen Guilded and paynted with resemblances of warfare'. Such Oriental lacquer screens, however, remained a rarity in this country until well into the second

XIV (right) Tapestry-woven panel of a firescreen designed by Jean Bérain and woven at Beauvais late in the seventeenth century.

256

half of the century. There were several such 'Indian screens' at Ham House in the 1670s, for instance, and a number were cut up to panel rooms in Dutch palaces.[51] At Ham in 1679 there was an 'Indian paper screen' and in the inventory of 1683 mention was made of 'a litle Indian screen'; perhaps these entries concern a Chinese painted silk screen of four folds that still survives.[52] It is about thirty inches high.

From mediaeval times until the mid-seventeenth century the standard firescreen was of basketwork and seems usually to have been circular.[53] They came in different sizes and grades.[54] Several specimens may be seen at Hardwick, at least one of which may well date from around 1600 (Plate 243). The circular wicker firescreen was originally an adaptation of the hand-held bat-like implement which was often used for fanning the fire—and still is in many countries (Plate 84).[55] Randle Holme illustrates the pattern of 'hand-screen' current in his day in England; it was circular but of pleated paper. He explains that it 'is a thing made of crisped paper and set in an handle to hold before a ladies face when she sits neere the fire in winter tyme'.[56] The wicker firescreen went out of fashion in the second half of the century.[57]

When Horace Walpole visited Hardwick in 1760 he noticed some 'screens like stands to brush cloaths, with long pieces of carnation velvet hanging over them, fringed with gold; the velvet now turned yellow'.[58] There did in fact stand in the best bedchamber at Hardwick in Elizabethan times 'a skreyne with a cover for it of carnation velvet imbrodered with golde and a golde frenge' and there was a similar item in the Gallery.[59] Some T-shaped stands with tripod bases are still in the house and may be the supports for the screens in question (Plate 244). Maybe many of the references to 'screen cloths' in seventeenth-century inventories concern screens of this form.[60]

Although some 'screen cloths' were embroidered, little attention was paid to the decoration of firescreens until the second half of the century. Even the inventories of Ham House, taken between 1677 and 1683, say nothing about the leaves of the firescreens there listed although they linger lovingly over their descriptions of the stands, which were quite elaborate.[61] Tapestry-woven firescreen-leaves were being produced by 1700 at Beauvais and perhaps elsewhere (Colour Plate XIV), and it was only at this time that firescreens seem to have become an acceptable vehicle for domestic embroidery.[62]

A new form of firescreen was introduced towards the end of the century. This was a version of what would today be called a 'cheval' firescreen and had a sliding leaf which could be set at different heights. In France this was known as an *escran à coulisse* (Plate 245). Five were provided for the principal rooms at Marly in 1698.[63] Several examples from the time of William and Mary survive in the English Royal Collection.[64]

Chimney-boards (see p. 264) were sometimes fitted with small feet so that they could stand out on the floor and serve as cheval firescreens (Plate 251). Several examples of this form survive in Sweden but the modification seems such an obvious one to make that it would be surprising if this variant had not been known elsewhere in Europe.

XV. (left) Several ways of arranging flowers—in a vase, in a basket, in shallow *tazze*, as a nosegay, wrapped in a handkerchief, and as a garland.

245. An *écran à coulisse* (cheval fire-screen with a sliding leaf) in a smart Parisian bedchamber in 1688. Note the firedogs, the fire-irons set upright and embraced by hooks, and the *garniture de cheminée*.

CHIMNEY-FURNITURE

The fireplace was the dominant feature of a room and the care therefore bestowed on chimneypieces is a theme explored in the chapter devoted to the rôle of the architect. In the present section I shall consider the various fittings, implements and decorative objects that might be associated with the fireplace.

In the centre of the back wall of a fireplace it was usual to have a cast iron fire-back decorated with some motif in relief (Plate 73). The subjects were sometimes topical but most consisted of coats of arms or cyphers, or of mythological figures.[65] When coal came to be more widely used and the fire was confined to quite a narrow area, fire-backs became correspondingly narrow but were usually taller in proportion because the coals were burned in a grate that was raised above the hearth.

No grate was needed until coal was introduced. The logs of a wood fire rested on fire-dogs or andirons (from the French *l'andier* or *landier*) which raised them off the hearth. During the late sixteenth and early seventeenth century andirons became larger and more decorative (Plates 43 and 227), and the task of supporting the logs was sometimes actually performed by a smaller pair of fire-dogs set between the main andirons and known as 'creepers'.[66] An andiron consisted of a massive front pillar, usually standing straddled on two feet, with an iron bearing-bar ('billet-bar') stretching backwards and ending in a third support. When the smaller fire-place openings came into fashion (see p. 66) there was no longer room for the large form of andiron (and certainly not for creepers as well) so a combined form evolved which had an additional billet-bar reaching inwards at right-angles (Plate 70). Just as andirons might in England be called 'fire-dogs', because they could have some resemblance to dogs, so the French called them *chenets* (from *chienette*), this being the usual term during the second half of the century.

The ornamental pillars of fire-dogs were mostly made of brass ('latten' as it was often called in the inventories) and the huge andirons, with their grotesque figures or handsome great ball-finials, must have produced a striking effect in the large fireplace openings of the first half of the century (Plate 246).[67] Brass fire-dogs came principally from Flanders[68] although indigenous brass foundries in France and England must also have turned them out in great quantities. A peculiarly English variant had crude but effective decoration of cloisonné enamel.[69] Cast or wrought iron fire-dogs were the commonest form but the 'paire of Andirons of Noremburg worke' in the Long Gallery at the Earl of Northampton's house in 1614 may have been of wrought steel like an impressive pair at Knole dating from the 1530s.[70] A rarity must have been the marble andirons at Kilkenny Castle but they clearly served no practical purpose as they flanked 'an iron stove in the chimney with a grate'.[71] Grandest of all were fire-dogs with silver pillars: Cardinal Mazarin had numerous

246. Fire-dogs (andirons) often formed striking ornaments. The magnificent brass specimens to be seen in this Dutch picture of the 1660s may have been cast at Dinant, the principal centre of production of brassware. Note the bow at the top of the frame of the looking-glass.

247. Proposals by Jean Cotelle for fire-dogs (*chenets*). Parisian; about 1640.

248. Design by Charles Le Brun for a fire-dog for use in a royal setting; 1660s.

pairs and they became fashionable in France, or in circles where French fashions were imitated, during the second half of the century.[72]

'None but people of the first quality burn wood in London,' noted a French visitor in the 1690s; others burned coal, or 'sea-coal' as it was called because it came to London by sea, and in order to distinguish it from 'coals' which meant charcoal.[73] In the 1570s it had been stated that 'sea-coal beginneth to grow from the forge into the kitchen and hall of most towns' near the coast but, by the turn of the century, the practice had spread deep inland—there was for instance 'an iron for seacole' at Hardwick in 1601.[74] Eventually it was only in the principal staterooms that wood was still burned in England.[75] In other European countries, where coal was hard to come by, wood remained the principal fuel.

When grates were a novelty, those compiling inventories were not always sure how to describe them. At Chatsworth in 1601 one was listed as 'a landyron for seacole'; at Tart Hall in 1641 there was 'in the chimney a great bowing iron to keep up the coales'.[76] When fireplaces became smaller, towards the end of the century, and the hearth-stone decreased correspondingly in area, there was a greater danger that burning coals would fall from the grate and out onto the floor. At Ham in the 1670s metal 'hearth-rods' were sunk into the hearth-stone but must have offered only a token protection against this danger. Fenders, which were taller and more effective, were evolved for positions where it really mattered. Once again, an early specimen (of pierced brass) is to be seen at Ham.

Charcoal was burned in 'fyre pannes' of which there was an example at Henham

Hall at the beginning of the century, and of which several specimens (one with silver mounts) still survive at Ham.[77] Braziers of all kinds, often on stands and with pierced lids, were available and could be brought in to warm a room in much the same way as we can plug in an electric fire. Related to these braziers were the small chafing-dishes on which food could be kept warm at the table. And then there was the foot-warmer consisting of a small box-like wooden housing with one side left open, into which one inserted an earthenware container, with tiny peg-feet and a loop handle, that could hold the burning coals. These were especially favoured in Holland but must have been known all over Europe (Plates 93 and 283).

With wood fires one needed a 'fire fork' and a 'billet hook' with which to manipulate the logs. For coal one required a fire-shovel and a poker.[78] Tongs were needed for both.[79] Optional seems to have been 'one stiffe brush', or 'a haire broome' as it was called at Ham.[80] Bellows were fairly common in the seventeenth century but were not obligatory. They were often decorative and sometimes seem to have been carefully cherished.[81] Fire-irons generally tended to be largely ornamental and were stood or hung upright at the side of the fireplace (Plate 245). They often came in matching sets. Most had decorative handles of brass, because this metal reflected the heat, but the cheaper sort could be of iron, and especially grand ones had mounts of silver.[82] There were no coal-scuttles; fuel was kept in baskets (Plate 319[83]) in an adjacent locker awaiting the time when the fire needed topping up.[83]

Fireplaces should be 'garnished with green bowes or flowers' in summer, maintained the author of *The Rules of Civility* which appeared in 1671.[84] These *feuillards*, as the French called them, could be quite elaborate screens of verdure which, in the large fireplaces of the sixteenth and first half of the seventeenth century, incidentally provided effective hiding places, as several stories of the time make clear.[85] Right through the century, and irrespective of the size of the opening, large vases of flowers were often stood in the fireplace in summer (Plate 43).

249 & 250. Two French designs for fire-dogs; late-seventeenth-century.

251. Painted chimneyboard from a country house in Sweden. The two brass knobs are for lifting it into position in the fireplace opening and for removing it later. The small cross-pieces form feet that enable this screen to double as a firescreen. The decoration may well be based on a French design for such screens. The room whence this board came was decorated in a similar style. About 1690.

252. The title-sheet of a French suite of engravings of chimneypieces set in a cartouche which could be used as a model by an artist faced with the task of decorating a chimney-board.

Sometimes even a *jardinière* with a flowering bush might be placed there (Plate 253). If flowers were not available, handsome porcelain or delftware jars distracted the eye from the empty hearth quite effectively (Plate 238).

An even more effective way of filling the fireplace opening was to fit it with a chimney-board, which could either be a board made up with planks set side by side or it might be composed of a canvas nailed to a stretcher in exactly the same manner as a picture-canvas (Plates 251–3). The large flat surfaces of both the boarded and the canvas forms lent themselves well to decoration, which was usually painted but could consist of applied carving. Most of the paintings were of fairly simple motifs rendered with strict symmetry; sometimes they amounted to a true easel-painting, like the 'grand tableau peint sur toile representant un paysage et eaux jaillissantes, servant de devant de cheminée' [a large painting on canvas representing a landscape with fountains, serving to set before the fireplace] which was at the Château d'Humières in 1694.[86] From the closet fireplace in some House of Orange dwelling must come the two canvasses each painted with representations of an orange tree in a *jardinière* standing on a simulated hearth, one of which is in a Dutch collection (Plate 253), and one in an English collection. They probably date from the 1690s and may conceivably have been designed to go in some interior by Daniel Marot. Because chimney-boards were sometimes designed to go with the décor of a particular room, surviving examples can occasionally still provide information about the decoration of the room concerned. This is especially the case in the eighteenth century but it can anyway be well worth while searching the attics of ancient houses for what may look like paintings of no especial distinction but may turn out to be chimney-boards. Instead of canvas, chimney-boards could also be faced with tapestry, embroidery, gilt leather, or paper.

Dutch chimney-pieces of the seventeenth century consisted of a hood-like over-mantel protruding from the wall over the actual fireplace which was mostly recessed into the wall. Smoke from the fire had to rise to about the height of a man before it was trapped by the hood of the chimney but, to assist in the trapping, a narrow textile hanging was often fixed like a pelmet all round the lower edge of the hood (Plate 241). Such features seem also to have been known in northern France where they were called *tours de cheminées*. They could be highly decorative, one mentioned in an inventory of 1628 being of 'tapisserie de Rouen'.[87] Close inspection of contemporary illustrations suggests that a detachable lining was often fitted behind these pelmets to ward off smoke and dirt. It seems possible that these small hangings were also known in England, for we find 'a chimneycase of ye same worke' as the 'Arras round ye chamber', but here the reference may simply be to a facing for the chimney-breast that was en suite with the other wall-hangings.[88] The same could be the case with the 'little peece on the chimney' that was in the principal bedchamber at St Giles House in 1639, and with the 'fowr chymey peeces valued att £13' which belonged to Charles I, but it would not be surprising if the *tour de cheminée*, which was so practical and decorative for large fireplaces, was also used in this country as well.[89]

Some chimney-pieces had a shelf or 'mantel-tree' in their composition. This was to become a notable feature of the *cheminées à la royale* of the last decades of the century (see p. 66, f.n. 24). For such shelves, special ornaments were devised. When they comprised a set of vases or jars, groups of such ornaments were called *garnitures de cheminée* (Plates 70 and 245). They usually consisted of five pieces and the potters at Delft produced sets specially designed for this purpose, or for standing in a row on the tops of cupboards. Small pieces of sculpture and busts were also sometimes stood on mantle-shelves (Plate 241). In a closet at Tart Hall, for instance, there stood 'eight brasse pieces' which are likely to have been small bronzes. Perhaps Lord Arundel had acquired them in Italy.[90] At Ham House, there were 'brasse figures' on the shelf over the withdrawing room fireplace, along with two brass candlesticks and two 'Indian boxes'.[91] The use of massed porcelain and delftware as decoration for chimneypieces was discussed in an earlier section of this chapter.

FLOWERS AND PLANTS INDOORS

People in the seventeenth century used flowers indoors in much the same way as we do today but they seem to have been more casual about it; they did not go in for 'flower arrangement' when it came to placing vases of flowers about the house. They mixed blooms of different kinds and no special care seems to have been given to achieving a balanced effect.[92] When one occasionally sees a vase of flowers standing on a piece of furniture in a contemporary illustration, it is there as a charming addition to the decoration and not as a significant feature (Colour Plate XIII). Only when the vase (then usually a large one) is standing in the hearth does it form a complement to a dominant feature of the room, but even then the flowers do not seem to have been arranged in any formal manner (Plate 43). Flowers seem only to have been used formally as components of garlands and similar motifs contrived for

253. Chimneyboard from one of the residences of William III, Prince of Orange, decorated with a *trompe l'oeil* representation of an orange-tree in a vase.

the bedecking of buffets, banqueting halls and settings for weddings (Plate 229).

Shrubs, on the other hand, might be dragooned most rigorously, and were thus often placed in precise rows so as to form part of the interior architecture—in a gallery, for instance, in covered 'walkes' and orangeries. Such regular arrangements of carefully trimmed shrubs standing in tubs or urns were an extension indoors of the formal garden which surrounded the house. This is not the place to discuss the formal garden, with its *parterres*, its carefully manicured hedges, its rows of urns and statues, and its strategically placed fountains: suffice it here to remind the reader that these regimented schemes were seen as an extension of the interior organisation of the house, the central axis of the gardens commonly passing through the principal or focal room in the house, so that it was not only the interior that was planned round this room but the exterior was focussed on it as well. Particularly favoured for putting indoors in tubs were small orange-trees, myrtle, jasmine, yew and certain conifers.

In the seventeenth century a 'flower pott' could be a large urn with two handles or it could be a vase (Plates 253 and 254).[93] In French a distinction was sometimes made between a *pot à bouquets* or a *vase à fleurs* on the one hand and a *pot à fleurs* which was usually an altogether more substantial vessel,[94] but the distinction is often blurred.

At Ham House in 1679 there were some 'boxes carved & guilt for tuby roses' and these small marbled and gilded *jardinières* are still in the Long Gallery although it is not today possible to keep them filled with sweet-smelling tuberoses.[95] There was incidentally a 'guardiniare' in the Earl of Kildare's house in Dublin in 1655.

At the end of the century Celia Fiennes reported that a pair of tables in the Gallery at Hampton Court was flanked by 'two great jarrs on each side of each table . . . to putt potts of orange and mirtle trees in', while at Chippenham 'there was a great flower pott gilt each side of the chimney in the dining roome for to sett trees in.'[96] In both instances, these were containers or *jardinières* in which one placed small trees or shrubs growing in flower pots. But what can have been the nature of the 'iron for a flower pott to stand in' which was at Tart Hall before the Civil War?[97]

According to Havard artificial flowers were much used during the seventeenth century.[98] Savary des Bruslons informs us that one made artificial flowers of paper, of feathers and of the cut open cocoons of silkworms.[99] He says nothing of those made of wax, glass, straw, or silk although they certainly existed.[100] A small silk rose may still be seen between the fingers of the wax effigy of Frances Stuart at Westminster Abbey. 'La Belle Stuart' died in 1702.

254. Proposal for a vase or urn suitable for shrubs, drawn by Charles Le Brun; about 1670 (?).

CHAPTER XI
Lighting

IT IS difficult for us to conceive how little light there normally was in a seventeenth-century house after dark (Plates 255 and 256). Good wax candles were expensive and other forms of lighting—tallow candles and rush lights—were either smelly, quickly consumed, or both.[1] The mathematician William Oughtred had a wife who was 'a penurious woman and would not allow him to burne candle after supper, by which means many a good [mathematical] notion is lost' wrote Aubrey.[2] Mrs Oughtred was no doubt excessively mean but extravagance in this direction was confined to a relatively small circle. When a large number of candles was lit for some special occasion, it was invariably remarked upon with wonder and delight.[3] For the rest of the time, lights were conserved[4] and life was lived as far as possible in the daylight hours.

In fact, the strongest light in a room after dark would mostly come from the fire. It was an exceptional occasion when the candles were so numerous that they equalled the fire in brightness. With the firelight playing so important a part, the surroundings of the fireplace became a focal point of the décor of the room in the evening. Masks and figures on the chimneypiece and firedogs came alive, marble glowed and brass andirons seemed liquid in the flickering firelight.

Candles did not burn steadily either; they moved and pulsed, and what they illuminated seemed to come alive in a manner quite unknown to generations familiar only with the unwinking stare of the electric-light bulb. When the level of light in a room is low, moreover, reflecting surfaces seem relatively bright. Gilding, particularly, stands out in the surrounding half-light; gilt picture frames sparkle (if they are not dulled with age), gilded mouldings on panelling shimmer, a glow emanates from the gilt leather, mounts and handles play counterpoint. Because they had to be lit and snuffed out, candles were normally set at a convenient height, usually between table height and shoulder level, and light from such a source was reflected more directly into the eye and thus revealed the fronts of objects (cabinets, vases, tables)rather than their top surfaces as is so often the case with modern gallery-type lighting which is usually set high up under the ceiling. When the light-source is low and not too powerful, the whole appearance of a room is altered.

There are three principal types of candle-holder. The candlestick which may be placed on a flat surface, the sconce which hangs on the wall, and the chandelier which is suspended from the ceiling. The French word *chandelier* originally meant a holder for *chandelles*, the name for tallow candles, wax candles being called *bougies*. However, by the seventeenth century *chandelier* had become the name for a holder of wax candles, but a holder of no specific kind and certainly not necessarily of the suspended type. Chandeliers with rock crystal or glass components came to be called *lustres* in France[5] and this subsequently became the generic term for all chandeliers. An arm with a nozzle at one end was called a 'branch' in English and a *bras* in French, but branch could be the generic term for all suspended candle-holders, whether of sconce or chandelier form. A candlestick with several branches might be known in

255 & 256. Writing by candlelight, one candle being in a lantern. It is worth remembering how very dark it was indoors in most houses except on special occasions. In such circumstances any reflecting surface would catch the light and stand out brilliantly in the surrounding darkness.

France as a *candelabre*, literally, a tree of candles—in England this became 'candelabrum'— although it came to be called a *girandole*, (from the Italian *girare*, to turn, and *girandola*, a pyrotechnic device that revolved like a horizontal Catherine wheel). There were usually six arms radiating from a central pillar (Plate 269), but half this amount (i.e. a *demi-girandole*) could be set on the wall against a back-plate of mirror-glass so that the candles were reflected to appear like a whole *girandole* (Plates 34 and 202).[6] Such multi-arm sconces were mostly called *bras* but, in the eighteenth century, the English adopted the form (enlarging the glass plate in the process) and then called it a 'gerandole' even though it was strictly speaking only half of one. A tall candlestick for a thick candle (*torche* because it had originally been composed of

269

257. Numerous candles used on a festive occasion. 'In the midst were four lustres, or christal candlesticks', the describer of this scene at The Hague in 1660 says of the four rock-crystal chandeliers, and adds that 'many other candlesticks, arms of silver, and a great number of torches, enlightened all corners much better than the Sun could have done at Midday. They gave, particularly, a most marvellous lustre to the bottoms of the chimney . . .' which must have been of polished marble. The 'arms of silver' are shaped like fore-arms protruding from mask-like bosses; they may be seen flanking the windows but are shown without candles. Some similar sconces are at Hardwick (see Plate 262).

several rods of wax twisted together—*torse*) was called a *torchier* or *torchère*. Particularly tall candlestands also came to be known as *torchères*, and some *torchères* actually sprouted candle-branches of their own.[7]

This is not the place to discuss the various forms of candlestick. Suffice it to say that, in a house of any standing, they were mostly of brass or pewter but wooden candlesticks were still to be found in the kitchens and working quarters of great houses, early in the century.[8] During the second half of the century, it became fashionable to have candlesticks of silver and occasionally they were made of rare materials that were hard to work—amber, lignum vitae and rock crystal, for instance. There were many variants of the standard form, including the chamber candlestick which stood in a large drip-pan with a handle, and the miniature taper-stick. Cardinal Mazarin had some 'chandeliers à la financière' which were presumably specially suited for office-work and he owned a candlestick which was fitted with 'une feuille d'argent servant entre le feu de la lampe et la veue' [a leaf of silver to set between the flame of the candle and the eyes],[9] in fact a shade. Shades that clipped onto the light-holder were not all that uncommon, it would seem; one is to be seen in Plate 111 and there was 'a shadowe of mettle gelt' in the study at Marton Hall in Yorkshire, early in the century.[10] At the end of the previous century, Gabrielle d'Estrées had owned some 'chandeliers à tapisseries' which Havard suggests could be hung inside the bed-curtains.[11] One does sometimes see what looks like a lamp (perhaps an oil lamp in a glass container) suspended under the tester of a large bed—quite a sensible idea if one considers how difficult it would have been to obtain a light at night and that some people may have preferred to 'sleep with the light on'. In fact, it was common to place a candlestick in the hearth at night (Plate 258) and of course the fire, if it was lit, provided light after dark. A stubby form of night-light known as a 'morter' was provided at night for grand bedchambers.[12] These could have special holders to ensure they could not be knocked over, and to screen the light from the bed. The pierced metal holder shown in Plate 259 is probably for such a night-light. Among the Dauphin's silver plate at the end of the century were some silver-gilt *mortiers* which must have been particularly splendid versions of such functional light-fittings.[13]

The standard form of sconce at the beginning of the century had one or more branches springing from the lowest point of a reflecting back-plate which often took the form of a *repoussé* brass or copper dish that was suspended on the wall by a ring at the back (Plate 260). The 'fyftene plate candlesticks of copper to hang on the wales' of the Hall at Hardwick in 1601 will have been of this type; there were more in the Hall at Hengrave and at Marton there were some 'plate candlesticks of latten' (i.e. of brass).[14] In the Elizabethan period 'Candle plates of latten' of all sorts carried an

258. (below left) A candlestick on the hearth-stone serving as a night-light.

259. (below right) Holder for a night-light (morter). Of uncertain date but probably seventeenth century. Sheet iron, painted green. There is a ring fixed to the base-plate that locates the morter which must have been a stubby-shaped candle.

260. A 'plate candlestick'. A brass sconce with dish-shaped reflector. It bears the profile portrait of Queen Marie Thérèse of France and the date 1660 (the year in which she married Louis XIV). Presumably French and of that date.

261. Candlesticks on a dressing-table and an elaborate sconce on the wall. Paris; 1630s. This gives a good idea of normal lighting in a fairly luxurious house at the time.

import duty of three shillings a dozen when brought into England (presumably from Flanders), according to a tariff of duty-rates. Only items that were being imported in considerable quantities will have been included on such a list.

The 'plate candlestick' went out of fashion soon after the middle of the century (a late specimen is shown in Plate 260) and various forms of sconce became popular. Back-plates (*plaques*) of elaborate shape were evolved (Plate 189).[16] Sometimes they were fitted with reflectors of mirror-glass (Plates 34 and 202). The single 'hanging brass sconce' in the Earl of Arundel's own room at Tart Hall in 1641 is likely to have been something rather special.[17] Cardinal Mazarin owned in 1653 some sconces of polished tin-plate—'plaques de fer blanc avec leurs chandeliers' [back plates of tin-plate, with their branches]—and a decade later we find 'cinq petitz mirouers garnis de leur plaques et chandeliers' [five small mirrors with their back-plates and branches] in Fouquet's possession in 1661, which were presumably early versions of the 'six pettites plaques à miroir à huit angles' [six small octagonal back-plates of mirror] with copper-gilt frames surmounted by the royal cipher listed in the French royal inventories for 1673, each of which had two branches of copper-gilt (Plate 202).[18] But increasing use was now made of wood, painted or gilt, for sconces. At first they appear in halls and passageways like the 'foure wooden guilt candlesticks

262. A sconce or candle-branch in the form of a fore-arm protruding from a grotesque mask. Similar sconces are to be seen in Plates 257 and 33. Apparently of gilt *carton pierre*.

263. (right) Design for one of the 'beaux lustres d'argent' which Nicodemus Tessin saw in each of the state rooms (the *Grands Appartements*) when he visited Versailles in 1687. The preliminary sketch was no doubt made by Le Brun but this drawing is probably by Claude Ballin (compare with Plates 9 and 10, and 25).

fa[s]tned on the sides of the ffoure walles' in the Footmen's Hall at Tart Hall and those 'upon ye staires' at the Duke of Lauderdale's house in Westminster.[19] But then they begin to vie with metal sconces for grander positions; one 'large guilded skonce of wood' was to be seen in a bedchamber at Cowdray in 1682, for instance.[20] Carved and gilt wood was a substitute for gilt bronze, copper or silver, and a material known as *carton pierre* was a substitute for them all. This material was composed of moulded paper in layers and was the precursor of papier mâché (Plate 262). It already makes its appearance in the second quarter of the century at Fontainebleau where there were thirty-six 'bras de moullures de carton, dorez d'or brun, chacun de deux piedz de longueur ou environ pour . . . servir de chandelliers à porter des flambeaux' [branches moulded in *carton pierre*, gilded with dark gold, each two feet long or thereabouts . . . serving to carry candleholders for candles] and Mazarin had some 'bras de carton dorez avec leurs bobeches de fer blanc' (branches of *carton pierre* with nozzles of tinplate).[21] At Ham House there were 'four sconces of brasse hung with gould and silke strings with tassels',[22] which must have been early examples of the sconce suspended by a tasselled cord or a gathered ribbon with bows— a practice taken up enthusiastically by Daniel Marot and depicted in many of his engravings at the end of the century in which he shows sconces introduced for their decorative effect, hanging against the wall-hangings at regular intervals (Plates 95 and 141).

Chandeliers are not mentioned at all frequently in English inventories of the seventeenth century and it is probable that they were indeed by no means common over here. The same probably applies to France. In the Low Countries, on the other hand, brass chandeliers were popular (Plates 43 and 267) and one has of course to remember that the principal centres of the production of brassware lay in that part of the world. They came in many varieties and in several qualities; their radiating branches sprang from a central body of baluster or globular form. The brass type was exported all over northern Europe and was subsequently imitated in the other countries. The 'too great copper candlesticks' hanging in the Hall at Hardwick and the single 'great brannche of copper which hangs in the midst of the hall for lights' at Hengrave were all probably chandeliers of 'latten' imported from Flanders.[23]

Chandeliers, whether lit or not, could constitute an important decorative feature in a room, so considerable attention was paid to their embellishment. In order to obtain as much sparkle as possible, reflecting surfaces were increasingly introduced. The great polished globes and balusters of the brazen type glowed handsomely but the effect was sometimes enhanced by small plates set so as to catch the light. The most striking seventeenth-century innovation in this direction sprang from the use of rock crystal which was found to reflect light in a delightful manner. Beads of this material (globular or faceted) were threaded onto wire armatures to form arms, or were linked together to form chains (Plates 257 and 266). Plates of the material, with bevelled edges, were later suspended from the arms to increase the reflections. Rock crystal was principally worked at Milan but it seems to have been the French who developed the chandelier of rock crystal to its fullest splendour.[24] Four impressive specimens may be seen in the view of the King's Bedchamber at Fontainebleau in 1645 reproduced in Plate 33, and Madame de Rambouillet had a 'chandelier cuivre doré et cristal' [chandelier of gilt copper and crystal] in her famous *Chambre Bleue* in the 1660s;[25] it had fifteen branches. Rock crystal chandeliers were greatly admired and a few examples were brought over to England: the 'two crissal branches' listed

264. Chandelier of rock crystal which is said to have been presented by Louis XIV to the Danish Crown Prince Frederik (later King Frederik IV) when he visited France in 1693 although the tradition cannot be substantiated. It is nevertheless likely to date from the late seventeenth century and may well be French.

265. A Venetian twelve-branch chandelier with glass drops, some of them coloured. Perhaps among the glass objects given by the Venetian Senate to Frederik IV of Denmark when he visited Venice in 1709, although the style would appear to be that of the last decades of the seventeenth century.

266. A glass chandelier of an early form, now thought to have been made at a glassworks in northern Bohemia in the late 1680s but clearly inspired by the first glass chandeliers made in France, which in turn resembled those of rock crystal (see Plates 20 and 41). The conformation of the central pillar is reminiscent of that of brass chandeliers; it is however composed of large blue spheres alternating with small red ones.

in the inventories of goods that had belonged to Charles I are likely to have been French and may have been acquired through Henrietta Maria.[26] Charles II owned one for which his upholsterer provided a protective 'case of taffeter wth. ribbons' at a cost of two shillings in 1667.[27] The Duke of Ormonde also possessed a 'crystal chandelier' with ten branches which hung in his Drawing Room at Kilkenny Castle.[28] The 'guilt branche with crystall' in the grandly appointed Antechamber to the Queen's Bedchamber at Ham House in the late 1670s was perhaps also a chandelier although it could equally well have been a *girandole* (a candelabrum) since both forms of light-holder could have rock crystal components.[29] It is possible that this object was acquired when the future Duchess of Lauderdale was in Paris in 1670, for she can hardly have avoided being struck by the charming effect such lights were making in the most luxurious Parisian houses of the day, and she may well have decided that such an ornament would do much to lend a highly fashionable air to her own rooms back in England.

Rock crystal was expensive and hard to work but around 1670 chandeliers began to be produced in France which had components made of glass.[30] The general effect was the same and the conformation of the first glass chandeliers followed that of the rock crystal versions. The matter is further confused because clear glass went by the name of *cristal* in France.[31] The chandeliers to be seen in the engraving of 1682 reproduced as Plate 34 are likely to be early specimens of French glassware applied to this field. Some authorities believe that a handsome chandelier at Schloss Favorite, near Rastatt, may also be an example of French work in glass of about 1670 but others feel it is a more provincial expression of around 1690 (Plate 266).[32] In 1682 an Englishman could speak of a person 'living with lamps . . . intermixed with lustres or balls of glass', which indicates that the new type was then already familiar in England.[33] By the end of the century glass had almost totally supplanted rock crystal as the material from which such pleasing confections were made.

275

267. Candles were normally only fitted into the nozzles of chandeliers when they were about to be lit. Both the brass chandeliers in this charming picture are hanging empty. Dutch; 1670s.

268. Occasionally ones sees a single candle left in a chandelier, probably to serve in an emergency. A candle stub is to be seen in this brass chandelier hanging in a dentist's house. Note the adjustable double-branch candlestick on the table which only has a single candle. Dutch interior of the 1660s.

269. A *girandole* with a pyramid of glass drops and more drops below the branches. Probably French; 1680s.

270. A Venetian glass *girandole* or candelabrum, with six branches and a pyramid of glass reflectors of various kinds, some of them coloured. Probably part of the same gift from the Venetian Senate as Plate 265.

As has been pointed out, the French *girandole* of about 1670, with its short branches (usually six) radiating from a baluster stem, often had components of rock crystal. These were usually set in a pyramid round the central baluster so that they caught the light to advantage.[34] The glass models followed suit (Plate 269).

Such candelabra and ordinary candlesticks could be placed on any flat surface but these were not always in the right position or at the correct height. For this reason candlestands were devised. At first these were very simple structures. There are two early specimens (not a pair) at Knole, both crude constructions of wood, stained red (Plate 272). Red stands seem to have been popular at first; the Earl of Arundel had a pair in his room at Tart Hall in 1641, there was another pair at Edington in 1665 and at the Noordeinde residence at The Hague in 1632 there were two with gilding on a red ground.[35] Lady Arundel, on the other hand, owned 'a standard of greene for a candlestick to rest on'. The fact that it was still necessary to explain the purpose of her 'standards' suggests that they were still uncommon in England before the Civil War. Later, they simply called 'stands'. What may be a pair of stands dating from the 1640s is to be seen at Ham House. They are of gilded wood, carved with floral trails on spiral columns with tripod stands in the form of masks. However, their dish-like tops appear to be of rather later date and it is not at present clear what form their

271. Candelabrum for a chimney-shelf. The four branches subtend 180°; there are none at the back so it can stand close to the chimneybreast. Brass with glass drops. Although made in Sweden in the 1680s this was no doubt a form used in all countries under strong French influence.

272. A simple candlestand of wood painted red. English; perhaps from the second quarter of the seventeenth century.

original tops can have taken. If they do date from just before the Civil War, they represent an altogether grander class than the simple painted stands just described. It gradually became common to make candlestands very elaborate; this was especially the case when they came to form part of a triad comprising a side-table, looking-glass and pair of stands, which was to become a favourite decorative ensemble from about 1670 right through into the eighteenth century (Plate 218). A splendid pair of stands and associated table believed to have been made in Paris in 1670, may be seen at Knole. In this case no mirror originally accompanied the set which comprised a second table, eight *carreaux*, and a second pair of stands.[36]

The fashion for elaborately decorated candlestands originated in Italy where a long tradition of carving tall candlesticks and candlestands existed. By the early seventeenth century Italian carvers were producing splendid candlestands with stems in the form of exotic or grotesque figures.[37] A pair of painted and carved stands in the shape of blackamoors, which are believed to be Venetian and to date from the 1670s, are still to be seen at Ham House and there is an almost identical pair at Knole.[38] Clearly such figures were popular at the time and the French evolved the form in many imaginative ways from the 1660s onwards (Plate 24). Because so many of the French stands also took the form of negroes, the name of a negro mentioned in a popular vaudeville song of the period[39] was adopted as the generic term for this class of furniture. Anne d'Autriche (d. 1666) owned a pair of *guéridons*, the negro figures of which were lacquered black over silver (or silvered wood); they supported her coat of arms.[40] Actual silver *guéridons* were made in some quantity for the French royal palaces from about 1670 until the vogue for silver furniture was stifled in the tide of economic difficulties that beset France at the end of the century. The famous royal goldsmith, Claude Ballin, made some of solid silver 'habillez à la turque, posez sur les piedestaux en triangle' [dressed in the Turkish manner, standing on tripod pedestals] and Nicodemus Tessin, visiting Versailles in 1687, was extremely impressed (as was the intention) by the 'tables et guéridons d'argent avec leurs flambeaux dessus' [tables and candlestands of silver with their candlesticks on top] and the other silver items in the Salon de Mars which, he said, were 'd'argent d'une pesanteur et grandeur prodigieuse' [of silver of a prodigious weight and size].[41] He went on to describe minutely the furnishings of the Chambre du Roi, taking care to note that 'sur les grands guéridons', which were of silver, 'il y avoient des girandoles d'argent fort jolyment imaginées avec une hydre dont les sept testes soustenoit . . . les chandelles, l'une au milieu et les autres six à l'entour' [on large candlestands . . . there were candelabra of silver very charmingly contrived, with a hydra the seven heads of which each held aloft the candles . . . one in the centre and

273. The fashionable triad comprising a table, looking-glass and pair of candlestands set against a window-pier, which seems to have been the most usual position for such groups in the second half of the seventeenth century.

274. A French hall lantern of the late seventeenth century.
Presumably of sheet metal and glass.

the other six surrounding it]. *Guéridons* sometimes came in sets on their own but
mostly they were associated with a table (often but not always accompanied by a
looking glass) with which they were therefore made en suite (Plate 218). Many were
in consequence decorated with marquetry or japanning; the fashion for carved and
gilded *guéridons* or candlestands received much fresh impetus at the end of the
century when actual silver furniture was scarcely being made any longer (see p. 23).

Guéridons were primarily candlestands but they could also be used to support vases
or dishes of food.[42] They came in several heights: there were tall stands (*torchères*)
for use in large and formal rooms, there was a standard form about three feet high,
and a small type that was used with card-tables.[43] Care was taken to design
candlestands so that they were difficult to knock over but this hazard could also be
minimized by placing them close to the wall and especially in the corners of the
room.[44] This position also ensured that light (and a striking, side-light at that) fell on

the mural decorations—the chimneypiece, overmantel furniture, pictures and carved decoration. A variant of the standard forms was the *guéridon* in Cardinal Mazarin's possession which had 'bras qui s'allongent et accoursissent' (arms which lengthen and shorten).[45] The stand with branches that could be raised or lowered shown in Plate 17, is also noteworthy; it is there called a *chambrière*.

Chandeliers, incidentally, were probably not suspended as high up as they normally are today; it would have been difficult to light and snuff the candles if they had been hanging too high. La Bruyère tells the story of a man who 'passe sous un lustre où sa perruque s'accroche et demeure suspendu' [walks under a chandelier where his wig is caught up and held hanging], which could only have been possible if the chandelier was hanging fairly low down.[46] Chandeliers were usually suspended from a hook by means of a stout cord which could be decorative.[47] There is no indication that chains were used so the need to disguise them with an elaborate sleeve of silk had not yet occurred, but the brass chandelier shown in Plate 267 seems to be suspended with wire and this may well have been a common practice. Bows of silk were sometimes used to disguise the hooks and the rings at the top of the chandelier, as with picture frames.[48]

Lanterns were suspended in important passages. They were mostly made with small panes of glass (triangular or quadrangular) set in lead 'cames' or in a structure made of tinplate (Plate 274). At Hengrave Hall, however, the 'great lanterne of glasse' had a frame of 'Joyners worke, paynted', and was clearly a handsome affair.[49] On stairwells a modified form of lantern could be fixed to the wall; this form was essentially a glass housing for a candlestick. There are still some on a private staircase at Knole.

CHAPTER XII

Specific Rooms and their Decoration

ROOMS used for a specific activity tend naturally to assume a special character; they also require specialised equipment. In this last chapter I shall consider certain aspects of these matters and will thereby pick up various subjects that have not yet been touched upon.

Little would be gained from our here making general observations about the décor of the various types of reception room—the principal rooms in the house—because there was too much variety for such generalisations now to have much validity. However, the reader who has followed this survey through the last half dozen chapters will have formed some impression of how these matters were arranged and can supplement this impression by careful study of contemporary illustrations. It may, on the other hand, be rewarding to study in rather more detail the décor and furnishing of rooms like closets and libraries, and those set aside for dining, dressing, bathing, and so forth. Something further also needs to be said about bedchambers, for, while we have considered the bed itself and know something about the seat-furniture, the wall-hangings and floor-coverings that one could expect to find there, other specialised forms of furniture (here, used in its widest sense) associated with bedchambers deserve brief mention.

DINING-ROOMS

The unqualified term 'dining-room', used to signify a room where the family habitually dined, did not acquire its modern meaning until some time in the second half of the seventeenth century and this meaning was not generally accepted until well into the next century. Meals on ceremonial occasions had formerly either been taken in the hall or in the Great Chamber upstairs, while the family dined at less formal times in a parlour which was sometimes called the 'Dining Parlour' or 'Dining Chamber'.[1] We are often told, moreover, that the French term *salle à manger* was not coined until late in the eighteenth century but a room thus labelled is to be seen in a ground-plan published by Le Muet in 1647 (Plate 55) and the term occurs in an advertisement of a Parisian house that was for sale a decade before that.[2] But Frenchmen tended to dine ceremonially in the *salle* and less formally in a *salette* which was presumably the equivalent of a dining parlour.[3] As extra rooms, notably the *antichambre*, became interposed between the *salle* and the *chambre* (i.e. the chief reception room, and the bedchamber), it was often in one of these new rooms that the family dined, in the grander establishments. The 'Première Antichambre du Roi' at Versailles was also known as the 'Salle où le Roy mange' or the 'Salle du grand-couvert'.[4]

The important fact to remember is that one or more rooms in a seventeenth-century house would normally be equipped for dining; it was there that meals were normally taken, whatever the room's title may have been. One could not easily move the massive oak buffets and the heavy draw-tables of the early part of the seventeenth century; where they stood one dined. This was even more true of rooms, later in the century, which had built-in buffets. On the other hand, the owner or members of his family might decide to take a meal in some other room (a practice which seems to have been more common in France than in England), in which case light-weight tables (*tables volants*) were carried in and the chairs in the room were brought forward to it, in so far as was required.[5] It was anyway not apparently the practice, in the dining-rooms of the second half of the century, to leave the (usually oval) table standing out in the centre of the room. As it folded, it could either be removed entirely[6] or it could be stowed away against the wall along with the chairs. The floor was thus cleared and the room could serve other purposes. At Ham House the 'Marble Dining Room', the family's eating place, served as the central vestibule or salon of the domestic floor of the house, with the Duke and Duchess's respective apartments disposed symmetrically on either side. By the eighteenth century it had become the convention to hang family portraits in the dining-room (Long Galleries having gone out of fashion), and the late seventeenth-century dining-room was an obvious place to hang pictures so that, most of the day, they could be seen to advantage, without hindrance.

275. Different degrees of ceremony in dining are reflected in the names of the rooms given in a plan of Hampstead Marshall, built in the 1660s. To the left of the hall (a) lay a 'Little Parlour or Ordinary Roome to Eat In' (b) where the family presumably dined. Behind that was a 'Withdrawing Roome or Roome for the Lord to Eat In' (c), where the master of the household will have eaten when he wanted a higher degree of privacy. The 'Great Parlour' (d) was for grander occasions and had a 'Withdrawing Roome' beyond it (e). Quite separate, on the opposite side of the hall, were the dining quarters for two levels of servants—the 'Roome for the Gentlemen to eat in' and the 'Roome for Servants to eat in' ('f' and 'g'). If there was a suite of state rooms upstairs, there will have been a Great Dining Room among them.

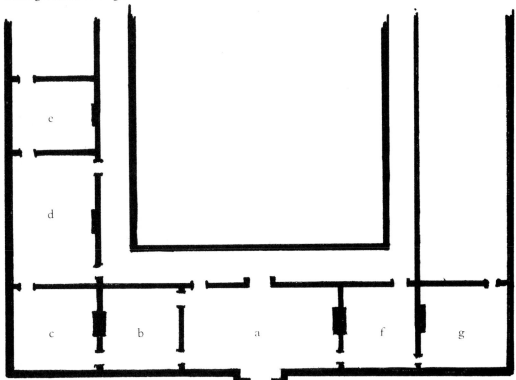

What primarily distinguished a dining-room, then, was the presence of a buffet (alias a cup-board, see p. 238) or sideboards at which drink could be dispensed or which would be of assistance to the servants in performing their duties during the meal. In Elizabethan times Lord Montagu ordered the Yeoman of his Cellar to 'stande att the . . . cupboorde and fill wyne wth. discretion to such as shall call for ytt' and, a little later, Fynes Moryson explained that one did not 'set drink on the table, for which no room is left, but the cups and glasses are served in upon a side-table, drink being offered to none till they call for it'.[7] By the cup-board or *buffet* there would in consequence stand 'a cistern of brass, pewter or lead to set flagons of beer or bottles of win in', as Randle Holme explained.[8] Today we call these cisterns wine-coolers and the French term for them was indeed *rafraichissoir*.[9] Such containers were mostly just filled with cold water but ice might be added if it could be obtained.[10] Adding camphor or saltpetre to the water also assisted refrigeration.[11] The contents of the flagons or bottles that stood in the coolant were then decanted into wine-jugs from which glasses were filled (Plate 160) and then taken on a salver to the individual diner who had asked for drink. Some of the large bottles to be seen standing in the cisterns shown in contemporary illustrations probably contained water, for watering one's wine was of course a widespread custom at the time. 'The Frenchman's glass is wrenched as often as he drinks,' Sir Balthazar Gerbier informs us;[12] if so, the French must also have had suitable containers for water in which to rinse the glasses. This practice may also have served to cool the glasses. It was anyway with this end in mind that the so-called 'Monteith' was evolved, a bowl with a notched rim that enabled glasses to be suspended bowl downwards in cold water.[13]

People in the seventeenth century might take supper seated at a small, often round, table that had been carried into a bedchamber or some other room but, for formal occasions, they at first dined at oblong tables (usually draw-tables, see p. 226) and this remained the fashion until well into the second half of the century. The table was usually placed across one end of the room and the diners sat at one of the long sides and perhaps also at the two ends, but the fourth side (that facing out into the room) was frequently left free so that the servants could wait on the table from the front. The principal diners sat at the centre of the long side, not at the ends. They might have armed chairs to set them apart from the diners of lower rank who sat on ordinary chairs or on stools.[14] Seniority was indicated by the relative heights of the actual seat. The position of the principal diners might in addition be marked out by a canopy hanging over the centre of the table (see p. 172 and Plate 257). At banquets, where large numbers of diners had to be accommodated, trestle- or folding-tables were commonly set together to form a 'U' or a 'T' (Plate 276).

During the second half of the century, when it became fashionable for the family and close friends to dine more informally in relatively small dining-rooms, oval and circular tables became common.[15] With them one no longer invariably needed special seating for the principal diners because one was eating with one's friends who all knew precisely what were the respective ranks of those present and there was therefore no need to stress precedence.[16]

The farthingale chair or back stool was the commonest form of chair from early in the seventeenth century until well into the last quarter, when it was supplanted by the cane-seated chair in England and by a variety of forms in France.[17] Chairs used for dining need to have backs that are almost upright and the back-stool was ideal for

A Paris Chez Melchior Tauernier Graueur et Imprimeur du Roy pour les Tailles Doulces demeurant en lisle du Pallais sur le Quay qui regarde la Megiserie.

Disposition du Festin fait par sa Majesté a M.rs les Cheualliers apres leurs Creations faitte a Fontaine bleau le 14.me May 1633. Auec Priuilege du Roy.

276. A banquet at Fontainebleau in 1633. Louis XIII dines alone at a table on a dais under a canopy. A servant with a covered cup on a salver stands by with drink for the monarch. The rest of the company sit along the outside of two long trestle tables covered with carefully creased linen cloths. A fresh course is being carried in by a file of servants led by the Gentleman Usher. In the foreground wine is being carried to one of the diners; no glasses are on the table.

the purpose. When used in dining-rooms it was commonly covered in leather or with turkeywork.[18] The latter was perhaps not especially practical for the purpose but it was comfortable to sit on, and one has to remember that meals often lasted a long time in those days.

Great Chambers, which were formal rooms where ceremonial banqueting took place, were often hung with tapestries.[19] They were decorative, the scenes depicted in them gave one food for thought, and they were impressive evidence of wealth. Unfortunately they tended to retain the smell of food. For this reason Robert Adam in the next century advised against tapestries in dining-rooms[20] and this is no doubt why the smaller dining parlours of the seventeenth century were usually panelled or hung with gilt leather.[21] As Cronström observed, with panelling 'l'odeur des viandes ne se sentiroit point' [the odour of food will not be smelt at all];[22] with textile hangings it would. The laying of the table, as well as the serving of the food and drink, was attended by much ceremony in big houses.[23] Something has already

285

been said about tablecloths. Those made of linen damask were usually provided with napkins en suite and sometimes a set might include a 'handcloth'—a long cloth which was carried by the servants waiting at table.[24] Napkins were normally placed across the knees but the young Henri III and his friends, who were notorious for their outrageous behaviour, used to tie their napkins around their necks so as to protect their monstrous ruffs—and, in consequence, looked 'as if they were being shaved' (Plate 290). Napkins usually measured 70 by 100 cm. during most of the seventeenth century but increased in size up to about 90 by 115 cm. towards the end of the century.[25] Some napkins were trimmed with lace.[26] A large seventeenth-century house would usually be stocked with prodigious quantities of linen,[27] all of which was meticulously listed and stored separately, like the household plate.[28] Both tablecloths and napkins were supposed to be pressed with sharp folds[29] and, to this end, the laundrymaids' workroom was often provided with large tables where the cloths could be folded and presumably also pressed with irons, while napkins might likewise be ironed, although a truly sharp crease could more readily be obtained by means of a napkin-press (Plate 320).[30] Not all tablecloths were of linen, incidentally; at a banquet given for the young Duchesse de Bourgogne in 1700, the cloths were 'des riches indiennes'—of Indian chintz.[31]

The French seem to have excelled at folding napkins into fancy shapes and a manual of the period provides instructions for twenty-seven ways of doing so.[32] Mention is fairly often made in contemporary literature of napkins shaped like birds or animals or fruit; Tallemant tells of a deaf-mute he had often seen 'pliant le linge admirablement bien en toutes sortes d'animaux' [folding linen astonishingly well into all sorts of animals].[33] Giles Rose, who was master cook to Charles II, explained to his own countrymen how napkins could be fancily folded in his book *The Perfect School of Instruction for Officers of the Mouth*, which was published in 1682.

Figures of various kinds, used as table decoration, were known already in the sixteenth century. Potters like Bernard Palissy and certain French silversmiths were already producing such *marmousets* well before 1600. The Italians were masters at such table ornaments which they called *trionfi* (Plates 277–80). When Marie de Medici was married at Florence in 1600, 'la table de la reine fut couverte d'un chasse de tous animaux avec grand arbres, partie faits de sucre et partie de linge ploie' [the queen's table was covered with a hunt of all kinds of animals with big trees, some made of sugar and some of folded linen].[34] No doubt Italians versed in these skills were brought into France to teach French pastry-cooks how to create such confectionary. At any rate, what would seem to have been Italian techniques were used to produce an astonishing table decoration for one of the *fêtes champêtres* held in the park at Versailles in 1668 which consisted of 'la face d'un palais basti de massepain et pastes sucrées' [the facade of a palace built with marzipan and sugar-paste].[35] Such *Schauessen*, as the Germans called them, often comprised mountains, trees and architectural features amid which the figures were placed, so that the table came to look like a park or landscape.[36] The earliest figures of porcelain, produced in Germany during the first decades of the eighteenth century, were generally made as table ornaments and were the direct descendants of the sugar-paste and wax *Schauessen* (Plates 279 and 280). Apart from figures made purely for show, there was of course a whole other form of *Schauessen* which was intended to be eaten after first having delighted the eye—the boar's head, the peacock with all its feathers put back,

277 & 278. Table decorations in 1667. The figures are of sugar-paste. The banquet in question took place in Rome where sculpture of an especially high order was executed in this medium at that period.

an ox head cooked and then entirely gilded, a seahorse of almond paste, a unicorn of butter.

Trionfi, marmousets and Schauessen are also closely related to centrepieces which were by no means a new invention in 1600. They had at first been associated with wine-fountains or containers of perfumed water; many groups of Schauessen and some of the early Meissen porcelain figures were likewise grouped round such fountains and all were prominent features of Baroque table-decoration on gala occasions.[37] The piling of dishes of food in decorative conformations was another popular form of table ornament that could also be indulged in at the sideboard (Plate 13). Randle Holme illustrates 'a stand for a dish' resembling a Victorian cake-stand, and comments that 'this is to set on a table full of dishes, to sett an other dish upon; which make the feast looke full and noble.'[38] Anthony Wood, describing a dinner given for Charles II at Oxford in 1687, records that the dishes were 'piled high, like so many ricks of high [hay]'. There were '24 little flat plates, like trencher plates, not piled: placed among the greater dishes scatteringly in vacant places to fill up the vacancies.'[39] Apparently also intended to raise dishes off the table were metal rings which are today sometimes known as 'potato rings' although they do not originally seem to have had anything to do with potatoes.[40]

A rather special form of seventeenth-century table decoration, reserved for royalty, was the cadenas, or 'caddinet' as it was called in English. This was a small platform of silver on which the royal person's cutlery was placed before the meal (Plate 281).[41] The cadenas had its origin in the custom of protecting the monarch from poisoning but became merely a symbol of rank. It had long been the practice to cover the monarch's bread and salt with a cloth.[42]

Many other items were used in the dining-room—cutlery, plates, salt cellars, chafing dishes and much else—but I should be drifting too far from the main theme if I pursued these subjects here. The same applies to the special equipment required

279 & 280. (far left) *Trionfi* executed in sugar-paste which formed part of the table decoration at a banquet held in honour of the English ambassador in Rome in 1688.

281. (left) A caddinet (*cadenas*) bearing the arms of King William III and Queen Mary engraved on the platform where the napkin would be laid. The receptacles are respectively for salt and for the royal cutlery. Bearing London hall-marks for 1683/4.

282. (below) Probably showing the gold *cadenas* provided in 1698 for the personal use of Louis XIV. Drawn by A. N. Cousinet in 1702.

283. A member of the supporting cast. A corner of the kitchen in a middle-class Dutch house in the 1660s. This servant is ironing linen coifs. An earthenware brazier standing on the table is probably being used for heating the iron. When the task was finished it was probably placed inside the foot warmer on which the girl has placed a foot (cf. Plate 93). Behind her stands the kitchen water-but. There is a pewter chamber-pot on the floor by the chicken coop.

XVI. (right) The Queen's Closet at Ham House was no doubt decorated in the most advanced taste when it was created late in the 1670s. The intricate marquetry floor must have been astonishing when it was new and the *scagliola* surround of the fireplace was presumably also a novel feature. The paintings set into the chimneybreast were provided specially for the purpose. The original wall-hangings may clearly be seen in this view; they are of brocaded satin bordered with a striped silk. The 'sleeping chayres' provided for the room about 1678, one of which is to be seen standing in the alcove, are covered en suite.

for serving tea, coffee and chocolate, although something has already been said about tea-tables (p. 230) and mention should perhaps just be made of *cabarets* which were small trays on which these exotic beverages could be served (Plate 30). They were often decorated in a correspondingly exotic manner, the most prized *cabarets* (comprising tray and cups) being of lacquerware and imported from the Far East.[43]

ACCESSORIES IN THE BEDCHAMBER[44]

People often received in their bedchambers (Plates 2 and 4) and the bedchamber was regarded as the innermost of the rooms of reception.[45] Bedchambers might be decorated in as many different ways as other reception rooms. As was pointed out at the beginning of this chapter, little would be gained from trying to analyse specifically the décor of seventeenth-century bedchambers, for they varied so widely, although it is true to say that principal bedchambers tended to be decorated in a rather formal manner and that the decoration of the room as a whole was usually governed by that of the bed itself (see Chapter VII).

XVII. (left) English fashionable decoration of about 1620 is reflected in this small library at Langley Marish, Bucks., which has miraculously been preserved largely untouched. The overmantel is delicately painted with grotesques on a gilt ground, there are Renaissance cartouches on the panels, and there is a frieze of small landscapes. The books are kept in cupboards, the inside of which are painted with open books *en trompe l'oeil*. In the now empty fireplace has been placed a board giving a catalogue of the contents of the shelves.

284. A French design for a bed-alcove with a balustrade across its mouth. Probably about 1640. Alternative treatments are offered. The balustrade has a hinged opening in the centre.

285. An engraved design for a bed-alcove published in Paris about 1660.

286. (right) Bed-steps with a pewter chamber-pot standing on them. Painted in 1671, the scene shows a Flemish bedchamber that seems rather old-fashioned.

In a royal bedchamber, or a State Bedchamber which was suitable for royalty to occupy if paying a visit to a house, there would often be a balustrade out in front of the bed to separate the area round the bed from the rest of the room and keep all but the most favoured at a distance.[46] The balustrade might run right across the room, cutting off the end where the bed stood (Plate 6). It could also run across the mouth of an alcove (Plate 284). In either case, the area enclosed was known in France as the *ruelle*[47] while the floor, which was often raised to form a daïs for the bed, was called the *parquet*. This term was subsequently used to describe the kind of ornamental woodwork that was commonly used to decorate this important floor area. (See also Colour Plate III.)

In most important seventeenth-century bedchambers there would usually be some form of storage furniture, not for clothes (which were rarely kept in an important bedchamber at night) but for the personal belongings of the owner of the room. During the first part of the century a buffet[48] with a cupboard-section below was often to be found in bedchambers; it was known as a 'livery cupboard' in England even though liveries were not regularly issued to a household much after 1600 (see p. 233). But there were no taps from which one could fetch water at night if one were thirsty, so it was common to have drink of some sort available and this could still stand on or in the livery cupboard, although it could of course equally well stand on a table. The livery cupboard was superseded by the ornamental cabinet which might also serve as a receptacle for valuables and personal possessions. In the sixteenth century chests had been common in bedchambers but they were fast going out of fashion by 1600 whereafter they were mostly to be found in farm-houses and the like (Plate 127).[49] Although one could use the chest as a seat (especially with a cushion) it was otherwise a rather impractical piece of furniture because one could not reach things stored at the bottom without first removing all the items lying above it; the difficulty could be mitigated by fitting drawers at the bottom and soon further tiers of drawers were fitted so that the chest eventually became a chest of drawers. This last class of furniture only came into its own at the end of the century but was then to be found in some important bedchambers. What were probably chests or coffers (the latter had rounded lids) of small size were the 'casette' of walnut

perched on a 'soubassement à colonnes torses' [stand with spiral columns] which was to be found in the bedchamber of a Breton country house in 1688, and the 'coffre de chambre' covered in black leather in the neighbouring bedroom.[50] Havard quotes a reference to a 'coffre de nuit de velours cramoisy rouge' [a night-box covered in crimson velvet] which contained a comb-case and 'un bonnet de nuit aussi de velours' [a nightcap also of velvet].[51] Lady Beauchamp had a 'velvett nighte-box and the cushionett of the same' in her bedchamber at Edington.[52] Maybe the 'cushionet' was a case for nightgown and nightcap, like the 'cover for nightgeere wth. checqr'd worke of several sorts in silver and gold' that belonged to Charles I.[53] Perhaps a night-box contained things that one might need at night. If so, it may have been placed alongside the bed, perhaps on a chair, so that one could reach it. There were no bedside tables in the seventeenth century.[54]

Other items commonly seen in bedchambers would have been portable candlesticks of various kinds—the morters, which were night-lights that could be left to burn right through the night, and chamber-candlesticks which had a dish-like base and handle (see pp. 270–271). But portable candlesticks are not listed in inventories of bedchambers because they were kept in a pantry or buttery during the day and only brought into the rooms where they were needed at nightfall. The same applies to chamber-pots. Warming-pans, those long-handled containers for hot coals, on the other hand, were sometimes kept in bedchambers (Plate 127). For this reason, they were often decorated. Some bed steps are shown in Plate 286; they do not seem to have been at all common.

CLOSETS

Any small room might be called a closet (*un cabinet* in French) but what concerns us here is the class of small room that was associated with a bedchamber.[55] The closet was a room to which the occupant of the bedchamber could retire and where he or she could normally expect to enjoy complete privacy to rest, read, study, write letters, or entertain intimate friends. When one recalls how very public a bedchamber could be in the seventeenth century, it is hardly surprising that there was a corresponding demand for a room of one's own.

When planning the principal apartments of a grand house, the closets were usually placed beyond the bedchamber with which they were associated (Plates 53–9), so that they formed the innermost and therefore most secluded room of the apartment concerned.[56] For although attached to the apartment, closets by their very nature were separate and were therefore freed from the conventions that governed the principal rooms. One could not only behave in them in a more relaxed manner, one could have them decorated and furnished in quite a different way. All formality was thrown to the winds and one could rig up these small rooms as one pleased, indeed, in as fanciful a manner as one liked (Plate 287). Thus it was often in closets that forms of decoration and furniture were first tried out that were subsequently to become widely fashionable—the setting of mirror-glass into pannelling, for instance, the display of precious vessels set on brackets in formal arrangements on the walls, and the facing of walls with panels of Oriental lacquer. The same applies to seat-furniture with truly accommodating upholstery which came into fashion in the last decades of the century, and probably also to tea-tables and other equipment necessary for the taking of the new exotic beverages.

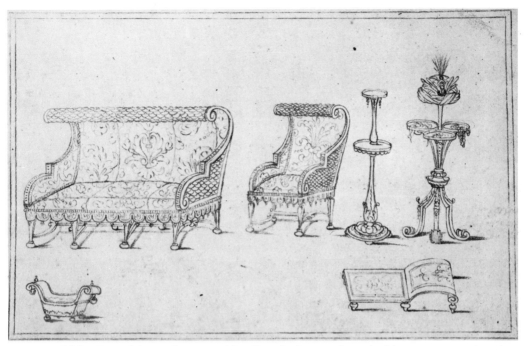

287. Fanciful furniture that may have stood in a French closet at the end of the century—perhaps in a *Cabinet turque* or one decorated in a *style indien* (note the turban on the stand). Certainly such crazy pieces would not have been suitable for any conventional room at the time. They include a footrest and a *jardinière*.

In closets one could display one's taste to advantage and, if one favoured exotic or advanced tastes, there was no better place in which to do so. We have many descriptions of particularly striking closets. The Dauphin's, which was designed by Jean Bérain and was executed by Boulle, had a floor worked in the most elaborate marquetry that seemed sensational to those who saw it. [57] By way of contrast the prince had another closet 'boisé à la capucine', faced with panels of untreated oak that were intended to conjure up a monastic atmosphere (see p. 71).[58] The Duchesse de Valentinois had what she called a 'cabinet de rocaille' that must have had rockwork and grotto-like elements in its décor. It was comfortably and charmingly furnished with 'piles de carreaux de drap d'or et de vases de porcelaine remplis de fleurs' [piles of squab-like cushions of cloth of gold and vases of porcelain filled with flowers]; (see p. 180).[59] And there was the *cabinet* of Madame de Rohan in the middle of the century which was unusual because its walls were clad with moquette (see p. 112). The favoured *habitués* of this apparently so delightful retreat were known collectively as 'La Moquette'. It would be interesting to know more about some of these charming little rooms which often had such a potent influence on the subsequent history of taste in Europe. It would also be pleasant to know what was so special about the panels 'which are to be seen at Paris in the Cabinets of the Palace called Orleans' that Sir Balthazar Gerbier, writing in 1664, clearly felt were remarkable.[60]

A gentleman's closet could be quite small: 'Nine feet upon three and a half deep . . . is the least you can allow to the Closet' maintained Sir Roger Pratt, writing in 1660.[61] Up to the end of the sixteenth century very little attention seems to have

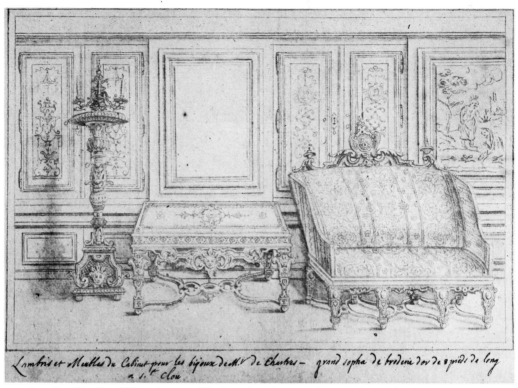

Lambris et Meubles du Cabinet pour les bijoux de M.r de Chartres — grand sopha de broderie d'or de 8 pieds de long a s.t clou

288. Details of the furnishings in one of the Duc de Chartres' closets at the Château de Saint-Cloud in the late seventeenth century. This shows his *Cabinet des Bijoux*, the collection of jewellery and other treasures no doubt being housed in the cupboards that may be seen in the *lambris* (panelling). Chartres became Duc d'Orléans in 1701 (and was later Regent). On the right Titian's *Noli me tangere* is set into the panelling. It remained in the Orléans collection until 1792 and is now in the National Gallery in London.

been paid to the decoration of closets; for the most part they were rather utilitarian rooms of no particular distinction.[62] But quite a different spirit is to be sensed in the descriptions of certain *cabinets* after the turn of the century. We then find Francis Bacon speaking of 'rich cabinets, daintily paved, richly hanged, glazed with crystaline glass, and a rich cupola in the midst', all of which betokens a certain opulence.[63] Somewhat later (1626–7) we hear of John de Critz painting the panelling in Henrietta Maria's closet at Denmark House (later Somerset House) with simulated graining in 'wall nuttree couloure', and decorating the panels with 'antique worke . . . with badges in the midst of them, they being guilded with fyne gold and shadowed'.[64] The Green Closet at Ham House, which was decorated in the 1630s, still gives us some idea of what a rich closet of the earlier part of the century might look like.

The select gatherings in Madame de Rohan's *cabinet* must have required a room of some size and it was indeed from about the middle of the century that the French evolved the concept of the *Grand Cabinet* which was no longer quite so private and served as a reception room for select company. One can follow the development by noting the seating arrangements in the *cabinets* of Louis XIV's mistresses. Louise de la Vallière could seat eighteen people in her *Grand Cabinet* which was furnished with no less than six armchairs, the rest of the seats comprising six ordinary chairs and six

298

folding stools (*pliants*); Madame de Maintenon at the end of the century had seating for up to twenty-nine people in hers.[65] As for the King's *Grand Cabinet*, this served as *Cabinet du Conseil* where his Privy Council (or Cabinet) met to discuss affairs of state. The fashion for having larger closets that served as small reception rooms was translated to England after the Restoration. There is a description of Catherine of Braganza's closet at Whitehall in 1669 which gives a vivid idea of how such a room was used 'as a place of amusement for their majesties and therefore they go into it every evening (unless particularly prevented) from the other apartments. The Queen sits in front of the door, and enters into conversation with the ladies who happen to be there, who form a circle round her Majesty'. A number of gentlemen were also present including most of the ambassadors and any distinguished foreigners visiting the English court. 'The King himself and the Duke [of York] are frequently seen there seeking relief from more mighty cares, and divesting themselves awhile of the restraint of royalty.' The King always stood or walked about, refusing to discuss affairs of state in these surroundings, 'those topics being always reserved for a proper and reasonable time'.[66]

Madame de la Vallière had to have a second and much smaller closet as well as the *Grand Cabinet* just mentioned, so that she still had somewhere truly private to which she could retire. Important apartments in the second half of the century anyway tended to be provided with two closets. For instance, the Duchess of Lauderdale had two closets lying next to each other at Ham House after she and her husband had extended the building in the 1670s. The 'White Closet' was a luxuriously appointed *cabinet* that was intended to impress visitors (there were six chairs in the room but only four people could ever have been in the room comfortably at a time) while her 'Private Closet' was in the nature of a study or office, although she also kept the equipment needed for drinking tea in this little room. These two small rooms survive and still convey much of the effect originally intended. The Duchess of Ormonde likewise had two closets at Dublin Castle at the same period, and 'My Lady's New Chamber' at Cowdray had one closet 'by My Lady's Chamber door' and another 'within My Lady's Chamber' (i.e. reached through the bedchamber).[67] Celia Fiennes noted that at Burfield there was 'within the dressingroome . . . a closset on one hand, the other side is a closet that leads to a little seate of easement'.[68] A description of Cardinal Mazarin's magnificent residence in Paris shows how, already before the middle of the century, the four principal apartments in this house, which had so many advanced features, were provided with 'des cabinets, des garde-robes, & des chambres de degagement' (Plate 58).[69]

A *garde-robe* was at first a place in which clothes were stored and the English word 'wardrobe' still carries the same meaning.[70] Both words can, by extension, also be used to designate a piece of furniture in which clothes are kept,[71] and this is indeed the common meaning in English today. In the seventeenth century, however, the *garde-robe* was not only a closet where clothes might be stored but was often also the place where the close-stool stood.[72] For this last reason *garde-robe* is in France today the term for what we equally euphemistically call a lavatory. The word 'wardrobe' also meant a room in which household effects, notably upholstery (in its widest sense), were stored and repaired.[73] At Chatsworth, in Elizabethan times, there were three wardrobes, one for her Ladyship's clothes, a 'Middle Wardrop' in which some dismantled beds and their bedding were stored along with a pair of virginals, some

Femme de qualitez a sa Toillette.

289. *Femme de qualitez à sa Toilette* in the late 1680s, showing her luxuriously appointed dressing-room. Her dressing-table is covered with a *toilette* (apparently of silk) trimmed with a wide lace border. On the table is her dressing-set including a looking-glass, trays for bottles and boxes, and a folding comb-case. The man seated on a comfortable chair of ultra-modern form appears to be reading a book of music and singing.

chairs, some coffers and some presses, and there was a 'Lowe Wardrop' for such things as chamber-pots and candlesticks.[74] When beds were not in use they were often dismantled and the grandest beds sometimes had sets of both summer and winter hangings, so a considerable amount of storage space was needed for these prominent items of furniture in the seventeenth century; indeed, at Lady Leicester's house there was a special 'Bed Wardrobe'.[75] The French, more logically, called such a room a *garde-meuble*—a room where furniture was stored.

Garde-robe might also be the name for a dressing-room which would usually be a fairly small room, a closet, leading off a bedchamber (Plates 54, 55, 57 and 58). Evelyn saw the Duchess of Portsmouth 'in her dressing-roome within her bedchamber, where she was in her morning loose garments, her maids combing her, newly out of bed, his Majesty and the gallants about her'.[76] This room must have been of some size to have held so many people; no doubt it was really a *cabinet* of the large type then fashionable in France. The morning toilet of such a lady could be a social occasion of some importance; news and gossip was exchanged, new ideas were discussed, and new fashions tried out. It was, for instance, at 'la grande toilette chez M. la duchesse de Bourgogne' on Friday, 25 September 1699, that the new lower hair-style which was to reign through the first half of the eighteenth century was first seen.[77]

The term 'dressing room' does not occur before the middle of the century, an early mention being that which occurs in an inventory of the Earl of Kildare's house in Dublin in 1656.[78] Anne of Denmark, however, had an '[At]Tiring Chamber' already in 1610.[79]

We have already in this chapter touched upon some of the more extraordinary forms of mural decoration to be seen in fashionable seventeenth-century closets, but most closets, even of the most luxurious class, had textile hangings on the walls that in no way differed from those on the walls in other fashionable rooms of the time, except perhaps in their scale. Catherine of Braganza's large closet mentioned above had hangings of 'sky blue damask . . . with divisions of gold lace'. A closet at Ham House furnished to receive the same queen still has on the walls its hangings of red satin brocaded with gold, empaned with a striped silk (Colour Plate XVI). Madame de la Vallière's two *cabinets* were respectively hung with 'broderie fond d'or, manière de velours à arabesques, rouge cramoisy' [crimson arabesques rendered in needlework on a gold ground, also embroidered] and 'velours rouge et brocat lamé d'or'[red velvet and brocade with gold thread]. At about the same period the 'inward chamber to Lady Isabella's Bedchamber' at Edington was hung with green

290. The man about town also needed a dressing-table. The table-carpet is protected by a *toilette* while his moustache is being curled. A small brazier or chafing-dish is being used to heat up curling tongs. On the floor stand a ewer, a barber's bowl and a sponge.

dornix while the 'Petit Garderobbe atenant ladite chambre' at a house at Rheims in 1621 was hung with *tapisserie de Bergame*.[80] In store at Lady Dorchester's was '1 sute gilt leather and green cloth hangings for my Ladies Closett'.[81] In 1695, David Cronström wrote from Paris to advise Countess Piper in Stockholm to hang her closet in accordance with the latest French fashion which was with green Genoa damask divided into panels by simulated pilasters cut out (*découpé*) of some rich material.[82] With the letter he sent some proposals for the scheme drawn by Jean Bérain himself, together with some sketches by an upholsterer of a similar scheme which had actually been carried out already in Paris.

Since ease, comfort and relaxation were sought in closets, it was also there that was first to be seen the truly comfortable seat-furniture that was so striking a product of the late seventeenth-century upholsterer's skills (see Plate 202). The two 'sleeping chayres' with adjustable backs in the Queen's Closet at Ham House are famous and early examples of this phenomenon, as is that with castors which formerly stood in the Duke's Closet and is now in a private collection. Such *fauteuils de commodité* and the related easy chairs, as well as well cushioned couches and sofas, formed focal points in these delightful rooms (Plate 208).

According to Cotgrave (*Dictionnarie of the French and English Tongues*, 1632) the French word *cabinet* could mean 'a closet, little chamber, or wardrobe wherein one keeps his best, or most esteemed, substance', so one could expect to find there precious belongings of all kinds. I have already discussed 'Porcelain Cabinets' and closets where other kinds of precious vessels were displayed. At Burghley, Celia Fiennes saw a closet where there was 'a greate deale of worke under glasses and a glass-case full of all sorts of curyosityes of amber stone, curall and a world of fine things'.[83] Such 'Cabinets of Curiosities' or *Wunderkammern* were the ancestors of the modern museum (Plates 291–3); they were sometimes to be found attached to libraries, housing treasures other than the books which lived in the presses of the library itself. 'One's most esteemed substance' could also include important documents, jewellery, special articles of clothing, and mementoes of all kind—all suitable items for storage in the ornamental cabinets and writing-desks that are often listed in inventories as being in closets.

If, on the other hand, the closet was being used essentially as a dressing-room, a table of some kind that could serve as a dressing-table was of course needed, and an important feature of any luxuriously appointed *cabinet* being used in this way would have been the table-carpet laid over the dressing-table (Plate 309). Because this rich cloth needed protecting from spilt cosmetics, stray hairs and the like, it was usual to place over the carpet a *toilette* (see p. 243 and Plates 29, 131 and 309). Eventually complete sets, called *toilettes* collectively and comprising both the table-carpet and the toilette itself, as well as the full dressing set, all en suite, were produced for particularly splendid dressing-rooms. The dressing-table itself could be of any shape and, since it was covered with a cloth, did not need to be in any way elaborate.[84] Nevertheless, from about 1665 onwards, fancily-decorated dressing-tables were introduced.[85] The tables comprised in the ensemble of table, looking-glass and pair of candlestands, that I have called a triad might serve as dressing-tables in grand rooms, although it was probably only the plainer sets that were used, covered with a *toilette*, in this way. As these triads mostly stood against a pier between windows, daylight fell well on the sitter's face and the light from the flanking candlestands served the same purpose at night (Plate 94). The mirror had to be canted forward so the sitter could see herself in it. Later, a more solid form of bureau-like dressing table was evolved, as has already been noted (p. 231). Being steady, it was well suited for setting out the expensive dressing-sets that were fashionable at the end of the century,[86] and the dressing-mirror would henceforth invariably stand on the table and could be quite small (Plate 289). The large dressing-mirror hanging on the wall then went out of fashion. Once there, on the table, the small form of glass could be draped with a decorative cloth that fell down at the back and sides, integrating the glass with the table; this was the fashion in France at the end of the century.

The closet, then, was a highly personal room. Its decoration and furnishing varied widely according to the taste (one might even in some cases say whims) of the owner. The character of such rooms is well summed up by the list of the contents in the closet of the Princess Eléonore de Bourbon at Breda Castle taken after her death in 1619.[87] It lay next to her bedchamber and was hung with 'East Indian cloth of gold'. There was a large assortment of 'Indian' boxes and coffers of all shapes and sizes, some of them being of lacquer. An expensive piece of furniture was an ebony cabinet with silver-gilt figures and mounts, which probably came from Augsburg, as probably did her silver-mounted writing-desk. There was a plainer ebony cabinet and a coffer covered with velvet with a small looking-glass (in it?). Another cabinet, which was clearly quite large, contained numerous trinkets and treasured objects— some silk flowers, a turned ivory cup, a mother-of-pearl casket, some silver bottles, a silver-gilt bowl and cover set with pearls, and much else. On the walls were many small pictures, mostly of a religious nature, including a 'Last Supper' executed in silver relief. The list of '*porcheleyn*' is also long but one must not assume it all came from the Far East. It must have stood about on the various cabinets; no shelves are mentioned, and there were only two tables, one being a 'Spanish table' and therefore presumably folded. The table-carpets lying on them were of Oriental silk. There were two 'Spanish women's armchairs' (*twee vrouwe Spaens leynstoelen*) covered with green and white damask as well as six stools 'called tabourets' (*genoemt tamborees*). No floor-covers or window-curtains are listed. The room must have been crammed with small objects.

STUDIES AND LIBRARIES

'We doe call the most secret place in the house appropriate to our own studies . . . a closet,' explained a writer in 1586,[88] but he might have added that one could also call it 'a study'.[89] The 'Studdy Roome' at Cockesden in 1610 contained 'a fayer desk with his key' and 'a litle table, where uppon the desk doth stand'. On another table lay a second 'deske wereuppon the *Book of Martyrs* now standes'. There were also several maps, two 'fayre tronckes' with locks (which were probably for books and papers), a large chest, a standish for ink, etc., a chair with an embroidered seat and back, a looking-glass, a portrait of the owner's mother, twenty-four books, some almanacks and 'an ostrich egg hangs in the corner of the room'. With all this evidence of learning (the ostrich egg and the looking-glass would have been somewhat awe-inspiring items at the time) it comes as something of a surprise to find that there was also 'a black pyk for hay . . . behind the Study roome dore'. The

291–3. The Cabinet of Curiosities at one end of the Library
at the Monastery of Sainte-Geneviève in Paris; 1688. Note
how this wide variety of objects is organised in formal
patterns against the three walls. The open display-cabinet is
particularly noteworthy.

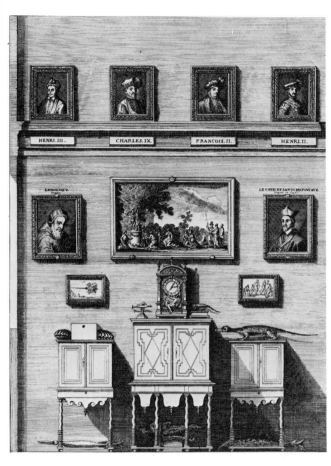

294. (below) The end wall of the Library outside the closet depicted in Plates 291–293. The room consisted of a long gallery flanked on both sides with bookcases separated by windows. The bookcases have doors with wire mesh and the shelves have dust-pelmets.

étude of the Archbishop of Bordeaux in 1680 was no doubt likewise a setting for intellectual pursuits but it seems to have had all the character of a large and luxurious French *cabinet*, with its hangings, chair-covers and table-carpet of red half-silk damask, its fifty pictures, its window-curtains of red serge, and its show of vessels of mother-of-pearl and porcelain.[90] The cabinet of purple wood, the red coffer containing cash, and the *prie-dieu* with a gilt crucifix hardly indicate that this was a room where studious activities were undertaken.

Studies were not only places in which to read and write, they were often also depositories for rarities of all kinds (e.g. the ostrich egg and mother-of-pearl vessels just mentioned). Books had of course also been rarities until the beginning of the seventeenth century[91] but when books became commoner, there was a tendency to separate them and house them in a library while the other rarities were kept in an adjacent small room (Plates 291–294).

When books had been very rare and costly, they were naturally stored with great care. It had been a common mediaeval practice to store one's books in a chest and this continued well into the seventeenth century. The Countess of Leicester was still keeping her books in a trunk by her bedside in 1634.[92] A gentleman living in Suffolk in 1648 owned 'a great chest of elming [elm] borde standing in the lower gallerie, for to put therein the bookes', while over in Ireland the Earl of Kildare still had 'a standard [massive chest] for bookes' as late as 1656.[93] These chests and trunks are all likely to have had locks.

As libraries grew, this form of storage became unpractical and proper book-cases began to be provided. The shelves behind lockable cupboard-doors that line the walls of the charming little Kederminster Library of 1623 at Langley Church in Buckinghamshire represent an early stage in this development (Colour Plate XVII Plate 301). Then, as book-bindings became increasingly attractive, it was desirable that at least the spines could be seen while the books rested on the shelves,[94] so bookcases fronted with wire mesh[95] or panes of glass came into being (Plates 294 and 295). The two original book-cases from Samuel Pepys' own house, which are now in the Pepysian Library at Magdalene College at Cambridge, are very early examples of such specialised cupboards with glazed doors.[96] They are markedly Dutch in character and are likely to have had Continental antecedents. These pieces of furniture were supplied in 1666 and Pepys had ten more made on the same model (with only minor differences) between that date and 1703 when he died.[97] Even the last in the series were still very early manifestations of the wish to have elegant and protective housing for a substantial number of books (Plate 303); the clerk drawing up a list of items destroyed when fire damaged Boulle's workshop in Paris in 1720 still felt obliged to explain that the three 'armoires en bibliothèques avec des glaces devant les portes' were 'servant à mettre des livres' [library cupboards with glass before the doors . . . used to put books in].[98] However, many libraries simply had shelves ranged against the walls, as is the case with the Library at Ham House that was fitted up in the 1670s (Plate 299). If one wanted to protect the books on such

295 & 296. (right) Samuel Pepys' library in London, about 1693. The first pair of bookcases was made in 1666 and those added subsequently vary only in points of detail. On the library-table (here shown entirely covered with a protective 'case') lies a reading desk. In the passage is a gate-leg table which might also serve as a desk. Note the fine looking-glass hanging against the window-pier, the portrait set into the chimneybreast, the other pictures canted forward, and the map of Paris.

297. The University Library at Leiden in 1610. The books are still chained to the presses which have reading desks below. There is a rail for the reader to rest a foot upon when standing at the desks. Note the globes with their protective covers, and the cupboard that presumably housed scrolls and other documents.

298. The 'Arts End' at the Bodleian Library, Oxford in 1675. Built in 1612 with an eye to the convenience and comfort of scholars. Note the seats where one may browse close to the shelves. The uprights of the benches are extended to form supports for a gallery. Beyond are book-presses and two library tables with a pair of globes presented by Sir Thomas Bodley who died in 1613.

299. (right) The library at Ham House, created in the 1670s. The book-shelves are simple structures and are not adjustable. The built-in writing cabinet of cedarwood is a delightful piece of furniture which has additional drawers superimposed. Originally there stood in the centre of the room a chest of drawers (no doubt a press for maps and the like) and a table. The globes, which still have their protective covers, formerly stood in the Gallery nearby.

shelves, one could fit a curtain in front (Plate 300).[99] With open shelves or bookcases with wire-mesh in their doors, a perennial problem was dust settling on the tops of the upright volumes—a problem that is still with us today. The eighteenth century often fitted a fringe or small pelmet below the front edge of the shelves to flick the dust off the volumes whenever they were withdrawn, but such a device seems to have been familiar in learned circles by the 1640s, as John Evelyn saw something of the sort in the Duke of Orléans' library in Paris in 1644.[100] The feature is to be seen in Plates 294 and 302 showing important French libraries at the end of the century. With such an arrangement it helps if all the volumes on a shelf are of the same height but a regular presentation of books in a library was anyway admired in learned circles towards the end of the century; Pepys actually had small pieces of wood, shaped and decorated to fit under his smaller volumes individually, so that they were raised and all the books on a shelf might seem to be of the same height.

'I can reach up to a shelfe 7 ft. high, from ye grounde,' wrote Sir Roger Pratt in a 'Mem[orandum] concerning shelves for my bookes of 20th August, 1671.'[101] 'From a chaire 18 ins. high consequently, $1\frac{1}{2}$ ft. higher, so yt. ye whole case may bee 9 ft. high an easy Joyners ladder may bee made about $4\frac{1}{2}$ ft. which be soe made as to thrust in at ye bottom of my table as part of it.' The table measured 5 ft 6 in. × 3 ft. and must have had solid stretchers near floor-level against which the foot of the ladder could be wedged. At Ham House there was 'one foulding ladder of cedar' in the Library but this was replaced by the massive eighteenth-century steps that are now there.[102] A late seventeenth-century pair of library steps is illustrated in Plate 302. An Oxford inventory of 1674 includes a reference to a 'boarded settle to reach down books' but exactly what this was like it would be difficult to say.

It was normal in libraries to have one or more sturdy tables on which large volumes could be opened or at which one could work. They were mostly simple structures without drawers, and were usually covered with a cloth.[103] As library bookcases became more architectural in character, so library tables also became more massive, the columnar legs being replaced by plinth-like pedestal supports which provided additional storage space inside. Pepys had a table of this type made for his library, probably not long before 1693, and several Continental libraries have substantial tables or presses of this kind dating from the late seventeenth century.

On the library table one could place the small portable desks (Plates 163 and 303) that remained common long after more substantial writing-cabinets of various kinds had become fashionable. Desks not only provided a conveniently sloping surface on which to write with a quill, they also served to prop up books—reading-desks. We have already noted a desk on which lay *The Book of Martyrs*; at Ingatestone the Bible in the chapel was provided with a similar 'deske for it to ly upon'.[104] These small desks could be richly decorated, like those Paul Hentzner saw at Whitehall Palace in 1598 in Queen Elizabeth's apartment and described as 'two little silver cabinets, of exquisite work . . . in which the Queen keeps her paper[s], and which she uses for writing boxes', or the 'little deske to write on guilded' at Marton Hall a few years later, and the 'escritoire de la Chine . . . vernie de couleur d'or' [writing-desk from China lacquered a gold colour] which belonged to Cardinal Mazarin.[105] Some desks at Hardwick were encased in leather but there was also 'a little deske of mother of pearle' in the best bedchamber.[106] Desks described as being covered with needlework are also likely to have belonged to this class of small

300. Books protected by a curtain. On the library table lies a large volume supported by a reading desk that cannot be seen. Alongside is a massive *torchère*.

furniture. In the inventories of Charles I's property appears the item 'A faire deske richly embroydered with silver and silk wherein is a silver inke pott and sand box' while the French royal inventory of 1673 notes 'une escritoire de petit point d'or et d'argent, enrichie de broderie d'or et d'argent' [a writing-desk of gold and silver tent-stitch embroidery, ornamented with embroidery in gold and silver] which had silver-gilt fittings.[107]

301. The Library at the Hôtel de Lauzun in Paris; about 1660. The books are housed in cupboards, the doors of which form an integral part of the richly decorated panelling.

At the end of the century, in England, these small desks were being placed on stands to serve as ladies' writing-desks and, when fitted with an adjustable looking-glass above, as dressing-tables.[108] Scaled up and furnished with more substantial stands, such desks finally evolved as the fall-front bureau so typical of the Georgian period. This is not the place to discuss in any detail the development of the writing-desk[109] but it needs to be said that the commonest form during the seventeenth century was that first evolved in Spain and called an *escritorio* (hence the French *escritoire* and English 'scriptor'). This was a box-like nest of drawers enclosed in the front by a flap that dropped down to form a writing-surface. Stands were often provided but small versions could stand on a table. There are four specimens at Ham House: two luxurious models with silver mounts which may be Dutch, a large utilitarian version which the Duchess used in her study ('Private Closet'), and the very handsome built-in cedarwood desk in the library which has sets of drawers above and below (Plate 299). During the second half of the century the French evolved quite a different form of desk (*bureau*) which was essentially a table with several stacks of drawers underneath, arranged so as to provide a 'knee-hole'. This is commonly called a '*bureau Mazarin*' today;[110] it served equally well as a dressing-table (Plates 31 and 195). A few desks of this type were made in England at the end of the century[111] and the form was subsequently developed into the 'knee-hole desk' with the flanking stacks of drawers forming pedestals. In France, on the other hand, the fully developed knee-hole form was not favoured. Instead of multiple drawers (which could be housed just as conveniently in a separate piece of furniture as a filing cabinet—a *cartonnier*) three wide drawers sufficed and the characteristic French writing-desk became little more than an extensive working-surface on four sturdy legs—the *bureau plât*.

Pauline Agius noted a 'turning desk' in an Oxford inventory of 1659. Maybe this was a reading-desk on a turntable base but it could also have been of the sturdy mediaeval type with a tall upright that stood on the floor supporting a swinging arm at the end of which was the reading-desk.[112] There was at Knole in 1645 'a deske upon a skreene' which would seem to have been a firescreen with a reading-stand attached.[113] In the Elizabethan period, use was still being made of 'book pillows' which were often elaborately decorated with needlework.[114] A favourite or special book might lie on such a pillow which had the advantage that it was more kind to delicate bindings than the hard surface of a desk.

Some portable desks were fitted with an ink-well and a pounce-box for sand, but it was more common to have these accessories assembled in a separate unit known as

302. 'La petite Bibliothèque . . . au Palais Royal' at the end of the seventeenth century showing built-in book-cupboards, the shelves of which are fitted with dust-pelmets. Curious is the fact that the inside of the doors are undecorated. The battens on the wall to the left are also difficult to explain; it is as if the room were not completed when the sketch was made. Note the decidedly functional library-steps.

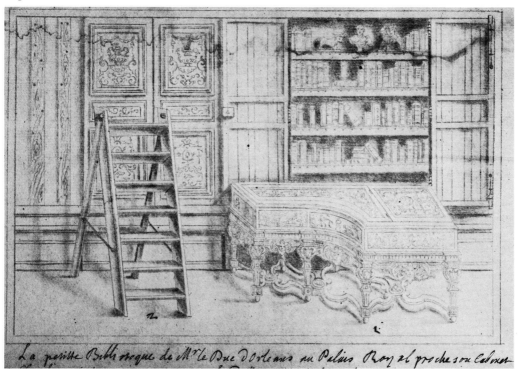

303. A library designed by Daniel Marot at the end of the century. The book-cases now form a prominent and fixed part of a unified scheme of decoration. Note the busts and globes used ornamentally, the barometer, the sturdy library table and comfortable chair with wings.

a 'standish' (Plates 109 and 163). Randle Holme, writing in the middle of the century, explained that ink-horns (hollowed horn-tips with a cap over the opening in which ink could be kept) were going out of use and being replaced by ink-wells of pewter or tin, and that a standish should 'have both inke place, sand box, candlestick and a long box to lay [sealing] wax' in.[115] A standish could either take the form of a small tray on which the various items stood, or could be a box with double lids swinging on a common hinge, covering two compartments, one of which could house the pens. Most pens were made from a quill but at Marton Hall there was apparently one made of brass.[116] This was listed among the writing materials in a Study which included another curious item, namely 'one bone to stirr incke'. A standish could be highly decorative: in his rooms at Oxford Lord Teviot had one of walnut and another that was inlaid; there was an 'Indian standishe' at Tart Hall which was probably lacquered, and at Kilkenny in the 1680s the Duchess of Ormonde had a 'standishe garnished with brass' which may very well have been French and perhaps of boulle-work.[117] They might also be made of silver. Another piece of equipment one might still find in a study early in the century was 'a little halff ynch board to cut parchement uppon'.[118] Parchment had of course long ago yielded to paper as the principal vehicle for writing but was still used for formal documents until well into the eighteenth century. As it was also quite expensive, one could cut slips of the size required from a skin.

314

Maps were popular in the seventeenth century, not merely for the information they gave but for their decorative effect. They are often to be seen in contemporary Dutch pictures of interiors and, because most maps were printed in Amsterdam, they may have been rather commoner in Holland than in other countries (Plate 231). But they are often mentioned in English inventories and were to be found in rooms of all kinds (Plate 296). Globes (normally in pairs, one terrestrial and one celestial) were also greatly in favour with those who could afford them. Once again, they had a fascination for the seventeenth-century mind as a revelation of Man's discovery of the physical world, but globes were also extremely pretty and it is quite obvious that they were treated equally as pleasing articles of decoration. The pair of large globes which are still at Ham House were not housed in the Library in the seventeenth century but were placed in the Gallery. They still have their original scorched leather protective covers (Plate 299).

Special lighting is required in places where people want to read after dark. This question is touched upon in Chapter XI. As I noted, some standishes were fitted with candle-holders, which would have provided a certain amount of light but would also have been useful for melting sealing-wax.

Baths and Cleanliness

How clean were our seventeenth-century ancestors? The evidence is scanty and one should not make sweeping statements on the matter. However, it is probable that many people were a good deal less dirty than is now generally supposed. It is not necessary to have a wash-basin in every bedroom and a bathroom next door in order to keep clean; it merely makes it easier.

On the days when he did not take a bath, Louis XIV wiped himself with a cloth moistened in spirits—probably a preparation akin to eau-de-Cologne or after-shave lotion. After meals he wiped both face and hands in a hot, damp napkin. Louis is not known to have been particularly fastidious in these matters and it is probable that many of his contemporaries took far greater pains to be clean than he. A seventeenth-century book on etiquette advises the gentry that 'tous les jours l'on prendra la peine de se laver avec le pain d'amande. Il faut aussi se faire laver le visage aussi souvent.' [every day one should take the trouble to wash with *pain d'amande*. It is also necessary to wash one's face almost as often.][119] The ewer and basin necessary for this last operation are to be seen in many contemporary illustrations, often standing on the dressing-table (Plates 29 and 309). The same equipment was brought in at meal-times so that the diners could rinse their fingers.[120] The staff were also expected to wash before the meal.[121]

Moreover, one must not think that, just because few houses had bathrooms in the seventeenth century, baths were not taken. All one needed was a tub—specially made for the purpose or cut from one end of a large barrel—and it was normally kept in the scullery or wash-house (Plates 305 and 319[58]).[122] This was carried into the room where the bath was to be taken and removed again afterwards. Most baths were of wood but they might also be of copper.[123] A few were of silver but then are likely to have been comparatively small—footbaths, perhaps, like that illustrated in Plate 304.[124]

Queen Elizabeth is said to have taken a bath once a month 'whether she need it or

Peint par I.D. De St. Iean.   *Gravé par N.Bazin.*

Femme de qualité déshabillée pour le bain.

304. A lady washing her feet in a vessel that
might equally well serve as a wine-cooler or
jardinière. This scene is a reminder that one
could keep clean without the full para-
phernalia of the modern bathroom. This
Femme de qualité sits in her shift on a highly
fashionable day-bed (the engraving is dated
1685) which seems to be set up in her
dressing-room. A perfume-burner (*cassolette*)
stands in the foreground.

305. Taking a bath. Note that the bath is no
more than a large laundry-tub and is probably
lined with a cloth. Over it is suspended a
pavillon embroidered with *fleurs-de-lis*. The
lady must be seated on a stool. As she is
wearing a bodice or shift it can only be the
lower half of her body that is intended to
benefit in this case. She may be enjoying a
kind of localised steam bath.

no'.[125] The young Louis XIII apparently took frequent baths, according to his personal physician, Héroard, who records how on one occasion in 1611 the king rose at 7 a.m. to watch his bath being filled when red rose-petals were scattered on the water. The next day he again took a bath and this time we learn the tub was placed in his bedchamber. He called for his model boats on this occasion, filled them with rose-petals and pretended that the vessels were returning 'from the Indies or from Goa'.[126] If one did not have facilities at home for taking a bath one could hire a bath-tub for no great sum[127] or one could go to a public bath-house. The book on etiquette mentioned above actually recommended its readers that 'l'on peut aller quelque fois chez les beigneurs pour avoir le corps net' [one can occasionally go to the bath-house to keep the body clean] in addition to the daily ablutions already noted (Plate 308).

There is no denying, however, that actual bathrooms remained few and far between right through till the end of the century. What is more, it must be admitted that some of the more splendid bathrooms were installed principally to impress visitors rather than through any strong desire for hygiene. Celia Fiennes records in some detail the splendid 'batheing roome' at Chatsworth which she was shown on her tour of the house.[128] It had walls

> all with blew and white marble the pavement mix'd one stone white another black another red rance [i.e. varigated]; the bath is one entire marble all finely white veined with blew and is made smooth . . . it was as deep as one's middle on the outside and you went down steps into the bath big enough for two people; at the upper end are two cocks to lett in one hott the other cold water to attempt it as persons please; the windows are all private [obscured] glass.

The Chatsworth bathroom must have been modelled on that in the *Appartement des Bains* at Versailles which, as I have noted, was a luxury flat fitted out for Madame de Montespan. Because this was the preserve of the King's mistress, it was probably more private than the Chatsworth bathroom that was shown to tourists, but it was appointed with the utmost luxury. The baths were hewn from single pieces of marble, the largest being ten *pieds* wide and three deep. The walls were faced with marble marquetry decorated with bronze reliefs (Plate 21).[129] There were less grand bathrooms in some of the other principal apartments at Versailles and similar rooms were installed at a number of noble houses in Paris towards the end of the century.

The *Appartement des Bains* was being installed in the second half of the 1670s and it cannot therefore have influenced the Duchess of Lauderdale or her architect when they were building the bathroom at Ham House in the very same years. However, as we have noted, the Duchess was in Paris in 1670, so she may have seen other bathrooms over there. But what is perhaps more remarkable about her bathroom is that it was intended for actually taking baths and was not for show. This is obvious from the fact that it is approached from her bedchamber by only a very narrow spiralling staircase down which it would never have been possible to take visitors. So the Duchess of Lauderdale clearly wanted to take baths and, if she did so, how many of her contemporaries were likewise inclined? The bathroom at Eriksberg in Sweden is roughly contemporary and is sumptuously decorated (Plates 306 and 307). It probably reflects the sort of bathroom to be seen elsewhere in Europe during the third quarter of the century. It has twin copper bath-tubs set in niches, and a fountain in the centre of the room. There are ducts in the balustrades for hot air

306 & 307. A bathroom of about 1670. Two copper baths stand in niches; they have festoons on a black ground. The baths are filled from taps. Hot air could be introduced from the boiler-room below by means of ducts in the balustrade and under the benches.

generated from the boiler-room below. In a small cupboard is a control panel where servants can adjust separately the flow of air and water.

Taking a bath in the seventeenth century may well have been a lengthy process, perhaps more akin to the sauna than to modern bathroom practice. The French ambassador to Sweden in 1634 noted that every house of any consequence in that country had its own bathroom, by which he meant a steam-bath, and Savot explained that next to a bathroom should lie what he calls an *étuve*, with a copper set over a fire, which must have served a similar purpose.[130] It may well be that such an amenity was not all that uncommon in England at the time, for Robert Herrick referred to 'a sweating closset' in a manner that suggests that everyone would have known what he meant (Plate 308).[131] Francis Bacon seems to have been advocating a sweat-bath when he wrote that one should 'first, before bathing, rub and anoint the body with oyle and salves, that the bath's moistening heate and virtue may penetrate into the body, and not the liquor's watery part: then sit two hours in the bath'.[132] The Duchess of Lauderdale had her 'bathing tubb & little stoole within it' which suggests she followed the practice outlined by Bacon, and we know that Louis XIV sat on a stool in his bath. Plate 305 shows a woman taking

319

308. Taking a bath in an elongated vessel lined with a cloth. The man lying on the covered staging behind is enjoying a steam-bath. Although this shows a Swedish sauna in 1674, 'sweating closets' were certainly known in other countries at the time.

309. A pewter chamber-pot stands in the foreground. Behind the bed is a cubicle set into the wall with a screening door housing a fixed close-stool. The circular dressing-table has a velvet table carpet protected by a white linen *toilette*. A wash basin and ewer stand behind the dressing set.

a bath in this way but she only seems to be interested in bathing the lower half of her body as she has a cloth across the mouth of the tub with a hole in the centre through which her upper torso protrudes. She anyway sits under a tent and it was apparently a common practice to envelop the bather in this way. For example, at Marly there were 'deux pavillons pour les deux baignoires' in 1684.[133] Such tents or *pavillons* would have kept the bather warm during a prolonged period of bath-taking and would have served to contain steam if the bath being enjoyed was of the sauna kind (Plate 305). At Ham House there is a rod fixed below the ceiling above the place where the bath-tub must have stood; this could well be to hold up a tent over the tub. There is also a large hook from which, presumably, a container of hot water could be suspended so that the bath could be topped up when it had cooled off. In the tub it was usual to place a cloth which reduced the cold touch of marble or metal, or the clammy feel of a wooden bath-tub.

Three steps down through a handsome pair of doors leading out of the Ham bathroom is a second room which housed an 'Indian painted bedstead' with painted satin hangings.[134] In this room one presumably relaxed after the bath, for, as Bacon recommended, one should 'after bathing wrap the body in seare-cloth made of mastiche, myrrh, pomander and saffron, for staying the perspiration or breathing of the pores, until the softening of the body, having layne thus in seare-cloth 24 hours [sic], bee growne solid and hard'. To complete the treatment one had to anoint oneself with more ointment. At Hampstead Marshall, built in the 1660s, there was not only a 'Roome to Bathe' but next to it lay a 'Roome for to Repose after Bathing' which is probably what the room at Ham might also have been called.

Randle Holme illustrates a small circular table with a tripod stand which he explains 'is used to stand a bason on whilest washing, or a candle to read by, with many other uses for the chamber' (Plate 319[91]). Basins for washing and the en suite ewers for water are rarely listed as being in bedchambers, however,[135] probably because they were kept with other plate or household vessels in the serving quarters and brought in when needed.[136] Some of the small tables that are often found listed in the contents of a bedchamber may also have served as wash-stands.[137] On the Continent, hand-washing was often performed under a small cistern of water mounted on the wall with a basin below (Plate 128). In a house at Rheims in 1621 there was a 'pied de bois servant à laver les mains' which must have been a stand supporting a wash-basin rather like that to be seen in the illustration.[138]

In the best circles soap was used, Venetian soap being particularly good 'pour les mains' [for the hands]. 'Boites de savon de Milan'[boxes of soap from Milan] were considered a very acceptable present for a lady in the sixteenth century and in 1630 the Elector of Brandenburg was given eight pieces of Turkish soap. But most soap was made locally. In any event soap came either in slab form or in balls. Spherical containers were made for these 'wash balls'.[139]

Also normally only brought into the room when needed were chamber-pots, which were otherwise kept with the candlesticks in the pantry. Chamber-pots might sometimes be called *Nebstschale* in German, a term which carries the implication that they were placed next to the bed rather than under it. In fact, the chamber-pot was sometimes placed on an adjacent chair (Plate 127) and a special low table covered with gilt leather, 'en kleyn taflken . . . met goude leer overtrocken', was provided in a Dutch palace in the 1630s 'diende om den pispot op te setten'

310. A *chaise percée* insultingly included in an anti–Spanish political tract of 1624.

311. A *chaise percée* being carried into a bedchamber in exceptional circumstances (the doctor is about to administer an enema). The padded ring and pewter pan are clearly shown.

312. Two mid-seventeenth-century close-stools of the box type.

313. (below left) A close-stool 'trunke fashion' covered with red velvet perhaps made for Charles I.

314. (below right) A japanned close-stool which was provided for the cubicle (stool room) set into the wall of the Antechamber to the State Bedchamber at Ham House late in the 1670s.

[serving as a stand for the chamber-pot].[140] Chamber-pots in the grander sort of house were commonly made of pewter in the seventeenth century; occasionally they were made of faience and perhaps also of porcelain, and more rarely of silver.[141] Pots of common earthenware were also used but the material was apt to be rather too brittle for the purpose.[142] Randle Holme illustrates a vessel of inverted conical form with a wide foot and turned over brim, which he calls a 'squatter' and explains was 'used by sick and infirm persons to ease nature in the bedchamber when they are not able to stire out'.[143] Bidets, incidentally, were unknown in the seventeenth century; Savary des Bruslons explains that a *bidet* was a small kind of horse and gives no other meaning.[144] The 'ewerinall' listed as being in the window-bay of a closet at Marton Hall will have been one of those long-necked flasks often illustrated in Dutch paintings being held up to the light by a physician who is usually shown in attendance on a sick woman (Plate 109).[145]

Altogether more substantial than the humble chamber-pot was the close-stool which took two distinct forms. What was presumably the earliest type consisted of an armchair with a padded ring-like seat (Plate 310). The term *chaise percée* accurately describes this form although it came to be used for both types of close-stool, under which the pewter pan fitted. The other type consisted of a box with a lid that closed over the ring-seat.[146] A few examples of the latter form survive (Plates 312–14).

Most close-stools were no doubt simple affairs but they could be quite elaborately decorated—like that at Hardwick which was inlaid, and the one at Ingatestone which was 'covered with black leather guilded in spotts'.[147] A handsome specimen covered in red velvet is at Hampton Court while one japanned black with chinoiseries

315. (below left) A 'lodging' or apartment in the late sixteenth century showing how the close-stool stood in a separate small closet or *garderobe* (c) behind the bedchamber (b). On the original plan the first room (a) is described as an 'Antecamera', using the Italian term. Room (c) is stated to be for 'Wood[,] cole and privy'. See also Plate 57 where a separate room for the close-stool is indicated.

316. (below centre) A privy in the thickness of the wall, approached from the alcove of a bedchamber. The Hôtel de Jars in Paris, designed by François Mansart about 1648.

317 (below right) The principal bedchamber at Kinross House with a 'stool room' in the thickness of the wall. Although Sir William Bruce, who designed the house for himself in the 1680s, admired French practice in the planning of buildings, there was nothing strange in thus placing the 'house of office' discreetly out of the way. It was the normal thing to do, not only in Scotland but all over the civilised world.

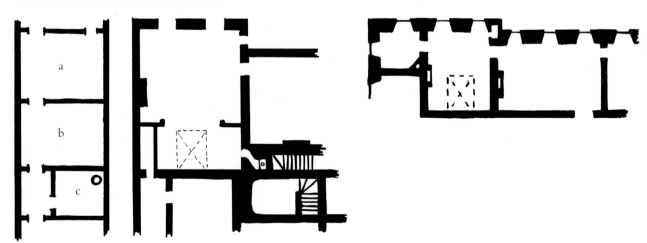

is to be seen at Ham House (Plate 314). Some close-stools were fitted with slip-over covers like that belonging to Cardinal Mazarin which had pendant flaps (à *pentes*) while another was covered with black leather and had an outer cover of red silk damask trimmed with silk fringe.[148] At Breda Castle in 1619 one close-stool had a red and yellow damask cover ['Eenen camerstoel met een behangsel van root en geel damast'] and the 'chaises d'affaires' at Marly were furnished with 'layettes de velour rouge' [loose covers of red velvet].[149] The inventories are rarely explicit about the actual seats but they must have been padded with straw or horsehair and covered with some material. At Ingatestone one had its 'seate lyned wth. yellow cotton' while one at Copenhagen Castle had red cloth on its seat-ring.[150] The pans or 'basons' fitted inside a close-stool were usually of pewter, but Mazarin had one of faience. Sometimes a stool was provided with two pans so that one served as a replacement while the other was being emptied.[152]

The close-stool is commonly listed in inventories among the contents of a bedchamber, but often it was in fact placed in a cubby-hole masked by a jib-door or disguised in some other way (Plate 309). The English version of Le Muet's work, published in 1670, tells us that 'the Privy shall be taken within the thickness of the wall' and such an arrangement can be seen in the plans reproduced in Plates 316 and 317. One sometimes also gets a hint that this was the practice from the inventories themselves. For example, the close-stool listed as being in Her Grace's Bedchamber at Kilkenny Castle in 1684 actually stood in such a cubicle, for we learn that there was 'a picture with flowers over the stool door'.[153] At Ingatestone right back in 1600 two bedchambers each had 'a little house of office within'.[154] The close-stool might also stand in a separate small room. At Ingatestone there was 'a little Stool house' containing a close-stool; at Petworth in 1670 there were 'two Close Stoole Roomes on the Middle Staires', at Tart Hall in 1641 a close-stool was located 'in ye lobby at ye back stayres', and Dr Thomas Lockey had his close-stool 'in a little place by . . . the parlour', while the close-stool at the Lauderdales' London house stood in a place known as 'The Hole'.[155] At Ham House one may still see two cubicles where close-stools once stood set in the walls behind the hangings in two antechambers, as the inventory proves: one of these rooms was called 'the Withdrawing Roome' and at Petworth there was likewise 'a Stoole Roome w'th[in] the Withdrawing Roome'. In his rooms at Oxford, Lord Teviot kept his close-stool 'in the Passage next the Dining Room'.[156]

Exactly the same may be seen on the Continent. The *camerstoel* in one of the principal apartments at the Noordeinde residence of the Prince of Orange stood in a special small closet [Het kleyn secreet camerken].[157] In a house at Rheims two close-stools were placed in a room called the *Garde-robe* and Louis XIV had his standing in a *garde-robe* off the closet known as the *Cabinet des Perruques*.[158] It was 'placée dans une niche garnie de gros de Tours rouge avec galon d'or' [placed in a niche faced with red *gros de Tours* taffeta trimmed with red galloon]. Although Louis XIV, who was old-fashioned in matters of court ceremony, revived the old tradition of receiving honoured callers while seated on his *chaise d'affaires*, it was no doubt all managed very discreetly.[159] The Noordeinde close-stool stood in a *secreet camerken*; in Germany such closets were also known as the *secret* or *das heimliches Gemach* [the secret room], in Sweden as the *privet* and in England as a 'privy'. The evidence all points to the conclusion that our seventeenth-century ancestors were a good deal

318. A French perfume-burner or *cassolette* on a stand. Apparently dating from the last quarter of the seventeenth century this design was probably for an important object, perhaps to be made of silver. It may well have been quite large—up to 100 cm high.

more discreet about these matters than one is often led to suppose. Only in rather special circumstances (as that depicted in Plate 311 where an enema is about to be administered by the doctor) were close-stools brought right into an important bedchamber. At Burfield Lodge at the end of the century Celia Fiennes saw a closet that 'leads to a little place with a seate of easement of marble with sluices of water to wash it all down'.[160] She was clearly impressed by the arrangement which was no doubt a very early example of the water-closet. By the eighteenth century such an amenity was known in France as 'un lieux à l'anglaise' [an English place] which suggests that it was an English invention, although this may be just a further example of that long-standing and childish Anglo-French animosity which has, for instance, led one nation to speak of 'taking French leave' while this in French is called to 'filer à l'anglaise'. Incidentally, a common French name for the close-stool house or *lieu d'aisance* was simply *le lieu*—from which derives our own corruption, 'the loo'.

All this said, one could still cite many tales of dirty habits but the very fact that they were remarked upon suggests that the writer expected the reader to disapprove and at least indicates that a certain fastidiousness prevailed in some quarters.[161] It may well be that people in the seventeenth century were in general not so very different from what we would be if we did not have running hot and cold water freely available.

There was, whatever the case, incentive enough to surround oneself with fragrant

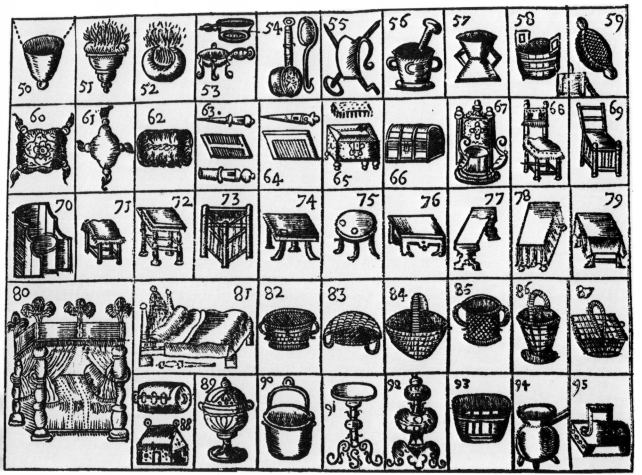

319. Mid-seventeenth-century English household furniture and utensils.

50–52   lamps
53   colander and chafing-dish. The purpose of the latter was 'to hold hot coales of fire in, and to set dish-meates thereon, to keepe them warme till the tyme of serving them up to the table . . .'.
54   warming pan and frying pan. The former was for airing beds.
55   a 'steel to strike fire', used in association with a tinder-box, and two spits for roasting.
56 & 57   mortars, one with its pestel
58   'A tub or turnell with handles' of the sort used by laundry-maids. It could also be used as a bath.
59   'a twiggen basket'
60 & 61   cushions
62   bolster, laced lengthways 'for the greater adornment and beauty of it'
63   two-sided head-comb and a bodkin, the latter to hold up long hair
64   single-sided comb and a bodkin
65   'a Bristle brush' and a 'kind of cabinett . . . such as ladyes keep their . . . jewells in; it stands constantly on the . . . dressing table . . .'.
66   coffer (with a curved lid). 'If it have a flat cover, it is called a Chest'.
67   throne 'or a cathedre'
68   'a stoole-chair, or back stoole'. If all made of joiner's work, then called 'a Joynt chaire, or a Buffet chaire'.
69   a 'turned chaire'
70   ancient form of chair, sometimes called a 'settle chair'. A variant made of osiers was a 'twiggen chaire'.
71   stool
72   'Joynt stoole', has wooden seat. In Cheshire called a 'buffit stool'.
73   'turned stoole'
74   'country stoole', also called a 'plancke or blocke stoole'
75   round 'country stoole'
76   nursing stool
77   'Joint forme, or bench'
78   long table
79   square table covered with a carpet
80   'a bed royall'
81   bed without a tester. Below is a 'bed staffe'.
82   'voyder basket' for carrying delicate clothes
83   'cloathes basket'; rough versions were for coal.
84   'hand basket'; might be coloured
85   fruit basket
86   'twiggen basket' for collecting eggs
87   egg or butter basket; has two lids and a partition
88   'port manteau' of tanned leather and an ark 'of wood and covered with haire cloth', which could be suspended from ceiling to 'secure all things . . . from the cruelty of devouring rates, mice, weesels and such like vermine'. Instead of horse-hair, panels of pierced tin might be used.
89   covered cup
90   hanging kettle or cauldron
91   'little round table . . . for to set a Bason on whilest washing, or a candle to read by, with many other uses for a chamber. Some call it a dressing table.'
92   andiron, 'for ornament more than profitt'.
93   tub
94   'posnett', used for boiling liquids
95   smoothing iron.

smells. Fragrant herbs were cultivated assiduously. The proper drying of such plants and the making of *pot-pourri* were subjects a young lady was expected to master. 'Swetebages' (sweet smelling bags or sachets) filled with lavender and other pleasant-smelling products of the garden[162] were laid among the clean sheets and clothes in their presses (see p. 299). Scented leather gloves and fans from Spain and Italy were much in demand, as were exotic confections like pomanders. Ladies sucked aniseed pastilles to sweeten the breath and covered themselves in scents imported from far afield. It is when one remembers how essential it was to kill the numerous malodours of daily life that one comes to realise why cargoes of spices and perfumes were so valuable and why so much money could be made when an East Indiaman loaded with such goods had braved the many hazards of the long journey from the Orient and succeeded in reaching port.

One of the principal ways of perfuming the air in a room was to install a perfume-burner. These took many forms and could be decorative (Plate 318). The huge specimens of silver that stood in the *Grande Galerie* at Versailles were especially striking. In French inventories the larger versions are called *cassolettes*. They were more commonly of brass or faience. Such 'perfuming pannes' or 'perfuming dishes'[163] had a shallow upper container in which the scented pastille was placed under a pierced lid which let out the scent. In the lower container hot coals could be placed to make the pastille give off its scent (Plate 304). Candlesticks could be adapted to function in a similar manner.[164]

If all these devices had still not killed an evil smell, the final weapon in the perfumer's armoury, at Versailles at any rate, was the scent-spray. Louis had one described as 'une seringue, avec son manche d'ebenne garny d'argent' [a spray, with its ebony handle and silver mounts]. This must have resembled a modern bicycle-pump and was clearly a new invention, for it was necessary to explain that it was 'pour jetter des eaues de senteurs' [to spray scented waters].[165]

320. A Dutch dolls' house, about 1700. As this is a contemporary painting it records the actual state of the dolls' house at the time; a real dolls' house can lose its furnishings, they can be arranged quite incorrectly, and can be added to.

Top left:	Linen Room. A laundry-maid irons linen at a table. Opposite is a napkin-press and a *bakermat* hangs on the wall (see Plate 197).
Top centre:	Landing. A spinning-wheel and sconce for lighting the stairs.
Top right:	Nursery. The nurse has a canopy bed. Wicker cradle. Painted sashes in windows. Rush-bottomed chairs.
Centre left:	Parlour. Verdure tapestries. Sconce above the table. Painted tea-table withdrawn to side of the room with top tipped forward.
Centre:	Hall with view of garden. Hall bench and candlestands.
Centre right:	Bedchamber with box bed. Dressing table forming part of a triad. Sconces. Rush-bottomed chair with cushion. Six-leaf screen.
Lower left:	Dining Parlour? One wall fitted with a glass-fronted cupboard for chinaware; some of it is ranged on top. Brass birdcage. Painted sashes. Nursemaid making pillow-lace.
Lower centre:	Kitchen area. *Couvre feu* in corner fireplace. Cupboard. Waiter's table?
Lower right:	Closet or Library? Gilt leather hangings. Japanned cabinet with porcelain on top. The turned and black-stained chairs have slip-over covers with lappeted edges. An open door seems to reveal bookshelves.

The whole is housed in a fashionable cabinet with glazed doors that is furnished with a fitted protective cover. With its finials and valance, the whole piece would have looked very much like a contemporary bed when the curtains were drawn round it.

Abbreviations

In the notes references to works frequently cited are given in the following abbreviated forms. Occasionally, a slight but unmistakable variant has been used where the context so demands.

Agius	Pauline Agius, 'Late 16th and 17th century Furniture in Oxford', *Furniture History*, Vol. VII, 1971.
Bishop of Winchester's Invt.	Evelyn Philip Shirley, 'The Will, Inventories and Funeral Expenses of James Montague, Bishop of Winchester, anno 1618', *Archeologia,* Vol. XLIV, Pt. II, 1873
Books of Rates, 1582	T. S. Willan, *A Tudor Book of Rates (1582)*, London, 1962.
Celia Fiennes	*The Journeys of Celia Fiennes*, ed. Christopher Morris, London, 1947.
Charles I Invts., 1649–51	'The Inventory and Valuation of The King's Goods, 1649–1651,' ed. Oliver Millar; *Walpole Society Journal*, Vol. XLIII, 1973.
Chatsworth Invt., 1601	Transcript deposited in the Department of Textiles, Victoria and Albert Museum, London; from the archives of the Dukes of Devonshire.
Chenies Invt., 1585	'Inventory of Household Goods, etc. at Chenies, Com. Bucks., on the Death of Francis, 2nd Earl of Bedford, 1585.' From a typescript deposited with the Department of Furniture and Woodwork in the Victoria and Albert Museum by Miss Scott Thomson with the knowledge of the 11th Duke of Bedford.
Clonmell Invt., 1684	National Library of Ireland, MS. 2522. Kindly communicated to me by Desmond Fitz-Gerald, Knight of Glin. Clonmell belonged to the Duke of Ormonde.
Cockesden Invt., 1610	Inventory of a house at Cockesden, 1610; James O. Halliwell, *Ancient Inventories of Furniture, Pictures, Tapestries, Plate etc. illustrative of the domestic manner of the English in the 16th and 17th century*, 1854. The property concerned was probably one belonging to the Earls of Leicester.
Cockesden Invt., 1626	From the same source as the previous item and concerning the same house.
Countess of Leicester's Invt., 1634	Inventory of the effects of Lettice, Countess of Leicester, 1634; J. O. Halliwell, *op. cit.*, under

'*Cockesden Invt., 1610*' above.

Cowdray Invt., 1682	Francis W. Steer, 'A Cowdray Inventory of 1682', *Sussex Archeological Society*, Vol. CV, 1927, pp. 84–102. Taken on the death of Francis, 3rd Viscount Montagu.
D.E.F.	Ralph Edwards, *The Dictionary of English Furniture*, 2nd edition, London, 1954.
Du Boisgelin Invt., 1688	Inventory of Monsieur Gilles Dubois Geslin, Seigneur de la Sourdière in Brittany; manuscript in the possession of Mr Cyril Staal who has generously allowed me to quote from it.
Devon Invts.	'Devon Inventories of the 16th and 17th Centuries,' *Devon and Cornwall Record Society*, New Series, Vol. II, Torquay, 1966.
Dublin Castle Invt., 1679	'Inventory of Dublin Castle, seat of the Duke of Ormonde, Lord Lieutenant of Ireland, 1679,' *Historical Manuscripts Commission*, New Series VII, 1912.
Duke of Norfolk Invt., 1684	'Inventory of the goods and Chattels of His Grace Henry Duke of Norfolk deceased taken at the house at Wabridg . . . 1684.' Arundel Castle Archives (MS.IN53). Quotations published by kind permission of His Grace the Duke of Norfolk. I am much indebted to Mr Francis Steer for drawing my attention to this inventory.
Dyrham Invt., 1703	An Inventory of all the Goods and Furniture in Dirham House, 1703. Gloucestershire Record Office. Copy in the Victoria and Albert Museum.
Easton Lodge Invt., 1637	Francis W. Steer, 'The Easton Lodge Inventory, 1637', *The Essex Review*, Vol. LXI, January, 1952.
Ebba Brahe's Invt., 1665	William Karlson, *Ebba Brahe's Hem. Ett herremans inventarium från 1600-talet*, Lund, 1943. (Inventory of this powerful lady's house in Stockholm, made in 1665).
Edington Invt., 1665	Anne, Lady Beauchamp's Inventory at Edington, Wiltshire, 1665; *Wiltshire Archeological and Natural History Magazine*, LVIII, No. 211, 1963, pp. 383–93.
Evelyn's Diary	*The Diary of John Evelyn*, ed. by E. S. de Beer, Oxford, 1955.
Faringdon Invt., 1620	*An Inventairie of all such Implements and Household goods as allso Jewells, Plate and other Ornaments of the right honble the Ladie Dorothy Shirley . . . att Farringdon, in the countie of Barkes . . .*, 1620. See *The Unton Inventories . . . 1596 and 1620, with a Memoir by John Gough Nichols*, printed for the Berkshire Ashmolean Society, London, 1841.
Gilling Castle Invt., 1594	'Inventories made for Sir William and Sir Thomas Fairfax, Knights of Walton, and of Gilling Castle',

	Yorkshire, *Archeologia*, Vol. XLVIII, 1884.
Gosfield Invt., 1638	F. W. Steer, 'Inventory of Anne, Viscountess Dorchester', *Notes & Queries*, March, April, September, October, November and December 1953 and January 1954 (the last being a transcription of her will). Gosfield Hall was in Essex.
Guiffrey, Inventaire	Jules Guiffrey, *Inventaire Général du mobilier de la couronne sous Louis XIV*, Paris, 1885.
Ham Invt., c. 1654	Unpublished inventory of the contents of Ham House, probably taken in 1654. The Victoria and Albert Museum intends to publish this in due course.
Ham Invt., 1677	Unpublished inventory of the house taken when much of the extension and re-decoration carried out by the Duke and Duchess of Lauderdale was largely completed. To be published (see previous note). It differs in several respects from that of 1679 (see below).
Ham Invt., 1679	The unpublished but well-known inventory of the house then recently enlarged by the Duke and Duchess of Lauderdale. To be published (see previous note).
Ham Invt., 1683	The inventory taken after the Duke's death. See previous note.
Hampton Court Estimates, 1699	'Estimates for Furniture, Upholstery, etc. for Hampton Court Palace, 1699, signed by the Earl of Montague, Master of the Great Wardrobe.' Photographic copy in the Victoria and Albert Museum Library.
Hardwick Invt., 1601	Lindsay Boynton (commentary by Peter Thornton), 'The Hardwick Inventory of 1601', *Furniture History*, Vol. VII, 1971
Hatfield Priory Invt., 1629	'Inventory of the Household Goods of Sir Thomas Barrington, Bart., at Hatfield Priory, 1629' [not 1626 as stated in title], *Transactions of the Essex Archeological Society*, III, New Series, 1889.
Havard	Henry Havard, *Dictionnaire de l'ameublement . . .*, Paris, 1887–90, in four volumes.
Hengrave Invt., 1603	John Gage, *The History and Antiquities of Hengrave in Suffolk*, London, 1822; p. 21 *et seq.*; inventory of Hengrave Hall, 1603
Henham Invt., 1602	A. Suckling, *The History and Antiquities of the County of Suffolk*, London, 1848; inventory of Henham Hall, 1602.
Ingatestone Invt., 1600	'Inventory of the furniture etc. at Ingatestone Hall, Essex,' typescript in the Victoria and Albert Museum Library; see also *Ingatestone Hall in 1600: an Inventory*, Essex Education Committee, 1954.

Karlson	William Karlson, *Stât och Vardag i Stormakstidens herremanshem*, Lund, 1945. A major survey of seventeenth-century furnishings in Sweden.
Kensington Palace Invt., 1697	T. Lunsingh Scheurleer, 'Documents on the Furnishings of Kensington House,' *Walpole Society*, Vol. XXXVIII, 1960–62.
Kensington Palace Invt., 1699	As for the previous entry.
Kildare Invt., 1656	'An Inventory of the Earl of Kildare's goods which is left in his house at Dublin, 1656.' Communicated to me by Desmond Fitz-Gerald, Knight of Glin. By kind permission of the Marquess of Kildare.
Kilkenny Invt., 1684	'Inventory of Kilkenny Castle, 1684', *Historical Manuscripts Commission*, New Series VII, 1912. The seat of the Duke of Ormonde, Lord Lieutenant of Ireland.
Knole Invt., 1645	Chas. J. Phillips, *History of the Sackville Family*, London, *c.* 1928, p. 353 'An Inventory of Goods at Knole, 1645.'
Lauderdale London Invt., 1679	Inventory of the house in Whitehall, London, of the Duke and Duchess of Lauderdale, 1679; included with the *Ham Invt., 1679*, see above.
Lockey Invt., 1679	'Inventory of Dr Thomas Lockey, 1679'; *Bodleian Library Record*, 1954–6, p. 82. Lockey was Bodley's Librarian 1660–5 and then Canon of Christ Church until his death.
Marton Invt., 1605	'An inventory of the goodes moveable and imoveable within the house at Marton, 1605.'
Mazarin Invt., 1653	Henri d'Orléans, *Inventaire de tous les meubles du Cardinal Mazarin*, London, 1861; the inventory was made in 1653.
Montague Household Book, 1595	Sir William St John Pope, *Cowdray and Easebourne Priory*, London, 1919. Appendix II.
Noordeinde Invt., 1633	'Inventaris van de Meublen van het Stadhouderlijk met het Speelhuis en van Huis in het Noodeinde te s'Gravenhage, 1633,' C. Hofstede de Groot and C. H. de Jonge (eds.), *Oud Holland*, 1930. Inventory of the Stadholder's Residence in the Noordeinde at The Hague. Possibly made in 1632. See also the *Orange Invts.* below.
Northampton Invt., 1614	'Inventory of the . . . Earl of Northampton . . . 1614,' *Archeologia*, Vol. XLII, Pt. II, 1862.
Northumberland House Invt., 1670	'Inventory of Northumberland House, 1670,' Jocelin, Earl of Northumberland's estate (see *Petworth Invt., 1670*, below).
Orange Invts.	*Inventarissen van de Inboedels in de verblijven van de Oranjes . . . 1567–1795*, ed. S. W. A. Drossaers and

	Th. H. Lunsingh Scheurleer (Rijks Geschiedkundige Publication), in three vols., The Hague, 1974–6. Inventories of members of the House of Orange.
Pepys' Diary	*The Diary of Samuel Pepys.* For the years 1660–1669, Robert Latham and William Matthews' edition was consulted; for subsequent dates, that of H. B. Wheatley of 1904.
Petworth Invt., 1670	'Inventory of the Rt Hon. Jocelin, Earl of Northumberland's Personal Estate at Petworth, 1670'; Manuscript shown to me by the Lady Victoria Percy, the quotations from it being published here by kind permission of His Grace, the Duke of Northumberland.
Princess Palatine's Letters	*Letters from Liselotte (Elizabeth Charlotte, Princess Palatine and Duchesse d'Orléans)*, ed. Maria Kroll, London, 1970.
Provost of King's Invt., 1660	J. W. Clark, 'On the Old Provost Lodge of King's College, with special reference to the furniture,' *Cambridge Antiquarian Society*, Communications, IV, 1876–80, 1881.
Randle Holme	Randle Holme, *The Academy of Armory or a Storehouse of Armory and Blazon*, 1688, The Roxburghe Club, London, 1905. Holme was writing in the middle of the century (see the note to Plate 319); he was a 'Deputy for the Kings of Arms' and well versed in heraldry.
Rambouillet Invt., 1652	*Deux inventaires de l'Hôtel de Rambouillet, 1652 & 1665; Bulletin Archéologique du Comité des Travaux Historiques et Scientifiques*, Paris, 1892.
Rambouillet Invt., 1665	See previous item.
Savary des Bruslons	Jacques Savary des Bruslons, *Dictionnaire universel de commerce*, Paris, 1723.
Standon Lordship invt., 1623	Sir Ambrose Heal, 'A Great Country House in 1623. The Inventory of Standon Lordship, near Ware, Herts.,' *Burlington Magazine*, May 1843.
Stengel	Walter Stengel, *Alte Wohnkultur in Berlin und der Mark*, Berlin, 1958.
Syon Invt., 1670	'Inventory of Syon House, 1670', Jocelin, Earl of Northumberland's estate (see *Petworth Invt., 1670*, above).
Tart Hall Invt., 1641	'A Memoriall of all the Roomes the Household Stuffe at Tart-Hall: and an Inventory of all the goods there belonging to The Rt. Hon. The Countess of Arundel ... 1641'. Lionel Cust, 'Notes on the Collections formed by Thomas Howard, Earl of Arundel and Surrey, K. G.,' *Burlington Magazine*, 1911, Pt. II, pp. 97–100; pp. 233–6; Pt. IV, p. 341–3.

334

Tessin-Cronström Correspondence	*Les Relations artistiques entre France et Suède, 1693–1718. Extraits d'une correspondance entre l'architecte Nicodème Tessin le Jeune et Daniel Cronström.* Ed. R. A. Weigert and C. Hernmarck, Stockholm, 1964.
Tessin's Visit, 1687	Ragnar Josephson and Pierre Francastel eds., 'Nicodème Tessin le Jeune. Relation de sa visite à Marly, Versailles, Clagny, Rueil et Saint-Cloud en 1687.' *Revue de l'histoire de Versailles et Seine et Oise*, 28 Année, 1926, pp. 149–67.
Thiret Invt., 1621	'Inventaire des Meubles de l'Hôtel de Mr. Claude Thiret . . . Rheims . . . 1621.' *Travaux de l'Académie, Nationale de Reims*, LXXV (1883–84), Nos. 1–2, Rheims, 1885.
Tredegar Invt., 1688	Inventory of Tredegar House, 1688; manuscript in the National Museum of Wales (Tredegar Papers; MSS. 315).
Tredegar Invt., 1698	As previous item.
Turenne Invt., 1615	J. Deville, *Dictionnaire du tapissier, critique et historique de l'ameublement Français*, Paris, 1878–80; Inventaire des meubles du Chàteau de Turenne, 1615.
Walton Invt., 1624	Household stuff at Walton, 1624; see *Gilling Castle Invt., 1594*, above.

Notes to the Text

NOTES TO THE INTRODUCTION

1. Henry Kamen, *The Iron Century. Social Change in Europe, 1550–1660*, London, 1971, p. 1.
2. In his Slade Lectures held at Oxford in January and February 1976 under the title 'The Power Houses', published as *Life in the English Country House: A Social and Architectural History*, New Haven and London, 1978.
3. 'All authority . . . belongs to us. We hold it of God alone, and no person, of whatever quality he may be, can pretend to any part of it.' (Royal Declaration of Louis XIV, 31 July 1652). 'When Kings come to the crown, they swear on the Holy Gospels that they will maintain the Church of God to their best ability; that they will observe the fundamental laws of the State, and they will protect their subjects according to God and reason, as good Kings should do; in consideration of this oath, the people are obliged to obey them as Gods on earth . . .' (*Lettre d'avis à messieurs du Parlement de Paris*, 1649, see P. R. Doolin, *The Fronde*, Cambridge, Mass., 1935, pp. 79 and 135.)
4. In his *Instructions destinées au Dauphin*, Louis XIV explained how the endless round of parties, balls, *carrousels* and spectacles would serve this end, for one should always seek to entertain and please one's people so that by 'ces divertissements . . . nous tenons leurs esprits et leurs cœurs quelquefois plus fortement peut-être que par la recompense et les bienfaits' [these entertainments . . . we sometimes hold their imagination and their hearts more strongly perhaps than by rewards and favours]. With regard to foreign visitors, 'ce que se consume en ces depenses, qui peuvent passer pour superflues, fait sur eux une impression très advantageuse de magnificence, de puissance, de richesse et de grandeur' [what is spent on these occasions, which might be thought to be extravagent, makes on them a very favourable impression of magnificence, power and greatness]. (R. A. Weigert, Introduction to the catalogue to the exhibition *Louis XIV : faste et décors*, Musée des Arts Décoratifs, Paris, 1960, p. xv.)
5. Sir William Cavendish, for example, extended Bolsover in order to entertain Charles I and his Queen in the hope of being granted the guardianship of the young Prince of Wales, and wrote to a friend in 1634 that 'I have bent my estate with the hope of it.' (O. Hill and J. Cornforth, *English Country Houses, Caroline 1625–85*, London 1966, p. 9.)
6. See Girouard (note 2, above) and Penelope Eames, 'Furniture in England, France and the Netherlands from the twelfth to the fifteenth century', *Furniture History*, XIII, 1977.
7. One is reminded of the mobile character of ancient furniture by the Italian word for furniture, both in the modern narrow sense and in that embracing all furniture that is movable, which is *i mobile*. The French, German, Dutch and Scandinavian words for furniture (*les meubles, die Möbel, meubelen, møbler*) carry the same reminder.
8. A Swedish historian has concluded, however, that it was probably still uncommon in Sweden as late as 1640 for a noble family to keep all its houses fully furnished. (*Ebba Brahe's Invt., 1665*, p. 27.)
9. 'What has been created in the past is small in comparison with our own time, since we see the quality of buildings and the number of those who build them far exceed any yet known particularly among the nobility, who devote themselves to it more for glory than out of necessity', wrote La Noue in 1587. Francis Bacon could likewise say in 1592 that 'there was never the like number of fair and stately houses as have been built and set up from the ground' since the beginning of Queen Elizabeth's reign. A generation later another writer claimed that 'No kingdom in the world spent so much on building as we did in [King James'] time' although the phenomenon was not in fact confined to England (Kamen, *op. cit.*, pp. 144–5). So much building was being carried out in Paris early in the century as the result of new prosperity that Malherbe claimed that someone returning after a two-year absence would find the city unrecognisable (*Oeuvres*, letter of 3 October, 1608).
10. A. Blunt, *Art and Architecture in France, 1500–1700*, London, 2nd edition, 1970; J. Summerson, *Architecture in Britain 1530–1830*, London, 5th edition, 1969; O. Hill and J.

Cornforth, *op. cit.*; J. P. Babelon, *Demeures parisiennes sous Henri IV et Louis XIII*, Paris, 1965; L. Hautecoeur, *Histoire de l'architecture classique en France*, Paris, n.d.; and J. Rosenberg, S. Slive and E. H. Ter Kuile, *Dutch Art and Architecture, 1600–1800*, London, 1966.

11. There was of course still no special course of training for an architect in 1600 in France or England. The first architectural academy of all was that of San Luca, established in Rome in 1577. Before that, as Vasari pointed out in 1550, 'Architecture is to be adequately pursued only by such men as possess an excellent judgment, a good knowledge of design, or extensive practice in some such occupation as painting, sculpture, or woodwork, and have been thereby led to the habit of measuring figures, edifices and bodies of similar character in their several members . . .' Among the leading architects active in England during the seventeenth century we find a former painter (Inigo Jones), an astronomer (Wren), a military engineer (Winde) and a diplomatist-courtier with an interest in buildings (Gerbier). Only Webb had been brought up to practice in the profession, according to H. M. Colvin (*A Biographical Dictionary of English Architects*, London, 1954). The *Académie Royale d'Architecture* that was to offer French architects a formal training and provide a sound basis for future practice was established in 1671 but English architects had to rely on picking up what they could at schools of drawing or from older, practising architects until late in the next century. However, the Office of Works acted as a sort of academy for those whom the Surveyor of the King's Works selected to join his staff and, as those attached to the organisation had time to undertake private work as well as their official duties, the influence of this institution was considerable. As we shall see, the French equivalent of the Office of Works, the *Surintendance des Bâtiments Royaux*, also became a cradle of influential and advanced ideas. This and related questions are also surveyed by Frank Jenkins in *Architect and Patron. A Survey of Professional Relations and Practice in England from the Sixteenth Century to the Present Day*, London, 1961 and in Malcolm Airs, *The Making of the English Country House, 1500–1640*, London, 1975.

12. R. Gunter, *The Architecture of Sir Roger Pratt*, Oxford, 1928, p. 60.

13. A list of the principal architectural books

published before 1685 and probably known in England is given by Hill and Cornforth, *op. cit.*, pp. 250–1.

14. Clarendon House, for example, provided an especially favoured model that was imitated all over England. Erected between 1664 and 1667 in Piccadilly, admired by Pepys as 'the finest pile I ever did see in my life' and by Evelyn as 'the best contriv'd, the most usefull, graceful and magnificent house in England', and demolished already in 1683, its influence lived on and can still be traced in a great many country houses.

NOTES TO CHAPTER I

1. Harold Nicolson, *Good Behaviour, being a Study of Certain Types of Civility*, London, 1955, p. 164. Sauval, writing in the mid-seventeenth century, claimed that the Hôtel de Rambouillet was 'the most celebrated in the kingdom' and that 'every day there gathered a group of eminent people . . . only those of exquisite and refined taste met there'. (Henri Sauval, *Histoire et recherches des antiquités de la ville de Paris*, Livre III, Vol. II, pp. 200–1.) This work was first published in 1724 but Sauval died only four years after the Marquise and seems to have known her.

2. 'Nous ont appris qu'elle en a fait & donné le dessein, qu'elle seule l'a entrepris, conduit & achevé.' [We have been told that she actually made and provided the design, that she alone undertook, directed and brought about its execution.] (Sauval, *loc. cit.*)

3. Of the house Sauval (*loc. cit.*) said that 'one will not find many in Paris which equal it or surpass it'.

4. She placed the staircase to one side so that visitors, as they approached, might see the whole suite of state rooms through the *portes en enfilade*. Neither the siting of the staircase, however, nor the arrangement of doors in enfilade were entirely novel features. As Sir Anthony Blunt has pointed out, doors thus arranged had been known in the sixteenth century ('The Précieux and French Art', in *Fritz Saxl . . . A Volume of Memorial Essays*, London, 1957, pp. 326–38). See also J. P. Babelon, *Demeures parisiennes sous Henri IV et Louis XIII*, Paris, 1965, pp. 189–95.

5. Sauval, *loc. cit.*

6. *Ibid.*

7. G. Tallemant des Réaux, *Historiettes* (*c.* 1657–9), II, p. 216.

8. Sauval (*loc. cit.*) speaks of the room being

'parée de son tems d'un emmeublement de velours bleu, rehaussé d'or & d'argent' [dressed at the time in an *ameublement* of blue velvet, enriched with gold and silver]. The term *ameublement* was normally applied to the complete textile furnishings of a room (i.e. wall-hangings, chair-covers, table-carpets, window-curtains if any, and bed-hangings if it was a bedchamber). But Babelon (*op. cit.*, p. 211) claims to have found the bill of 1620 for the wall-hangings which, he says, were of brocatelle with white and gold scrollwork on a blue ground. But he suggests this was for the summer hangings. Maybe in winter the wall-hangings were of the blue velvet while the chair-covers and other items remained unchanged all the year round.

9. Penelope Eames, 'Furniture in England, France and the Netherlands from the twelfth to the fifteenth century', *Furniture History*, XIII, 1977.

10. Babelon, *loc. cit.* He provides a reconstructed plan of the house, showing the layout of the main floor.

11. Sauval, *loc. cit.*

12. Tallemant des Réaux, *loc. cit.* Rosalys Coope, in her excellent monograph on the architect of the Luxembourg, Salomon de Brosse (London, 1972, p. 131), discounts this story, however, but it must surely have some foundation.

13. Work on the Luxembourg started in 1615 and the main building seems to have been roofed in 1616 but the Queen could still apparently not stay in the building by 1623. The rebuilding of the Hôtel de Rambouillet was started in 1619 and it was again altered in 1627.

14. *Parentalia; or Memoirs of the Family of Wrens . . . but chiefly of Sir Christopher Wren . . . compiled by his son Christopher. Now published by his grandson, Stephen Wren, Esq.*, London, 1750, p. 261, quoting a letter of 1665 from Paris.

15. *Tessin-Cronström Correspondence*, letter of 3 Jan., 1694.

16. Le Comte de Laborde, *Le Palais Mazarin . . .*, Paris, 1846, pp. 166–8. He quotes a pamphlet of 1649 entitled *Inventaire des merveilles du monde recontrées dans le palais de Cardinal Mazarin* which describes the superb tortoiseshell cabinets, the tables of Italian work in *pietre dure*, the statues, the silk damask on the walls, an ivory couch and a particularly noteworthy painting of the Virgin Mary which were among the wondrous objects to be seen in the *Galerie*. Next door was a second gallery, the *Galerie des Antiques*, where were displayed the Cardinal's rich collection of Classical sculptures. See in addition the *Mazarin Invt., 1653*, for a detailed description of the furnishing of this sumptuous building.

17. R. A. Weigert, Introduction to the Catalogue of the exhibition *Louis XIV : faste et décors*, Musée des Arts Décoratifs, Paris, 1960, p. xv.

18. *Ibid.*, p. xviii.

19. No other building can have been studied so much or written about so often as the Palace of Versailles. The history of its building in the seventeenth century is summarised by Sir Anthony Blunt, *op. cit.*, Chapter 7. A masterly and entertaining survey is Pierre Verlet's *Versailles*, Paris, 1961. But anyone seriously interested in the history of this important building in the seventeenth century should read Alfred Marie's *Naissance de Versailles*, Paris, 1968, and *Mansart à Versailles*, Paris, 1972.

20. 'Je me paroit qu'il y a quelque chose à changer, que les sujets sont trop sérieux, qu'il faut qu'il y ait de la jeunesse mêlée dans ce que l'on ferat . . . Il faut de l'enfance répandue partout.' F. J. B. Watson, *Wallace Collection Catalogue : Furniture*, London, 1956, p. xxvi.

21. The building of the *Trianon de Porcelaine*, which was seemingly created to please Madame de Montespan, began in 1670. Félibien spoke of it as 'un enchantement' because it sprang up so quickly. He mentioned the blue and white walls of the *salon* 'travaillé à la manière des ouvrages qui viennent de la Chine', i.e. in the Chinese manner. (See Alfred Marie, *Naissance de Versailles*, Vol. II, Paris, 1968, Chap. XI.)

22. The *Pavillon de la Ménagerie* was built in 1663–4 and had various novel features including several chimneypieces of rather low proportions (Marie, *op. cit.*, Vol. I, Chap. III). Le Vau created an Orangerie in the 1660s: this was replaced by the present building in the mid-1680s (see Alfred and Jeanne Marie, *Mansart à Versailles*, Paris, 1972, pp. 279–300). The *Trianon de Marbre* was begun in 1687.

23. Saint-Simon's account of how the King sought out the site for Marly is amusing. It was written in 1715, long after the event. 'The King, tired of elegance and of the crowd, became convinced that he needed a small place and privacy on some occasions. He searched around Versailles for something to satisfy this new fancy. He visited several places . . . He found . . . a narrow, deep valley, with steep sides, inaccessible on account of the boggy ground,

without any view, closed in by hills on all sides.' (Saint-Simon, *Mémoires*, ed. Pléiade, Vol. IV, p. 1008.) See also Jeanne and Alfred Marie, *Marly*, Paris, n.d.

24. 'The King never allowed ceremony at all at Marly. No ambassadors or envoys were permitted to come there; there was no etiquette and everything was higgledy-piggledy—in the *salon* everyone, right down to the captain and sub-lieutenants of the guard, was allowed to sit down', wrote the King's sister-in-law (see *Princess Palatine's Letters*, 11 August, 1716).

25. 'There is to be a further expenditure of a hundred thousand *livres*; Marly will soon be a second Versailles,' wrote Madame de Maintenon in 1698. France was at the time in a desperate financial state and the Marquise tried to remonstrate with the King at this enormous fresh outlay on such a frivolous exercise but 'I have not pleased [the King] in my conversation about the buildings and my sorrow is that I have offended without profit... One can only pray and grieve ... But the People, what will become of them?' (A. Genevay, *Le Style Louis XIV: Charles Le Brun, décorateur*, Paris, 1886, p. 104.)

26. The Château de Clagny was built between 1674 and 1678. On a contemporary engraving it is described as 'Clagny, maison des délices'. Madame de Sévigné reported in 1675 that the Queen had visited Madame de Montespan at Clagny where 'elle trouvèrent la belle si occupée des ouvrages et des enchantements que l'on fait pour elle...'. There was a special room set aside for dining and actually called the *salle à manger* and some of the chimneypieces were of the new low proportions. (See Alfred and Jeanne Marie, *Mansart à Versailles*, Vol. I, Paris, 1972, Chap. I.)

27. The *Appartements des Bains* was created in the early 1670s. (See Alfred Marie, *Naissance de Versailles*, Vol. II, Paris, 1968, Chap. XIII.)

NOTES TO CHAPTER II

1. *Parentalia: or Memoirs of the Family of Wrens*, London, 1750, p. 261.

2. *Ibid.*, p. 262.

3. Philibert de l'Orme, *Le Premier tome de architecture*, 1567; Pierre Le Muet, *Manière de bien bâtir pour touttes sortes de personnes*, 1623, enlarged with *Augmentations de nouveaux bastimens* in 1647; Roland Fréart, *Parallèle de l'architecture antique et de la moderne*, 1650; Jean Marot,

L'Architecture François ou recueil des plans... bâtis dans Paris et ses environs, c. 1670.

To be fair, however, it must be said that Jean Marot was also the publisher of suites of engravings of ornamental features and it is interesting to note that de l'Orme was tempted to give information about the interior decoration of palaces but felt his book was not the right place to do so. 'Ce lieu n'est à propos pour parler des mesures des chambres & dedans des logis, ny moins des meubles & ornemens des salles & chambres des Roys & Grands Seigneurs, veu [sic] que telle matiere est assez suffisante pour en faire un livre à part... peu de personnes... sçachent bien orner & decorer les logis des Roys & Princes' [This is not the place to discuss the size of rooms and the interiors of apartments, nor even the furniture and decoration of the great chambers and bedchambers of kings and great noblemen, since the subject is so great that it would fill a separate volume... few people really understand how properly to decorate and furnish the apartments of kings and princes] (*Libre IX*). It would seem that already by the middle of the sixteenth century the French were more interested in such matters than other people.

4. Published in 1670 under the title *The Art of Fair Building*. Incidentally, John Evelyn translated Fréart's work in 1664.

5. See R. A. Weigert's introduction to the Catalogue of the exhibition entitled *Louis XIV: faste et décors* held at the Musée des Arts Décoratifs in Paris in 1960. This gives an excellent survey of the output of ornamental engravings in Paris during the period. It would be impossible to list here the huge number of sets of engravings available at the time.

6. John Harris, 'Inigo Jones and His French Sources', *Bulletin of the Metropolitan Museum*, New York, May 1961, discusses the use made by Jones and his pupil, John Webb, of Barbet's *Livre d'architecture, d'autels, et de cheminées* of 1632 in devising chimneypieces for Greenwich House and at Wilton in the late 1630s and 1640s. Several chimneypieces of the 1660s and early 1670s at Skokloster are modelled on plates in Barbet's work (see Erik Andrén, *Skokloster*, Stockholm, 1948, pp. 254, 267, 281, 287, 298 and 302). Some ceilings at Skokloster, incidentally, are based on engravings by Le Pautre.

7. Published by Cornelius Danckerts (*c.* 1603–56).

8. Robert Pricke, *The Architect's Store-house*, 1674. Pricke published and sold translations of many of the principal works on architecture and ornament including those of Vitruvius, Le Muet, Barbet and Francini. He advertised the 'choice of Mapps, Copy Books, chimney peeces and ceiling peeces' available at his shop near Cripplegate where he was established shortly after the Great Fire had destroyed much of the City of London and guidance was being eagerly sought by architects and decorators busy making good the devastation. In 1675 he advertised the wide selection of 'Italian, French & Dutch Prints, Books of Geometry, Perspective and Architecture' he had for sale (see L. Rostenberg, *English Publishing in the Graphic Arts 1599–1700*, New York, 1963, pp. 55–60).

9. Sir Roger Pratt, *Certain Short Notes Concerning Architecture*, 1660 (see R. T. Gunther, *The Architecture of Sir Roger Pratt*, London, 1928, p. 23).

10. The most obvious example is Ralph, Duke of Montagu (1638?–1709) who was Ambassador to the French court between 1669 and 1672, and again between 1676 and 1678.

11. See P. Thornton, 'The Parisian Fauteuil of 1680', *Apollo*, February 1975, and G. Jackson-Stops, 'The 6th Earl of Dorset's Furniture at Knole', *Country Life*, 2 and 9 June 1977, for further information on acquisitions by ambassadors to the French Court.

12. Karel van Mander, describing the way Michelangelo had freed Classical architecture from its bonds and of the 'free rein' and 'licence to invent' that architects had as a result been given, lashed out at his own countrymen in sharply critical terms, saying that now 'this rein is so free, and this licence so misused by our Netherlanders, that in the course of time in Building a Great Heresy has arisen among them, with a heap of craziness of decorations and breaking of pilasters in the middle, and adding, on pedestals, their usual coarse points of diamonds and such lameness, very disgusting to see' (*Schilderboeck*, fol. 168v).

13. Early in the seventeenth century the 9th Earl of Northumberland had in his library the works of Vitruvius, Alberti, Serlio, Vignola, Du Cerceau, de l'Orme, and Dietterlin. They must all have been in the original. (Frank Jenkins, *Architect and Patron*, London, 1961, p. 49).

14. Hans Vredeman de Vries, *Architectura, de oorden Thuschana . . .*, Antwerp, 1578.

15. For example, the cove in the Single Cube Room at Wilton and that in the Queen's Bedchamber at Greenwich are painted with grotesques in the Netherlandish Mannerist style (by Matthew Gooderick or John de Critz?). Those at Greenwich are rather more Italian in conception than those at Wilton which have pinnacles and all the 'craziness of decoration' about which van Mander was so scathing (see note 12).

16. Jean Cotelle, *Livre des Ornemens pour Plafonds . . .*, Paris, about 1640. A number of the original drawings for these ceiling designs are incorporated in a volume of mostly coloured drawings of interior architecture by various hands now in the Ashmolean Museum (see K. T. Parker, *Catalogue of the Collection of Drawings in the Ashmolean Museum*, Oxford, 1938, No. 395). Apart from a few interpolations they all seem to be Parisian and to date from the second quarter of the century. Several are for royal buildings, others bear ciphers with coronets indicating that they too are for decorative schemes of importance. It has very plausibly been suggested that the drawings come from the drawing-office of Inigo Jones or his pupil and successor John Webb (see John Harris, 'Inigo Jones and His French Sources', *Bulletin of the Metropolitan Museum*, New York, May 1961). What is more likely than that Jones and/or Webb made considerable efforts to acquire drawings of this sort which provided such helpful and vivid information about the newest schemes of interior decoration in important buildings·in the French capital?

17. Franz Cleyn was a German who was taken into the service of Christian IV of Denmark whose sister Anne was married to James I of England. James persuaded his brother-in-law to release Cleyn who finally came to England in 1624 or 1625, the year Charles I came to the throne. In Denmark he had been a decorative painter (e.g. at Rosenborg Castle) and had apparently provided patterns for some rich cupboard carpets (see p. 241) that were made—woven or embroidered, it is not clear which—in Copenhagen in 1622. (I am indebted to Mrs Vibeke Woldbye for this information.) It is probable that James had intended that Cleyn should decorate rooms for Anne of Denmark but she died in 1619. Instead he executed work for Queen Henrietta Maria who arrived in England at about the same time as he did. He was apparently responsible for designing the tri-

umphal arches erected for her entry into the City, under the general supervision of Inigo Jones, and carried out decoration in her apartment at Somerset House. He also worked at Holland House, Carew House, Bolsover Castle and Ham House. Although he was primarily a painter, he was obviously capable of designing ornament and may even have devised quite extensive schemes of decoration. The chimneypiece in the North Drawing Room at Ham is plausibly attributed to him and he may well have designed the rich panelling still in that room, as well as the fireplace in the Hall which is in the current 'court style' of Inigo Jones—with which he must have been entirely familiar by the 1630s when Ham was being done over by William Murray. Some shell-back *sgabello*-type chairs to be seen in a view of the garden at Ham in the 1670s probably date from Cleyn's period and resemble closely a set which stood in the Gilt Room at Holland House that he is known to have decorated (Plate 52). This suggests that Cleyn could design Italianate furniture suitable for Classical interiors. If so, his services could well have been much in demand by Inigo Jones and his clients.

18. James Howell, in his *Instructions for Furreine Travel* of 1642, likewise claimed that 'commodity, firmness and beauty' were 'the three maine principles of Architecture'. These qualities were embodied, he claimed, in the buildings erected for the Earl of Arundel (1586–1646) who 'observing the uniforme and regular way of stone structure up and down Italy, hath introduced that forme of building to London and Westminster, and elsewhere'. He was presumably referring to buildings designed by Inigo Jones who had accompanied the Earl to Italy and certainly worked at Arundel House.

19. Katharine Fremantle, *The Baroque Town Hall of Amsterdam*, Utrecht, 1959, p. 99.

20. *Ibid.*, p. 101.

21. Letter of 2 July, 1639. (*Ibid.*, p. 98.)

22. Letter of 11–21 November, 1637. (*Ibid.*, p.102.)

23. D. F. Slothouwer, *De Paleizen van Frederik Hendrik*, Leiden, 1945, is the principal source of information on this matter. See also Fremantle, *op. cit.*, pp. 102–8.

24. Sir William Brereton, *Travels in Holland . . .*, Chetham Society, London, 1844, p. 33.

25. Fremantle, op. cit., p. 107.

26. Sir William Temple, *Observations on the United Provinces*, 1673.

27. *Ibid.*

28. John Harris, 'Inigo Jones and His French Sources', *Bulletin of the Metropolitan Museum*, New York, May 1961 (see notes 6 and 16).

29. At the Palais du Luxembourg her mother had several rooms with floors of marquetry of oak laid so as to form interlacing patterns which were 'merveilleuse & admirée de tous les gens du metier' [marvellous and admired by all those in the profession], that is, by other joiners and people who knew the trade and could appreciate how skilfully the joints were disguised (Sauval, *Antiquités de Paris, Livre XIV*, 1724, p. 8). An English visitor noted in particular the Queen's Closet which was 'floored with Wood wrought in little workes all Severall forms pitcht in with Silver' (O. Millar, 'The notebooks of Richard Symonds', *Studies in Renaissance and Baroque Art*, London, 1967). Dr Martin Lister commented in his *Journey to Paris* of 1699 that 'inward knots were inlaid with threads of silver' although it is likely that the metal was in fact pewter. He remarked on the astonishing 'firmness . . . after so long laying' of these floors. At the Palais Royal, Anne d'Autriche in the 1640s had some parquet floors laid by the exceptionally skilful joiner, Jean Macé (see D. Alcouffe, 'Les Macés, ébénistes et peintres', *Bulletin de la Société de l'Histoire d'Art Français*, Paris, 1972). Henrietta Maria's floors were considered so remarkable in their time that engravings of them were available for sale shortly after their completion. In the English translation of Palladio's *First Book of Architecture* (published in 1663) designs of these floors were included and it is stated that the floors had been 'lately made in the Palace of the Queen Mother at Somerset-House. A curiosity never practised before in England' (see L. Rostenberg, *English Publishing in the Graphic Arts 1599–1700*, New York, 1963, p. 54); the designs are composed entirely of straight lines.

30. Information kindly provided by H. M. Colvin.

31. The inventory was drawn up by Murray's daughter, the future Duchess of Lauderdale, probably in 1654. See *Ham Invt.*, c. 1654.

32. In the parlour, for instance, the gilt leather hangings were red and gold, the covers of the couch and the eighteen chairs were of scarlet cloth bordered with the same gilt leather, while the window-curtains and table-covers were made up in the same fashion. It will be remembered that Francis Cleyn was responsible

for some of the decoration at Ham at this stage (see note 17, above).

33. It is noteworthy that Paul Vredeman de Vries' influential *Verscheyden Schryn werck* was only published in 1630. The style embodied in the many designs it offers its readers is only a slight modification of that brought forward in the *Variae Architecturae Formae* that his father, Hans, had published in 1560.

34. Sir Roger Pratt went abroad, as he said, 'to give myself some convenient education'.

35. *Memoirs of the Verney Family*.

36. Sir Roger Pratt, *Certain Short notes concerning Architecture*, 1660 (see R. T. Gunther, *The Architecture of Sir Roger Pratt*, London, 1928).

37. However, Montagu himself was a confirmed francophile. When his house was gutted in the 1680s he had a French architect reconstruct it. He is identified as Pierre Pouget by G. Jackson-Stops in 'The Building of Petworth', *Apollo*, May 1977. He is said to have been assisted by the French painter James Rousseau who was responsible for much of the interior decoration.

38. The facts supporting the assertions made in these passages may be found in the appropriate entries in H. M. Colvin's *Biographical Dictionary of English Architects, 1660–1840*, London, 1954.

39. Verrio had arrived in Paris by 1671 where he became a friend of Molière. He was invited to England by Lord Montagu. His main occupation between 1675 and 1684 was executing decorative work at Windsor Castle under Hugh May and, in 1684, he was created 'first & chief Painter to his *Matie*'. He worked with a troupe of foreign craftsmen including Grinling Gibbons (who was supported by two other Dutchmen), Jean-Baptiste Monnoyer (the flower-painter), René Cousin (gilder) and John Vanderstaine (stone carver). Clearly this band was able to create complete schemes of fixed decoration. Verrio's group, plus or minus a few members, also worked at Burghley and Chatsworth, and apparently also at Ham House (E. Croft-Murray, *Decorative Painting in England*, Vol. I, London, 1962).

40. John Casbert is mentioned in the royal accounts between 1667 and 1673, John Poitevin in the 1670s, 'Monsieur La Grange' in 1674, and Francis La Pierre and Philip Guibert in the 1690s. La Pierre worked also for the Duke of Devonshire and Guibert for the Duke of Leeds. Some of the chairs Casbert supplied were described as 'French' but this clearly refers to

their style (see the *Dictionary of English Furniture*; R. W. Symonds, 'Charles II: Couches, Chairs and Stools', *The Connoisseur*, January and February, 1934; and notes in the Department of Furniture and Woodwork, Victoria and Albert Museum). Incidentally, the principal upholsterer in The Hague serving William III was named Pierre Courtonne and died in 1714 (see *Orange Invts.*, I, p. 554).

41. *Evelyn's Diary*, 9 June, 1662. He tells us that the bed had been bought originally for the king's sister, the Princess of Orange (i.e. Maria Stuart, sister of Charles I, who died in 1660) but that the Estates General had then bought it back and presented it to the King. He must then in turn have given it to his bride on their marriage in 1662. Its high cost lay chiefly in the rich embroidery on a crimson velvet ground but the bed undoubtedly was accompanied by a set of seat-furniture and possibly also by a set of wall-hangings—all en suite.

42. See P. Thornton, 'The Parisian Fauteuil of 1680', *Apollo*, February 1975.

43. An account of money 'payed out for the Lady Dutchess of Lauderdale in Holland by Mistress v. der Huva' includes as its first item 'for a cabinet of black ebonie with a table and two Gadons [*guéridons*] cost . . . 440 Guilders'. The French term for a candlestand at this date was *guéridon* (Scottish Record Office, Lauderdale Papers, 6/11).

44. See G. Jackson-Stops, 'The 6th Earl of Dorset's Furniture at Knole', *loc. cit.*

45. There is a splendid illustration of this cabinet in colour in Nancy Mitford's *The Sun King*, London, 1966, facing p. 192. The almost identical pair to this cabinet, which must also have belonged to Louis XIV will come to form one of the glories of the J. Paul Getty Museum in California not long after this book is published.

46. I am grateful to Professor Lunsingh Scheurleer for providing me with additional information about the Golle family.

NOTES TO CHAPTER III

1. See Chapter II, note 17.

2. Francis Bacon, *Essayes*, 1625, XLV, 'Of Building'.

3. Published in *Archeologia*, Vol. CI, 1967.

4. M. Girouard, 'The Power Houses', Slade Lectures, Oxford 1976. Published as *Life in the*

English Country House: A Social and Architectural History, New Haven and London, 1978.

5. J. Fowler and J. Cornforth, *English Decoration in the 18th Century*, London, 1974, Chap. 3.

6. A writer in 1700 described the apartments at Dyrham as being 'more for State than use except upon Extraordinary occasion' (see Fowler and Cornforth, *op. cit.*, p. 60, and the Guide to Dyrham).

7. Bacon, *op. cit.*

8. Girouard (see note 4) has drawn attention to the two royal apartments created at Hatfield House early in the century.

9. Among the upper classes married couples did not share a bedchamber. Marriages were mostly arranged for dynastic reasons and while they might sometimes grow into love-matches, this was the exception.

10. In former times such sets of rooms had been called lodgings. The term apartment, and more especially the French *appartement*, has more stylish connotations but was essentially a lodging in a new guise.

11. A pallet was a small straw mattress. A pallet-bed usually consisted of three such pallets. Sometimes there may have been a very simple wooden framework underneath, to raise the mattresses off the ground.

12. The household regulations of the period give a good idea of the involved ceremonies that were associated with the laying of the table, the decking out of the cup-boards with splendid plate, the taking of seats, the testing of the food and drink and the serving of it, the bringing on of the various courses and their subsequent removal. See, e.g., Viscount Montagu's House-hold Book of 1595 (Sir William H. St. John Hope, *Cowdray and Easebourne Priory*, London, 1919, pp. 119–34) and also 'A Breviate touching the Order and Governemente of a Nobleman's house ... 1605' communicated by Sir Joseph Banks, *Archæologia*, XIII, 1800, pp. 315–89. Miss Rachel Cooper has informed me, it should be noted, that no date 1605 is actually given at the head of the manuscript and how Banks arrived at this date is at present a mystery. Other details have not been accurately transcribed either but there is no reason to doubt that the date is about right.

13. How far a person penetrated along the sequence of rooms leading to the bedchamber in a grand house was an indication of his standing with the owner. The greater the honour one wished to bestow on the visitor to the apartment, the further he was allowed to come. Especial honour was signified when the owner advanced to meet the visitor at the entrance and escorted him deep into the apartment. Intimate friends of the owner might be allowed to join him (or her) in the privacy of the closet that lay beyond the bedchamber. These are complicated questions and the etiquette varied somewhat from country to country. The reader is referred to the works of Murray Baillie and Girouard already mentioned.

14. Sir Henry Wotton was however not impressed with this arrangement which he will have seen in Italy. In his *Elements of Architecture* of 1624 he wrote that 'They do cast their partitions as when all doors are open, a man may see through the whole house, which doth necessarily put an intolerable servitude upon all the chambers save the innermost, where one can arrive but through the rest ... I cannot commend the direct opposition of such overtures, being merely grounded upon the fond ambition of displaying to a stranger all our furniture at one sight.'

15. Sheraton, writing at the beginning of the nineteenth century, summed up the practice which was still current in his day. 'The chimney should always be situated so as to be immediately seen by those who enter the room. The middle of the partition-wall is the most proper place in halls, saloons, and other rooms of passage; but in drawing-rooms, dressing-rooms, and the like, the middle of the back wall is the best situation. In bed-rooms, the chimney is always in the middle of one of the partition-walls; and in closets and other very small places, to save room, it is put in a corner.' (T. Sheraton, *The Cabinet Maker, Upholsterer and General Artists Encyclopaedia*, London, 1804, 'Architecture'.) These rules were being formulated in the seventeenth century. Le Muet was more specific about the siting of the fireplace in a bedchamber which 'ought not be situate in the midst but distant therefrom about two feet, whereby place be allowed for the bed', unless the room was very large. The bed being about six feet square and standing with its head against the inner wall, it was naturally desirable to have the chimneypiece well to the window-side of the foot of the bed, allowing plenty of space round the fireplace (P. Le Muet, *The Art of Fair Building*, 1670, p. 2; translated from the original French version of 1623). Savot also discusses the best position for chimneypieces (L. Savot, *L'Architecture Française*

des Bastimens Particuliers, Paris, 1624). Evelyn remarked of Charles II's house at Newmarket that 'many of the rooms had chimnies plac'd in the angles and corners, a mode now introduced by His Majesty which I do at no hand approve of . . . It does only well in very small and trifling rooms, but takes from the state of Greater' (*Evelyn's Diary*, 22 July 1670). However, some chimneypieces were set in strange places. Celia Fiennes saw one 'just under a window' at Wilton at the end of the century, arranged so that 'the tunnells [flues] runnes upon each side'. In another room she saw one alongside a window (*Celia Fiennes*, p. 9).

16. P. de l'Orme, *Le Premier Tome de l'Architecture*, 1567.

17. Apart from Barbet's work, there were those of Pierre Collot, Jean Le Pautre, L. Francart, Jean Marot, Antoine Perretz, Jean Bérain, Pierre Cottart and Pierre Le Pautre, together with quite a few anonymous sets brought out by the print-seller, Langlois.

18. Barbet's book actually contains more than just designs for chimneypieces but it was for these that it became famous. The engravings were by Abraham Bosse whose genre-scenes of Parisian interiors are famous. The 1641 edition was published by Frederik de Wit, a prominent print-seller of Amsterdam, with fresh engravings based on Bosse's by Cornelis Danckerts. 'Mr de Witt, ein alter mann, hat die besten zeichnungen undt kupffer stijckke zu verkauffen, wohnet neben den Statthaus . . .' [Mr de Witt, an old man, has the best drawings and engravings for sale and lives next to the Town Hall] wrote Tessin in 1687 (Gustav Upmark, 'Ein Besuch in Holland 1687', *Oud Holland*, Vol. XVIII, 1900, p. 127).

19. Published by F. de Wit (see previous note) and presumably drawn by C. Danckerts. These simpler designs would have been better suited to a middle-class purse than Barbet's original proposals.

20. *Princess Palatine's Letters* 27 November 1717. One must remember, however, that a charcoal-burning brazier gave off much heat and these could easily be brought into a room when needed.

21. In his foreword, Barbet states that his designs are based on 'ce qu'il y a de beau dans Paris'. The book, incidentally, is dedicated to Cardinal Richelieu.

22. François Blondel, in his *Cours d'Architecture* of 1683, claims that *cheminées à la Romaine* were 'prises entierement dans l'épaiseur du mur' [entirely built into the thickness of the wall] while those *à la Lombarde* were partly so. Those called *à la Française*, however, stood out from the wall. None the less those called by Jean Le Pautre 'à l'Italienne' certainly protruded from the wall and were characterised by their wealth of ornament.

23. Blondel, *op. cit.*

24. See Fiske Kimball, *The Creation of the Rococo*, Philadelphia, 1943. See also his 'The Development of the "Cheminée à la Royale"', *Metropolitan Museum Studies*, Vol. V, 1934, where this phase is surveyed. A piece of bevelled mirror-glass is set into the chimney-breast (beneath a painting) in the Duchess's Private Closet at Ham House, a room created in the 1670s. If it is original, which seems possible, the fashion may have begun earlier than Kimball supposed.

25. *Tessin-Cronström Correspondence*, letter of 2 March 1697. On 11 October Cronström sent from Paris to Tessin in Stockholm 'quelques nouveaux desseins de cheminées' which may very well have been the set of which one is illustrated here (Plate 70).

26. *Pepys' Diary*, 19 January 1666.

27. R. T. Gunther, *The Architecture of Sir Roger Pratt*, Oxford, 1928, p. 192. Incidentally, Pratt gave instructions that the fireplace in his Great Parlour was 'for whiting' (i.e. to be white-washed) and this was probably the normal treatment for fireplaces in his day.

28. *Chetham Society Journal*, 1844. 'Travels in Holland . . . of Sir William Brereton, Bt.' Brereton explains how to mend any tiles that get chipped. 'if any part of the corners break out, there is plaister of Paris powder, which is to be made as it were pap, and instantly with the point of a knife laid on; let it dry, and when it is dry, form it and scrape it even with a chisel or sharp knife. To cleanse it and even it, use a dog-fish's skin, or for want thereof, hair-cloth [i.e. horse-hair cloth].'

29. Geoffrey Beard, *Decorative Plasterwork in Great Britain*, London, 1975; G. Bankart, *The Art of the Plasterer*, London, 1909; Mr Jourdain, *English Decoration and Furniture . . . 1500–1650*, London, 1924; A. Blunt, *Art and Architecture in France, 1500–1700*, 2nd edition, 1970; J. Rosenberg, S. Slive, E. H. Ter Kuile, *Dutch Art and Architecture, 1600–1800*, 1966; J. Summerson, *Architecture in Britain, 1530–1830*, 5th ed., 1969.

30. *Livre de divers ornemens . . . de l'invention de Jean Cotelle, peintre ordinaire du Roy*, was published about 1640 but a group of his actual drawings for ceilings (some of them subsequently engraved for the book) may have been in the possession of Inigo Jones or John Webb (see Chapter II, note 16).

31. It is possible that the Parlour at the old house at Chatsworth which was 'fayre waynscotted with whitewood' (*Chatsworth Invt., 1601*) may have had untreated white pine panelling. What is more, the room from Haynes Grange, which probably dates from about 1620 and may have been designed by Inigo Jones, is entirely faced with red pine that seems never to have been painted. If so, it must be exceptional. Could Inigo Jones, if it was he, have been thinking of rooms he had seen in Italy panelled with cypress wood? (The room is now in the Victoria and Albert Museum; see H. Clifford Smith, *The Haynes Grange Room*, London, 1935.)

32. When varnished, oak retains its light honey-colour and does not turn grey, as happens if it is left to itself, or go dark brown like molasses, which is the result of dirt becoming embedded in layers of polishing wax. Celia Fiennes saw panelling at Broadlands that was 'wanscoated and varnished' while the drawing room at Lady Donegal's house was likewise finished. (*Celia Fiennes*, pp. 85 and 90). Some panelling at Wimbledon House in 1649 was varnished green and decorated with golden stars and crosses. Was the varnish tinted or was there a green ground under a clear varnish? (See M. Jourdain, *English Decoration and Furniture of the Early Renaissance*, London, 1924, p. 96.)

33. John Evelyn, *Sylva*, London, 1664.

34. The Grand Dauphin had a closet made for his personal use at Meudon which was panelled in this manner in the 1690s (Comte Paul Biver, *Histoire du Château de Meudon*, Paris, 1923, Chap. XI).

35. *Chatsworth Invt., 1601*.

36. One of the most ambitious surviving schemes in this technique is the Inlaid Room from Sizergh Castle which dates from prior to 1582. When a panel was cleaned in 1968, the original contrast between the woods forming the white tendrils and black leaves, all set in the honey-coloured grounds, appeared decidedly bold. (See the Victoria and Albert Museum monograph, *The Inlaid Room from Sizergh Castle*, London, 1928.)

37. *Chatsworth Invt., 1601* and *Cockesden Invt., 1610*. It has been suggested (*Country Life*, 8 December, 1928, p. 813) that 'French panell' had mitred joints instead of the older mortised joints but compilers of inventories normally pick on some obvious feature to help identify an object. This tends to mean that they pick on a decorative characteristic rather than a technical feature.

38. *Celia Fiennes*, p. 153.

39. William Lower, *A Relation . . . of the Voiage and Residence which . . . Charles II . . . hath made in Holland . . . 1660*, The Hague, 1660. The Mauritshuis, built for Johan Maurits who was known as 'the Brazilian' on account of his exploits in that part of the world, was gutted by fire in the eighteenth century. I am grateful to Professor Lunsingh Scheurleer for throwing light on this matter.

40. *Celia Fiennes*, p. 56.

41. R. T. Gunther, *The Architecture of Sir Roger Pratt*, Oxford, 1928.

42. Sir Balthazar Gerbier, *Counsel and Advise to All builders*, 1663.

43. E. Croft-Murray, *Decorative Painting in England*, Vol. I, London, 1962, p. 199.

44. *Celia Fiennes*, pp. 85 and 90.

45. An important survey is being carried out by Mr Ian Bristow at the Institute of Advanced Architectural Studies at York University under the enlightened patronage of Messrs. Berger Paints, Ltd. Interesting work is also being done at the National Museum in Copenhagen and at several centres in the United States. A helpful but still very tentative essay appeared in J. Fowler and J. Cornforth, *English Decoration in the 18th Century*, London, 1974, Chap. 5, but great advances in this field can be expected soon.

46. *Tessin-Cronström Correspondence*, letter of 19 April 1693.

47. *Hardwick Invt., 1601* and Gunther, *op. cit.*, p. 189.

48. See Anne Berendsen and others, *Fliesen*, Munich, 1964, which has a chapter on wall-tiles and many excellent illustrations. See also Arthur Lane, *A Guide to the Collection of Tiles* (Victoria and Albert Museum) London, 1960; Dingeman Korf, *Dutch Tiles*, London, 1963; and C. H. de Jonge, *Oud-Nederlandsche Majolica en Delftsch Aardewerk*, Amsterdam, 1947.

49. See Arthur Lane, 'Daniel Marot: Designer of Delft Vases . . . at Hampton Court,' *The Connoisseur*, March 1949.

50. For information about the *Trianon de*

Porcelaine, see Alfred Marie, *La Naissance de Versailles*, II, Paris, 1968, pp. 197–225; see also note 19 to chapter 1.

51. *Havard, 'Miroir'*.

52. S. Roche, *Miroirs*, Paris, 1956, p. 22. The mirror was presented to the Queen (herself an Italian princess, of course) by the Republic of Venice in celebration of the birth of her son, the future Louis XIII.

53. Francis Bacon, *Essayes*, 1625, XLV, 'Of Building'.

54. *Havard, 'Miroir'*.

55. Elphège Frémy, *Histoire de la manufacture royale des glaces au 17e et 18e siècle*, Paris, 1909, p. 16.

56. *Ibid*., p. 17.

57. *Havard, 'Glace'*.

58. Geoffrey Wills, *English Looking-glasses*, London, 1965, p. 16.

59. *Tessin-Cronström Correspondence*, letter of 22 March 1697.

60. *Celia Fiennes*, p. 153.

61. G. Upmark, 'Ein Besuch in Holland 1687 . . .,' *Oud Holland*, 18, 1900.

62. The tariff in 1682 in France was:

10 × 10 *pouces* . . .	9 *livres*
20 × 20 *pouces* . . .	24 *livres*
30 × 30 *pouces* . . .	70 *livres*

In 1699 it was as follows:

15 × 12 *pouces* . . .	7 *livres*
40 × 30 *pouces* . . .	150 *livres*
70 × 45 *pouces* . . .	750 *livres*
90 × 55 *pouces* . . .	3,000 *livres*

A *pouce* was approximately equal to an inch. When one considers that the services of a good cook could be had for 300 *livres* per annum while a serving girl would work for 30 *livres*, and a shop with a room over is known to have cost 348 *livres*, one can more easily appreciate how the Comtesse de Fièsque came to sell an unfruitful estate in order to buy a mirror and why Louis XIV, who spent no less than 56,653 *livres* on mirror-glass in the year 1671 alone, arranged to pay for it at a 30 per cent discount. At least one lady sought the King's permission to buy her mirrors at the royal rate.

63. J. Barralet, *La Verrerie en France*, Paris, 1953, p. 83.

64. For information on this whole matter, see the works of Frémy and Barralet mentioned above.

65. Frémy, *op. cit*., p. 197.

66. The Venetian Ambassador to England at the time commented that 'by this order they also mean to prohibit looking-glasses, of which they make a quantity here' (Wills, *op. cit.*, p. 42).

67. Wills, *op. cit.*, pp. 43–6.

68. The French royal manufactury was permitted to make 'ornements composés de glaces plates'. The flat pieces of glass could be 'coupées par bandes et par morceaux, figurez et taillez à facettes ou à bizeaux avec baguettes mince ou tortillés, colonnes torses, frontons et couronnements de toutes sortes de figures sur fonds colorez ou autrement' [cut into strips and small pieces, shaped and facetted or bevelled, with narrow or twisted beading, spiral columns, pediments and crestings of all kinds of figures on coloured or other grounds]. (Frémy, *op. cit.*, p. 78.) There are inset mirrors with such slips still to be seen at Hampton Court, some being of blue glass.

69. Cronström reported to Stockholm that in Paris there was a craftsman who knew the secret of how to 'creuser dans la glace: cela fait un assez joly effet' [engrave the glass: this produces a very pretty effect] and was known as 'ouvrage à la Mayenne' (*Tessin-Cronström Correspondence*, letter of 19 April 1693). Gerreit Jensen supplied 'a Peer Glass for ye Great Closett [at Hampton Court] with wrought work and Ingraved . . . £55' (R. W. Symonds, 'English Looking-glasses', *The Connoisseur*, May 1950).

70. *Havard, 'Miroir'*.

71. *Havard, 'Glace'*.

72. *Havard, 'Miroir'*.

73. R. Edwards, 'A Mirror with Painted Decoration', *Country Life*, 26 October 1935, quoting Faulkener's *History and Antiquities of Kensington*, 1820. Vertue also mentions 'the most curious of all is the Looking-Glass at Kensington House, which he [Monnoyer] painted for the late Queen Mary, of Glorious Memory, her Majesty sitting by him all the While'. A panel of what could be an example of Monnoyer's work is in the Victoria and Albert Museum; there are other sections in a closet off the Gallery at Syon House, and at Melbourne House.

74. H. Sauval, *Histoire et recherches des antiquités de la ville de Paris*, 1724 (but written before 1670), Livre VII, Vol. II, pp. 200–1.

75. See J. P. Babelon, *Demeures Parisiennes sous Henri IV et Louis XIII*, Paris, 1965, p. 190. Le Muet illustrates such a window, and explains how to calculate its proportions, in his *Divers Traictes* of 1646.

76. L. Savot, *L'Architecture Francoise des bastimens*

particuliers, Paris, 1624, Chapter VII, entitled 'De la position des membres du bastiments'; and Sir Henry Wotton, *Elements of Architecture*, 1624.

77. 'Three window shutes' (*Walton Invt., 1624*), '2 shuting windowes' (*Marton Invt., 1605*), 'wainscott shutts to both ye windowes' at King's College, Cambridge (*Provost of King's Invt., 1660*). '2 wyndow leaves and there wooden barres' are mentioned in the *Cockesden Invt. of 1610*, one only needs a locking bar for an interior shutter. In the same inventory mention is made of the 'double leaves to the wyndowe' in the Hall, which seems to indicate a paired arrangement rather than two tiers, while there was only 'one leafe to the other wyndowe'. 'Wyndowe levys of tymbre be made of bourdis joyned together with keys of tree let into them,' tells W. Horman, *Vulgaria*, 1619.

78. *Hatfield Priory Invt., 1629*. Also 'The wyndow wainescotted wth. two drawing wyndowes' (*Ingatestone Invt., 1600*); 'a draw window' (*Provost of King's Invt., 1660*; bill of 1616–17); 'drawers for the windowe (*Standen Lordship Invt., 1623*). The analogy is presumably with 'drawing the curtains' but it may be that the term was used in reference to some form of sliding shutter. Horman (*op. cit.*) says he had 'many prety windowes shette with levys going up and downe . . .'.

79. *Havard*, 'Abat-jours'.

80. That certain windows at Ham House were double-glazed can be deduced from the accounts for 1674, the number of glass panes supplied being far greater for the rooms where the windows were thus furnished.

81. *Tessin's Visit, 1687* and *Celia Fiennes*, p. 339. The earliest mention of double glazing in Stockholm dates from 1729 (see G. Hazelius Berg, *Gardiner och Gardinuppsättningar*, Nordiska Museet, Stockholm, 1962, p. 12). An *Ode à l'Hiver*, written by Chapelle in 1520, tells how:

> On garnit les appartments
> De doubles chassis et de nattes,
> Et les grands foyers s'allumants.

[Apartments are furnished with double window-frames and mats, fires in the great hearths are kindled.] Although these 'double window-frames' may *both* have contained panes of glass, it is more likely that the inner frame had matting stretched over it.

82. In 1579 there was a legal wrangel as to whether glass windows were fixtures or movable chattels, and it was then claimed that 'without glass is no house perfect' (Nathaniel Lloyd, *History of the English House*, London, 1931, p. 71). However, stables, out-houses and many places in the country no doubt still had less expensive forms of 'glazing'. The stables at Versailles had panes of oiled cloth. Animal membrane (the diaphragms of cattle were best), oiled cloth and oiled paper (strengthened by two wires fixed diagonally from opposite corners of the frame) were all used for this purpose. 'Horne in windows is now quite laid downe in every place, so our Lattices [of thinly riven oak woven chequerwise, or of wicker] are also growne into lesse use because Glass is become so plentiful . . .' wrote William Harison in his *Description of England* in 1577, and by the beginning of the seventeenth century such wooden lattice-work can only have been used in humble dwellings. Nevertheless, it needs to be noted that the inventory of a house in Oxfordshire, drawn up in 1583, still drew attention to the fact that there was glass in three of the windows—implying that this was rather special. The fact that the glass windows at Alnwick Castle and at the Earl of Northumberland's other northern houses were 'taken doune and lade up in safety' when his lordship was not in residence has, incidentally, been taken to show that glass was rare even in grand establishments in sixteenth-century England but the actual passage from the survey of Alnwick in 1567 explains that it was because of the 'extreme winds' of Northumberland which caused the glazed windows to 'decay and waste'. It was cheaper to 'set uppe of newe with smale charges to his Lp. [Lordship] wher[eas] now the decaye thereof shall be verie costlie and chargeable to be repayred'. (*The Regulations and Establishment of the Household of Henry Algenon Percy, the Fifth Earl of Northumberland . . .*, London, 1827.)

83. Walter Gedde, *A Book of Sundry Draughts principally serving for Glaziers*, 1613. Many large houses at this period (see e.g. *Chatsworth Invt., 1601*) had a 'plumerie' and it is noteworthy that the task of a plumber in those days was as much concerned with repairing leaded windows as with the roofs and drainpipes.

84. M. Jourdain, *English Decoration and Furniture of the Early Renaissance*, London, 1924, p. 127. Some specimens may be seen in the Victoria and Albert Museum.

85. J. P. Babelon, *Demeures Parisiennes sous Henri IV et Louis XIII*, Paris, 1965, p. 78.

86. *Havard*, 'Chassis'.

87. *Tessin-Cronström Correspondence*, letter of 19 April 1693.

88. The author's translation from the original German which is given by Gustav Upmark, 'Ein Besuch in Holland, 1687', *Oud Holland*, Vol. XVIII, 1900, pp. 123–4.

89. Ada Polak, *Glass, its Makers and its Public*, London, 1975, Chap. 13: 'a Sash Window and Frame with Weights lynes and Pullies' (Windsor Castle Accounts, 1686–88).

90. According to Nathaniel Lloyd, *History of the English House*, London, 1931, p. 118. It will have been noticed that Cronström explained how the counter-balanced form could be fixed 'sans l'accrocher'.

91. R. K. Marshall, *Life in the Household of the Duchess Anne* [of Hamilton], London, 1973, p. 174; and Lloyd, *loc. cit.* Sash-windows with 'brass pulleys' were fitted at Ham House in 1673, incidentally, but no mention is made of weights there either.

92. R. K. Marshall, *loc. cit.*

93. Martin Lister, *A Journey to Paris*, London, 1691, p. 191. Publication of the researches of Mr H. J. Louw, a Dutch architectural historian, into the early history of the sash-window is eagerly awaited as this work goes to press. He is convinced that references to strings and pulleys do concern counter-balanced sashes in spite of the fact that weights are not mentioned, and he may well be right. He believes counter-balanced sashes were invented about 1670.

94. William Harison, *op. cit.*

95. R. T. Gunther, *The Architecture of Sir Roger Pratt*, Oxford, 1928, p. 72. Sir Roger Pratt was writing in 1660. In 1664 the rate was much the same, according to Sir Balthazar Gerbier, *op. cit.*, p. 83: The best French glasse . . . sixteen pence a foot

The best Englishe glasse . . . seven pence a foot
Ordinary glass for quarries . . . five pence half penny a foot.

Savot, in *L'Architecture Françoise des bastimens particuliers*, Paris, 1624, has a section on glass made in Normandy and in Lorraine. The former was of better quality and was sold in baskets each containing twenty-four circular pieces of blown glass about 70 centimetres in diameter.

96. Sir Balthazar Gerbier, *Counsel and Advise to All Builders*, 1663, p. 22. He lists the prices per square foot of various types of stone paving then commonly used in England:

Portland stone . . . 8d.
Black and White marble, laid in London . . . 2s. 6d.
Black and White marble, laid in the provinces . . . 3s. 6d.
Namur stone, grey and white . . . as above
Rans[rance] . . . 5s. mixed with white
Rans and Purple . . .
White marble pavement . . . 3s.
Black marble pavement . . . 1s. 6d.
Black and White polished . . . 5s.
Red and White polished . . . 5s.
Black glazed Holland pan-tiles . . . £6 per 100.

97. 'Hollandische Floorsteenen' and 'neiderländische Flores' are terms occuring in late sixteenth and seventeenth-century German documents. Perhaps the 'steentjes' of Dutch sources were identical. Gerbier (see previous note) spoke of 'black glazed Holland pan-tiles'.

98. Chas. Phillips, *History of the Sackville Family*, London, *c.* 1928, p. 391; and *Havard* 'Carreau'. The tiles at Knole cost 6s. 8d. each so were probably rather handsomely decorated.

99. See C. H. de Jonge, *Oud-Nederlandsche Majolica en Delftsch Aardewerk*, Amsterdam, 1947; M. Boyken, *fliesen . . . de 17de und 18de Jahrhundert*, Darmstadt, 1954; and Anne Berendsen, *Fliesen*, Munich, 1964. The last has excellent illustrations in colour of tiled floors.

100. F. H. Garner, *English Delftware*, London, 1948, p. 2.

101. M. Jourdain, *English Decoration and Furniture of the Early Renaissance*, London, 1924.

102. This recipe was given me by Mrs Ellen Sørensen who had treated floors in this manner as a girl in provincial Denmark.

103. 'Fuller's earth and fine sand preserves the original colour and does not leave a white appearance as soap does,' advised Susanna Whatman in her *Housekeeping Book (1776–1800)*, edited by Thomas Balston, London, 1956. All her rooms were to be dry-scrubbed with white sand regularly. An American, writing of the town of Boscawen in 1800, states that no carpets were used there but the floors were 'strewn with clean white sand . . . and swept into curved lines, scrolls, and whorls, by a broom'. Another American, writing in the 1880s, tells how 'many years ago the kitchens and perhaps the sitting rooms were sanded over after

being scoured with sand and water. The sand, when the floor was dry, was scattered all over the floor and the next day was carefully and lightly swept in herringbone shape—this looking quite pretty' (see Nina Fletcher Little, *Floor Coverings in New England before 1850*, Old Sturbridge Village, Massachusetts, 1967).

104. *Tessin-Cronström Correspondence*, letter of 10 July 1693.

105. *Tessin-Cronström Correspondence*, letter of 22 May 1693.

106. 'Cette manière de placage est venue d'Italie' [This form of veneering comes from Italy] (Sauval, *Antiquités de Paris*, [written 1669–70], Paris, 1924, XIV, p. 17). A new monograph on decorated floors, H. Kier, *Schmuckfussboden in Renaissance und Barock*, Munich, 1976, does not seem to contradict what has been said in the present section but complements it substantially.

107. O. Millar, 'The Notebooks of Richard Symonds', *Studies in Renaissance and Baroque Art*, London, 1967. The floor is also described by Martin Lister (see note 108).

108. Dr Martin Lister, *A Journey to Paris*, London, 1699, p. 41. He adds that parquet floors 'in London and elsewhere in Paris . . . prove so noisy to tread on and faulty that they are in a few years intolerable'.

109. P. Verlet, *Versailles*, Paris, 1961, p. 33. See also D. Alcouffe, 'Les Macés, ébénistes et peintres', *Bulletin de la Société de l'Histoire de l'Art Français*, Paris, 1972, in which he assembles much information about the marquetry floors of Macé and others. Noteworthy are the careful instructions given for the laying of the intricate marquetry floor in the *Petite Galerie* at Versailles in 1685 (p. 63, f.n. 6); the marquetry of some dozen sorts of wood was to be laid over a complete new sub-floor of ancient oak boards and no singeing or dying was to be used.

110. See Gillian Wilson, 'Boulle', *Furniture History*, Vol. VIII, 1972. He also made floors for the Queen and the Dauphin.

111. *Orange Invts.*, I, p. 267).

112. John Aubrey, 'The Natural History of Wiltshire', Bodleian Library MSS. Aubrey 1 & 2.

113. The bill for laying this floor survives. The floor of the raised bed-alcove was provided with 'two leather covers for the step' by way of protection for this expensive feature when the room was not in use. The Closet also had a 'leather cover for the flore.' Evelyn noted that some floors at the Duke of Norfolk's new house at Weybridge were 'parqueted with cedar, yew and cypress' but, since he does not bother to describe them more fully, it seems probable that they were not as elaborate as those at Ham. (*Evelyn's Diary*, 23 August 1678).

114. *D.E.F.*, Illus. 8, 'Tables, Side-, Console-, and Pier-.'

115. See Fowler and Cornforth, *English Decoration in the 18th Century*, London, 1974, Plate 193.

116. The December issue of the *Mercure Galant* for 1673 told its readers that 'les gens de qualité ne veulent plus de tapis de pied dans leurs alcoves à cause de la poudre qu'ils conservent. C'est pourquoy ils les font parqueter de bois de diverses couleurs et de pieces de rapport' [people of quality no longer want foot carpets in their alcoves on account of the way they harbour dust. That is why they have them parquetted with wood of different colours and with marquetry].

117. In the introduction to G. Lizzani's *Il Mobile Romano*, Milan, 1970, A. Gonzalez Palacios discusses certain furniture designed by Roman architects and illustrates a design for candlestands by Algardi (Plate XIV).

118. See p. 37 and note 17 to Chapter II and also p. 185.

119. When Nicodemus Tessin visited Versailles in 1687 he was much impressed by the silver furniture—as was the intention. The *Grande Galerie* (*des Glaces*) contained no less than seventy-six pieces comprising massive tables, candlestands, great urns and basins, stools and benches. Some were up to nine feet high. Tessin lists 167 items of silver furniture as being in the State Apartments (*Tessin's Visit, 1687*, p. 29). However, it must not be thought that it was only the King who had silver furniture in France. La Grande Madamoiselle had several imposing pieces in her apartment at the Palais Royal in 1679 and Monsieur, the King's brother, had more at Saint-Cloud; Madame du Lude is reported to have owned silver furniture which had cost her no less than 27,000 *écus* and Monsieur de Lavardin, according to Madame de Sevigné, had tables, candlestands, chandeliers and fire-dogs of this precious metal (*Havard*, 'Argent'). Earlier in the century, Sully saw some silver furniture at the house of the Comptroller-General of Castile and Cardinal Mazarin also owned several pieces. The fashion had spread to

England. Charles I owned a folding table 'covered all over with silver plate ingraved' (C. C. Oman, *English Domestic Silver*, London, 1965, p. 183) and this is a reminder that most silver furniture consisted of thin sheets of the metal riveted to a wooden structure. A table, looking-glass and pair of candlestands given to Charles II by the City of London and now at Windsor Castle belongs to this category (Oman, *op. cit.*, pp. 183–4; see also his 'An XVIIIth Century Record of Silver Furniture at Windsor Castle', *Country Life*, 6 December 1930). What was remarkable about the Versailles furniture, on the other hand, was that it was apparently all of solid or 'massy' silver. Celia Fiennes visited the 'Silver Roome' at Lord Chesterfield's house at Bretby in 1696 and noted that the 'stands, table and fire utensils were all of massy silver' (*Celia Fiennes*, p, 171) and a table and looking-glass presented to William III by the City of London is of the same solid class. But a tax was introduced in Great Britain in 1697 which made it prohibitively expensive to have large objects of silver. As Celia Fiennes said of the Bretby items 'when plate was in nomination to pay tax, the Earle of Chester-field sold it all' (see J. F. Hayward, 'Silver Furniture', *Apollo*, LXVII, pp. 71, 124, 153 and 220). In France in 1690 it was even forbidden by law to cause large items of silver to be made. The result of these measures was two-fold: it gave an immense impetus to the faïence industry that now found great incentive to produce large, showy dishes, ewers and basins which could stand on buffets, replacing the silver pieces that had been melted down. And it greatly encouraged the production of carved furniture with silvering or gilding that looked tolerably like real metal furniture but was more sympathetic to the touch and tended to be more graceful. For information on Dutch silver furniture, incidentally, see the article by Th. H. Lunsingh Scheurleer in *Opusculum in Honorem Carl Hernmarck*, Stockholm, 1966, pp. 141–158.

120. 'Devant les deux pilliers entre les croisées' of the Salon de Mars at Versailles, for instance, 'il y a de grands miroires, tables et guéridons d'argent avec leurs flambeaux dessus . . .' [In front of the two piers between the windows . . . there are large looking-glasses, tables and candlestands of silver with their candelabra on top . . .], wrote *Tessin* on his *Visit in 1687* (p. 25). These great mirrors, then, were pier-glasses with console-tables below; they were flanked by candlestands

with candlesticks standing on them; and it was all of silver. In addition '. . . la salle est toutte entourée des grands pièces, comme vases, cuves, cassettes et chesnests d'argent d'une pesanteur et grandeur prodigieuse . . .' [the room is furnished all round with large pieces, including urns, cisterns, chests and fire-dogs of silver of prodigious weight and size . . .].

NOTES TO CHAPTER IV

1. Penelope Eames, 'Furniture in England, France and the Netherlands from the Twelfth to the Fifteenth Century', *Furniture History*, XIII, 1977.

2. The contents of each of the twenty-four 'cariages' in the Earl of Northumberland's baggage-train are listed in *The Regulations . . . of the Household of . . . Earl of Northumberland begun in Anno Domini M.D.XII* (1512), London, 1827, pp. 386–91. After 'my Lordes Chariot', the first three carts carried respectively the 'Stuf of the Dynyng Chambre and Gret Chambre,' that of 'my Ladies Chambre' and that of 'the Chambre wher my Lord makes him[self] redy' together with the Gentlewomen's belongings, and 'such Stuf remaynynge in the Wardrobe'. Each class of officer was allocated a cart onto which the appurtenances of their office or the tools of their trade, their beds and bedding, and their personal belongings were packed.

3. One Gentleman Usher was instructed to 'oversee the continewall furnisheinge and cleanely keepinge of all lodgeinges, galleryes, greatchambers, dyneinge rooms, parlours, &c.', although the lord's own lodging was the particular responsibility of the Gentleman of the Chamber. (Viscount Montague's Household Book, 1595, see Sir William H. St. John Hope, *Cowdray and Easebourne Priory*, London, 1919, Appendix II.)

4. The Yeoman Usher of the Great Chamber (the site for ceremonial dining and banqueting) was expected to see that the room was 'orderly prepared . . . wth. tables, stooles, and chayres necessarye for the companye and after dynner, and supper to see them bestowed agayne decentlye into their several rooms [i.e. replaced where they belong]'. (Viscount Montague's Household Book, 1595, *op. cit.*).

5. The Yeoman of the Wardrobe was responsible for the 'furniture of all the chambers in the house, as they be furnishede, and what soever ells

is in the wardrobe [i.e. in store, not in use], and all these things to keepe well, and see there bee noe defectes in any of them, but to be presentlie amendede' ('A Breviate Touching the Order of a Nobleman's House . . . 1605', *Archæologia*, XIII, 1800, pp. 315–89).

6. The Yeoman of the Wardrobe who received the instructions in the previous note was expected to mend all the furnishings 'unlesse it bee joyners woorke as tables, stooles, bedsteedes, etc. which hee is to cause a joyner to mende'.

7. A law was enacted in 1750 granting certain privileges to the 'Art, Trade or Mystery of an Upholder otherwise called Upholsterers within the said City' of London. (See Karin Walton, 'The Worshipful Company of Upholders of the City of London', *Furniture History*, IX, 1973.)

8. 'This man Francis Oddy was servant to my father many years & hath since served me . . . He serves me in the way of upholsterer when there is a need to furnish the Lodging rooms and dress them up . . .' (written in 1638, *The Diary of Sir Henry Slingsby of Scriven . . .*, ed. Daniel Parsons, London, 1836, p. 5).

9. In 1613, for example, a payment is recorded to 'the uphoulster for sylck ffringe and making up chaires and stooles and window cusshen of damask', while Lord Cork paid 'Mr Argyll the uphoster' for wall-hangings, bedding and cushions in 1628. (*D.E.F.*, 'Upholder').

10. We do not yet know sufficient about the careers of any seventeenth-century upholsterers to give concrete examples but we know, for example, that Chippendale started off as a cabinetmaker but, in his will, he called himself 'upholsterer'. The latter was generally a far more lucrative trade.

11. *Ingatestone Invt., 1600.*

12. *Northampton Invt., 1614.*

13. *Havard, 'Broderie'.*

14. *Historical manuscripts Commission*, Vol. VI, p. 275, De L'Isle and Dudley 1955; letter from the Countess of Leicester to W. Hawkins, Paris, 1640. She was describing the kind of *ameublement* to be seen in fashionable interiors like those illustrated by Bosse, comprising a bed, arm-chairs, 'backstools' and stools.

15. *Ham Invt., c. 1654.*

16. *Devon Invts.*

17. *Easton Lodge Invt., 1637.*

18. For example, Madame de Maintenon's bedchamber at St Cloud, furnished at the end of the century, had a bed hung with a green and gold damask lined with red damask, and these two materials were used for all the other furnishings in various ways. The counterpoint had a green and gold panel with red pendant edges (*pentes*) falling down the sides. The wall-hangings were of the two materials made up in alternating bands. The day-bed was dressed *en suite* and stood in a niche hung like the walls. The seat-furniture (three armchairs, twelve folding stools and four benches) were covered with the red damask framed (impaned) with a border of the green and gold. The window-curtains, portières and a five-leaf screen were likewise made up with the two materials, as was the small coverlet she used for covering her legs, as it was seemly for a woman to do when reclining on a day-bed. The only items that broke the sequence were the red cloth put on the table when the King had a Cabinet meeting, and the red velvet covering of the close-stool. The rest of the furniture comprised two small walnut desks inlaid with pewter, the writing-table of *bois de violette* (kingwood?) and two looking-glasses hanging on the wall (see *Havard*, 'Chambre'). So greatly did Madame de Maintenon love this room that the Duc d'Antin had an exact replica of it made in order that she would feel quite at home when she visited his château in 1707. He even had the markings in her favourite books copied.

19. The *Ham Invts.* of 1677, 1679 and 1683 are to be published by the Victoria and Albert Museum.

20. For example, the Duchess had a red and yellow damask *ameublement* in her Bedchamber in 1677 and 1679. By 1683 the whole set had been exchanged for a set that was red and black, fringed blue and black. The hangings from the first set were used in the Duke's Dressing Room next door while the rest of the set was sent up to the Lauderdales' house in Whitehall. The Lauderdales were in the height of fashion; the Provosts of King's College, Cambridge, were probably not. At any rate the bed-hangings in the Provost's Lodge that had been acquired in 1609–10 were not replaced until 1631. *Provost of Kings Invt., 1660.*

21. For example, a silk damask might cost between 20 and 25 *livres* an ell (say 1.20 metres) in Paris (G. Mongrédien, *La Vie quotidienne sous Louis XIV*, Paris, 1948) while crimson damask suitable for use in the royal apartments at Hampton Court cost 22 shillings in 1699 and

green taffeta, a plain material, cost 16 shillings a yard (*Hampton Court Estimates, 1699*). A very richly brocaded silk, with much gold thread, might cost anything up to 100 shillings a yard. It is recorded that a certain French silk-weaver completed four pieces of silk totalling 393 *aunes* (one *aune* or ell equalled about 46 inches) in nine months—say 11 els per week or 84 inches a day. This was good going for a figured material; a plain material could be woven much more speedily but a complicated one with much brocading might proceed at the rate of only a few inches a day. The weaver concerned was working in the eighteenth century but there is no reason to suppose a seventeenth century weaver could work any faster. (See L. Bosseboeuf, 'La fabrique de soieries de Tours au XVIII et XIXe siècles', *Mémoires de la Société Archéologique de Touraine*, XLI, 1900, p. 349).

22. At Hardwick an embroidered bed had 'a curtain of darnix and a peece of buckerom about the bed to cover yt'. (*Hardwick Invt. 1601*). Daniel Marot shows an iron curtain rod protruding conspicuously round the tester of some of his beds from which the 'case-curtains' could be hung, 'pour conserver le lit contre la poussière' [in order to protect the bed from dust] as it says on the drawing reproduced in Plate 144.

23. The French called such cases *housses* and this term occurs in the *Cowdray Inventory of 1682* as 'a housse of printed paragon'.

24. At Chatsworth, *Celia Fiennes* (p. 100) saw that 'there were no beds up'. Presumably this means that their hangings had been removed and only the wooden structures remained in place.

25. The *Cockesden Inventory of 1610* records that one bed had its 'testerne and valence covered with a sheet', while *Celia Fiennes* (p. 100) saw 'clean sheets pinn'd about the beds and hangings' when she visited Ashstead Park at the end of the century.

26. Le Comte de laborde, *Le Palais Mazarin*, Paris, 1846, p. 299.

27. William Karlson, *Ebba Brahe's Hem . . .*, Lund, 1943.

28. *Ham Invts. 1677, 1679 & 1683*.

29. Laborde, *op. cit.*, p. 301.

30. *Hardwick Invt., 1601*.

31. *Havard*, 'Lit'.

32. *Cockesden Invt., 1626*.

NOTES TO CHAPTER V

1. Mrs Florence Montgomery, formerly curator of textiles at the Henry F. du Pont Museum at Winterthur, Delaware, and now textile consultant at the Metropolitan Museum, New York, has in manuscript form a glossary of historic textile terms which it is to be hoped will soon be published. The Department of Textiles at the Victoria and Albert Museum have a working index of such terms. Mrs Montgomery made numerous helpful comments on this chapter before it went to print, for which I am exceedingly grateful. The responsibility for all the statements made here nevertheless rests entirely with me.

2. This technique is described in most books on historic textiles. For this and related technical questions, see *Notes on Carpet-Knotting and Weaving* (which includes tapestry-woven carpets), Victoria and Albert Museum Handbook, London, 1969. See also François Tabard, 'The Weaver's Art' in *The Art of the Tapestry*, (ed. J. Jobé), London, 1965.

3. See P. Thornton, 'Tapisseries de Bergame', *Pantheon*, VI, XVIII Jahrgang, March, 1960. 'Une pièce de tapisserie de Bergame' is listed in a storeroom at the House of Nassau's residence in Brussels in 1618 (*Orange Invts.*, I, p. 118).

4. The French royal inventories list 160 pieces of hangings of this material 'dont la plus grande partie a esté employée à Versailles et pour les ballets' [of which the majority have been used at Versailles and for ballets] but they were probably not in any of the principal rooms (*Guiffrey, Inventaire*, II, p. 277). *Savary des Bruslons* claims that all artisans or 'gens de basse condition' had this material in their chambers—presumably only in Paris.

5. The crowned 'L' form is illustrated by Thornton, *loc. cit..* *Savary des Bruslons* (1723) states that *tapisseries de Bergame* also came 'à grandes barres chargées de fleurs & oiseaux, ou d'autres animaux; d'autres à grandes & petites barres unies, sans aucune façon . . .' [with wide stripes on which are flowers and birds; others with plain wide and narrow stripes, without any decorative motives].

6. Hangings thus described were in the room of Monsieur Mancini, in Cardinal Mazarin's apartment at the Louvre (*Mazarin Invt., 1653*).

7. *Savary des Bruslons* says they were also made at Toulouse.

8. The 'Roanischen Tapeten' on the walls of the Palace of Potsdam in the late seventeenth century (*Stengel*, p. 36) were presumably 'hangings from Rouen'. Other German inventories refer to 'geflammte Teppiche' (flamed hangings) which presumably means they had a *point d'Hongrie* pattern that we know was much woven as *tapisserie de Bergame*. At Oranienstein, near Koblenz, there was in 1696 a 'kamer behangsel [set of wall-hangings] Rouans gevlamd tapeet' which must have been of the same class (*Orange Invts.*, II, p. 226). At Copenhagen Castle in 1688 there was likewise some 'fransk kammer haengsel' (French chamber hanging; G. Boesen, 'Kongelige Slotsinteriører omkring 1700', *Til Knud Fabricius*, Copenhagen, 1945) while Swedish inventories of the period make occasional reference to 'franska tapeter' (French hangings), some being specified as having violet stripes or bands while others are described as 'stora, nya grofva franska tapeter' (large, new, coarse French hangings; *Karlson*, p. 41). Some are listed as having silk details (medh silke in Wäfvet) and others had silver and gold flowers (med sölver och guld blommerat). These French hangings were evidently quite elaborate. There is also reference to 'flamska rums tapeter' (Flemish room hangings) which may concern actual Flemish tapestries but could just as well have to do with coarse woven materials of this kind, especially as some are described as being 'hemväfna' (home woven) which suggests these materials were of a relatively simple character.

9. Many hangings listed among the belongings of Charles I are called 'course Elizens' and a reading of the original manuscript shows that this spelling is correct. Could they, all the same, be a mis-transcription of Elbeuf, for no other reference to 'coarse Elizens' seems to have been noted (*Charles I Invts.*, 1649–51)? Maybe the 'Dover stuff' also mentioned in these royal inventories in the same way came from Douai rather than from Dover Castle, as has been suggested. This is pure conjecture but the terms have never been satisfactorily explained.

10. The *Book of Rates of 1582* lists the duties payable on three types of dornix:

Dornix called French dornix . . . 15d/ell.

Dornix with caddas [caddis = linen thread] . . . 10/- the piece of 15 yds.

Dornix with silk . . . 13/- the piece of 15 yds.

The material 'called French Dornix' may have been of a distinctive type, perhaps with large patterns, and may not necessarily have been French in origin. It cost more than the other two classes (20 ells equalled about 15 yards). An Act of 1678 regulating the London cloth markets listed 'Dornix' with 'Birdsey[e] Carpeting, Bristol Carpeting and all sorts of Carpeting' on the one hand and as 'Darnix, narrow, for Garments' on the other—indicating a wide range of qualities (I am grateful to Miss Wendy Hefford for drawing my attention to this reference in W. Maitland, *The History of London*, 1761, Vol. I, p. 465).

11. Hangings of 'stript darnax' are mentioned in the *Cockesden Inventory of 1626*, as well as a dornix table-carpet 'of blue and white birdwork' and a coverlet of 'birdwork'. A room at Clonmell in 1684 was hung with yellow dornix 'with white flowers'. As shown in note 5 above, *tapisserie de Bergame* could be striped, or decorated with birds or flowers. (*Clonmell Invt.*, *1684*, National Library of Ireland, MS 2522, kindly communicated by Desmond Fitz-Gerald, Knight of Glin).

12. For example, the *Countess of Leicester's Invt.*, *of 1634* shows that her ladyship had true tapestry in her own chamber but her daughter had hangings of dornix.

13. See the *Countess of Leicester's Invt.*, *1634*. The material is also mentioned in the *Charles I Invts.*, *1649–51*. Samples of eighteenth-century Kidderminster stuffs are to be seen in the Berch Collection in the Nordiska Museum, Stockholm; some are strongly banded by coloured wefts and have a warp pattern.

14. *Tart Hall Invt.*, *1641* and *Dyrham Invt.*, *1703*.

15. A 'table-carpet' might be an Oriental knotted-pile rug but it might equally well be an embroidered cloth or of a rich velvet trimmed with fringe. There was a 'carpet of black velvet for the little bord' in the 'Chiefe Chamber' at *Hengrave Hall* (*Invt.*, *of 1603*), for instance.

16. See note 2 above.

17. It is recorded that the Elector of Brandenburg still kept his Turkish rugs in his *Wunderkammer*—in his Cabinet of Curiosities—in 1617 (*Stengel*, p. 50).

18. In an inventory of a house at Marseilles in 1587, mention is made of 'trois masquetz neufs' (*Havard*, 'Moquette'). *Savary des Bruslons*, under the heading 'Tapis', lists *mosquets* as one of the three types of Oriental carpet available in Paris in his day (1723), the others being 'tapis de pic' and 'Cadene', but he fails to explain what they were

like. Several 'Musketta carpets' are listed in the *Gosfield Inventory of 1638*; some had 'redd grounds'. They seem to have been small; one lay on a table and two together were valued at only £1.

19. There is a famous example at Hardwick (see M. H. Beattie, 'Antique Rugs at Hardwick Hall', *Oriental Art*, Vol. V, No. 2, 1959). In the *Charles I Invts., 1649–51* we find 'two verie rich carpetts of Persian makeing, the ground of them gould & silver, wrought in workes of silver and silkes of sundry collors'. Some of Louis XIV's 'tapis de Perse' were also described as being 'estoffe razé, le milieu fonds d'or, avec quatre tigres qui devorent quatre cerfs' [a flat material i.e. with only a shallow pile], the centre with a gold ground, with [representations of] four tigers devouring stags] (*Guiffrey, Inventaire*, I, p. 381). Fouquet likewise had a 'tapy de Perse de soye' (*Havard*, 'Perse') which he very sensibly had lined with black cloth (doublé de thoille noire).

20. Lady Dorchester, for instance, owned several Eastern carpets but only one 'long Pertian carpett of 6 yards long and two and a half broad'. It was valued at £38, which was a lot of money. (*Gosfield Invt., 1638*.)

21. Sir Philip Sidney wrote to a friend in 1602 that he had 'brought a Turkey carpet for my Lord Bergavenny, seven Dutch ells [about sixteen feet] long; it cost £27 sterling but is esteemed very fine and well worth the money' (S. W. Beck, *The Draper's Dictionary*, 1884, 'Carpet'). If it really was Turkish and not Persian, this might well have been an Ushak carpet. Lady Dorchester owned '2 Egiptian carpetts' valued at £10.10s. od. (see the previous note); Louis XIV owned a 'tapis du Kaire' (*Guiffrey, Inventaire*, I, p. 378) and *Charles I (Invt., 1659–51)* had 'one ould Carew Carpett' in his collection, valued at only £4. Carpets described as *Cairine, Kerrein*, and *Querin* occur in English and French inventories every now and then. For surveys of the use of Near Eastern carpets in Europe during the Middle Ages and later, see K. Erdmann, *Europe und der Orientteppich*, Mainz, 1962 and P. M. Campana, *Il Tappeto Orientale*, Milan, 1945.

22. They were made principally at Lahore (see J. Irwin, 'The Indian Textile Trade in the Seventeenth Century', *The Journal of Indian Textile History*, Vol. I, 1958).

23. See E. Kuehnel, *Catalogue of Spanish Rugs*, The Textile Museum, Washington, 1953.

24. See C. E. C. Tattersall, *A History of British Carpets*, revised by S. Reed, Leigh-on-Sea, 1966, pls. 2, 3 and 5.

25. *Havard*, 'Tapis'.

26. *Guiffrey, Inventaire*, I, p. 387. The bill for the *Galerie d'Apollon* carpets was paid in 1666. One is illustrated by M. Jarry, *The Carpets of Manufactory de la Savonnerie*, Leigh-on-Sea, 1966, fig. 11. Some of the carpets 'façon de Perse' woven at the Louvre (before the two factories were merged) were, however, of silk with gold brocading— like actual Persian court carpets.

27. Jarry, *op. cit.*, figs. 13–17.

28. A document of the 1680s refers to chairs of 'setwork (commonly called Turkey-work chairs)', see R. W. Symonds, 'English Cane Chairs', *The Connoisseur*, March and May 1951.

29. *Northampton Invt., 1614*. In the same room was 'a foot carpett of Turky Worke, the ground redd and yelowe' which may, on the other hand, actually have been Anatolian, as it is not specified as being 'of Englishe worke' like the large carpet, and red and yellow are colours characteristic of a well-known class of Anatolian rug.

30. *Gosfield Invt., 1638*. Frith's long carpet must have been English but the other four may well have been Oriental. Lady Dorchester also had '1 small Turkie carpett of English worke', valued at £1. 10s. od.

31. *Ingatestone Invt., 1600*.

32. Tattersall, *op. cit.*, figs. 14 and 15.

33. A Durham merchant owned 'ij carpetes noryshe wourke' in 1596 (*Surtees Society*, XII, 1906 'Durham Wills and Inventories', p. 260), while an inventory of 1584 includes a reference to a 'Turquey carpett of Norwiche work (J. O. Halliwell, *Ancient Inventories...*, London, 1854).

34. Tattersall, *op. cit.*, fig. 15.

35. *Havard*, 'Tapis'. This authority, however, suggested that 'tapis d'Angleterre' was a kind of moquette (see p. 112) although moquette was woven in France in great quantity so there would have been no need to import it to the extent that the introduction of an import-duty would imply. Turkeywork was certainly used both for chairs and floor-covering. Seventeenth-century chairs covered with what looks like English turkeywork are to be seen in several Scandinavian collections.

36. *Kilkenny and Clonmell Invts., 1684*.

37. See note 2, above.

38. *Savary des Bruslons*, (1723) had a heading 'Moquette, Mocade, Moucade'. 'Mockado of

Flaunders making' is listed in the *Book of Rates, 1582*.

39. In the Bibliothèque Forney, Paris, is an Italian sample-book of *c.* 1760 with specimens of 'Mocchetta unita denominata trippa' which are woollen-pile velvets. In 1601, 10,805 pieces of *trippe de velours* were woven at Lille. So excellent were the Lille products that the Procureur Générale of Tournai obtained from Lille in 1590–91 'une demi pieche de tripe de haultliche fin ouvrage' which he hoped would inspire the local weavers to do better (E. Houdoy, *Tapisseries de haute-lisse, . . . la fabrication Lilloise*, Lille, 1871, p. 70; note that at Lille and Tournai the *hautelisseurs* were not weavers of tapestries but made large-scale upholstery materials on a wide loom. This is made clear by E. Soil, *Tapisserie de Tournai, les tapissiers et hautelisseurs de cette ville*, tournai, 1891, who quotes many sixteenth-century references to *trippe* including one to 'pieces de haultliche . . . appelées trippes'). In the inventory of the Princess Albertina Agnes' possessions (1696) note is made of some flowered Tournai *trippe* (*Doornicks gebloemd trip; Orange Invts.*, II, p. 226).

40. In 1606 Claude Dangon, an inventive weaver of Lyons, devised a method of making a velvet with a shaggy reverse of 'panne ou pelluche' (Le Comte d'Hennezel, *Claude Dangon*, Lyons, 1926) but this was probably of silk, and there were certainly also 'pluches de soye' (silk plushes) available in the eighteenth century. Under 'Manufactures de Paris', *Savary des Bruslons* (1723) lists together 'velours, trippes de velours, pannes, pluches'. Savary, under 'Panne', also explains that 'pannes de laine' (woollen plushes) are usually known as *tripes* or *moquette*. At Marly some stools were covered 'de tripe ou peluche cramoisie' (D. Pitoin, *Marly-le-Roi*, Paris, 1904, p. 174). There was a room completely dressed with 'stript plush' at Dyrham at the end of the seventeenth century (*Dyrham Invt., 1703*) and at *Tredegar* (*Invt., of 1692*) some cane chairs had cushions of 'flowered plush'.

41. There are some seventeenth-century armchairs at Boughton still covered in a plain red woollen velvet that are described in an inventory of 1718 as being 'cover'd in vallure'. Whether this material was on the chairs when they were new (*c.* 1670?) has not yet been established but it is certainly possible. Some chairs of *c.* 1720 at Erthig have 'caffoy' covers (see J. Fowler and J. Cornforth, English Decoration in the 18th

Century, London, 1974, fig. 90); the material originally had a bright yellow satin ground and a pattern rendered in red pile. 'Caffa' is mentioned in sixteenth-century records. In the eighteenth century, 'Caffoy paper' was a flocked wallpaper.

42. The '*Cafawerkers*' combined to form a guild with the '*Tripmakers*' at Hamburg in 1609 (K. Germann, *Die Deutsche Möbelplüsche*, Leipzig, 1913, p. 18). These names reflect the fact that the trades were run by immigrant Netherlandish craftsmen; there were *caffawerkers* at Tournai in 1532, for instance. There is a Swedish reference to a room being hung with red 'Harlemer trip' in 1706 and 'Harlemer plyss' occurs in another Swedish document of 1677 (*Karlson*, p. 276). In the *Orange Inventories* one finds 'Haarlems fluweel' (Haarlem velvet; I, p. 276) and 'Haarlems caffa' with black flowers on an orange ground (II, p. 226). Some accommodating chairs were provided at Versailles 'pour servire dans les chambres des seigneurs' [for use in the bedchambers of [set aside for] noblemen] and these were covered in 'panne d'Hollande couleur de feu' while some others had striped material of the same kind (*Guiffrey, Inventaire*, p. 414 and 433).

43. *Agius*, p. 76.

44. There is reference to 'a rugg coverlet' in the *Henham Inventory of 1602*.

45. A duty of no less than five shillings each was payable on the importation of 'Mantles, called Irish mantles' in 1582 (*Book of Rates, 1582*). An even higher duty (10/- to 13/4d) was paid on 'blankets called Paris mantles' which came white or coloured (often red, which is specifically mentioned).

46. In 1585 there was a 'checkey' Irish rugg at Chenies. 'Chicker' and 'chequered' ruggs are mentioned in the inventories of *Gilling Castle, 1594* and of *Marton, 1605*.

47. *O.E.D.*, 'Cadow'.

48. *Ibid*. Mr John Nevinson has kindly informed me that in an inventory of Worksop Hall of 1591 in the Sheffield Public Library there is a reference to 'Waterford ruggs'. Presumably these materials were exported from that port on the southeast coast of Ireland.

49. The Yeoman of the Wardrobe in Lord Montague's household had to see that 'the lodgeinges reserved for strangers' staying in the house were in proper order, making sure to remove the quilts at night and to have 'yrishe rugges lay'd in their places' (*Montague Household Book, 1595*).

50. *O.E.D.*, 'Cadow'. 'Outlandish' meant foreign but the implication is that the cadow was by this time strange and unfamiliar.

51. For instance, Spanish blankets are listed after ordinary blankets in the *Ham Inventory of 1679* but before silk blankets.

52. *Havard* and *Savary des Bruslons*, both under 'Castelogne'. Savary says they were woven in many parts of France in his day (1723).

53. *Hengrave Invt., 1603.*

54. *Mazarin Invt., 1653.*

55. *Ingatestone Invt., 1600.*

56. *Havard*, 'Blanchet'.

57. *Ham Invt., 1679.*

58. *Hampton Court Estimates, 1699.*

59. *Kensington Palace Invt., 1699.*

60. *Savary des Bruslons* says fustian was of cotton, sometimes with a linen warp, and a writer of a pamphlet on *Treasure and Traffic* of 1641 explained how Manchester bought in London 'cotton wool' from Cyprus and Smyrna 'and perfects it into fustians, vermillions, dimities and other such stuffs'; but in 1604 it was stated in an Act of Parliament that 'in Norwich, time out of mind, there had been a certain craft called Shearman, for sheering as well worsteds, stamins and fustians, as also all other woollen cloths' ('The House and Farm Accounts of the Shuttleworths of Gawthorpe Hall . . ., Pt. III, Notes, 'Fustian'' *Chetham Society*, 1857). 'Jeans fustian' (i.e. from Genoa) is often mentioned in seventeenth century inventories; 'jeans' is and was a cotton material. Fustian also came from Milan, Naples, Ulm (called Holmes) and from Holland.

61. *Ingatestone Invt., 1600.* A blanket at *Hatfield Priory* (*Invt., 1629*), perhaps one of fustian, was 'napte on both sides'. A charter of 1641 mentions 'Naples Fustian Tripp, or Velvet' which must have been a cotton velvet (Beck, *Draper's Dictionary*). This material became popular in the late eighteenth century as 'Manchester velvet', now called velure and a ribbed version of which we still have as corduroy.

62. *Chetham Society*, 1861, 'Lancashire and Cheshire Wills and Inventories'.

63. 'whole clothes of fledge to make fledges of' occurs in an inventory of Sheffield Castle, taken in 1582, Mr John Nevinson has very kindly told me.

64. I am indebted to Professor Garnet Rees for suggesting this interpretation which I feel sure is correct.

65. *Celia Fiennes*, p. 339.

66. A seventeenth-century tariff of import duties lists together 'Sayes, Double Serges, or Flanders Serges, Double Saye or Serge . . .'.

67. Berch Collection, Nordiska Museet, Stockholm. W. Karlson (*Ebba Brahe's Hem . . .*, Lund, 1943) explains that perpetuana was a broad serge.

68. *Tart Hall Invt., 1641.*

69. From the Danish *'vadmel'*, homespun. See *Ingatestone Invt., 1600* and *Knole Invt., 1645.*

70. A document of 1732 in the Bibliothèque Centrale, Lyons, refers to 'crêpes appellé estamines' (*Inventaire Chappe*, Vol. VII, p. 591). Other authorities speak of it being 'slight' and suggest it had rather an open texture.

71. *Countess of Leicester's Invt., 1634.*

72. Evelyn 'went to see . . . the pressing and watering . . . [of] chamblettes' in 1644 (*O.E.D.*). *Savary des Bruslons* (1723) differentiates between *'camelots à eau'* which were pressed with a hot plate to impart a glaze, *'ondez'* which had waves imparted by pressing to give a 'watered' or 'moiré' effect, and *'gauffrez'* which had a figure imprinted on the surface by pressing it with a hot plate against a wood block carved with a pattern in intaglio. It should be noted that the watered or *moiré* effect was called 'waved' in England, whereas the plain, glazed sort of camlet was apparently called 'water camlet' because the process involved the application of water.

73. Velvets made of wool have been discussed above (p. 111). Velvet can also be made of cotton, as were 'Manchester velvets' in the eighteenth century (see note 61).

74. We have already considered the technique of weaving damask in connection with damasks made of worsted (see p. 113).

75. Brocading, as well as other weaving processes, is explained in many readily obtainable books. One of the most recent is Verla Birrell, *The Textile Arts*, New York, 1973.

76. Satin is a weave that gives the resulting material one shiny face. Although one can make satin of cotton, it is a weave that is particularly well suited to silk since it allows the shiny quality of the thread to come to the fore. See note 75.

77. 'Formerly the term restrained to cloths woven either wholey of gold . . . or of silver . . .' (*Chambers' Dictionary*, 1786).

78. Gold thread was in fact a narrow strip of silver-gilt metal wound on a silken core. It came in several sorts—straight (*filé*) or spiralling (*frisé*). It could also take the form of flat strips which could be woven into the ground.

356

79. A rich bed at *Ingatestone* (*Invt., 1600*) had its tester and valances of 'tysshew layde with crimson silke and goulde lace'. These were the richer components; the curtains were of taffeta (i.e. plain silk). Presumably the silver cloth was embroidered with red silk and trimmed with gold lace.

80. Lady Dorchester had a bed with a set of summer hangings of 'white tinsell wrought with flowers of several colours of silke', i.e. the white, shimmering material was embroidered with coloured silks (*Gosfield Invt., 1638*).

81. It is occasionally called 'taffeta sarsnett' (*Ingatestone Invt., 1600*) or 'taffety sercenet' (*Cockesden Invt., 1626*).

82. *Tabis à fleurs* was a major product of the Tours silk-weaving establishments in the later decades of the seventeenth century. The imparting of the 'tabby' (*tabisé*) effect is described in a document of 1638 (L. A. Bossebeuf, *La fabrique de soieries de Tours*, Tours, 1900, p. 257).

83. *Ham Invt., 1679*.

84. Given thus in the *Tredegar Invt., 1688* and the *Dyrham Invt., 1703*, and as 'Blak silk moyhair' in the accounts of John Clerk for the year 1649 (Register House, Edinburgh), a reference to which my attention was kindly drawn by Griselda Chubb. *Savary des Bruslons* (1723), under the heading 'Mohère, mouaire ou moire', explains that this is 'une étoffe ordinairement tout de soye . . . un espèce de gros de Tours mais plus faible'. When given a *moiré* or watered effect by being crushed in a calendering machine, it came to be known as *mohère tabisée*. In German and Scandinavian, watered silk is called '*Mohr*' in seventeenth-century inventories; some hangings of this material thus described are still to be seen on the walls of a room at Rosenborg Castle, Copenhagen, for instance. William III's bed at Honselaarsdijk at the end of the century was hung with blue English mohair (*blau Engels moor*; *Orange Invts.*, I, p. 462). The Countess of Manchester in 1675 had a room 'hung with six pieces of haire, called silk watered moehaire' (J. Fowler and J. Cornforth, *op. cit.*, p. 132): The Duchess of Lauderdale had the hangings of her bed and of her closet made of 'morello mohair' (*Ham Invt., 1679*). One might think that morello was the colour but the hangings are respectively described as being red and black, and white. Could 'morello' be a corruption of the Italian for watering 'marrezzo'? In 1646 Tours produced 'moires de soye' but also 'moires' of wool, cotton

and camel hair (Bossebeuf, *op. cit.*). Article LXXVIII of the *Regulations* of the Lyons silk-weavers, issued in 1737, concerned 'les moires de soye'. Beck's *Draper's Dictionary* (1884) explains that 'mohair' was in his day a cloth of mohair yarn but reminds his readers that Chambers' *Cyclopoedia* of 1741 describes it as 'A kind of stuff, ordinarily of silk . . . There are two kinds, the one smooth and plain, the other watered like tabbys'. Today the term is often used to describe a woollen velvet and is no longer associated with a silk material.

85. Apparently quite exceptional was the bed at Knole which had hangings of 'yellowe cotten trymde with blew and yellow silke fringe and lace sutable [i.e. matching blue and yellow lace]' (see Charles J. Phillips, *History of the Sackville Family*, London, *c.* 1928, p. 317; 'Household stuff sent . . . to Knole in 1624').

86. Chintzes began to come through the port of Marseilles in the 1570s and 1580s (see J. Irwin and K. Brett, *Origins of Chintz*, London, 1970, p. 4). They were subsequently imported through Lisbon and Antwerp—and then London. The name 'pintado' comes from the Portuguese likening these colourful materials to the speckled plumage of a peahen (*pintade* in French).

87. In 1609 a factor of the East India Company in Surat was writing about 'pintadoes of all sorts, especially the finest . . . I mean such as are for quilts and for fine hangings', (Irwin and Brett, *op. cit.*, p. 4).

88. One of the Company's factors actually stated that the *chintes* he was having made in 1619 were 'for hangings in England'. In 1630 a set of 'pintado hangings . . . for fitting a gallery or room' cost £30 (Irwin and Brett, *op. cit.*, p. 3).

89. *Tart Hall Invt., 1641*.

90. *Pepys's Diary*, 5 September 1663.

91. *Cowdray Invt., 1688*.

92. A bed at *Syon* House (*Invt., of 1670*) had hangings of 'white tufted Holland' and there was a bed with white linen hangings in a Prussian castle in 1695 but such examples are difficult to find. *Randle Holme* (Bk. III, Chap. XIV, p. 16) speaks of inner valances on beds being 'generally white silk or linen' but this is not borne out by contemporary inventories. The bed of John Evelyn and his wife had hangings lined with printed linen at the very end of the century (Inventory of Wotton House taken in 1702; deposited in the Library at Christ Church, Oxford).

93. e.g. 'two great southege curtyones for ye great windowe' (*Hengrave Invt., 1603*). Soultwich is listed among linen materials in seventeenth-century Books of Rates; so is buckram. There was a buckram curtain 'within the window' at *Hatfield Priory* (*Invt., 1629*).

94. See F. W. Steer, *Farm and Cottage Inventories of Mid-Essex, 1635–1749*, Colchester, 1950. 'Dowles & Centin [Kenting]' sheets are listed separately from those of Holland in the *Tredegar Invt., 1688*.

95. e.g. *Hardwick Invt., 1601*.

96. At *Ham House* (*Invt., 1679*) the diaper cloths have patterns described as 'paviour work' (presumably chequered like marble paving), 'little rose', 'double rose' and 'holly'.

97. At Ham (see previous note) there were diaper table-cloths decorated with the Imperial crown, with 'flower and festoon border', with 'vine and grape', with 'fruit work', with 'forest worke' and with 'flowerpots'. The cloths with the Imperial crown were probably from Courtrai which lay in the Hapsburg territories; the same applies to the cloths 'wrought with a Spread Eagle' which are listed in the *Gilling Castle Inventory of 1594*, where there were also cloths with 'ye marigold and rose', and others 'with pictures'. At the same house in *1624* were some cloths 'wrought with mulberyes'.

98. *Chenies Invt., 1585, Dublin Castle invt., 1679*, and *Gosfield invt., 1638*.

99. *Ingatestone Invt., 1600*.

100. For instance, girthweb and sackcloth are among the materials listed in the bill John Casbert rendered after delivering a fine couch for use at Whitehall Palace in 1660–61 (R. W. Symonds, 'Charles II Couches, Chairs and Stools, Pt. I', *The Connoisseur*, February 1934).

101. *Ingatestone Invt., 1600*. 'The chamber [is] matted wth. cornishe matt somewhat worne.' Several other rooms in the house were fitted with Cornish matting.

102. *Johnson's Dictionary*, 1765, 'Mat'.

103. *Havard*, 'Natte'.

104. *Dyrham Invt., 1710*.

105. *Orange Invts.*, I, p. 114, and *Mazarin Invt., 1653*. The Dutch mat was large; it measured $5\frac{1}{2} \times 2\frac{3}{4}$ ells.

106. *Pepys' Diary*, 15 June, 1666. Miss Juliet Allan informs me that a bill for furnishing His Majesty's Bedchamber at Hampton Court in 1715 includes reference to a 'large Barbary mat' on which the bed stood.

107. *Kilkenny Castle Invt., 1684*. Kilkenny was rather grandly appointed at this time.

108. There were many Portugal mats at Kensington Palace (*Invt., 1699*) including one in the 'King's Low Bed Chamber'. In 1699 '4 larg Portugall Matts' were ordered for the Presence Chamber at Hampton Court for the throne to stand on (*Hampton Court Estimate, 1699*). Under William's bed in the Binnenhof at The Hague in 1700 was another (*Een Portugalise mat onder t' bedde*; *Orange Invts.*, I. p. 428). It is curious that nothing seems to be known of a great trade in mats in the seventeenth century although mats of *jonco* are still laid in Portuguese houses in summer. Perhaps 'Portugal mats' came from Africa, via Lisbon. *Savary des Bruslons* ('Jonc') says that 'nattes de jonc' were imported in his time from the Levant but makes no mention of Portugal.

109. *Tart Hall Invt., 1641*. The Arundel's matting was rolled up as it was not in use but Fouquet, not long after, had 'un roulleau de bande de jong [jonc] servant à faire des tapis de pied' [a roll of rush runner for use as a foot carpet] (*Havard*, 'Natte').

110. At *Hardwick* (*Invt., 1601*) there were in store fifty pieces of 'wrought' gilt leather which presumably had a pattern and were finished, while there were thirty-four more pieces that were 'silverd but not fynished', which suggests they were blanks that could be used to repair existing hangings and merely had to be painted with a design to match.

111. Such trimming-strips may be seen on the gilt leather hangings in the Marble Dining Room at Ham House which were hung in the 1670s.

112. J. W. Waterer's excellent *Spanish Leather* (London, 1971) surveys the history of this material and explains the technique in greater detail. At Breda Castle in 1618 there were in store twenty-four skins of 'tapisserie de cuir d'Espagne' while the Audience Chamber had hangings of this material with a blue ground (*Orange Invts.*, I, p. 118).

113. In the splendidly furnished Gallery at Tart Hall (*Invt., 1641*) there were twelve black wooden chairs which had backs and seats covered in 'Rushia leather'. On the other hand an Oxford inventory of 1664 shows that eight chairs covered with 'Russia leather' cost only £1. 6s. 8d. (*Agius*, p. 78) while chairs thus covered were to be found in the 'Gentlewoman's

Eating Room' at Chapelizod (*Invt., 1679*). 'Turkey' leather was on some chairs at Oxford in 1669 (*Agius*, p. 78) and there were a dozen at Cowdray (*Invt., 1682*). A mattress (squab) of 'maroquin' is mentioned in the French royal accounts in 1681 (*Havard*, 'Maroquin').

114. *Northampton Invt., 1614.* The leather is stated to have been 'lined with silver and golde'; this can hardly be a reference to a lining and must mean it had lines on it of silver and gold—which suggests the 'printing' was in the same finish.

115. *Hardwick Invt., 1601.*

116. M. A. Havinden, *Household and Farm Inventories in Oxfordshire, 1550–90*, London, 1965, p. 113.

117. *Guiffrey, Inventaire*, p. 425. The silk was woven with flat silver strip in the ground.

118. *Hardwick Invt., 1601.*

119. 'Painting on Cloth is decayed,' wrote an observer in 1601, 'and not one hundred yards of new painted cloth made here in a year, by reason of so much Flanders pieces brought from thence.' (E. Croft-Murray, *Decorative Painting in England*, London, 1962, p. 30).

120. *Dyrham Invt., 1703.*

121. Waterer, *op. cit.*, p. 63.

122. *Ibid.*, p. 63.

123. *Ibid.*, p. 57.

124. *Ibid.*, fig. 47.

125. C. A. Weigert, *La tapisserie francaise*, Paris, 1956; also the Catalogue of an exhibition of French drawings from the Bibliothèque Nationale held in 1950 at the National Museum, Stockholm. *Savary des Bruslons*, under 'Tontisse', says Audran's establishment was at the Luxembourg.

126. *Havard*, 'Papier Peint'. See also C. C. Oman, *Catalogue of Wall-papers*, Victoria and Albert Museum, London, 1929, pp. 10–11.

127. E. A. Entwisle, *The Book of Wallpaper*, Bath, 1970, p. 22.

128. There was, for example, The Blew Paper Warehouse at Aldermanbury, in the City of London, at the end of the century which claimed that it 'sold the true sorts of figured paper hangings in pieces of twelve yards long, and others of the manner of real tapestry, and in imitation of Irish stitch [see p. 127] and flowered damask and also of marble & other coloured wainscot . . .' (Oman, *op. cit.*, pp. 2–4). Flemish and English harpsichord-makers frequently used papers for dressing the insides of the cases of their instruments in the seventeenth century. The formal pattern of confronted dolphins printed in black on white paper which was used by the Antwerp firm of Ruckers on the keyboard-surrounds of their harpsichords and spinets is well known, but papers grained like wood and strips of gilt embossed paper resembling gilt gesso ornament that may be seen on such instruments also help to give us some idea of what seventeenth century wallpapers looked like.

129. *Pepys' Diary*, 8 January, 1665–6.

130. Edward Phillips, *New World of Words, or, Universal English Dictionary*, 1706.

131. C. R. Rivington, *The Stationers' Company*, London, 1883.

132. See *D.E.F.*, 'Beds' fig. 25, and J. Fowler and J. Cornforth, *op. cit.*, Pl. IX.

133. Very many of the textile materials we have been discussing could be embroidered. However, embroidery is usually most effective on a plain ground, rather than one with a pattern.

134. e.g. A. F. Kendrick, *English Needlework*, London, 1933; J. L. Nevinson, *Catalogue of English Domestic Embroidery of the 16th and 17th Centuries*, Victoria and Albert Museum, London 1938; P. Wardle, *Guide to English Embroidery*, Victoria and Albert Museum, London, 1970; G. F. Wingfield-Digby, *Elizabethan Embroidery*, London, 1963; L. de Farcy, *La Broderie du XIe siècle jusqu'au nos jours*, Paris, 1890.

135. Viscountess Dorchester bequeathed to her daughter 'my Irishe stitched furniture for a bedd' (*Gosfield Invt., 1638*).

136. Inventory of Chastleton House, Gloucestershire, 1633, kindly shown me by Mrs Alan Clutton-Brock. We have also the evidence of the Blew Paper Warehouse (see note 128), the trade-plate of which mentions 'Irish Stitch' as being one of the wallpaper patterns they sold while a roll of zig-zag patterned paper is displayed prominently on the counter.

137. Professional embroidery was not in those days anything like the female preserve that it was to become.

138. *Randle Holme*, Bk. III, Chap. XIV, p. 16.

139. Some fringe at Ham House, which is almost certainly the 'gould embroidered fringe' from the Queen's State Bed, has rosettes and bows of white vellum strip amid the rich spirals and loops of metal thread and the tufts of salmon-pink and cream-coloured silk.

140. e.g. The Duchess of Lauderdale's bed at *Ham House* (*Invt., 1679*) had 'campaign fringe'.

However, *campanes* could also mean the baggily gathered pleat hanging down between swags of material on valances or pelmets (see Plate. 144).

141. *Savary des Bruslons*, 'Frange'. See also *Havard*, 'Crépine' and 'Mollet'.

142. Thus a French inventory lists some red cloth bed-hangings that were trimmed with 'grand et petit frange' (*Du Boisgelin Invt., 1688*).

143. A Parisian bed in Sweden has rich silver lace trimming along the lower edges of its valances and these are described in a Swedish inventory of the period as '*krepiner*' (Åke Setterwall, 'Ulrika Eleonora d.ä's. paradsäng', *Gripsholm och des Konstskatter*, Stockholm, 1956).

144. Gabrielle d'Estrées had a splendid bed that was 'tout passementé de clinquant d'argent'. *Clinquant* was flat metal strip and the *passementerie* on her bed was therefore presumably of lace made up with such strip (*Havard*, 'Clinquant').

145. Some black and white damask hangings on a bed at *Hardwick* (*Invt., 1601*) were 'layde about with golde lace and golde frenge, and golde lace down the middest', while the 'Best Bed' was likewise 'layde with golde lace about the edges', while it had 'twist downe the seames' which probably means 'snailing fringe'.

146. The Countess of Shrewsbury's bed at *Hardwick* (*Invt., 1601*) had hangings 'stript' with lace; the bed-hangings in the Duke's Chamber at *Cockesden* (*Invt., 1626*) were 'stript with yealloew and redd lace'. At the end of the century, *Celia Fiennes* (p. 256) saw the State Bed at Windsor and described its green velvet hangings as 'strip'd down very thick with gold . . . lace of a hands breadth'.

147. The invalid chair specially created for Philip II of Spain (d. 1598) was padded with horsehair and quilted. John Casbert was supplying Charles II with chairs which had 'curled haire to fill the chaire backs' in 1660–61 (R. W. Symonds, 'Charles II Couches, Chairs and Stools', *The Connoisseur*, January and February, 1934) and Parisian upholsterers were certainly using *crin* for stuffing chairs by the 1670s (*Havard*, 'Crin'). The best horsehair apparently came from Ireland or from Holland; the Muscovite produce was thought to be less good. The curling of horsehair was most successfully carried out in Paris and at Rouen although the French conceded that the Dubliners were also good at it. (*Savary des Bruslons*, 'Crin' and 'Crespir de Crin').

NOTES TO CHAPTER VI

1. e.g. 'History of Vulcan' (*Ham Invt., 1679*); five pieces of 'new Flanders hangings with a storye' (*Ingatestone Invt., 1600*); 'tapestries of imagery' (*Lauderdale London Invt., 1679*); 'with personages' (*Hardwick Invt., 1601*).

2. 'foure pieces of fforrest worke hangings' were in Colonel Tollemache's room at Ham House (*Invt., 1679*) which was not one of the principal bedchambers. The Earl of Northampton (*Invt., 1614*) had some hangings of 'buskedge with redd and white and yelowe roses and bunches of grapes in the borders' as well as some 'busted hangings of a larger sort' and others 'of hunting worke'. It is possible that these were in fact of the dornix or *tapisserie de Bergame* class but they could also have been tapestries decorated with *boscage*(or *bocage*, as it is rendered in modern French). Some 'buscage tapestry' is listed with other tapestries in the *Syon Inventory of 1670*, although the collection also included some 'greenworke hangings' and some 'greenleafe hangings'. *Bossages* or *boschagies* are often mentioned in Dutch inventories of the late seventeenth century in a context where 'verdure tapestries' would seem an appropriate translation.

3. Painted hangings might also fall into the same category. The rooms of the Grand Apartement at Versailles, and the Grande Galerie, all apparently had alternative sets of tapestry hangings and painted hangings. They were designed specially to fit the rooms concerned. In the cases where large scenes painted on gilt leather were special commissions, they too fall into this small category (see note 14, below).

4. Pictorial tapestries were usually designed in a series with different scenes. Numerous weavings could be executed from these designs, or 'cartoons' as they were called, and a series might remain popular for many decades. A set of tapestries woven after the designs might not necessarily comprise all the scenes of the original series.

5. Cronström informs us that one could obtain half-width borders of *brocatelle de Venise* (*Tessin-Cronström Correspondence*, letter from Paris, 7 January, 1695).

6. The 'pane' or rectangle of the field of such hangings was 'impaned' with the secondary material but it is by no means always clear which of the two materials mentioned in an entry

concerning this kind of hanging is the main one. Did the room 'hanged with payned red and yellow damaske hangings' (*Tart Hall Invt., 1641*) have a panel of red damask framed by yellow or the reverse? Or was the damask red and yellow, with a framing of some quite other and unspecified material? At Ham House the 'Yellow Bedchamber' had hangings of yellow damask, fringed '& paind with blew mohair', i.e. empaned with blue silk (*Ham Invt., 1679*). Some of the Ham hangings are described as being 'paned and bordered' which suggests that 'paned' essentially meant that the rectangular panels were produced by alternate bands of material. But even so they are likely to have had a border at the bottom and probably at the top as well.

7. The hangings at Ham (*Invt., c. 1654*) were of 'blew perpetuanae' and gilt leather. At Gosfield (*Invt., 1638*) there was 'a sute gilt leather and greene cloth hangings for my Ladies closett', and the Banqueting House in the garden at Cowdray (*Invt., 1682*) had similar hangings made up with green printed paragon.

8. Le Comte de Cosnac, *Les riches du Palais Mazarin*, Paris, 1884, p. 787. Mazarin had several such sets with columns. They were so valuable that they were provided with loose covers of 'toile rouge' (a red material of linen or cotton rather than wool) and with a set of Beauvais serge covers in which they could lie when folded away in store.

9. Daniel Cronström, advising Count and Countess Piper in Stockholm in 1695, told them that 'l'on pourroit prendre un camelot couleur de feu et y faire des pilastres, ou montans, de brocatelle vert et aurore, ou violet et aurore, ou bleu et aurore, ou blanc au lieu d'aurore. L'on pourroit aussi prendre des satins de Turin et y faire des colonnes torses et des bordures ou frises, découppées suivant le dessein de M. Bérain. Tout cela seroit propre, nouveau et d'un goût nouveau' [one might take a flame-coloured camlet and on it make pilasters of green or pink brocatelle, or of blue and pink, or white instead of pink. One might also take a Turin satin and on it set spiralling columns or friezes cut out after designs by Mr Bérain. All this would be appropriate, new and in the latest taste] (*Tessin-Cronström Correspondence*, Letter of 7 January 1695).

10. Exceptions would be tapestry, *tapisserie de Bergame*, gilt leather and chintz.

11. *Tart Hall Invt., 1641*. It was of 'red & red and yellow damaske with a deep Fringe at the bottome & a narrow one at ye top'.

12. It is scalloped and has a border of braid accentuating the lobed edges, while a gathered band is stitched across the face of each lappet to form a simple pattern. Cronström (see note 9, above) advised that 'Si les découpures ou gallons vous paroissent trop riches nous ne ferons qu'une campane,' which was a gathered valance 'qui regnera sous la corniche en haut, tout au tour de la chambre, galonné d'un petit bordé et d'un petit gallon d'argent, et qui sera couppée en festoon ou portique . . . Les campanes faites et gallonnées sont maintenant si fort à la mode qu'on voit quasy que cela.' [If the cut-out ornaments or galloons seem too overloaded, we will merely make a *campane. . .* which runs round the cornice at the top, right round the room. It is trimmed with a narrow edging and a narrow silver galloon, and will be cut out like a festoon or arcading . . . Made up valances with galloon are nowadays very much in fashion so that one hardly sees anything else.]

13. Cronström (see note 9, above) maintains that 'le velours n'est pas de toute saison' although perhaps in Stockholm 'nostre climat froid pourroit vous permettre l'usage du velours en hyver comme en esté'.

14. Cronström (see note 9, above) wrote that 'Mon avis n'est point de meubler la salle de cuir doré . . . Parce que cela n'est point de toute saison, du moins selon la mode d'icy.' [My advice is not to hang the main room with gilt leather . . . Because it is not at all suited for all seasons, at least, not according to the fashion here.] He advises the Pipers to use instead brocatelle or tapestry, or the camlet hangings with *découpage* mentioned in note 9. Mention should here be made of the large hangings, made up of many skins of gilt leather, on which large scenes similar to those on pictorial tapestries were painted. There is a famous set at Dunster Castle which includes a scene related to one designed for a Brussels tapestry by Justus van Egmont in 1661 but one does not get the impression such hangings were at all common in Britain. A Flemish artist arrived in Scotland in 1638 claiming that he had been trained in Rome in a new method of 'making great designs and representing histories upon leather hangings in chiaro scuro' but whether he produced anything of the sort in this country is not known (R. K.

Marshall, *Life in the Household of the Duchess of Hamilton*, 1636–1716, London, 1973, p. 41). In the Swedish Royal collection there is a superb set of gilt leather hangings with scenes depicting the Siege of Vienna by the Turks in 1688. One of the Dunster hangings is illustrated in Plate 105.

15. At Cowdray, which was appointed in an old-fashioned manner when the *Inventory* was taken *in 1682*, there were turkeywork hangings in four important rooms including the Great Dining Room, the Great Withdrawing Room and her ladyship's chamber. Tallemant de Réaux (*Historiettes*, written 1657–59, Paris, 1834–40, III, p. 69) tells of Madame de Rohan's closet which was 'tout tapissé par haut et par bas de moquette'. For a while, he tells us, 'c'etoit là que la société faisoit ses conversations . . . et on appeloit cette cabale La Moquette'. There was a room at Dyrham (*Invt., 1703*) which was hung with 'striped plush'; and a Swedish account of 1706 refers to hangings for a room of red Haarlem *trippe* (see p. 112) but this was not a common material for wall-hangings.

16. *Tart Hall Invt., 1641*. The Great Chamber, for instance, had 'freeze hangings . . . laced with two gold galowne [galloon] laces in each space' which suggests they were plain with a panelled effect created with the gold braid. The frieze hangings in the Withdrawing Room were 'laced with parchment lace of gold' while those in 'My Lady's Chamber' had 'little silver laces in each seame and round the top.'

17. There was one in the old building at Tart Hall (*Invt., 1641*) and another at Dyrham (*Invt., 1703*).

18. *Havard*, 'Paillassons'.

19. *Havard*, 'Natte'.

20. *Ibid.*

21. J. Evelyn, *Kalendarium Hortense*.

22. *Havard* 'Matlassé', quoting Dufort de Cheverny.

23. Some gilt leather hangings from the 1670s and still on the walls at Ham House are fixed in this manner. The silk hangings painted by Bailly with 'toutes les victoires du Roy tres bien representé' which were provided for some of the principal rooms at Versailles had frames made for them by the joiner Prou (*Havard*, 'Peintre sur toile'). Some gilt leather hangings were put up at Dyrham in 1703 after instructions had been given that 'the opportunity of wett weather be taken'. In early August it must have been raining for we learn from a letter of 8 August that 'this is very good weather to putt up gilt leather'. (J. W. Waterer, *Spanish Leather*, London, 1971, p. 65.)

24. Mrs Delany tells us in 1750 that 'when you put up paper the best way is to have it pasted to the bare walls; when lined with canvas it always shrinks from the edges (*The Autobiography and Correspondence of Mary Granville, Mrs Delany*, ed. Lady Llanover, London 1861–62, p. 562). See also E. A. Entwisle, *The Book of Wallpaper*, London, 1954, p. 83. A writer in 1699 explained that, by his time, some wallpapers came in rolls and were therefore 'managed like wollen hangings' which means pasted to canvas and nailed to stretchers (Entwisle, p. 22).

25. See *Havard*, 'Dessus de Porte.'

26. *Cowdray Invt., 1682* and *Hardwick Invt., 1601*.

27. In the Gage inventory of 1556 (*Sussex Archaeological Collections*, XLV, 1892).

28. *Mazarin Invt., 1653*.

29. *Celia Fiennes*, p. 153.

30. *Dyrham Invt., 1710*.

31. In the early part of the century, when window curtains were still comparatively rare, there was a tendency to spell it out—two dornix curtains 'for the windows' were in 'The Nobleman's Chamber' at Chatsworth (*Invt., 1601*), and at Cockesden (*Invt., 1610*) there were 'for the wyndoes, 2 curteans of greene cotton'. Later the entries are made quite simply as 'window curtaines'.

32. 'Windowe peeces' are listed with window-curtains in the inventory of Kenilworth of 1584 (J. O. Halliwell, *Ancient Inventories . . .*, London, 1854). A distinction is made between the 'window-cloths' of 'arras' in the Great Chamber at Hengrave (*Invt., 1603*) and the 'two great southege [a linen material] curtyons for ye great window' in the same room. The 'sarges de Reins pour fenestres' (Rheims serge) mentioned in a French document of 1316 as well as the 'toile pour les fenestres de la chambre du Roy' required in 1359–60 for King Jean of France when he was held captive in England could both have been for window-pieces rather than curtains as we would understand them (*Havard*, 'Rideau' and 'Courtine'). Note is made in the English royal accounts in about 1470 of a payment to 'Rauf Underwood, wyre drawer, for iij and a quart'on of wyre for to hang verdours against the grete bay windowe in the Quenes old chamber' (S. W. Beck, *The Draper's Dictionary*, London, 1884, 'Verdure'). These

verdure tapestries could hardly have been made to draw on rings so were presumably hooked in place. The 'window cloth' of arras at Hengrave was probably fixed in a similar manner. The same applies to the 'two wyndow clothes of tapistry worke' at Henham (*Invt., 1602*), and to the 'rideau de tapisserie unie, servant au devant d'une croizée' [a curtain of plain tapestry for use in front of a window] mentioned in a French inventory of 1628 (see *Havard*, 'Rideau').

33. The earliest certain reference so far published seems to be in a French inventory of 1380 where a 'courtine bleue de toille, qui se tire devant le fenestre' [blue curtain of linen [?] which may be drawn in front of the window] is mentioned (*Havard*, 'Courtine'). The word 'rideaux' came into general use in France early in the seventeenth century.

34. For example, at Ingatestone (*Invt., 1600*) there were 'three curtaines of grene saye to the wyndowes' in the Garden Chamber with 'three curtaine rodds to them'. Likewise at Walton (*Invt., 1624*) there was 'a dornix window curtaine & an iron rod for it'.

35. The *Inventory of Ham House*, drawn up about *1654* when the house was probably very much in the state it had been in before the Civil War, shows that several rooms there had window-curtains *en suite* with the wall-hangings. The fact that unity was stressed at Ham at that stage may reflect a connection with the thinking of Inigo Jones, working through Francis Cleyn (see p. 54). When the house was re-decorated in the 1670s, the curtains were not made to match the hangings (see *Ham Invt., 1679*).

36. See *CIBA Review*, No. 126.

37. *Ham Invt., c. 1654* (see note 35 concerning its date). In the Parlour, which was one of the principal rooms, there was a pair of window-curtains of red cloth bordered with gilt leather 'and the curtaine rod'. The Countess of Dysart, later to become the Duchess of Lauderdale, likewise had a pair of divided curtains (with only one rod) in her bedchamber. There was apparently a set of divided curtains at Ingatestone already in 1600 (*Invt.*), which are described as old and with 'a curtaine rodd the length of the wyndow', but this is likely to have taken this form for purely practical reasons.

38. *Le Mercure Galant*, 1673, III, p. 203.

39. *Dublin Castle Invt., 1679*, and *Ham Invts., 1677, 1679* and *1683*.

40. A series of cords attached to the lower edge of the curtains passed loosely through guide-rings at the back of the curtain and up over pulleys at the top of the window embrasure, or through a pulley-board, and then down to a cleat or pair of 'cloak pins' to which the cords could be tied so as to adjust the curtains at the right height when pulled up.

41. P. Verlet, *Versailles*, Paris, 1961, p. 258.

42. *Hampton Court Estimates, 1699*. One item concerns some white silk damask for window-curtains that were being ordered for His Majesty's Closet. In addition ninety-seven yards of 'white small silk stringe to drawe them up' were required together with two large white tassels which must have gone on the ends of the draw-strings.

43. The estimate mentioned in the previous note also referred to 'covering cornices'. Thirty yards of edging were required for this in addition to the silk damask that would have been needed.

44. *Havard*, 'Rideaux'. In a Swedish inventory of 1689 a window-curtain is described as being 'with a pelmet to it' (*Medh en kappa der til; Karlson*, pp. 49–50). There were matching 'window-curtains & Valens' at Dyrham in 1703 (*Invt.*).

45. *Celia Fiennes*, p. 345.

46. Dornix window-curtains are mentioned, for instance, in the *Hardwick, Chatsworth, Cockesden* and *Walton Inventories* of *1600, 1601, 1610* and *1624* respectively.

47. *Ingatestone Invt., 1600*.

48. See note 32, above.

49. *Hardwick Invt., 1601*. This double set of curtains was in The Shipp Chamber, a relatively splendid room.

50. *Hengrave Invt., 1603*; see note 32, above.

51. *Hatfield Priory Invt., 1629*. The large curtain and rod may have been across the mouth of a window bay. Clive Wainwright has drawn my attention to a note by John Evelyn concerning the 'great bay windows jetting out within' gentlemen's houses in former times which had 'commonly a curtaine to draw before them for privacy'. Apparently people laid large cushions on the window-seats and used to retire there and 'discourse in private of business' (J. Aubrey, 'Monumenta Brittanica, MS Top Gen C.25, f.164 verso; Bodleian Library, Oxford).

52. *Cockesden Invt., 1610* and *Edington Invt., 1665*. The 'ffrench . . . curtaines' must have been in some way distinctive: could they possibly have been early specimens of the pull-up variety?

53. *Tart Hall Invt., 1641.*

54. Silk curtains were most frequently made of taffeta, especially the thin version known as sarcenet. Particularly grand rooms might have curtains of silk damask or, more rarely, of satin.

55. White sunlight-excluding curtains were not always plain white. A set at Ham House (*Invt., 1679*) was of grey and white striped taffeta and the stripes were no doubt intricately patterned; another was of white and purple chequered Indian sarcenet.

56. *Cowdray Invt., 1682.* The bed-hangings, wall-hangings, chair-covers and carpet, as well as the window-curtains, were all of the same material.

57. *Dyrham Invt., 1703.*

58. *Havard,* 'Damas'.

59. *Mazarin Invt., 1653.*

60. *Kilkenny Invt., 1684.*

61. In 1642 one could apparently order sets of rings by post—according to G. Hazelius Berg whose *Gardiner och Gardinuppsättningar*, Nordiska Museet, Stockholm, 1962, is still by far the best survey of the history of window-curtains. Being in Swedish and with only a very short English summary the information in it is unfortunately not readily accessible to most people.

62. At Copenhagen Castle in 1669, the windows of the Queen's Bedchamber were fitted with eight rollers 'on which are to roll the Dutch mats that shield the Queen's Chamber against the sun' (Hazelius Berg, *op. cit.*, p. 87).

63. *Ibid.* The blinds seem to have been of blue linen and had two cords.

64. Ambrose Heal, *The London Furniture Makers . . .*, London, 1952, p. 15 (illus.). John Brown's painted blinds must have been the successors of the 'painted sashes' that are discussed in the next paragraph, and the ancestors of the roller blinds printed with scenes that were so popular in the nineteenth century.

65. *Tessin's Visit, 1687*, p. 35. His description reads 'couverts d'satin sur lequel l'on a peint des branchissages et que se ferme à ressort, et que l'on tire en haute par moyen d'une corde à costé' [covered with satin on which scrollwork is painted and which are closed with a spring [catch?] and which may be pulled up by means of a cord at the side].

66. *Havard,* 'Jalousie'.

67. Smith states that the materials were wetted and then strained onto the frame, after which they were varnished 'so that they may appear all over clear and transparent'. Krünitz, in his *Oeconomiske Encyclopaedie* of 1777, explains how linen was treated with a mixture of Venetian turpentine, wax and tallow. Sashes covered with white silk were still being provided for windows at Osterley in the middle of the eighteenth century.

68. John Garret published in about 1670 *A Book of Six Large Land-skips* said to be 'fitting for sashes of windows' (see Leona Rostenberg, *English Publishers in the Graphic Arts, 1599–1700*, New York, 1963, p. 45). One could imitate stained glass windows, even down to the 'cames' of lead framing each quarry.

69. *Havard,* 'Chassis'. He also notes that, when the City of Lyons wished to honour a citizen in 1643, they undertook to do up his house in the smartest manner 'comme encores que les chassis tant de bois, pappier que vittres' [with, in addition, frames of wood fitted with paper and glass].

70. Hazelius Berg, *op. cit.*, p. 6. Dr Lars Sjöberg kindly informed me about the entry in the Stenbock accounts.

71. Andrew Clark, *The Life and Times of Anthony Wood, Antiquary, of Oxford, 1654–1695, described by himself*, Oxford, 1891, III, p. 271 and index, V, p. 208.

72. *The Spectator*, No. 510.

73. *Havard,* Paille'.

74. W. B. Rye, *England as seen by Foreigners*, London, 1865, p. 104.

75. Rye, *op. cit.*, p. 80.

76. Rushes are still strewn on the floor of the Council Chamber on important occasions at Trinity House, Hull, as they have been since time immemorial. The rushes were originally cut from reed-beds on the Humber but now have to come from further afield.

77. See *Havard,* 'Natte'. Matting was also much used in Sweden at the time (see *Karlson*, pp. 52–3) and one may presume that the fashion was widespread on the Continent.

78. *Walton Invt., 1624* and *Chatsworth Invt., 1601.* We are told that at Ingatestone (*Invt., 1600*) 'the chamber [is] matted wth. Cornishe matt somewhat worn'.

79. Rye, *op. cit.*, p. 204. The Duke's actual words were 'alle Gemächer und Galerien waren mit geflochtenen Decken aus Wintzen belegt'.

80. *Cowdray Invt., 1682.*

81. Listed together with a coarse cloth covering

the stairs at Dyrham (*Invt., 1710*) was 'a flore matt' which was clearly an insignificant object. There were also '2 church flore matts' in the Chapel.

82. *Pepys' Diary*, 15 June 1666.

83. For example, the Duke and Duchess of Ormonde had two 'Portugal mats' in the Drawing Room at Kilkenny Castle (*Invt., 1684*) and William III had one in his 'Low Bed Chamber' (i.e. his private bedroom) at Kensington Palace (*Invt., 1699*). '4 larg Portugall Matts' were laid on the daïs in the Presence Chamber at Hampton Court in 1699 (*Estimates*) and nailed to the flooring round the edge through a galloon.

84. There was, for instance a 'tapis de moquette de trois lais de large et trois aulnes et demye de long, fon[d]s jaune' at the Château de Turenne (*Havard*, 'Moquette'). The three widths were stitched together (making a total of about a yard and a half) while the carpet was three and a half ells wide. Cardinal Mazarin (*Invt., 1653*) had 'un grand tapis de moquette de quatre aunes trois quart de long, large de trois laiz, faisant une aune et demie'.

85. *Guiffrey, Inventaire*, II, p. 304.

86. *Hardwick Invt., 1601*

87. *Cockesden Invt., 1626.*

88. *Dyrham Invt., 1610* and *Guiffrey, Inventaire*, I, p. 414.

89. The equivalent German word is *Teppich*. When Constantijn Huygens visited Postdam in 1686, he saw there a workshop producing 'Tisch und Fussteppichen' (Table and Foot Carpets); they were presumably of moquette (*Stengel*, p. 52).

90. *Stengel*, p. 50.

91. The four Oriental carpets (two Turkish, one Persian and a silk carpet that must have been Persian, see p. 109 at Ham House were all in the Wardrobe Room when the Inventory was taken in 1679 although one was for a while noted as being in the drawing room.

92. In 1578 the King of Navarre had 'neuf tapis velus [i.e. pile carpets], desquels les deux sont grand pour servir soubs les pieds, et les aultres sept estoient pour servire à la table et buffet' [nine pile carpets of which two are large for laying on the floor, the other seven being for laying on tables and buffets] (F. Michel, *Recherches sur le commerce, la fabrication, et l'usage des etoffes de soie, d'or et d'argent . . . pendant le moyen age*, Paris, 1852–4, p. 165). The Duke of Pomerania asked

the art-dealer and agent, Philip Hainhofer, to secure for him some Turkish carpets of such a size that two or three would cover the entire floor of a room ('in der grösse dass zwei oder drei ein Ganzes Zimmer an der Erde bedeckten'; see *Stengel*, p. 50).

93. See pp. 110–111.

94. e.g. the thirteen 'grand tapis . . . facon de Levant, faits à la Savonnerie pour servir à la Gallerie d'Apollon du Louvre' (*Guiffrey, Inventaire*, p. 387).

95. In 1633 the King of Denmark ordered ten large chairs to be brought from Holland for some special festivity and apparently had each chair placed on its own individual carpet of tapestry (G. Garde, *Danske Silkebroderede Laeredsduge fra 16 og 17 arhundrede*, Copenhagen, 1961, p. 186).

96. *Mazarin Invt., 1653*. See p. 355 for a note on 'hautelisse'.

97. *Savary des Bruslons*, 'Tapis'.

98. *Hengrave Invt., 1603* and *Gosfield Invt., 1638.*

99. *Guiffrey, Inventaire*, II, p. 304.

100. *Ham Invt., 1679*. This was rendered as 'Two leathers to cover ye inlaid floore' in 1677.

101. *Tart Hall Invt., 1641.*

102. *Mazarin Invt., 1653*. It is unlikely the carpet was of scorched leather (see p. 120).

103. *Kensington Palace Invt., 1697.*

Notes to Chapter VII

1. Penelope Eames ('Documentary Evidence Concerning the Character and Use of Domestic Furnishings in England in the Fourteenth and Fifteenth Century', *Furniture History*, Vol. VII, note 10) has explained that, during the late mediaeval period, the 'tester' was the upright piece at the head (*tête* or *teste* in French) of the bed while the roof-like component above the bed was called the 'ceilour'. The French still called the latter the '*ciel*' in the seventeenth century. By this period, the English word 'ceilour' had largely fallen out of use and what had formerly been the 'tester' then became the 'head-cloth' or 'head-board'. That there was room for confusion even at the time is shown by the note concerning a set of bed-hangings that were sent down to Knole in 1624 which comprised five curtains, the valances and the 'test and tester' (see Charles J. Phillips, *History of the Sackville Family*, London, 1928, p. 317). Nevertheless there is absolutely no doubt that the word 'tester' almost invariably

meant the roof-like component in the seventeenth-century parlance. A 'half-tester' bed was one in which the tester only projected so far from the wall as to cover half the length of the sleeping-surface.

2. 'Quant les lits ne portoient que six pieds de long, sur autant de large, on leur donnoit le nom couchettes; mais lorsqu'ils étoient de huit pied et demi sur sept et demi, ou be onze sur dix ou de douze sur onze en ce cas là on les appeloit des couches' [When beds were only six feet long, by as much wide, they were simply given the name *couchettes*; but when they were eight and a half feet by seven and a half or eleven by ten or twelve by eleven, in that case they called them *couches*] (Sauval, *Antiquités de Paris*, written before 1669–70, Paris, 1724, II, p. 230).

3. *Charles I Invts., 1649–51* and *Havard*, 'Couches'.

4. *Havard*, 'Couche'.

5. *Turenne Invt., 1615*.

6. It was 'façon de camp', i.e. a field bed (see below) which 'se ploye et ferme' [which folds and shuts up] and was 'femant à quatre vis' [closed [locked in position?] with four screws] (*Havard*, 'Couche'). At the Brussels residence of the Prince of Orange in 1568 two ladies attending the Princess had 'Deux litz de camp en fachon de couches, avecq leurs fers de gordines, de bois' [two campbeds of wood in the form of *couches* with their iron curtain-rods] (*Orange Invts.*, I, p. 33).

7. The Germans called it a *Schaub-bette*, a 'shove-bed'. A French mediaeval inventory of 1471 refers to 'une petite couchete rouleresse' and another to 'une petite couchete roulante' (*Havard*, 'Couche'). The inventory of the Prince of Orange, mentioned in the previous note, refers to 'une couche rollé', 'une petite rolette' (pp. 29 and 32). The inventory of Breda Castle of 1597–1603 notes a gilt bed 'met rollebedt', with its rolling-bed (p. 76).

8. *Havard*, 'Couche'.

9. In the best bed the squire must lie,
   And John in truckle-bed hard by
a contemporary poet tells us, while another speaks of a servant who 'lay at his master's feet in a truckel bed' (*O.E.D.*, 'Truckle bed').

10. *Du Boisgeslin Invt., 1668*. Cardinal Mazarin's guards also had beds consisting of a plank laid on trestles (*Mazarin Invt., 1653*).

11. *Hardwick Invt., 1601* and *Knole Invt., 1645*.

12. *Tart Hall Invt., 1641*.

13. *Mazarin Invt., 1653*. Was the 'sempter [sumpter] hanging upp by the bedd' listed with the 'standing bedsted ... wth. a waneskote tester' at Marton Hall (*Invt., 1605*) a similar embellishment? And what about the 'French bedd, the tester and vallance of fugured [figured] sattin ... with a French canopie suteable to it'? Was this also such a double-tiered affair (*Gosfield Invt., 1638*)?

14. Gabrielle d'Estrées' bed 'façon de camp' has already been mentioned. Cardinal Mazarin also owned a very splendid 'lict de campagne' of red damask (*Mazarin Invt., 1653*). Louis XIII was forced to sleep on a plain straw-filled palliasse on one occasion in 1622 when he had arrived at some place in the evening and 'son lit n'etoit pas venu'. In 1608 he is recorded as having helped his servants to 'plier son lit' before moving off to Saint-Cloud (*Havard*, 'Lit', quoting from Héroard's life of Louis XIII).

15. Mazarin's bed (see previous note) had its own leather-bound travelling coffer. At Copenhagen Castle (F. R. Friis, *Kjøbenhavn's Slots Inventarium, 1638*, Samlinger til Dansk Bygnings- og Kunsthistorie, Copenhagen, 1872–8) there was an old box (ein alter Kasten) with 'darin ein Reise bette'—in it a travelling bed. *Karlson* (p. 135) mentions several such containers including one of sealskin.

16. For example, the Earl of Northampton (*Invt., 1614*) had a 'field bedstead of China worke blacke and silver with the arms of the Earle of Northampton upon the head-piece, the toppe and valance of purple velvett striped downe wth. silver laces and knottes of silver'.

17. e.g. 'the vallans wth. bells' on a field bed at Marton Hall (*Invt., 1605*).

18. A splendid field bed with black velvet and silver-lace hangings at Hardwick (*Invt., 1601*) had five 'guilt knops to stand on top of the bed'. It is difficult to imagine five finials being disposed otherwise than on a tester of hipped conformation like that shown in Plate 122.

19. The Earl of Northampton's field bed (see note 16 above) had eight cups with plumes as finials. Had it been a bed with a single slope, it would only have needed six finials.

20. e.g. the inventories of *Hatfield Priory (1629)*, the *Countess of Leicester (1634)* and *Knole (1645)*.

21. *Randle Holme*, Bk. III, Chap. XIV, p. 16.

22. e.g. at Hardwick, Henham, Marton, Cockesden (*Invts. of 1601, 1602, 1605* and *1610*).

23. *Dyrham Invt., 1703*, and Martin Lister, *A Journey to Paris*, London, 1699, p. 191.

24. The chief groups of designs were those published by Jacques Androuet Ducerceau and by Hans Vredeman de Vries (see S. Jervis, *Printed Furniture Designs before 1650*, Furniture History Society, 1974, pp. 25 and 29).

25. e.g. the 'standing bedstead ... wth. a waneskot tester' at *Marton* (*Invt. 1605*).

26. The Duke's bed at Cockesden (*Invt. 1626*) was inlaid, for example. There were several carved and gilt bedsteads in important rooms at Hardwick (*Invt., 1601*), while at Chatsworth (*Invt., 1601*) a splendid bed is described as being 'with sondrie coulers and golde'.

27. *Karlson*, p. 149, believed that the *Ståndsäng* of contemporary Swedish inventories was a bed without a superstructure but this hardly squares with the evidence.

28. The bed mentioned in note 25, above, seems to confirm this.

29. *Unton Invt., 1595.*

30. *Marton Invt., 1605.*

31. *Kilkenny Invt., 1684.* There was a *lit en dome* in the French royal collection in 1675 (*Guiffrey, Inventaire*, p. 263).

32. Could the 'Dutch bed' mentioned in the will of Mary, Countess Rivers (1644) have been of this sort? (J. Watney *Sole Account of St Osyth's Priory, Essex*, London, 1871.)

33. An upholsterer working for the royal household in 1595 was engaged on 'new guilding the bolle of a canopie' (information kindly given me by Mr John Nevinson) while there was 'a greate guilt demi ball for a canopy' at Tart Hall (*Invt., 1641*), and 'one round canopy head' at Knole (*Invt., 1645*).

34. 'One Crimson velvett Canapie ... wth. two rich Tafata changeable Trayned Curtaynes to it' (*Easton Invt., 1637*), and '2 longe traynes of greene taffety sarcenet ... belongeinge to the canopy' (*Cockesden, Invt., 1626*). The same term occurs in the *Gilling Invts., 1594*.

35. In the *Turenne Inventory of 1615* the beds are listed in groups, one of them being headed 'Pavillons'. One, of red damask trimmed with silver, had 'le chapiteau de velours Cramoisy' [the cap of crimson velvet] and a deep fringe 'en rond' [all round] as well as a 'pomme paincte de rouge ... avec son cordon de soie' [finial painted red ... with its red silk cord]. Another French inventory refers to 'ung pavillons' which had a 'pomme dorée au dessus'—a gilt knob on top

(*Thiret Invt., 1621*).

36. A. C. Fox-Davies, *The Book of Public Arms*, London, 1894, p. 816.

37. See Penelope Eames, *Mediaeval Furniture*, London, 1977, p. 83; also published as Vol. XIII of *Furniture History*, where this question is also discussed.

38. *Charles I Invts., 1649–51*. One could of course fit pull-up curtains to beds of a more elaborate nature. The Duchess of Ormonde's domed bed at Kilkenny (*Invt., 1684*) had 'nine pairs of strings and tassels to tie the curtains'.

39. The beds in the *Turenne Invt., of 1615* are grouped under 'Litz Completz', 'Litz à housse', 'Pavillons' and 'couchettes'. The first group presumably concerned beds of the massive kind; *pavillons* and *couchettes* have already been discussed.

40. *Havard*, 'Couchette'.

41. *Havard*, see under 'Linomple', because the bed had hangings of linen.

42. *Havard*, 'Bonnegraces' and 'Cantonnières'. A 'French bed' with 'cantoons' is listed in the *Charles I Inventories of 1649–51*. A royal bed in Sweden, that was apparently imported in 1620, was noted as having 'corner-pieces' (*hörn-styckar*) in 1655 (Åke Setterwall, 'Gustaf II och Maria Eleonoras Bilägersäng', in *Uppländsk Bygd*, Stockholm, *1940*).

43. *Ham Invt., 1679.*

44. William III's ambassador in Paris in 1698 reported home to his royal master that 'les lits ... que l'on fait ici ... sont tous carré par dehors, jusques au haut' [the beds ... that are made here ... are all square outside right to the top] and went on to stress that 'en haut ... ils ne sont pas plus large qu'au bas' [at the top ... they are no wider than at the base], unlike the fashionable form of bed in England which had a spreading cornice as well as furbellows and excrescences of all kinds (G. Jackson-Stops, 'William III and French Furniture', *Furniture History*, VII, 1971).

45. The famous cloth-of-gold bed at Knole which probably belonged to James II is of the French type, with no cornice but with valances that are fanciful in outline. Whether it was made in Paris or London is a question that has not yet been settled. See G. Jackson-Stops, 'The 6th Earl of Dorset's Furniture at Knole, II', *Country Life*, 9 June 1977. See also Plate 140 here.

46. '2 halfe headed bedsteads' are listed as being in the 'Gentlemen's Chamber' (i.e. the gentle-

men servants) in the Earl of Northampton's *Inventory of 1614*, and there was such a bed in a 'Servant's Chamber' at Knole (*Invt., 1645*).

47. e.g. 'a halfe headed bedstead with a canopie' (*Northampton Invt., 1614*); 'A half headed bedstead . . .,' 'A featherbed' etc., 'A watchett [light blue] perpetuana cannopie[,] Curtaynes of the same . . .' (*St Giles Invt., 1639*); at Gosfield (*Invt., 1638*) a bed of this sort had a 'round canopie' which was presumably of the normal conical form.

48. *Noordeinde Invt., 1633*.

49. *Tessin's Visit, 1687*.

50. *Havard, 'Lit'*.

51. There was a bed of this sort in Mazarin's collection (*Invt., 1653*). The tester was held up by means of 'quatre cordons servans à attacher le dict lict' [four cords serving to suspend the said gauze bed]. It had six curtains. A bed at Meudon was described as 'un lit a l'Impérial et à la duchesse' but it is not easy to say precisely what the last term meant (*Havard, 'Imperiale'* and *'Duchesse'*).

52. *Celia Fiennes*, p. 277.

53. Dean Goodwin provided a livery bedstead for his maid; it had a separate canopy. 'Inventory of W. Goodwin, Dean of Christ Church, Oxon., 1621' (Manuscript in the Bodleain Library; by kind permission of the Keeper of the Archives, Oxford University). The same combination was to be seen at Henham (*Invt., 1602*). The Bishop of Winchester (*Invt., 1618*) had a livery bed among his household goods valued at 3s. 4d. while his half-headed beds cost between 2s. and 3s.

54. *Hardwick Invt., 1601*. A pallet normally lay on the floor, perhaps on a mat, but the Hardwick pallets seem to have had some sort of framework because the bedclothes are listed as being 'in ye pallet[s]'.

55. *Countess of Leicester's Invt., 1634* and *Tart Hall Invt., 1641*. At the Prince of Orange's residence at The Hague in 1632 there was a servant's 'sleeping bench' or couch (*Een Slaepbanck voor Dunois, camerdiener; Orange Invts.*, I, p. 235).

56. *Dean Goodwin's Invt., 1618 loc. cit.* and *Havard, 'Banc'*.

57. *Ham Invt., 1683*.

58. *Stengel*, p. 138. There is an engraving by Abraham Bosse showing the beds (of the 'French bed' type) standing in rows in one of the wards. Incidentally, Hans Fugger's sons each had an 'eysernes Pettstatt' (an iron bedstead) when they attended the University of Padua in the fifteenth century.

59. *Copenhagen Castle Invt., 1638*.

60. *Knole Invt., 1645* and *Guiffrey, Inventaire*, p. 122.

61. At Knole (*Invt., 1645*) there were three, for instance.

62. An Italian visitor to Sweden in 1674 noted that even quite humble citizens might sport a canopy; it was not a sign of rank (L. Magalotti, *Sverige under år 1674*, ed. Carl Magnus Stenbock, Stockholm, 1912).

63. A rich canopy bearing the arms of Anne of Denmark, the consort of James I who died in 1619, had as its complement a chair and long cushion with a footstool, two other ceremonial chairs and their footstools, six back chairs and twenty-two high stools—all with painted and gilded frames (*Charles I Invts., 1649–51*).

64. Cotgrave in fact explains that the French word 'daïs' meant a 'cloth of estate, canopie or heaven, that stands over the head of Princes' thrones' but could also mean 'the whole state or seat of estate'. He does not mention platforms at all.

65. In her will, Lady Dorchester mentioned her 'canopie couche . . . which did stand on my Gallerie att Westminster' (*Gosfield Invt., 1638*); there was a 'coutch . . . wth. 2 taffeta curtaines & a canopie to it' in the Lower Gallery at Hatfield Priory (*Invt., 1629*) and, at Tart Hall (*Invt., 1641*), a couch with canopy stood in the North Gallery. At Knole (*Invt., 1645*) one of the couches was described as having not only a tester and a head-cloth (but no curtains?) but had a separate and additional canopy with a pair of curtains and double valances over it. An inventory of the possessions of Amalia van Solms, Princess of Orange, of about 1654–58, refers to a canopy belonging to a couch of red velvet which had two ball-finials above (*Een canaby offte rustbedde van root flueweel . . . twee gardijnen . . . twee bollen bovenop't caneby; Orange Invts.*, I, p. 275).

66. Charles I had 'one seate couch fashion' with a canopy (*Charles I Invts., 1649–51*). At Cockesden (*Invt., 1626*) the 'fayre couch chaire of black feegurd sattin' was furnished with a single footstool (as well as two small stools, presumably to flank the couch) which suggests that one sat centrally and with a support for the feet. The 'couch of crimson leather printed borderwise' in the *Northampton Inventory of 1614* had a long

cushion (the mattress or squab) and two short cushions which were probably disposed, one at each end, as in the Hardwick drawing. At Tart Hall (*Invt., 1641*) the 'couch of painted wood on some partes thereof' (i.e. partly painted, like the Hardwick couch) likewise had 'thereon a couch bed [mattress or squab] & two long cushions'.

67. Some couches that started life as double-ended ceremonial couches have had one end sawn off so as to turn them into day-beds, when the ceremonial form went out of fashion. This has happened to a couch in the Victoria and Albert Museum, for instance (W. 57–1953).

68. Molière, for instance, had a *lit de repos* with a *pavillon* of Indian chintz (*Havard*, 'Pavillon').

69. See P. Thornton, 'Couches, Canopies and Chairs of State', *Apollo*, October 1974, pp. 292–9.

70. *Thiret Invt., 1621.*

71. e.g. The 'Pearl Bed' at Hardwick (*Invt., 1601*) had 'tester, bed's head and double vallens of black velvet imbroidered with silver, golde and pearle' but the five curtains were of a black and white damask. Lady Dorchester (*Gosfield Invt., 1638*) bequeathed to her daughter 'my white taffeta satten flowered piece of stuffe and cloake of the same for a valance and cantoones for a bedd, and thirtie pounds in money to buy her damaske' which must have been to make up the remaining hangings. Incidentally, *Randle Holme* states that the inner valances of beds in his day were 'generally white silk or linen' although this is not confirmed by the evidence of inventories. (Bk. III, Chap., XIV, p. 16).

72. Examples from the end of the seventeenth century survive (Plate 98) but inventories confirm that the counterpoint was habitually richly ornamented. At Gilling Castle (*Invt., 1594*) his Lordship slept in a bed with 'a fayre counter pointe shadowed with silke' while the 'Best Bed' at Hardwick (*Invt., 1601*) had a counterpoint 'payned with cloth of gold and silver, and a brode golde lace and golde fringe about it, lyned with crimson sarcenet.'

73. The *Thiret Inventory of 1621* refers to a brown serge coverlet on a bed 'pendante jusques en bas avec les courtines' (i.e. hanging down to the same level as the lower edge of the curtains) but such an arrangement would of course disguise the base valances. Normally their lower edges lined up with those of the curtains while the counterpoint reached down only over the top of the base valances. Elaborate beds of the Marot

type sometimes had the edges of the bed-stock accentuated by a textile-covered board of fancy shape. In such cases the counterpoint was tucked in under the mattresses and did not hang down.

74. *Mazarin Invt., 1653.*

75. *Randle Holme* (Bk. III, Chap. XIV, p. 16) explained that the tester of a bed might have 'bobbs of wood gilt, or covered sutable to the curtaines'. Charles I ordered that 'five gilt cupps for a feild bedd' be sent for melting down in 1626 (C. C. Oman, *English Domestic Silver*, London, 1963, p. 183).

76. Mazarin had a bed of embroidered velvet topped with four *panaches* each consisting of fifty large, twenty-two medium, and twenty-three small ostrich plumes 'blanches fines' as well as four *aigrettes* (*Havard*, 'Aigrette').

77. A bed at Versailles in 1682 had plumes that were white and *couleur de feu* while the Maréchale de Humières had green, yellow and white feathers on her bed (*Havard*, 'Bouquet de Plume').

78. Madame de Maintenon's bed at Saint-Cloud was surmounted by four carved vases of flowers which were gilded and 'glacé de rouge'—probably lacquered with a red-stained varnish (*Havard*, 'Chambre'). In the Thiret mansion (*Invt., 1621*) there was in store a special case containing 'quatre boucquets en feuilliage servans à mectre sur le lict' [four bouquets with foliage for putting on the bed] which must have been of artificial flowers. *Havard* ('Bouquet de Plume') mentions a bed of 1694 with metal flowers: they were presumably painted.

79. Apart from the one illustrated, which is at Cotehele in Cornwall, a pair from a bed that no longer survives is at Skokloster in Sweden, and the form may be seen in several contemporary illustrations.

80. A rare instance was the bed with 'three peeces of Arras hangings' at Edington (*Invt., 1665*).

81. Several 'Arras Coverletts' were on beds in the house of a West Country squire in 1641 (*Devon Invts.*). It is possible that they were specially woven as coverlets but the 'large counter pointe of verders' on a bed at Gilling Castle (*Invt., 1594*) must have simply been a verdure tapestry laid over the bedclothes.

82. There were 'green and white Broccadella' hangings on a bed at Petworth (*Invt., 1670*), however.

83. e.g. Lady Dorchester had a fine bed of 'purple

cloth embroydred in spaces' line with yellow taffeta that was valued at £150 (*Gosfield Invt., 1638*) and in 'My Lady's Old Chamber' at Cowdray (*Invt., 1682*) the bed was 'hung with embroidered cloth lined with clouded sattin'.

84. Lady Dorchester bequeathed to her daughter, among other items that she seems to have treasured, 'my tawny imbroidered cloth bedd which was wrought in my house' (*Gosfield Invt., 1638*). Celia Fiennes (p. 68) noted that Lady Burghley 'used to lye in winter' in a green velvet bed embroidered by her mother, the Countess of Devonshire.

85. The bed-hangings of 'wrought greene usted [worsted]' in the 'Greene Wrought Chamber' at Tredegar (*Invt., 1688*) and those of 'white dimity wrought wth. green worsted' in 'Young Master's' room ten years later (*Invt., 1698*) may have been of this distinctive class, as may have been another set of 'dymathy' hangings at Syon House (*Invt., 1670*) that were 'wrought with redd worsted'.

86. *Ham Invt., 1683*. The bed was the eldest son's; it had six main curtains along with the other bed-hangings of blue velvet and a 'tower de leet' of blue taffeta. A bed at Dieren in 1683 had silk hangings and a 'tour de lit' as well (*Orange Invts.*, I, p. 388).

87. Hans Andersen's fairy-tale about the princess who could feel a pea through twenty-four matresses was only a slight exaggeration. Many fine beds had four but lowly people had to make do with one filled with rough materials.

88. The Great of Bed of Ware, in the Victoria and Albert Museum, has holes bored into the side rails of the bedstock, through which the cords were threaded. Many early seventeenth-century beds have this feature.

89. *Randle Holme* (Bk. III, Chap. XIV, p. 16) lists the parts of a bed and mentions 'Mat or sackcloth bottom.' There was a 'London mat' on a bed at Marton Hall (*Invt., 1605*) and a Cornish one on a bed at Ingatestone (*Invt., 1600*).

90. When a German prince slept in what must have been the 'Great Bed' at Ware in 1612, he told how 'je fus couché dans un lict de plume de cigne qui avoit huict pieds de largeur' [he slept in a bed of Swansdown which was eight feet wide] (W. B. Rye, *England as seen by Foreigners*, London, 1865, p. 62). See also *Havard*, 'Coite'.

91. King Christian IV, the brother of Anne of Denmark (the wife of James I of England) had an eiderdown on his camp-bed during his campaigns in Germany during the Thirty Years' War (E. Fischer, *Linväverämbetet i Malmö*, Lund, 1959), and Pepys (*Diary*, 9 September, 1605) records how he 'lay the softest I ever did in my life, with a down bed after the Danish manner *upon* me' (my italics).

92. *Havard*, 'Matelas' and 'Bourralisse'. He cites a reference of 1697 to 'un matelas de bourralisse couverte de toile rayé' [a mattress of flock covered with striped linen]. In the *Du Boisgeslin Inventory of 1688* a bed is described as having both a wool and a 'boure' mattress.

93. *Devon Invts.*

94. The island of Chios apparently produced 'cotton wool etc., and also coarse wool, to make beds' (Gasper Campion, *Discourse of the Trade of Chio*, 1569).

95. It was remarked upon at the time when Henri IV had had to sleep on a straw-filled mattress on one occasion in 1598, and French courtiers considered it almost insufferable that one should have to sleep on such mattresses when staying at Saint-Germain in the middle of the century. By the end of the century such a thing would have been inconceivable (*Havard*, 'Paille').

96. *Havard*, 'Matelas'.

97. *Turenne Invt., 1615*.

98. *Princess Palatine's Letters*, letter of 8 December 1697.

99. *Havard*, 'Draps de Lit'.

100. One sees striped sheets in Dutch paintings of the period. *Stengel* (p. 171) states that blue and white striped sheets remained common in Berlin, even in quite grand houses, even in the eighteenth century, and quotes several references to checked bed linen.

101. *Savary des Bruslons*, 'Courtepointe'. He was probably describing quilting executed with a double running stitch where two threads appear alternately on the two faces to form a continuous line. Quilting is of course reversable.

102. There was a coverlet at Ingatestone (*Invt., 1600*) of 'taffeta sercenett ... ymbrodered all over with yellow twyst, and lyned with fyne crimson wollen' while a handsome quilt at Hardwick (*Invt., 1601*) must have been that of 'India stuff imbroidered with beasts with frenge and tassells of white silk'. Counterpanes of 'painted quilted caleco' were on three beds at Cowdray (*Invt., 1682*).

103. Listed among Cardinal Mazarin's linen (*Invt., 1653*) are some 'couvertures de drap de toile d'Hollande fines'. There was a 'Hollon

quilt' at Edington (*Invt., 1665*) and a 'Holland quilt' at Chenies (*Invt., 1585*).

104. *Guiffrey, Inventaire*, III, p. 110; and *Gosfield Invt., 1638*.

105. Molière had a 'sommier de crin' which seems to have been a form of bolster filled with horsehair and may have been wedge-shaped so as to tilt upward the top half of the body. Such 'triangular bolsters' were still to be found on many German beds until recently and the 'Kopfmatratze' (head-mattress) on the Queen of Prussia's bed in 1705 is likely to have been of a similar nature. English farmers occasionally had straw-filled bolsters but these were always used in conjunction with a feather bolster (*Havard*, 'Couche'; *Stengel*, pp. 146–8; *Devon Invts.*).

106. Lady Maynard, for instance, had two pillows while her lady-in-waiting had only one (*Ham Invt., 1679*).

107. La Comte de Laborde, *Le Palais Mazarin*, Paris, 1846, p. 301.

108. *Randle Holme*, Bk. III, Chap. XIV, p. 16.

109. e.g. 'Sixe colored turned bedstaves in a case of wood' (*Ingatestone Invt., 1600*).

NOTES TO CHAPTER VIII

1. *Hardwick Invt., 1601*. Note particularly the detailed description of the nineteen 'long cushions' that were in the Gallery. See also G. F. Wingfield-Digby, *Elizabethan Embroidery*, London, 1963. In the *Easton Lodge Inventory of 1637*, the cushions are listed separately as well; most of them were richly decorated and all must have been showy.

2. Lord Teviot (*Invt., 1694*) had two caned couches in his rooms at Oxford furnished with 'Irish Sticht squabs & six cushons of ye same' while a pair of 'Dutch chaires' (which had rush seats; see p. 206) had 'two Irish stitcht cushions'.

3. The mattress of Russia leather 'garni de petites touffes or et argent et d'un galon tout autour' mentioned in the French royal inventories of 1681 (*Havard*, 'Matelas') would seem to have been a squab with tufting (see p. 128).

4. *Kilkenny Invt., 1684*.

5. *Havard*, ('Carreau') quotes a reference of 1471 to 'carreaulx longs'.

6. A royal easy chair in 1693 was described as a 'grand fauteuil de commodité ... avec son carreau separé' (*Guiffrey, Inventaire*, II, p. 416);

Havard, ('Fauteuil') refers to several 'fauteuils de paille' [rush-seated chairs] with 'leurs carreaux'. Easy chairs are discussed on p. 195.

7. *Havard*, 'Carreau'. Mazarin (*Invt., 1653*) owned a *carreau* which had 'cuir rouge par dessous'.

8. *Ibid.*

9. It is illustrated in the *D.E.F.* under 'Stool', Plate 22.

10. *Ham Invt., 1683*.

11. *Ingatestone Invt., 1600; Hatfield Priory Invt., 1629*.

12. *Mazarin Invt., 1653*.

13. *Randle Holme*, Chap. XIV.

14. 'One forme with a back benshe of waynskot' and 'one forme with a bench bord' are quotations from inventories of 1619 cited by S. Wolsey and R. W. P. Luff, *Furniture in England, The Age of the Joiner*, London, 1968, p. 72.

15. Records of the Court of the Joyners' Company, Guildhall, London, Mx. 8046/2, 27 November 1694; and Ipswich Court Record, 26 March 1661 (both kindly communicated to me by Mr Benno Forman).

16. 'One forme with a joyned back' (*Agius*; given in the original typescript but deleted from the published version).

17. The 'settee' at Hatfield Priory (*Invt., 1629*) was probably of this class.

18. *Havard*, 'Archebanc'. An *arche* was a box-like container like our 'ark'. The 'banc de noyer à deux couverceaux et fermatures fermans à clef' [walnut bench with two lids with locks closed with a key] will have been an *archebanc* (*Thiret Invt., 1621*). The scene of the Assumption was painted on it, presumably on its panelled back.

19. 'Ung grand banc à coucher, en forme d'archebanc, bois noguier garny de couitte, cuissin, rempli de plume, couverte blanc' [A large sleeping bench in the form of a *archebanc*, of walnut, furnished with a mattress, cushion, filled with feathers with a white cover] (*Havard*, 'Archebanc'; inventory of 1635).

20. *Randle Holme*, Bk. III, Chap. XIV. 'Six joyned buffett stooles' were in the Parlour at Bramfield which was in Suffolk, for instance (Inventory of Arthur Coke of Bramfield, 1629, ed. F. W. Steer, *Proceedings of the Suffolk Institute of Archaeology*, xxv., p. 13, 1951); there were others at Tart Hall (*Invt., 1641*) which was in London.

21. *Havard*, 'respect'.

22. *D.E.F.*, 'Stool', fig. 5. See also G. Jackson-Stops, 'The 6th Duke of Dorset's Furniture at

Knole II', *Country Life*, 9 June 1977, fig. 3, where they are dated to the 1620s—in which case they may have been part of Queen Henrietta Maria's furniture; she arrived in this country from Paris in 1625. Some folding stools are mentioned in the *Petworth Inventory of 1670*.

23. *Havard*, 'Pliant'.

24. Furetière, in his *Dictionnaire* of 1690, states that *perroquets* were 'des sièges pliants' which 'ont un dossier'.

25. Furetière, *op. cit.*, also says that 'ils servent à s'asseoir à table' [they serve as seats at the table]. See *Havard*, 'Perroquet'.

26. What follows in this paragraph is a summary of an article on the identity of the 'back stool' (see P. Thornton, 'Back-stools and Chaises à Demoiselles', *The Connoisseur*, February 1974).

27. 'Low-back chairs' are mentioned in several inventories including that of Tart Hall of 1641. 'Half back chairs' (*Cockesden Invt., 1626*) and the 'two lowe chaires with lowe open backs' at Ingatestone (*Invt., 1600*) are likely to have been of the same class, the word 'open' presumably referring to the gap between the seat and the back-rest.

28. Contrasted with some 'chaize à bras' [armchairs] covered with embroidery in a room in a house at Rheims in 1621 were 'six chaises basses à dam[ois]elle' covered *en suite* (*Thiret Invt., 1621*). In another room were twenty-one 'chaizes a bras' of walnut covered with moquette and 'une autre chaize de bois a dam*elle*', covered in the same material. Women were being provided with low chairs well back in the sixteenth century; an inventory of 1568 refers to 'Une chayere basse pour dames à doz garny de volours rouge, viel' (*Orange Invts.*, I, p. 27).

29. Gabrielle d'Estrées had some gilt walnut chairs, four of which had arms while the rest were 'à vertugadin' (*Havard*, 'Chaise'). The farthingale itself had gone out of fashion by 1620 yet the hey-day of this type of chair was only reached about 1635; so, strictly speaking, it is only early versions which have a right to the name 'farthingale chair'.

30. An inventory of 1611 refers to some 'petites chaizes caquetoires en tapisserie' (E. Bonnaffé, *Le Meuble en France au XVIe siecle*, Paris, 1887, pp. 216–19). In 1580 the new regulations of the Parisian Guild of Huchiers-Menuisiers [Joiners] stipulated that those seeking to become masters of the Company had to make and submit for examination a 'chaise basse appellée caquetouère'

[low chairs called *caquetoires*]. It may well be that, at this early date, such chairs did not have padded backs but the sort of chair today mis-named 'a *caquetoire*' can certainly not be called low. This question is discussed by Thornton, *loc. cit.*

31. Bonnaffé, *loc. cit.*

32. e.g. in the *Du Boisgeslin Invts., 1688*.

33. In the Great Chamber at Faringdon (*Invt., 1620*), for instance, there was a 'greate chaier', a red velvet chair and a 'red velvett back chaier imbroydred' and seven more 'back chaiers'. There can be little doubt that, in such a setting, the fashionable chair of the day—the 'farthingale chair'— would have been present in some numbers. 'A little back chaire embrodred' was bought for the Provost's lodge at King's College Cambridge in 1609–10. (*Provost of Kings Invt., 1660*).

34. e.g. the famous set of 'dolphin chairs' at Ham House (see Plate 40, here) comprise armed and armless versions; the latter are called 'back stools' in the *Inventory of 1678* although they have little resemblance to the sort of chair we have been discussing. The term seems to have become synonymous with 'a chair without arms' during the last three decades of the century.

35. The type of 'farthingale chair' covered with turkeywork was probably always an exception to this general rule, for the uprights could not be conveniently covered in this thick material. In fact, rectangular panels of turkeywork with borders were made specially to go on the seats and backs of such chairs, the woollen manufacturers claiming towards the end of the century that '5,000 dozen' turkeywork chairs were produced in England each year. This is no doubt an exaggeration but it indicates that a lively industry existed and that the output was considerable (See R. W. Symonds, 'Turkey Work, Beech and Japanned Chaires', *The Connoisseur*, April, 1934). See Plate 103, here.

36. Mrs Eames has done much to clarify this subject, explaining how precedence rather than rank governed the use of chairs in mediaeval society (see P. Eames, 'Furniture in England, France and the Netherlands from the Twelfth to the Fifteenth Century', *Furniture History*, XIII, 1977).

37. In the Victoria and Albert Museum is a X-frame chair of state in which, tradition has it, Charles I sat during his trial in 1648 (see *D.E.F.*, 'Chairs', Plate 38).

38. It is curious that the chair-makers still bothered to make them foldable until well into the seventeenth century and still incorporated the scissor-action in the X-frame even after having made all movement impossible by introducing front and back seat-rails, and rails at the top and bottom of the back-support, thus effectively locking the frame in the open position. The late specimens of X-frame chairs of state at Knole exemplify this phase in the chair's development.

39. Jean Nicot, *Thresor de la langue francaise . . .*, 1606.

40. See 'Inventaires de la Royne Descosse Douairière de France, Catalogues of the . . . Furniture . . . of Mary Queen of Scots, 1556–1569', *The Bannantyne Club*, Edinburgh, 1863, Inventory of 1561.

41. The word appears in a French inventory of 1626. In one room were 'six chaires à vertugadin . . ., quatre chaires de bois de noier à dossier, façon de fauteuil, couverte de velours vert à ramages, trois chaires à bras et dossier de bois de noier . . .', i.e. six 'farthingale chairs' four walnut X-frame chairs covered with green velvet, and three walnut armchairs (*Havard*, 'Fauteuil').

42. P. Biver, *Histoire du Château de Meudon*, Paris, 1923, p. 141.

43. Some authorities have maintained that a *fauteuil de commodité* was a form of close stool (e.g. *Karlson*) but this was not the case. Eight chairs thus designated in the French royal inventories (*Guiffrey, Inventaire*, p. 433) had a leaf for writing at the end of one arm. It is unlikely that a close stool would have been fitted with such an accessory. What is more, no reference is ever made to pewter pans and the like in connection with such chairs.

44. *Guiffrey, Inventaire*, p. 368. A few years later (p. 433) were listed 'huit grands fauteuils de commodité à cremillières et joues', i.e. they had 'cheeks' or 'wings' against which one could rest the head—these were undoubtedly 'sleeping chairs'. The 'sleeping chayres' at Ham occur in the inventory of 1679 but not in that of 1677.

45. *Ibid.*, p. 414. The state bed at Clandon, dating from about 1700, is accompanied by a pair of easy chairs *en suite* (see J. Fowler and J. Cornforth, *English Decoration in the 18th century*, London, 1974, Plate 142). *Havard* ('Commodité' quotes a late seventeenth-century complaint about the fashionable young gentlemen at the French court who, 's'il y a des grandes chaises de commodité, ils s'en saisissent d'abord et ils auront l'incivilité de ne les pas offrir à une dame: ils s'y étendent, ils s'y renversent à demy couchez, ils s'y bercent, ils mettent leur jambes sur d'autre sièges ou sur l'un des bras de fauteuil où ils sont assis, ils les croisent et se mettent quelque fois en des postures encore plus indécentes croyant que cela a l'air de qualité d'en user ainsi' [if there are large easy chairs, they commandeer them straightaway and are so uncivil as not to offer them to a lady [first]; they stretch themselves upon them, they throw themselves back half lying down, they cradle themselves, they put their legs up on other seats or over one of the arms of the chair, they cross them and sometimes adopt postures that are even more indecent, believing that it lends an air of quality to use the chairs in this way].

46. *Evelyn's Diary*, 10 November, 1644.

47. *Charles I Invts., 1649–51.*

48. R. W. Symonds, 'Charles II couches, Chairs and Stools', *The Connoisseur*, January and February, 1934.

49. *Ham Invt., 1679 and 1683.*

50. Some indication of how great had been the advances made by the Parisian chairmakers in the 1670s is provided by the fact that both the English and the Swedish ambassadors to the French court took the trouble to take home sets of French chairs for the furnishing of their own homes (see P. Thornton, 'The Parisian Fauteuil of 1680', *Apollo*, February 1975).

51. Symonds, *loc. cit.*

52. *Ibid.* Casbert also supplied a chair for use at Whitehall which was 'round in the back and quilted' while at about the same time Richard Price, another craftsman working for the royal household, supplied some 'elbow chaires with compass backs'; these were probably both descriptions of the same 'hollow back' form.

53. *Ibid.*

54. *Ibid.* Richard Price provided some chairs in 1677 which had 'compass heeles and crooked backs'. These chairs had to be particularly stable as they were for the royal yacht.

55. R. W. Symonds, 'English Cane Chairs', *The Connoisseur*, March and May, 1951.

56. Under the heading 'Rotin', *Savary des Bruslons* (1723) tells us that this is a form of cane 'dont on fait en la fendant par morceaux, ces meubles de canne dont on fait un si grand usage et un si grand commerce en Angleterre et en Hollande, et qui commence a passer en France'

[of which have been made, by splitting it into pieces, the cane furnishings for which there is so much use and such a large trade in England and Holland, and which are beginning to enter France]. The Cane-chair Makers claimed that they exported some 2,000 dozen such chairs. So popular were they in Germany and Scandinavia that the indigenous makers of such furniture called themselves 'Englische Stuhlmacher' (or 'Engleske Stolemagere' in Danish).

57. *Havard*, 'Paille'.

58. An inventory of 1627 refers to 'une chayre de Flandre viele, garnye de paille' [an old Flanders chair, garnished with straw [i.e. rushes]] (*Ibid.*).

59. *Agius*, p. 78. There were three 'flagg bottomed chaires' in the housekeeper's room at Cowdray (*Invt., 1682*) which may have been Dutch, as may have been the four 'wooden chayres with bulrush bottoms' under the stairs at Tart Hall in 1641 (*Invt.*).

60. *Cowdray Invt., 1682* and J. Watney, *Sole Account of St Osyth's Priory, Essex*, London, 1871 (Will of Lady Rivers, 1644).

61. e.g. *Guiffrey, Inventaire*, II, pp. 241 and 243.

62. There are some black-japanned chairs of this sort at Boughton which may possibly have been imported from France along with some of the other furniture that the Duke of Montagu brought back from his embassies to that country between 1669 and 1672, and between 1676 and 1678 (see note 50). They were furnished with cushions of red damask. At Skokloster in Sweden there are some similar chairs.

63. 'garnis de carreaux et dossiers picquez' (Guiffrey, *loc. cit.*). An inventory of 1677 lists 'cinq petites chaises de bois tourne e garni de paille, et chacune de leur oreiller [here meaning a cushion rather than a pillow] et dossier rempli de plume et crain [crin, meaning horsehair, an early reference], couverte de brocatelle' (*Havard*, 'Chaise'; see also 'Fauteuil' for further examples).

64. *Agius* (p. 78) mentions one in a document of 1639. Steer (*Devon Invts.*) found another in an inventory of 1675. As Mrs Agius also found references to 'wicker rodds', she cautiously avoids drawing any firm conclusion about the nature of 'rodden chairs', but that primitive 'staked' chairs were being made at the time seems probable.

65. Lady Rivers' Will, 1644 (see note 60, above); see also *Ingatestone Invt., 1600* and *Edington Invt., 1665*.

66. e.g. a 'wicker chaire wth. a cover over the head' (*Hatfield Priory Invt., 1629*).

67. *Randle Holme*, Bk. III, Chap. XIV, p. 14.

68. I am indebted to Mrs Patricia Griffiths for this information.

69. *Agius*, loc. cit.

70. *Gilling Castle Invt., 1624.*

71. *Knole Invt., 1645.* Many of those mentioned in the *Orange Inventories* (e.g. p. 120, *passim*) had black leather covers; others were covered in cloth of gold or with silk damask. Some were specially for women (*2 Spaensches vrouwestolen*; p. 148) and some were for men (p. 153). They came with and without arms. In the Gage Inventory of 1556 (*Sussex Archeological Collections*, XLV, 1892) two chairs 'of Spanyshe making' are noted; one was 'garniyshed with collored woode' the other with coloured bone. There is no reason why all chairs from Spain should have been of the same class, but there was probably a distinctive form known as a 'Spanish chair'.

72. *Gosfield Invt., 1638*

73. *Tart Hall Invt., 1641.* Oriental furniture was still very rare in Europe at this date.

74. At the Vyne in 1541 there were some 'Flanders chairs covered with leather' (M. Jourdain, *English Decoration and Furniture of the early Renaissance 1500–1650*, London, 1924, p. 244), while some early seventeenth century French inventories have 'chaises de Flandres' that were 'basse, couverte de cyre' and others that were 'garnye de paille' (*Havard*, 'Chaise').

75. They occur, for instance at Hengrave (*Invt., 1603*) and in the Earl of Northampton's inventory of 1614. In Charles I's inventories (1649–51) mention is made of 'two scrowle or backed chaires'. Was the 'lowe role back chaire without armes' at Ingatestone (*Invt., 1600*) similar?

76. See also *D.E.F.*, 'Couch', Pl. V.

77. *Thiret Invt., 1621.*

78. *Guiffrey, Inventaire*, II, p. 346.

79. An item referred to as a *canapée* in a Dutch inventory of 1657 had mattresses and pillows, and seems to have had a canopy over it (*een geborduerd canopé met gehemelt*, a bordered canapée with a heaven; *Orange Invts.*; II, p. 77). presumably this was a couch and canopy (see p. 172) but it is here called a *canapée*. It may be worth recording that the earliest reference to a *Kanapee* in Germany so far noted occurs in a document of 1663 (P. W. Meister and H.

Jedding, *Das Schöne Möbel im Lauf der Jahrhunderts*, Munich, 1966, p. 21).

80. *Ibid.* p. 356.

81. *Havard*, 'Sopha'. Maybe the writer was thinking more of a kind of 'ottoman', for Saint-Simon some years later described something very like this piece of furniture that one tends to associate with the early nineteenth century. 'La sofa est une manière d'estrade,' he says, 'couverte de tapis, au fond de la chambre d'audience du grand vizier sur la quelle il est assis sur des carreaux' [The sofa is a kind of platform, covered with carpet, at the end of the audience chamber of the [Turkish] grand vizier, on which he is seated on squabs.]

82. *Tessin-Cronström Correspondence*, letter of 7 January, 1695.

83. See P. Thornton, 'Couches, Canopies and Chairs of State', *Apollo*, October 1974, where this question is discussed at greater length.

84. *Ibid.*, Plate 12. Some sofa-like settees standing under canopies, are illustrated in the article; they are presumably French and date from the 1690s.

85. *D.E.F.*, 'Settees and Sofas', Plate 51. This piece so closely resembles a sofa that its true nature is usually forgotten.

86. *D.E.F.*, 'Settees and Sofas'.

87. Among the upholsterers working for the royal household in the time of Charles II and William III, occur French-sounding names like Casbert, Paudevine, Guibert and 'Monsr. Le Grange'.

88. Having drawn his attention to this reference, it was gratifying that Mr Christopher Gilbert subsequently found the name 'Gilbert' (for Guibert) in the Duke of Leeds' accounts.

89. The future king Charles X of Sweden, who came to the throne in 1654, was provided with some stuffed chairs by the Court Saddler, it may be relevant to note in this connection. He stuffed the chairs in question with reindeer hair (see *Karlson*, p. 281).

90. Here again is an indication that the easy chair was evolved from the invalid chair rather than from standard forms of armchair, all of which had the gap at the back.

91. See R. W. Symonds, 'The Royal X Chair', *Apollo*, May 1937, Plate VII. It is at present covered in a green velvet which is itself fairly venerable but the red velvet, bearing the imprint of the applied lace, can be seen underneath. The double-ended couch at Hardwick (Plate 147) is painted with imitation embroidery which gives a very clear indication of what the textile covering of the mattress, valances, and two large cushions was like.

92. See Thornton, 'Backstools . . .', *loc. cit.*, Plate 6.

93. The folding stools were 'marbrez de diverses couleurs' (*Mazarin Invt., 1653*). The marbling of carcase furniture was common in the seventeenth century but it seems rather perverse to marble the slender wooden members of folding stools.

94. An important set of English armchairs at Ham House make a case in point. They were supplied about 1680 and the black areas were painted green (bronzed) in the Regency period, but the black paint may still be seen in places (P. Thornton, 'Some neo-Carolean Chairs at Ham House', *Furniture History*, Vol. X, 1974). The French armchairs at Salsta, in Sweden, also have black and gold frames (see P. Thornton, 'The Parisian *fauteuil* of 1680', *Apollo*, February 1975), and there were two black and gilt carved armchairs (*swarte vergulde gesneden armstoelen*) in William III's closet at Honselaarsdijk around 1695 (*Orange Invts.*, I, p. 470). See Plate 39, here.

95. At Hardwick (*Invt., 1601*) only one chair was gilt. Of the various chairs in the Leicester Gallery at Knole (*Invt., 1645*), several were painted but only one, with its accompanying pair of stools, was gilded and even that was only 'painted gold'. Daniel Cronström, advising Countess Piper on how to do up her house in Stockholm in close imitation of the latest Parisian fashion, suggested that 'les chaises du Cabinet de Madame seront à bois doré' [the chairs for My Lady's closet should be of gilded wood] but none of the other chairs in the house, which was to be very richly appointed, were to be gilded (*Tessin-Cronström Correspondence*, letter of 7 January 1695). As for silvering, no doubt considerable impetus was given to the fashion when Louis XIV in 1673 acquired 'un grand fauteuil de bois taillé de plusieurs ornemens et argenté, pour servir de trosne au roi lorsqu'il donne ses audiences aux ambassadeurs' [a large armchair of wood carved with many ornaments and silvered, to serve as a throne for the King when he gives audience to ambassadors] (*Havard*, 'Argenture'). The Duke of Lauderdale had silvered chairs in his closet at Ham House in the late 1670s.

96. See Catalogue of the Exhibition, The Golden Age of English Furniture Upholstery, 1660–1840,

Temple Newsam, Leeds, 1973, Plates 31 and 32.

97. If the reader doubts this assertion, he or she should think of the many seventeenth-century cane chairs that survive; they all have backs that are rough and unfinished, while their fronts are handsomely carved.

98. The royal accounts for 1617–18 include an item for providing some armchairs, footstools and stools covered with crimson velvet and 'for making . . . cases of bayes for the same . . . and for the stringes & other necessaries to them (R. W. Symonds, 'The Craft of the Coffer and Trunk Maker . . .', *The Connoisseur*, March 1942).

99. The taffeta 'cases' of some chairs supplied for Hampton Court (*Estimates, 1699*) were closed in this way.

100. At Walton (*Invt., 1624*) there were six high stools with leather seats which in addition had 'covers of green cloth & fringe on them, which may be taken of at pleasure'. Was the 'mante verte' [green mantle] on a chair mentioned in a French inventory of 1621 (*Thiret*) also some form of slip-over cover?

101. *Ham Invt., 1679*. See P. Thornton, 'The Parisian fauteuil . . .', *loc. cit.*, where it is suggested that these chairs may be French.

102. *Mazarin Invt., 1653*.

103. *Kilkenny invt., 1684*. In the *garderobe* next to the Princess of Orange's Closet in the Noordeinde residence at The Hague, there stood an armchair on wheels (*Een armstoel staaende op rollen*; *Orange Invts.*, I, p. 206).

104. There were some tapestry-woven cushion covers at Cockesden in 1610 (*Invt.*).

105. F. R. Friis, *Kjøbenhavn's Slots Inventarium, 1638*, Samlinger til Dansk Bygnings- og Kunsthistorie, Copenhagen, 1872–8.

106. 'Four squobbs wth. covers of tapistry . . .' (*Ham Invts. 1679* and *1683*). The two surviving covers are, however, now too delicate to be shown on the squabs which are today covered in a checked cotton reflecting the fact that in 1679 the covers were protected by cases of purple and white chequered Indian sarsnet. The squabs *may* already have been present in the Gallery in the 1640s if they are identical with the 'three couches and their silk furniture on them' and a fourth in the adjacent closet which are listed in the Ham inventory of about 1654.

107. *Tessin-Cronström Correspondence*, letter of 7 January 1695.

108. There were '3 small stools covered with dorney' at Cockesden (*Invt., 1610*) but no other reference has been noted.

109. *Tart Hall Invt., 1641*.

110. *Dyrham Invt., 1703*.

111. This statement was made in a petition laid before Parliament by members of the woollen industry who were seeking to curb the manufacture of cane-chairs. The cane-chair makers naturally disputed the matter and pointed out that the chairs concerned were anyway pretty humble confections (see note 56). The actual figure is given as '2000 dozen'.

112. *Thiret Invts., 1621* and *Havard*, 'Moquette'.

113. 'Twee oude spaensche stoelen van coleur kaffa . . .' (*Orange Invts.*, I, p. 198). In the Dieren inventory of 1683, for instance, mention is made of twelve 'gebloemde trijpe stoelen' in the dining-room (*Orange Invts.*, I, p. 389).

114. *Havard*, 'Chaise'.

115. See C. Pitoin, *Marly-le-Roi*, Paris, 1904, p. 174, and *Havard* 'Tabouret'. Of the 1,323 *tabourets* listed in the French royal inventoires under Louis XIV, 514 were covered in *moquette*, 24 with *panne* and 246 with 'peluche ou tripe'.

116. *Dyrham Invt.*, and *Tredegar Invt., 1692*.

117. *Hardwick Invt., 1601*.

118. The woollen industry (see note 111) claimed that 'there were yearly Vended in this Kingdom about five thousand dozen of Setwork (commonly called Turkey-work chairs though made in England)'.

119. The Crown acquired two dozen turkeywork chairs for Hampton Court in 1699, for instance, at a cost of £14. 8s. 0d. Similar orders were being placed for Holyrood Palace in Edinburgh right through the last decades of the century (see M. Swain, 'The furnishing of Holyrood House in 1668', *The Connoisseur*, February 1977).

120. *Mazarin Invt., 1653*. The frames of these pieces were 'façon d'ebeine à colonnes torses', i.e. of imitation ebony (probably black-stained pearwood) with spiral turning.

121. Le Comte de Biver, *Histoire du Château de Meudon*, Paris, 1923, p. 1495 *et seq.*

122. *Havard* ('Chaise') quotes an early seventeenth century reference to some 'chaises de Flandres . . . basse, couverte de cuyr' (see also p. 210).

123. The accounts of the Provost of King's College, Cambridge, for the year 1609–10 include a reference to 'le great red-leather chaire printed with gould, et 2 low-stooles eiusdem

operis' which cost 16 shillings (*Provost of King's Invt., 1660*). The Earl of Northampton's couch with its 'crimson leather printed border wise . . . lined with silver and gold' was probably likewise tooled and gilded (*Northampton Invt., 1614*; see p. 119).

124. *Cowdray Invt., 1682, Ham Invt.*, c. *1651*, and *Orange Invts.*, II, p. 70 (*Acht goldenleeren manstoelen ende een groot Engels goldenleeren stoell*).

125. *Tessin-Cronström Correspondence*, letters of 4 May and 29 July, 1965. Clearly the *tapissiers* (upholsterers) had these particular embroiderers working for them. Charles II acquired '2 large elbow chairs of needlework richly wrought, one of blue and gold, the other of silver and pincke' in 1672 at a cost of £60 which was also a considerable sum (R. W. Symonds, 'Charles II Couches, Chairs and Stooles', *The Connoisseur*, January and February, 1934).

126. Symonds; *loc. cit.*

127. *Mazarin Invt., 1653.*

128. The Marquis de Sourches, *Mémoires*, Vol. I, p. 82. He tells us that others blamed the malady on excessive consumption of *ragouts*, while some even suggested it could have been due to 'des debauches ultra montaines' [outlandish debauches]. The Marquis, however, felt that 'ce dernier avis n'etoit pas si bien fondé que les deux autres'.

NOTES TO CHAPTER IX

1. Presumably the tables 'appliquées sur des tréteaux qui se brisent' [laid on trestles which fold] which were in Catherine de Medici's possession in 1589 were of this kind (E. Bonnaffé, *Le Meuble en France au XVIe siècle*, Paris, 1887, p. 185).

2. A seventeenth-century Spanish specimen is represented in *St Bonaventura* by Zurbaran, painted in 1623 and now in the Gemäldegalerie Berlin-Dahlem. It is likely that the 'petite table à la mode d'Espaigne, qui se ouvre et clot' [small table in the Spanish style, which opens and closes], listed in the inventory of Marguerite d'Autriche of 1523, was of this type (Bonnaffé, *loc. cit.*).

3. Mr Francis Steer, in his excellent introduction to the *Cowdray Inventory of 1682*, suggested that the 'Spanish tables' there mentioned might have been made of mahogany (the early shipments of which came from Spanish Honduras) but the inventory of Tart Hall (*1641*) included references

to 'Spanish tables' of walnut and of oak. The term 'Spaens tafelken' [small Spanish table] occurs several times in the inventory of Breda Castle of 1619 (*Orange Invts.*, I, p. 150); this and the French reference of 1523 mentioned in the previous note, suggest that this type of table was in widespread use. They do not seem to have been regarded as of any importance. They came both with oval and with rectangular tops. The 'litle fir table with feet to fould up', mentioned in the *Walton Inventory of 1624* was very likely of the same class, as may have been the 'large table behind the hangings' at Marton Hall (*Invt., 1605*) which was fitted 'with iron hooks'.

4. Several oak tables of this type survive at Cotehele in Cornwall. Only one retains its original iron bracing-hooks which are secured by ingenious catches (Plate 213).

5. At Ingatestone (*Invt., 1600*) there was a little table which had 'two falling leaves', while the Countess of Shrewsbury had a 'little folding table' in her bedchamber at Hardwick (*Invt., 1601*). A 'foulding field table' is listed in the *Charles I Inventories* (1649–51); this echoes the description of a table that belonged to Catherine de Medici (1589; see Bonnaffé, *op. cit.*, p. 184) which is listed as 'une table de camp brisé'. She also had a 'table de camp pozée sur un pied brisé' which may have consisted of a top resting on an X-frame stand.

6. e.g. 'two longe Tables in the hall fastened to Tressells set in the ground' (*Easton Lodge Invt., 1637*).

7. In former times, when grand people still dined in the hall, the large trestle-tables had often been capable of being taken to pieces. In the late fifteenth century *Bokes of Keruyne and Curtasye*, the servants are instructed to 'lay some of the tables [tops] on the floor, and remove the trestles'. There is a seventeenth-century description of James I standing on a dismantled table-top and rinsing his hands after a meal. The long tables in early seventeenth century halls were no longer of the kind that could be dismantled. While it would appear that a static table might be called a 'table dormant' in the Middle Ages (see *D.E.F.*, 'Dining Table'), it is clear that trestles might be called 'dormants' or 'dormers' in the seventeenth century (e.g. 'one planke table wth. the Dorments' and 'a long thick elme planke for a table lyinge upon iiii dormers'—respectively from F. W. Steer, *Farm and Cottage Inventories of Mid-Essex, 1635–1749*,

Colchester, 1950, p. 12, and *Ingatestone Invt., 1600.*

8. When Jacques Wecker, native of Colmar, published his *De Secretis* at Basle in 1582, he included a drawing of the construction of such a table 'qui se redoublent' [which doubles itself], as he put it. He stated that the invention had been made in Flanders and that he had seen many such tables at Ghent. The implication would seem to be that they were still not all that common by the 1580s. However, Jacques Androuet Du Cerceau published several designs for such tables in about 1560, so they must have been familiar in French court circles by then. Bonnaffé (*op. cit.*, p. 186) cities early French references to tables 'qui se tire' [which draw out] or 'tirant par les deux bouts' [drawing out at the ends] in 1566 and 1577. The standard description was to become 'une table à ralonge' [a table that extends] (e.g. in the 'Sale où mange Son Ex[cellen]ce' the Prince of Orange in his residence at Brussels in 1618: see *Orange Invts.* I, p. 121). Many designs for this kind of table appeared in Holland, principally in the works of Hans Vredeman de Vries (*c.* 1586), of Paul, his son (1630), and of Crispin van de Passe (1621 and 1642) (see S. Jervis, *Printed Furniture Designs before 1650*, London, 1974). In the dining parlour ('Op de eetsael') in the Stadholder's residence at The Hague there was a large oak table of this type ('een groote wagenschotten uyttreckende tafel') but the form went out of fashion in about the 1640s (see *Orange Invts.*, I, p. 189).

9. It is an indication of the prominent position in important rooms which such tables often occupied that designers of the calibre of Du Cerceau and the de Vries, father and son, should have published proposals for them (see the previous note). Clearly they realised it was desirable that such a feature should be decorated as far as possible in a manner consonant with the décor of the room concerned.

10. *Randle Holme* (Bk. III, Chap. XIV), listing the 'things necessary for and belonging to a dineing roome' maintains that there should be a 'large table in the middle, either square to draw out in leaves, or long, or round or oval with falling leaves'. He was writing just at the time when the change-over was becoming apparent.

11. *Ham Invt., 1679.* 'A Lauderdale Table-Board ... 4 feet long, 3 feet Broad with twist-leggs all of Walnut-tree wood' and costing twelve shillings was in the 'little Parlour' of Dr Morris of Wells in 1686 (G. Olive, 'Furniture in a West Country Parish, 1576–1769', *Furniture History*, Vol. XII, 1976); could this have been some form of gate-leg dining-table, perhaps oval rather than square?

12. At Dublin Castle (*Invt., 1679*) there was in a closet 'another table to lengthen the other in the dining-room'.

13. There was 'une ralongement de table' [table extension] of oak in the Thiret mansion at Rheims (*Invt., 1621*) which was 'garni d'un pied'. Likewise, in the Gilt Parlour of Breda Castle around 1600, two long tables were described as being 'met een reloenje' [with an extension-piece] (*Orange Invts.*, I, p. 75).

14. We learn that oyster tables had a 'hole in the middle' and were circular from a reference in a Restoration comedy. (A. Scouten and R. Hume, 'A lost Restoration comedy, *The Country Gentleman* (1669)', *Times Literary Supplement*, 23 September 1973). In the *Easton Lodge Inventory of 1637* there is mention of a basket 'to stand under the oyster table'.

15. There were two oyster tables 'on folding frames' at Ingatestone (*Invt., 1600*), while 'one litle joyned bord, wth. feete to terne in, for oysters' was to be found in the Winter Parlour at Hengrave Hall (*Invt., 1603*). The latter may have had an action like a 'Spanish table'.

16. M. Jourdain, *English Decoration and Furniture of the Early Renaissance*, London, 1927, p. 5.

17. *Ham Invt., 1679.*

18. *Ham Invt., 1683.* It may also be identical with the 'One table painted black and gould' that was in the room in 1679. In the adjacent closet (an altogether grander room) there was 'One Indian furnace for tea garnished with silver' which may have been a kind of *samovar*. The tea-table stands on six red and gold legs carved in the East Indian taste; it was obviously found to be too low for use with European chairs so an under-frame with spiral-turned legs was added.

19. The Dyrham table was to be flanked by a paid of stands in the form of kneeling black-amoors for, as the owner's clerk told him in a letter of 1700, 'the two black boys have a proper place on each side of the Indian tambour in one of the best rooms' (*National Trust Guide to Dyrham*). In the inventory of Dyrham made in 1703 the ensemble is described as 'a large tea table and 2 blacks'. It stands on taller legs than did the Ham table in its original guise. The Charlottenburg tables also stand somewhat taller. Some of them are octagonal and drum-like (see

Catalogue of the Exhibition 'China und Europa', Schloss Charlottenburg, Berlin, 1973, p. 53). There was also, incidentally, an East Indian tea-table at the Binnenhof at The Hague in 1700 (*Orange Invts.*, I, p. 434). It may also be relevant to note that a red and gold '*teetrommel*' (lit. tea-drum) was at the palace of Soestdijk in 1699–1712 (*ibid.*, II, p. 623). Th. Lunsingh Scheurleer discusses other examples in 'The Dutch at the Tea-Table', *The Connoisseur*, October 1976.

20. Scheurleer, *loc. cit.*, illustrates an early specimen in a painting of 1689, with a circular tray-like top.

21. C. Pitoin, *Marly-le-Roi*, Paris, 1904, pl 174.

22. *Turenne Invt.*, 1615.

23. *Easton Lodge Invt.*, 1637. Had there been only two, one might have suspected that these tables were for dressing food in the dining parlour—that they were '*dressoirs*' or dressers. But the fact that there were no less than sixteen indicates that they were indeed what they seem. The *Ham Inventory* of c. 1654 probably reflects the state of the house before the Civil War broke out. A dressing-table is also mentioned in the *Edington Inventory of 1665*.

24. Of the several triads at Ham House in the 1670s, no complete set survives. There is a delightful black lacquered ensemble painted with flowers at Hopetoun House, near Edinburgh, and there is a famous silver set at Knole, Sevenoaks. William III acquired for one of his Dutch residences two complete silver ensembles (i.e. two looking-glasses, two tables and four candlestands) from Paris in 1697 (*Orange Invts.*, I, p. 421). It should in parentheses be added that the triad seems to have evolved from a group comprising a table and pair of candlestands only. For instance Amalia van Solms, the widow of Frederik Hendrick, Prince of Orange, owned a pair of candlestands and small table that was new in the period 1654–1668 (*Orange Invts.*, I, p. 279), and the well-known black table and stands at Ham House, with their strange caned tops, which were probably bought in Holland, do not seem from the outset to have had a looking-glass *en suite* although one was always hung above them.

25. The French royal inventories of 1686 note 'une table en forme de bureau . . . avec un petit bord d'or pour y mettre une toilette de vermeil doré . . .' [a table of desk shape . . . with a small gallery of gold on which to stand a toilet set of silver gilt] (*Guiffrey, Inventaire*, II, p. 165). The red tortoiseshell 'bureau Mazarin' at Erthig in Denbighshire is listed as being in the state bedchamber in 1726 and is described as a dressing-table (see J. Hardy, Sheila Landi and Charles D. Wright, *A State Bed at Erthig*, Victoria and Albert Museum, 1972).

26. A few random examples can be given, however. There was the red coral table decorated with Latin sayings that a Danish visitor saw at Windsor Castle in 1613 (W. B. Rye, *England as Seen by Foreigners*, London, 1965, p. 164; see also p. 45 for a note on elaborate tables at Theobalds in 1592). At Tart Hall (*Invt., 1641*) there was an ebony table 'inlayde with torteaux shells' in the Drawing Chamber. In the Long Gallery at Northumberland House (*Invt., 1670*) stood a table of 'agott' as well as three tables of marble, all of which were presumably acquired in Italy. At Ham House (*Invt., 1679*) there stood in the Long Gallery a table and pair of candlestands of 'counterfeit marble' (i.e. of *scagliola*), of which the tops of the stands survive. And in the Hall at Dyrham (*Invt., 1703*) there was a table with a hone-stone top which is likely to have come from Solnhofen in Germany. Specimens survive in several German collections; they have ornament carved in shallow relief (see H. Kreissel, *Die Kunst des Deutschen Möbels*, I, Munich, 1968, Plates 71 and 271).

27. *The Walton Inventory of 1624* contains a reference to 'a paire of white & black checkered tables'. For further information on this matter see Julia Raynsford's forthcoming book on Gamesboards to be published shortly by George Bell & Sons.

28. *Knole Invt., 1645*. An early reference to a billiard-table is to be found in the *Hengrave Inventory of 1603*. It had 'two staves of bone, and two of wood, and four balls'. There was a billiard-table in the hall at *Ham House* in the 1670s (*Invt., 1679*).

29. See *D.E.F.*, 'Tables, Shovel-board'.

30. There was a table for this game at Hatfield Priory in 1629 (*Invt.*) and 'one table to play Trolle Madame at' is listed in the Charles I inventories (*1649–51*).

31. *Ingatestone Invt., 1600* and *Chatsworth Invt., 1601*.

32. 'Her mistress . . . set all her plate on the cubboorde for shewe' (1592; *O.E.D.*, 'Cupboard'). Lord Montague instructed the Yeoman of his Cellar to 'carrye uppe his plate . . . and

place ytt upon the cupborde' before dinner (*Montague's Household Book, 1595*). William Harrison, in his *Description of England* of 1577, speaks of the recent great increase in wealth and how the nobility now owned such great quantities of 'silver vessels, and so much other plate, as may furnish sundrie cupboards, to the summe oftentimes of a thousand or two thousand pounds at least'. The *Walton Inventory of 1624* includes a 'Note of Plate which stood upon the cupboard in your own Chamber' (i.e. the owner's bedchamber).

33. See Penelope Eames, *Mediaeval Furniture*, London, 1977, where the cup-board as a symbol of status in mediaeval times is discussed. The number of stages signified the owner's rank and was governed by an elaborate code of practice.

34. Cupboards created solely for storage (e.g. wardrobes and similar mostly rather large pieces of furniture) were generally known as 'presses' in the seventeenth century. The French term was 'armoire'.

35. The Earl of Northumberland set out in very specific detail 'the Order of all such Lyveryes of Breid Bere Wyne White-lights and Wax as shall be allow'd Dayly' in his houses (*The Regulations . . . of the Household of . . . The Fifth Earl of Northumberland . . ., begun in 1512*; London, 1827).

36. Lord Montague, in his *Household book of 1595,* instructed the Yeoman of his Wardrobe to see that the rooms in which visitors were staying were kept in proper order and to 'give his attendance to the servinge of lyveryes (if any be to be served)'. His Gentleman Usher was likewise to 'after supper . . . cause all lyveryes to be served' to the household, adding 'if any ought to be'. A year later Edmund Spenser seemed to find it surprising that in great Irish houses 'the lyverye is sayd to be served up for all night, that is theyr nyghtes allowance of drinke' (*View of the State of Ireland*, 1596).

37. I once put forward a rather different interpretation of the term (P. Thornton, 'Two Problems', *Furniture History*, Vol. VII, 1971) but now entirely accept that given here and proposed by Mrs Eames (*op. cit.*, p. 59, n. 154). In all other respects, I believe my suggestions in this direction remain acceptable.

38. See Elias Ashmole, *The Institution, Laws and Ceremonies of the Most Noble Order of the Garter*, London, 1672, p. 592, where is illustrated a banquet given by Charles II at which a series of plain tables standing against the window-piers are described as 'court cupboards'.

39. *Randle Holme, loc. cit.*

40. *Hatfield Priory Invt., 1629* and *Ham Invt., c. 1654*. The term 'cupboard table' occurs in a number of inventories from the 1620s until the middle of the century. At Cockesden (*Invt., 1626*) one was described as being 'with falling leaves' while at Tart Hall (*Invt., 1641*) there was one 'inlayde with bone and some slight stones' while another had a lock to a container (cupboard?) housing a box of oyster knives. Both were clearly distinguishable from ordinary tables, of which there were many in the house.

41. Nicot, in his dictionary of 1606, states that a 'Dressoir n'est jamais à armoire ne tiroir' (i.e. it had neither a cupboard or a drawer) and 'c'est le meuble qui est en chambre ou salle sur laquelle on estalle la vaiselle d'argent aux heures de disner ou de souper' [it is the piece of furniture that stands in the bedchamber or parlour on which one displays the silver vessels during dinner time or supper].

42. Furetière's dictionary of 1690 gives 'buffet' as 'un meuble qui sert pour mettre les pots et les verres, la vaiselle et autres choses nécessaires pour le service de table' [a piece of furniture on which are placed the jugs, glasses, plate and other things necessary for serving at table]. This piece of furniture often had 'numerous small columns' (Furetière died in 1688 so was probably writing this some years earlier). Cotgrave, in his French-English dictionary of 1632, gives 'buffet' as 'a court-cupboard, or high-standing cupboard'. It is interesting to note that, at Ingatestone in 1600 (*Invt.*), there were two 'courte buffett cupbourdes' as well as a 'high buffett lyerrie cupbourde' which indicates that both the 'court cupboard' and the 'livery cupboard' were variants of the buffet. When Marie de Medici was married in Florence in 1600, a Frenchman recorded that there was a 'credence ou buffect . . . qui montait jusqu'au plancher, garni tout de vases d'or et d'argent, de porcelaines, d'agathes, d'esmeraudes, rubis, saphirs et diamans par dedans, de la valeur de dix huit cent mil escus' [which reached up to the ceiling, decked all over with vases of gold and silver, porcelain, agates, emeralds, rubies, sapphires and diamonds inside, to the value of eighteen hundred thousand *écus*] (A. Lebault, *La Table et le repas à Travers les siècles*, Paris, 1910, p. 462). The term 'credence' was not much used in France; it derived from the

Italian word 'credenza' which not only means a buffet but carries implications of the owner's high standing, the wealth of plate displayed on it being his 'credentials'.

43. In the *Thiret* mansion at Rheims (*Invt., 1621*) there stood 'ung grand dessert de bois de noyer à quatre grand colonnes et quatre petites' [a large buffet of walnut with four large columns and four small] which had a back-board painted with a scene of Susannah and the Elders. The dessert, a last course of sweetmeats, was brought on once the table had been cleared (thus from *de-servir*) after the main course.

44. See Jervis, *op. cit.*, Plate 438, where the type is described as a '*Buffet*'. One has a 'petit Cabinet, ou Armoire . . . au milieu' (i.e. a small enclosed section with a door between the top and middle shelves). The same illustration was published in 1672 by Robert Pricke in an English translation of de Breuil, where they are described as 'court cupboards'.

45. *Tessin-Cronström Correspondence*, letter of 1 October, 1700.

46. See *D.E.F.*, 'Buffet' (illus.).

47. An exception may have been the long tables still to be seen in many halls during the early part of the century. As we noted (p. 226), the lower servants dined at these tables which were probably just scrubbed. But it is possible that even these were usually covered with the cloths of coarse linen which are often listed in inventories.

48. The ebony table with silver mounts which is and was a notable feature of the decoration at Ham House (*Invt., 1679*) had a 'green sarsenet case for it fring'd'. Some of the magnificent tables that stood in Cardinal Mazarin's famous Gallery (*Invt., 1653*) had special covers of 'maroquain du Levant rouge cramoisy' that were trimmed with gold fringe.

49. At Kilkenny (*Invt., 1684*) there were some 'cases' of 'black leather to cover the table and [candle] stands' while other tables had 'printed leather carpets' which were perhaps tooled round the edges. A long table in the house had a cover of 'damask leather' (see p. 120). Several 'scorched leather' covers for tables were found at Ham House when the attics were cleared out around 1950. Some have now returned to the house, others are at Colonial Williamsburg.

50. For instance, a draw-table at Ingatestone (*Invt., 1600*) had two carpets of green cloth, one of which was for use when the table was 'at the shortest' (i.e. closed). At Hengrave Hall (*Invt., 1603*) there was in the 'Chiefe Chamber' a 'carpet of black velvet for the little bord' which was 'laced and fringed with silver and gould, [and] lyned with taffita'. Table-carpets of velvet are frequently to be seen in contemporary illustrations; it is possible that not a few of these were of woollen rather than silk velvet.

51. In 1596 Richard Bellasio made a specific bequest of his 'best Turquey carpett for the long table, and other carpets for cobbarts'. The latter need not necessarily have been Oriental rugs at all (William Beck, *The Drapers' Dictionary*, 1884, 'Carpet'). In the 'Dyneing chamber' at Cockesden in 1610 (*Invt.*) there was a side-table with 'thereupon a very good Turkey-carpett large'. The change from using Turkish rugs on tables to laying them on the floor in England is reflected in the list of carpets in the *Easton Lodge Inventory of 1637* where some 'little Turkey Carpitts' are described as being 'for foote Carpitts or side Tables' or 'for foote Carpitts or side Bordes'.

52. e.g. there was a turkeywork cup-board cloth at Hengrave Hall (*Invt., 1603*), while Lady Beauchamp owned a square table with 'one Turky worke carpett with a false [protective] bayes carpet' (*Edington Invt., 1665*). At Syon House (*Invt., 1670*) there was in the Wardrobe a 'Yorkshire carpett of Turkey-worke'. There were still some turkeywork table-covers at Woburn in 1703 (typescript in the Department of Textiles in the Victoria and Albert Museum) but these must by then have been old-fashioned.

53. In the Thiret mansion at Rheims in 1621 (*Invt.,*) there was a 'tapis de mocquette de couleur jaulne et rouge fasson de Turqy'.

54. In England such tapestry-woven carpets were called 'Arras Carpets' (see p. 108). The Provost of King's College, Cambridge, acquired '2 tapetis communiter vocat arrace carpetts' in 1610 (*Provost of King's Invt., 1660*).

55. In the French royal inventories of the Louis XIV period are mentioned 'cinq tables de bois avec leurs tapis de Bergame' (*Guiffrey, Inventaire*, p. 240). There were cloths of 'Darnicks' and 'darnax', the latter being 'of bleu and white birds worke' at Marton (*Invt., 1605*) and Cockesden (*Invt., 1610*) respectively. In the inventory of Breda Castle, taken in 1619 (*Orange Invts.*, I, p. 131), one also finds mention of 'Dornicxse tafelkleedekens' (small Dornix table covers), while the inventory of the House of Nassau residence at Brussels of a year earlier (*ibid.*, p.

108) includes a note of some 'tapitz de table' of 'ouvrage de Tournay' (it will be remembered that Doornik was the Flemish name for Tournai). Some Tournai table-carpets, however, had a woollen pile and could thus be classed with moquettes. An inventory of 1654, for instance, notes a table covered with 'un tapis velu de Tournai, le fond bleu' (This reference and the whole question of Tournai table-covers is discussed by E. Soil, 'Tapisserie de Tournai', *Mémoires de la Société de l'Histoire de Tournai*, 1891, Vol. 22).

56. At Tart Hall (*Invt., 1641*) there was a closet where the floor was covered with white leather while a small table 'of firre' in the room was covered in the same material. On the table lay a cushion embroidered with the arms of Philip and Queen Mary—a treasured possession of fine workmanship, then already more than a century old, and deserving fine display.

57. The fitted table-carpet with four *pentes* was probably not uncommon (there is a dressing-table cover of the 1720s at Ham House with these features) and it was perhaps therefore not necessary to specify its character in inventories. A red damask cover which 'hangs down on four sides' (henger neder på fyrra sijdor) was in a house in Stockholm in 1665 (*Ebba Brahe's Hem*) and the 'three French gilt leather carpets fitted to the tables' in the Great Dining room at Kilkenny (*Invt., 1684*) were presumably of this form.

58. e.g. In the parlour at Ham House in the middle of the century (*Invt., c. 1654*) there were carpets on the two round tables and the sideboards made of green cloth bordered with gilt-leather. At Tart Hall (*Invt., 1641*) a large oval table with folding leaves standing in the hall had 'thereon a cover of red leather bordured with blew guilt leather'.

59. *Cockesden Invt., 1610* and *Tart Hall invt., 1641*. 'Six stayned Callico Carpitts' are listed in the *Easton Lodge Inventory of 1637*.

60. See G. F. Wingfield Digby, *Elizabethan Embroidery*, London, 1965. Of the forty-eight 'carpitts' at Easton Lodge in 1637 (*Invt.*), six were embroidered and it is clear that three of these were important items. The embroidered cloths are listed after the valuable Turkish and Persian rugs but before the plainer cloths.

61. At Gilling Castle (*Invt., 1594*) some 'newe cubberde clothes' were listed among the linen damask and there were several more of the rather coarse linen diaper. There were 'diaper sideboard clothes' at Dyrham a century later (*Invt., 1703*).

62. An Italian describing a French banquet in 1625 explains that 'sur la table était d'abord une nappe [linen tablecloth] ordinaire et sur cette dernière une seconde nappe damassée, très fine, pliée en deux et tombant jusqu'à terre formant ainsi nappe et tapis pour recouvrir la table' [on the table lies first an ordinary linen tablecloth and on this last lies a second damask cloth, very fine, folded in two and reaching to the ground thus forming cloth and carpet to cover the table] (*Havard*, 'Nappe'). This seems to imply that he would have expected a *tapis* to be left under the linen damask upper cloth. Lord Montague (*Household Book, 1595*) does not mention any table-carpet. On special occasions he wanted a second tablecloth which was revealed when the uppermost cloth was removed after the main courses had been cleared away. In Germany and other parts of Central Europe, however, it seems that it was normal to leave the carpet in place. Rumpolt, in his *Neu Kochbuch* of 1587 and 1666, (the second edition contained only minor changes), explains very carefully how two tablecloths should be laid over the table-carpet. The cloths should be so laid that a hand's breadth of the carpet shows all round, just above the floor. Comenius, writing in 1631, confirms what Rumpolt says (*Janua Linguarum Reserata*, 1631).

63. The French royal *toilettes* of 1673 were of brocade with a silver ground, trimmed with silver fringe and lace. They usually comprised three widths of material and were one ell long (about a yard). At each corner was an elaborate tassel or a bow.

64. Louis XIV gave Mary of Modena a rich *toilette* when she was living in exile at Saint-Germain. It was of green satin trimmed with lace, with borders of gold and silver galloon, and with a red taffeta lining.

65. *Havard* ('Toilette') cites a reference in an inventory of 1705 to 'une petit table de toilette de sapin, avec son Toilette, composée d'un dessous de toilette d'étoffe de soie, avec un dessus de toilette de mousseline à falbalas' [a small dressing-table of firwood with its *toilette* comprising an underlay of silk material with an overlay of muslin with furbellows].

NOTES TO CHAPTER X

1. A well-defined class of sixteenth-century

writing-cabinet that was popular in Spain (today often called a *vargueño*) had sometimes been furnished with a stand but these seem to have been exceptional in their day.

2. Such a high degree of craftsmanship was otherwise only bestowed on tables of special richness and on games-boards. The very fact that 'cabinet-maker' is the English term for a craftsman who creates fine furniture by means of skilfully applied woodworking techniques is evidence enough of the prestige cabinets enjoyed in former times.

3. See S. Jervis, 'A Tortoiseshell Cabinet and its precursors', *Victoria and Albert Museum Bulletin*, Vol. IV, No. 4, October 1968.

4. For example pearwood stained black was often used instead of the far more expensive ebony of the best cabinets; and rather than having the gilt mounts cast in bronze, they could more cheaply be stamped out of sheet copper and gilded, or they might be cast in brass and merely varnished.

5. In 1679 (*Ham Invt.*) it had stood in the North Drawing Room, one of the principal state rooms; it had been moved to the 'Queen's Bed Chamber' by 1683 (*Invt.*). It was furnished with a protective case of green paragon.

6. For instance there were 'Japan cabinets with frames' in the Green Closet and also in the Gallery and Antechamber, all of which formed part of the sequence of state rooms. At the time a stand for a cabinet was described as 'a frame'.

7. *Northampton Invt., 1614.* This cabinet was presumably of black lacquer with gilt decoration.

8. *Mazarin Invt., 1653.* The cabinet in question was 'en forme d'un temple d'ordre et structure du pays, vernis et peint de paysages, d'animaux et autres choses . . .' [in the form of a temple of the style and conformation of that country, lacquered and painted with landscapes, animals and other things]. To be fair, it must be added that Mazarin owned some lacquer boxes including a magnificent chest now in the Victoria and Albert Museum.

9. *Orange Invts.*, the residence at the Noordeinde, I, p. xxv; see also p. 193, a 'Jappaens cabinet met een tafelken daer't op staet . . .' [a Japan cabinet with a small table to stand it upon], p. 204, two 'cabinetten van Oostindien', one with a red and one with a black ground, and one Japan cabinet inlaid with mother-of-pearl.

10. *Orange Invts.*, I, p. 191. Noordeinde inventory, 1632; 'Een cabinet van buyten becleet met Parsiansch stoff met een gouden gront ende versheyde blomkens, staende op een vergulde schabelle.'

11. John Stalker and George Parker's *Treatise of Japaning . . . Together with . . . Patterns of Japanwork . . . for . . . Cabinets, Boxes, etc.*, 1688. A Parisian harpsichord decorated with gilt *chinoiseries* on a black ground and dated 1681 (in the Victoria and Albert Museum) represents the parallel development in France, and Dutch equivalents could certainly be found.

12. This was especially so in royal circles in France as the *Comptes des Bâtiments* of the period show.

13. Jervis, *loc. cit.*, illustrates the tortoiseshell group.

14. In the French royal collection there were some 'guéridons de marqueterie' made to accompany a cabinet ('pour mettre au costé dudit cabinet' [placed on either side] *Guiffrey, Inventaire, II*, p. 144). *Havard* (Guéridon) cites a reference to a lacquer suite in Paris in 1694. A magnificent cabinet which is still associated with its pair of stands is at Knole (see G. Jackson-Stops, 'The 6th Earl of Dorset's Furniture at Knole', I, *Country Life*, 2 June 1977, Plate I).

15. *Savary des Bruslons*, 'Cabinet'.

16. *Gosfield Invt., 1638.*

17. Inventory of Claudine Bouzonnet Stella, neice of Jacques Stella, *Nouvelles archives de l'art Français*, 1877.

18. *Orange Invts.*, I, p. 162.

19. See Fritz Heikamp, 'Zur Geschichte der Uffizien-Tribuna', *Zeitschrift für Kunstgeschichte*, 1963.

20. *Orange Invts.*, I, Inventory of the Oude Hof at the Noordeinde, 1632, pp. 204–206. The list is repeated in the *Nordeinde Invt., 1633*.

21. Some of the pottery is stated to have come from Fontainebleau and will therefore have been what is today called Palissy ware. The rest is described as '*porceleyne*' although whether all of it came from the Far East is not clear. Since the quantity of 'porcelain' in the room was so large, it is likely that some of it was in fact European but this is by no means certain. Some of the supports are described as '*richels*' although precisely what these were like has not yet been discovered.

22. This 'Inventory of all the parcels of purselin, glasses & other goods now remayning in the Pranketing Roome at Tart Hall', taken on 8 November 1641, is unpublished (archives of

Arundel Castle, Ms.L.M.1). I am much indebted to Mr Francis Steer for drawing my attention to this important document and to His Grace the Duke of Norfolk for allowing me to quote from it here. Reference is made in the *Tart Hall Iventory of 1641* to the Banqueting Room, where it is specifically called 'Dutch', but the inventory concerned is a separate document. Among the porcelain items were '3 white little purselin figures, the first a man and a woeman; the second a dolphin' as well as 'a lyon on a pedestall of white purselin' which could be early specimens of Fukien *blanc-de-chine* ware.

23. *Orange Invts.*, I, pp. 250–2. See also pp. 310–11, for a later list.

24. See Th. H. Lunsingh Scheurleer, 'Stadhouderlijke Lakkabinetten', *Opstellen voor H. van der Waal*, Amsterdam/Leiden, 1970, p. 166. Marot may also have seen the drawing reproduced as Figure 236 here.

25. See G. Upmark, 'Ein Besuch in Holland, 1687; Aus der Reise schilderungen des schwedischen Architekten Nicodemus Tessin d.J.,' *Oud Holland*, 18, 1900.

26. Le Comte Biver, *Histoire du Château de Meudon*, Paris, 1923, p. 443 et seq. It may well be that the vessels of Siamese porcelain in the Dauphin's collection had been presented to him when the Siamese ambassadors were received at the Court of Versailles in 1686. Siamese porcelain was rather coarser than that of China but was technically similar. It is interesting that contemporary French connoisseurs could tell the difference. Clearly there were discriminating collectors at the time. Dr Martin Lister met one in Paris at the very end of the century and reported that this man owned 'the greatest variety, and best sorted China ware I ever saw, besides pagods and China pictures' (*A Journey to Paris*, London, 1699, p. 35).

27. See Fiske Kimball, *The Creation of the Rococo*, Philadelphia, 1942, Plate 22.

28. See Arthur Lane, 'Queen Mary II's Porcelain Collection At Hampton Court', *Transactions of the Oriental Ceramic Society*, 1945–50; also Joan Wilson, 'A Phenomenon of Taste; The Chinaware of Queen Mary II', *Apollo*, August 1973.

29. An illustration of the 'Porzellankammer' at Oranienburg was published in I. B. Broebes, *Prospect des Palläste . . .*, 1733. See also H. Kreisel, *Deutsche Spielgelkabinette*, Darmstadt, *c.* 1953.

30. See *Orange Invts.*, II, cf. 1684 inventory of Oranienstein with the 1695 inventory (pp.

121–33 and 159–203). The inventory of the Nassau-Dietz residence at Leeuwarden (pp. 147–52) also shows how extensive were these Dutch princely collections of porcelain.

31. *Kensington Palace Invts., 1697* and *1699*.

32. D. Defoe, *A Tour through England and Wales* (1724–27), Everyman edn., London, 1948, pp. 165–6. However, when the expense became prohibitive, painted wooden or plaster of Paris imitations of Chinese porcelain jars and vases could be used, at least in the less conspicuous corners. Such deceits 'mit blau und weissen Figuren auf Porcellanahrt' [with blue and white figures like those on porcelain] were noted in a Berlin inventory (*Stengel*, p. 73).

33. For example the Duchess of Ormonde had '4 pedestalls gilt for china' at Kilkenny Castle in 1684 (*Invt.*) which indicates that she had at least four groups of china ware forming conspicuous features in the décor of one room.

34. Heikamp, *op. cit.*

35. In the *Kilkenny Inventory of 1684* are listed many 'knots' of ribbon of various colours which must have been such bows. Fifteen were 'of several colours for the glass and sconces' in the Drawing Room. In Her Grace's Bedchamber there were 'three knots of ribbon to the looking glass'.

36. William Salmon, *Polygraphice, or the Arts of Drawing, Engraving, Etching, Limning, etc.*, London, 1675, III, Chap. XV. I am indebted to Mr Benno Forman for drawing my attention to this amusing passage.

37. 'An Inventory of the Pictures . . . Ham House . . . 1679'. This unpublished document was acquired by my colleague, Mr John Hardy, and presented to Ham House where it may now be seen.

38. When the Duke and Duchess subsequently exchanged bedrooms, it proved impossible to swap the fixed paintings over, so she ended up sleeping in a room with some 'masculine' pictures. The movable pictures of course presented no problem.

39. A thoughtful essay on this question by Sir Oliver Millar is to be found in *The Destruction of the Country House*, London, 1974, pp. 103–6, ed. Roy Strong, Marcus Binney and John Harris. See also J. Fowler and J. Cornforth, *English Decoration in the 18th century*, London, 1974, Chap. 8, 'Attitudes to pictures and picture hanging'.

40. Was the Earl of Northampton's 'skreene of

tabine fringed' which stood in a very grand bedchamber in 1614 (*Invt.*) an *écran* or a *paravent*? Tobine was a silk material.

41. *Hengrave Invt., 1603.* Six-leafed screens were commonest; many examples could be cited including the four at Marly which were fourteen feet high (Pitoin, *op. cit.*, p. 174). At Tart Hall (*Invt., 1641*) there was a screen of eight leaves in the Gallery.

42. The folding screen at Hengrave Hall (see previous note) had 'a skreene cloth upon it of green kersey'. In store at Easton Lodge (*Invt., 1637*) were some 'skreene Clothes for Foldinge skreines'.

43. Leather-covered screens survive in some quantity and are invariably faced on one side only; the framing may be seen at the back. There is no reason to suppose other sorts of screen were normally treated differently although Cardinal *Mazarin* had 'une sorte de paravent à double face de serge cramoisy, garnie de petit passement d'argent[,] clouée' [a kind of screen with two faces of crimson serge, trimmed with a narrow silver galloon, nailed] (*Invt., 1653*).

44. The eight-leafed screen in the Gallery at Tart Hall (see note 40 above) was covered with blue baize.

45. Late seventeenth-century screens seem often to have been faced with silk damask. Those in the Council Chamber at Kensington Palace (*Invt., 1697*), for instance, were blue and one had a protective 'baize screen bagg'.

46. *Ham Invt., c. 1654.* This screen was in Elizabeth Dysart's own room so was presumably a valued object.

47. An early example would seem to be that at Tredegar in 1688 (*Invt.*); there was also one in the gilt leather Parlour at Dyrham in 1703 (*Invt.*) which may be that still in the house.

48. *Ham Invt., 1679*; it was in the Withdrawing Room and was probably quite a notable item in that reception room.

49. Nicodemus Tessin gave the Swedish Countess Piper a Savonnerie screen (*écran* or *paravent*?) in 1700; he felt that such 'ouvrages paroissent d'une grande durée' [such work seems to be exceptionally durable] (*Tessin-Cronström Correspondence*, letter of 31 January 1700).

50. See J. Irwin, 'A Jacobean Vogue for Oriental Lacquer-ware', *The Burlington Magazine*, December 1953, pp. 193–4. Scriptors were writing cabinets (*escritorios* in Spanish); *beobee* was the Japanese for a screen.

51. e.g. at Honselaarsdijk (see p. 78), and at Leeuwarden (*Orange Invts.*, pp. xxix and II, p. 147).

52. *Ham Invts. 1679* and *1683*.

53. One At Tart Hall is actually described as being circular (*Invt., 1641*). The lack of specific descriptions suggests that they were all the same shape and such evidence as we have all points to their having been circular.

54. At Hengrave Hall there was a 'little fine wicker skrene, sett in a frame of walnut tree' (*Invt., 1603*) and the Arundels had 'in the chimney, hanging on a rod with iron feete, a little wickar skreene' at Tart Hall (*Invt., 1641*). Was the 'wandel screen' at Gilling Castle in 1624 (*Invt.*) of a coarser sort, and how did the 'twiggen skreyne' at Hardwick (Old Hall) differ from the wicker ones also mentioned in the inventory of 1601?

55. There was a 'wicker fan for the fire' at Cockesden in 1610 (*Invt.*).

56. *Randle Holme*, Book III, Chap. 16, p. 83.

57. They may have lingered on in Ireland for, even at Kilkenny Castle (*Invt., 1684*) in the time of the great Duke of Ormonde, there was a wicker screen on 'a steel stem'.

58. *Walpole's Letters*, Walpole to Montague, 1 September, 1766.

59. *Hardwick Invt., 1601.*

60. For example, the several screen cloths listed in the *Charles I Inventories, 1649–51* were of two widths of material and were mostly $3\frac{1}{2}$ yards long although one was only $2\frac{1}{2}$ yards long. This last was embroidered with the arms of the Knights of the Garter within a circle. But we have shown that some screen cloths were for folding screens (see note 42).

61. 'One screen with a screen stick garnished with silver' is still in the house. It now has a tapestry-woven leaf which appears to date from the eighteenth century and may have replaced an original leaf of no great distinction.

62. Lady Johanna St John made a specific bequest of her 'crosstich screen' which stood in her dining room, when she wrote her will in 1705 (Somerset House, Gee 40; kindly communicated by Mr Frank Smallwood).

63. *Havard*, 'Ecran'.

64. *D.E.F.*, 'Screen', Plate 5. In the King's Library at Kensington Palace in 1697 (*Invt.*) there stood a 'sliding fire-skreen, one side embroidered with silke'.

65. See *D.E.F.*, 'Chimney Furniture'.

66. A satirical pamphlet of 1642 likens bishops to 'andirons of state, standing in the chimney for show; but if a heavy block or red billets are brought to the fire there are four little creepers or cobirons underneath [i.e. the lesser clergy] who must bear all the weight' ('Threefold Discourse Between Three Neighbours'; quoted by F. Lenygon, *Decoration in England from 1640-1760*, London, 1927, p. 231). When creepers were present, a pair would normally have sufficed and it is not clear why the satirist speaks of four; maybe he wanted to exaggerate the difference.

67. So familiar were these objects that a writer in 1650 could make a comparison with 'brazen andirons in great men's chimnees' and expect to be understood (*O.E.D.*, 'Andiron'). References to andirons of brass or latten are so common that to cite any here is unnecessary but there was a splendid pair at Tart Hall (*Invt., 1641*) of which 'the upper part thereof [was] of cast brass pt. guilt'.

68. At Cockesden in 1610 (*Invt.*) there was a 'payre of Flaunders cobirones . . . and a payre of creepers'.

69. See *D.E.F.*, 'Chimney Furniture', Plate 7. At Cowdray (*Invt., 1682*) there were some 'brass andirons enamelled' with a set of fire-irons *en suite*.

70. *Northampton Invt., 1614* and *D.E.F.* 'Chimney Furniture', Plate 2.

71. *Kilkenny Invt., 1684*. Stoves, incidentally, were not common in the British Isles but seem to have been familiar in Holland and to have gained some favour in France during the third quarter of the century (see *Havard*, 'Poële').

72. *Mazarin Invt. 1653*. A particularly early example was the 'paire of andirons garnished with silver' that were listed in the *Charles I Inventories, 1649-51*.

73. *D.E.F.*, 'Chimney Furniture' (Misson's *Mémoires*, 1698). Already by 1606 one could speak of something being 'as common as coales from Newcastle' and the well-known proverb about people who 'carry coals to Newcastle' was certainly current by the middle of the century. (*O.E.D.*, 'Coal'; that 'coals' were charcoal is borne out by a reference of 1628 to the 'turning of trees to coals for fuel . . .').

74. William Harison, *Description of England*, 1577, and *Hardwick Invt., 1601*.

75. At Hengrave Hall (*Invt., 1603*) it is evident that coal was burned in the Hall but logs were burned in the Great Chamber.

76. *Chatsworth Invt., 1601* and *Tart Hall Invt., 1641*.

77. *Henham Invt., 1602* and *Ham Invt., 1679*.

78. At Hengrave Hall in 1603 (*Invt.*) there was a 'fier sholve made like a grate to seft the seacole with'.

79. *Randle Holme* (Bk. III, Chap. XIV, p. 7) claims that the more ornate forms of tongs were 'for ladys chambers and seldome used there, but hung by the fire-side more for shew and ornament then use'. He called the more serviceable sort 'useing tonges' or 'kitchen tongues'. There was a small-sized kind known as 'brand tongs' with which a live coal could be picked up for lighting a pipe although it is not certain this variant existed before 1700; perhaps it was identical with the '*tirebraize*' that was included in a set of fire-irons that belonged to Cardinal Mazarin (*Invt., 1653*).

80. *Edington Invt., 1665* and *Ham Invt., 1679*.

81. Nell Gwynn was given a pair of bellows decorated with marquetry which had silver mounts. A pair belonging to the Earl of Northampton (*Invt., 1614*) was inlaid with mother-of-pearl. A pair similarly decorated belonged to Lady Dorchester who kept hers with other valuable objects, including an ivory cup, some linen, 'certen beads' in a small box, some small cabinets and a 'tostinge forke', 'in the Deale chest' (*Gosfield Invt., 1638*). The silver-mounted pair at Ham is well known; at Hatfield Priory (*Invt., 1629*) there was a carved pair which is likely to have been Italian.

82. The status of the rooms at Ham House can be guaged by the richness of the fire-irons allocated to the respective fire-places, the grandest rooms have silver-mounted irons while those in less important rooms have mounts of brass.

83. At Ingatestone (*Invt., 1600*) in two instances the 'skepp baskett for cooles' was placed in the 'House of Office', the small closet where the close-stool lived. *Randle Holme* illustrates such a skep (Fig. 319[83]).

84. By Antoine de Courtin, originally published as the *Nouveau Traité de la Civilité*. The Yeoman Usher of the Great Chamber of an important household in 1605 was instructed to attend to the fire 'at the season of the yeare, or ells the chemney to bee garnished with greene bowes, or flowers' ('Breviate touching upon the Order and governmente of a Noblemans House', *Archæologia*, XIII, 1800, p. 332).

85. Brantôme, for instance, tells of a certain

Admiral Bonnivet who one evening was surprised in the room of a lady of the court on whom King François I was also at the time wont to bestow his favours. The Admiral only just had time to scramble behind the foliage in the fireplace before the King came into the room and himself climbed into the bed alongside the lady. Later, the King felt a need to relieve himself and proceeded to do so in the fireplace. As Brantôme puts it, he 'la vint faire dans la cheminée, et arrousa le pauvre amoureux plus que si l'on luy eust jetté un seilleau d'eau' [came to do it in the fireplace, and soaked the poor lover more than if a bucket of water had been thrown on him].

86. *Havard*, 'Devant de Cheminée'; see also 'Papier de Cheminée'.

87. *Havard*, 'Tapis' and 'Cheminée'.

88. *Provost of King's Invt., 1660.*

89. 'Two 17th century Dorset inventories', ed. Lettice Ashley Cooper, *Dorset Record Society*, Publication No. 5, 1974 and *Charles I Invts., 1649–51.*

90. *Tart Hall Invt., 1641.*

91. *Ham Invt., 1679.* These may have been the bronzes after Giovanni Bologna and others which were still in the house at the beginning of the present century. Above the corner chimneypiece in the Duchess of Lauderdale's White Closet at Ham stood, and still stands, the gilded full-size bust of 'Her Grace's mother' now attributed to Dieussart.

92. Dutch flower-paintings may not always be strictly accurate (blooms that flower at different times of the year are sometimes depicted together) but probably convey the general spirit of seventeenth-century flower-arrangements. See R. Warner, *Dutch and Flemish Fruit and Flower Painters of the XVII and XVIII centuries*, London, 1928, and M. L. Hairs, *Les peintres flamands de fleurs au XVIIe siècle*, Paris and Brussels, 1955; also W. Blunt, *The Art of Botanical Illustration*, London, 1950.

93. The trade-plate of a Nottingham pottery dating from the late seventeenth century shows a massive bucket-shaped vessel with a pair of handles in which a shrub is growing (orange tree?); it is described as a 'flower pott' (see *World Ceramics*, ed. Robert Charleston, London, 1968, fig. 386). At Dyrham (*Invt., 1703*) there was in one room a 'Delf[t] flower pot in ye chimney'.

94. Cardinal Mazarin had 'quatre pots à bouquets d'argent blanc, façon de Paris' [four bouquet vases of silver in the Parisian taste] (*Invt., 1653*).

In the *Du Boisgeslin Inventory of 1688* mention is made 'vases à bouquets de terre blanche' [vases for bouquets of white ware] which were painted and gilded; there were also some 'petits vases à fleurs et un grand de fayence' [small flower vases and a large one of fayence]. These all seem to have been for cut flowers. The 'pots à fleurs' in the French royal collection (*Guiffrey, Inventaire*, I, p. 44, 1673) which were one and a half *pieds* high may have been tall vases but could equally well have been containers for flower-pots. Some 'pots à fleurs' were of metal, in which case they must surely have been in the nature of *jardinières*, but the *pot à fleur* made of engraved rock crystal in the French royal collection (*Ibid*, p. 222) can only have been a vase for cut flowers.

95. *Ham Invt., 1679.*

96. *Celia Fiennes*, p. 154 and p. 355.

97. *Tart Hall Invt., 1641.* This does not seem to have been a *jardinière* for there were several 'flower potts' in the house, two of which were 'leaden . . . gilded' while others were of 'letany' (i.e. brass), and can only have been containers for actual pots with plants growing in them.

98. *Havard*, 'Fleur'.

99. *Savary des Bruslons*, 'Bouquets'. Artificial flowers were made in nunneries and sold by the *marchands merciers*.

100. The Swedish Countess Brahe owned a beadwork basket filled with wax fruit and silk flowers, as well as a glass vase in which stood some white lillies of silk. In a closet she had a glass vase with glass flowers, and a basket with straw flowers. When one of her sons got married she gave his wife some small silver vases filled with artificial flowers. At one of her country farms some delftware vases on the chimneypiece were filled with paper flowers (W. Karlson, *Ebba Brahe's Hem*, Lund, 1943, p. 47 and inventory of 1665).

NOTES TO CHAPTER XI

1. J. du Pradel, in his *Traité contre le luxe* of 1705, contrasts the simple tastes of yesteryear when people had been content to burn *chandelles* (tallow candles) at four *sous* per pound with the present extravagant age when one had to burn wax candles (*bougies*) costing twenty-two *sous* the pound. The cost of lights in England at the beginning of the seventeenth century is discussed in 'The House and Farm Accounts of the Shuttleworths of Gawthorpe Hall . . .' (ed. J.

Harland), *The Chetham Society*, 1857, Pt. III, Notes, 'Candles'). Rush lights were made of peeled meadow rushes (with a strip left to give strength) soaked in fat. A rush light fourteen inches long would burn in about half an hour. Tallow candles were made half of beef fat and half of mutton, refined; in Paris, at any rate, one was not permitted to add pork fat which was particularly smelly, but tallow candles were always smelly and gave an uneven light. 'Base and unlustrous as the smoky light that's fed with stinking tallow' is a passage that occurs in Shakespeare's *Cymbeline* (Act 1, Scene 7). Beeswax candles were brighter and burned evenly; moreover they did not smell, and their wick required little snuffing as they did not 'gutter' or dribble down the sides. Samuel Pepys 'began to burn wax candles in my closet at the office [the Admiralty], to try the charge [expense], and to see whether the smoke offends like that of tallow candles' (*Pepys' Diary*, 15 December 1664). *Bougies* were normally tapered but 'bougies de table' were cylindrical. The whitest candles were called 'bougies de Venise' but some candles were 'citronnée' (see *Savary des Bruslons*, 'Bougies' and 'Chandelles'). At Somerset House in 1650 there was a 'chest of yellow wax lights' and another of white (*Charles I Invts.*, 1649–51).

2. John Aubrey, *Brief Lives*, written between 1667 and 1680 (ed. O. L. Dick, Penguin Books, London, 1972). Madame de Maintenon's brother used only one pound of *chandelles* (tallow candles) a day—one in the *antichambre*, one in the kitchen and one in the stable (G. Mongrédien, *La vie quotidienne sous Louis XIV*, Paris, 1948).

3. For instance, at the banquet given for Charles II at the Mauritshuis at The Hague in 1660 (Fig. 257), there depended from the ceiling 'four lustres, or christal candlesticks [chandeliers]; which with many candlesticks, arms of silver, and a great number of torches, enlightened all the corners much better than the sun could have done at midday' (William Lower, *Voiage and Residence which . . . Charles II . . . hath made in Holland . . . 1660*, The Hague, 1660). At a ball given in the Galerie des Glaces at Versailles there were 7,000 candles. With the lights multiplied over and over again by the mirror-glass panelling, the effect must have been breath-taking and extremely impressive—as was the intention (see *Tessin-Cronström Correspondence*, letter of 29 November 1695).

4. The same care was bestowed on candles as on the household linen. The Yeoman of the Ewery at Lord Montague's house (*Household Book, 1595*) was instructed to look after the linen, the candlesticks and the 'torches, lynkes and candles'. At Ingatestone (*Invt., 1600*) there was not only a 'plaine longe chest to laye linnen in' in the Buttery but 'a long shelfe to sett candlestickes upon', as well as a candlebox and a 'lock to the candle-house' door. Candle chests and candle boxes are listed quite frequently in seventeenth century inventories. Lady Rivers made a specific bequest of her 'cofer with partitions wherein my lights doe lye' J. Watney, *Some Account of St Osyth's Priory, Essex*, London, 1871. Incidentally, candles were never fitted in chandeliers except when actually needed, as numerous illustrations of the period show. A single candle at most was left in one of the branches to serve in an emergency.

5. Furetière (*Dictionnaire, 1690*) explains that a *lustre* could be a sconce with a mirror-glass backplate and also a 'chandelier de cristal qu'on suspendu au plancher' [a candle-holder of crystal [glass] that one suspends from the ceiling].

6. At a ball given for the Duchesse de Bourgogne at Versailles in 1700 'il y avoit sur tous les pilastres des demi-girandoles à cinq branches d'argent. Ces girandoles . . . ont été nouvellement inventées par M. Bérain' [there were on all the pilasters demi-girandoles with five branches of silver. These girandoles . . . have been designed by Mr Bérain] (*Havard*, 'Girandole').

7. The Dictionary of the French Academy of 1696 explains that a *torchère* was 'une éspèce de guéridon fort eslevé, sur lequel on met un flambeau, une girandole . . . dans les sales des . . . grandes maisons' [a kind of very tall *guéridon* on which one places a candlestick or *candelabrum* . . . in drawing rooms . . . in great houses]. However, the royal silversmith, Claude Ballin, provided 'une grandissme torchère à cinq bobeshes [a very large torchère with five nozzles] for use in the French royal household in 1673.

8. Wooden candlesticks probably dropped from fashion because nozzles of wood have very little strength so, for a wooden candlestick, it was best to retain the old pricket form with an iron spike onto which the candle was fixed. Only thick candles could be used with a pricket. There were several wooden candlesticks in the kitchen at Ingatestone (*Invt., 1600*). The 'paynted candlesticks' in the High Great Chamber at Chatsworth (*Invt., 1601*) may also have been of wood and

will certainly have been very splendid (consonant with the richly inlaid panelling and the valuable contents of the room) but were probably old-fashioned and may anyway have been sconces rather than candlesticks as we understand them.

9. *Mazarin Invt., 1653. Havard* ('Chandelier') suggests that 'à la financière' implied adjustable in height.

10. *Marton Invt., 1605*

11. *Havard*, 'Chandelier'.

12. 'When your Soveraigne is in bed, draw the curtaines and see there be mortar of wax or perchours ready', advises J. Murrell in his *Cookery and Carving* of 1641. A 'percher' was a small candle that could be fixed to a stand called a perch.

13. Comte Paul Biver, *Histoire du Château de Meudon*, Paris, 1923, p. 395, inventory of 'Vaiselles de chambre de Monseigneur le Dauphin' taken in 1702.

14 *Hardwick Invt., 1601, Hengrave Invt., 1603*, and *Marton Invt., 1605*. The last were of 'latten' but although the others were both described as being of copper it is almost certain they too were of brass.

15. *Book of Rates, 1582*. Brassware was primarily made at Dinant and was particularly popular in the Low Countries. There were, for instance, no less than seventy copper (brass?) plate candlesticks (*pannecandelaers*) at Breda Castle in 1597–1603 (*Orange Invts.*, I, p. 75).

16. The back-plates might be decorated 'with Faces, others with Birds, Beasts, Fish, Trees and Flowers, some round or oval embossed works' (*Randle Holme*; see *D.E.F.*, 'Sconces' where this passage is quoted and some examples are illustrated).

17. *Tart Hall Invt., 1641*.

18. *Mazarin Invt., 1653*, and *Havard*, 'Plaques'.

19. *Tart Hall Invt., 1641*, and *Lauderdale London Invt., 1679*.

20. *Cowdray Invt., 1682*.

21. *Havard*, 'Carton Pierre', and *Mazarin Invt., 1653*.

22. *Ham Invt., 1679*.

23. *Hardwick Invt., 1601*, and *Hengrave Invt., 1603*. The Hardwick pair may be those now hanging in the bays of the Long Gallery.

24. The French royal inventories for 1685 include a specific reference to a 'chandelier . . . de cristal de Milan' (*Guiffrey, Inventaire*, II, No. 199). See J. Holey, 'Der Kristalkronleuchter;

seine Entstehung und Engwicklung', *Stifter Jahrbuch*, VIII, Locham bei München, 1964; he illustrates a splendid rock crystal chandelier of about 1690 in Genoa as well as two in Vienna which are likely to be Milanese. See also C. Waage Petersen, *Lysekroner*, Copenhagen, 1969, and the *D.E.F.* 'Chandelier'.

25. *Rambouillet Invt., 1665*. From about this time onwards, crystal chandeliers were commonly called *lustres*.

26. *D.E.F.*, 'Chandelier'.

27. *Ibid*. When the King gave Cosimo III a farewell banquet at the end of the Grand Duke's visit to this country in 1669 there was a 'chandelier of rock crystal with lighted tapers . . . suspended from the ceiling' (*The Travels of Cosmo the Third . . .*, London, 1821). It was very probably the identical piece.

28. *Kilkenny Invt., 1684*. The Ormondes owned several pieces of French furniture and this chandelier probably came from France as well.

29. *Ham Invt., 1679*.

30. See Holey, and Waage Petersen, *op. cit.*; also A. Polak, 'Om glas-lysekrone', Oslo Kunstindustrimuseum's *Yearbook*, 1943–9. There is a fine glass chandelier at Skokloster, Sweden, which was apparently in place by 1672 (E. Andrén, 'Melchior Jung's glasbruk i Stockholm . . .', *St Eriks Årsbok*, 1972).

31. e.g. the French royal inventory for 1684 includes the item 'une chandelier de cristal de Venise' which it is reasonable to suppose was composed of Venetian glass.

32. See Holey, *op. cit.*, and D. Rentsch, 'Bedeutung und Restaurierung des grossen Glaskronleuchters in Schloss Favorite', *Jahrbuch der Staatlichen Kunstsammlungen in Baden-Württemberg*, Bd, 12, 1975.

33. *O.E.D.*, 'Lustre'.

34. Perhaps Cardinal Mazarin's 'chandeliers à pyramides' were early versions of these.

35. *Tart Hall Invt., 1641, Edington Invt., 1665*, and *Orange Invts.*, I, p. 195 'twee flambeaupilaeren, vergult ende met rooden gront' [two candlestands, gilded and with a red ground].

36. See G. Jackson-Stops, 'The 6th Earl of Dorset's Furniture at Knole', I, *Country Life*, 2 June 1977, and illustrated in colour on the cover. What was apparently the payment for these items appears in the French royal treasurer's accounts for February 1671.

37. A drawing for four magnificent candlestands by Alessandro Algardi, the Roman sculptor, is

illustrated in G. Lizzani, *Il mobile Romano*, Milan, 1970, introduction by G. Gonzales-Palacios, Plate XIV.

38. 'Two Blackamore Stands' (*Ham Invt., 1679*).

39. The song had been current in the second half of the century. One heartless verse ran as follows:

> Guéridon est mort
> Depuis plus d'une heure,
> Sa femme le pleure,
> Hélas, Guéridon.
>
> [Guéridon has died
> more than an hour ago,
> his wife weeps,
> alas, Guéridon]

People at first gave the name to their negro servants and some wag then gave it to candlestands in the form of negroes. *Havard* ('Guéridon') noted an early use of the word in this sense in 1650.

40. *Ibid.*

41. *Ibid.*, and *Tessin's Visit, 1687*, p. 25.

42. The description of a party given by Madame de Chaulnes for Anne d'Autriche in 1651 makes this clear.

> A l'entour de la même sale,
> Et dans une distance égale,
> Des Mores noirs et non pas blonds,
> Fais en forme de guéridons,
> Chacun portant dessus sa teste,
> Un grand plat de viande preste,
> Et des autres entre leurs mains,
> Les uns remplis de massepains,
> Et les autres de marmelades
>
> [Around the same room,
> and at equal distances,
> black Moors and none fair,
> made in the shape of *guéridons*,
> each carrying on his head
> a large dish of prepared meat,
> and others in their hands,
> some filled with marchepain
> and others with marmalade.]
>
> (*Havard*, 'Guéridon').

43. At Marly there were some 'paires de guéridons de 3 pieds de haut', which was an average height, and some smaller pairs 'pour tables de jeux' (C. Pitoin, *Marly-le-Roi*, Paris, 1904, p. 174). Three *pieds* would be roughly 91.5

cm. The heights of the *guéridons* shown at the Exhibition 'Louis XIV: Faste et Décors' (Musée des Arts-Décoratifs, Paris, 1960) ranged in height from 98 to 120 cm with three pairs being 175 cm and one 170 cm.

44. A drawing showing a room in a Roman *palazzo* with mural decoration couched in an ebullient Baroque style and attributed by Gonzales-Palacios (see Lizzani, *op. cit.*, Plate XXXVI) to G. P. Schor shows a candlestand placed in the corner of the room. Judging by the costume, this composition dates from about 1670. The Duc d'Orléans had some japanned (*vernis de Chine*) *guéridons* standing in the same position in his bedchamber at Versailles in 1708 (*Havard*, 'Chambre'), and there is a description of a masqued ball given in 1706 where 'the Duc de Bourgogne and three others—le Vidame, the Prince de Rohan and young Seignelay—were wittily dressed; they were in gold with golden masks and silver sashes like carved gilt guéridons. They wore candelabra on their heads and stationed themselves at the four corners of the room' (*Letters from Liselotte*, the letters of the Princess Palatine, ed. Maria Kroll, 1970; letter of 25 February 1706).

45. *Mazarin Invt., 1653*.

46. Jean de La Bruyère, *Charactères*, 1688.

47. The crystal chandelier at the Hôtel de Rambouillet (see note 25 above) was suspended with a 'cordon or et soie' [silk and gold cord], while *Mazarin* (*Invt., 1653*) owned several 'cordons d'argent et soie couleur de feu, garnis de boutons d'or et d'argent par les bouts, servant à suspendre les chandeliers' [cords of flame-coloured silk, furnished with gold and silver buttons [pom-poms?] at each end, used for hanging chandeliers].

48. At Kilkenny Castle (*Invt., 1684*) the crystal chandelier (see note 28 above) had 'a knot of ribbon on top'. The gold and silver 'boutons' mentioned in the previous note will also have served to disguise the hooks.

49. *Hengrave Invt., 1603*.

NOTES TO CHAPTER XII

1. Already in 1618 we find the Bishop of Winchester (*Invt.*) distinguishing between his Great Chamber and his Dining Parlour, calling them respectively the 'Great Dining Room' and the 'Little Dining Room'; but for a long time there was always a qualifying word. For in-

stance, the senior staff at the Countess of Leicester's (*Invt., 1634*) ate in 'The Mens Dyninge-roome' and those at Ham (*Invt., 1679*) in 'The Gentlemen's Dining Roome'. On the other hand, the 'Corner Dineing Room' at Cowdray in 1682 (*Invt.*) and the 'Marble Dining Room' at Ham (*Invt. 1679*) were both used solely by the family, the qualifying word having nothing to do with their size or purpose. A similar room at Petworth in 1670 (*Invt.*) was called the 'Supping Room', however, and the nomenclature was by no means firmly established by the end of the century when *Celia Fiennes* (p. 24) could still speak of 'The large dineinge roome or great parlour' at Coleshill.

2. J. P. Babelon, *Demeures Parisiennes sous Henri IV et Louis XIII*, Paris, 1965, p. 196. When the ambassadors from Siam visited Paris and Versailles in 1686 they were provided with an apartment that included a 'salle à manger' (Deville, *Dictionnaire du Tapissier*, Paris, 1878–80). There was also a room so entitled at the Mme. de Montespan's Château de Clagny (see A. and J. Marie, *Mansart à Versailles*, Paris, 1972, p. 31). *Havard* ('Salle à manger') noted what he called an early reference to the term in 1787 (*sic*) and even this was to 'une anti-chambre servant de salle à manger'.

3. In the Thiret mansion at Rheims in 1621 (*Invt.*), for example, 'La Grande Salle' was clearly intended for use as a dining-room—and was presumably the equivalent of a Great Chamber—while there was both a 'Salle Basse' and a 'Salette Basse' equipped for dining. The latter was next to the main bedchamber and seems to have been the family's private dining parlour, but maybe they normally dined in the 'Salle Basse', and only used the *salette* for informal *soupers*.

4. See P. Verlet, *Versailles*, Paris, 1961, p. 248, for further details. On less formal occasions the King dined in his closet 'à petit couvert'. Saint-Simon records having dined in the *anti-chambre* of the Cardinal de Rohan.

5. There are numberous references in the contemporary French literature to dining in bedchambers and closets. The poet Scarron wrote a charming verse inviting Pierre Mignard, the painter, to join him and dine 'dans ma chambre' (*Havard*, 'Salle à manager'). When Queen Christina of Sweden visited the French court it was noted that she 'ne dinoit pas souvent en public servie par ses officiers, mais presque toujours dans son petit cabinet servie par ses femmes' [did not often dine in public attended by her officers, but almost always in her private attended by her ladies] (*Ibid.*). Queen Elizabeth also preferred to dine in her 'inner and most private chamber', according to Paul Hentzner who visited England in 1598 (W. B. Rye, *England as Seen by Foreigners*, London, 1865, p. 100). Dr Martin Lister saw an Orangery in Paris which was 'the most beautiful room . . . I make no doubt it served to eat in in Summer when cleared of trees' (M. Lister, *A Journey to Paris*, London, 1699, p. 139).

6. Already in 1641 at Tart Hall (*Invt.*) there was an 'ovall Table of Wanscote wth. falling sides' in the Waiters' Room 'next the Little Parler' into which it could presumably be carried. In the Little Parlour itself stood a French draw-table and a small round table with 'falling leaves', so the oval table will have been for use when the company was large.

7. *Montague Household Book, 1595*, p. 129, and Fynes Moryson, *Itinerary, 1617*.

8. *Randle Holme*, Bk. III, Chap. XIV, p. 15. At Hengrave (*Invt., 1603*) there was 'a great coppr. sestourne to stand at the coobard'. At Ham (*Invt., 1679*) the wine-cooler of white marble is still in the house.

9. Near the 'grand dessert' or *buffet* in the Thiret mansion (*Invt. 1621*) stood 'ung rafrechissoir de cuivre avec le pied de bois' [a wine-cooler of copper with its stand].

10. So much ice was required in French fashionable circles that it was regarded as a valuable concession to be granted the monopoly of supplying ice to the whole of France, as happened to a certain Louis de Beaumont in 1700 (A. Lebault, *La Table et le repas à travers les siècles*, Paris, 1960, p. 136).

11. *Ibid.*

12. Balthazar Gerbier, *A Brief Discourse concerning the three Chief Principles of Magnificent Building*, 1662, p. 35.

13. 'This year [1683] came up a vessel or bason notched at the rim to let drinking glasses hang there by the foot, so that the body or drinking parte hang in the water to coole them' (Anthony à Wood, quoted by C. C. Oman, *English Domestic Silver*, 7th edn., London, 1968, p. 136).

14. 'Quand sa Mté. [i.e. Louis XIV] mange à Versailles en famille' he dined with considerable formality in the ancient tradition (*de l'ancienne institution*), we are told by Cronström. 'La table y

est d'un quarré long; le Roy et la Reine seuls ont des fauteuils . . .' [The table is oblong; only the King and Queen have armchairs] (*Tessin-Cronström Correspondence*, letter of 24 February 1702).

15. 'Quant le Roy mange à Marly, Trianon ou quelque autre maison de plaisance, alors la table est grande et ovalle . . . parce que les dames de la cour mangent avec le Roy' [When the King dines at Marly or some other *maison de plaisance*, then the table is large and oval . . . because the ladies of the Court dine with the King] (*Ibid*.). In fact the oval table measured 3 metres by 1.9 and sat eighteen, allowing 50 cm (19 pouces) per diner. This table seems to have been installed in 1699; previously there had been two circular tables each seating fourteen or fifteen people (see C. Pitoin, *Marly-le-Roi*, Paris, 1904, p. 157, with diagrams).

16. William III in 'The King's Pryvat Eating Room below stairs' at Kensington Palace also had 'a large oval table' accompanied by sixteen black leather chairs 'wth. ye large back' (i.e. with tall backs; see *Kensington Palace Invts. 1697 and 1699*). At Ham there were twelve chairs with cane seats in the family dining room; none of them had arms (*Ham Invt., 1679*). Likewise at Cowdray (*Invt., 1682*) the family dining-room contained twelve ordinary chairs, but there were 'two armeing chaires' along with twelve plain chairs in the 'Great Dineing Room'.

17. Louis XIV invariably dined seated in an armchair while those around him sat on stools (*tabourets*). This practice was maintained even at the Trianon where the atmosphere was supposed to be more relaxed ('un fauteuil pour Sa Majesté et vingt-quatre tabourets' [an armchair for His majesty and twenty-four stools] were provided for the Trianon in the 1680s; *Guiffrey, Inventaire*, II, p. 382).

18. *Randle Holme*, Bk. III, Chap. XIV, states that the chairs and stools in a dining-room should be 'of Turky work, Russia or calves leather, cloth or stuffe or needle work. Or els made all of Joynt work or cane chairs.'

19. e.g. The High Great Chamber at Hardwick (*Invt., 1601*), the 'Grande Salle' in the Thiret mansion at Rheims (*Invt., 1621*), the Great Dining Room at Ham (*Invt., 1651*) and the Great Dining Room at Edington (*Invt., 1665*). Large dining parlours like the Low Great Chamber at Hardwick and the Great Parlour at Edington might also be so hung.

20. Robert Adam, 'Instead of being hung with damask or tapestry etc.,' the walls of a dining-room should be of 'stucco, and adorned with statues and paintings, that they may not retain the smell of victuals.' (Robert and James Adam, *The Works in Architecture . . .*, Vol. I, 1773, p. 9.)

21. *Randle Holme* (Bk. III, Chap. XIV) stated that the walls of dining-rooms ought to be 'well wanscoted about, either with Mountan [muntin, the upright members between the panels] and panells, or carved as the fashion was; or else in large square panell'. The 'Little Dyning Chamber' at Hardwick (*Invt., 1601*) had 'waynscott rownde about the . . . roome'; the walls of the dining parlour at Ingatestone were likewise faced (*Invt., 1600*). As for gilt leather, we find it in the 'Salle basse' which served as dining-room in the Thiret mansion (*Invt., 1621*), in the family dining-room at Ham House (*Invt., 1679*) where it is still to be seen on the walls, and in the *Eetsael* at Dieren, the small residence in Holland that Queen Mary II liked so much (*Orange Invts.*, I, p. 289; inventory of 1683). There was also gilt leather on the walls of the 'Banqueting House in the garden' at Cowdray (*Invt., 1682*).

22. *Tessin-Cronström Correspondence*, letter of 24 February, 1702.

23. The 'household books' setting out instructions for the officers of important households mostly give information on these matters. Many survive but only a few have been published. Useful are 'Viscount Montague's Household Book, 1595', Appendix II to Sir William St John Hope, *Cowdray and Easebourne Priory*, London, 1919; and 'A Breviate touching the Order of Governemente of a Nobleman's House, etc.' *c.* 1605, *Archæologia*, XIII, 1800).

24. The cloth might be carried over the arm but could also be worn ceremonially round the neck or over the shoulder, it seems. The cloth was used for drying the hands after the hand-rinsing that followed the meal. A set comprising two tablecloths, thirty-two napkins and a handcloth, all marked with the owner's initials and dated 1638, is cited by C. A. Burgers ('Tafelgoods in vroeger tijd', *Voedings niews*, No. 60, 1969; 'Twee taffeltiens en 32 servetten int Jaer van 1638 getekent met EVK en d'handdoecken oock').

25. Burgers, *loc. cit.*

26. At Marton Hall (*Invt., 1605*) some napkins were 'wth. coventre thread wrought by the weaver at thende'. Coventry-thread was blue so

this set had an in-woven border of blue at each end.

27. At Breda Castle in 1618, for instance, there were no less than four hundred tablecloths, 3,600 napkins and forty-three handcloths (Burgers, *loc. cit.*).

28. The linen at Marton was wrapped in a worn linen diaper cloth and kept in an iron-bound chest (*Invt., 1605*) while Lady Dorchester kept her linen 'in the deale chest' at Gosfield in 1638 (*Invt.*). There is a famous painting by Pieter de Hoogh showing folded linen being carefully put into a large oak cupboard that stands in the main part of the house.

29. The creases usually formed squares (Plate 276) but fanciful patterns could also be produced like that 'ployée d'une certaine façon, que cela ressembloit fort à quelque rivière andoyante, qu'un petit vent fair doucement sous lever' [folded in a certain fashion so as to look very like some flowing river that a gentle breeze gently lifts] (*Description de l'Isle des Hermaphrodites nouvellement découverte*, 1605). According to G. P. Harsdörfer's *Vollständiges Trichir-Büchlein* of about 1650, linen with a fine damask figure ought not to be pressed with patterns as well.

30. In the Buttery at Hatfield Priory in 1629 (*Invt.*) there was a 'skrew presse for napkins'. The napkins were carefully folded, a small board was placed between each one, and the whole assemblage was compressed with the aid of the screw-thread.

31. *Havard*, 'Nappe'.

32. G. Mongrédien, *La vie quotidienne sous Louis XIV*, Paris, 1948, p. 95.

33. Gédéon Tallement des Réaux, *Historiettes*, (written 1657–9), Paris, 1834–40, VI, p. 96).

34. *Havard*, 'Nappe'. This presumably means that some of the figures were sculpted in sugar-paste, the rest were of folded linen.

35. P. Verlet, *Versailles*, Paris, 1961, p. 81.

36. An excellent survey of table ornament is provided by S. Bursche, *Tafelzier des Barock*, Munich, 1974. He quotes (p. 78) the description of a banquet held at Stuttgart in 1609 where the *Schauessen* were of wax and included scenes of Adam and Eve in the Garden of Eden, The Rape of the Sabines, Diana and Acteon, The Nine Muses with mount Helicon and a spring that ran with water for over an hour, and Jonah and the Whale where a splendid ship floated on a miniature pond with live fish, letting off squibs

that released perfume. Incidentally, when the pie was cut open, birds flew out.

37. *Ibid; passim.*

38. *Randle Holme*, Bk. III, Chap. XIV.

39. Andrew Clark, *The Life and Times of Anthony Wood . . .*; Oxford, 1891, Vol. III, p. 236.

40. At the King's table at Versailles, 'les plats sont servys sur des colliers, ou *ringar*' [the dishes were set forth on collars or rings] as the Swede, Daniel Cronström reported (*Tessin-Cronström Correspondence*; letter of 24 February 1702). At the Duke of Norfolk's house at Weybridge in 1684 (*Invt.*) there were in the Wardrobe Room '2 pewter rings to putt dishes upon'. There were two more at Dyrham in 1703 (*Invt.*). Modern caterers sometimes use tinned iron rings when they have to stack plates of food. Collectors of antique silver are familiar with rings, often of great elaboration, and always bearing Irish hall-marks—a fact that has led to the seemingly mistaken view that they have something to do with that Irish staple food, the potato.

41. See C. C. Oman, 'Caddinets . . .', *Burlington Magazine*, December 1958, 'Le Roy et la Reine seuls ont des fauteuils et des cadenas' [The King and the Queen alone have armchairs and caddinets] said Cronström in the same letter from Paris as that quoted in the previous note. A *cadenas* of gold 'garny de sa cuillier, fourchette et cousteau' [furnished with its spoon, fork and knife] with the arms of Anne d'Autriche in enamel is listed in the French royal inventories of 1673 (*Guiffrey, Inventaire*, p. 10).

42. Charles I (*Invts. 1649–51*) owned a 'rich scarfe . . . to cover ye bread and salt'. At the Palace at Leeuwarden there was 'a silver-gilt caddinet on which to lay bread' ('een vergult candinae om broot op te legen'; *Orange Invts.*, list of silver made in 1681, p. 94).

43. *Savary des Bruslons*, 'Cabaret'.

44. See also Chapter VII on Beds, bed-hangings and bed-clothes, and sections relevant to the furnishing of bedchambers in Chapters VI, VIII and IX.

45. So common was the fashion of receiving in the bedchamber that Molière, in his *Les Précieuses Ridicules* (1659) makes a character say that 'ils me rendent tous visite' [they all pay me a visit] and that 'Je puis dire que je ne me lève jamais sans une demi-douzaine de beaux éprits' [I may say that I never get up without half a dozen men of wit] being present in the bedroom. Saint-Simon (*Mémoires*, ed. La Pléiade, Vol. I, Chap. XV, p.

229) tells of a lady who on one occasion 'reçut . . . sur son lit toute le France' [received . . . on her bed the whole of France]. Many other instances could be cited.

46. *Celia Fiennes* (p. 277), describing an unusual balustrade she had seen at Windsor Castle round the state bed there, said that 'this was insteade of the raile use to be quite round the king and queen's beds to keep off companyes coming near them'. At the French court, those permitted access beyond the balustrade were referred to as 'seigneurs à balustrade'.

47. 'Ruelle se dit . . . des alcoves et des lieux parés ou les dames reçoivent leurs visites, soit dans le lit, soit sur les siéges' [*Ruelle* means . . . the alcoves or separated areas where ladies receive their visits, either in bed, or on chairs] (Furetière, *Dictionnaire*, 1690). It was incidentally, 'une très grande indécence de s'asseoir sur le lit, et particulièrement si c'est d'une femme' [it is a great indelicacy to sit on the bed and particularly if it is that of a woman] (N. Courtin, *Traité de la civilité*, 1671).

48. For example at Breda Castle at the beginning of the seventeenth century the principal bedchamber contained a 'buffet van schreyn-werck' [a buffet of joiner's work] *Orange Invts.*, I, p. 75; many more references could be cited from this source alone).

49. We know that there was still a coffer in the bedchamber of the King of France in 1594 because the Maréchal de Biron is reported to have been so tactless as to fall asleep while sitting on it (*Havard*, 'Coffre'), but they were not to be seen in such places much after that.

50. *Du Boisgelin Invt., 1688.*

51. *Havard*, 'Toilette'. Amalia van Solms, Princess of Orange, owned a 'nacht-coffer' covered with a Persian silk material which stood in her closet at the Noordeinde residence at The Hague (*Orange Invts.*, I, p. 191).

52. *Edington Invt., 1665.*

53. *Charles I Invts., 1649–51.*

54. Rather exceptional may have been the Earl of Arundel's splendid bedchamber at Tart Hall (*Invt., 1641*) which had 'on the further side of the Bed a little square Table . . . on the other side of the Bed, a little Narrow table . . .'. The tables had carpets of Indian quilting *en suite* with the bed-hangings.

55. Sir Roger Pratt (1660) insisted that each bedchamber should have 'a closet, and a servant's lodging' (R. T. Gunther, *The Architecture of Sir Roger Pratt*, Oxford, 1928, p. 27).

56. As one often reached the closet through the bedchamber, the former are commonly described in English seventeenth-century inventories as being 'within the bedchamber'. At Ham House, for instance, the future Duchess of Lauderdale, wrote of 'the Closet within my bedchamber' (*Invt., 1654*). The 'inward chamber to Lady Isabella's bedchamber' was likewise a closet, and the inventory (*Edington, 1665*) goes on to describe how 'the closet there [is] hanged with g[r]een dornex'. As both the chamber and the closet were particularly personal to the occupant of the apartment, the contents of the two rooms are not infrequently listed together.

57. Miss Gillian Wilson has assembled all the relevant material in her article on Boulle (*Furniture History*, Vol. VII, 1972). The room was decorated in 1683. The Dauphin's uncle also had a *cabinet* decorated in this manner while the Duc de Chartres had his decorated with 'menuiserie' which also suggests marquetry of some kind (*Havard*, 'Marqueterie').

58. *Havard*, 'Capucine'.

59. *Havard*, 'Porcelaine'.

60. Sir Balthazar Gerbier, *Council and Advise to all Builders*, 1664, p. 108.

61. R. T. Gunther, *The Architecture of Sir Roger Pratt*, Oxford, 1928.

62. For instance, the very splendid 'Shipp Bedchamber' at Hardwick (*Invt., 1601*) had a closet which only contained bedding and a stool, while that next to the 'Prodigall Chamber' housed only a close stool and a chamberpot. On the other hand, the closet next to 'The Noblemans Chamber' (i.e. the owner's room) at Chatsworth (*Invt., 1601*) was 'waynscotted and shelfed' which suggests a certain refinement.

63. Francis Bacon, essay 'On Building'. The last authorised edition of this essay was published in 1625, the year Bacon died. It presumably reflects fashionable taste of about 1610.

64. E. Croft-Murray, *Decorative Painting in England . . .*, Vol. I, London, 1962, pp. 198–9. The chimneypiece of the Kederminster Library at Langley, Buckinghamshire, probably gives a good impression of the style of the Somerset House decorations (Col. Pl. XVII); see also John Harris, 'A Rare and Precious Room', *Country Life*, 1 December 1977 with colour illustration.

65. *Havard*, 'Cabinet'.

66. *The Travels of Cosmo the Third, Grand Duke of*

Tuscany, through England during the reign of Charles II [1669], London, 1821, p. 177. *Celia Fiennes* (p. 345) noted seeing 'a large closet or musick room' at Lady Donegal's when she paid a visit at the end of the century.

67. *Dublin Castle Invt., 1679* and *Cowdray Invt., 1682.*

68. *Celia Fiennes*, p. 358.

69. Sauval, *Antiquités de Paris*, Vol. VII, p. 173.

70. At Chatsworth (*Invt., 1601*) the room called 'My Lady's Wardrop' does not seem to have lain anywhere near 'My Lady's Chamber' but it was 'waynscotted with fayre presses rownde about' and these cupboards were presumably for her ladyship's clothes. At Ham there was a room called the 'Wardrobe' on the second storey containing 'two great presses for clothes', two 'standers' and some other large chests (*Invt., c. 1654*). In the French royal inventories of the time of Louis XIV mention is made of 'deux armoires de bois de noyer pour servir dans des garde-robbes' [two cupboards of walnut for use in *garderobes*] and of three other 'grands armoires qui sont posées dans les embrazures des croisées de la garde robbe du Roy' [large cupboards which were placed in the window embrasures of the King's *garderobe*] which were mounted on brass casters and were so formed that they blended with the panelling during the day (*Guiffrey, Inventaire*, p. 156 and p. 166).

71. 'Ung garde robe bois noyer à quatre portes et deux tiroirs' [A wardrobe of walnut with four drawers and two doors] is listed in a Lyons inventory of 1633 (*Havard, 'Garde-robe'*). Wardrobes were, however, normally called presses in the seventeenth century. In the 'Chamber under my mrs [mistress's]' at Ingatestone (*Invt., 1600*) there were, for instance, 'two great open joyned presses with three rayles in them wth. turned pynns to hange gownes upon', while at Walton (*Invt., 1624*) there was 'a presse wherein hanges my lady's clothes' in the 'Middle Nursery'. Madame de Mercoeur, who formed part of Cardinal Mazarin's retinue (*Invt., 1653*) had 'deux grands amoires de bois de chesne à mettre des habits' [two large cupboards of oak in which to keep clothes] which were seven feet high and five wide.

72. e.g. The *garderobe* at the Thiret mansion at Rheims in 1621 (*Invt.*) contained two close-stools but apparently no storage for clothes. It did have two tables, however, and probably served mainly as a dressing-room (see below).

73. At Hengrave Hall in 1603 (*Invt.*), for instance, one notes that there were 'divers tents to serve for the embroyderers'. 'Tents' were frames on which work to be embroidered could be stretched (Fr. 'tendre', to stretch, hence 'tentures', wall-hangings).

74. *Chatsworth Invt., 1601.*

75. *Countess of Leicester's Invt., 1634.*

76 *Evelyn's Diary*, 4 october 1683. A *garderobe* with a table that probably served as a dressing-table is mentioned in note 72 above.

77. *Havard*, 'Toilette'.

78. *Kildare Invt., 1656*. The dressing-room also contained a still and one may be forgiven for at first suspecting that this was some ingenious Irish arrangement; but there was a 'clocke om water in te distilleren' [a vessel for distilling water] in a closet at Breda Castle in 1597/1603 (*Orange Invts.*, I, p. 82). Perhaps distilling was associated with the preparation of certain cosmetics.

79. Croft-Murray, *loc. cit.*

80. *Edington Invt., 1665.*

81. *Thiret Invt., 1621.*

82. *Tessin-Cronström Correspondence*, letter of 23 August 1693.

83. *Celia Fiennes*, p. 69.

84. Some were portable and could fold (e.g. the 'huit tables brizées pour des toilettes' listed in the French royal inventory for 1685: *Guiffrey, Inventaire*, II, p. 165). The cedarwood tables noted in several rooms at Ham House probably also served as dressing-tables and/or wash-stands.

85. Plain dressing-tables still continued to be used nevertheless; e.g. *Havard*, 'Toilette', cites an inventory of 1705 which notes 'une petite table de toilette de sapin, avec son toilette, composée d'un dessous de toilette d'étoffe de soie, avec un dessus de toilette de mousseline à falbalas' [a small table of pinewood, with its *toilette* comprising an underlay of silk and an overlay of muslin with furbelows].

86. See C. C. Oman, *English Domestic Silver*, 7th edition, London, 1968, p. 190. John Evelyn's amusing verse, *Mundus Muliebris, or the Ladies Dressing-room Unlock'd and her Toilette Spread* (1690) describes the furnishings of a dressing-table in a most entertaining way. See also *Havard*, 'Toilette'.

87. *Orange Invts.*, I, pp. 160–2. Although married to Philip Willem, Prince of Nassau-Orange, this French princess no doubt maintained strong links with her French background and the

arrangements in her rooms could well reflect contemporary Parisian taste.

88. *O.E.D.*, 'Closet'.

89. There was a room called 'The Studdy' at Marton Hall (*Invt., 1605*); James Montague, the Bishop of Winchester who died in 1618 (*Invt.*) had both a 'great' and a 'Little Study'. On the other hand the owner's own closet at Walton (*Invt., 1624*) in which it is recorded that he kept his 'own cabinet & bookes' was not graced with such a title.

90. *Havard*, 'Etude'.

91. The Countess of Shrewsbury kept her small personal library in her bedchamber at Hardwick (*Invt., 1601*). 'My Ladie's bookes' numbered only six titles and, while there may have been other books in the house, there was no separate library; since Hardwick seems to have represented the most advanced thinking on architecture and planning in this country when it was built in the 1590s, this dearth of books is revealing. At Gilling Castle in 1624 (*Invt.*) there were thirty-nine books in 'My Master's Closet', but George Marshall, the Warden of New College, Oxford, had a rather more substantial library when he died in 1659. It comprised sixty-five volumes in folio, 124 quarto, seven English Bibles, six translations of the Bible into different languages, some stitched books, nine other books, and a small group valued at 11s. 2d. The painter, Philippe de Champaigne, according to an inventory of 1674, owned sixty-five volumes in folio, 105 octavo and four in *douze*, 'le tout relié tant en veau qu'en parchemin' [all bound either in calf, or in parchment]. Inventaire des biens de Philippe de Champaigne, *Nouvelles Archives de l'Art Français*, 3rd series, VIII, 1892. The books at Petworth (*Invt., 1670*) were valued at no less than £600, while the Canon of Christ Church who was also Bodley's Librarian between 1660 and 1665 owned books to the value of £200 (Invt. of Dr Thomas Lockey, 1679, *Bodleian Library Record* 1954–6, p. 82). No firm basis for comparison is provided by these figures but they reflect the fact that the size of private libraries increased strikingly during the seventeenth century.

92. The *Countess of Leicester's Invt., 1634*.

93. *Camden Society*, Wills and Inventories from the Registry of the Commissary of Bury St Edmunds, ed. Samuel Tymme, London, 1851, p. 209; and the *Kildare Invt., 1656*.

94. In earlier centuries particularly fine bindings had been displayed lying flat, on tables or sloping shelves and desks. Their spines were then of less consequence. When first set up on shelves they were placed with the spines inwards but the advantages of reversing them gradually became apparent, and the spine then became an important feature. When the effects of Henry Cooke, a painter who died in 1700, were put up for sale, it was pointed out that his books were in volumes 'most of them gilt on the back' (*The London Gazette*, 16/19th December 1700; Mr G. Jackson-Stops very kindly drew my attention to this reference).

95. The bookcases in the Ambrosian Library at Milan, built between 1603 and 1609, have wire mesh in their doors which is said to be original (J. W. Clarke, *The Care of Books*, London, 1901, pp. 260–5).

96. *D.E.F.*, 'Bookcase', Plate 5.

97. The bookcases were moved from Pepys' house in London to Magdalene early in the eighteenth century. My study of this furniture was greatly assisted by Mr Robert Latham, the well-known Pepys scholar to whom I am much indebted. Some very similar bookcases are at Dyrham (*A Short History of English Furniture*, Victoria & Albert Museum publication, London, 1966, Plate 221).

98. *Havard*, 'Bibliothèque'.

99. In the 'Boekcabinet' at the Binnenhof at The Hague in 1700, there were white damask curtains with pelmets in front of the books (*damast gardijnen met rabaten voor de boecken; Orange Invts.*, I, p. 434).

100. He describes 'The Valans of the shelves being greene Velvet, fring'd with gold' (see *Evelyn's Diary*, Vol. II, p. 128, 1 April 1644).

101. R. T. Gunther, *The Architecture of Sir Roger Pratt*, Oxford, 1928, p. 174.

102. *Ham Invt., 1679*.

103. The cloth made the table pleasanter to use and prevented the desk from sliding about. A rough woollen cloth named *bure* in France was often used for this purpose in earlier times and it was from this practice that the term *bureau* was coined for a writing-table or desk. According to *Havard* ('Bureau') the cloth had often been blue in former times but by the seventeenth century it had already been discovered that green was kinder to the eyes. At Marton (*Invt., 1605*) a table in the Study had a green cloth cover and the tables in Mazarin's library had covers 'de drap vert avec mollet de soye mesme couleur' [of

green cloth with a short silk fringe of the same colour] (*Invt., 1653*).

104. *Ingatestone Invt., 1600.*

105. W. B. Rye, *England as Seen by Foreigners*, London, 1865, p. 258; *Marton Invt., 1605*; and the *Mazarin Invt., 1653*. It is possible that the Queen's cabinets were of ebony with mounts of silver, of the kind produced by the silversmiths of Augsburg at that period.

106. *Hardwick Invt., 1600.*

107. *D.E.F.*, 'Desks'; and *Guiffrey, Inventaire*, II, p. 103.

108. What must have been quite a large desk on a stand was the 'deske and a frame' which was noted at Marton already in 1605 (*Invt.*) which contained many items in the 'rowmes' underneath it, but this seems to have been an exceptional object. The 'mettle writing box table' at Kensington Palace (*Invt., 1697*) was probably a sloping-topped desk on a gate-leg stand, faced with boullework marquetry of the sort produced in this country by Gerreit Jensen. Two less elaborate versions are illustrated in the *D.E.F.*, 'Bureau', Plates 3 and 4.

109. The article on Bureaux in the *D.E.F.* sums up the development in England admirably.

110. However, Mazarin (*Invt., 1653*) did own a strange desk described as being 'en forme de tombeau' (tomb-shaped). It was made of black touch-stone (*pierre de touche noire*), enriched with semi-precious stones, and was surmounted by the figure of a sphinx. It had feet in the form of four silver-gilt bats and the whole curious affair was housed in a case of red velvet. It may not have been very large and there is no cause to equate it with what is today called a *bureau Mazarin*, a form that can hardly have been evolved until well after the Cardinal's death.

111. *D.E.F.*, 'Bureau', Plate 2.

112. *Agius*, p. 81. The form was revived again in the second half of the eighteenth century and became popular in Regency England. No seventeenth-century specimens seem to survive but it would be surprising if this useful fitting had been totally abandoned by the studious during the intervening centuries.

113. *Knole Invt., 1645.*

114. See G. Wingfield Digby, *Elizabethan Embroidery*, London, 1963, pp. 107–8. At Tart Hall (*Invt., 1641*) there lay on a table in a closet a pillow embroidered with the arms of Philip I of Spain and Mary, by then a treasured antique, which is likely to have been a book-pillow.

115. *Randle Holme*, Bk. III, Chap. XIV.

116. *Marton Invt., 1605*. It is of course possible that a quill was fitted into this brass pen which should then have been described as a pen-holder.

117. 'Inventory of Robert, Viscount Teviot "lately deceased in his lodgings in Christ Church, Oxford" 1694', (Manuscript in the Bodleian Library, transcript shown me by Mrs Pauline Agius; by kind permission of the Keeper of the Archives, Oxford University); *Tart Hall Invt., 1641*; and *Kilkenny Invt., 1684*.

118. *Cockesden Invt., 1610.*

119. *La Loi de la Galanterie Française*, 1640. See G. Mongrèdien, *op. cit.*, p. 71. 'Pain d'amande' was a paste. 'On sçait assez que les pâtes pour laver les mains, se font avec des amandes douces ou amerés, & quelques autres ingrédiens' [It is well known that the pastes used for hand-washing are made from sweet or bitter almonds, and various other ingredients] *Savary des Bruslons*, 'Amandes'.

120. 'The dynner beinge done ... [the Gentleman Usher] shall come towards the table wth. a towell (gentlemen following wth. basons, and ewers) ...' *Montague Household Book, 1595*. 'Quand les napes furent levées et que les mains furent lavées ...' [when the tablecloths have been removed and the hands rinsed], wrote Loret in 1649 (*Havard*, 'Nappe').

121. 'When ... I am redye for my dinner or supper, then my Gentleman Usher shall see the Carver and Sewer to washe att the ewerye table' where there were basins and ewers for the purpose (*Montague Household Book, 1595*).

122. In most cases there was probably no difference between a bath-tub and a wash-tub for laundry, so no distinction would have been made in an inventory.

123. *Savary des Bruslons*, 'Baignoires', confirms that these could be of copper or wood, the latter being made by members of the Coopers' Guild (*Tonneliers*).

124. Louis XIV had 'une grande cuvette d'argent qui sevoit au roi à laver les pieds' [a large silver basin for the king to wash his feet in] (*Havard*, 'Cuvette'). The English royal accounts for 1623–4 refer to a payment for 'one large flatt coffer covered with leather lyned with bayes for the carriage of his higs. [His Highness, later Charles I] silver bathine sestorne [cistern]' (R. W. Symonds, 'The Craft of the Coffer-maker', *The Connoisseur*, March, 1942).

125. Lawrence Wright, *Clean and Decent*, London, 1960.

126. See P. Négrier, *Les Bains à travers les Ages*, Paris, 1925, quoting from Jean Héroard's journal of the life of the young Louis XIII.

127. Mongrédien, *loc. cit.*, states that a copper bath could be hired for 20 *sous* in Paris.

128. *Celia Fiennes*, p. 99.

129. *Havard*, 'Baignoire' and 'Salle des Bains'; and P. Verlet, *Versailles*, Paris, 1961, p. 102. One of the baths cost 15,000 *livres*. The ceiling of the Cabinet des Bains was painted and gilded, the cost of the gilding alone amounting to 24,000 *livres*. Along with two bronze figures by François Anguier, there was an imposing looking-glass. The bronze reliefs were by the famous *fondeur*, Domenico Cucci.

130. *Karlson*, pp. 620–2. This is confirmed by Lorenzo Magalotti who visited Sweden in 1674 and made a drawing of a sauna with tiered platforms on which the bathers reclined (C. M. Stenbock, *Sverige under År 1674*, Stockholm, 1912; see Plate 308, here). See also L. Savot, *L'Architecture Françoise des Bastimens Particuiliers*, Paris, 1624, Chap. XVIII.

131. Robert Herrick, 'Panegerick to Sir Lewis Pemberton'. When Paul Hentzner visited Windsor Castle in Elizabeth's reign he remarked on the magnificent bedchambers, halls and 'hypocausts' (using the ancient Latin term for baths with ducted heating). Horace Walpole, editing his travelogue a century and a half later, translates this as 'bathing rooms' but adds that it might mean bedchambers equiped with stoves. It seems more likely Hentzner really meant that there were a number of steam-baths or 'sweating closets' at Windsor (P. Hentzner, *A Journey into England . . . in the year 1598*, translated by H. Walpole).

132. Francis Bacon, *The Historie of Life and Death*, London, 1638, pp. 249–250. Bacon died in 1626.

133. *Guiffrey, Inventaire*, II, p. 379. These tents were of a striped cotton material known as *bazin*.

134. *Ham Invts., 1677, 1679* and *1683*.

135. Lady Dorothy Shirley mentioned in her will 'my silver livery bason and ewer which are usually sett upon my cupboard in my chamber'. (Will proven in 1634; *Faringdon Invt., 1620*). The Bishop of Chester (Inventory of Hugh Bellot, Bishop of Chester, 1596, *Chetham Society*, Lancashire and Cheshire Wills and Inventories, Pt. III, ed. The Rev. G. J. Piccope, 1861) likewise had his pewter 'bason and laver' standing on a 'livery cupboard' which had a red cover.

136. At Henham (*Invt., 1602*) there were ten 'washing basons' in the Pantry and there were two pewter basins and ewers (with lids) in the Pantry at Ingatestone (*Invt., 1600*).

137. For example, the cedarwood tables that were in the Duke's dressing-room at Ham (*Invt., 1679*) and in that of Lady Maynard. Can the oak table 'covered with letaine' (laiton = brass) at Tart Hall (*Invt., 1641*) and the 'little table tinned-over' at Tredegar (*Invt., 1688*) also have been washstands?

138. *Thiret Invt., 1621*.

139. *Stengel*, p. 185. At Marton (*Invt., 1605*) there was a box with three 'washinge balls and one of them is a camphyre ball'.

140. *Noordeinde Invt., 1633*.

141. *Stengel*, p. 173, mentions a chamber-pot of 'porzellan' which may possibly have been of Oriental porcelain but was more likely of faience. Lady Joanna St John made a specific bequest of 'my oval silver chamber pott' in her will dated 17 February 1705 (Somerset House, Gee 40; kindly communicated by Mr F. T. Smallwood through my colleague Mr Simon Jervis). Mazarin (*Invt., 1653*) seems to have had a pot of glass ('un couverture de pot de chambre de verre de velours . . .').

142. The hazards of using an earthenware pot are vividly described by the Princess Palatine (*Lettres de Madame Palatine*, Le Club du Meilleur Livre, ed. H. Juin, Paris, 1961, p. 21; translated from the German). Finding that the close-stools in charge of the *garçon du château* at Saint-Germain were all too foul, she demanded a chamber-pot which turned out to be a humble vessel of earthenware. She placed it on a rush-seated chair but the pot unfortunately broke in two at the crucial moment. The Princess only saved herself from disaster by clutching at a nearby table. 'Je serais tombée, mollement si vous voulez, mais peu proprement' [I would have fallen gently, if you like, but hardly elegantly], she added.

143. *Randle Holme*, Bk. III, Chap. XIV; he spells 'squatter' with only one 't'.

144. *Savary des Bruslons*, 'Bidet'.

145. *Marton Invt., 1605*.

146. The form was probably new in the middle of the century when one in the royal palaces was described as a 'close stoole trunke fashion of redd velvet' (*Charles I Invts., 1649–51*).

147. *Ingatestone Invt., 1600*.

148. *Mazarin Invt., 1653*. At Ingatestone there

was a 'high close stoole with a lose cover all covered wth. black leather'.

149. *Orange Invts.*, I, p. 149 and C. Pitoin, *Marly-le-Roi*, Paris, 1904, p. 174.

150. *Ingatestone Invts., 1600* and F. R. Friis, *Kjøbenhavns Slots Inventarium, 1638*, Samlinger til Dansk Bygnings- og Kunsthistorie, Copenhagen, 1872–8.

151 *Mazarin Invt., 1653.*

152. This was the case with the close-stool in the Countess of Shrewsbury's own apartment at Hardwick (*Invt., 1601*) and in the King's apartment at Hampton Court (*Estimates, 1699*), for instance. Incidentally, the Marquis of Hertford's accounts for 1641–42 include the item 'given to the woman who empties my Lordes close-stool ... twentie shillings' (*Antiquaries Journal*, XXV, p. 23).

153. *Kilkenny Invt., 1684.* The close-stool in question was covered with Turkey leather.

154. *Ingatestone Invts., 1600.*

155. *Ingatestone Invts., 1600*; *Petworth Invt., 1670*; Invt. of Dr Thomas Lockey, *loc. cit.*, *Lauderdale London Invt., 1679.*

156. Teviot Invt., 1694, *loc. cit.*

157. *Noordeinde Invt., 1633.* A close-stool in the palace at Leeuwarden in 1633 is called a *secreetstoel* (*Orange Invts.*, II, p. 50).

158. Verlet, *op. cit.*, p. 264. Savot, *op. cit.*, p. 97, explains that 'L'arriere-garderobe n'est necessaire que pour y retirer une chaise percée' [the back *garderobe* is only necessary as a housing for the close-stool] and need only be four feet deep 'si ce n'est en celle des Princes, où il est besoin de plus de grande place' [unless it is in a princely house, in which case it needs to be larger].

159. The niche may well have had curtains behind which the King could retire. Lady Dorothy Shirley, whose husband had been our ambassador at the French court in the 1590s, had a curtain to hide the close-stool in her 'Close Rome' (*Faringdon Invt., 1620*).

160. *Celia Fiennes*, p. 358.

161. For example, the Princess Palatine writes that 'The Dutch understand cleanliness better than anyone in the world. Things are very different in France; there is one dirty thing at Court that I shall never get used to; the people stationed in front of our rooms piss in all the corners. It is impossible to leave one's apartments without seeing somebody pissing.' (*Letters from Liselotte*, ed. M. Kroll, London, 1970, letter of 23 July 1702).

162. G. Wingfield-Digby, in his *Elizabethan Embroidery*, (London, 1963, pp. 20–71) describes some richly decorated sweet-bags but suggests they were made to hold confectionery. Bulwer (*Artificial Changling*, 1653) refers to Montaigne's story of a man who was 'wont to find fault with Nature she had not made provision for a sweet-bag to hang under our noses ... alleadging that his mustachoes served him to that purpose in retaining the sent of his perfumed gloves'. 'One sweett bage' is listed among the bedclothes in a chamber at Edington (*Invt., 1665*). Madame de Rambouillet (*Invt., 1665*) kept '2 petits sachets de parfums' trimmed with silver lace in a coffer in her bedroom. A recipe for 'a pouder for sweet baggs' dating from the late seventeenth century included 'orris' (ground up rhizomes of a type of iris), benhemen (a resinous gum), calamus (the rhizomes of sweet flag), lignum vitae sawdust, rosewood, musk, civet, ambergris, oil of orange-flowers, 'labdanum' (a sticky substance obtained from rock-roses) and 'chypre'. These were all 'separately beat by themselves and then mixed together, and to a pound of these pouders take a pound of roses dried' (see Beryl Platts, 'The Perfume and the Potters', *Country Life*, 2 June 1977).

163. 'A perfuming panne of brass with figures' (*Tart Hall Invt., 1641*).

164. *Walton Invt., 1624.*

165. *Guiffrey, Inventaire*, p. 63, 1673. The Dauphin had a 'seringue pour les eaux de senteurs' of silver-gilt in his bedchamber at Meudon (Le Comte de Biver, *Histoire du Château de Meudon*, Paris, 1923, p. 395).

Notes to the Plates

I (opposite p. 52) *The Music Party* by Pieter de Hoogh.
The Wellington Museum, Apsley House, Victoria and Albert Museum photograph.
II (opposite p. 52) Attributed to David des Granges (1611–*c*.75) who is said to have been a friend of Inigo Jones. Sir Richard Saltonstall (d. 1650) stands by the bed in which his wife has recently given birth to the baby held by the woman seated in the chair. What may be a turkeywork carpet lies on the floor.
The Tate Gallery, London, Victoria and Albert Museum photograph.
III (opposite p. 55) Model made in 1976–7 by Miss Lucy Henderson working under the guidance of the Department of Furniture and Woodwork in the Victoria and Albert Museum. On show at Ham House, near Richmond.
Victoria and Albert Museum photograph.
IV (opposite p. 86) See Marcus Binney, 'The Hôtel Lauzun, Paris', *Country Life*, 11 May 1972. The parquet and chimneypiece in the second *salon* are of later date; the damask on the right is modern.
Country Life photograph.
V (opposite p. 89) From the volume of drawings, largely by French architects, which may have belonged to Inigo Jones (see note to Plate 44). Perhaps by Pierre Collot, about 1620.
The Ashmolean Museum, Oxford.
VI (opposite p. 120) From the album discussed in the note to Plate 44.
The Ashmolean Museum, Oxford.
VII (opposite p. 123) Victoria and Albert Museum, London.
VIII (opposite p. 154)
A, Red worsted cut pile on a linen ground.
B From Chastleton, Gloucestershire, where an inventory of 1633 mentions hangings of 'dornix' in one of the principal rooms, and hangings of this material are still on the walls of a landing to which position they may have been moved. It has thin linen warps; the yellow sprigs are brocaded. Some similar material, without the brocaded detail, is on a wall at Skokloster, Sweden.
C The patterns are produced by woollen wefts (in two cases organised in bands) on the white linen ground. Such materials are usually called Italian and Mr Donald King informs me that the few specimens which have a firm provenance come from southern Europe.
Victoria and Albert Museum, London.
IX (opposite p. 157) From Hornsberg manorhouse in Kalmar County, Sweden. See also note to Plate 105.
Kulturhistoriska Museet, Lund, Sweden.
X (opposite p. 188) The Drawing Room at Penshurst, Kent. The *appliqué* work suite may have been made for Leicester House which was re-decorated between 1698 and 1700. An early photograph of the daybed shows that it originally had a row of heavy tassels beneath the seat-rail. A similar daybed was at Beningbrough.
Country Life photograph.
XI (opposite p. 191) *Richard Sackville, Third Earl of Dorset*, Miniature by Isaac Oliver.
Victoria and Albert Museum, London.
XII (opposite p. 222) Perhaps made for Kiveton, the great house built by the Duke of Leeds (created 1694) between 1697 and 1702. Mr Christopher Gilbert informs me that a payment was made to 'Gilbert ye Joyner' in 1703 which is probably a reference to Philip Guibert who in 1697 had provided the Crown with a 'fine black soffa of a new fashion, filled with hair', its cushion 'filled up with downe, the frieze and cheeks all molded and fringed'.
Temple Newsam House, Leeds.
XIII (opposite p. 225) By Emanuel Witte.
Photograph by courtesy of the Terry-Engell Gallery, London.
XIV (opposite p. 256) Specially commissioned for Countess Piper who was re-decorating her town house in Stockholm in the fashionable Parisian manner, guided by the Swedish Court Architect, Nicodemus Tessin, and through the agency of Daniel Cronström in Paris (see *Tessin-Cronström Correspondence, passim*).
Now at Sövdeborg, Sweden (photograph by courtesy of Messrs Allhem, Malmö).
XV (opposite p. 259) By Frans Francken (1581–1642). Dutch; second quarter of the seventeenth century.

Photograph generously provided by Mr and Mrs Frank Woods (I am greatly indebted to Mr Brian Koetser for assisting me by tracing the painting which passed through his hands some years ago).

XVI (opposite p. 290) Ham House, Richmond. Victoria and Albert Museum photograph.

XVII (opposite p. 293) The Kederminster Library, Langley Marish, Buckinghamshire, about 1625(?); completed by 1631. Photograph by permission of the Buckingham County Council.

BLACK AND WHITE PLATES

1. Engraving from the suite by Abraham Bosse (1602–76) entitled *Les Vierges folles*. While purporting to show frivolous girls, the artist in fact depicts with obvious delight an interior of considerable opulence. Note what appear to be sash-windows; also early parquet flooring and a chimney piece after a design by Barbet (1632). By courtesy of the Trustees of the British Museum, London.

2. *Le Retour du baptême*, engraving by Bosse from a suite entitled *Mariage à la ville*. The bed has pillows for two; the counterpoint lies on the bed while occupied. By courtesy of the Trustees of the British Museum, London.

3. Engraving from the same suite as Figure 1. A lighted sconce is masked by the chimneypiece but the principal light comes from the fire. Note how the fire-dogs catch the light. The decorative cup-board cloth forms a prominent feature.

4. *La Visite à l'accouchée*, engraving from the same suite as Figure 2. The cabinet with a 'carpet' may be a house-altar. The tapestry is pulled back so that the door can open.

5. See catalogue of the exhibition *Charles Le Brun* (Versailles, 1963, No. 96). The author is indebted to Mme. L. Buffet-Challie for information about this drawing. National Museum, Stockholm (Cronstedt Collection).

Two extensive collections of drawings, now in the Print Room at the National Museum, were amassed by a succession of Swedish Court Architects, starting with Nicodemus Tessin the Younger (1654–1728) who formed the substantial nucleus of the first collection in the late seventeenth century. He was in France in 1687 (see *Tessin's Visit, 1687*) and made detailed notes

of what he saw. He no doubt also brought back drawings on that occasion but he remained avid for fresh information and obtained many further drawings from Paris later in the century (see the *Tessin-Cronström Correspondence*). The collection was subsequently much increased by his son, Carl Gustav Tessin (1695–1770), who was in Paris in 1728 and was ambassador there in 1735–36, and later became effectively *Surintendant des Bâtiments* in Sweden. Further additions were made by Carl Hårleman (1700–53) who visited Paris in the 1720s and succeeded C. G. Tessin as *Surintendant*. He was again in Paris in 1731–2 and 1744–5. The second collection was formed by C. J. Cronstedt who succeeded Hårleman as Court Architect and had himself been in Paris between 1732 and 1735. These men were all extremely well informed about artistic affairs in Paris between 1680 and 1770, and the drawings they assembled in Stockholm are all likely to have been of some special significance to the understanding of contemporary French taste and fashions. The author is much indebted to Dr Ulf Johnsson for his great help in selecting the drawings from these collections that are reproduced in the present work.

6. The audience given to Cardinal Chigi, the Papal Legate, on 29 July 1664 in the State Bedchamber at Fontainebleau. It is not known exactly when Le Brun drew the scene but it is likely that a designer of his standing would have shown furnishings in his latest style when composing such a scene. The tapestry was woven between 1671 and 1676. On the walls, three silver sconces may be seen. A carpet, which may have been woven at the Savonnerie factory or at Dupont's *atelier* at the Louvre, lies on the *parquet* behind the balustrade. Behind is a splendid cabinet. The richly-trimmed state bed is of simple outline. Mobilier Nationale, Paris.

7. See catalogue of the exhibition *Charles Le Brun* (Versailles, 1963, No. 120). Musée du Louvre, Paris.

8. Perhaps the design for the 'trois guéridons dont le corps est de trois figures de femmes qui portent le plâteau, posées sur un pied à trois consoles terminées en patte de lion pesans ensemble 1263 marcs, 5 onces, 0 g[ros]' [three candlestands of which the stem represents a female figure holding the plateau, standing on a tripod with lions-paws weighing . . .] listed in the French royal inventory in August 1685

(*Guiffrey, Inventaire*, pp. 347–8). The designer, working to Le Brun's preliminary sketch, has provided alternative proposals for the base.
National Museum, Stockholm (Cronstedt Collection; see note to Plate 5 above).

9. Musée du Louvre, Paris.

10. The central support under the top table suggests it was very heavy, as would have been the case if it was made of silver. These are likely to be some of the tables that were melted down in 1689.
National Museum, Stockholm (Cronstedt Collection; see note to Plate 5 above).

11. Engraving by Sébastian Le Clerc in Mlle de Scudéry's *Conversations nouvelles sur divers sujets, dédié au Roy*, Paris, 1684.
Bibliothèque Nationale, Paris.

12. Brussels tapestry, probably designed by Louis van Schoor; late seventeenth century.
By courtesy of Messrs. Sotheby, through the kindness of Mr Michael Webb; sale of 10 October 1969.

13. By A. F. Desportes (1661–1743). Note the pyramid of fruit.
The Metropolitan Museum, New York.

14. The complete *ameublement* for the bed-chamber, which is described in the French royal inventory (*Guiffrey, Inventaire*, II, p. 263), included four *carreaux* (see p. 181), four large *fauteuils de commodité* (see p. 195), four *portières* and a table with flanking candlestands (see p. 231). The 'enfans' supporting the looking-glass at the headboard were of *papier mâché* (*carton*). The Trianon de Porcelaine was destroyed in 1687.
National Museum, Stockholm (Tessin-Hårleman Collection; see note to Plate 5 above).

15. National Museum, Stockholm (Tessin-Hårleman Collection: see note to Plate 5 above).

16. Engraving by J. D. de St Jean; 1680s. Perhaps based on knowledge of the *Chambre des Amours* at the Trianon de Porcelaine. Madame de Montespan, for whom this *maison de plaisance* was built in 1672, fell from royal favour in 1682 and the cipher over the bed is certainly not hers.
Bibliothèque Nationale, Paris.

17. Inscribed 'à Trianon' which must be in reference to the Trianon de Marbre (Grand Trianon) which was begun during the winter 1686–87, replacing the demolished Trianon de Porcelaine. The inscription concerning the sofa reads 'Les 2 grands canapez de la Chambre du Roy garnis de velours bleu à frange et galons

d'or' [The two large sofas in the King's Bed-chamber covered with blue velvet with gold fringes and galloons] and gives their dimensions (eight feet long). It would seem that the crestings of the two sofas differed somewhat. The arm-chair is described as a *fauteuil* and the adjustable *torchère* is called a 'chambrière à 4 bougies à la mode' [a fashionable chamber light with four candles]. It was five feet high. The King's Apartment was completed in 1692.

This is one of a group of drawings in a volume belonging to the Bibliothèque de la Con-servation of the Château de Versailles which Monsieur Gérald van der Kemp, Conservateur de Versailles, has most generously given me permission to publish here. A few have already been published by Monsieur Alfred Marie ('Louis XIV avait déja du mobilier Napoléon III', *Connaissance des arts*, February 1970; also in his *Mansart à Versailles*, Paris, 1972). Although the unidentified draughtsman seems to have been particularly interested in uphol-stery, he has drawn details of every kind (parquet patterns, iron grilles, topiary, etc.); he was clearly concerned to record items that struck him as strange or significant in the décor at the French royal palaces and other grand houses at the end of the seventeenth century. The drawings are not dated but are datable on internal evidence to somewhere between 1687 (or 1692) and 1701, the present drawing providing the evidence for the earliest date and Plate 288, which mentions the Duc de Chartres who became Duc d'Orléans in 1701, gives us the last possible date. Such sketches were probably drawn by architects and designers visiting Paris and Versailles, to record what they saw and in order to help them reproduce the latest French fashions in this field when they returned home. However, it may be that a Frenchman made these particular sketches for sale to such visitors; perhaps the fact that they are actually off-sets (produced by pressing down sheets of soft damp paper onto the original red-chalk drawings, the impressions thus being in reverse) may be significant. Some of the images have subsequently been inked in and the in-scriptions re-written. (I am much indebted to Mme Simone Hoog for the assistance she has given me in connection with my study of this material).

18. Inscribed 'A Marly dans le petit apparte-ment'. The *Pavillon Royal* at Marly was largely completed by 1682–3 and the furniture illus-

trated in this drawing probably dates from that phase. The *fauteuil* and *chaise* were covered with green silk damask and stripes of galloon, trimmed with a silver rod (*tringle d'argent*). On the table of 'bois de violette' stand a 'coffre' and some Siamese vases. The latter may have been among the presents brought by the Siamese Ambassadors who visited Versailles in 1686.
Château de Versailles (see note to Plate 17).

19. Engraving by Pierre Le Pautre (1660–1744). Victoria and Albert Museum, London.

20. Clagny was being built between 1674 and 1680 (Mme de Montespan fell from favour in 1684). The architecture visible in the background only agrees very approximately with the published plans and the scene is probably to a great extent imaginary (even a royal mistress would not set up her daybed at the top of stairs leading down to a large and no doubt draughty room, and even she cannot have persuaded cherubs to hold up its curtains). The furniture and costume otherwise seem totally plausible and are likely to be of the kind used to decorate this 'maison de délices' as it was called at the time. In the left foreground is a *carreau* on its stand, its second cushion supports her feet.
The Uffizi Gallery, Florence (Alinari photograph).

21. Probably by Antoine Desgodetz. An alternative proposal did not have the bath sunk so deeply into the floor (see Fiske Kimball, *The Creation of the Rococo*, Philadelphia, 1943, Plate 3; and A. Marie, *Naissance de Versailles*, Paris, 1968, Plates CXXIII and CXXIV).
Les Archives Nationales, Paris.

22. 'Chez Monseig[neu]r à Versailles' [In the Dauphin's apartment at Versailles]. The inscription under the *canapé* explains that it was covered with *damas bleu* and that 'le dossié' was of 'brocard d'or piqué et d'or[,] le falballa aussi bleu brodé de fleurs' [the back covered in gold brocade quilted with gold thread, the furbellow also being embroidered with flowers]. The dolphins forming armrests are an allusion to the prince's title. The rooms were being decorated in November 1684 and were so greatly occupying the time and energies of the best royal craftsmen that the exasperated King dropped a strong hint that his son should bring the work to a prompt conclusion (see A. and J. Marie, *Mansart à Versailles*, Paris, 1972, pp. 265–72 and 589–607).
Château de Versailles (see note to Plate 17).

23. Once again Mme Simone Hoog has greatly assisted me with information about this picture which belongs to the Musée du Château de Versailles. When acquired in 1898 it was thought to depict the *Cabinet du Régent* at Versailles, a room decorated by Boulle between 1682 and 1685, having originally been set up on the first floor and then moved downstairs. When the Dauphin died in 1711, the apartment was given to Philippe d'Orléans who became Regent in 1715. The boy standing on the left would then be the young Louis XV and the French authorities still adhere to this view. Fiske Kimball (*The Creation of the Rococo*, Philadelphia, 1943, pp. 64–5), on the other hand, advances cogent reasons for supposing that it shows the Dauphin's Closet at Meudon which was completed in 1699, with the Dauphin and his third son, the Duc de Berry who was born in 1686. If we accept this latter view, we here have a French royal prince in his ultra-fashionable room rather than one in a setting that was twenty years old. The fact that one can see a painting of *Mars and Venus* by Lanfranco, which is known to have been at Meudon, suggests that Kimball was correct. At any rate, the picture gives a convincing impression of a rich closet at the end of the seventeenth century.

24. From Jean Le Pautre's *Livre de miroirs[,] tables et guéridons*; about 1675?
Victoria and Albert Museum, London.

25. Daniel Cronström wrote to Tessin (*Tessin-Cronström Correspondence*, letter of 19 April, 1693) that he was sending him 'certains dessins de feu Baslin . . . ils sont veritablement de Baslin . . .' [certain drawings by the late Baslin . . . they really are by Baslin]. Tessin wrote back on 26 July concerning the 'table et guéridon avec des mors qui servent des soutiens' [the table and candlestand with blackamoors serving as supports]. No reference is made to the melting down of the silver furniture in 1689; can this set have been so important that it was allowed to survive a few years longer?
The National Museum, Stockholm (see note to Plate 5 above).

26. Note how the mouldings of the ceiling are shown in section.
Victoria and Albert Museum, London.

27 & 28. From a series of *Alcoves* which had immense influence all over Europe. For instance there is a painting of a Danish countess at Gisselfeld Kloster which is dated 1682 and shows a bed and alcove exactly like that illustrated in

Figure 27, while Robert Pricke in 1674 published a re-engraving of Figure 28 in *The Architects Store-house*.
Victoria and Albert Museum, London.

29. *Dame de qualité à sa toilette*, engraving by N. Bonnart (1636–1719); 1690s. Note the folding dressing-mirror, the *toilette* over the table-carpet.
The Pierpoint Morgan Library, New York.

30. *Un Cavalier, Et une Dame beuvant du Chocolat*, engraving *en suite* with Plate 29. The chocolate is being whipped in a special pot; glasses of cold water are brought by the negro servant (who might have been called *un guéridon* at the time). Note the fitted table-carpet.
The Pierpoint Morgan Library, New York.

31. Engraving by J. D. de St Jean; about 1690.
Bibliothèque Nationale, Paris.

32. By courtesy of the Trustees of the British Museum, London.

33. The signing of the contract of marriage between King Vladislas IV of Poland and Princess Louise Marie de Gonzaga on 25 September 1645, in the *Chambre du Roi* at Fontainebleau; engraving by Abraham Bosse. The young King Louis XIV, who had acceded to the throne only two years before, stands with his mother (Anne d'Autriche) and brother (Duc d'Anjou, later Duc de Chartres, then d'Orléans) 'enclos de la Balustrade'. A list of those who were not permitted beyond the balustrade is given in the inscription; they include Cardinal Mazarin, several dukes and ambassadors, and the 'dames de la Cour'.
Bibliothèque Nationale, Paris.

34. The engraving entitled *Bal à la Française* celebrates the return of Louis XIV and his Queen from Strasbourg in that year.
Bibliothèque Nationale, Paris.

35 & 36. From a series of engravings by Jean Le Pautre entitled *Differens desseins d'alcauve*, one edition of which was sold by Le Blond in 1667.
Victoria and Albert Museum, London.

37. 'Madame de Seignelay, dans ses plus magnifiques et propres cabinets[,] faits apres la mort de son mary [d. 1670], et, qui sont des chefs d'oevres, n'a point voulu de serrurerie de cuivre doré n'y d'Angleterre; tout est de fer, mais d'une propreté qui passe tout ce qu'on a encore veu.' [Madame de Seignelay, in her most sumptuous and neatly-contrived closets, which she has created since her husband's death, and which are veritable masterpieces, did not want any locksmith's work of gilt copper or of the English type; all is of iron [steel] but of a finish that surpasses anything one has ever seen before.] wrote Cronström (*Tessin-Cronström Correspondence*, letter of 11 September 1693). He added that he was sending a specimen of the work of the locksmith who had executed the Seignelay fittings; presumably this was in the form of the drawing here reproduced.
The National Museum, Stockholm (Tessin-Hårleman Collection).

38. Acquired by Count Niels Bielke, who was Ambassador to the French Court between 1679 and 1682, probably in 1680 according to surviving documents (see P. Thornton, 'The Parisian Fauteuil of 1680', *Apollo*, February, 1975).
Photograph from the Archives of the Nordiska Museum, Stockholm.

39. Acquired together with the preceding item. An old photograph shows that the modern re-upholstery of this chair has been carried out faithfully although the back is now perhaps a little too flat.
Photograph by courtesy of Bukowski Konsthandel, Stockholm.

40. The chairs were in the house by 1677 when they are listed in an inventory. The 1679 inventory describes the red and green material as a 'rich Brocard', using the French term for brocade; in 1727 it was described as being Venetian.
Photograph; Victoria and Albert Museum, London.

41. Given to Count Niels Bielke while Ambassador to the French Court between 1679 and 1682. Crimson velvet with *appliqué* ornament executed in white and light blue silk edged with silk cord.
The National Museum, Stockholm.

42. By Bartolomaeus van Bassen (1590–1652). This exercise in perspective is likely to be imaginary but is composed with elements in the fashionable style then current in the Netherlands. The architectural elements may in fact have been drawn by Paul Vredeman de Vries.
Hessisches Landesmuseum, Darmstadt.

43. By Nicholaes de Giselaer (1583–1654). Another exercise in perspective. As with the previous illustration, the architectural components may have been drawn by Paul Vredeman de Vries; these are anyway in the style he favoured.
The Fitzwilliam Museum, Cambridge.

44. The volume containing this drawing belonged to James Gibbs (1682–1754) but Mr John Harris has suggested that the volume had formerly belonged to John Webb and perhaps even to Inigo Jones—in fact that it belonged to the Office of Works. Some of the drawings are signed by Cotelle and a number (not the present subject) were published in his *Livre de divers ornemens pour plafonds* . . . in about 1640, a work that was dedicated to Anne de Rohan, Princesse de Guémené. The monogram on this ceiling occurs in conjunction with hers on another drawing in the volume.
The Ashmolean Museum, Oxford. (I am greatly indebted to Sir Anthony Blunt for drawing my attention to this extremely important album.)

45. This bedchamber lay in 'King Charles Block' (i.e. Charles II who was entirely familiar with French practice in this field) at Greenwich Hospital (then Palace). Engraved and mistakenly attributed to Webb's master, Inigo Jones, by John Vardy, *Some Designs of Mr. Inigo Jones and Mr. William Kent*, 1744.
The Devonshire Collection, Chatsworth. Reproduced by permission of the Trustees of the Chatsworth Settlement. (Courtauld Institute photograph.)

46. By Bartolomeus van der Helst (1613–70).
Rijksmuseum, Amsterdam.

47. By courtesy of Messrs Thomas Agnew and Sons, Ltd., London.

48. By Pieter de Hoogh (1629–88). On top of the handsome oak cupboard (note its light colour) stand some Japanese lacquer coffers—expensive exotica.
The Cleveland Museum of Art, Cleveland, Ohio.

49. By J. van den Aveele, active in his native country from 1678 until he went to Sweden in 1698. The chairs have deeply skirted seat-covers.
Victoria and Albert Museum, London.

50. From the *Second livre d'appartemens inventé par Marot, architecte du Roy Guillaume III* (d. 1702). According to C. W. Royards (*Het Loo*, The Hague, 1972) this shows a bedchamber in that palace, which was begun in 1694.
Victoria and Albert Museum, London.

51. The architrave of the flanking window (*moulure de la Croisée*) is indicated. The sheet of glass is '96 pouces de hauteur—ce qui est 8 pieds' which does indeed make the plate a 'grande glace' as the inscription claims. Marot gives careful instructions concerning its proportions.
The Rijksmuseum, Amsterdam.

52. Victoria and Albert Museum, London.

53. Based on an original plan of Combe Abbey of about 1682 reproduced by Hill and Cornforth, *English Country Houses; Caroline*, Plate 243.

54. Based on a plan of the Château de Chavigny by Le Muet in his *Nouveaux bâtimens faits en France*, 1647.

55. Based on the plan of the Château de Pontz given by Le Muet (see previous note).

56. Based on a plan given by Th. H. Lunsingh Scheurleer, 'De Woonvertreken in Amalia's Huis ten Bosch', *Oud Holland*, LXXXIV, 1969.

57. Based on a plan reproduced by A. Blunt, *Art and Architecture in France, 1500–1700*, 1970 edn. The architect was Louis Le Vau.

58. Based on a plan reproduced by Blunt (see previous note). The design is by Jules Hardouin Mansart.

59. The Duchess of Lauderdale had been to Paris in 1670. Shortly afterwards, she began to modernise Ham House.

60. Based on Verlet, *Versailles*, Paris, 1961, and H. Murray Baillie, 'Etiquette and Planning of the State Apartments in Baroque Palaces', *Archæologia*, Vol. CL, 1967.

61. Based on the same sources as Figure 60.

62. Collot's compositions often include rather graceful female figures in Classical dress.
Victoria and Albert Museum, London.

63. From the same album as Figure 44.
Ashmolean Museum, Oxford.

64. J. Harris, 'Inigo Jones and his French Sources', *Metropolitan Museum Bulletin*, May 1961, suggests the drawing is by François Derand the Elder, but makes no positive identification. The present attribution is the author's.
Royal Institute of British Architects, London.

65 & 66. Sold by C. Danckerts.
Victoria and Albert Museum, London.

67. From F. de Wit's *Poorten en schoorsteenmantels en Autare*, Amsterdam, 1640s. Based on a design in Barbet's *Livre d'architecture*, 1632.
Victoria and Albert Museum, London.

68. This seems to be fitted with a pair of doors across the opening, acting as a chimney-board.
Victoria and Albert Museum, London.

69. By Jean Le Pautre. The cartouche supported by putti was a motif no doubt intended to provide a source of inspiration for the decorators of chimney-boards (see Plate 252).
Victoria and Albert Museum, London.

70. The title-page of a suite of *Cheminées et lambris à la mode* by Pierre Le Pautre (1660–1744). Published in the 1690s and purporting to show chimneypieces that had been 'executez dans le nouveaux Batimens de Paris'.
Victoria and Albert Museum, London.
71. All but one design does indeed have a panel of mirror-glass inset.
Victoria and Albert Museum, London.
72. A perfume-burner (*cassolette*) is represented in relief on the fire-back.
Victoria and Albert Museum, London.
73. Published in Holland, presumably in the 1690s (William III, to whom Marot was architect, died in 1702), this illustration is presumably based on schemes he had already devised in one of the Dutch residences of the House of Orange.
Victoria and Albert Museum, London.
74. From the same suite as Plate 73.
Victoria and Albert Museum, London.
75. In the same album as Plate 44.
The Ashmolean Museum, Oxford.
76. The attribution to Webb was made verbally to the author by Mr John Harris, the chief authority on the architectural drawings of Inigo Jones and his school. The style is Webb's and an earlier attribution to Inigo Jones can hardly be sustained on account of the late date (Jones died in 1652 and does not seem to have been an active architect during his last years). Inserted in the album discussed in the note to Plate 44.
The Ashmolean Museum, Oxford.
77. Ham House, Richmond (Victoria and Albert Museum, photograph).
78. From the same album as Plate 44.
The Ashmolean Museum, Oxford.
79. From the same album as Plate 44.
The Ashmolean Museum, Oxford.
80. See note to Colour Plate IV for information about the Hôtel Lauzun.
Country Life photograph.
81. The magnificent state rooms at the Château de Maisons bear eloquent witness to the sobriety and well-mannered reticence of the French Classical style as handled by its most talented advocate, François Mansart (d. 1666). This closet lies beyond the *Chambre du Roi*.
Country Life photograph.
82. At this stage the framing of the glass panel is still rectangular; soon, much attention was to be paid to framings of fanciful outline.
Archives Nationale, Paris.

83. The group is playing *trou-madame*, a game somewhat like the modern *bagatelle*. Later, special tables were made for the game.
From Matthäus Merian, *Emblemata Amatoria*, Paris, about 1614. (See note to Plate 133.)
The National Museum, Stockholm.
84. *L'Hyver* from a suite of Seasons by Abraham Bosse. The company is making apple fritters at the fireplace (the apples await peeling on the stool; batter is in a bowl on the floor).
The Bibliothèque Nationale, Paris.
85. 'Maturity' from a series Depicting *Les Quatre ages de l'homme*.
By courtesy of the Trustees of the British Museum, London.
86. From C. A. d'Aviler *Cours d'architecture . . .*, 1738 (first published in 1691).
The Victoria and Albert Museum, London.
87. Published in the English translation of Le Muet's *Palladio*, 1670, when the floors were described as having been 'lately made at Somerset House'.
The Avery Memorial Architectural Library, Columbia University, New York.
88 & 89. From the same collection as Plate 17.
Château de Versailles.
90. The *Cabinet Doré* was created to house the Dauphin's collection of bronzes and gemstone vessels which are said to have rivalled the King's and were likewise displayed on giltwood brackets on the white walls (see A. and J. Marie, *Mansart à Versailles*, Paris, 1972, p. 271).
Musée des Arts-Décoratifs, Paris.
91 & 92. Published at Amsterdam in 1630. Paul Vredeman de Vries was the son of Hans Vredeman, architect and designer. He collaborated with his father on the important *Architectura . . .*, published in 1607. See also Plates 42 and 43.
Victoria and Albert Museum, London.
93. *The Van Goyen Family* by Jan Steen (1626–79). Jan van Goyen was dead (1656) by the time his close friend Steen painted this picture but it no doubt gives a faithful impression of a well-to-do Dutch parlour of the 1660s.
The William Rockhill Nelson Gallery of Art, Kansas City, Missouri.
94. Probably French, about 1690; artist unknown. X-ray photographs show that the curtains have been repainted and formerly were shown pulled back to reveal a couple on the bed, having retired there after a scuffle at the dressing-table where they had been playing cards. Only

one candlestand is shown although there would normally have been a pair flanking the table.
Victoria and Albert Museum, London.

95. From a suite of engravings entitled *Nouveaux livre de paramens inventée et gravée par D. Marot, architecte de sa Majesté Britannique* (i.e. before 1702 when William III died). The word *croissée* at the front indicates the position of windows.
Victoria and Albert Museum photograph (from P. Jessen, *Daniel Marot*, Berlin, 1892).

96. The decoration resembles that on the Bielke Bed (see Plate 41) and the design may even be a proposal for it.
National Museum, Stockholm (see note to Plate 5 above).

97. The main hangings are of oyster-coloured Chinese silk damask. The bed-head is composed of a shaped three-dimensional wooden ground to which silk is pasted. The outlines are trimmed with red silk braid and 'campaign fringe'. It is possible that the bed was designed by Daniel Marot; it is anyway entirely in his style.
Victoria and Albert Museum, London.

98. Victoria and Albert Museum, London.

99. See Plate 137 where the complete bed is shown.
The Swedish Royal Collection (Gripsholm Castle).

100. The National Trust, Cotehele. (I am indebted to Mr Cyril Staal for answering technical enquiries about this important survival.)

101. A bed with cups of this sort may be seen in Figure 136.
Skokloster, Sweden.

102. On the sheet of paper with this heading is a memorandum dated 1694.
The National Trust, Dyrham (Victoria and Albert Museum photograph; I am indebted to Mr Anthony Mitchell for help in obtaining this photograph).

103. Mounted on a canvas backing awaiting restoration. The panel is now on a chair in the Victoria and Albert Museum.
Victoria and Albert Museum, Department of Furniture and Woodwork Archives.

104. By Gonzales Coques (1614–84). The wooden floor is bare (a common enough feature at the time). The painted harpsichord was an expensive item.
Staatliche Kunstsammlungen, Kassel.

105. *Anthony and Cleopatra*, one of a set at Dunster Castle. One of the scenes closely resembles that on a tapestry hanging designed by Julius van Egmont in Brussels in 1661; maybe the designers of tapestries were also prepared to provide the painters of this class of leather hanging with compositions to copy.
The National Trust, Dunster Castle (I am indebted to the late John Waterer for providing me with this photograph).

106. The bed was made for Queen Christina the Elder of Sweden (1573–1625). Daughter of the Duke of Holstein-Gottorp, she married Charles IX of Sweden in 1592.
The National Museum, Stockholm.

107. The National Museum, Stockholm.

108. By Pieter de Hoogh (1629–83).
Photograph from the Rijksbureau voor Kunsthistorische Documentatie, The Hague (by courtesy of the Frick Art Reference Library).

109. By Gothfried Schalcken, dated 1669.
Photograph by courtesy of Messrs. Christie, Manson and Wood (I am indebted to Mr Anthony Coleridge for his assistance in locating this picture which was in the sale of 1 May 1964).

110. By Pieter Janssens (1612–72), probably painted in the 1660s. The artist has had trouble with the scale; the catches of the windows are shown as being at eye level while the door seems too low. This may explain why the figure of the sweeping maid was painted out until recently again revealed.
The Städelsches Museum, Frankfurt-am-Main.

111. By Wolfgang Heimbach.
The Danish Royal Collection; Rosenborg Castle, Copenhagen.

112. By Jan Verkolje.
Photograph by courtesy of Messrs. Christie, Manson and Wood (sale of 28 November 1975).

113. From a suite of engravings of *Les quatres ages de l'homme* by Abraham Bosse; about 1640 (Plate 85 is from the same suite).
By courtesy of the Trustees of the British Museum, London.

114. This shows the closet at Ter Nieuburch at Rijswijk at the time of the signing of the Treaty of Ryswick in 1697 and furnished in a late seventeenth-century manner. However, the building was erected in the 1630s and 1640s to the designs of Jacques de la Vallée, architect to the House of Orange-Nassau. The drawing is faulty; the room is quite small. Engraved by J. van Vianen, published by Anna Beek.
The Rijksprentenkabinett, Amsterdam.

115. *Sir Thomas Aston at his Wife's Deathbed*, by

John Souch (1616–36). The picture is not painted from life, as the black hangings would not have been present at the event. The deceased wife is also depicted seated at the foot of the bed. The boy holds a fore-staff, an aid in surveying and navigation.

The City of Manchester Art Galleries.

116. By Jan Steen.

The Royal Collection; by Gracious permission of Her Majesty the Queen.

117. The Infanta Maria, sister of Philip IV of Spain and wife of Ferdinand III of Hungary (1606–45); painter unknown.

The National Trust, Knole, Sevenoaks. (I am indebted to Mr R. St John Gore for providing me with information about this picture.)

118. This sketch by the author is not to scale nor is it based on any particular contemporary illustration.

119. Probably from the 1660s; see the following note.

The National Museum, Stockholm (Tessin-Hårleman Collection; see note to Plate 5).

120. This may be the silver bed designed in 1669 by Charles Le Brun for the royal palace of Saint-Germain (see catalogue of the exhibition 'Versailles et les châteaux de France', held at Versailles in 1951, no. 125). This is no state bed; such a fanciful confection can presumably have been made only for a royal mistress. Louise de la Vallière became mistress to Louis XIV in 1668. Parts of this coloured design are rendered in silver which has since tarnished.

The National Museum, Stockholm (Tessin-Hårleman Collection; see note to Plate 5).

121. From a suite entitled *Livre de lits à la Romaine*.

Victoria and Albert Museum, London.

122. Made either at Augsburg or in Italy. Walnut inlaid with ivory. A very similar bed, still with its curtains, is at Gripsholm Castle in Sweden; it belonged to the father of Queen Eleonora of Sweden (born 1636) who was a Duke of Holstein-Gottorp.

Bayerisches Nationalmuseum, Munich.

123 & 124. Of oak with tinned iron mounts. Perhaps Swedish.

Eskilstuna Museum, Sweden (photograph by Lars Rannegårdh, kindly provided by Dr Carl Braunerhielm).

125. Originally the field bed of Count Carl Piper, the powerful minister of Charles XII of Sweden. He acquired it in Paris through the agency of Nicodemus Tessin. It was probably in

reference to this bed that, on 8 May 1695, the latter wrote to his agent in Paris that 'Mr. Piper vous fait faire ses compliments et protestation d'amitié plus que jamais, et il vous recommande fort son petit meuble du lict . . .' [Mr Piper sends you his compliments and expressions of friendship more than ever, and praises exceedingly his small bed]. *Tessin-Cronström Correspondence*.

The Royal Armoury, Stockholm.

126. From *Dend hyrdinde Astrea* by Søren Terkelsen, Copenhagen, 1645.

The Royal Library, Copenhagen.

127. From Johannes de Brune's *Emblemata of Zinnewerck*, 1624.

Victoria and Albert Museum, London.

128. From the family sketchbook of Gesina Terborch (1633–90).

The Rijksprentenkabinett, Amsterdam.

129. Sketches by the author.

130. Sketched from A. C. Fox-Davies, *The Book of Public Arms*, London, 1894, p. 816.

131. *La Veue* from a suite of engravings representing the Senses by Abraham Bosse. Paris; about 1635.

By courtesy of the Trustees of the British Museum, London.

132. *Le Touché* from the same suite as Plate 131.

Bibliothèque Nationale, Paris.

133. From an *Emblemata Amatoria* by Matthäus Merian (1595–1650) which appeared between 1612 and 1614 in Paris (see L. Wüthrich, *Das Druckgraphische Werk van Matthaeus Merian de. Ae.*, Basle, 1966).

The Bibliothèque Nationale, Paris.

134. From the same work as Plate 127.

135. From the same work as Plate 126.

136. The Lying-in-State of the Landgraf Wilhelm VI von Hessen-Kassel. Engraving by Elias von Lennep. 1663.

Staatliche Kunstsammlungen, Kassel.

137. A detail of the valance from this bed is shown in Plate 99. The property of the Danish princess Ulrika Eleonora who married Charles XI of Sweden in 1680. An inventory of that year describes 'the fine state and ordinary beds that have come out of France, with the great hangings belonging thereto, and their white plumes, the hangings of the former being trimmed with very rich gold and silver lace, both on the inside and outside and on the *cantonnières* and *bonnegrâces* . . .' (see Åke Setterwall, 'Ulrika Eleonora d. ä's. paradsäng' in *Gripsholm och des Konstskatter*, Stockholm, 1956; I am much

indebted to Dr Setterwall for providing information about this bed).

The Swedish Royal Collection, Gripsholm Castle.

138. From the French Royal Drawing-office, probably drawn by Antoine Desgodetz (see A. and J. Marie, *Mansart à Versailles*, Paris, 1972, pp. 340–6).

Archives Nationale, Paris.

139. Sketches by the author based on rather indistinct representations of the bed in paintings by F. Marot and A. Dieu (at Versailles) of scenes that took place respectively in August 1682 and May 1683.

140. Of cloth of gold (cream-coloured silk brocaded all over with two kinds of silver-gilt thread) lined with salmon-pink silk embroidered with couched decoration, trimmed with a rich 'campaign' fringe in places producing a three-dimensional effect. The sixth Earl of Dorset, who was Lord Chamberlain at the time, probably removed this suite from Whitehall Palace by way of a perquisite. An inventory of 1701 shows it formerly had a gilded rod running round the outside of the tester to support a dust-curtain like that shown in Plate 144. See G. Jackson-Stops, 'The 6th Earl of Dorset's Furniture at Knole', *Country Life*, 2 and 9 June 1977, I, Plates 2, 3 and 5; II, Plates 6 and 9.

The National Trust, Knole, Sevenoaks (*Country Life* photograph).

141. From the *Second livre d'appartements inventé par Marot, Architect du Roy Guillaume III* (i.e. published before 1702).

Victoria and Albert Museum photograph (from P. Jessen, *Daniel Marot*, Berlin, 1892).

142. Victoria and Albert Museum, London.

143. From the *Nouveau livre de licts de differentes penseez fait par Daniel Marot, Architecte du Roy Guillaume Troisième*.

Victoria and Albert Museum photograph (from Jessen, *op. cit.*).

144. The Biblioteca Comunale, Siena (I am indebted to the late Professor Robert C. Smith for providing me with this photograph which he published in *Furniture History*, III, 1967).

145. Sketches by the author. The bed is one of several currently in store at Hardwick.

146. From the same collection as Plate 17.

147. Drawn by Samuel Hieronymus Grimm in 1775 in the Long Gallery at Hardwick.

By courtesy of the Trustees of the British Museum, London (Add. Mss. 15537).

148. Photograph from the Archives of the Department of Furniture and Woodwork, Victoria and Albert Museum, London.

149. Formerly at Forde Abbey; present whereabouts unknown.

150. The National Trust, Knole Park, Sevenoaks.

151. The Rijksmuseum, Amsterdam.

152. The National Trust, Knole.

153. *The Comtesse d'Olonne*, by A. Trouvain. French, 1694.

Victoria and Albert Museum, London.

154. By Dirck Hals, 1626.

National Gallery, London (by courtesy of the Trustees).

155. *La Visite à la nourrice* from the same suite of engravings as Plate 2. The servant in the background is using a stick to even out the bedclothes.

By courtesy of the Trustees of the British Museum, London.

156. From Hendrik Hondius, *Instruction en la science de perspective*, The Hague, 1623.

Victoria and Albert Museum, London.

157. From the series of drawings associated with Plate 17.

158. From the sketch book of Gesina Terborch. Note the pierced doors of the food cupboard. I am greatly indebted to Mr C. A. Burgers for drawing my attention to this important source of information about the Dutch interior around 1670.

The Rijksprentenkabinett, Amsterdam.

159. Much of the embroidery has disintegrated since this photograph was taken in 1912. Ancient upholstery has been treated with far too little respect in the intervening years.

Victoria and Albert Museum, London.

160. Parlour scene by Jan Steen; 1660s.

Museum Boymans van Beuningen, Rotterdam.

161. Portrait by Philippe de Champaigne of Jacques Tubeuf who was at this time *Surintendant des Finances* of Anne d'Autriche and Louis XIV as well as *Ordonateur* of the King's works.

Château de Versailles.

162. Sketch by the author after an engraving by J. D. de St Jean.

163. Portrait by Gerhard Terborch of Gosewijn Hogers who was elected to the city council of Deventer in 1668 and represented that city at the States General in 1672. It has been suggested that the furniture was painted in by Terborch later but the chairs would anyway have been up-to-

date in the late 1660s. See also Plate 186.
Private collection (photograph by courtesy of the National Gallery, London).

164. Powis Castle, Montgomeryshire (photograph kindly provided by the late J. W. Waterer).

165. By kind permission of the Governing Body of Christ Church, Oxford.

166. Engraving by Renold Elstrack (?) in Robert Glover's *Nobilitas Politica Civilis*.
Victoria and Albert Museum, London.

167. Susan Villiers, Countess of Denbigh, by Daniel Mytens, about 1625. (Mytens painted the lady's brother in 1626).
From the Collection at Parham Park, Sussex. (I am indebted to Miss R. Courcier for providing information about this portrait.)

168. The National Trust, Knole.

169. The National Trust, Knole.

170. From the same collection as Plate 17.

171. From the same collection as Plate 17.

172 & 173. Said to be in the Royal Library, Brussels, but not located there. Taken from *Havard*.

174. Illustrated in Mathurin Jousse, *La Fidelle ouverture de l'art de serrurerie*, La Flèche, 1627.
Victoria and Albert Museum, London.

175 & 176. Skokloster, Sweden.

177. Colonial Williamsburg Foundation, Virginia, U.S.A.

178. Victoria and Albert Museum. London.

179 & 180. Now in a private collection. Old photograph, taken before restoration, in the archives of the Department of Furniture and Woodwork, Victoria and Albert Museum.

181. Mentioned in the *Inventory of 1679* but not in that of *1677*. In that of *1683* they are called 'reposing chayres'. The royal accounts show that John Paudevine supplied Charles II with a sleeping chair 'neatly carved and the irons all gilt with gould' in 1677 at a cost of £6.
Victoria and Albert Museum photograph.

182. Sketch by the author.

183. Victoria and Albert Museum, London.

184. Sketch by the author from a painting at Clandon Park (The National Trust).

185. Sketch by the author from an engraving by Blooteling after a portrait by Lely (*The Connoisseur*, December 1944).

186. Gosewijn Hogers' wife; the pendant to the portrait shown in Plate 163.

187. Portrait of the brothers Henri and Charles Beaubrun by Martin Lambert, 1675.
Château de Versailles.

188. Portrait of Louis XIV based on an engraving by J. de St Jean (inscribed 'pinxit', suggesting he painted the original picture).
Esplunda, Närke, Sweden (photograph by courtesy of Messrs Allhem of Malmö).

189. *The Lying-in* by Mathys Naiveu (1647–1721). Although said to date from the early eighteenth century, the furnishings point to a rather earlier date.
Stedelijk Museum 'De Lakenhal', Leiden.

190. Based on Largillière's portrait of Charles Le Brun, painted in 1686 (see P. Thornton, 'The Parisian Fauteuil of 1680', *Apollo*, February 1975, where the portrait is illustrated).

191. Sketch by the author based on a portrait of Madame de Maintenon by Louis Elle, painted in 1687.

192. The woodwork is stained black. This chair is from a set en suite with a state bed at Drayton House, Northamptonshire.
Victoria and Albert Museum, London.

193. On loan from Lord Newton to The National Trust, Lyme Park (*Country life* photograph).

194. Sketch by the author based on a self-portrait of Pierre Mignard, the French court painter, executed in 1696.

195. From the same collection as Plate 17. The inscription under the 'Bureau' is unfortunately indecipherable.

196. From the same work as Plate 156.

197. From the same work as Plate 127.

198. *Nursing Twins* by Esias Boursse (1631–72). Photograph by courtesy of Messrs Appleby Bros Ltd, London.

199. From the same collection as Plate 17.

200. From the same collection as Plate 17.

201. It may be that the furniture shown here was made for the Dauphin; it is in a similar taste to that shown in Plate 22. From the same collection as Plate 17.

202. The identity of this room is unfortunately not indicated but it is likely to have been one of great importance, perhaps in the Dauphin's apartment.
From the same collection as Plate 17.

203. On loan from Lord Newton to The National Trust, Lyme Park (*Country Life* photograph).

204. Victoria and Albert Museum, London.

205. From the same source as Plate 133.

206. Engraving by Jacob van der Heyden.

Photograph by courtesy of Nordiska Museet, Stockholm.
207. Formerly at Nether Winchendon, Buckinghamshire.
(Photograph by kind permission of Mrs Spencer-Bernard).
208. From the same collection as Plate 17.
These pieces are stated to be 'chez Madame Boquemar', whose identity has not been established. Maybe whoever inked in the inscription misread the name Roquelaure.
209. Sketch by the author based on a painting in the London art-market in 1969.
210. Sketch by the author based on several Vermeer paintings, notably one in the Kunsthistorisches Museum, Vienna.
211. Miniature portrait of Sir Anthony Mildmay by Nicholas Hilliard (1547–1619), probably painted in 1596 when Mildmay was knighted. He died in 1617. The trunk covered with black leather and protected by tinned iron bands would have been for Mildmay's new suit of Greenwich armour, elements of which he is wearing (I am indebted to Mr John Hayward for making this observation).
The Cleveland Museum of Art, Ohio, (purchased from the J. H. Wade Fund).
212. The National Trust, Cotehele (I am greatly indebted to Mr Cyril Staal for helping me to obtain this photograph).
213. Sketch by the author.
214. From Gripsholm Castle, Sweden. Branded HERS GRIMSHOLM showing it was made for Queen Hedvig Eleonora who died in 1715.
Nordiska Museet, Stockholm.
215 Provided for the same Queen of Sweden as the table shown in Plate 214. Many tables of this highly serviceable type are still to be found in the Swedish palaces.
The Swedish Royal Collections, Gripsholm Castle (I am indebted to Dr Åke Setterwall for providing information about these tables).
216. Part of the furniture of the Duchess of Lauderdale's apartment at Ham House. Perhaps bought in Holland.
Victoria and Albert Museum, London.
217. It is certainly mentioned in an inventory of 1718. Veneered with ebony; decorated with floral marquetry and ivory stringing. Probably made in Copenhagen, perhaps by an immigrant Dutch craftsman.
The Danish Royal Collections, Rosenborg Castle.

218. By Jean Le Pautre (d. 1682). Perhaps inspired by a triad of silver in a French royal palace and certainly in the general style of Charles Le Brun.
Victoria and Albert Museum, London.
219. From the same work as Plate 114.
220. This is probably one of 'deux ou trois desseins de pièces d'orfèverie du Sr. Balin' that were sent to Stockholm on 10 July 1699 (see Plate 25 and Tessin-Cronström Correspondence; also C. Hernmarck, 'Claude Ballin . . .', Gazette des Beaux-Arts, 6e., XLI, 1953). The table is probably identical with item 926 in the French royal inventories (made between 1673 and 1681) which concerns 'une grande table d'argent, faite par Baslin . . . entourée d'une campanne, et portée par quatre cupidons assis sur des dauphins . . .' [a large table of silver, made by Baslin . . . with a lappeted apron all round, supported by four cupids seated on dolphins] (Guiffrey, Inventaire, p. 86). The Grande Galerie was not completed until 1684.
The National Museum, Stockholm (Tessin-Hårleman Collection; see Plate 5).
221. Made by Jean-François Cousinet between 1697 and 1707, under the guidance of Nicodemus Tessin, the Swedish Court Architect who had seen the silver furniture at Versailles in 1687.
The Swedish Royal Collection, Stockholm Palace.
222. Engraving by Pierre Le Pautre (1660–1744). Victoria and Albert Museum, London.
223. The inscription states that this furniture was to be seen 'au petit Sallon'; this presumably means a room in the Dauphin's apartment, perhaps his Grand Cabinet or even the Cabinet doré next door (see Plate 90; also Marie op. cit., pp. 265–72 and 589–607).
From the same collection as Plate 17.
224 & 225. The National Museum, Stockholm (Tessin Collection; see Plate 5).
226. Banquet given by Charles II (seated under the canopy at a high table behind a barrier) for the Knights of the Garter. From Elias Ashmole, The Institutions, Laws and Ceremonies of the Most Noble Order of the Garter, London, 1672.
Victoria and Albert Museum, London.
227. A room in Rubens' house at Antwerp in the 1620s, painted by Frans Franken II (1581–1642). Strictly speaking this shows a Flemish interior but a grand Dutch room of the same date would have differed in no significant manner.

The National Museum, Stockholm.

228. Family portrait by Pieter Pieters. (1543–1603). Two children who died before this family portrait was painted are shown with palm fronds in the foreground.

American private collection (photograph by courtesy of the Isaac Delgado Museum of Arts, New Orleans).

229. Musée des Arts Décoratifs, Paris.

230. Engraving by M. Daigremont, about 1700. The inscription states that this had been executed 'chez Monsieur Thévenin à Paris'.

Victoria and Albert Museum, London.

231. From the album of watercolours by Gesina Terborch. See Plate 158.

232. By Gonzales Coques (1614–84).

Musée d'art et d'Histoire, Geneva (Fondation Lucien Baszanges).

233. From the same collection as Plate 44.

234. By Jean Le Pautre (d. 1682).

Victoria and Albert Museum, London.

235. By George Hainz of Altona; dated 1666.

The Kunsthalle, Hamburg (photograph by courtesy of the Museum für Kunst und Gewerbe).

236. Nicodemus Tessin saw the panels of this elaborate scheme of mural decoration set up at the Gobelins in 1687. In 1706 some panels were erected at the Tuileries when they were described as a 'tres riche lambris que l'on avoit destiné pour la petite galerie de Versailles, orné de glaces et de moulures de bronze doré, sur des fonds d'écaille de tortue et d'un lapis assez bien Contrefait' [very rich panelling which had been intended for the small gallery at Versailles, decorated with mirrors and with gilt bronze mounts, on a background of tortoiseshell and of a lapis lazuli that is exceedingly well counterfeited] (see Marie, *op. cit.*, p. 291).

Les Archives Nationale, Paris.

237. It may well be that the arrangement is partly imaginary but the concept is characteristic of the period.

Metropolitan Museum, New York (Whittlesey Fund).

238. From Marot's *Nouveaux livre de paremens*, published before 1702. Victoria and Albert Museum, London (from P. Jessen, *Daniel Marot*, Berlin,

239. By Simon Renard de Saint-André (1613–77). If the inscription on the letter refers to the artist himself, he seemed to have served the Crown, as the words 'du Roy' are legible.

Staatsgemäldesammlung, Munich (displayed at Schloss Aschaffenburg).

240. Sketches by the author.

241. By Hieronymus Janssen.

The Liechtenstein Collection, Schloss Vaduz, Duchy of Liechtenstein.

242. By Gerhard Terborch (1617–81).

The Wallace Collection, London.

243. The National Trust, Hardwick Hall.

244. The National Trust, Hardwick Hall.

245. *Femme de qualité en deshabillé sortant du lit*; engraving by J. D. de St Jean.

Victoria and Albert Museum, London.

246. Delft School; 1650–55.

The National Gallery, London (by courtesy of the Trustees).

247. Engraving from a suite entitled *Livre de chenets*.

Victoria and Albert Museum, London.

248. Musée du Louvre, Paris.

249 & 250. National Museum, Stockholm (Tessin-Hårleman Collection; see Plate 5).

251. Salsta, Uppland, Sweden (photograph by courtesy of Messrs. Allhem, Malmö).

252. From a suite of *Cheminées à l'italienne nouvellement inventées* by Jean le Pautre; about 1670 (?).

Victoria and Albert Museum, London.

253. A similar chimneyboard, with an orange-tree growing in an urn in the style of Daniel Marot, is in a private collection in London.

Stedelijk Museum, Amsterdam.

254. Musée du Louvre, Paris.

255 & 256. By Gerard Dou (copy by W. J. Laquy); 1660s.

The Rijksmuseum, Amsterdam.

257. Banquet given at The Hague in honour of Charles II in 1660. The King is seated under a canopy, with his two brothers, his aunt (Elizabeth of Bohemia), his sister, and the young Prince of Orange, later William III. From William Lower's *A Relation . . . of the Voiage and Residence which . . . Charles II . . . hath made in Holland . . .*, The Hague, 1660.

Victoria and Albert Museum, London.

258. From the same work as Figure 127.

259. The National Trust, Knole (photograph from archives of the Department of Furniture and Woodwork, Victoria and Albert Museum).

260. Almnäs, Västergötland, Sweden (photograph by courtesy of Messrs Allhem, Malmö).

261. *La Rentrée des Mariées*, from the same suite as Plate 2.

Bibliothèque Nationale, Paris.

262. The National Trust, Hardwick Hall. (I am indebted to Air-Commodore C. C. M. Baker for his help in procuring this photograph.)

263. Probably identical with the 'deux très grands chandeliers d'argent, à six branches [only two are shown] en cornets, d'ou sortent six thermes de femmes qui portent chacun trois bobesches [nozzles]; les corps desdits chandeliers portez sur six consoles et couronnez d'une couronne royalle soustenüe par trois Amours, [the drawing suggests there were to be six] lesdits chandeliers faits par Ballin, pesans ensembles 216 marcs, 5 onces, 4 g[ros]' which are listed in the French royal inventories as being in existence by February 1681 (*Guiffrey, Inventaire*, item 954–5). The figure of Fame seems to have been omitted. The National Museum, Stockholm (Cronstedt Collection; see Plate 5).

264. The Danish Royal Collections, Rosenborg Castle (I am greatly indebted to Dr Gudmund Boesen for providing information about this handsome object and that shown in Plate 265).

265. See G. Boesen, *Venezianske glas paa Rosenborg*, Copenhagen, 1960.
The Danish Royal Collections, Rosenborg Castle.

266. See D. Rentsche, 'Bedeutung und Restaurierung des grossen Glaskronleuchters in Schloss Favorite', *Jahrbuch der Staatlichen Kunstsammlungen in Baden-Württemberg*, Bd. 12, 1975.
Schloss Favorite (photograph by courtesy of the Badisches Landesmuseum, Karlsruhe. I am very grateful to Dr Rosemarie Stratmann for helping me to obtain this photograph on completion of the restoration).

267. By Emanuel de Witte (1617–92).
The Museum Boymans-van Beuningen, Rotterdam.

268. By Gerard Dou (associated with Plates 255 and 256).

269. The Royal Danish Collections, Rosenborg Castle.

270. From the same collection as Plate 265.

271. Made in Stockholm and paid for in December 1684 (see E. Andrén, 'Melchior Jung's glasbruk i Stockholm . . .', *St Erik's Årsbok*, 1972).
Skokloster, Sweden.

272. The National Trust, Knole (a second stand, not a pair, is at the house).

273. From the same work as Plate 114.

274. No information accompanies this drawing but it must have seemed significant to Nicodemus Tessin, probably as evidence of the modern taste in such fittings in Paris at the time.
The National Museum, Stockholm (Tessin-Hårleman Collection; see Plate 5).

275. Based on a plan reproduced by Hill and Cornforth, *English Country Houses: Caroline*, Plate 227.

276. By courtesy of the Trustees of the British Museum, London.

277 & 278. Decorations at the banquet given by Pope Clement IX for Queen Christina of Sweden.
The National Museum, Stockholm (Tessin Collection; see Plate 5).

279 & 280. From Michael Wright, *An Account of His Excellence Roger Earl of Castlemaine's Embassy . . . to His Holiness Innocent XI*, London, 1688.
Victoria and Albert Museum, London.

281. The Earl of Lonsdale (Victoria and Albert Museum photograph).

282. Two other royal *cadenas* are illustrated in Marie, *op. cit.*, pp. 327–328.
The National Museum, Stockholm (Tessin-Hårleman Collection; see Plate 5: I am indebted to Dr Carl Hernmark for providing information about this drawing).

283. By Jacob Duck.
Central Museum, Utrecht.

284. Marked in *pieds*. Drawn in red chalk. From the collection that may have been in Inigo Jones' drawing-office (see Plate 44).
The Ashmolean Museum, Oxford.

285. From the same suite as Plates 27 and 28.

286. By Jan Siberechts, Antwerp.
The Royal Museum of Fine Arts, Copenhagen.

287. From the same collection as Plate 17.

288. From the same collection as Plate 17.

289. The Bibliothèque Nationale, Paris.

290. *Le Barbier* by Abraham Bosse; 1630s.
By courtesy of the Trustees of the British Museum, London.

291–4. From R. P. Claude du Molinet, *Le Cabinet de la bibliothèque de Sainte-Geneviève*, Paris, 1692.
Victoria and Albert Museum, London.

295 & 296. Pen and ink drawings in Pepys' own manuscript catalogue to his Library, now set up at Magdalene College, Cambridge.
Reproduced by courtesy of the Master and Fellows of Magdalene College, Cambridge (I am greatly indebted to Mr Robert Latham for

providing me with much information about the Pepys Library and its furniture).

297. Leiden University.

298. Reproduced by the courtesy of the Curators of the Bodleian Library.

299. This library originally housed a valuable collection of books which was subsequently sold.
Ham House, Richmond (Victoria and Albert Museum photograph).

300. Painted by Jan van der Heyden when he was seventy-four (i.e. about 1711).
Reproduced by courtesy of Messrs Christie, Manson and Woods (I am indebted to Mr Anthony Coleridge for securing this photograph for me).

301. See Colour Plate IV.
Country Life photograph.

302. The harpsichord is shown in reverse because the illustration is an off-set image (see Plate 17 for an explanation concerning this and the related drawings). It is gilded and decorated with grotesques. The Duc d'Orléans died in 1701 and was succeeded by his son, the Duc de Chartres (see Plate 288).

303. From the *Nouveaux livre de paramens inventée & gravée par D. Marot, architecte de sa Majesté Britannique* (i.e. published before 1702). This no doubt reflects the general appearance of William III's library at Het Loo and perhaps also of libraries at Kensington Palace and Hampton Court.
Victoria and Albert Museum (from P. Jessen, *Daniel Marot*, Berlin, 1892).

304. Engraving by H. de St Jean. The *garniture* over the door-case is noteworthy, as are the bowls of flowers above the cornice.
The Bibliothèque Nationale, Paris.

305. A sixteenth century drawing said to represent a scene connected with the birth of François II in 1559.
Present location unknown (photograph from the archives of the Department of Furniture and Woodwork, Victoria and Albert Museum.

306 & 307. Eriksberg, Södermanland, Sweden (photographs by courtesy of Nordiska Museet, Stockholm).

308 From Lorenzo Magalotti's description of Sweden published by C. M. Stenbock (*Severige Under År 1674*, Stockholm, 1912). Already in 1634 a French ambassador noted that the *sauna* attendants were women—a tradition that still pertains today.
Photograph by courtesy of Nordiska Museet, Stockholm.

309. By Jacob Ochtervelt (1634/5–1708/10). About 1670?
The Minneapolis Institute of Arts (The Putnam Dana McMillan Fund).

310. Title page by Crispin van de Passe in Part II of *Vox populi, or Gondomar appearing in his likeness of Mackiavell in a Spanish Parliament*, 1624.
By courtesy of the Trustees of the British Museum, London.

311. *Le Clystère* by Abraham Bosse; about 1635.
The Bibliothèque Nationale, Paris.

312. Skokloster, Sweden.

313. Hampton Court Palace (reproduced by gracious permission of Her Majesty the Queen).

314. Ham House, Richmond (Victoria and Albert Museum, photograph).

315. Based on a plan reproduced in 'The Book of Architecture of John Thorpe in Sir John Soane's Museum', ed. by Sir John Summerson, *The Walpole Society*, 1966.

316. Based on a plan given by Blunt, *Art and Architecture in France 1500–1700*, 1970 edn.

317. Based on a plan in the care of the Royal Commission on the Ancient Monuments of Scotland.

318. The National Museum, Stockholm (Tessin Collection; see Plate 5).

319. From Randle Holme, *An Academie or Store of Armory & Blazon*, Book III, Chapter XIV, apparently published in 1688 although the title-page bears the date 1682 while the manuscript edition in the British Museum is dated 1649. Holme was born in Chester in 1622 and died in 1700. Some of the motifs would seem highly unsuitable for heraldry.
Victoria and Albert Museum, London.

320. The Rijksmuseum, Amsterdam.

Note. All Victoria and Albert Museum photographs are Crown copyright.

Index

415

420